Medical Device Accidents and Illustrative Cases

Second Edition

Leslie A. Geddes

Lawyers & Judges Publishing Company, Inc.

Lawyers & Judges Publishing Company, Inc.

P.O. Box 30040 • Tucson, AZ 85751-0040
(800) 209-7109 • FAX (800) 330-8795
e-mail: sales@lawyersandjudges.com

Library of Congress Cataloging-in-Publication Data

Geddes, L. A. (Leslie Alexander), 1921-
Medical device accidents and illustrative cases / Leslie A. Geddes.
p. cm.
Includes index.
ISBN 1-930056-36-2
1. Products liability--Medical instruments and apparatus--United States. 2. Evidence, Expert--United States.
I. Title.
KF1297.M4 G43 2002
614'.1--dc21

2002000927

ISBN 1-930056-36-2
Printed in the United States of America
10 9 8 7 6 5 4 3 2 1

online
www.lawyersandjudges.com

Table of Contents

Preface

This book is written for all who are concerned with medical device accidents, primarily, attorneys, expert witnesses, clinical engineers, nurses, physicians and manufacturers. Designers of new medical devices will find useful information on how to avoid product misuse or how to identify a design defect. The materials presented in the various chapters were drawn from the author's experience preparing and testifying as an expert witness, from the published literature and from teaching biomedical engineers, medical students and physicians during the last five decades. Much material has been derived from teaching a graduate course entitled, "Medical Device Accidents and Their Engineering Analysis," which has been presented three times at the time of this writing (2001).

The general plan of each chapter is similar. First, the basic principles of a device or a procedure are presented. Then accidents caused by malfunction or misuse or negligent use of a device are described. The cause of an accident is identified and explained insofar as possible. Also presented are ways of preventing such an accident.

The objective of Chapter 1 is to introduce the reader to many important aspects of medical devices. The chapter starts with a discussion of the evolution of medical devices through the Golden Era of Medical Electricity, which ended in 1938 when the FDA was given limited authority to seize fraudulent devices. In 1976, this authority was expanded by passage of the Medical Device Legislation Amendment. Subsequent amendments increased FDA's authority to require reporting of all medical device accidents in the form of Medical Device Reports (MDR's), now Manufacturer and User Device Experience (MAUDE) reports. Because medical malpractice is sometimes associated with a device, this topic is covered briefly. The chapter identifies the intended use of a product, negligent use and misuse, along with the criteria for establishing a product defect and a design defect. The text stresses the requirements for a carefully constructed instruction manual. The concept of variability of products made in the same way is introduced by the distribution curve, which leads to a discussion of the safety factor, which in turn, leads to the concept that the creation of a perfect product is an unrealizable goal. Product life and failure modes are also discussed. The chapter concludes with a description of the responsibility of the manufacturer and the consumer's expectations and behavior.

Chapter 2 deals with the effect of electromagnetic interference (EMI) on medical devices. With the ever-increasing use of electronic controls (analog and digital) in medical devices, their susceptibility to electromagnetic energy is becoming a serious problem. With the rapid growth in the use of high-frequency energy in devices such as cellular telephones, pagers, emergency communications equipment, remote controllers, electronic surveillance systems, etc., the amount of EMI in the environment is increasing at a very rapid rate and medical device malfunction due to EMI is on the increase. A section describes the effect of electronic surveillance (antitheft and metal-detecting) systems on pacemakers, implanted cardioverter defibrillators and other implanted electronic devices. Patient telemetry systems in hospitals are being interfered with increasingly and many examples are presented. New sources of EMI from TV monitors, slot machines, loudspeakers, bingo wands etc. are identified and the type of device malfunction that they can cause are explained. The effect of electrostatic discharge (ESD) on medical devices is described along with the procedure for testing susceptibility to ESD.

Electrosurgery, electrocautery, and laser surgery are described in Chapter 3. These three modalities are used to cut and coagulate tissue. The first uses radiofrequency (0.5–2MHz) current; the second employs electric current to heat a filament and the third uses radiant energy in the ultraviolet, visible and infrared spectral regions; the principles underlying the use of each are described in detail. The use of high-frequency electric current to cut and coagulate tissue entered surgery in the late 1920s and revolutionized it. Electrosurgery disrupts patient monitors and some types of implanted electronic devices; many examples are given. Despite the continued improvements in equipment and techniques, electrosurgical accidents are still quite common, ranging from muscle stimulation, skin burns, fires, to bowel-gas explosions and circumcision accidents. The various electrosurgical techniques and effects are described and explanations of the various accidents are presented in this chapter.

Disposable, battery-operated electrocauteries are seeing increased use and are described in detail. Although their use does not interfere with monitoring equipment, they do not eliminate a fire hazard. Many such accidents are described.

Lasers entered medicine in the mid-1960s and their use is steadily increasing in medicine and surgery. Lasers present hazards to environmental personnel and to the patient if used without adequate training. Fire hazard accompanies laser use and precautions must be taken to guard against this risk. Although the delivered energy can be controlled precisely, it has the capability of stimulating excitable tissue (e.g. nerve and muscle, including heart muscle). Another hazard is overlasing, i.e. the use of excessive laser energy, which can penetrate tissue beyond the target site. Wherever appropriate, standards of performance for these three surgical systems have been provided in this chapter.

General anesthesia entered medicine in the mid-1800s with ether (a flammable substance) as the anesthetic agent. Nonflammable gases replaced ether which resulted in creation of the anesthesia machine. To it were added many monitors and alarms. With over 20 million anesthetic procedures in the U.S. annually, the opportunity for mishaps is considerable. Moreover the patient is unconscious and cannot complain; therefore severe accidents can occur. Chapter 4 describes the two types of anesthesia machine and the monitors that have been added. Despite these improvements, accidents still occur with disturbing frequency. Valves malfunction, the anesthetic circuit develops leaks, disconnects, and carbon dioxide absorbers become exhausted. Fires occur when oxygen comes in contact with flammable materials that are ignited by a spark from an electrosurgical electrode, an electrocautery or a laser beam; such airway and other fires are described. In addition to the monitoring and alarm devices on the anesthesia machine, monitors are applied to the patient, the most important of which is the pulse oximeter which measures oxygen saturation (blood redness). This device also indicates pulse rate and is an excellent monitor of the function of the cardiorespiratory system. The principles underlying operation of the pulse oximeter and the hazards and accidents with its use are detailed. Blood pressure is monitored indirectly and sometimes directly during anesthesia. The types of mishaps associated with the use of such devices are described. Patient injuries have resulted from the use of warming devices; such accidents are described in this chapter, which includes a large number of case studies.

Muscle relaxants are used during anesthesia and their effect is monitored by transcutaneous electrical motor-nerve stimulation and observing the ensuing muscle twitches. The type of accident that sometimes occurs with this technique is described. Likewise, the integrity of the central nervous system (brain and spinal cord) is sometimes assessed by applying electrical stimuli to the skin and recording the evoked potential with scalp electrodes; the types of accidents that have occurred are described. Likewise, cardiac output is sometimes measured noninvasively with chest-surface electrodes that measure conductivity changes due to the heartbeat. The small current injected to make this measurement can cause malfunction of some devices; such mishaps are described.

Chapter 5 deals with intravascular catheters and catheter electrodes. Sections on catheter whip and mishaps with the Swan-Ganz (balloon-tipped) catheter for cardiac output are presented. Catheter electrodes and the mishaps and failures are covered extensively and the clavicular crush and twiddler's syndromes are explained fully. The three types of catheter- electrode extractor (mechanical, laser, and electrosurgical) are described, along with the risks and accidents associated with their use. The hazards of leakage current flowing in fluid-filled catheters are explained fully. A section describing balloon angioplasty is included; with this technique a catheter-borne balloon is used to expand the lumen of a blood vessel. Frequently the catheter delivers a stent to hold the vessel open. The hazards and accidents associated with these two techniques are described.

Chapter 6 is devoted to transdermal drug delivery which can be effected by: (1) placing the drug in a skin patch, (2) driving a drug with a charged molecule into the skin using a direct current (iontophoresis), (3) increasing skin permeability with low-frequency ultrasound (sonophoresis or phonophoresis), and (4) using a high-voltage pulse to make a pore in a cell membrane (electroporation). These four techniques are described in Chapter 6, along with the risks, side effects and hazards.

Chapter 7, entitled "Pain Suppression by Electrical Stimulation," includes sections on transcutaneous electrical nerve stimulation (TENS), peripheral nerve stimulation (PNS) and dorsal column stimulation (DCS). These techniques are increasingly used for pain control. PNS and DCS employ electrodes in direct contact with nerve fibers and use implanted stimulators. The effficacy, safety and complications associated with use of these devices are described in detail. Also there are sections on electroacupuncture and stimulators that are used to stun subjects to gain control of their behavior.

Chapter 8 (Tissue Injury) contains many accident reports. The relationship between temperature and exposure time for discomfort, complete transepidermal necrosis and full dermal thickness injury are included to quantify the conditions for second-, third- and fourth-degree burns. A section on tap-water burns and burns from microwave-oven heated packs is included. Ischemic injuries (pressure sores etc.), along with class)fication information is included, along with examples of nerve injury due to improper posturing a patient on the operating table during anesthesia of long duration. A section on reflex sympathetic dystrophy (RSD) describes this disabling and longlasting pain syndrome. Chemical injury and allergic responses are described along with many case reports.

The last chapter (Chapter 9), entitled "Important Information for the Technical Expert," is designed to alert the reader to many facts that attorneys and judges require in discovering the truth. The material on accident investigation identifies what is expected of a technical expert from a legal viewpoint. Because medical devices can be associated with a death, a section on ascertaining the time of death is included. A section on the admissibility of evidence included to identify the requirements deriving from the *Frye*, *Daubert*, *Joiner*, and *Kumho* landmark cases. Coverage is given to patents (infringement and invalidation) and includes the criteria for patentability and defines "one of ordinary skill in the art." Material is presented on the criteria for infringement, including case citations as well as the value of the doctrine of equivalents. The anatomy of a patent is described and includes definitions of each section of a patent, along with pointing out that the specification (text) must support the claims. Patent infringement criteria are discussed extensively.

The requirements for an expert's report illustrates what is essential and what is supplemental; a typical report example is given to illustrate these points.

The "Deposition" section explains how the technical expert can aid the court reporter as well as describing the nature of interrogation during a deposition. A section describes appropriate courtroom behavior in which the expert is a teacher who explains the complex in easily understood language. This section also presents the relative values of the spoken word, visual aids, demonstrations and videotape presentations.

A paragraph on attorney styles is included. A section on billing is provided and a paragraph on my experience with the small claims court should aid those who may select this route for securing payment.

Sections that cover expert witness malpractice and liability, including the desirability of having errors and omissions (E&O) insurance are presented.

A "Where-to-Find-It" section presents a worldwide listing of government agencies concerned with medical device performance. Also, in the reference list, are the names and addresses of standards-promulgating organizations, including professional societies, relevant books, journals, and computer accessible databases.

One of the diffficulties the author encountered in writing this book was what to put what where. For example cardiac pacemakers and other implanted electronic devices can be interfered with by electrosurgical current, antitheft devices, communications equipment of various kinds, etc. Likewise patients can be injured by electrosurgical current, hot packs, and Iying immobilized for prolonged periods (which produces pressure sores). Obviously, each of these items can fit into several chapters. To avoid repetition and to eliminate the need for the reader to search through all of the relevant index listings, entries are made in each chapter referring to other chapters where additional information on a particular subject can be found. The author hopes that this technique will make this book more user friendly. After all, a book that contains inaccessible information is of limited value to the reader.

Finally, no work of this breadth represents the efforts of a single person. I am indebted to my Ph.D. graduate student, Rebecca Roeder, who was my teaching assistant in "Medical Device Accidents," and a helper with investigation of many accidents. I wish to acknowledge the assistance of Cheryl Haines and Stacey Coar, who faithfully typed my lecture notes that ultimately became this book. Lastly, I must acknowledge the valuable assistance of Coni Boss, my former secretary, who prepared the final manuscript that was submitted to the publisher.

L.A. Geddes
Purdue University

Chapter 1

Product Liability and Medical Technology

Synopsis

1.1 Introduction

The law imposes burdens not only on the medical professional who uses technology, but also on the manufacturer, seller, installer and repairer of technological equipment to insure patient safety. A patient has the right not to be harmed as a result of the use of a medical device, which can be defined as something created to produce a benefit to the patient; it is operated by trained personnel and must not be adversely affected by its working environment.

According to Enghagen (1992), product liability lawsuits generate more million-dollar-plus judgments than any other class of personal injury, except medical malpractice cases. Therefore, when medical device product liability is associated with medical practice, the stakes can be high and medical device incidents become very serious business. The law imposes burdens to ensure patient safety.

1.2 Medical Device Evolution

Since the late 1600s, a variety of electrical and magnetic devices were claimed to have a therapeutic effect and were applied widely. The electrostatic machine was used to charge the Leyden jar (capacitor) in 1745, which was then discharged into the body. The discharge was supposed to cure paralysis, diseases of the internal organs, impotence, infertility, psychoses and a variety of other ailments. Static-electric therapy was succeeded by galvanotherapy, which used direct current, which appeared in the early 1800s. This current was also believed to cure a variety of ailments. Then followed faradic therapy, which employed single or a train of induction coil shocks to cure illnesses. Then, at the turn of the 20th century, high-frequency current was used to heat body segments to increase blood flow. So popular were these electrical devices that two medical textbooks on their use were published: the first was entitled *A Treatise on Medical Electricity*, authored by J. Althaus and published in Philadelphia in 1873; the second was entitled *On the Medical and Surgical Uses of Electricity*, authored by C. M. Beard and A. D. Rockwell, the eighth edition being published in New York in 1891. Geddes (1984) reviewed the history of these electrotherapeutic techniques.

In this, the Golden Era of Medical Electricity, anecdotal reports were all that was needed to show efficacy and safety. During this time the attitude of the law was *caveat emptor* (let the buyer beware). Accidents and failed therapeutic claims resulted in the Pure Food and Drug Act of 1918 in federal regulatory law. In common law, a number of court decisions began to recognize the right to recover monetary damages for injuries caused by products at this time.

By 1938 in the U.S. it became recognized by the lawmakers that the public needed protection against unscrupulous vendors of a variety of medical products. The main concern at that time related to labeling, that is, claims made for the product and the need to remove fraudulent items from the market. In 1938, the Food and Drug Administration (FDA) was given the authority for seizure, injunction, or criminal prosecution with respect to adulterated or misbranded devices. Although numerous cases were tried and many products were removed from the market, the postwar medical instrumentation boom created new jurisdictional problems. After the mid-1940s an enormous variety of medical devices became available to physicians and a large number of these made no claims regarding safety and efficacy. It is important to note that many of these devices played lifesaving roles in the hands of competent physicians. However, many devices had technological flaws. For example, the *Federal Register* of March 9, 1976 noted that "a committee chaired by Dr. Theodore Cooper, the director of the National Heart Institute, issued a report indicating that in the ten years prior to 1969, medical devices caused 10,000 serious injuries and over 750 deaths." An intrauterine device marketed in the early 1970s was linked to sixteen deaths and twenty-five miscarriages. Significant defects in cardiac pacemakers had resulted in thirty-four voluntary recalls, involving 23,000 units.

Taking note of these facts, the lawmakers passed the Medical Device Legislation Amendments Bill of 1976 (HR-11124, *Federal Register*, March 9, 1976), which was signed into law. The bill amended the federal Food, Drug and Cosmetic Act to give it jurisdiction over the safety and effectiveness of medical devices intended for human use in the U.S.

A special feature of this bill allows the FDA to exempt a device from the requirements of the bill if the device is intended solely for investigational use and if the proponent of the device submits a plan demonstrating that the testing of the device will be supervised by an institutional review committee, ensures appropriate patient consent, and maintains certain records and reports. The protocol must be scientifically sound and the benefits and knowledge to be gained must outweigh the risks to the patient. This provision thereby provides a means for the creation of new medical devices.

1.3 Medical Malpractice

Medical malpractice involves a breach of the standard of care, which is generally defined as what is to be expected of any given physician based upon that physician's training and experience under a particular set of circumstances. The standard varies whenever the circumstances change. For example, a physician may be held to one standard of conduct under elective conditions, and another under emergency conditions. The law recognizes that in an emergency situation there is not as much time to obtain consultations, tests, or to evaluate the patient's reaction to treatment. Similarly, a physician practicing in a rural hospital with limited resources is not held to the same standard as the same physician practicing in an urban environment at a large medical center. Because the standard is constantly changing, depending upon the circumstances, there are an infinite number of variables as to the exact standard to which any physician may be held at any given time. The standard to be applied is based upon the opinions of medical experts.

Malpractice judgments involve large sums of money. According to the Health Care Liability Alliance, in 1996 the median medical malpractice award was $568,000 and the mean (average) award was $4,494,064. Million dollar verdicts increased by 40 percent for 1995–1996 combined, up from 34 percent in 1993–1994. The median settlement in 1996 increased by 13.3 percent to 455,000. According to the American Medical Association (AMA), the average annual rate of lawsuits filed against physicians remained at or above 9.5 percent for 1993 and 1994, the latest years for which data are available, which is 50 percent greater than the 1988 claims rate. Nearly 40 percent of all physicians are sued at least once in their careers. Failure to diagnose and diagnostic errors constitute the largest proportion of malpractice lawsuits.

Medical malpractice lawsuits often involve medical devices that are used negligently, misused, fail or have a design or manufacturing defect. Negligent use can involve inadequate training or unfamiliarity with the indications and contraindications for use of a device. Failure to read the instruction manual is very common among physicians. A device may fail and in rare instances the failure may not be noted at the time of use. The failure may not be obvious, and if it involves a diagnostic or monitoring device it can provide an incorrect reading, leading one to an inappropriate action. A design defect may not be apparent until circumstances conspire to make it obvious because of an accident. Environmental factors or use of a device with other devices connected to a patient can produce misleading function or harm to a patient. All of these scenarios are discussed in this chapter and it is the task of the biomedical engineering expert to identify which of these factors are relevant in a particular case.

1.4 Medical Technology

Medical technology is advancing at an ever accelerating rate. New devices and the procedures that they permit are improving the quality of life and prolonging it. Associated with use of the new devices is an increasing number of product liability lawsuits, often not related to a product defect, but because of new technologies coming together, the patient being the interface. Situations are arising in which two or more medical devices are used on a patient and injury or death results, despite the fact that when tested, the individual devices function normally. In other words, accidents can result from the use of multiple devices connected to a patient.

Despite the fact that there are now rigidly enforced standards for all medical devices, accidents do occur due to medical device malfunction. According to Silberberg (1995) the FDA receives over 95,000 medical device problem reports per year. Many of the incidents that generated the reports involved injury or death to a patient. An increasing number of these incidents involve environmental electromagnetic interference (EMI), which causes medical devices to malfunction. Silberberg (1995) stated: Between 1979 and 1995, the Center for Devices and Radiological Health (CDRH) of the U.S. Food and Drug Administration (U.S. FDA) has received over one hundred reports alleging that electromagnetic interference (EMI) resulted in malfunction of electronic medical devices.

Although medical device accidents are covered in detail elsewhere in this book, a few examples will illustrate the foregoing.

About 100,000 cardiac pacemakers are implanted annually. These sophisticated stimulators can be interrogated and programmed by an external device that uses a radiofrequency link. Patients with pacemakers often undergo surgical procedures that employ electrosurgery, which uses radiofrequency current. There have been cases in which pacemakers caused serious arrhythmias and were reprogrammed, inhibited, and even destroyed when the electrosurgical unit was employed. While the two technologies are safe and effective when used alone, their combination has resulted in injury.

Cellular telephones are used by more and more people, some of whom may be hospitalized and connected to a drug-infusion pump, a dialysis machine, or a monitor. Because the patient has little to do, he or she can pass the time using the cellular phone to talk to friends or family. There have been many instances of malfunction of drug-infusion pumps and patient monitors associated with the use of a cellular telephone. To solve this problem, many hospitals have banned the use of cellular telephones in some areas. Again each technology is safe and effective when operated alone, but malfunction occurred when the technologies come together.

Electrical impedance-based respiration monitors pass a low intensity, high-frequency current through the chest and detect the increase and decrease in impedance with inspiration and expiration. Such devices alarm when the respiratory rate exceeds a preset low and high breathing rate. However, some such apnea monitors are sensitive to environmental electromagnetic interference

(EMI) and fail to alarm. Although safe and effective in low EMI environments, they are not in a high EMI environment.

An example of a potentially serious ECG misdiagnosis was reported by Capuano et al. (1993), who described an ominous arrhythmia in the ECG of a patient whose urine output was being measured by an electronic device. When the urine monitor was turned off, the "cardiac arrhythmia" disappeared. The "arrhythmia" resembling ventricular tachycardia, was traced to beat frequencies between the isolation methods used in the ECG and the urine monitor. Again, each monitor functioned normally, but the combination, when connected to the patient, produced what mimicked a dangerous cardiac arrhythmia. There is therefore an urgent need to "harden" medical devices so that they will be immune from interference sources that are likely to be encountered in the vicinity of a patient. The term "harden" is well known to the military and describes their efforts to make electronic military devices immune from EMI generated by the enemy as well as from environmental sources. Such hardening techniques are well known to civilian engineers and may become a requirement as more EMI-generating equipment appears.

A most important factor in reducing medical device related accidents is the education of those who use them. The delivery of appropriate education has not kept pace with the appearance of new medical devices that are susceptible to environmental factors. It should not be concluded that education has been totally neglected; it has not. Manufacturers present in-service courses that relate to the proper use of their equipment, but they now need to educate about the hazards of combinations of technologies as well as environmental factors.

It has been said that the best way to keep information away from users of medical devices is to place it in the instruction manual. It has been a constant surprise to the author to discover, during litigation, that many users of medical devices have never read the instruction manual. It should be a rule that before operating a medical device, the operator should be required to prove that he or she has read the manual, no matter how good the in-service training may be or no matter how obvious it is to use the device.

Too little attention is paid to misuse and the effect that environmental hazards may have on a given medical device. Attention to these two factors may well reduce the number of lawsuits; it will certainly reduce the number of defendants per lawsuit.

1.5 Misuse

The dictionary definition of misuse is wrong or improper use, misapplication or used wrongly. In the case of a medical device, the intended use appears on the device label, package insert, or in the instruction manual in the form of "instructions for use."

When harm results from the misuse of a product, it is assumed that the product was without a manufacturing or design defect. Therefore, the issue becomes one of user behavior. The Supreme Court held that foreseeability is significant in product liability cases when the product is what it is intended and known to be, but injury is suffered because the product is misused. A product is not misused merely because the manufacturer intended that it be used in a different manner; the manufacturer must show that the use which caused the injury was not reasonably foreseeable. Therefore the manufacturer is responsible for designing a product with reasonable misuse in mind, as well as communicating the features of the product and indications for use to the user. It is in this area that the instruction manual can play an important role.

There are two elements in misuse: contributory negligence and assumption of risk. In the former case, the test of reasonableness applies. In other words, did the user act as a reasonable person in the same or similar circumstances? In the latter case, the assumption of risk is evaluated on the basis of what the user knew just before the incident. In assessing the assumption of risk, there are three elements the user must be shown to have: (1) known about the risk before the incident, (2) voluntarily acted, and (3) unreasonably acted.

It should be borne in mind that tampering or sabotage could have occurred to cause an accident. Tampering is defined as meddling for the purpose of altering, damaging, misusing, etc. Sabotage is malicious injury to work, tools, machinery, etc.

Several scenarios can arise in which a well-designed product is misused. For example, if the user, with good intentions, does something to the product to make it safer or more easily used in his or her view, the product is no longer what the manufacturer intended it to be; it has been adulterated. If an accident occurs with the adulterated product, the manufacturer can claim no liability.

1.6 Negligence

Negligence is the failure to conform one's conduct to that of a reasonable and prudent person. If such conduct results in harm to a person or property a lawsuit can be filed. The purpose of negligence law is protection from unreasonable risks or harm and four elements must be proven: (1) the existence of a duty of care, (2) breach of that duty, (3) proximate cause, and (4) damage establishment. The duty of care refers to behavior as a reasonable and prudent person; breach of that duty is obvious. Proximate cause establishes the value of personal injury, property damage, emotional stress, lost wages and so on which resulted from the negligent behavior.

Negligence lawsuits are usually characterized by "failure to . . . ." Common examples are failure to perform a test, failure to use a technique, failure to monitor, failure to timely perform an act, failure to properly interpret information, failure to diagnose properly, and so forth. In this series of "failures to," a medical device may be involved. If it provides misleading or erroneous information, or fails to perform according to specifications must be established to reveal the cause of an incident.

The following case reported by *Medical Malpractice* (2000) raises the issues of misuse and negligence. On May 27, 1997, the plaintiff, a fifty-three-year-old retired firefighter received electrical muscle stimulation therapy for a previous lower back injury. Dr. X administered the treatment by applying four electrode pads to the plaintiff's lower back. One of the pads caused a third-degree burn about the diameter of a quarter that allegedly damaged the L-4 nerve root, resulting in residual impotence, necessitating Viagra. The manufacturer of the machine settled for $5,000 prior to trial. The plaintiff's wife sued for a loss of consortium. The plaintiff contended that Dr. X failed to apply a conductive agent; that she reused disposable pads; that she told him "the more he could take the better;" and that she tried to cover up her error by saying that it looked as though the plaintiff had an irritated pimple on his back. The defendants contended that an accident such as this can happen absent negligence; that Dr. X at all times followed the applicable standard of care for administering electrical muscle stimulation therapy; that the plaintiff was negligent in failing to call for help when he was burned; and that the plaintiff did not become impotent as a result of his burn. According to *Jury Verdicts Weekly*, this action resulted in a $35,000 gross total award, but the jury determined the plaintiff to be three percent comparatively negligent for a net award to plaintiff of $33,950.

The foregoing case raises the issue of negligent use of electrodes. Because they were available commercially, it is assumed that the manufacturer obtained a 510(K) permission from the FDA. The electrodes were not at fault,- because if they were, there would have been four burns. Moreover the standard of care, which includes adequate patent supervision, does not result in a third-degree burn.

1.7 Product Liability

Product liability is the term used to describe the litigation in which a complaining party (the plaintiff) alleges that a product caused personal injury, property damage, or both, and wants to be compensated for the loss by one or more parties (the defendants), who may be, and usually include, the manufacturer, contractor, assembler, distributor, vendor, or practitioner who used the product. Product liability is under the purview of civil law, and to prevail requires that proof be established by a preponderance of the evidence. The dictionary definition of preponderant is "superior in weight, number, or power." A loose definition of adequate proof would be "more likely than not." This is a lesser requirement than is needed in criminal law where the plaintiff (state, people, or government) must prove its case beyond a reasonable doubt.

Product liability extends into three areas: (1) manufacturing, (2) design, and (3) misrepresentation. To prevail it must be proven that (1) the defect existed when the product left control of the manufacturer or vendor, (2) the provider knew (or should have known) the existence of the defect, (3) there were feasible alternatives that would have eliminated the risk, and (4) the product caused the injuries or damages complained of. In essence, by selling a product, a manufacturer accepts an obligation to the consumer.

1.8 Elements of a Product Liability Case

In a product liability case, four categories of complaint can be identified: (1) manufacturing or production defect, (2) design defect, (3) failure to adequately instruct and (4) failure to adequately warn. Each or all of these factors can present danger and harm can result. The theory of strict liability is associated with these issues; under the theory of strict liability, for manufacturing or design defects, it is no defense that the manufacturer acted reasonably. In a negligence action, the duty to warn in strict liability arises only if the danger is known or should have been known.

A. Manufacturing or production defect

The simplest definition of a defective product is one that is unreasonably dangerous when put to its intended use. A product is defective when it emerges with characteristics that are different from the provider's own specifications and applicable industrial and governmental standards. However, meeting the requirements of such standards is not enough; it must be shown that the product is safe for any reasonable and foreseeable use. For a product to be classified as defective, it is necessary to prove that the defect was present when the product left the manufacturer's premises. Inspection and test records are needed to prove this point. The issue of adequacy of the tests is a legitimate point to raise.

B. Design defect

If a product is produced exactly to the manufacturer's specifications, but when put to its intended use is deemed to be unreasonably dangerous, then it has a design defect. The final design of a product is a trade-off between many factors. The design must be such that the product is safe for any reasonably foreseeable use. Conversely, a design defect exists if use of the product creates an unreasonable risk of injury. An important aspect of a satisfactory design is recognition of foreseeable misuse. In essence, the design process ends with the application of the warning label which transfers the risk to the user.

To establish that a design defect exists involves the following elements: (1) identification of the design defect, (2) establishing a link between the design defect and the harm done, (3) identification of alternate designs that would have prevented the harmful incident, and (4) comparing the product performance with like products offered by other manufacturers.

In design defect cases, the issue of the availability of an alternate design can be raised. Therefore, the designer of the accused product is called upon to review and defend his or her risk/utility decisions. The availability of a competitive product that performs the same function but does not have the hazard of injury offers proof that an alternate design is available.

Environmental conditions can be an important factor in a design defect. For example, a product is designed to operate in its intended environment. If it fails to do so, the issue of a design defect can be raised. The following examples will illustrate this point.

Sattari (1999) reported a malfunction associated with the use of an anesthesia machine in the operating room. Two of the coauthors sought to report their separate views in the same paper. Sattari reported that a malfunction of the volume monitor sensor of a [manufacturer's name] anesthesia machine after overhead surgical lights were directed toward the volume sensor. The surgical lights were aimed at the head of the operating room table after the patient was prepared for surgery. Within one minute, the anesthesia machine spirometer indicated apnea volume, and no tidal volume or respiratory rate appeared on the monitor. The lights were then directed away from the anesthesia machine, and within one minute, the readings returned to normal. Sattari stated that no warning pertaining to this malfunction was found in the anesthesia machine's instruction manual. He concluded that intense lighting can affect the volume monitor sensor and this led to spurious data. He added that this problem does not affect newer models provided by the same manufacturer. A representative of the anesthesia machine manufacturer (Richard) replied that extremely intense lights can affect the readings of the volume monitoring function of this anesthesia machine and other products that use the same infrared light/turbine vane volume measurement technique. He stated that the manufacturer has revised its operation and maintenance manuals to warn users of this malfunction. Richard stated that newer surgical lights are designed to filter out infrared light.

It is useful to discuss this incident, which, happily enough, did not lead to injury due to personnel vigilance. Nonetheless, it is a reasonable expectation that an anesthesia machine should operate normally in the operating room environment, which is characterized by high illumination. It is difficult to argue that the volume sensor could not have been designed to eliminate this malfunction. Surely optical shielding would solve this problem. Alternately, the use of a narrowband optical source and detector, operating at a safe wavelength, is another alternative.

An unusual accident associated with dental anesthesia was reported by McCaughey (1992) who stated:

> During a recent anesthetic session in a dental surgery, I anaesthetized a child in an electrically operated dental chair, in the horizontal position. Immediately after induction of anesthesia, the chair, apparently spontaneously, resumed the upright position and refused to respond further to its controls. The anesthetic and extraction were, fortunately, completed successfully, and it then became apparent that the child had a full bladder which had emptied on loss of consciousness and "shorted" the chair electrics.

Urine is one of the most highly conductive fluids in the body, it is five times more conducting than blood and twice as conductive as physiological saline. When it is spilled on electric circuits, the circuits malfunction.

McCaughey continued by stating, "After replacing burnt-out parts at some expense, my dental colleagues have now waterproofed the vital regions of the chair, and I hope that the telling of this tale will encourage others, like myself, to check patient preoperative fluid balance more carefully in future."

This accident clearly raises the issue of the environmental use of a product. Was it foreseeable that the controls of the dental chair should be protected so that conducting fluid cannot access them? Bladder evacuation during anesthesia is not unknown.

Another example of a design defect is a product that functions normally under restricted circumstances. For example, if an apnea monitor operated properly in one environment, but failed to alarm cessation of breathing in another environment, the issue of design defect is raised. If the reason for failure were electromagnetic interference (EMI), it would be fruitful to inquire if similar apnea monitors provided by competitors also failed in the same environment or an equivalent environment. If they did not, it shows that there is technology available to eliminate this hazard. If the manufacturer of the monitor that failed was unaware, or chose to ignore the available technology, a case can be offered for a design defect.

In the chapter on anesthesia, a case is described that the author investigated in which a nerve stimulator, which contained a battery, provided jacks for testing the battery voltage. Unfortunately, these jacks were the same as those that delivered the stimulus output. During the course of an operation, the stimulating electrode plugs became dislodged and the technician plugged them into the battery-test jacks. After the operation, deep skin lesions were found at the site of the stimulating electrodes.

A similar but less disastrous case was reported by the FDA in a MAUDE report (7/6/98):

> The patient was connected to a ventilator. When the [manufacturer's] connector was connected to the ventilator circuit the nurse connected the ventilator to the suction port instead of the ventilator port. The ventilator did not alarm, but the nurse noticed and reconnected the ventilator to the correct port. No injury occurred.

The manufacturer's comment was reported in *Health Devices* (9/24/99):

> The [manufacturer's] device is a closed suction airway connector. The connector is designed with three ports. One port [the patient port] is 17 mm OD, the other two ports have 15 mm OD dimensions. One port is open and should connect to the ventilator; the other port is the suction port. The suction port has a cap over it and has a valve system inside which keeps the circuit closed. The user connected the ventilator to the suction port. The ventilator did not alarm because the valve systems inside the port presented enough resistance for the ventilator not to alarm. Corrective action: Company modified the suction port's outside dimension to 16.5 mm so ventilators/resuscitators cannot connect to this port.

A disastrous case, which on first examination would appear like the failure of a life-support device, was described in the *South African Cape Times* (1996):

> For several months, our nurses have been baffled to find a dead patient in the same bed every Friday morning, a spokeswoman for the Pelonomi Hospital (Free State, South Africa) told reporters. "There was no apparent cause for any of the deaths, and extensive checks on the air conditioning system, and a search for possible bacterial infection, failed to reveal any clues."

Although device failure could cause such deaths, why they occurred on Fridays is difficult to understand. The hospital investigated further and the *Cape Times* reported:

> It seems that every Friday morning a cleaner would enter the ward, remove the plug that powered the patient's life-support system, plug her floor polisher into the vacant socket, then go about her business. When she had finished her chores, she would plug the life-support machine back in and leave, unaware that the patient was now dead. She could not, after all, hear the screams and eventual death rattle over the shirring of her polisher.
>
> We are sorry, and have sent a strong letter to the cleaner in question. Further, the Free State Health and Welfare Department is arranging for an electrician to fit an extra socket, so there should be no repetition of this incident. The inquiry is now closed.

The foregoing incidents raise many questions, such as "Shouldn't all life-support devices have loud alarms? Shouldn't all life-support devices have a backup battery supply? Why was there not a central monitoring station that exercised surveillance over all such patients?"

The issue of product design defect could well be raised because technology exists to prevent such deaths, either by alarming or provision of a built-in backup power supply. Any attorney involved in such a case would raise the issue of foreseeability, and would be correct in doing so. Finally, it may be appropriate to raise the issue of what minimal training should all have who are in an area where patients are on life-support equipment. Even a nonmedical person could sound an alarm or seek emergency assistance.

C. Failure to adequately instruct

If there is a failure to warn of a hazard or danger, it will be revealed in the instruction manual which extols the virtue of the product, the principle of operation and instructions for its intended use. The manual also contains warnings and identifies risks and hazards. A well composed manual should contain much more information.

We live at a time when many products that we purchase are so well designed that an instruction manual is ignored if we turn on the device and it operates like we think it should. For example, we purchase a refrigerator, plug it in and if cooling occurs, we ignore the manual. Other familiar examples could be cited, such as the purchase of an AM /FM radio. An industrialist friend of mine used this situation as a measure of the quality of a product's design. He defined the instruction manual as the booklet that comes with the product and is ignored when the purchaser operates the device successfully for the first time. If it operates according to expectations, he claimed the design was satisfactory.

Not reading an instruction manual is not confined to the general public; medical personnel are equally guilty. It has been said "If you want to hide information from medical personnel, put it in the instruction manual." I have yet to meet a surgeon or a surgical nurse who uses electrosurgery and who has read the instruction manual, despite the fact that these manuals contain much information on proper surgical techniques.

D. Instruction manual

The foregoing clearly calls attention to the need for a carefully designed instruction manual. Such manuals vary widely in their form and content and depend greatly on the nature of the product; however a few common ingredients are worthy of note. Although the author's expertise is in the area of medical devices, the following list of ten elements for an instruction manual may be widely applicable. Therefore the instruction manual should contain:

1. Copyright information and date
2. Introduction—indications and contraindications
3. Principle of operation
4. Operating instructions
5. Warnings and safety considerations
6. Technical specifications
7. Troubleshooting
8. Warranty
9. Educational material available
10. How to contact the company

The copyright information is important because it identifies the owner of the text and illustrations. In addition, the date specifies the time when the information was current; i.e., it identifies the state of the art to the copyright date.

The introduction points out the features of the product and often distinguishes them from competitors' products. It also provides the indications for the intended use, thereby directing one away from unintended uses.

The principle of operation tells how the device operates and is written in easily understood language. In essence, it is a tutorial for the user and will give him or her confidence in using the device.

The operating instructions constitute the most important part of the instruction manual. The language should be easily understood and supported by sketches or line drawings with only enough detail as is needed to establish proper procedure. One set of instructions for each procedure, with accompanying sketches, are highly desirable if many procedures can be performed with the same device. Here is where the user can be guided to the use of a procedure that will not lead him or her to harm or danger. A few don'ts and why nots or the consequences thereof are useful and protective for the manufacturer. To test the clarity and comprehensibility of the instructions, it is useful to select volunteers to read the instructions, then apply a test to determine the comprehension. Warnings and safety considerations are essential in every instruction manual. The text should enhance and explain any warning or hazard labels on the device. Sketches showing undesirable procedures and their consequences are valuable. This is the place to state "this device is to be operated only by authorized personnel" if it is applicable. Some medical devices can only be obtained with a physician's prescription; if this is applicable, it should be clearly stated.

The technical specifications are usually a laundry list of size, weight, power requirements (e.g. 60 Hz 117 V), current and power consumption, range of environmental temperature for operation, output power (if applicable), altitude restriction (if applicable), and susceptibility to other environmental factors (noise, vibration, humidity, barometric pressure, electromagnetic interference, etc.). Listing these factors may eliminate or reduce misuse.

The warranty statement is a guarantee that the manufacturer provides a product that is free from defects and will perform according to existing standards. Prominent in a warranty statement is a guarantee and the duration of the guarantee. It is usually stated that the warranty is void if repairs are made by unauthorized personnel.

Most modern manuals state that there are training materials available from the manufacturer. Often representatives provide in-service training courses.

Available video tapes are listed along with a bibliography of published papers relative to the field of the product are often identified.

The provision of a contact telephone number or department in the manufacturer's company lets the customer know that he or she does not have to face unforeseen problems alone. This feature is an excellent device for gaining customer loyalty and avoiding lawsuits.

E. Failure to adequately warn

The courts have held that the lack of an adequate warning renders a product defective and unreasonably dangerous even if there is no manufacturing or design defect in the product. It is therefore the obligation of the manufacturer to place adequate warning labels on the product.

The Fifth Circuit Court has held that in order for a warning to be adequate, it must provide "a complete disclosure of the existence and extent of the risk involved." The question of whether or not a given warning is legally sufficient depends upon the language used and the impression that such language is calculated to make upon the mind of the average user of the product.

An adequate warning label is a defense against liability by informing the user about a potential hazard in using a product. However, a warning label cannot protect a bad product, that is, one whose use is associated with an unreasonable danger. Even a well crafted warning label cannot make such a product reasonably safe.

We can summarize the criteria for an adequate warning label as follows: (1) it should catch the attention of the reasonably prudent person who uses the product, (2) it should be comprehensible to such a user and (3) it should convey the nature and extent of the danger to such a user. Prudent derives from the Latin *prudens* which means foreseeing or knowing. Reasonable is defined as agreeable to reason or sound judgment.

Regarding "catching the eye of the user," location of the warning label is important. I have seen warning labels adjacent to the on/off switch and on the power cable. Obviously a prominent site is essential. The use of some devices requires special training and the label "to be used only by authorized personnel" is common. Some products have finite life and carry an expiry date, either in numerical or pictogram format. For example, I have encountered one product whose expiry date was January 2000; the pictogram showed an hour glass and below it was 1/2000. Pictograms are good provided that they are easily understood by the average person. One in this category is the skull and crossbones on a bottle containing poison.

The nature and extent of the danger needs to be identified by the warning label, such as "electric shock hazard" or "fumes are irritating to the eyes." The instruction manual should elaborate on the dangers identified by the warning label.

F. A too-well-designed product?

An interesting case of a too-well-designed product raises several product liability issues. The Institute of Safe Medication Practices (ISMP) reported that a manufacturer's transdermal nitroglycerin patches are clear and blend with skin color so well that they may be missed or forgotten. ISMP stated that two days passed before a long-term care nurse noticed and removed a previously applied patch on a patient. ISMP concludes that the manufacturer confirmed similar reports and continues to monitor the situation, but that no changes have been implemented.

The potential hazard is that a patch may not be removed and a subsequent patch or patches could be applied, thereby increasing drug delivery. Issues to be debated are: (1) Is the design defective? (2) Can the design lead to misuse or negligent use? (3) Is the warning on the package insert adequate? (4) Does the insert identify this hazard?

One way of solving this problem would be to require placement of each removed patch in the patient's record.

1.9 The Untested Product

Two types of product can be purchased: (1) tested and (2) untested. In the latter case, a sample number is selected from a production run and tested. Such testing provides performance information on a typical product of that production lot. This procedure is used for several reasons; for example, often the volume of production is so great that it would be uneconomical to test each product sold. Also the product may lend itself to reasonably uniform production. In some cases, testing of each product could reduce its lifetime. In the case of some medical devices, testing would destroy the sterility.

A. Performance level safety factor and testing

In addition to being safe, products are designed and produced to function reliably at a specified advertised performance level. However, a well designed product will perform well beyond the advertised performance level. The ratio of failure level to the advertised performance level may be called the apparent safety factor, the magnitude of which may range from 2 to 10, depending on the type of product and its arena of application. When a product fails, the result can range from mild annoyance, property damage, bodily injury to death. Encountering a product failure raises the issue of reliability, with the circumstances surrounding the failure being scrutinized carefully by attorneys, expert witnesses and manufacturers. To investigate the failure, often a product identical to the failed product is selected and tested to failure. Figure 1.1 illustrates the type of result, which indicates an apparent safety factor of 2P / P = 2, where P is the advertised performance level. Although a useful concept, there is much more to the safety factor as will be demonstrated and we will show that there is a range of safety factors and the term itself is not easily defined.

B. Product variability

Even if the identical procedure is followed in making a product, no two units will be identical. Whether one is stamping out coins with a punch press or assembling components to create a device, the resulting products differ (e.g., in size, performance, etc.). The underlying principle is described by the distribution curve, which is a plot of the number (#) of units having a given performance level versus the performance level. The following simple example will illustrate this very useful concept.

Let us assume that we are making a product that has a design performance goal of 100. We make twenty units and measure the performance of each unit; Table 1.1 presents the result, revealing performance levels ranging from 50 to 155, the mean value being 108. If we had chosen a safety factor of 2.0, the simple advertised performance level would be 54, but there is more to the story. Although the mean performance value of 108 exceeds the design goal of 100, the mean value does not describe the range of performance level of each of the tested units.

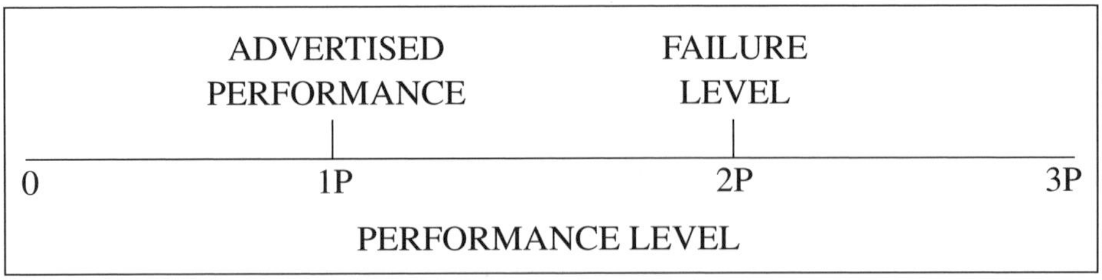

Figure 1.1 *Simplest concept of safety factor. The advertised performance level is P. The failure level is 2P; therefore the apparent safety factor is 2P / P = 2.0.*

A better way of examining the production result is shown in Figure 1.2 which is a bar graph (histogram) that arranges the measured performance levels into classes, e.g., 40 to 60, 60 to 80 etc. to 140 to 160. The vertical axis represents the number (#) of units falling in each class. The resulting histogram characterizes the performance distribution of all of the tested products.

There is a simple quantitative mathematical way of expressing the range of variability among the tested specimens. Note the bell shape of the curve in Figure 1.2, obtained by joining the mid points of the summits of the bars that represent the magnitudes in each performance class interval. Such a curve is known as a distribution curve, the width of which identifies the range of performance values.

C. Distribution curves

A large number of manufactured products fit what is called the normal Gaussian distribution curve. Such a curve gives equal weight to all measurements and assumes that small variations are more probable than large ones. Figure 1.3A illustrates the normal distribution curve which is a plot of the number (#) of samples having the value on the X axis. The mean is represented as zero to accommodate the definition of standard deviation (SD), to be defined subsequently. Note the general similarity of the curve in Figure 1.3A to that in Figure 1.2 in which the middle of the summits of the bar graphs have been

Table 1.1
Measured Performance Values

MEASURED VALUES	
50	113
65	117
75	121
82	126
85	130
90	135
101	139
103	145
105	155
107	Mean Value = 108

joined. Referring to Figure 1.3A, the important concept is the standard deviation (SD) which is a measure of the breadth of the distribution curve. The SD is defined as the square root of the sum of the squared individual differences from the mean, divided by the number of measurements (*n*), minus one. If many measurements, are made (*n*>>1), the divisor can be n. Figure 1.3A shows that between 1 and -1 SD from the mean (represented as zero), 68.27 percent, or roughly two thirds, of the measured values can be found. Obviously, the smaller the SD, the narrower the distribution of values about the mean. The factor that identifies the width of the distribution curve with respect to the mean is the coefficient of variance, defined as the ratio of the SD to the mean. A low value for this coefficient indicates a narrow distribution curve and reflects tight production control.

Not all production runs result in a normal distribution curve, as shown in Figure 1.3A, in which the curve is symmetrical about the mean. Distribution curves can be skewed to the right or left, as shown in Figures 1.3B and 1.3C. There are mathematical techniques for describing the breadths of these skewed curves. However, the important point to be recognized is that there is a performance distribution curve and its nature merits close examination when considering product safety.

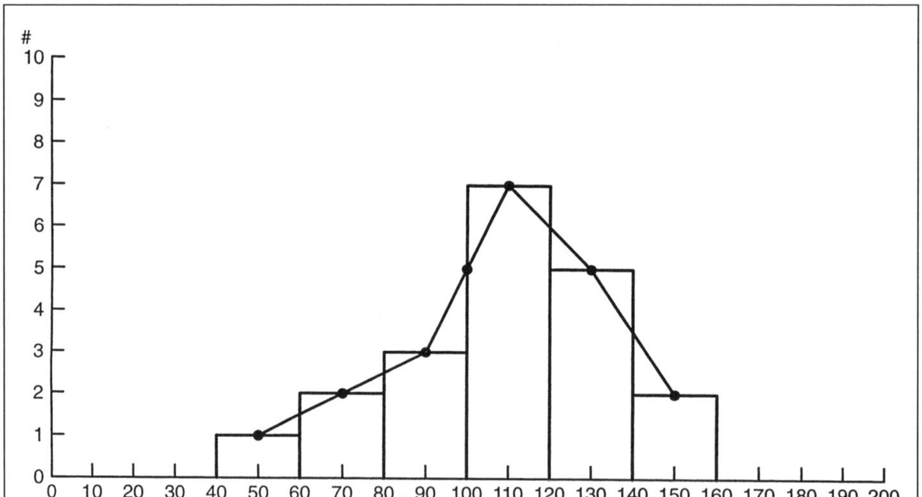

Figure 1.2 *Distribution of product performance levels represented by a histogram, in which the number (#) of units with a measured performance level is plotted against the performance level divided into classes of 20-unit intervals.*

D. Practical application of the distribution curve

We will now determine the SD for the performance data in Table 1.1. Table 1.2 summarizes the procedure and shows that the mean value is 108 and the sum of the squared deviations from the mean is 14,275. The number of units is 20; therefore, the

$$SD = \sqrt{14275 / (20 - 1)} = 26.1$$

Consequently, the coefficient of variance is 26.1/108 = 0.24.

The standard deviation of 26.1 means that if the values are normally distributed, 68.27 percent of the values will fall between the mean (108) ± 26. 1,

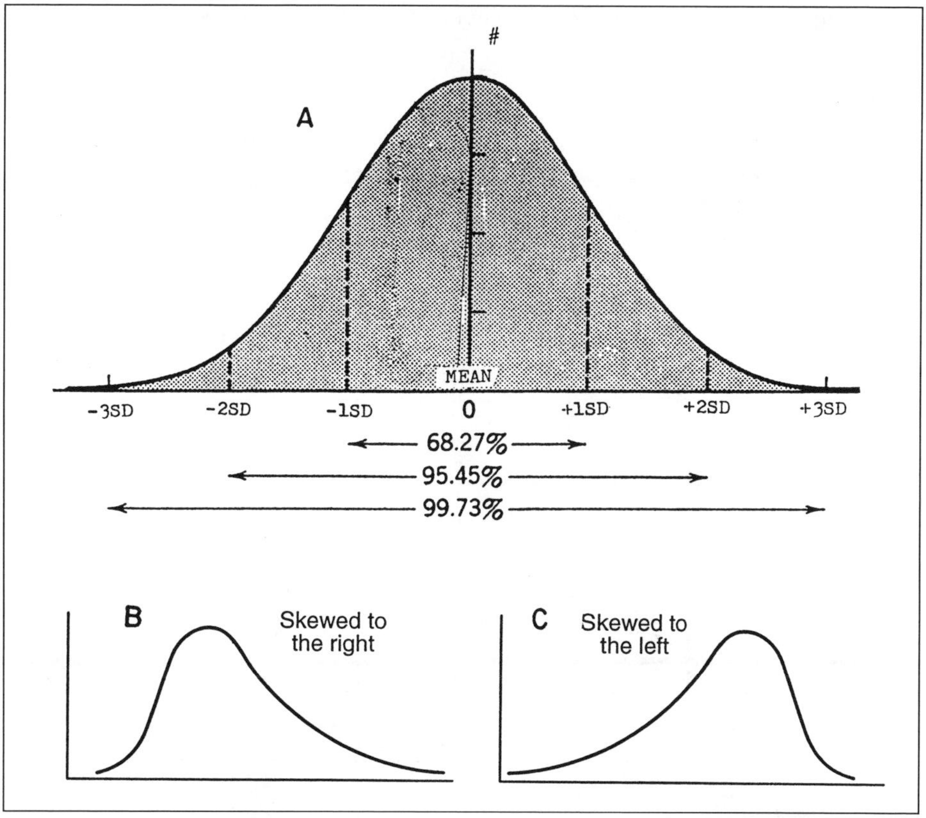

Figure 1.3 *The normal distribution curve (a) which represents the number (#) of units (Y axis) having the values on the X axis. The mean value is represented by zero and the spread of values about the mean is represented by the standard deviation (SD). When the SD is 1.0, 68.27 percent of the values will fall between the mean and ± one SD. Distribution curves skewed to the right (b) and left (c)*

namely 134 and 81.9; Figure 1.4 shows this result. It also means that there are products that lie outside of this range; 95.45 percent of the products are expected to lie between $108 \pm 2 \times 26.1$, namely 55.8 and 160. Similarly 99.73 percent of the products are expected to lie between $108 \pm 3 \times 26.1$, namely between 29.7 and 186; these values are shown in Figure 1.4.

It is now of value to compare the measured values presented in Figure 1.2 with those represented by the normal distribution curve. Figure 1.4 shows that 68.27 percent of the values are expected to fall between 81.9 and 134. From Figure 1.2, it is seen that 15/20 or 75 percent of the values fall between. 80 and 140. Similarly 95.45 percent of the values are expected to fall between 55.8 and 160 (Figure 1.4). In point of fact, (Figure 1.2), 19/20 or 95 percent of the values fall between 60 and 160. However, it also means that 5 percent will fall below 60 and above 160.

Table 1.2
Calculation of Standard Deviation (SD)

MEASURED VALUES	DIFFERENCE FROM MEAN	DIFFERENCE SQUARED
50	-58	3364
65	-43	1849
75	-33	1089
82	-26	676
85	-23	529
90	-18	324
101	-7	49
103	-5	25
105	-3	9
107	-1	1
111	+3	9
113	+5	25
117	+9	81
121	+13	169
126	+18	324
130	+22	484
135	+27	729
139	+31	961
145	+37	1369
155	+47	2209

$$\text{Standard Deviation} = \sqrt{14275/(20-1)} = 26.1$$

Recall that the design goal for the tested samples was 100 and the mean production value was 108. One standard deviation was 26.1; therefore these facts can be used to illustrate the choice of all advertised performance levels. Recognizing the bell shape of the distribution curve, it is desirable that a product with a performance level lying on the far left of the distribution curve should have a performance level exceeding the advertised performance level (P) for the product. Choosing three standard deviations from the mean (i.e,. $108 - 3 \times 26.1 = 29.7$), 30 would be a reasonable advertised performance level (P) where very few products would fail. Figure 1.5 shows that 29.1 (three SD below the mean) is very low on the left skirt of the distribution curve. However, it is necessary to remember that the distribution curve asymptotes to the *X* axis and although three standard deviations (i.e. where 99.72 percent of the samples lie), 0.27 percent of the specimens will fall outside of this range. Assuming symmetry to the distribution curve, one half (0. 135 percent) will have a performance level less than 29.7 which is encroaching on the advertised performance level (30). It follows therefore that a few samples will have a performance level less than 30, indicating that there is no perfect product and a choice must be made for the advertised performance level with the knowledge that a few products will ultimately fail. Figure 1.5 generalizes the concept in which the mean value is NP, N being the safety factor for an advertised performance level of P.

From the foregoing, two rules can be stated for the untested product: (1) the mean value for the tested specimens should be much higher than the adver-

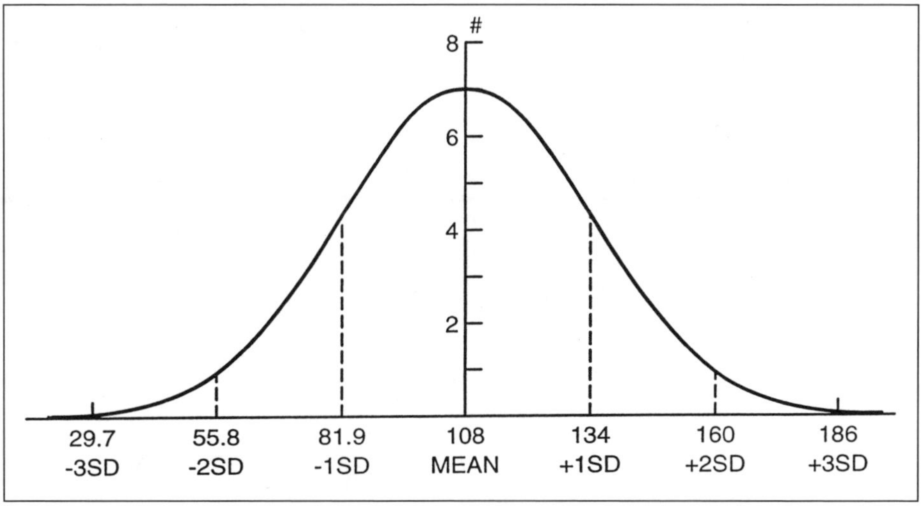

Figure 1.4 *Normal distribution curve applied to the measured data in Table 1.1*

tised performance level, and (2) the ratio of one SD to the mean, which is the coefficient of variance, should be small to assure a narrow distribution curve.

E. Choice of a safety factor

From the foregoing discussion, the choice of a mean safety factor involves many considerations that will be dependent on cost; that is, the higher the safety factor, the higher the cost of a product. Balanced against the desire to produce the best product is the price that competitors charge for the same product. Selling a product with a low safety factor invites the return and replacement to the customer. It also invites the cost of litigation due to possible harm, injury or death. Producing a product with a high safety factor may make the product noncompetitive in the marketplace. These are serious decisions that a manufacturer must face. In making such a decision, the manufacturer should recognize two scenarios: (1) use of the product is under control of the user, and (2) the user has no control over use of the product. In the first case, in which the user has control of use of the product the safety factor may be chosen on the basis of foreseeable misuse. If the likelihood of foreseeable misuse is high, it may be desirable to choose a high safety factor. If the user has no control over use of the product, as in the case of an automatic implanted device such as a cardiac pacemaker or ICD, the choice would favor a high safety factor.

1.10 Product Life

The earlier section on safety factors did not address the issue of product life. Although it maybe true that a high safety factor is expected to be associated with product longevity, this is not necessarily true. In fact, longevity and safety factors may be orthogonal quantities. What follows will address the issue of product lifetime and identify product history as an important predictor.

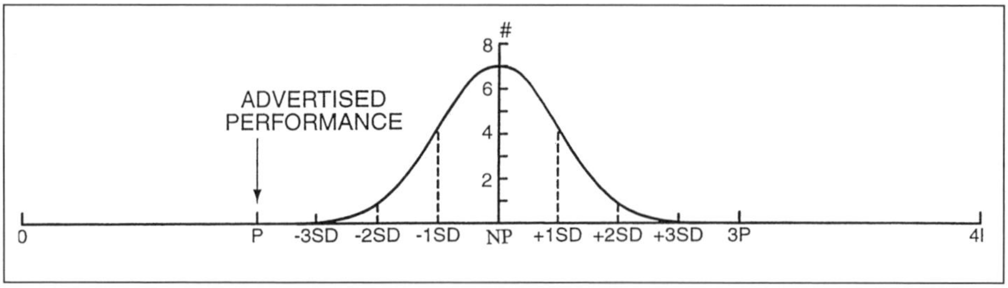

Figure 1.5 *A normal distribution curve placed with its mean centered on NP, N times the performance level. Note that if the standard deviation (SD) is large, some units may have a performance level less than P, the advertised value.*

We live at a time when products are used only once and then discarded, examples of which are disposable syringes, needles, examining gloves, razors and electrodes. Reuse invites the risk of accident or injury. Other products must be used before all expiry dates, familiar examples being drugs, photographic and x-ray film and items in sterilized packages. Some products have a limit on the number of uses, labeling in such cases state "good for X activations or uses;" this caution may or may not include an expiry date. The term half life may appear on a label and means that by the indicated time, half of the activity or potency will have been lost. Because such degradation tends to be exponential in nature, the term time constant (τ) is used and is defined as the time (τ) taken for the quantity to fall to 37 percent ($1/e$) of its initial (time zero) value. The half-life time is equal to 70 percent of the time constant τ.

Some products degrade in other ways. The term shelf life is frequently applied and refers to the fact that after the indicated time on the shelf, the product will not perform as a new product, despite the fact that it has never been used. This term arose in the early days of electrochemical batteries (dry cells).

Notwithstanding the foregoing situations, many products can be purchased with no time limit label and the purchaser's expectation is that the product will last and perform for a long time without attention. However, a different example is the automobile, which requires maintenance and repair for long-term service. The issue of expected lifetime for a product arises when it fails to meet the user's expectation for service. Statements such as "I only used it X times" or "I only had it for Y weeks and used it once" are common complaints. Dealing with these situations requires careful scrutiny of the warning and cautionary labels and the instruction manual.

Many medical products last a very long time, examples being common surgical instruments such as hemostats, clamps, clips and scissors. However many medical devices such as electrical cables and endoscopes, have a shorter life, especially those subject to steam sterilization. An interesting category of medical devices, which has a life expectancy that depends on the amount of therapy that it delivers to a patient, is the cardiac pacemaker and the automatic implanted cardioverter defibrillator (ICD), the latter being designed to deliver a specified number of shocks (typically 100). Performance history of prior units is a useful tool in predicting probable life.

Life expectancy analysis resides in the field of industrial engineering which provides mathematical tools for estimating the probable life expectancy based on historical data. However, life expectancy is defined as the time when one half of the original group of identical products produced by the same manufacturer will fail and this time does not pertain to an individual product. The life span for an individual product is as difficult to quantify as it is to predict the lifetime of an individual human. However, statistical analysis of the life spans of previously sold, individual products produced by the same manufacturer provides the best assessment of the range of life spans. One hundred percent reliability is an unattainable goal.

Performance history data are available for a large variety of devices from the U.S. Returned Product Analysis files. To illustrate the type of information, the data for single-chamber cardiac pacemakers was selected. The modern single-chamber cardiac pacemaker delivers a stimulus to the ventricles only on demand, i.e. it monitors the electrical activity of the ventricles on a beat-by-beat basis, and if a beat does not occur at a preselected time after the last beat, it delivers a stimulus. This device is called a demand (VVI) pacemaker. Obviously, if no spontaneous beats occur, the pacemaker keeps on delivering stimuli to pace the heart. Therefore the life of the battery contained therein will be very long if the pacemaker does not deliver many stimuli and shorter if it stimulates frequently. The battery is never replaced; the pacemaker is replaced and the time for replacement is determined by the end of life (EOL), which is identified in either of two ways: (1) by the magnet rate which is determined by placing a magnet on the skin over the pacemaker and measuring the resulting pacing rate. The manual that accompanies the pacemaker identifies the magnet rate for pacemaker replacement. (2) Programmed interrogation of the battery voltage is achieved by placing a programming wand on the skin over the pacemaker and reading the display on the programmer. The instruction manual identifies the voltage when the pacemaker should be replaced. Battery depletion is not a pacemaker failure; it is a natural accompaniment to pacemaker use.

Actuarial pacemaker survival rates have been selected from data for over one million registered pacemaker implantations. Only data from manufacturers who reported over 5,000 implants have been included. Table 1.3 presents the summary for different models (A–Z) of single-chamber pacemakers. The number of implants and the percent survival rates are shown for one, five, ten, twelve, fourteen and sixteen years. It is evident that with the passage of time, the percent survival decreases, but very little out to five years. By ten years, the survival rates decrease noticeably.

The foregoing clearly illustrates that modern cardiac pacemakers are extremely well made and reliable, despite the fact that they operate in a hostile environment, i.e. body fluids at 37°C.

In conclusion, the best predictor for the lifetime of a product is its past history. Actuarial data of the type presented here for cardiac pacemakers needs to be sought for the product of interest.

Table 1.3
Percent Survival for Single Chamber Pacemakers

Product	Registered Implants	Percent Survival (Years 1-16)					
		1	5	10	12	14	16
A	24,911	99.9	99.6	95.8	90.5	87.2	
B	107,190	99.9	99.4	93.1	84.7	77.2	66.9
C	111,157	99.9	99.6	95.3	89.7	82.0	75.6
D	5,270	99.9	93.8	73.9	69.4		
E	27,876	99.9	99.0	89.9	81.9		
F	58,452	99.9	99.5	94.6			
G	6,919	99.9					
H	52,456	99.9	99.4				
I	26,649	99.9	97.7	47.0			
J	57,041	99.9	99.2	92.0			
K	58,434	99.9	99.6				
L	14,016	99.9					
M	41,381	100.					
N	14,466	99.9					
O	12,436	100.					
P	45,524	99.9	93.5	47.2	28.0		
Q	8,360	99.9	94.1	40.0			
R	21,635	99.9	95.2	44.2			
S	47,673	99.9	99.6				
T	57,297	99.9	95.3				
U	16,731	100.	99.5				
V	29,443	99.9	99.1				
W	102,953	99.9					
X	26,448	99.9					
Y	18,546	100.					
Z	19,063	99.9					

1.11 Medical Device Reports

In 1990, the U.S. Congress passed the Safe Medical Devices Act (SMDA), which went into effect on May 28, 1992 and was amended in 1995. This act and amendments mandated the reporting of incidents associated with medical devices. Such incidents must be reported to the FDA in the form of a Medical Device Report (MDR). In 1999 the name of the report was changed to MAUDE (Manufacturer And User Device Experience). MDRs and MAUDE reports are available from the FDA and contain a wealth of information on medical device accidents.

The FDA regulation for reporting incidents was published in the Federal Register of December 11, 1995 (21 CFR 803 and 807). This document clarifies and expands existing requirements for medical device manufacturers and health care facilities. Failure to comply with this rule can result in increased risk of liability and civil penalty.

In February 1996, the Emergency Care Research Institute (ECRI) summarized the reporting requirements mandated by the Safe Medical Devices Act. The highlights of the reporting requirements are:

Health care facilities must submit a report whenever they receive or otherwise become aware of information, from any source, that reasonably suggests that a device has or may have caused or contributed to a death or serious injury.

The term "serious injury" is defined as an injury or illness that:

1. Is life threatening
2. Results in permanent impairment of a body function or permanent damage to a body structure or
3. Necessitates medical or surgical intervention to preclude permanent impairment of a body function or permanent damage to a body structure

Required to report are the following:

1. Hospital, ambulatory surgical facilities, nursing homes, home-health agencies, ambulance providers, rescue groups, skilled nursing facilities, rehabilitation facilities, hospices, psychiatric facilities, and all other outpatient treatment and diagnostic facilities that are not a physician's office
2. Manufacturers of medical devices
3. Distributors of medical devices (at present, covered by a different regulation)

Special forms are used to report device-related incidents. The report must be made within ten working days of knowledge of the incident.

1.12 Chemical Accidents

Sometimes an accident is associated with the use of a chemical compound or a substance classified as a drug. Such accidents must be reported. In such cases, valuable information can be found in the Materials Safety Data Sheet (MSDS), the Drug Insert (DI), and the *Physician's Desk Reference* (PDR). The address for the latter is P.O. Box 10689, Des Moines, IA, 50336-0689. The MSDS can be obtained directly from the manufacturer or the following:

Canadian Center for Occupation Health and Safety
CCOHS
250 Main Street, E.
Hamilton, Ontario, Canada L8N 1H6
1-800-668-4284

Genium Publishing Corp.
145 Catalyn Street
Schenectady, NY 12303
1-518-377-8854

The MSDS provides the correct name of the chemical substance, along with any synonym and brand name, the chemical composition, and physical and chemical properties. Fire, explosion and health hazards are given, along with first aid information. Reactivity and environmental factors, along with disposal techniques, are described. The sheet concludes with special precautions regarding use, storage, and handling procedures.

The Drug Insert is the data sheet that comes in the drug package. It lists indications, contraindications, side effects, toxicity, and antidotes. The PDR contains similar indicators and is indexed alphabetically by product name, product category, generic name, and chemical name. The PDR also provides an alphabetical listing of drug manufacturers.

The information provided by the sources identified may allow consideration of the foreseeability of an accident, the possibility of misuse, or uninformed use of a chemical substance.

1.13 The Incident Report

An incident report is a document that describes an event or events that caused harm, injury, or death to a patient. Such a report is composed at the time of or just after the incident by those present. The incident report does not assign culpability to anyone. On the contrary, it describes the incident in unambiguous language and often includes sketches showing the location of equipment and personnel. Healthcare facilities routinely complete and file incident reports, which are used by the institution to investigate the incident and promulgate rules or procedures to avoid such incidents. Because this document is composed by personnel on the scene at the time of the incident, it is very useful in contributing to an understanding of how the incident occurred. Incident reports are generally available to attorneys in a lawsuit. Over a fifteen-year period I have been denied an incident report only once.

1.14 Product Liability Future

In the ideal world, the manufacturer provides a product that meets all applicable standards and is safe to use. It has been designed to avoid all foreseeable hazards in use and the instruction manual describes the intended purpose and use. The manual also contains a warranty, appropriate cautions, and warnings, along with information on service. There is no misrepresentation in the advertising. The vendor receives the product and conveys it to the customer in the same condition that it left the manufacturer's supervision. The manufacturer exercises a duty of due care to the customer.

The customer, who is a prudent and reasonable person, reads the instruction manual then becomes a user of the product with safety and satisfaction. However, we live in a real world of rapidly expanding technology and a breakdown of one or more of the foregoing steps originates litigation.

It is likely that product development rate will exceed the recognition of a foreseeable hazard despite the regulatory requirements for inspection and testing. It often takes a long time for a defect to be revealed. It takes even longer to promulgate regulations that will eliminate the defect and the hazard.

References and Bibliography

AAMI (Association for the Advancement of Medical Instrumentation). 3330 Washington Blvd., Arlington, VA 22201-4598.

Althaus JA. Treatise on Medical Electricity. 1873. Presley Blakiston, Philadelphia.

American National Standards Institute. 11 W. 42nd Street, New York 10036.

American Society for Quality Control. 161 West Wisconsin Avenue, Milwaukee, WI 53203.

Beard GM and Rockwell AD. On the Medical and Surgical Uses of Electricity. 8th edition. 1891. W. Wood & Co., New York.

Canadian Standard Association. 235 Montreal Road, Ottawa 7, Ontario, Canada.

Capuano M, Misole P and Davidson D. Patient coupled device interaction produces arrhythmia-like artifact on electrocardiographs. Biomed. Inst. Technol. 1993, November–December: 475–483.

Department of Health and Human Services, FDA. Docket 91N-0295. Federal Register. 1995, 60(237) December 11.

ECRI Emergency Care Research Institute ECRI Advisory. February 1996. Safe Medical Device Act. ECRI, 5200 Butler Pike, Plymouth Meeting, PA 19462

Enghagen LK. Fundamentals of Product Liability Law for Engineers. 1992, Industrial Press, Inc., New York.

FDA MAUDE Report July 6, 1998.

Federal Register. March 9, 1976.

Food and Drug Administration (FDA), Gaither Rd., MD 20850.

Geddes LA. A short history of electrical stimulation of excitable tissue including therapeutic applications. Physiologist (Suppl.) 1984, 22(l):S1-47.

Health Devices Alert 1999, 23, R9: 7–8. ECRI, Plymouth Meeting, PA.

International Electro Technical Commission (IEC). Centre du Service Clientele (CSC) Commission Electrotechnique Intenationale 3, rue de Varembe Case postale 131 CH I211, Geneve 20 (Geneva) Suisse (Switzerland.).

ISMP. See ECRI Health Devices, 2000, 21:11, ECRI, Plymouth Meeting, PA.

McCaughey W. A wee problem in dental surgery. Anesthesia. 1992, 47 (3):280.

Medical Malpractice Verdicts, Settlements and Experts 2000. 16(5):7–8.

National Electrical Code, National Fire Protection Association (NFPA). Battery Park, P.O. Box 9146, Quincy, MA 02269-9959.

Sattari R. Temporary malfunction of the Ohmeda Modules (1) series volume monitor caused by the overhead surgical lighting. Anesthesiol. 1999, 894–895.

Silberberg J. What can/should we learn from reports of medical device electromagnetic interference?, at Electromagnetics, Health Care and Health, EMBS 95. September 19–20, 1995. Standards Promulgating Organizations, Montreal, Canada.

Underwriters Laboratories, Inc. 207 East Ohio Street, Chicago, IL 60611.

U.S. Food and Drug Administration. Center for Devices and Radiological Health. 12720 Twinbrook Parkway, Rockville, MD 20857.

Chapter 2

Electromagnetic Interference and Electrostatic Discharge

2.1 Introduction

Electromagnetic interference (EMI) is the term used to describe malfunction of a device exposed to electromagnetic waves which have the property of propagating through space. That such high-frequency waves have this property was predicted by Maxwell in 1873. In 1888, Hertz demonstrated the accuracy of this prediction by generating them with a spark-gap transmitter. It was Marconi in 1903 who put this property to practical use to create wireless telegraphy, followed in 1906 by the first transmission of the human voice by Fessenden. Both events gave rise to modern communications.

The frequency spectrum for electromagnetic waves ranges from the low-kilohertz range to thousands of gigahertz. The term hertz (Hz) replaced the old term "cycles per second." Table 2.1 identifies the terms used to designate the spectral bands. Various services are assigned to operate in these bands. In the U.S., the Federal Communications Commission issues the licenses to use the assigned frequencies. There are international treaties regarding the use of frequencies.

Table 2.1
Nomenclature of Frequency Bands

Frequency Range		Designation
30 to 300 hertz	ELF	Extremely low frequency
300 to 3000 hertz	VF	Voice frequency
3 to 30 kilohertz	VLF	Very low frequency
30 to 300 kilohertz	LF	Low frequency
300 to 3000 kilohertz	MF	Medium frequency
3 to 30 megahertz	HF	High frequency
30 to 300 megahertz	VHF	Very high frequency
300 to 3000 megahertz	UHF	Ultra high frequency
3 to 30 gigahertz	SHF	Super high frequency
30 to 300 gigahertz	EHF	Extremely high frequency
300 to 3000 gigahertz	—	—
3 terahertz		

EMI is ubiquitous; the intensity is measured in volts/meter at a particular frequency. EMI is strongest in the urban areas where there is a plethora of communications equipment. Bassen et al. (1992) stated:

> More than 1 percent of the U.S. population is exposed to ambient field strengths of more than 2 V/m by FM radio and VHF television broadcast transmitters operating in the 54 to 108 MHz frequency range. This information is especially significant in light of the existing requirements for RF susceptibility of medical devices. Present and proposed new Electromagnetic Compatibility (EMC) standards require immunity to field strengths of 1 to 3 V/m in this frequency range. Therefore, the effects of patient connection need to be accounted for in new medical device EMC standards.

Medical devices can be influenced in many ways by electromagnetic radiation. Such devices can fail to operate or operate improperly, depending on the intensity, frequency, and type of modulation. EMI can be produced by communications equipment (radio, TV, cellular phones, pagers, etc.), arcing contacts, flashing lights, household appliances, video monitors, computers, electro-surgical and diathermy machines, etc. Those devices that produce intermittent bursts of EMI are the most troublesome; however, those that produce a constant level of EMI can also cause device malfunction by saturation.

It is not difficult to test a device for susceptibility to EMI. By such tests it can be determined to what frequency range it is sensitive and at what intensity (volts/meter). With this information, it is useful to determine if emitters producing this spectral range are in the environment, thereby making it possible to launch a fruitful investigation.

EMI can enter an electronic device by many different paths. For example, if the device is battery operated, EMI can gain easy access to electronic circuits if the cabinet housing is unshielded. If a cable or a fluid-filled catheter connects the patient to the medical device, the patient and the connections can constitute an antenna. If the device is power-line operated, EMI can enter via the power line. If the device is battery operated and connected to a power-line-driven battery charger, EMI can enter via the power line.

2.2 Sources of EMI

Any emitter of radio frequency (electromagnetic) energy is a potential source of EMI. As stated previously, whether the source interferes or not depends on the frequency, type of modulation, intensity at the medical device, and its susceptibility. Various types of emitters are in the environment and the following identifies some of the more common types.

A. Radio broadcasting

Although the first radio broadcasts used 50 and 100 kHz, the present amplitude modulation (AM) broadcast band extends from 535 to 1605 kHz, each station being spaced by 10k Hz. Below 535 kHz is reserved for navigational aids. There are numerous short-wave broadcast bands that employ AM; these range in frequency from 5.95 to about 60 MHz.

The frequency modulation (FM) broadcast band extends from 88 to 108 MHz. Radio station WWV broadcasts (AM) standard time and frequency information day and night; 1/sec pulses and several constant tone frequencies are emitted at 2.5, 5, 10, 15, and 20 MHz.

B. Television

The frequencies allocated for television broadcasting are designated as channels. The picture information is transmitted using amplitude modulation and the sound channels employ frequency modulation. Channels 1 to 6 occupy the frequency range from 54 to 88 MHz; channels 7 to 83 broadcast in the frequency range of 174–890 MHz. Each channel is separated from its neighbor by 5 MHz.

C. Public safety (police, fire, highway, forestry, and emergency services)

Public safety services have assigned frequencies from 1605–2850 kHz, 3.1–3.4 MHz, and channels assigned in the frequency range of 30.56–459 MHz.

D. Land transportation (taxis, trucks, buses, railroads)

These services have channels assigned in the frequency range from 30 to 458 MHz.

E. Amateur radio

Table 2.2 identifies the frequencies assigned to amateur radio operators. Many different types of modulation are permitted in the amateur bands, providing the sidebands are limited to those specified by the FCC. Amateur radio operators require a license.

Table 2.2
Amateur Radio Frequencies

1800–2000 kHz	420.0–450.0 MHz
3.500–4.000 MHz	1215–1300 MHz
7.000–7.300 MHz	2300–2450 MHz
14.00–14.35 MHz	3.300–3.350 GHz
21.00–21.45 MHz	5.650–5.925 GHz
28.00–29.70 MHz	10.00–10.50 GHz
50.00–54.00 MHz	21.00–22.00 GHz
144.0–148.0 MHz	40.00-88.00 GHz
220.00–225.0 MHz	Above 90.00 GHz

F. Cellular phones and paging systems

In 1996, Hayes et al. reported that there were 50 million cell phone subscribers in the USA and predicted that this number would increase to above 100 million by the year 2000, thereby increasing the amount of environmental EMI. The frequency spectrum for cell phones extends from 824 to 893 MHz. Paging systems occupy the 35-454 MHz range; some are one-way and others are two-way systems; all are potential EMI sources.

G. Industrial, scientific, and medical

Radio frequency current is used for a variety of purposes in industry and medicine and specific frequencies have been allocated for these uses. Table 2.3 identifies these frequencies. The lower frequencies (13.56 and 27.12 MHz) are used for short-wave diathermy in which body segments are heated. In some countries 915 MHz is used for diathermy. Microwave diathermy uses 2450 MHz; this frequency is also used for microwave ovens.

Electrosurgical units emit frequencies ranging from 0.5 to 2 MHz. This frequency range covers the standard AM broadcast band and there is no assigned frequency for this intermittent medical use.

Table 2.3
Industrial, Scientific and Medical Equipment

MHz
13.56
27.12
40.68 (government)
915.0 (government)
2450

H. Citizens' band (CB) radio

The FCC has assigned two frequency bands for citizens to use for communication; they are 26.96 to 27.23 MHz and 462.525 to 467.475 MHz. A license is not needed to operate a CB radio but the power is limited to permit only short-range communication.

I. Radar

Radar employs repetitive short bursts of high-frequency electromagnetic radiation to locate the distance of a target using the pulse-echo technique. The frequencies used range from 3 MHz to 110 GHz, depending on the type of information sought. However, frequencies from 1 to 100 GHz are common. The pulse repetition rate used depends on the target distance. Electromagnetic waves travel in space at the rate of 186,000 mi/sec, or 982 ft/μsec. Therefore, a target at a 982-ft distance would return an echo in 2 μsec. In general, the pulse repetition rate in most cases is low.

2.3 Frequency, Wavelength, and Antenna Effect

Associated with frequency is wavelength, which in meters equals 300/frequency in MHz. The significance of wavelength becomes important when the length of the conductor approaches one quarter wavelength or more, which creates a reasonably good antenna. One meter is equal to 39.4 inches.

2.4 Skin Depth

In a uniform conductor direct current is distributed evenly over the cross section of the conductor. When sinusoidal alternating current flows in a uniform conductor, the current distribution becomes nonuniform As the frequency is increased, the current density at the perimeter increases. The term "skin depth" is used to quantitate this phenomenon. Skin depth is that distance from the perimeter where the current density has fallen to 1/e, or 37 percent of that at the surface. Skin depth has nothing to do with the dermis. Skin depth (*S*) is calculated:

$$S = \frac{1}{2\pi}\sqrt{\frac{10^8 \rho}{\mu f}}$$

where ρ is the resistivity (ohm-cm), μ is the permeability (1.0), and f is the frequency (Hz). Rearranging this expression yields:

$$S = 5033\ \sqrt{\rho / f}$$

Note that the skin depth depends on the resistivity (ρ ohm.cm) of the conductor and inversely with frequency (f in Hz). It is of more than passing interest to calculate skin depth for a metal, such as copper, and for biological material. Copper has a resistivity of 1.6×10^{-6} ohm-cm; therefore the skin depth in centimeters is $6.36 / \sqrt{f}$. Consequently, the skin depth is small in good conductors. In fact, high-frequency conductors are often made of tubing.

It is of interest to calculate the skin depth for tissue ($\rho = 500$ ohm-cm) exposed to a typical radar frequency (2.5×10^9 Hz). Entering these values into the skin-depth equation yields a skin depth of 2.25 cm.

2.5 Modulation

Information is superimposed on a radio frequency carrier and recovered at the receiving site. In general, there are two types of modulation: (1) amplitude and (2) frequency. Figure 2.1a illustrates an unmodulated carrier of frequency f_c and Figure 2.1b illustrates the signal that is to be applied to the carrier. Figure 2.1c illustrates the resulting 100 percent amplitude-modulated carrier. In this case, the peak amplitude of the modulated carrier is twice that of the unmodulated carrier. The modulation amplitude can range from 0 to 100 percent. At the receiving site, the modulation is stripped from the carrier, the radio frequency energy that travels through space.

Another type of amplitude modulation is shown in Figure 2.1d in which the carrier is turned on and off. This is the kind of signal used in wireless telegraphy and radar. Figure 2.1d represents the letter S in the Morse code (three dots). The spacing and duration of the modulated carrier can be selected to conform to any desired coding scheme.

There is an inconsistency in modulation terms that arose with the passage of time. Originally a carrier that was modulated by the voice was designated

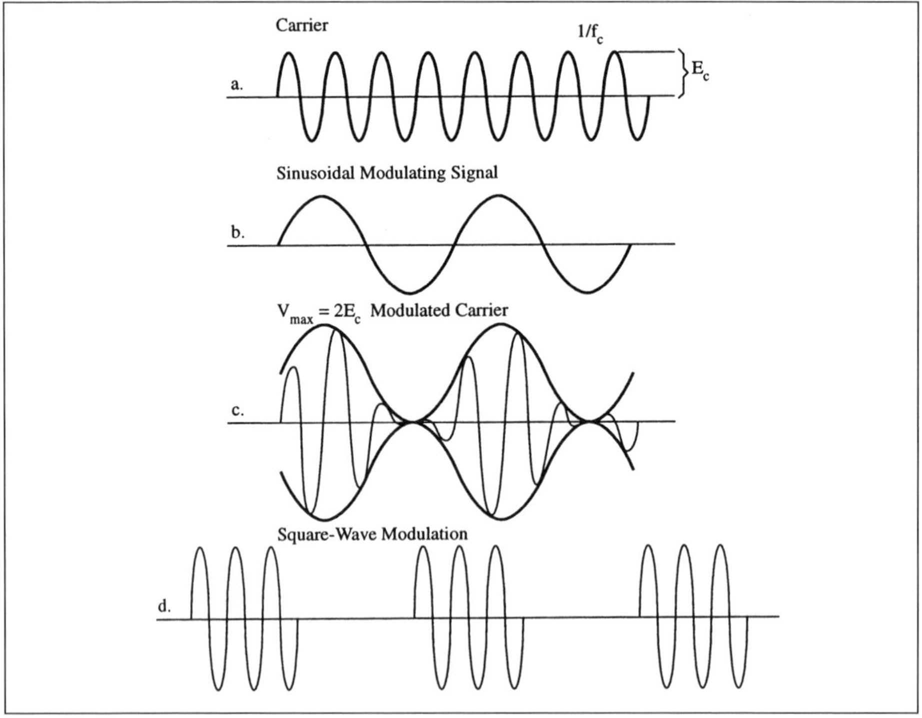

***Figure 2.1** Amplitude modulation*

wireless telephony. A carrier that was keyed on and off (Figure 2.1d) was called continuous wave (CW) by the radio amateurs and others. Nowadays continuous wave is used for an unmodulated carrier (Figure 2.1a).

Figure 2.2 illustrates frequency modulation of a carrier (a) by a sinusoidal modulating signal (b), resulting in the frequency-modulated carrier (c). In this case the frequency of the carrier is linearly related to the amplitude of the modulating signal, increasing and decreasing as the modulating signal goes positive, then negative. If the modulating signal is a rectangular pulse, the carrier frequency will suddenly increase, then decrease. In all cases, the amplitude of the carrier is constant.

2.6 Examples of Device Malfunction Due to EMI

The type of EMI produced by the various emitters of radio frequency energy varies widely. Those sources that are turned on and off are the most troublesome. For example, cellular and mobile telephones, paging systems, emergency services (ambulance, fire and police), amateur radio, taxi radio, walkie-talkies, and several other types of communications are characterized by frequent, short periods of communication. Diathermy is turned on for about

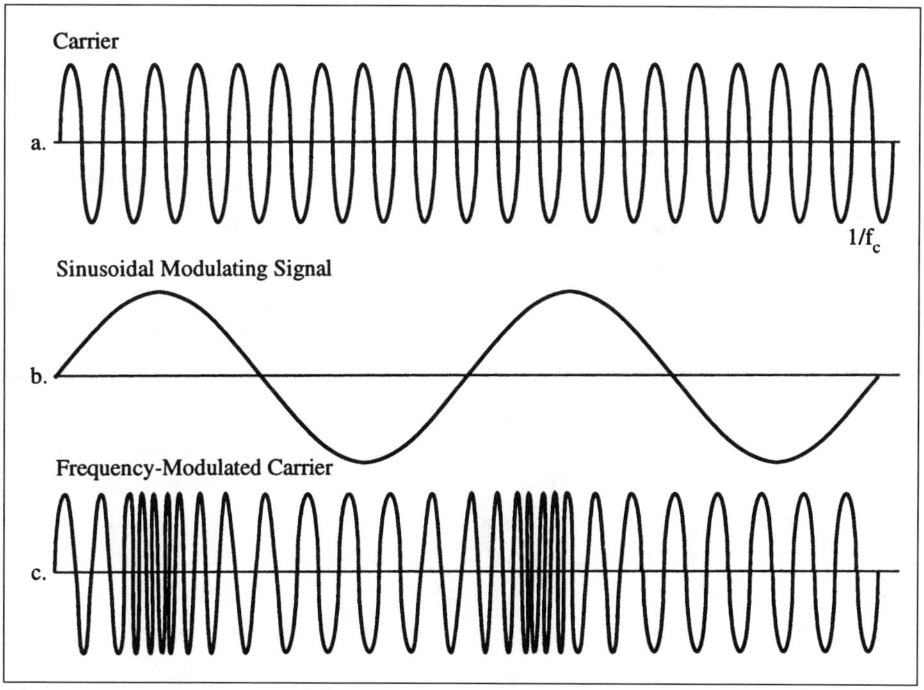

Figure 2.2 *Frequency modulation*

twenty to thirty minutes, whereas electrosurgical units are activated for only a few seconds each time cutting or coagulation is desired. Navigational devices vary widely in the type of radio frequency signals that they emit; some operate at relatively low pulse frequencies, while others use high-frequency bursts of carrier. Devices that emit bursts of radio frequency energy can simulate heartbeats, respiration, brainwave signals, or can even reprogram devices such as pacemakers, drug-delivery devices, ventilators, etc.

A. Patient simulator

EMI can be detected and interfere with devices connected to electrodes on a patient; examples of such are the EEG, EMG, ECG, impedance-based apnea monitors, etc. To investigate the susceptibility of such devices to EMI where they are used, it is practical to connect a patient simulator to the device. A simulator could be as simple as a resistor, or a calibrator that produces a known voltage or resistance change. The simulator should be capable of producing no signal as well as the signal appropriate for the device being tested. When the simulator is connected and no simulator signal is applied, the device should register no output; if it does, EMI is suspected. In the absence of a patient simulator, it is practical to use an easily created circuit, which, of course, produces no output, and when connected to the device, no signal will be registered in the absence of EMI. The following describes such passive simulators.

B. Electrical equivalent for a subject

For a variety of reasons it is useful to have an electrical analog for the circuit formed when electrodes are placed on a subject. Such an analog (Z) evolved from 60-Hz leakage testing and it is sometimes called a patient dummy load or a patient simulator. The simplest equivalent for Z (Figure 2.3a) is a 500- or 1000-ohm resistor. The 500-ohm value was derived from the 60-Hz impedance of the body in good contact with ground. The 1000-ohm value was recommended by the National Fire Protection Association (NFPA, 76BM-3042).

The Association for the Advancement of Medical Instrumentation (AAMI) developed a standard circuit (Figure 2.3b) which exhibits a decreasing impedance with increasing frequency, as shown in Figure 2.4. At DC, the impedance is 1000 ohms; the impedance is very slightly less than 10 ohms at infinite frequency. The impedance at 60 Hz is a fraction of a percent below 1000 ohms.

Figure 2.3a illustrates the circuit recommended by the Canadian Standards Association (C22.2, 1979). The impedance-frequency characteristic of this cir-

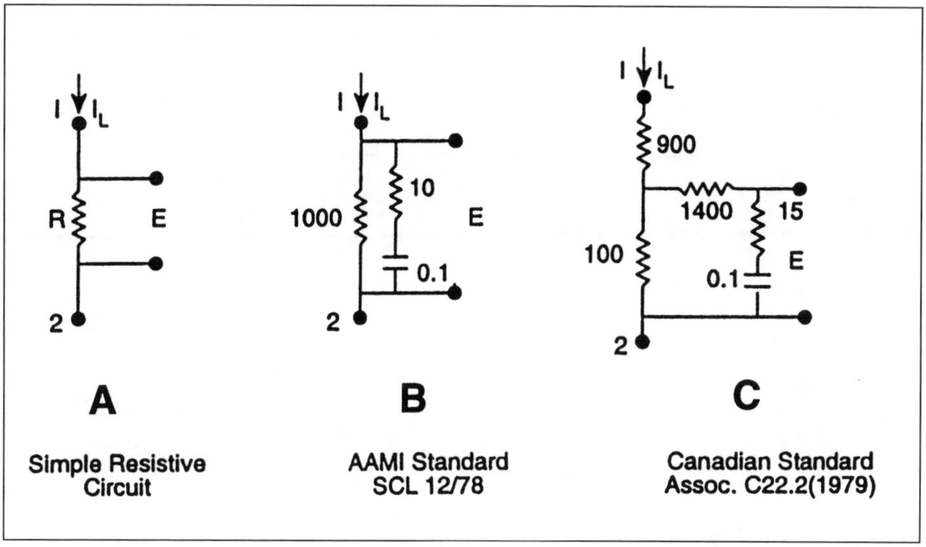

Figure 2.3 *Equivalent circuits for a pair of electrodes on a subject*

cuit is illustrated in Figure 2.4. The impedance decreases only slightly with frequency, starting out at 1000 ohms at 0 Hz and decreasing to 993 ohms at infinite frequency.

Not only are the circuits shown in Figure 2.3 useful for leakage-current testing, they are of value as a patient dummy connected to an ECG or impedance-respiration monitor. Because these three circuits are entirely passive—no output, i.e., a flat line will appear when connected to patient monitors. These equivalents do not apply when high current is applied to electrodes such as in defibrillation.

A saline filled, full-sized, plastic torso model of the body was described by Bassen et al. (1992). The model consisted of a plastic rectangular box (80 × 40 × 22 cm) with two cylindrical legs. Each leg had a diameter of 13 cm and a length of 86 cm. These legs were parallel to each other and attached to one end of the box in which 13-cm-diameter holes were cut. The model was originally developed for testing the susceptibility of pacemakers to electromagnetic pulses. Bassen et al. (1992) used the model to test the susceptibility of apnea monitors to EMI.

C. Electroencephalographic interference

Silbert et al. (1994) reported the first instance of EMI interference while recording the EEG:

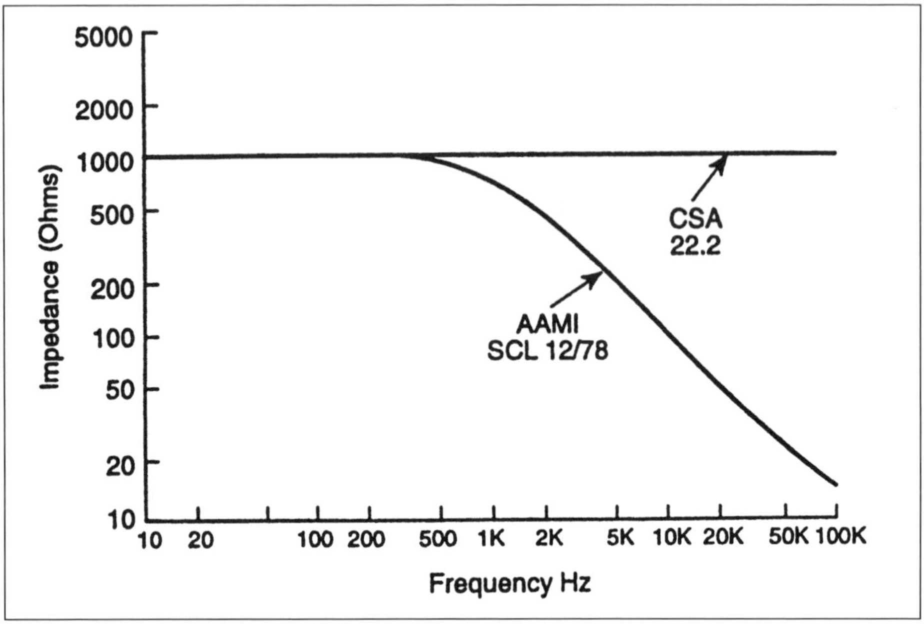

Figure 2.4 *Impedance-frequency characteristics of the AAMI SCL 1278 and the CSA 22.2 equivalent circuits*

> A four-year-old boy was referred to the Mayo Clinic EEG laboratory for evaluation of generalized tonic-clonic seizures. The recording was performed on a 16-channel Grass electroencephalograph, using collodion application of electrodes, a high frequency filter of 70 Hz, a low frequency filter of 1 Hz, and a paper speed of 30 mm/sec. During the procedure both parents were present in the same recording room as the patient and the technologist. After approximately three minutes of recording, an unusual artifact appeared, which then recurred approximately every 40–120 seconds. The technologist was suspicious of an extrinsic electrical artifact, although no obvious source in the vicinity was apparent. She then asked the parents if they were carrying anything unusual. In fact, both had cellular telephones which were turned on, but had not rung or otherwise been used. Upon removal of the cellular telephones from the recording room to approximately twenty feet away, no further artifacts occurred. The recording, which demonstrated generalized epileptiform activity, was completed without further incident.

Silbert et al. carried out additional studies with different types of EEG machines using a Motorola DPC 550 cellular telephone. They stated that similar EEG artifacts were observed with other cellular telephones. They reported that:

> When the telephone was turned off, no artifact could be identified. When the telephone was turned on, but not otherwise being used, an "autonomous registration artifact" was seen recurring up to every forty seconds. The artifact was present in several widely separated derivations (leads), varied in duration from 0.5 to 1.5 seconds, and was characterized by a series of spikes of 50 msec duration separated by 70–100 msec.

The foregoing demonstrates that when a cellular telephone is on and awaiting a call, it emits EMI autonomous pulses. Pulses are also emitted when the telephone is turned on and off. Such spikes occurring in an EEG record could lead to misdiagnosis.

Additional information on the effects of EMI on medical devices due to cellular telephones will be presented elsewhere in this chapter.

D. Electrocardiographic interference

ECG recordings are susceptible to EMI from a variety of sources. The type of malfunction ranges from artifacts that resemble cardiac excitations to complete inhibition of the recording. The reporting sources range from investigative journalism to clinical engineering and medical records.

Writing in the *Wall Street Journal* on ECG malfunction, Knutson and Bulkeley (1994) reported:

> Michael Willingham, director of regulatory affairs for Physio-Control, says the radio waves were the source of the problem. He says company engineers discovered that the ambulance maker had replaced the metal roof of the vehicle with a fiberglass dome that didn't block radio waves well—then placed a powerful, long-range radio-transmission antenna atop it. Mr. Willingham says this is the only incident of its type involving LifePak (a defibrillator that contains an ECG).
>
> In 1992, a doctor installed an apparently unnecessary pacemaker in a patient's chest after an electrocardiogram telemetry system made by SpaceLabs Inc., also of Redmond, displayed "long periods of flat line." That evening, the same phenomenon recurred. Nurses discovered that the patient was next to a TV set when the flat line occurred. "Current labeling has warning about TV interference with telemetry signals," SpaceLabs reported to the FDA.

> "We've had only two or three instances of problems with EMI," says John Hall, vice president of quality assurance at SpaceLabs. "Another kind of diagnostic would normally be done before implanting a pacemaker", he adds, "but the company can't tell people how to practice medicine."
>
> Physio-Control Corp., then an Eli Lilly Corp., Redmond, WA reported medical technicians taking a ninety-three-year-old heart-attack victim to a hospital in 1991, attached her to one of the company's LifePak monitor/defibrillators to track and try to revive her failing heart. But they said the heart machine shut down every time the technicians turned on their radio transmitter. The woman died.

An unusual case of EMI interference was reported by ECRI (1999) in which a patient was being monitored with an ambulatory telemetry transmitter when the display of the patient's ECG rhythm at the central station monitor changed from normal sinus rhythm to ventricular tachycardia and then to ventricular fibrillation. A defibrillator was rushed to the patient's room, but the patient did not appear to be in distress. When a portable bedside monitor was connected to the patient, it displayed a normal sinus rhythm. The telemetry transmitter was disconnected from the patient and the batteries were removed, but the abnormal rhythm was still displayed on the central station monitor for that telemetry channel. Further investigation revealed that another telemetry system from the same supplier had just been introduced in another care unit two floors below the room where the incident occurred and that a training class on the system was being conducted at the time of the incident. Apparently, a telemetry transmitter being used for the training class had been programmed to the same frequency as the transmitter involved in the incident. Consequently, the simulated electrocardiogram arrhythmias used with the training transmitter were overriding the signal transmitted from the patient.

Telemetry from a bedridden patient to a central nursing station is becoming more common and can be associated with interference from other transmitters. A MAUDE report filed with the FDA (7/22/98) stated that the U.S. distribution of a foreign-made patient telemeter reported that a patient died while connected to the telemetry system. The report stated that a signal from another transmitter overpowered the signal from the patient's transmitter and was received and displayed at the central station. The signal detected and displayed was interpreted as "normal." No alarms were sounded.

The manufacturer stated that the initial information reported does not indicate that the system was working according to specifications. Data received also indicates that the signal strength at the receiver may have been too high. The age of the system does indicate that further investigation is required. The company is requesting additional information from the United States and is evaluating the results of testing on similar devices. The results of these investigations will be described in a follow-up report. Transmitter signals to a level that would have greatly increased the likelihood of interference. The data from the site indicates that the amplification of the antenna system exceeds what is currently recommended. The report from this site does indicate that when adjusted to the current requirements that no interference was noted. A review of complaints available on similar systems does not show any trends. This appears to be an isolated incident. Adjustment of the antenna system has corrected the problem. In addition, the transmitter frequencies that have been assigned to this site are being changed to further reduce the possibility of interference and the overall system will be verified. Finally, additional training has been provided to this site to assist the operators in making the most of this system and alerting them to possible problems and their solutions. This report is closed with no further action required.

E. Impedance-based apnea monitor mishaps

Many patient monitors use the small inspiratory-induced increase and decrease in transthoracic impedance to monitor respiratory rate. This technique was originally developed to monitor astronauts during spaceflight (Geddes et al., 1962). Typically, a low-intensity (e.g., 50 μA), high-frequency (10 to 100 kHz) current is applied to transchest electrodes, as shown in Figure 2.5. Because these electrodes are in an excellent location to detect the electrical activity of the heart, it is easy to obtain respiration and heart rate from the same pair of electrodes (Geddes et al., 1962). Figure 2.5 presents a record of these two events from the same pair of electrodes. Note the small rhythmic changes in heart rate with breathing. This normal event is called sinus arrhythmia. With slow breathing, heart rate increases slightly during inspiration and decreases slightly during expiration.

With apnea monitors, dry electrodes are usually employed and are located in a belt wrapped around the chest. The size of the impedance change depends inversely on the size of the subject (Valentinuzzi et al., 1971). The maximum impedance change is obtained when the electrode pair is at about the level of the bottom of the sternum (xiphoid process). Dry electrodes, when first applied to the skin, exhibit a high impedance owing to the high skin resistance. This makes it difficult to obtain clean respiration and electrocardiac signals. Tap water or an electrode paste can be used to reduce the skin impedance. However, when a dry electrode is placed on the skin, perspiration can no longer evaporate from the site and with the passage of time, the skin becomes hydrated and the electrode impedance becomes less (Geddes and Valentinuzzi, 1973).

Impedance respiration and heart-rate monitors are appropriately band-pass filtered to accept these two signals. However, because the beating heart is between the transchest electrodes, there is a small pulsatile nonrespiratory (cardiac) signal in the respiration channel. Between breaths in Figure 2.5, these small cardiac impulses can be identified. To illustrate them better, Figure 2.6 is presented in which the recording sensitivity has been increased. In the center of the record, the subject stopped breathing and the cardiac impulses are clearly visible. Thus, with impedance respiration, cardiac impulses could be counted as breaths during apnea if the recording sensitivity is increased excessively. Such a condition could arise if the electrodes are not placed in the optimum location and the recording sensitivity is increased to detect breaths.

1. Monitor alarms

All cardiorespiratory monitors are equipped with alarms that sound for a

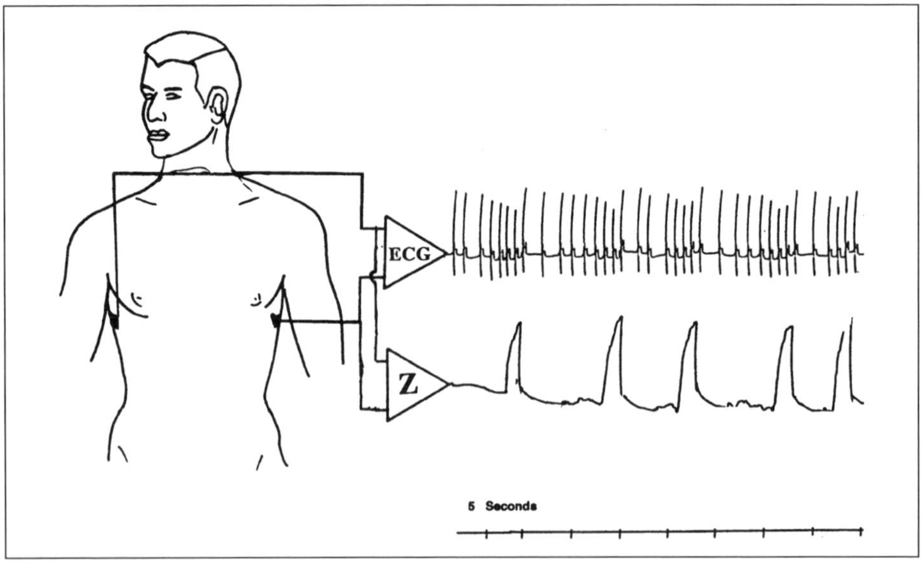

Figure 2.5 *Method of obtaining the electrocardiogram (ECG) and impedance respiration (Z) from a pair of transchest electrodes*

preset low and high heart rate and a preset low and high respiratory rate. Impedance and ECG-based monitors also have an electrodes-off (lead-off) alarm. These alarms are designed to alert the caregiver that the monitored patient needs prompt attention.

2. Mechanism of death due to apnea

Respiration is neurogenic and the heartbeat is myogenic in origin. In other words, central nervous system integrity is needed for rhythmic breathing. No neurogenic activity is needed for the heartbeat because the heart's natural pacemaker (the S-A node) is in the heart—this is why transplanted hearts beat spontaneously.

A patient is usually placed on a cardiorespiratory monitor because there is a risk of respiratory arrest (apnea). If apnea occurs, the heart continues to beat and circulates blood with less and less oxygen. Very soon the oxygen delivery is inadequate and the heart rate gradually slows and ultimately stops beating.

If, in the scenario just described, the patient was connected to an impedance-based apnea monitor with the breathing sensitivity set too high, the cardiac impulses could be counted as breaths and the breathing-rate alarm would fail to sound. The result would be increasing hypoxia (blueness) and likely brain damage and/or a failure to resuscitate when the low heart-rate alarm ultimately sounds.

To address the problem of counting a cardiac impedance impulse as a breath, Birnbaum and Stasz (1986) developed circuitry that sounds an alarm

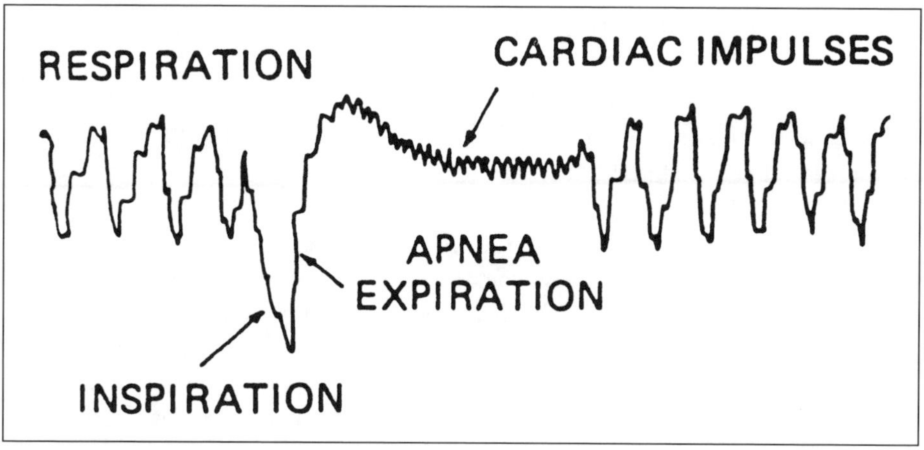

Figure 2.6 *Impedance respiration during quiet breathing (left) and during apnea (center) showing cardiac impulses*

when the respiratory impedance-signal frequency was equal to the ECG heart-rate frequency. In the patent issued to them, it states, "It is another object of the present invention to detect apparent heartbeat and respiration signals occurring at the same frequency and to generate an apnea alarm when such conditions exist."

3. Susceptibility to EMI

Impedance-based apnea monitors, although designed to accept their own signals, are not immune from environmental EMI, the amount of which is increasing as new communications devices are introduced. Most existing apnea monitors were not designed to operate in areas where pulsating EMI signals are found. In fact, many ordinary devices emit EMI when turned on and off.

Ruggera and O'Bryan (1991) constructed a test chamber which provided controlled electromagnetic fields with frequencies ranging from 0.5 to 220 MHz. Into this chamber were placed several models of apnea monitors. The patient cable was connected to an ECG and breathing simulator, with the breathing signal inhibited. The field was 100 percent modulated at 0.5 Hz. Their study revealed:

> EMI can cause disruption of apnea monitors at relatively low field strengths and at common communication frequencies. We also determined the field strength and frequency-dependent failure sensitivity of the monitors tested. The most sensitive model failed to alarm at a field strength below 0.1 V/m at a frequency in the FM broadcast band when 0.5 Hz 100 percent square-wave amplitude modulation was used.

Ruggera and O'Bryan carried out field-strength surveys in Washington, D.C., Omaha, NE, and Portland, OR, sites where apnea monitor failures had been reported. They stated that:

> Some sites at which several of the monitors failed had high total field strengths, on the order of a few volts/meter. This supported laboratory findings that all monitors would fail when exposed to sufficient field strengths. A more typical situation at the survey sites was the existence of total RF field strengths of 0.4 to 1.0 V/m and "naturally occurring" modulation of the ambient fields. It was found that very low frequency amplitude modulation could be induced on RF fields at user sites by nearby moving objects such as people, pets, and cars. This produces time-varying multipath interference of the RF fields. Exposures to "moderate" strength RF fields that are intermittently am-

> plitude modulated are potentially more of an EMI threat to apnea monitors than continual higher exposure since the former type of interference may be unsuspected.

It is important to note that the study by Ruggera and O'Bryan was published in 1991, when awareness to EMI was beginning to be recognized. However, apnea monitors made at that time are still in use and the need for EMI susceptibility testing is still present.

Ruggera et al. (1992) evaluated the susceptibility of nine impedance-based apnea monitors to EMI:

> Exposing the monitor to 100 percent square-wave modulated RF fields can cause the monitor to "think" it is sensing breath and/or ECG and not sound an alarm, even though no signals either from an infant or a patient simulator are being received.

Using a uniform radio frequency field presented to the monitor, they found that:

> The fully extended (patient) leads became a much more effective receiver of RF interference over the frequency range of 10–53.5 MHz compared to earlier data taken in a TEM cell in the laboratory. Over this range the leads were approximately 0.1 to 0.5 wavelengths of the exposure frequency. An example of the data obtained was presented as an EMI threshold field-strength vs. frequency plot from 1 to 220 MHz. Also, a field-strength average was calculated for three frequency bands in this range to summarize EMI threshold data for all nine of the apnea monitors tested. The high sensitivity of all monitors in a frequency band of 10 to 54 MHz used by CB radios, land-mobile communications, walkie-talkies, and amateur radio again emphasizes the need for the monitors to be hardened to withstand these common sources of ambient RF fields.

Figure 2.7 illustrates the EMI sensitivity of all nine monitors. Field strengths above the bars represent the values that will interfere with monitor operation.

Geddes (1995) investigated the susceptibility of three different impedance-respiration recorders, operating at 15, 35, and 45 kHz to EMI produced by arcing room thermostat contacts, a soldering gun, a hot-air gun, a fluorescent lamp, and electric hair clippers. Two types of tests were performed using

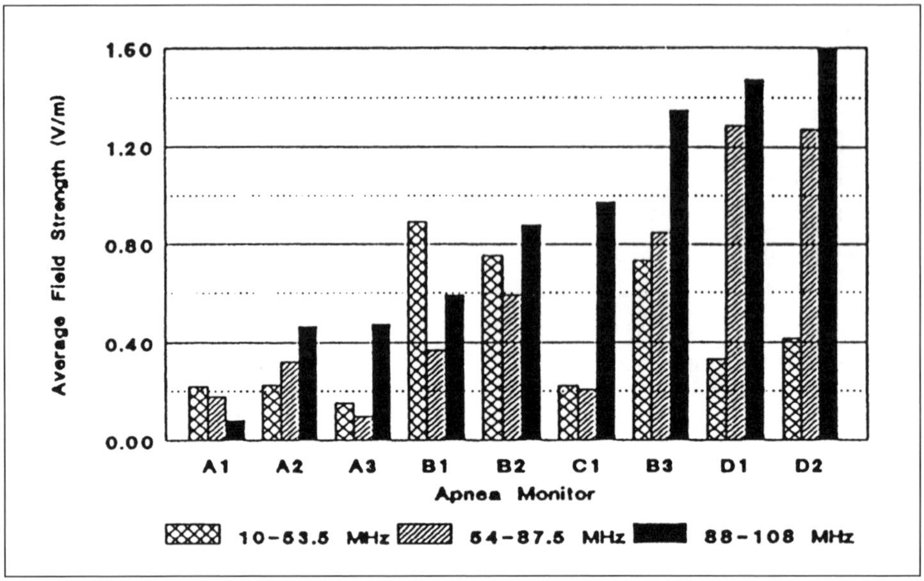

Figure 2.7 *Field strengths for malfunction of nine apnea monitors (Redrawn from Ruggera PS, O'Bryan R and Casamiento JP. Proc. IEEE EMBS Conf. 1992, 2839–2840)*

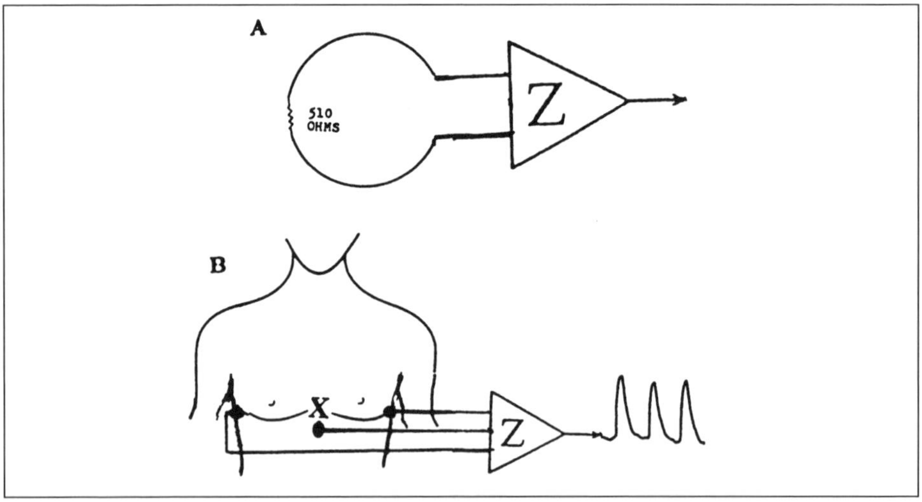

Figure 2.8 *Impedance recording methods. (a) shows the impedance recorder (Z) connected to a 2-sft-diameter loop antenna with a 510-ohm resistor to simulate a subject. (b) shows the method used to record the respiratory-induced impedance change with transthoracic electrodes. The central electrode (X) serves to ground the subject to reduce susceptibility to electrostatic discharges.*

(1) a loop antenna two feet in diameter with a 510-ohm resistor (dummy subject), shown in Figure 2.8a, and (2) a subject with transthoracic electrodes and a central ground (X), as shown in Figure 2.8b. The use of a ground (X) on the subject reduces the susceptibility to electrostatic discharge (ESD).

Figure 2.9a illustrates the output of an impedance recorder, operating at 33 kHz, connected to the loop antenna (Figure 2.8a) as the thermostat contact arced periodically. On the right is a 5-ohm calibration signal.

Figure 2.9a shows the output of an impedance recorder operating at 33 kHz connected to the loop antenna (Figure 2.8a) placed two feet from arcing thermostat contacts.

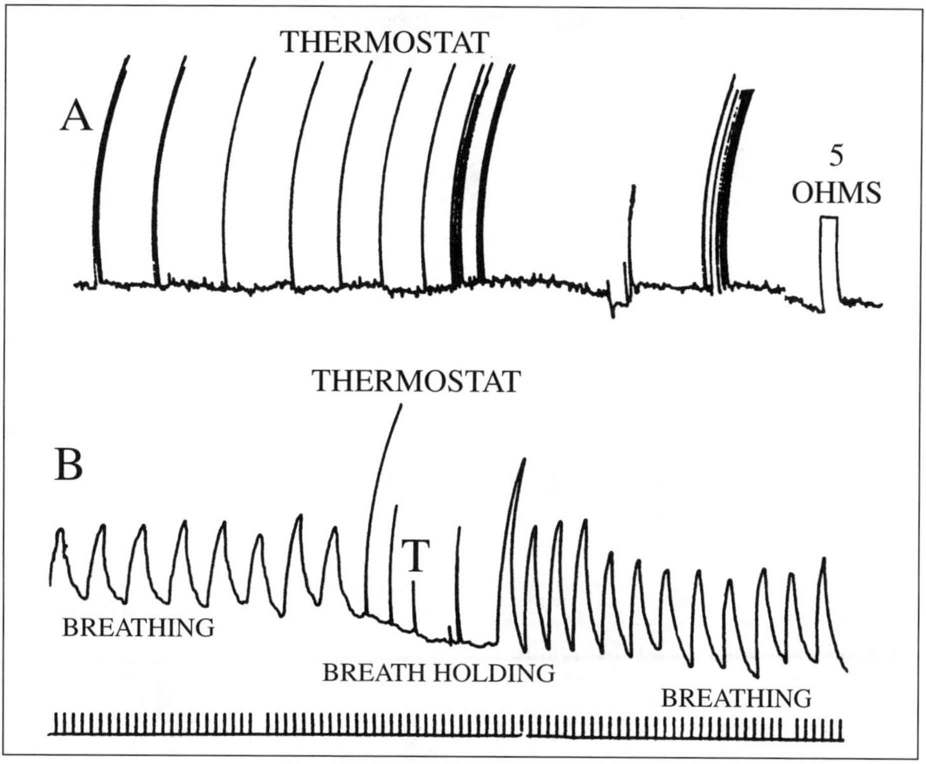

Figure 2.9 *(a) shows the output of an impedance recorder operating at 33 kHz connected to the loop antenna (Figure 2.8a) placed two feet from arcing thermostat contacts. (b) shows spontaneous breathing (left) and breath holding (center), during which time the thermostat contacts were arcing. The transient T was produced when the room fluorescent lights were turned on. On the right, spontaneous breathing as resumed. (Time marks one second)*

Figure 2.9b shows spontaneous breathing (left) and breath holding (center), during which time the thermostat contacts were arcing. The transient T was produced when the room fluorescent lights were turned on. On the right, spontaneous breathing was resumed. (Time marks one second)

Figure 2.9b is a record of spontaneous respiration (left), breath holding (center), with transients from the thermostat during the twenty-second period of breath holding and the resumption of spontaneous breathing (right) in a subject monitored as in Figure 2.8b at a distance of two feet from the thermostat. The small transient (T) during breath holding was produced by turning on the roof fluorescent lights.

Similar breath-size responses were obtained with the soldering gun, hot-air gun, fluorescent lights, and electric hair clipper.

Silberberg (1993), of the Center for Devices and Radiological Health (FDA), stated that:

> Because there had been numerous reports of unexplained failure of apnea monitors to alarm upon death, the susceptibility of these monitors to radiated RF was evaluated by CDRH. After both laboratory and field testing, CDRH engineers determined that most commercial apnea monitors could erroneously detect respiration when exposed to relatively low field strengths, which could result in failure to alarm during apnea. Most monitors were found to be susceptible above 1 V/m when the field was pulsed or when an ambient FM field was incidentally amplitude modulated at a low rate of movement of objects and humans.
>
> One model was susceptible to pulsed fields above 0.05 V/m, and the manufacturer performed a recall to improve the immunity of its monitor, particularly in the FM broadcast band (88 to 108 MHz) . . . The same model was found to be unusually sensitive to quasi-static fields, detecting respiration when the monitor or cables were touched or when an electrostatically charged fabric was waved over the monitor.

Silberberg (1993) reported three other instances of mishaps with apnea monitors:

> Neonatal monitors were interfered with when placed in close proximity to similar models of neonatal or adult monitors while operating in the shallow breathing mode at high gain.
>
> Transmissions from an amateur radio station interfered with an infant monitor only when the remote alarm was attached.

> A combination pulse oximeter and capnograph, which used a switching power supply with a frequency of 62.5 kHz, interfered with the impedance measurement circuit of respiration (apnea) monitors, resulting in false readings. The oximeter power supply frequency was close to the frequency used to measure transthoracic impedance in respiration monitors from three different manufacturers. The manufacturer of the pulse oximeter has issued a safety alert and will change the power supply frequency of the oximeters to prevent recurrence.

The foregoing indicates the need to test the susceptibility of apnea monitors for EMI at the site where used, by connecting a patient dummy load to the monitor which should show no breathing and sound the no-breathing alarm.

F. Ventilator mishaps

A ventilator is a device that inflates the lungs by providing intermittent air flow, usually delivered to an endotracheal tube; a tightly fitting face mask can also be used. The old name for a ventilator is a respirator. Because there is the need to control ventilation depth, rate, and the duration of inspiration, electronic controls are used, some of which can be quite sophisticated. Because such controllers are electronic, they are not immune from EMI.

Silberberg (1993) described a variety of ventilator mishaps due to EMI:

> A ventilator experienced keyboard lockup, due to interference from a guard's walkie-talkie.
>
> Two ventilators that were within twenty feet of each other alarmed simultaneously. That day the ventilators alarmed frequently; it was discovered that the power company was using walkie-talkies in the area. The hospital staff was able to duplicate the problem using walkie-talkies in the hospital.
>
> The operation of a particular model of ventilator was disrupted, resulting in cessation of ventilation, inoperative monitoring functions, display or error messages, or display of unintelligible messages. The disruptions were caused by "extreme events" of EMI or power-line disturbances, possibly resulting from the use of electrosurgical, laser, x-ray, or other equipment.
>
> A ventilator went into "safety valve open" and displayed an error code during a chest x-ray.
>
> A microprocessor-based intensive care ventilator ceased operating and alarmed, and microprocessor-based infusion pumps stopped working when a portable x-ray machine was turned off in the vicinity.
>
> The operation and readouts of ventilators were affected by keying of two-way handheld FM radios, both in the same room and in the next room.

The low minute volume alarm would sound, the analog display would indicate an exhaled minute volume of zero, and the digital display would indicate negative values of exhaled minute volume.

Four-watt walkie-talkies used for communication within a hospital interfered with the operation of high-frequency ventilators up to a distance of ten feet, causing the bar graph display of piston location and amplitude to be driven out of the display window, and the pressure readout to decrease enough to trip low pressure alarms, which caused the piston to stop. The manufacturer found that replacing the plastic cover of the electronic control assembly with a metal cover would result in only a 2-cm error in the displayed mean pressure and no error in the actual delivered mean pressure.

RF transmission from a hospital source (handheld, two-way radio) or an outside source caused a ventilator to activate alarms. The hospital was able to duplicate the event. While in use during a flight, a portable ventilator operating on battery power stopped cycling and alarmed several times. Factory evaluation revealed that radio frequency interference caused false signals. The unit was updated and the cable was shielded.

G. Drug-infusion pump mishaps

Drugs are often injected into the vascular system via a programmable infusion pump. Typically, a sterile syringe containing the drug is inserted into the pump and the delivery program is entered by a keyboard. Such devices are typically microprocessor controlled and can be susceptible to EMI.

Silberberg (1993) cited the following cases of infusion-pump malfunction:

An infusion pump changed rate when a cellular phone was placed on the instrument stand.

An infusion device on an isolated circuit (high source impedance) behaved erratically due to conducted EMI at 33 MHz.

H. Powered-vehicle mishaps

Motor-driven wheelchairs and scooters used by patients contain electronic controls which have malfunctioned in the presence of electromagnetic radiation. Silberberg (1993) reported:

A quality assurance manager who had previously worked for a large wheelchair manufacturer, in a letter dated June 26, 1992, inquired about the status of medical device EMC standards. As a side issue, he reported that in his previous position he had received reports of powered wheelchairs driving off

> curbs and piers unintentionally when a police or fire vehicle, harbor patrol boat, or CB or amateur radio was in the vicinity. The reporter had reproduced the phenomenon under controlled conditions and had observed powered wheelchairs "go by themselves" within fifteen or twenty feet of a police or fire truck radio. [EMC = electromagnetic compatibility.]
>
> The CDRH databases were checked for reports of electromagnetic interference problems with powered wheelchairs. While several reports of unintended motion were found, several involving serious injury, none had been attributed to electromagnetic interference in the report.
>
> CDRH engineers investigated the EMI susceptibility of the motion controllers of several makes of powered wheelchairs and scooters. The powered wheelchairs tested were found to be susceptible to field strengths in the range of 5 to 15 V/m. At the lower end of the susceptibility range, the electric brakes would release, which could result in a hazard of rolling if the chair were stopped on an incline. As the field strength at a susceptible frequency was increased, the wheels would begin turning, with the speed of rotation a function of the field strength.
>
> CDRH engineers also measured the emissions from police and fire radios. A 100-watt state police radio transmitting at 39 MHz was found to have a field strength of 41 V/m at a distance of 0.9 m. CDRH also learned that a small number of manufacturers of wheelchair controllers supply much of the powered wheelchair and scooter industry.

Further studies on the effect of EMI on wheelchairs were reported by Witters (1995), who stated that the FDA became aware of this problem in 1992 and launched a susceptibility investigation over the frequency range from 50 to 90 MHz. He stated that the wheel speed was measured over a range of field strengths. For these tests, the wheelchair controller was turned on with the "joystick" in the neutral position (wheelchair stationary). The wheel speed was monitored in revolutions per minute (rpm). If there were no EMI-induced movements, the wheels would have remained stationary at 0 rpm. In this case the wheels were induced to move at several different speeds, some quite fast.

He stated: "One of the main observations made was that the device would react differently for the different field strength levels of EM energy, creating windows of effects." He concluded:

> The CDRH laboratory results clearly indicated an EMI problem for these devices. Further testing revealed that the EMI seemed to affect the control system of the powered wheelchairs. In many cases, motorized scooters utilize the

same type of control systems, thus there was concern for EMI with these devices. Testing indicated the scooter devices could exhibit EMI problems.

2.7 Cellular and Mobile Telephone-Generated EMI

Bren (1996) estimated that by the end of the 1990s there will be over 60 million users nationally. With this tremendous expansion in service the opportunity for interaction with medical devices will increase dramatically. At present there are two technologies employed: analog and digital. In the U.S. the NATEL-C system employs frequency modulation operating in the 824- to 849- and 869- to 894-MHz bands. It is important to note that even when the cellular telephone is not being used (but is turned on), it emits signals that are identified by the base station. The method used in Europe is digital and is designated GSM (Global Standards for Mobile Communication), which emits 8/sec pulses in the 890- to 915-MHz band for signal transmission to the base station and in the 935- to 960-MHz band from the base station. Two types of digital phones are being introduced in the U.S.: one is called Code Division Multiple Access (CDMA) and the other is designated Time Division Multiple Access (TDMA). The latter technology is similar to that used in the GSM. Therefore, when investigating the performance of medical devices exposed to electromagnetic radiation emitted by cellular telephones, it is essential to identify the type of technology used by the telephone.

A. Infant radiant warmer mishaps

An AAMI (1996) committee is drafting a list of incidents in which EMI has caused dysfunction in medical devices. One entry in this preliminary report states the following:

> On December 1, 1994, the television program *Eye to Eye with Connie Chung* aired a story on the EMI effects of wireless transmitting devices on medical devices. In January 1995, at a hospital in the Southwest, testing was performed in an effort to duplicate the effects reported on the program. The testing involved a similar type of infant radiant warmer and its response to an imposed electromagnetic field produced by (1) a hand-held transceiver and (2) a cellular telephone. It was found that the handheld transceiver affected the infant warmer at distances up to ten feet away, depending on the transceiver's battery charge. The cellular telephone affected the device only if it was located within eighteen inches of the infant radiant warmer.

The report concludes:

> As a result of these tests and others performed on infusion pumps, PCA pumps, infant ventilators, and certain monitors, the Safety Committee decided, upon recommendation by the Clinical Engineering Department, to restrict the use of handheld transceivers and cellular telephones in the critical care, labor and delivery, nursery, respiratory care, EEG, EMG, and cardiology areas of the hospital. (Handheld transceivers can be used to receive in those areas, but can be used to transmit only in unrestricted areas. Cellular telephones must be turned off. Memos and letters were sent to physicians and to the directors of the affected departments to explain the need for the restrictions. Videos were presented to the Safety Committee to provide evidence of the interactions between handheld transceivers, cellular telephones, and medical devices.

B. Miscellaneous medical device mishaps

Clifford et al. (1994) investigated the effect of several mobile, handheld telephones on nearby medical devices. The study was performed in Australia using two different types of telephones: (1) Advanced Mobile Phone System (AMPS) and (2) Global System Mobile (GSM). The AMPS is an analog FM communication system operating between 825 and 845 MHz with a power of 0.6 W. The GSM is a digital communication system that operates in the 890- to 915-MHz band with 0.6-msec pulses having a repetition rate of 217 Hz. The output power ranges from 0.8 to 2 W. Handheld telephones of both types were brought close to the following medical devices: two patient monitors; six drug-infusion pumps; a defibrillator monitor; a cardiac monitor; a pulse oximeter; an oxygen monitor; a blood-pressure monitor; a fetal monitor with telemetry and an ECG telemeter. They stated their results as follows:

> The AMPS phone operating at 0.6 W affected only three pieces of equipment: the ECG trace was distorted on one of the patient monitors and two of the pumps initiated false alarms, though one of these pumps gave false alarms only when the antenna of the phone was within 50 mm of its case. This result suggests that manufacturers have generally adhered to the FDA standard and hardened their equipment to withstand fields of 7 V/m or greater.
>
> When the same pieces of equipment were tested with the (digital) GSM phones, seven of them operated normally. The other eight displayed the following symptoms: distortion or loss of ECG traces, false alarms and halting/change of speed of infusion pumps and the introduction of severe distortion

> into the telemetry systems, including a 217-Hz audible interference tone on one unit. Increasing the power of the GSM phone did not change the symptoms, except in one case when the higher power phone triggered an alarm in addition to the other symptoms. Changing from the 2-W phone to the 8-W model doubled the distance within which interference effects were observed.
>
> Three of the pumps were not affected at all, and at distances greater than 200 mm, the other three were free from interference even from the 8-W phone. Within the critical distances, the three pumps displayed various error messages; two of them then ceased to operate and one continued to operate but at two-thirds of its selected rate.
>
> The ECG display in the defibrillator/monitor was free of interference, but the other three units with ECG monitors displayed a variety of symptoms including blanking of one CRT unit and/or horizontal lines, and high levels of noise on the ECG trace which initiated alarms in two of the units. In one of the units the distortion persisted at distances up to two meters with the 8-W phone.
>
> The pulse oximeter unit in one of the patient monitors showed a low signal at distances up to two meters with the 8-W phone.
>
> Both telemetry systems were affected by the GSM phones producing interference and large excursions of the trace. One unit had a 217-Hz interference which was audible. No interference was observed when the phones were more than two meters from both the transmitters and the receivers.

Of considerable value in the Clifford paper is a tabulation of the peak field strength (volts/meter) at different distances from the 0.6- and 2-W handheld telephones. These data are plotted in Figure 2.10. Although there is no universally accepted standard for the maximum permissible field strengths at different distances, Clifford et al. (1994) stated:

> It is our concern that the existing 1979 FDA standard can be exceeded at distances of up to two meters with an 8-watt transportable digital phone. The clear implication of this result is that digital phones will cause more EMI than the current analogue phones; this was confirmed in the interference tests with selected medical electrical equipment. It is also of concern that the IEC have set a standard of 3 V/m, rather than the FDA's 7 V/m.

Additional field-strength data for handheld cellular phones (0.6 W) and transceivers (5 W) were reported by Foster (1994). Table 2.4 lists the range of distances from a series of these instruments for field strengths of 1 and 3 V/m.

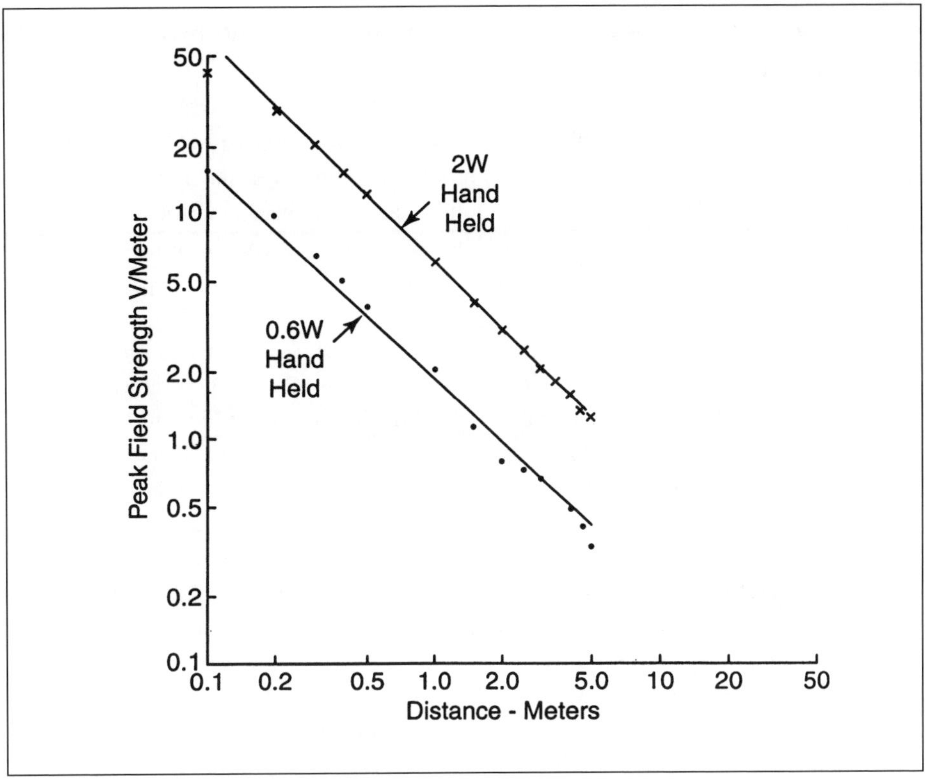

Figure 2.10 *Field strength (V/m) vs. distance (m) for handheld phones (0.6 and 2 W). (Data from Clifford KJ, Joyner KH, Stroud DB et al.* Austral. Phys. Eng. Sci. Med. *1994, 17(1): 23-27)*

Table 2.4
Distance from Personal Communications Devices for Field Strengths of 1 and 3 V/m

Instrument Type	Distance[a] 1 V/m	In feet for 3 V/m
Cellular phone (0.6 Watts)	1–8	0.5–3
Transceiver	3–25	1–8

[a] Expected range for different units

Data from Foster, K. Sci. Eng. Biomed. 1994, December.

Bostrom (1991) reviewed a series of European incidents involving mobile telephones and medical devices:

> One of the first reports was from Denmark, where a single-patient hemodialysis monitor stopped working when a mobile telephone was used on the floor under the dialysis department. In another case a dialysis monitor malfunctioned in Sweden when a patient used his own mobile telephone during dialysis in a hospital. The patient noticed the alarm from the monitor stopped when using his telephone.
>
> Several problems with different kinds of electromedical equipment in Norway have been reported in *Hyhetsrevy*, which is a Norwegian newsletter about accidents and incidents with medical devices published by the Norwegian Institute for Hospital Research in Trondheim. Incubators, syringe infusion pumps, infusion controllers, dialysis equipment, and defibrillators have been reported to malfunction due to interference from mobile telephones.
>
> So far only a few incidents have been documented, but some of them have been rather serious. In one case a home patient's lung ventilator changed its function in a serious way; in another case an infusion pump, used for administration of a potent drug, switched to the maximum infusion speed. I have been told that the death of a patient due to electromagnetic interference with an infusion pump has occurred in Japan. But since no report about this accident has been written in English it has not been possible for me to check the circumstances of that specific case.

Bostrom concluded:

> Many hospitals in the Scandinavian countries have now prohibited the use of mobile telephones (and radio transmitters) within the whole hospital area. Other hospitals have prohibited the use of such equipment only in certain zones with susceptible electromedical devices, e.g., intensive care units, operating theatres, and dialysis departments. Still other hospitals have only informed the medical staff and clinical engineers about the risks and warned about the use of mobile telephones within certain distances (e.g., 5 m) from electromedical devices. The nations' authorities for health and welfare in Sweden, Norway, and Finland have also sent out alerts with information about the safety risks with mobile telephones.

C. Health effects

Because cellular phones are held close to the head, some concern has been raised about potential health effects. The research to date was summarized by

Bren (1996), who stated, "Thus far, no supportable evidence has been brought forth to show that exposure to non-ionizing radiation from cellular telephones causes adverse health effects."

D. Blood pressure monitor

Paging systems vary in output power considerably and are capable of causing medical devices to malfunction. Silberberg (1993) reported the following incidents:

> The reading of all invasive blood-pressure monitors in an ICU/CCU jumped 3 to 10 mm Hg when a 150-W paging transmitter on the hospital roof was activated.
>
> Displays of a telemetry patient monitor would "flat-line" when a paging company transmitted digital control information to its remote sites.

2.8 Cardiac Pacemakers and EMI

A. Introduction

There are three types of cardiac pacemakers: (1) external, (2) temporary, and (3) implanted. The external type delivers pulses (20 to 40 msec) to transchest electrodes. The temporary type delivers pulses (<1 msec) to a catheter electrode passed down a vein into the right ventricle. The implanted type is contained in a metal enclosure (can), usually implanted in the chest, and delivers its pulses to the heart via a catheter electrode in the right ventricle and/or right atrium.

B. Closed-chest cardiac pacemakers

Cardiac pacing with chest-surface electrodes was introduced by Zoll (1952). Because transient cardiac arrest and/or atrioventricular block follows ventricular defibrillation, many of the early transchest defibrillators included a pacemaker. However, because the shocks used then were so unpleasant to the subject, these pacemakers were not included in later defibrillators. Zoll et al. (1981) found that by using a long-duration pacing pulse (20 to 40 msec), large-area electrodes, and a high-resistivity gel under the electrode, the skin sensation was markedly reduced. By mid-1982 closed-chest cardiac pacemakers became available commercially using self-adhering disposable electrodes (about 100 cm^2), long-duration pulses (20 to 40 msec), and a peak current of 60 to 100 mA. The high-resistivity gel reduces high-peak current density that is prominent under the perimeter of an electrode that uses a low-resistivity coupling agent. Typical pacing rates are seventy per minute and above.

To date the author has found only one report of malfunction of a closed-chest pacemaker due to EMI. DeBarros Moraes (1995) exposed a transchest cardiac pacemaker to the discharges of a stunning device, which he called an Autodefense Device. Such devices produce repetitive, high-voltage (tens of kilovolts) shocks and are designed to stun subjects for capture. The activation time used was five seconds and the device was activated at different distances from the external pacemaker. The response was described as reversal of working conditions, i.e. reversion to the fixed-rate mode, at a distance of 3 cm. When the device was deactivated, the external pacemaker reverted to operation in the demand mode.

There are reports of complications associated with long-term closed-chest pacing unrelated to EMI. For example, skin damage under the electrodes has been observed in human subjects when pacing has been applied for more than eight hours. For this reason some manufacturers place a pacing-time limit instruction on the electrodes.

A full-thickness skin injury due to prolonged closed-chest pacing (forty-five hours) of a seven-week-old child was reported by Pride and McKinley (1990). The pacing electrodes were designed for use on children less than 15 kg. In commenting on the electrodes, they stated, "Due to the child's very small chest there was little surface area available for the pacing pads."

After forty-five hours of pacing at eighty to eighty-five pulses per minute with a current of 40 to 60 mA, they reported, "When the pads were removed, a large bullous second-degree burn was noticed on the back. A 3-cm eschar covering a full-thickness burn penetrating to the pectoralis muscle was found anteriorly." Thus, injury occurred under both electrodes, but the degree of injury was slightly different.

It is of value to calculate the average current that flowed. Typically, the duration of a transchest pacing pulse is 25 msec. The total number of pulses delivered when pacing at eighty to eight-five per minute for forty-five hours is 45×60 (80 to 85) = 216,000 to 229,500 pulses. Each pulse is typically 25 msec; therefore, the equivalent duration of current flow is $25 \times 10 - 3$ (216,000 to 229,500), which is equal to 5400 to 5737 sec.

The charge transferred describes the electrolytic process at the electrode interface and is equal to the product of current and time. In this case the pacing current was 40 to 60 mA; therefore, the range of charge was $5400 \times 40 =$

216,000 to 5737 $\times$ 60 = 344,200 mA-sec or 216 to 344 (amp-sec). Clearly, this amount of charge produced skin lesions.

A high electrode current density, persisting for a long time, can cause tissue injury. In this case, it is not possible to calculate the current density accurately; but if the 3-cm lesion is taken as the effective electrode diameter, the current density is the current divided by the electrode area. In this case, the estimated current density is 40 to 60 mA divided by $0.785 \times 3 \times 3$ cm^2, or a current density range of 5.67 to 8.50 mA/cm^2. It is clear that this current density, when applied for forty-five hours at a pacing rate of 80 to 85/min, produced skin lesions.

Pride and McKinley (1990) pointed out that, "In contrast to adult skin, neonatal skin is thinner, has less hair, weaker intracellular attachments, fewer eccrine and sebaceous gland secretions and an increased susceptibility to external irritants." These factors may have contributed to the severity of the lesions.

In the introduction to their paper, Pride and McKinley (1990) stated that:

> After having received reports of burns during prolonged pacer use in neonates, the ZMI Corporation has issued a warning that pacing for one to two hours may cause thermal injury and that skin should be inspected every thirty minutes (unpublished FDA report distributed by Zoll, February 1988).

The nature of the skin lesions described by Pride and McKinley (1990) merits speculation regarding their possible cause. Note that the injury under the two electrodes was different, despite the fact that they both carried the same pacing current. If one electrode skin-contact area were smaller than the other, the current densities would be different and therefore the severity of the lesions would be different. The lesion on the back was described as "a large bullous second-degree burn" (a bullous is a blister filled with serous fluid). The lesion on the chest was "a 3-cm eschar covering a full-thickness burn penetrating to the pectoralis muscle" (an eschar is dead tissue cast off living tissue, produced by burning or the application of a corrosive substance). Thus the severity of the chest lesion was greater than that on the back despite the same total current flow at each site. However, we do not know the contact areas at both sites.

It was not proven that the "burn" was thermal in origin. The term "burn" is also used for chemical injury and it is logical to speculate on this point. When unidirectional (pulses or continuous) current flows through an electrode coupled to the skin via an electrolyte, local chemical injury can result from electrolysis of the electrolytic coupling agent, which is predominantly an aqueous solution of sodium chloride that provides Na^+, Cl^-, H^+, and OH^- ions. With a unidirectional current pulse, one electrode becomes positive and the other negative. Negatively charged ions (Cl^- and OH^-) are attracted to the positive electrode and positively charged ions (Na^+ and H^+) are attracted to the negative electrode and a variety of chemical reactions can occur. For example, gaseous oxygen, hydrogen, and chlorine can be liberated. Gaseous chlorine is soluble and is a strong bleaching agent. Sodium is a corrosive element which can combine with hydroxyl ions to form sodium hydroxide, which is corrosive to all tissues. The hydrogen ions can combine with the chloride ions to form hydrochloric acid, which is a corrosive agent. In general the environment of the negative electrode is acidic and that of the positive electrode is basic. This fact is easily proven by applying litmus paper at each site and noting the nature of the color change. Beyond these chemical compounds are those that may be formed by the material of the electrodes. Because one electrode is positive and one is negative, the chemical products at each are expected to be different and therefore the lesions are expected to be different. As yet, there has been no study that has quantitated the type of skin damage under the positive and negative electrodes having the same area carrying the same current.

Iontophoresis is another mechanism which could participate in skin damage when unidirectional current is passed through an electrode-skin interface. Iontophoresis is the process by which direct current is used to drive a charged substance into the skin. Typically the material to be transported is enclosed in a cup-shaped electrode applied to the skin. A large-area, distant-indifferent electrode completes the circuit. If the substance to be driven through the skin has a positive charge, the electrode in the cup is made positive. The opposite applies for negatively charged substances. Typically, a current density of less than $2 mA/cm^2$ is used. By identifying the charge on the substances in the electrolyte used with an electrode and knowing the electrode polarity, it is possible to predict which substances will be driven through the skin. More details on iontophoresis appear in the chapter on transdermal drug delivery.

One method of minimizing electrochemical decomposition at an electrode-electrolyte interface is to use a bidirectional wave in which there is no net current flow, i.e. the first current pulse is followed by an inverted pulse that has the same product of current and duration as the first pulse. This technique is used in TENS units and is called a balanced waveform. The method was first used by Lilly (1955).

C. Implanted pacemakers

There are many reports of implanted pacemaker malfunction due to EMI and the following paragraphs will provide illustrative examples. Several different types of malfunction can occur. For example, a pacemaker exposed to EMI may be inhibited and fail to deliver cardiac-pacing stimuli. It may revert to the fixed (constant)-rate pacing mode; it may be triggered to produce rapid pacing or even cause ventricular fibrillation. The internal program may be reset to an inappropriate pacing mode. Finally, a pacemaker can also be destroyed and cease to produce pacing stimuli.

Pacemaker manufacturers issue warnings against the use of pacemakers in the vicinity of radio frequency generators. Before describing pacemaker malfunctions it is useful to discuss the normal function of the heart.

D. The cardiac cycle

The origin of the heartbeat in a normal subject is in the sinoatrial (S-A) node, located in the upper right atrium (Figure 2.11). This region of modified cardiac muscle is really a chemical oscillator that has the interesting property of devel-

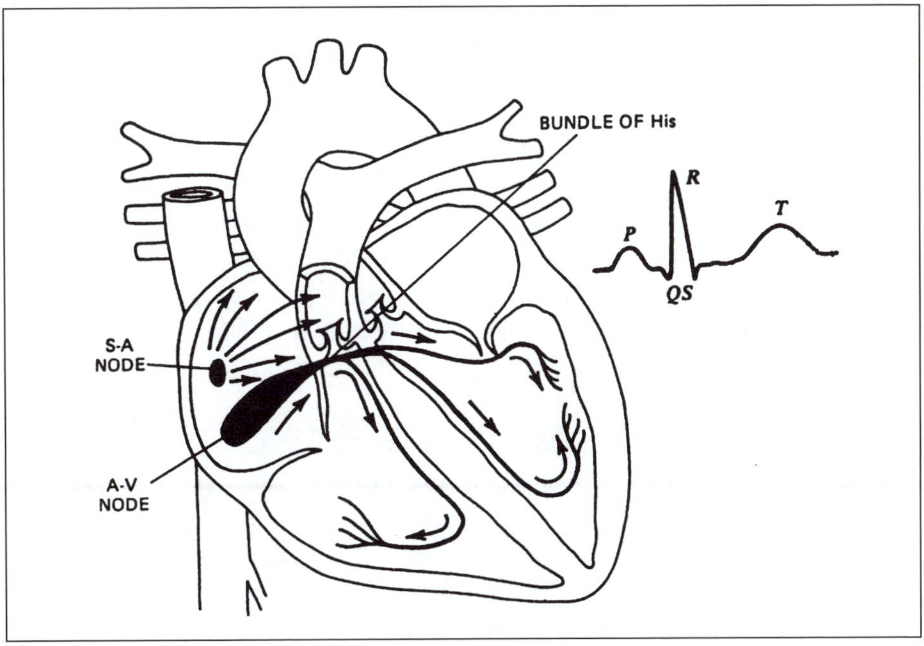

Figure 2.11 The pathways traversed by excitation that gives rise to atrial contraction and then ventricular contraction. In the normal heart, the sinoatrial (S-A) node is the pacemaker and the atrioventricular (A-V) node propagates excitation through the bundle of His and Purkinje fibers to the ventricular muscle.

oping rhythmic electrical activity which is propagated to the atria, causing them to contract and pump blood into the ventricles. The wave of propagated excitation, represented by the P wave of the ECG, travels over the atria and reaches the atrioventricular (A-V) node in the base of the right ventricle. The propagation velocity of excitation through the A-V node is slow; therefore, there is a delay in propagating excitation to the ventricles, thereby allowing them to fill. Excitation leaving the A-V node is propagated along the bundle of His and Purkinje fibers, ultimately arriving at the ventricular muscle, giving rise to the QRS wave, after which the ventricles contract. This arborizing network of fibers is called the conduction system, which serves to coordinate the spread of excitation so that a forceful ventricular beat ensues, thereby pumping blood from the ventricles. Relaxation of the ventricles is preceded by the T wave of the ECG; Figure 2.11 shows a complete electrical cycle of the heart (P, QRS, and T).

Normally the rate of the heart is determined by the rhythmicity of the S-A node. It is important to emphasize that the S-A node is spontaneously rhythmic. An excised heart will continue to beat for some time. The rhythmicity of the S-A node is influenced by temperature, nervous, and chemical (humoral) activity. Increasing temperature and an increase activity of the sympathetic nervous system increase the heart rate and force of ventricular contraction, thereby increasing blood pressure and cardiac output. Increase of activity of the parasympathetic nervous system decreases the heart rate, thereby decreasing blood pressure and cardiac output. These two branches of the autonomic nervous system are controlled by centers in the medulla and hypothalamus.

While it is true that under normal circumstances the heart rate is dependent on the activity of the S-A node, other areas in the heart can become pacemakers and originate a heartbeat. Atrial muscle fibers, the A-V node, the ventricular conducting system, and ventricular muscle fibers all have the capability of becoming rhythmic and acting as pacemakers. For this reason, it is possible that the heartbeat may not always consist of an orderly sequence of atrial contraction followed by ventricular contraction. In A-V block, the ventricles can become spontaneously active and beat rhythmically with no relation to atrial contractions. However, when this situation arises, the ventricular rate is usually so slow that an inadequate cardiac output results and a pacemaker is needed.

Advancing age and disease can disrupt the organization of the heartbeat. One of the most important cardiac impairments is atrioventricular (A-V) block. In this situation, the rhythmic excitations of the atria are not propagated through the A-V node. Sometimes two, three, or more atrial excitations occur before one ventricular beat occurs. This situation is called partial or second-degree A-V block. In many circumstances, none of the atrial excitations pass beyond the A-V node and the ventricles are thereby deprived of their normal pacemaker drive. In this situation, which is called total or third-degree A-V block, the most rhythmic region in the ventricles will start pacemaking and develop propagated excitation that will travel throughout both ventricles. However, in such a case the ventricular rate is often too slow to provide adequate cardiac output for consciousness or normal activity. Rhythmic stimulation of the ventricles by a cardiac pacemaker can provide adequate cardiac output.

From the foregoing it can be seen that although the atria and ventricles may lose their pacemaking drive, they can be made to contract by an electrical stimulus provided by a cardiac pacemaker. Thus, atrial or ventricular, or atrial and ventricular stimulation can be applied to restore cardiac output to a level compatible with the maintenance of a reasonable quality of life.

When an electronic pacemaker is used to evoke cardiac contractions, the ECG is different from that in a normal subject. For example, the pacemaker stimulus can be identified in the ECG as a spike followed by the wave of excitation that it produces. For example, Figure 2.12a shows a normal ECG, consisting of the P, QRS, and T waves. Figure 2.12b shows ventricular pacing; X identifies the pacing stimulus, followed by the ventricular QS-T complex.

E. Four-letter code

A four-letter code has been adopted to designate the type of pacemaker func-

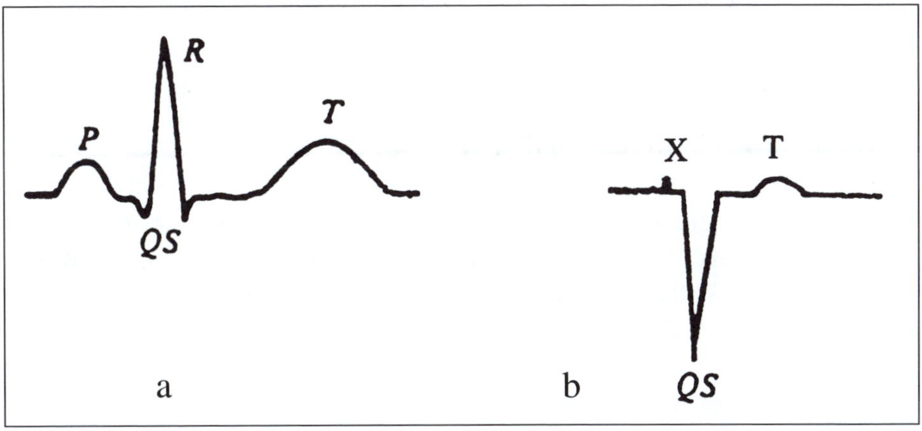

Figure 2.12 *(a) normal ECG and (b) the ECG in response to a pacing stimulus X*

tion. The first letter identifies the chamber that is paced, that is, atrium (A) or ventricle (V) or doubly (D). The second letter identifies the chamber sensed (A, V, D), and the third letter specifies the mode of operation, I being used to identify inhibited and T designating triggered. The letter O is used to identify that a particular descriptor is inapplicable. For example, the original (asynchronous), fixed-rate ventricular pacemaker would be designated VOO. The popular ventricular-demand pacemaker is identified by the letters VVI to specify that the pacemaker is inhibited by activity. The fourth letter R is used to identify rate sensitivity, i.e., the pacing rate increases in response to activity.

F. Communication with an implanted pacemaker

Two-way telemetry is possible between an implanted pacemaker and the programmer that is placed on the skin above the implant. The programmer can interrogate the pacing parameters, pulse current, duration, rate, battery voltage, electrode impedance, etc. The programmer can also set the mode of operation of the pacer. In addition, a magnet placed on the skin above the pacer can revert the pacer to a fixed-rate mode. This technique is used to identify the pacing rate which is indicative of battery voltage and thereby identify when pacemaker replacement is needed.

G. Failure modes

Before discussing pacemaker malfunction due to EMI, it is useful to recognize that implanted cardiac pacemakers and implanted cardioverter defibrillators can malfunction for other reasons. For example, the following can occur: (1) electrode lead fracture, (2) insulation fracture, (3) lead migration, (4) pulse generator failure due to battery depletion, and (5) pulse generator failure due to externally applied current (e.g. defibrillation).

H. Effect of EMI on pacemaker function

In reviewing the literature on the effect of EMI on cardiac pacemakers, it is important to recognize that the early units were not designed to reject EMI. Serious attention to the effects of EMI on pacemakers was slow to evolve and it is difficult to specify a date when improvements were made to attenuate this problem. However, an editorial by Furman (1982) provides insight:

> It has been recognized for at least two decades that electromagnetic signals exist which can interfere with pacemaker function. However, during most of this time the entire field, industry and professional alike, seems to have been

> bemused by the problem of nonphysiologic sources. Electrocautery, microwave ovens, electric shavers, and a whole host of exogenous electromagnetic interfering signals were recognized as potentially interfering with pacemaker function. This represented a challenge to the engineering-industrial community, which has been met well. Pacemakers were rapidly made substantially insensitive to the largely foreign signals of all the exogenous devices. That problem seems to be satisfactorily resolved.

While it is true that pacemakers produced in the last fifteen years are much less susceptible to EMI, they are not immune from many types found in the environment; particularly troublesome is the high-frequency current produced by electrosurgical and diathermy units as well as EMI from cellular phones, communications equipment, and the industrial environment.

I. Pacemaker malfunction due to electrosurgery

Wajsczuk et al. (1969) reported a case in which a demand pacemaker in a patient was inhibited when the electrosurgical unit was activated during a transurethral resection procedure. They reported that although the cutting current inhibited the pacemaker, the coagulating current did not. A similar case was described by Smith and Wise (1971) in which both the cutting and coagulating current inhibited a demand pacemaker. They found that locating the dispersive electrode under the buttocks and relocating the wires carrying the electrosurgical current distant from the heart eliminated inhibition of the demand pacemaker.

Greene and Meredith (1972) pointed out that the newer demand pacemakers revert to fixed-rate pacing when interference is present. In transurethral resection operations on twelve patients they recommended the following precautions: (1) use a copious amount of conducting gel on the dispersive electrode, (2) place the dispersive electrode under the buttocks, (3) arrange the wires to the ESU so that they are perpendicular to the axis of the pacing lead in the heart and (4) connect all equipment to the same ground. With these precautions, only one instance of pacemaker inhibition occurred when the ESU was activated.

Lerner (1973) reported another case of a bipolar demand pacemaker inhibition in which the dispersive electrode was on the low thigh. During transurethral resection, cutting current inhibited the pacemaker but coagulating current did not. In such cases, Lerner recommended activating the ESU using short bursts of current.

Inhibition of an implanted demand pacemaker by electrosurgical current was reported by O'Donoghue (1973):

> Six months later (after pacemaker implantation), the patient underwent a transurethral resection of the prostate gland. The ground of the Bovie CSV is placed under the patient's buttock. As expected, continuous ECG monitoring was impossible during electrosurgery, because of the electrical interference. On two occasions following four to five seconds of electrocuting, the patient was noted to have tonic-clonic movements of the head and arms, and the carotid pulse could not be felt at this time. A magnet was placed over the pacemaker converting it into a fixed-rate unit, and no further episodes of inhibition occurred for the remainder of the operation. The patient had a good result, and no sequelae from the temporary asystole.

O'Donoghue was aware of the need to direct the electrosurgical current away from the pacemaker and its leads when he wrote:

> Placing the indifferent electrode of the cautery under the buttocks of the patient should confine the current field to an area away from the pacemaker or endocardial electrodes, allowing electrosurgery to be carried out in safety, but as occurred in this patient, induction currents of sufficient magnitude to be picked up by the electrodes and inhibit the pacemaker can unfortunately still be generated.

In appraising the foregoing recommendations for placement of the dispersive electrode under the buttocks, it is useful to note that the surgical procedure was a transurethral resection and the buttocks location for the dispersive electrode directed the current away from the pacemaker. A better location for the dispersive electrode would be the thigh.

Domino and Smith (1983) elected to prevent electrosurgical inhibition of a demand pacemaker by placing a magnet on the chest to cause the pacemaker to operate in the fixed-rate mode. They reported:

> A fifty-nine-year-old man with cervical spondylosis and a vocal cord lesion was scheduled for direct laryngoscopy and cervical laminectomy.
>
> The patient had sick sinus syndrome "for which he had a permanent (manufacturer) right-ventricular, inhibited, unipolar, demand programmable pacemaker. Physical examination and preoperative laboratory studies were normal. An electrocardiogram revealed a paced rhythm at seventy beats per minute.

> A toroidal ceramic magnet was then taped over the pacemaker to prevent interference from the cutting and coagulating current of the (manufacturer) electrocautery used during the laminectomy and a grounding pad was placed on a leg. The electrocautery was used sparingly for the first forty-five minutes, during which time a spontaneous increase in heart rate to 100 beats/minute with clear pacemaker artifact and ventricular capture was observed.
>
> The pacemaker firing rate varied in multiples of ten (60, 70, 80, 90, 100), which corresponded to the possible programmable rate settings for this pacemaker.

From the foregoing it is clear that the pacemaker was variably affected by the electrosurgical current. Worthy of note is the fact that the active electrosurgical electrode was applied to the neck and the dispersive electrode was on a leg, placing the pacemaker lead directly in line with the electrosurgical current. Figure 2.13 illustrates this situation. Note that the pacing electrodes (P1, P2) are in line with the path taken by the electrosurgical current. The hazard is greater if a monopolar pacemaker is used because the spacing between the two electrodes is greater. Obviously, placing the dispersive electrode so that the electrosurgical current is directed away from the pacemaker lead is highly desirable.

Reprogramming of DDD pacemakers by electrosurgical current was reported by Bellott et al. (1984). In a study of 140 DDD pacer implants involving five different manufacturers, all pacemakers changed their mode of pacing to what is called the backup mode. All but one could be reprogrammed. They reported:

> All pacemakers were implanted via the percutaneous sheath set, retained guide-wire technique. Electrosurgery was used to effect hemostasis. On occasion, because of skin-edge bleeding, electrosurgery was used with the pacemaker in the pocket. At no time was electrosurgery applied directly to the pacemaker. Units were in the pocket and a two-layer subcutaneous closure effected prior to application of electrosurgery to the skin edge. The site of the dispersive electrode was not given. As stated above, all units (except one) could be reprogrammed to the desired pacing mode. The unit that could not, remained in the VVO mode.

A 1996 case investigated by the author provides another example of pacemaker malfunction due to electrosurgical current. A seventy-five-year-old white male was taken to the operating room for surgery to relieve the pain of

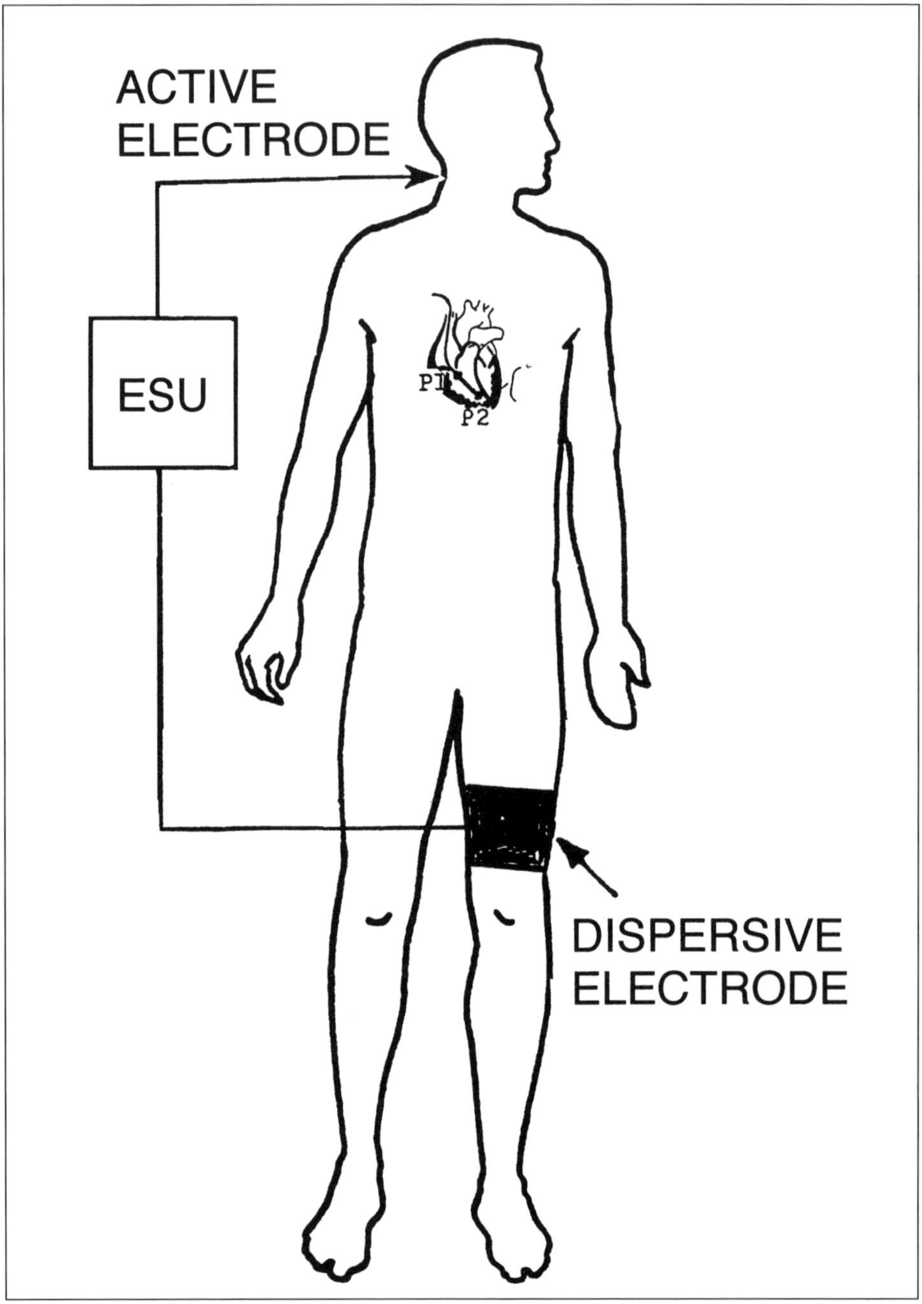

Figure 2.13 *Pacing electrodes (P1, P2) in the heart and electrosurgical current applied to the neck via the active electrode with the dispersive electrode on the thigh*

trigeminal neuralgia. He had an implanted cardiac pacemaker and had been pacemaker dependent since 1970 because of total A-V block. Full cardiorespiratory monitoring was employed during the procedure. The electrosurgical dispersive electrode was on the right thigh. When the active electrode of the ESU touched the skin of the back of the head, the patient became pulseless due to pacemaker failure. The patient was resuscitated with CPR and the application of a temporary cardiac pacer. The surgical procedure was abandoned and the patient was transferred to the ICU. Later a DDD pacemaker was implanted and the original (failed) pacemaker was not explanted. Radiographic evidence later revealed two implanted pacemakers. The patient recovered and the subsequent medical history will not be recounted.

In the foregoing case, the active electrode was applied to the back of the neck and the dispersive electrode was on the right thigh, placing the pacemaker lead directly in the path of the electrosurgical current, and the pacemaker was damaged irreversibly. This situation is that shown in Figure 2.13. If the dispersive electrode had been located to minimize the amount of electrosurgical current entering the pacemaker, it may well not have been destroyed. By placing the dispersive electrode over the left shoulder, the electrosurgical current would have been directed away from the pacemaker lead; in this case, the direction of current flow would be almost perpendicular to the axis of the pacemaker-catheter electrode axis.

In the early days of cardiac pacing, the occurrence of ventricular fibrillation associated with electrosurgery and pacemaker leads was quite well known. For example, Titel and El Etr. (1968) reported an incident at a time when pacing electrodes were sutured directly to the myocardium. Then it was customary to first use a battery-operated external pacemaker before implanting a permanent pacemaker. They wrote:

> Electrodes were implanted in the myocardium and connected to an (external) pacemaker power pack by extension wires and alligator clamps. The clamp of one electrode was inadvertently placed on a wet drape near the incision. A Bovie electrocautery was used to achieve hemostatis prior to closure; the ground plate was under the patient's buttock. Each time the electrocautery was used the heart was observed to fibrillate. The artificially-paced rhythm resumed immediately each time cautery was discontinued. An alligator clamp noted to be touching the wet drapes was moved, contact with the drapes thus broken, and cautery continued without the recurrence of fibrillation. The pa-

> tient required artificial pacing for about six hours postoperatively after which the rhythm returned to normal. He recovered without further difficulty.

It should be noted that it is more likely that ventricular tachycardia, rather than fibrillation, was produced because true ventricular fibrillation rarely ceases by itself in man. However, ventricular tachycardia is a dangerous rhythm.

J. Abandoned pacemaker lead accident

An abandoned pacemaker lead is one that is not connected to a pacemaker, usually due to lead breakage. Very frequently the lead is not removed because of extensive fibrous tissue that anchors it. Usually the lead is cut off and capped and a second pacing lead and pacemaker are implanted. Such an event is often discovered radiographically much later. Under some circumstances (e.g., the use of electrosurgery), this abandoned lead can induce serious cardiac arrhythmias, as the following example demonstrates.

Aggarwal et al. (1996) reported a case of ventricular fibrillation associated with a broken pacemaker lead and implantation of a new pacemaker. The patient, a twenty-two-year-old male, had the original DDD pacemaker implanted because of sick sinus syndrome. The leads of this pacemaker were broken and abandoned because of extensive fibrosis. Aggarwal et al. stated:

> Two epicardial screw-in leads (manufacturer) were placed on the inferior surface of the right ventricle via a subcostal approach. Threshold data for the replacement leads were 1.6 V, 3.1 mA with an R-wave of 7-8 mV and an impedance of 930 ohms. These leads were connected to a new VVI generator (manufacturer). The pacemaker settings consisted of a pulse amplitude of 3.7 V, a pulse width of 375 μsec, a rate of fifty beats per minute, a sensitivity of 2 mV, and a refractory period of 300 msec. The generator was replaced in the abdominal pocket of the old generator, and unipolar electrosurgery (manufacturer) was used to provide hemostasis. A disposable, pre-gelled dispersal pad was placed on the patient's left anterior thigh. The electrosurgery unit (ESU) was used in a blend mode with cutting set at twenty and coagulation set at thirty. The ESU had a return electrical monitoring system with an audible alarm for fault.
>
> During the use of the ESU, cardiac rhythm suddenly changed to ventricular fibrillation.
>
> Defibrillation was accomplished with external paddles at 300 joules, and a rhythm of ventricular tachycardia was then established. Ventricular tachy-

> cardia subsequently converted to sinus tachycardia following intravenous administration of a bolus of lidocaine (1.5 mg/kg). Heart rate subsequently decreased to eighty-five beats per minute.

They explained this incident by stating that:

> In the present case, we suggest that ventricular fibrillation occurred because of the direct conduction of current from the tip of the electrosurgery applicator to the surrounding tissues, and then via the exposed ends of the inner portion of severed pacing wires to the myocardium.

Removal of catheter electrodes is difficult and not without risk if they have been *in situ* for more than six months. There are several different types of lead extractors, these are described in the chapter dealing with catheter accidents.

K. Pacemaker malfunction due to paging systems

An interesting case of EMI with pacemaker malfunction was described by Duru et al. (1998), who reported that the hospital inductive paging system was a potential source of EMI that may disturb an implantable pacemaker and a pacemaker programmer. They observed, unexpected, an inaccurate battery voltage, current and impedance measurements when their pacemaker clinic was relocated to another room. They stated that there were disturbances in intracardiac electrogram tracings and occasionally telemetric communication was not possible. They discovered that the EMI was the result of the hospital paging system, which was installed in the ceiling of the pacemaker clinic. They stated that the reason for the EMI was an overlap of carrier frequencies of some pacemaker programmers with those of the pager system. They stressed that awareness of this particular type of EMI may have practical applications when selecting carrier frequencies for inductive hospital pager systems and pacemaker programmers.

L. Effects of mobile-phone EMI on pacemakers

The possibility that mobile telephones may interfere with the operation of DDD pacemakers was investigated by Nowak et al. (1996). The authors studied thirty-one consecutive patients, fourteen female, age range 61 ± 18 years, with high degree A-V block and a single-lead VDD pacemaker. Twelve patients had a Unity 292-07 (Intermedics), ten with a Thera 8949/8961 (Medtronic) and nine with a Sahir 600 (Vitatron) VDD pacemaker. After a complete pacemaker check the atrial and ventricular channels were programmed to minimum sensitivity thresholds (A: 0.1 = 0, 25 mV; V: 1.0 mV) and to unipolar ventricular sensing to simulate worst-case conditions. During continuous ECG recording, the antenna of a mobile phone (Orbitel 902.2 W, digital D-net) was brought in direct contact with the patient's skin, parallel to the pacemaker lead. Then the following operations were performed: connection to the net, making a call, ringing phase, receiving a call, and leaving the net. Thereafter, the pacemaker was interrogated and checked for any change of the programmed parameters. They concluded that in this group of patients with VDD pacemakers, no case of interaction was observed with the mobile phone. Although tested at minimum sensitivity thresholds with direct skin contact of the antenna, the single-lead VDD pacemakers examined were free from interference with a 2-W mobile phone in the digital D-net.

M. Pacemaker malfunction due to cellular phones

Naegeli and Burkart (1996) investigated the effect of three handheld and one transportable digital cellular telephones (GSM) on implanted cardiac pacemakers in thirty-nine patients using the following pacemakers: fourteen dual-chamber [DDD], eight atrial-synchronized, ventricular-inhibited [VDD(R)], seventeen ventricular-inhibited [VVI(R)], and four mobile phones with different levels of power output (2 and 8 W) in the standby, dialing, and operating modes. During continuous electrocardiographic monitoring, 672 tests were performed in each mode with the phones positioned over the implanted pacemaker and over the atrial and the ventricular electrode tip. The tests were carried out at different pacemaker sensitivity settings and, where possible, in the unipolar and bipolar pacing modes.

Each patient was tested with each type of mobile phone at maximal power output. In each operating mode, first the antenna and then the body of the mobile phones were placed (1) directly over the implanted pacemaker, (2) over the atrial electrode tip, and (3) over the ventricular electrode tip. Then they were moved slowly over the whole chest to detect possible interference with the pacemaker. Direct contact with the skin was avoided.

For each test series, the pacemakers were set to both the nominal and the maximal sensitivity settings. In a subset of fourteen patients with VVI(R) pacemakers with programmable lead polarity, the whole test series was carried out in both the bipolar and unipolar pacing modes. All VVI(R) pacemakers were additionally tested in the rate-adaptive (R) mode with the nominal and most sensitive sensor settings. To avoid possible pacemaker inhibition due to myopotentials, the patients were asked to hold the phone with the hand opposite to the pacemaker implantation site. Each time that noise sensing was documented, the patient was asked to repeat the test without a phone to rule out myopotentials as the source of sensing. Then the test was repeated with the investigator holding the phone in the same position to prove reproducibility of the test result. Only reproducible results were considered to be due to electromagnetic interference.

The results of this carefully controlled study with digital communications (GSM) equipment revealed that in seven (18 percent) of thirty-none patients, a reproducible interference was induced during twenty-six (3.9 percent) of 672 tests with the operating phones in close proximity (<10 cm) to the pacemaker. In twenty-two dual-chamber (14 DDD, 8 VDD) pacemakers, atrial triggering occurred in seven (2.8 percent) of 248 and ventricular inhibition in five (2.8 percent) of 176 tests. In seventeen VVI(R) systems, pacemaker inhibition was induced in fourteen (5.6 percent) of 248 tests. Interference was more likely to occur at high power output of the phone and at maximal pacemaker sensitivity (maximal versus. nominal sensitivity, six versus 1.8 percent positive test results, $p = 0.0009$). When the bipolar and unipolar pacing modes were compared in the same patients, ventricular inhibition was induced only in the unipolar mode (12.5 percent positive test results, $p = 0.0003$).

The authors concluded that digital mobile phones in close proximity to implanted pacemakers may cause intermittent pacemaker dysfunction with inappropriate ventricular tracking and potentially dangerous pacemaker inhibition. Further, they recommended:

> Pacemaker-dependent patients should be tested by their physicians for possible interferences before they use digital mobile phones. Furthermore, to minimize the risk of potentially dangerous pacemaker inhibition, their patients should be advised to hold the phone opposite to the site of implantation and not to carry it in a breast pocket close to the generator.

The testing referred to above involves recording the ECG with the telephone in the standby, dialing, receiving, and off modes.

In a similar multicenter study, the pacemaker response to cellular phones was determined in 980 patients using four types of digital and one type of analog cellular telephone. The ECG was monitored on all patients. Hayes et al. (1997) reported:

> The incidence of any type of interference was 20 percent in the 5533 tests, and the incidence of symptoms was 7.2 percent. The incidence of clinically significant interference was 6.6 percent. There was no clinically significant interference when the telephone was placed in the normal position over the ear. Interference was more frequent with single-chamber pacemakers (6.8 percent, P = 0.001) and more frequent with pacemakers without feed-through filters (28.9 to 55.8 percent) than with those with such filters (0.4 to 0.8 percent, P = 0.01).

Hayes et al. concluded, "Cellular telephones can interfere with the function of implanted cardiac pacemakers. However, when telephones are placed over the ear, the normal position, this interference does not pose a health risk." They added, "Placement of the telephone over the pacemaker should be avoided. While the telephone is on, it should not be carried in a pocket over or close to the pacemaker."

N. Pacemaker malfunction due to magnetic resonance imagers

In magnetic resonance imaging (MRI) there are three electromagnetic fields: (1) a high-intensity static field (1.5 T), (2) a high-frequency (64 MHz) field, and (3) gradient-coil fields (kilohertz). All of these fields are capable of interfering with the operation of cardiac pacemakers. Pacemaker manufacturers advise against placing patients with implanted pacemakers in MRI devices.

A study was carried out by Erlebacher et al. (1986) to investigate the type of pacemaker malfunction that resulted from exposing several different pacemakers to MRI fields. They studied four different DDD pacemakers (Cordis 233F, Intermedic 283-01, Medtronic 7000A, and Pacesetter 283) in a saline phantom under several conditions and with various imaging fields. Pacemaker output was monitored using electrocardiographic telemetry. All units paced normally with only the static magnetic field present. During imaging, all units malfunctioned, with total inhibition of atrial and ventricular output in three of the pacemakers. In the fourth, ventricular backup pacing was activated at high radio frequency pulse repetition rates. However, the MRI scanner could trigger atrial output in this pacemaker at rates of up to 800/minute. All malfunctions were a result of radio frequency interference, whereas gradient and static magnetic fields had no effect. Despite magnetic field strengths adequate to close pacemaker reed switches, radio frequency interference during MRI may cause total inhibition of atrial and ventricular output in DDD pacemakers, and can also cause dangerous atrial pacing at high rates. They concluded that MRI should be avoided in patients with these DDD pacemakers.

O. Pacemaker malfunction due to microwave-oven EMI

Rustan et al. (1973) investigated the 2450-MHz power density levels required to cause pacemakers to malfunction. The study involved nine dogs with implanted pacemakers and ten unimplanted pacemakers exposed to power density levels ranging from 1 to 10,000 μW/cm². Demand and P-wave-triggered pacemakers were used. Table 2.5 identifies the types, many of which are no longer available. To simulate the emission from microwave ovens, a double modulation method was used. The main modulation was either 120 or 60 Hz; the second modulation ranged from 0.6 to 10 Hz. Each animal or unimplanted pacemaker was placed 370 cm from a pyramidal horn antenna that delivered the 2450-MHz electromagnetic energy. Electrocardiograms were obtained from the dogs and the frequency of the pulses from the unimplanted pacemakers was measured.

Table 2.5
Pacemaker Types Exposed to Microwaves*

A — Biotronik	K — General Electric A2072D
B — Device Implanted 3821	L — American Optical 281013
C — Cordis Stanicor	M — American Optical 281003
D — Cordis Atricor	N — Medtronic 5942
E — Vitatron	O — Medtronic 5942
F — General Electric A2072D	P — Medtronic 5942
G — American Optical 281013	Q — Medtronic 5842
H — Medtronic 5943	R — Medtronic 5842
I — Medtronic 5842	S — Medtronic 5842
J — Cordis Stanicor	

*Data from Rustan et al. 1973

There was considerable variability in the responses of the various pacemakers, ranging from no effect at low power densities to reduced pacing rate, inhibition, and increased pacing rate. Figure 2.14 (A to I) presents the results for the implanted pacemakers and Figure 2.14 (J to S) presents the results for the unimplanted pacemakers. Two pacemakers (C and I) were inhibited at

8 μW/cm². Three unimplanted pacemakers (Q, R, S) were inhibited by 0.8 μW/cm². Rustan et al. stated that the maximum permissible level of radiation from microwave ovens is 5 mW/cm².

It is useful to note that this study was carried out in 1973 and some of these pacemakers are no longer in production. In addition, microwave ovens have improved, as have pacemakers. However, electromagnetic radiation from microwave ovens is still present and the degree to which it affects modern pace-

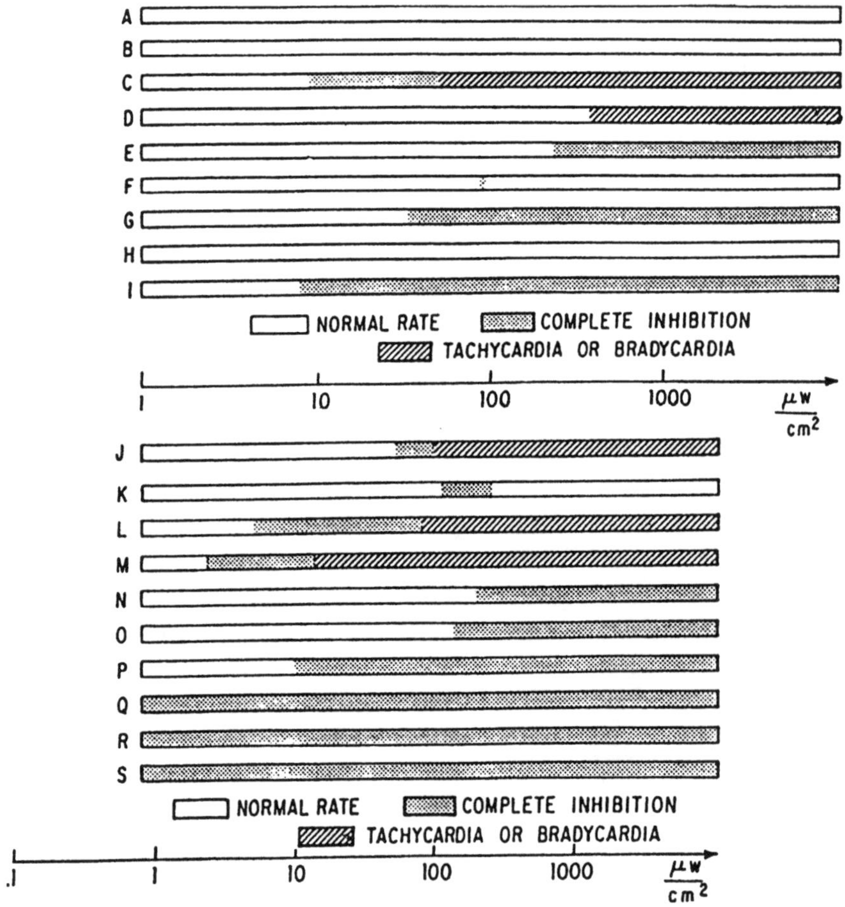

Figure 2.14 *Responses of pacemakers (a–i) implanted in dogs and responses of unimplanted pacemakers (j–s) exposed to simulated microwave-oven energy (Redrawn from Rustan PL, Hunt WD and Mitchell JC.* Med. Instr. *1973, 7: 185-188)*

makers is unclear. Hauser (1994) classifies microwave ovens as an unlikely source of pacemaker interference and microwave oven interference "has not been a concern for many years."

P. Pacemaker malfunction due to low-frequency EMI

In the earliest days of pacemaking, it was suspected that environmental signals could cause a ventricular pacemaker to malfunction. Calling attention to the paucity of literature on this subject, Carleton et al. (1964) tested a homemade pacemaker and a commercially available unit of the type that had been implanted in twenty-six patients. Testing in the laboratory consisted of monitoring the pacemaker output on an oscilloscope. Another test consisted of placing the pacemaker electrodes on the tongue to feel the stimuli. Field tests were made with the oscilloscope powered by a portable alternator used to drive the oscilloscope.

The environments and the manner in which the pacemakers were tested are interesting and clearly demonstrated the need for improved pacemaker designs at that time. For example, they reported:

> The distributor of a 6-volt automobile electrical system produced acceleration of the pacemaker rate when the pacemaker was brought to within 6 cm of the distributor. An increase in the rate up to 450 impulses per minute occurred when any of the pacemakers was moved to within 1 cm of the distributor. Upon their withdrawal from the distributor field, however, a difference was noted between the two types of pacemakers; the locally made type produced no impulse for seven to ten seconds, while the commercially available pacemaker promptly resumed the original rate. The distributor of a 12-volt automobile electrical system produced similar alterations in pacemaker performance. The ignition coils of both automobiles produced occasionally sporadic, premature impulses without a fixed acceleration of rate in either type of pacemaker.
>
> The spark plugs on a gasoline-powered lawn mower and a gasoline-powered alternator were tested. The spark plug of each was shown to alter pacemaker activity when the spark plug-pacemaker separation was less than 8 cm. As demonstrated with the distributor, a progressive acceleration of pacemaker rate occurred as the pacemaker was brought closer. All three pacemakers responded similarly.

Carleton et al. (1964) identified fifteen environmental items that did not affect the pacemakers. They even exposed their pacemakers to defibrillating current caused to flow through saline in which the pacemaker leads were immersed; transient arrest of pacing was encountered. With the highest defibrillator output, one pacemaker stopped permanently.

It is to be noted that these early pacemakers were not in a metal container; this issue was discussed as follows:

> In most of these tests the pacemakers were covered only with three to four layers of towel wrapping. However, completely covering the pacemaker with the hands, thus interposing tissue of the approximate thickness of the usual subcutaneous pocket, did not protect against the effects of diathermy or automobile distributors.
>
> The inherent electrical characteristics of oscillating circuits make them vulnerable to interference by electromagnetic activity in the environment. Since metals of high magnetic permeability, such as alloys with 80 percent nickel, have been used in other applications to provide electromagnetic shielding, a pacemaker was tested after its complete encasement in such an alloy. No protection from the effects of diathermy was observed, but the malfunction induced by automobile electrical parts was attenuated. With such shielding, the pacemaker output was stable at distances greater than 2 cm from distributors or spark plugs.

Modern pacemakers are in metal containers, only the leads protrude. Although the container affords shielding from much environmental EMI, high-frequency (electrosurgical and diathermy) radio frequency current can still gain entry via the leads and cause pacemaker malfunction.

Several studies have been carried out in which pacemakers have been exposed to 50-, 60-, and 400-Hz fields. Some of these studies submerged the pacemakers in saline; others exposed patients with implanted pacemakers to these fields. In both cases, it was desired to determine the field strengths that would cause the pacemaker to malfunction. The following paragraphs summarize these studies.

A study designed to determine the susceptibility to electric and magnetic fields was reported by Jenkins and Woody (1978). Fifty-seven monopolar pacemakers, submerged in a nonconducting tank filled with 0.03M saline, were exposed to 50, 60, and 400 Hz electric fields. Twenty-six pacemakers, submersed in saline, were exposed to a 60-Hz magnetic field. In both cases the field strength could be increased until the pacemaker malfunctioned, as judged by oscilloscopic monitoring of the output pulses. In both cases, the voltage presented to the pacemaker electrodes was measured. The criteria for malfunction were (1) reversion from its normal mode of pacing to a fixed-rate mode, (2) inhibited, or (3) change of pacing rate beyond a range of 50 to 150/min. It was found that for directly injected interference (pacemaker in the saline tank), all of the pacemakers were susceptible to voltages ranging from 0.1 to 11.5 mV. The susceptibility for malfunction was greater for 50 to 60 Hz than for 400 Hz.

For the magnetically induced signal (pacemaker in saline tank surrounded by a Helmholtz coil), 30 percent malfunctioned when exposed to a field of 4 G. There was a nonlinear relationship between failure rate and magnetic field strength; about 4 percent failed when exposed to about 1.2 G.

When viewing the results of Jenkins and Woody (1978) it should be recognized that few, if any, of these early pacemakers are in patients today. Since then, pacemakers have been designed to reject such external signals. However, the test methods described by Jenkins and Woody are still applicable.

The effects of 50-Hz electric fields on implanted pacemakers was reported by Butros et al. (1983). The study involved thirty-five patients with sixteen different types of pacemakers provided by six manufacturers. All were monopolar units and implanted in the pectoral region. Each patient stood between two electrodes that provided a uniform electric field, variable in intensity from 0 to 20 kV/m (rms). The current flowing through the subject was measured at each field strength and the pacemaker behavior was evaluated by the telemetered ECG.

As the field strength was increased, four types of response were noted: (1) normal sensing and pacing (i.e., no effect), (2) reversion to a fixed-rate mode, (3) slow and irregular pacing, and (4) slow and irregular pacing preceded by reversion to a fixed-rate mode. There were large differences among the different pacemakers for the field strengths required to produce these effects. Body current due to the electric fields in the range of 0 to 20 kV/m was measured because it is this current, flowing through the resistive tissues of the body, that develops a potential that enters the pacemaker via its electrodes. There was a linear relationship between body current and field strength. For a 172-cm subject, the body current was 200 μA (rms) for 20 kV/m. The body current for a taller subject was slightly higher and slightly less for a shorter subject. The body current required for reversion to a fixed-rate mode ranged from 37 to 200 μA. One pacemaker functioned normally at 200 μA of body current. The field strengths equivalent to these body currents are about 4 and 24 kV/m. Increasing the sensitivity of the pacemaker detection circuit lowered the field strength required for reversion. Commenting on their findings, Butros et al. (1983) concluded:

> The differences in behavior between different pacemaker models must be due to differences in the design of their sensing and filtration circuitry. It is encouraging that some models appear to be completely immune to interference by electric fields as high as 20 kV/m.
>
> Despite the abnormal behavior seen with some pacemaker models it should be stressed that power transmission lines, even those operating at the highest voltages (400 kV in the U.K.), should not be considered potentially hazardous to members of the general public who are fitted with pacemakers.

Butros et al. went on to state that the general public may be exposed rarely to in excess of 5 kV/m. It was observed from this study that all pacemakers tested (with the exception of two) needed more than 5 kV/m to change their behavior. They hastened to point out, however, that the electric field did not affect the programmability of the pacemakers, which functioned normally when the field was removed.

To determine the level of 50-Hz body current required to produce malfunction in implanted monopolar VVI pacemakers, Kaye et al. (1988) placed electrodes on the dorsal shoulders and on the feet of eighteen patients and slowly increased the current. The pacemakers were manufactured by six different companies and the ECG was recorded during the trials. While increasing current, they reported:

> There was an initial period of normal pacemaker function followed by a variable period of mal-sensing, inappropriate pacing and intermittent complete inhibition. The duration of the period of inappropriate pacemaker behavior we have called the inappropriate window (I.W.) and have defined it as the difference between the minimum current producing inappropriate pacing and the minimum current producing reversion to fixed-rate pacing (interference mode). For all pacemakers the minimum current producing inappropriate pacing during bilateral current injection in the supine position occurred in the range 27–246 μA (median 88 μA). The width of the I.W. was in the range 2–90 μA, (median 15 μA). Further increase in the current produced reversion to interference or asynchronous mode in the range 29–255 μA (median 145 μA).

Q. Implanted cardioverter defibrillator (ICD)

1. Ventricular defibrillation and cardioversion

Because ventricular fibrillation (VF) has been associated with pacemaker and ICD function, and especially as a complication in electrosurgery, the nature of VF and the method of terminating it will be described briefly.

Ventricular fibrillation (VF) is a condition in which all of the muscle fibers of the ventricles, the main pumping chambers of the heart, contract and relax randomly and there is no cardiac output. Defibrillation is achieved by passing a high-intensity pulse of current through the ventricles via chest-surface electrodes. Patients with pacemakers are defibrillated and in this process the pacemaker can be damaged.

Figure 2.15 illustrates the ECG and blood pressure before the induction of VF (left) and during VF. Note the dramatic change in the ECG and the immediate fall in blood pressure. VF does not stop spontaneously in man and it is necessary to restore the circulation immediately by instituting cardiopulmonary resuscitation (CPR) and then defibrillate the ventricles. Typically, anterior-chest electrodes (D1D2), as shown in Figure 2.16, are used and a pulse of current (e.g., 40 to 50 amps, 5 to 10 msec) is passed through the adult thorax. Defibrillation is immediate, as shown in Figure 2.15b, and the heart usually starts to beat. If not, CPR is instituted until the heartbeat is restored or a higher energy shock is used to achieve defibrillation. Sometimes temporary pacing is needed if defibrillation is achieved and the ventricles do not start to pump blood.

Cardioversion is the term used when a pulse of current is delivered to chest electrodes to arrest atrial fibrillation. The term is also used when atrial tachycardia and ventricular tachycardia are treated.

Giedwoyn (1971) reported a case in which a patient was implanted with a cardiac pacemaker and subsequently went into ventricular fibrillation. Five 400-J shocks were delivered with paddle electrodes and the pacemaker ceased to function.

When a patient with a pacemaker is defibrillated with anterior-chest electrodes (paddles), the pacing catheter electrodes (P1, P2, Figure 2.16) are virtually in line with the current flow between the defibrillating electrodes (D1, D2). Therefore, a substantial current can be delivered into the pacemaker via the pacing electrodes (P1, P2) and the pacemaker can be damaged.

A study of the amount of current entering a pacemaker due to defibrillating energy was reported by Lau et al. (1969). In his paper he stated that only one

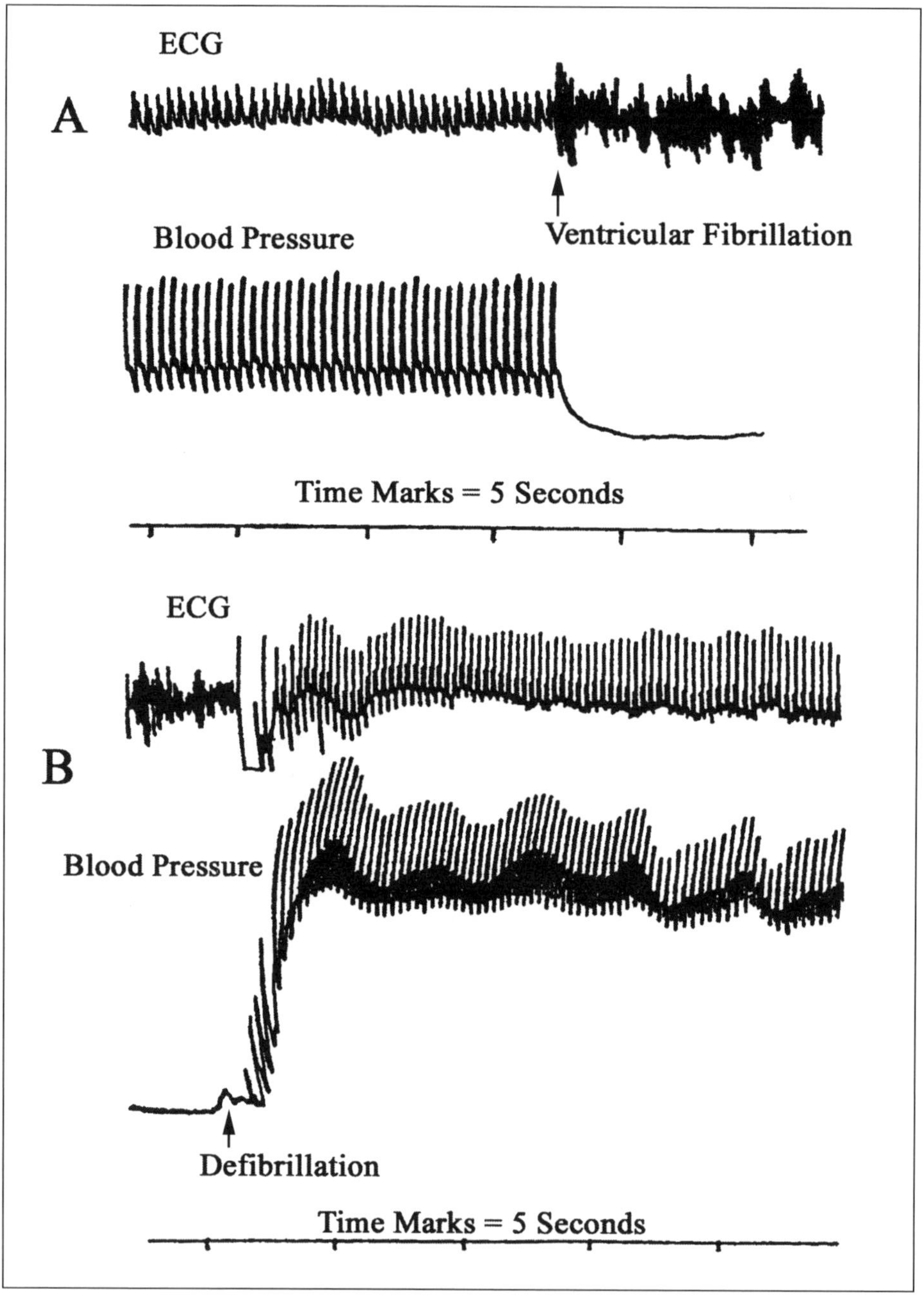

Figure 2.15 *(a) the ECG and blood pressure before the induction of ventricular fibrillation (VF) (left of arrow) and during VF (right of arrow); (b) the delivery of a defibrillating shock and restoration of the ECG and blood pressure*

manufacturer (at that time) had placed protective circuitry (zener diodes) in the pacemaker. Since then pacemakers have been equipped with various types of protective circuitry. The amount of current entering the pacemaker depends on the type of protective circuit, the intensity of the defibrillating current pulse, the location of the chest electrodes, and the location and spacing between the pacing electrodes (P1, P2). If the pacemaker lead is monopolar, i.e., one electrode on the catheter and the pacemaker case is the other electrode, the spacing between the electrodes is larger and the risk of pacemaker damage is greater. Although anterior-chest electrodes are used routinely for ventricular defibrillation, chest-to-back electrodes deliver current to the ventricles in a direction that is nearly at right angles to the axis of the pacing electrodes (P1, P2), and consequently much less current will enter the pacemaker via the pacing electrodes. Hauser (1994) made such a recommendation:

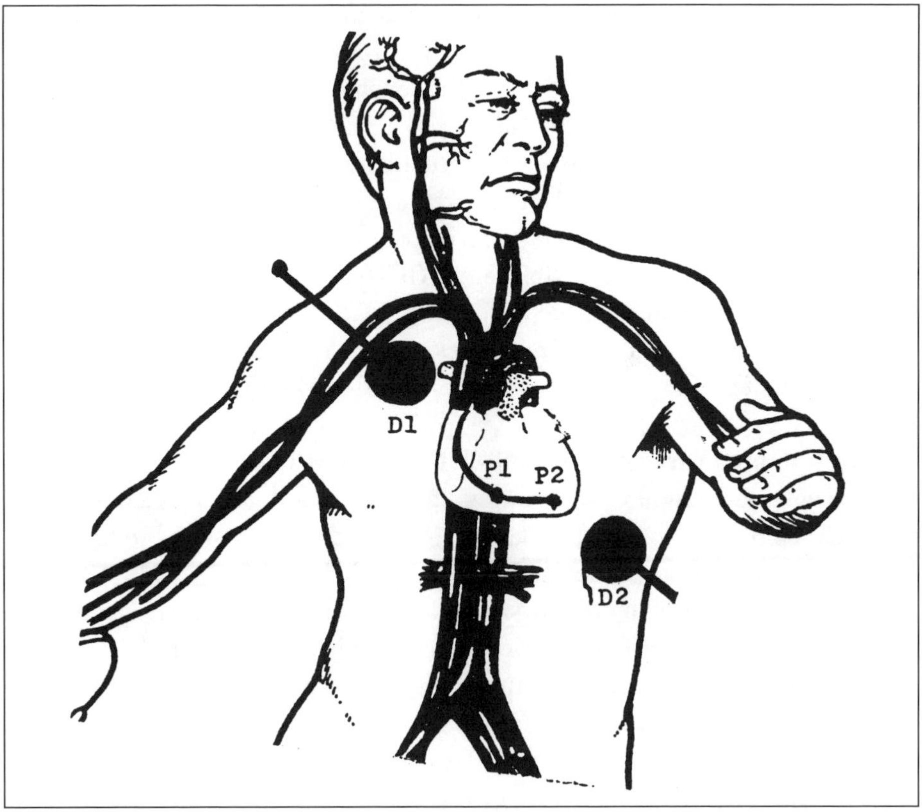

Figure 2.16 *Location of anterior-chest defibrillating (paddle) electrodes (D1, D2) and a pacing catheter with electrodes (P1, P2) in the right ventricle*

> The main concern during cardioversion and defibrillation (in a patient with a pacemaker) is the potential for circuitry damage. Also, energy may be coupled to the lead, causing myocardial damage. Another possible occurrence is inadvertent resetting of the pacemaker's programmed parameters.
>
> In order to minimize these possibilities, anterior-posterior paddles should be used rather than two anterior paddles. With anterior-posterior paddles, the energy is perpendicular to the plane of the lead and less energy is coupled to the lead. The paddles should be placed at least five inches from the pacemaker.

The myocardial damage referred to by Hauser results from high-current density at the interface between the pacing electrodes and myocardium due to the defibrillating current. The consequence of such damage is an increase in pacing threshold and loss of capture. When protective circuitry (Zener diodes and/or a low-loss capacitor) was placed in pacemakers in the early 1980s, the output impedance of pacemakers became low for the high-intensity defibrillating pulse of current; therefore, the current density at the pacing electrodes (P1, P2) becomes high during defibrillation and cardioversion. The price paid for pacemaker protection is temporary or permanent threshold increase and potential loss of capture. Levine et al. (1983) reported transient or permanent loss of capture in six pacemaker patients experiencing cardioversion or defibrillation.

Implanted cardioverter defibrillators (ICDs) have been implanted in patients with an implanted pacemaker and malfunction resulted when the defibrillating shock was delivered. These cases are described in the section dealing with the ICD.

2. Implanted cardioverter defibrillator operation

The automatic implantable cardioverter defibrillator (ICD) is a device that detects a rapid electrical ventricular rhythm and delivers a shock to terminate the arrhythmia. Originally devised by Mirowski et al. (1972), its first clinical feasibility was reported by Mirowski et al. in 1973. Now on the horizon is the implantable atrial defibrillator, which is in preliminary clinical trials. Although effective, ICDs are not without complications, in the form of failure to deliver a shock, delivery of an inappropriate shock, complications following delivery of a shock, and susceptibility to EMI. The following paragraphs describe these complications, not all of which are device related.

Several different electrode systems, including catheter electrodes, transventricular patch electrodes, or a catheter electrode paired with a subcutaneous electrode, are used to detect the ventricular arrhythmia and to deliver the therapeutic shock. Sometimes a separate pair of electrodes is used to detect the electrogram.

Several different algorithms have been used to identify the type of ventricular arrhythmia (Jenkins and Caswell, 1996); however, at present, most are based on a rate criterion, the key requirement being detection of only the ventricular excitation waves. A few examples will be presented to illustrate the detection problem.

Figure 2.17a illustrates two normal ECG complexes, consisting of P, Q, R, S, and T waves. The P wave is produced by the atria; the Q, R, S, and T waves are produced by the ventricles. The three horizontal lines (1, 2, 3) identify three

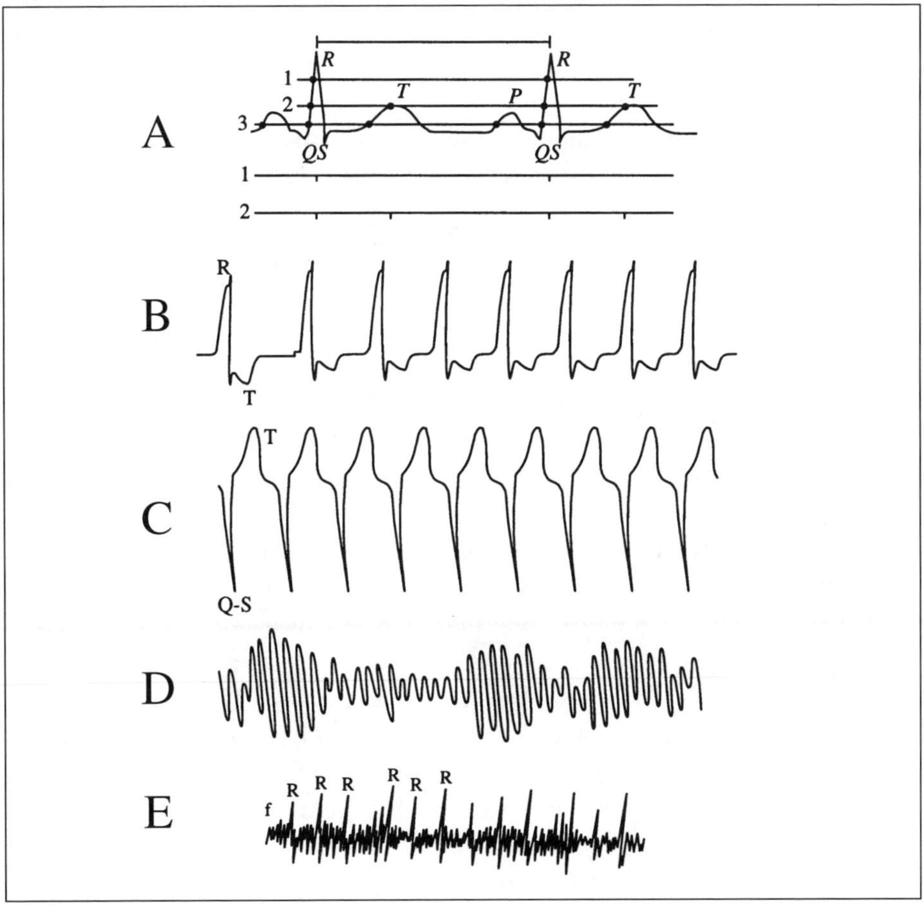

Figure 2.17 (a) Normal sinus rhythm with three levels of sensing (1, 2, 3); (b and c) ventricular tachycardia; (d) ventricular fibrillation; (e) atrial fibrillation

different sensing thresholds. Level 1 illustrates a threshold that detects only the R waves. Level 2 illustrates what is known as double counting, i.e., a threshold that detects both R and T waves, a situation that could cause the ICD to deliver an inappropriate shock if the R-wave rate is elevated. Level 3 illustrates gross oversensing in which the P, R, and T waves are sensed and the ICD is informed that the ventricular rate is three times the true rate, a condition that is very likely to result in delivery of an inappropriate shock to the ventricles. Obviously, single counting of the QRS wave is desirable to identify ventricular rate. The various waveforms that an ICD must distinguish will be described next.

Figures 2.17b and c illustrate ventricular tachycardia, a rapid ventricular rhythm that should be shocked; the shock strength required is less than that needed for defibrillation. Although Figures 2.17b and c both represent ventricular tachycardia, the focal origin of each is different.

Figure 2.17d illustrates ventricular fibrillation, a condition in which all cardiac pumping ceases and a defibrillating shock is mandatory. Note the high frequency and the waxing and waning of the amplitude of the fibrillation waves, making the detection task more difficult. The simplest algorithm for shock delivery is an electrogram frequency in excess of a preprogrammed value for a preprogrammed duration.

Figure 2.17e illustrates atrial fibrillation (f waves), a condition in which the ventricular (R-wave) rate is rapid and irregular. It is inappropriate for the ICD to deliver a shock to the ventricles because the arrhythmia is in the atria.

Despite the sensing difficulties just outlined, there is no doubt that for selected patients the ICD is a lifesaving device, with over 75,000 implants to date (Jenkins and Caswell, 1996). However, problems are beginning to appear in the form of failure to deliver a shock or delivery of an inappropriate shock. EMI can be implicated in these malfunctions. However, other complications exist which cannot be blamed on EMI.

It is important to recognize that not all ICD malfunction is due to EMI. There are circumstances that cause an ICD to deliver an inappropriate shock or fail to deliver a shock. For example, Jenkens and Caswell (1996) reviewed the literature and stated that atrial tachycardia and atrial fibrillation, both of which drive the ventricles at a rapid rate, often cause an ICD to deliver an inappropriate shock. Figure 2.17e shows atrial fibrillation; note the rapid ventricular (R-wave) rate and the variability in the amplitude of the R waves. Because the arrhythmia resides in the atria, it is inappropriate to deliver a shock to the ventricles.

3. ICD control and monitoring

Two-way communication is provided with an ICD via a telemetry link with the programmer that is placed on the skin above the implant which may be in the abdominal or pectoral region. The programmer can interrogate circuit function, e.g., sensing sensitivity and rate, energy setting and delivery, number of activations to date, etc. The programmer can also sense certain operating parameters such as electrode impedance and battery voltage. In addition, an implanted ICD can be activated or deactivated by placing a small permanent magnet on the skin over the implant. Accidental deactivations are by no means unknown.

4. Effect of EMI on ICDs

An unusual case of EMI was reported by Hunn et al. (1998) who interrogated the ICD of a fifty-seven-year-old man. The interrogation caused delivery of shocks. Hunn et al. investigated the cause of this abnormal response by stating:

> The only abnormality detected was a loose sensing lead connection at the time of explantation. The presumed origin of the signals that resulted in inappropriate discharges was current induced in the sensing lead by radio frequency energy emitted by the programming wand during interrogation. These signals are normally below the maximum sensitivity of the ICD, but were probably enhanced because of the loss of a low impedance current path due to the disconnected sensing lead. The resultant signal was sensed by the ICD as R waves and led to oversensing and inappropriate discharges.

Kim et al. (1987) reported the inadvertent delivery of shocks from an ICD in a patient with an implanted pacemaker. They stated:

> A patient with an automatic implantable cardioverter defibrillator (AICD) received two inadvertent shocks when a magnet was placed over the pacer during a routine permanent pacer check. Analysis of the rhythm strip suggested that both patient's QRS complexes (133 beats/minute) and asynchronous pacer artifacts (70 beats/minute) were counted by the AICD sensing system and exceeded the rate criteria of 153 beats/minute. This resulted in shocks from the AICD during sinus rhythm at 133 beats/minute. To avoid possible inadvertent shocks, an AICD should be deactivated while a magnet is placed over the pacemaker during a permanent pacer check.

During a routine follow-up, Bonnet et al. (1990) found five patients in whom the ICD was in the inactive state because of prior exposure to magnetic fields of various origins. They stated:

> Four of the five unsuspected deactivations clearly appeared to be from accidental contact with magnets in the everyday environment—two from magnetic bingo wands, one from a magnet placed in a jacket pocket next to the ICD, and one from a magnet inside a large stereo speaker which was carried by the patient. Once reactivated, interrogation revealed normally functioning devices without evidence of battery depletion. Fortunately, none of our patients had recurrent arrhythmias while their ICDs were inactivated. (The cause of the deactivation in the fifth patient was not identified.)

Another case of deactivation of an ICD by a loudspeaker was reported by Karson et al. (1989). The incident involved a patient who presented for a routine follow-up which revealed that the ICD had been deactivated. Karson et al. stated:

> On careful questioning, however, he recalled that about ten days earlier he had moved his large stereo speakers. In moving them, he had grasped the speaker cabinet from behind, put his arms around the unit, and lifted it up against his body. He remained in contact with the equipment for at least thirty seconds.
>
> Checking with the manufacturer of the stereo speaker, we learned that the strength of the magnetic field at the speaker gap is rated at 1160 gauss. A handheld gauss meter measured the magnetic strength in various places. With the probe in contact with the speaker cabinet: top, 6.1 gauss; bottom, 39.5 gauss; grill, 36 gauss; and baffle board, 48 gauss. The manufacturer of the cardioverter defibrillator, indicated that a magnetic intensity of 10 gauss at the surface of the device is required for deactivation.

Another ICD deactivation due to the magnetic field of a loudspeaker was reported by Schmitt et al. (1991). The patient was a sixty-year-old male who had a coronary artery bypass at which time an ICD was implanted. They reported:

> Since then, spontaneous discharges had not occurred. Upon follow-up in December, 1989, the device was deactivated and in standby function. A few days earlier, the patient had worked with a loudspeaker of his radio that came in

> close proximity to the ICD, thus deactivating the device. Positioning the loudspeaker approximately 20 cm in proximity to the ICD pocket reproducibly activated and deactivated the device. The magnetic field strength generated by the loudspeaker was 295 gauss at the surface, and 11 gauss at a distance of 5 cm. In October, 1990 the ICD was explanted and sent to the manufacturer for evaluation of possible reed switch problems. According to their information the activation/deactivation switch operated normally.

Another deactivation case was reported by Ferrick et al. (1991) which involved a seventy-six-year-old lady bingo player who had an ICD implanted. Upon routine follow-up, the ICD was found to be deactivated and was promptly reactivated. She returned two months later for checkup and the ICD was again found to be deactivated. In pursuing the cause, Ferrick et al. (1991) stated:

> Only after an on-site review failed to detect a source of electromechanical interference did the patient's family allude to her routine of resting a "bingo wand" in her lap during weekly bingo tournaments. The wand was described as a small magnet encased in plastic that was designed to retrieve bingo chips. The recovered wand was shown to generate a magnetic field sufficient to activate and inactivate the ICD. With subsequent follow-up the ICD has remained in the active mode and has exhibited appropriate charge times. The patient no longer rests her bingo wand near the defibrillator while engaging in bingo competition.

Three cases of ICD malfunction due to EMI were reported by Schmitt et al. (1991). The first case was a thirty-six-year-old male who experienced ventricular tachycardia and an ICD was implanted and functioned normally. Nine months later, a burst of ventricular tachycardia occurred which was not terminated by the ICD. Emergency transchest cardioversion was used to resuscitate the patient. Investigating this incident, Schmitt et al. reported:

> One month prior to his last VT episode, the patient was in close contact with magnetized screws needed for construction of book shelves. These magnetized screws, when in close proximity to the implanted device for thirty seconds reproducibly deactivated the ICD. The strongest magnetic field generated by the magnetized screws was approximately 30 gauss. In 1989 the ICD was replaced because of battery depletion. The device was sent to the manufacturer. According to information of the manufacturer this ICD had a random

> component failure: one of the reeds of the reed switch was bent at an incorrect angle causing the ICD to be more sensitive to magnetic fields.

The second case reported by Schmitt et al. (1991) was a sixty-six-year-old male with coronary heart disease and recurrent ventricular tachycardia. An anti-tachycardia pacemaker (with an externally inhibiting magnet) was implanted. Later, an ICD was implanted (August 1987). In a followup study Schmitt et al. (1991) reported:

> At the first one-month follow-up, the ICD was deactivated by the magnetic activator of the anti-tachycardiac pacemaker. This magnetic interference and disabling of the ICD occurred even at a distance of 40 cm. The patient had carried the activator in his pocket, thus deactivating the ICD. The magnetic field strength generated by the anti-tachycardia pacemaker magnetic activator was 630 gauss at the surface, and 2.4 gauss at 5 cm. The pacemaker was explanted and replaced by an automatic anti-tachycardiac pacemaker.

Schmitt's third case involved ICD deactivation by the magnetic field of a loudspeaker. This case was described earlier in this section.

Discharge of an ICD by a handheld radio frequency remote controller for a toy car was reported by Ching Man et al. (1993). The patient was a forty-six-year-old male with a history of ischemic heart disease. A third-generation, multiprogram-mable ICD was implanted. Ching Man et al. reported:

> One year after implantation, the patient reported an episode of defibrillator discharge while operating a handheld remote control to a radio frequency modulated toy car (2-Channel Transmitter, model #FP-2PBKA, Futaba Corporation of America, Irvine, CA, U.S.A., frequency 75.950 MHz, 12-volt battery source). The patient did not experience any symptoms prior to the defibrillator discharge. Investigation showed that: When the remote control was turned on and placed next to the pulse generator in the left upper quadrant of the abdomen, oversensing occurred. This oversensing was dependent on the distance between the remote control and the device, the orientation of the remote control in the frontal plane, and the length of the remote control antenna. Oversensing occurred only when the remote control was within 8 cm of the ICD. Interference was observed only when the antenna was angled between 60–120° in the frontal plane and when the antenna was extended >45 cm. Noise detection was eliminated when a ground wire was attached to the antenna and when the antenna was detached from the remote control. The

various features of the remote control transmitter such as the steering and speed did not affect the level of signal interference. Finally, no signal interference was detected when an aluminum shield was placed between the pulse generator and the remote control.

5. ICD malfunction due to arc welders

Embil et al. (1993) investigated a case involving a forty-eight-year-old male with dysplasia who received an ICD because of a drug-refractory arrhythmia. Following recovery the patient was anxious to return to work as an arc welder. The work site was evaluated for potential interference with the ICD and Embil et al. reported that:

> Telemetered intracardiac electrograms (EGM) and marker pulses (MP) were recorded while the patient used the arc welder (Model 250-DC-CP-TS, Auckland Canada Ltd., Miller Electric Co., Appleton, WI, USA) and performed spot welding (Rex Welding and Engineering Company, Type F.P.U., Markum, Ontario, Canada), and also while he stood near a high voltage transformer (Model DT3, Westinghouse Electric Corp., Somerset, NJ, USA). The sensitivity of the ICD was maintained at its usual maximum setting of 0.3 mV. During the course of his work, his lower thorax (where the ICD was implanted) came within 10 cm of the cable supplying electricity to the arc welding electrode holder, and between 10–50 cm from the spot welding electrode.

During arc welding the ECG telemetered from the ICD showed infrequent spikes with an amplitude of about half of that of the QRS wave, but they were not sensed by the ICD. No false (R-wave) marker pulses were sensed. Magnetic field strengths were measured in the environment of the arc welder. Embil et al. (1993) reported:

> The arc welder was operated at settings at the upper end of the operational range (200 A and 30 V, welding quarter-inch steel using a 0.035-mm [?] wire electrode). At a distance of 10 cm from the electrical cable supplying the welding electrode, the magnetic fields measured were typically 1 gauss (G), maximum 3 G. The measured frequency of pulsing was 70 Hz. The high-frequency component created by the arc was extremely small at 1–3 mG.

They continued:

> Magnetic field in excess of 90 G will definitely close the reed switch of this device, but constant DC magnetic fields of 20 G or more may result in closure. Among the items of equipment at the patient's work place, only the arc welding apparatus generated a DC magnetic field that, although pulsed rather than constant, could conceivably have caused the switch to close. Since the maximum DC field measured at a distance of 10 cm from the cable was only 3 G, its intensity was clearly insufficient to affect the reed switch. The measured field strengths at the patient's place of work were lower than expected. Levels of 3-10 G may be compared with the fields generated by such common household objects as electric shavers, microwave ovens, and hair dryers, which generate AC fields of up to 1.5, 2, and 20 G, respectively.

The decision in this case was that the patient could return to work as an arc welder. Nonetheless, the following caveat was offered:

> Nevertheless, the general ability of patients fitted with electronic devices to work in the presence of strong electromagnetic fields remains uncertain and our results are only directly applicable to patients fitted with an ICD who are exposed to these specific varieties of welding equipment kept in good repair.

The possibility that operating heavy industrial machinery (arc welders, 200-HP motors, and a locomotive starter) could interfere with an ICD was investigated by Fetter et al. (1996). The study involved eleven patients working about one foot from these devices, which draw substantial electric current and produce appreciable magnetic fields. In three of the patients the ICD was implanted pectorally and in the remainder the implants were in the abdomen. The ICDs used bipolar sensing with the electrodes spaced 1 cm. The emitted electromagnetic energy spectrum was measured from 0.01 Hz to 100 MHz. The counters in all ICDs were interrogated by telemetry to identify malfunction.

The measured electromagnetic spectrum was almost uniform over the frequency range, with a slight peak at 2 MHz. Commenting on the effects on the ICDs, they stated:

> At no time was any ventricular tachycardia or ventricular fibrillation counter activated by the radiated electromagnetic interference for any test conducted on any patient. There was no damage or reprogramming of any implanted defibrillator during the tests.

Mindful of the fact that the results were obtained with only eleven subjects and with only two types of ICD, Fetter et al. (1996) provided recommendations for others by stating:

> However, it would be prudent to provide an extra margin of safety before the patient returns to an electrically hostile work site by (1) having a technical consultant from the device manufacturer conduct a comprehensive electromagnetic interference test with patients at their site; (2) increasing the defibrillator sensitivity to 0.6 mV, programming the number of intervals to detect ventricular tachycardia to a minimum of sixteen, and programming the number of intervals to detect ventricular fibrillation to a minimum of eighteen; (3) determining the type of electrical equipment that the patient will be operating and assuring that appropriate electrical grounding is maintained in good condition; (4) ensuring that the patient's implantable defibrillator is two feet from the electrical source of the electromagnetic interference; (5) having patients wear gloves to avoid inadvertent contact with circuit electrical potentials; (6) advising patients to stop operating the electrical equipment if they experience a shock or lightheadedness and to immediately contact their primary physician.

6. Cell-phone EMI

The potential for cell-phone interaction with ICDs was studied in Italy by Ochetta et al. (1999), who investigated the two systems (GSM and TACS) used in Europe. Thirty patients, implanted with ICDs from five different manufacturers, were tested prior to the study and the ICDs were checked and functioned normally. The ICD with stored memory was interrogated to ensure that no prior events became part of the results. The following location protocol was used: (1) the telephone in direct contact with the ICD and the programming head, (2) the telephone in direct contact with the ICD alone (head of the programmer moved away), (3) the telephone positioned in the area of pacing/sensing ventricular lead, and (4) the telephone in the hands of the patient.

The procedures used with the two types of cell phones were the same and each procedure lasted 30 sec, namely: telephone in receiving and calling mode (frequency around 900 MHz); telephone in active conversation mode (speaking, frequency around 900 MHz modulated at 217 Hz) and telephone in passive conversation mode (listening, with activation for the digital transmission telephone of the discontinuous transmission mode—DTX—frequency modulated at 2–8 Hz). Each protocol step lasted for at least thirty seconds. During this period, intracardiac and surface electrocardiograms were observed and recorded if necessary.

After the tests, the ICD memories were interrogated for events such as reprogramming and pacing. A second study involved a subgroup of five patients who were tested during ICD implantation.

After performing standard pacing and sensing tests on the implanted lead(s), the ICD was connected and placed in a subcutaneous site. Using a sterile plastic sleeve, a TACS analog telephone in the receiving mode was then placed near the ICD. VF was induced and ICD detection time and shock interrogation were monitored. The test was repeated with the GSM digital telephone. Finally, a third VF induction was performed with the ICD functioning without any operating cellular telephone. The time from arrhythmia induction to ICD discharge, at same energy, was analyzed to identify any possible delay in VF detection or VF misdetection due to telephone interference.

From this extensive study, Ochetta et al. (1999) reported:

> All evaluated models showed significant noise in the telemetric transmission when the cellular telephone (both TACS and GSM) was located near the ICD and the programming head; noise was particularly significant during call and reception, in most cases leading to loss of telemetry. No false arrhythmia detections have been observed during tests with cellular telephones located on the ICD's. During tests performed with cellular telephones located near the leads or in the hands of patients, no telemetric noises or false arrhythmia detections were observed. During induced ventricular fibrillation and cellular telephones in reception mode near the device, the arrhythmia recognition was always correct and not delayed.

They concluded by stating:

> Present ICD models seem to be well protected from electromagnetic interference caused by European cellular telephones (TACS and GSM), without under-/oversensing of ventricular arrhythmias. However, cellular telephones disturb telemetry when located near the programming head. ICD patients should not be advised against the use of cellular telephones, but it has to be avoided during ICD interrogation and programming.

7. Slot-machine EMI

A report by Madrid et al. (1997), in Spain, who after interrogating the ICD memory in four patients, stated:

> The electrical interference occurred in all four of them, while they were playing with slot machines. The R-R interval history [and], irregular QRS sensing of variable frequency was documented in some episodes. The intervals were irregular and non-physiological, satisfying the rate cut-off criteria in an intermittent non-sustained way.

Although the authors used the term "electromagnetic energy" in their discussion, they also stated that the safe leakage current for such devices is 100-500 μA and reported, "It is advisable to avoid manipulating metallic can machines since they have more frequent electrical leaks than those without a metal can."

The foregoing indicates that the authors believes that power–line leakage current was the culprit; however this was not proven. That the interference occurred while playing the slot machines is not in doubt because of the ability to interrogate the ICD memory. What is in doubt is what agent caused the inappropriate sensing. It is useful to note that slot machines have numerous electromagnetic relays, solenoids and clutches that can emit electromagnetic energy. The resolution of this problem awaits future investigation. Nonetheless, the warning issued by the authors is appropriate when they stated: "Our experience calls for a warning to all defibrillator patients and, perhaps some regulatory intervention."

8. Pacemaker and ICD interaction

It is not surprising that patients with implanted pacemakers receive an ICD and the opportunity for interaction is omnipresent. The pacemaker could be a ventricular-demand type or a DDD type, which can pace both the atria and ventricles or be triggered by atrial activity. Regardless of type, the pacemaker stimuli (spikes) are delivered to the heart and the ICD monitors the ventricular activity. Echt (1984) pointed out that an ICD can sense a ventricular pacing pulse and the evoked ventricular response, especially if the intraventricular conduction time is long. This is an example of double counting. Likewise, if the atria and the ventricles are paced by a DDD pacemaker, the ICD may sense the atrial pacing spike, the ventricular pacing spike, and the evoked ventricular response; this is an example of triple counting and could cause delivery of an inappropriate shock. The likelihood of sensing pacing pulses is greater with a monopolar pacing system.

A remarkable record of pacemaker-induced ICD inhibition in a patient in ventricular fibrillation was published by Kim et al. (1986). The patient was a sixty-year-old lady who had a pacemaker implanted before ICD implantation. Kim et al. reported:

> The unipolar ventricular demand pacemaker implanted previously was not inhibited entirely during VF, presumably because of low amplitude of endocardial signals during VF. As a result, large unipolar pacer artifacts occurred randomly. The ICD failed to detect VF for more than forty-five seconds, and external direct current defibrillation was required. The unipolar pacemaker was replaced by a bipolar pacemaker, with resolution of the problem. The sensing time (from the onset of arrhythmia to discharge of the ICD) was twenty-two seconds.

Cohen et al. (1988) investigated the interaction between both monopolar and bipolar implanted pacemakers and the ICD in nine patients. Studies were performed by inducing ventricular fibrillation and observing the ICD response. They reported:

> Undersensing of ventricular fibrillation by the permanent pacemakers caused inappropriate pacemaker stimuli, which caused undersensing of ventricular fibrillation by the ICD in three of four patients with unipolar pacemakers. After an ICD discharge, pacemaker noncapture was seen in eight of twenty-two episodes for an average 4.9 seconds and inability to sense was seen in eleven of twenty episodes for an average 9.0 seconds. Counting of pacemaker stimuli and QRS by the ICD caused inappropriate discharges.

Worthy of note in the foregoing is the fact that the postshock pacing threshold increased, as evidenced by the temporary loss of capture. This phenomenon occurs with closed-chest defibrillation of patients with implanted pacemakers. Cohen et al. recommended that only bipolar pacemakers should be used in patients with ICDs.

Similar experiences with ICDs implanted in thirty pacemaker patients were reported by Calkins et al. (1990):

> Seventeen percent of patients receiving an ICD at The Johns Hopkins Hospital also had a permanent pacemaker implanted before (sixteen patients), at the same time as (two patients) or after (twelve patients) ICD implantation. Four types of interactions were noted: (1) transient failure to sense or capture immediately after ICD discharge (seven patients); (2) oversensing of the pacemaker stimulus by the ICD, leading to double counting (one patient); (3) ICD

failure to sense ventricular fibrillation resulting from pacemaker caused by ICD discharge (three patients).

Particularly interesting is their conclusion:

> Pacemaker system malfunction occurs frequently after an ICD discharge but is a transient phenomenon and does not appear to have clinical consequences. Double counting of pacemaker stimuli or both pacemaker stimuli and the evoked depolarization is unusual and the failure of the ICD to sense ventricular fibrillation has not been observed with bipolar pacemakers set at standard outputs. A previously unreported interaction, pacemaker reprogramming to a backup mode by an ICD discharge, occurs with an unexpectedly high frequency and may have important consequences. Although many of these potential adverse interactions may occur and must be screened for before discharge to minimize their occurrence, clinically important interactions between the two devices appear to be uncommon.

Khastgir et al. (1991) reported death due to ventricular arrest in two patients with ICDs caused by A-V block following delivery of the ICD discharge. They stated that presently FDA-approved ICDs do not have a backup pacing modality and reported:

> These cases illustrate the need for backup ventricular pacing and the ability to scan and retrieve the electrical events surrounding automatic implantable cardioverter-defibrillator discharges. Future technological advances addressing these issues will hopefully allow further decrease in sudden cardiac death incidence and enhance applicability to these high risk patients.

From the foregoing it is clear that there are many possible types of interaction between an ICD and an implanted pacemaker. Failure to sense ventricular fibrillation because of counting pacemaker spikes can prevent an ICD from delivering a shock. Counting pacemaker spikes and evoked ventricular responses can cause delivery of an inappropriate shock. Likewise, the rapid ventricular rate in atrial tachycardia, flutter, or fibrillation can cause an ICD to deliver an inappropriate shock to the ventricles. The increase in pacing threshold following a defibrillator shock is not uncommon and results in loss of capture. Moreover, A-V block often follows a defibrillating shock and emphasizes the need for backup pacing. Finally, the issue of an ICD shock reprogramming a pacemaker is a hazard that needs to be investigated.

It is clear that if an implanted ICD is to be used in a patient with a pacemaker, the preference is for a bipolar system. However, more important for the future is an ICD that contains a pacemaker so that the two devices can communicate with each other. Despite the future appearance of such a dual-function device, Spotnitz et al. (1992) cautioned:

> Even when dual-function devices become available, special situations will arise that require familiarity with the techniques described. Detection of pacemaker spikes by the ICD can lead to either inappropriate ICD discharges or failure of the ICD to detect and fire in ventricular fibrillation. These problems can be avoided by use of bipolar pacemakers and lead configurations physically separating the lead systems.

9. Improper electrode placement

The following incident associated with implantation of an ICD is self explanatory. The FDA MDR 211106, dated 10/2/90 stated:

> This event occurred during the implant of defibrillation patch leads. The Dr. attempted rescue via the leads with an external defibrillator. The defibrillator displayed an "open load" message. The Dr. tried a 15J-shock using a different defibrillator; it also failed to convert the arrhythmia. A rescue shock of 40 joules was delivered but did not convert the PT. At this time smoke was seen coming from the PT's chest. The PT. was rescued with an external defibrillator. The Dr. determined that the right ventricular anterior patch lead, positioned intrapericardially, was placed backwards so that the titanium mesh was against the pericardium. Since the chest retractors were in place during defibrillation, the patch was making intermittent contact, so that energy was dense at the contact points, causing burning of the pericardium. Dr. reversed the patch lead and the procedure continued without problem. The lead remains implanted and will not be returned for this event. There was no allegation of any device malfunction.

10. Powerline ICD accident

A most unusual electrical accident involving a patient with an ICD was reported by Mehdirad et al. (1997). The patient was a forty-nine-year-old male who had an ICD implanted one year earlier. While kneeling on damp ground in a utility tunnel, he accidentally grasped a 60V/30A alternating current (AC) power line with his bare left hand. He remained conscious but was unable to release the power line. He then received a shock from his ICD, causing him to be thrown back and as a result, the power line was released from his hand.

The patient was admitted to the hospital. His ICD was interrogated and the electrogram in memory revealed normal sinus rhythm at baseline followed by detection of 60 Hz electrical noise. The ICD then charged, and after confirmation that the detection criterion was satisfied, a 12-J shock was delivered. Upon release of the power line from his hand, the electrical noise detection was no longer present.

It is interesting in the foregoing case that the power line current did not induce ventricular fibrillation but it was strong enough to tetanize the hand and arm muscles preventing him from freeing himself. The large defibrillator shock supervened and released him from the power line.

R. Electronic surveillance systems

We live at a time when electromagnetic devices are widely used to interrogate persons carrying concealed items, to identifying thieves and catch those carrying concealed weapons. Retail stores, libraries, banks, courthouses, airports and many other institutions require patrons to pass through gates equipped with surveillance technology or require screening by a guard with a hand-held surveillance device. The need for such devices is on the increase and because they employ electromagnetic energy, there is the potential for interaction with implanted electronic devices such as cardiac pacemakers, cardioverter defibrillators, nerve stimulators, drug-infusion pumps, etc. and cause malfunction, injury, or death.

1. Types of surveillance systems

There are two basic types of electromagnetic surveillance systems: (1) those that require a tag placed in or on the object to be identified, and (2) those that do not require a tag. The former are called Electronic Article Surveillance (EAS) systems and are used as antitheft devices. The latter type is used to detect concealed metal objects, such as weapons, and are found in airports, banks, courthouses etc. This type of detector can identify any metallic object, whether magnetic or not.

2. Electronic article surveillance (EAS) systems

EAS systems are antitheft devices. According to Reuters Health of July 25, 1999, there are about 800,000 EAS systems in use worldwide. All of these systems require a person to pass through an electromagnetic field, typically produced by a coil in a gate.

There are three types of EAS systems, all of which require that a tag be in or on the item to be detected. Low and high continuous, pulsed and swept-frequency techniques are used. Table 2.6 presents a summary of the frequencies, modulation types and field strengths. In general, they are designated as follows: (1) low frequency, operating in the 200–900 Hz range, (2) the so-called magnetoacoustic operating around 65 kHz (there is no sound component), and (3) the radio frequency type operating in the 1.8–10 MHz range. In addition, there are UHF systems operating around 915 MHz.

The low-frequency systems operating in the 200–900 Hz region emit a continuous wave electromagnetic field. The tag contains a strip of magnetically permeable material that has a nonlinear (hysteresis) magnetic response to

Table 2.6
Characteristics of EAS Systems

EAS System	Operational Frequency	Modulation Type	Field Strength in Center (micro Tesla)	Coil Separation
Checkpoint QS-2000	7.2-9 MHz in 6 sec	FM 150 MHz/sec	0.32	36″
Sensormatic-Aisle Keeper	535.7 Hz	CW	107	29″
Sensormatic-Saver	7.6-8.9 MHz	FM 108 MHz/sec	0.3	36″
Sensormatic-Ultra-Max	58 kHz	Pulsed-1.66 msec Pulse width, 10% duty cycle	12.3 (39*)	72″
Sensormatic-Pro-Max	58 kHz	Pulsed-1.66 msec pulse width, 10% duty cycle	13 (39.7*)	108″
Knogo #1	1.83-2.11	FM 0.067	0.26	72″
Knogo #2	219 Hz 7-9 kHz 3.25 MHz 60 kHz	CW Dual freq Magnet???	220	32″
3-M	915 MHz 219 Hz 900 Hz 14 kHz	 CW Pulsed CW		

+ Data from FDA Office of Science of Technology (1997) and manufacturers' brochures
* Peak flux density

the transmitted field. Each time the transmitter-coil signal passes through zero in either direction, the tag emits a signal. Therefore the emitted signal has twice the frequency of the transmitted signal and the detecting coil identifies this second harmonic and the associated electronics signal an alarm.

According to O'Handley (1993), several different types of magnetic alloys are used for the tags, typical examples being Vicalloy, Amokrome and Crovac; these alloys are registered trademarks. In his paper, O'Handley discusses the requirements for tag materials.

With the second type of EAS system, (designated the acoustomagnetic), operating in the low-frequency range (14–65 kHz), employs a pulsed electromagnetic field that interacts with the material in the tag which emits a damped sinusoidal pulse that is detected and an alarm is sounded by the associated electronics.

The third type of EAS systems, which operates in the 1.8–9 MHz region, the tag consists of a flat coil and a capacitor connected in parallel that constitutes a tuned circuit and the electromagnetic field is swept through a given frequency range (typically 7–9 MHz). Resonance by the tag creates a phase shift, which is detected in the transmitting coil, and an alarm is sounded by the associated electronics.

It should be obvious that the institutions that employ the tag EAS system have deactivation means that are applied so that the bearer of the item can pass through the security gates without sounding the alarm. For obvious reasons, these deactivation methods will not be described here.

3. Interactions with implanted devices

There are reports of the three types of EAS systems interacting with cardiac pacemakers, implanted cardioverter defibrillators (ICDs), nerve stimulators and other devices. The following review was derived from the published literature, which did not always identify the type of EAS system. Nonetheless, the following will indicate the types of responses encountered.

a. Implanted cardiac pacemakers. Beaugeard et al. (1992), in France, tested the susceptibility of thirty-five pacemakers produced by eleven manufacturers to electromagnetic fields produced by four simulated antitheft devices, which produced the following electromagnetic fields: (1) 10 kHz modulated at 50/sec, (2) 73 Hz sine wave, (3) 3.3 kHz and 5 kHz amplitude modulated and (4) 218 Hz sine wave. The pacemakers were connected to coils and passed through the antitheft detector at typical walking speed, and then placed at different static positions in the detector field.

Their English-language summary stated:

> Of the thirty-five pacemakers tested, twenty-five developed serious dysfunctions: fourteen long-lasting inhibitions (over three seconds), two stimulations at maximal frequency, two electrical bradycardias and two permanent reprogrammings. These dysfunctions due to electromagnetic interference are observed in old or modern, monopolar or bipolar pacemakers, and seem to be influenced by the amplitude and complexity of the signals emitted by the detectors.

Dodinot et al. (1993), also in France, conducted *in vitro* and *in vivo* studies of twenty-four unipolar and four bipolar pacemakers exposed to synthesized fields to simulate those in EAS systems. The pacemakers were connected to a coil 570 cm^2 with a resistance of 510 ohms.

Two low-frequency constant electromagnetic fields, 300 Hz with intensity of 0.14 μT and 10 kHz with intensity of 1.3 μT, were used. No effects were produced on the pacemakers when they were stationary in these fields. However, more than one half of the pacemakers were affected when moved in and out of the fields at one to two times per second. The pacers were then tested in a pulsed 132 kHz field which was on for 33 msec and off for 33 msec; the field strength was 1.4 to 7 μT. The effects were observed on pacemaker function.

The pacemakers were then exposed to 7.4 to 9 MHz, swept eighty-two times per second; the field intensity was 3.5 μT rms. There was no effect when the pacemakers were stationary in the field. One was inhibited when moved in and out of the field at one to two times per second. However, when placed near the transmitting coil, two pacers switched to the fixed-rate mode, when removed, they reverted to normal function.

The *in vivo* study was performed on thirty-two volunteers with different pacemakers: twenty-two single chamber and ten dual-chamber. All patients had been monitored in the pacemaker clinic and all pacemakers were working well. Radio frequency and pulsed electromagnetic fields did not affect the pacemaker function. Magnetic interference evoked prolonged inhibition of seven out of the ten dual-chamber pacemakers, causing brief asystole in patients being continually paced. None of the dual-chamber pacemakers incorporated "safety stimulation intervals" after ventricular blanking. The EAS artifact was sensed after the ventricular blanking causing a cross-talk pattern. No reprogramming was induced by the electromagnetic fields.

Dodinot et al. (1993) concluded:

> Our study demonstrates that antitheft devices can be dangerous for pacemaker patients. Unipolar dual chamber pulse generators that do not incorporate a safety mechanism augmenting ventricular blanking after atrial pacing (safety or nonphysiological AV delay), are the most sensitive to interferences. In the absence of this protection, magnetic EAS may evoke potentials that are incorrectly interpreted by the ventricular sensing circuit after the end of the ventricular blanking, resulting in sustained ventricular inhibition.

Another *in-vitro* study on the effect of EAS systems of five pacemakers was reported by Lucas et al. (1994) who used four EAS systems: (1) low-frequency magnetic, operating at 218 and 875 Hz and a dual-frequency system operating at 7 and 9 kHz, (2) a so-called magnetoacoustic system operating at 60 kHz, (3) an RF system operating at 3.25 MHz, and (4) a UHF system operating at 915 MHz. Each pacemaker was connected to an ECG simulator by an 8-foot unshielded cable. They reported that no pacemaker was reprogrammed or damaged. The UHF (915 MHz) system had no effect on any pacemaker. However, there were interactions that were characteristic of each EAS system, as well as the location of the pacemaker within the field, e.g. center or near the transmitting coil. The effects were more prominent with monopolar, as opposed to bipolar pacemakers. Lucas et al. (1994) found that the low-frequency EAS system caused the greatest number of positive effects, with some observed in each pacemaker tested. Effects included inhibition, tracking, and noise reversion in four pacemakers (both unipolar and bipolar) when programmed to maximum sensitivity and when passed through or held stationary within the EAS field. At nominal sensitivity three pacemakers continued to be affected, while programming to minimum sensitivity completely eliminated sensing of EMI. Two pacemakers were unable to be tested at minimum sensitivity due to equipment limitations. When the magnet was placed over the pacemaker to cause it to revert to the fixed-rate mode, a response was noted only when the pacemaker was placed close to the transmitter coil. Pacemaker orientation was not a significant factor.

The EAS system operating at 875 Hz produced a magnet response with asynchronous operation in one pacemaker, but only when placed in close proximity to the EAS transmitter coil. The dual frequency (7–9 kHz) EAS system produced no response, except for noise reversion in two pacemakers when the pacemakers were programmed to maximum sensitivity and placed close to the EAS transmitter coil. In one case, when a unipolar pacemaker was placed in close proximity to the 7 kHz transmitter, the noise reversion mode was observed even at the pacemaker's minimum sensitivity. The 3.25 MHz EAS system caused transient inhibition of one pacemaker when it was placed in close proximity to the transmitting coil.

Lucas et al. stated:

> The magnetoacoustic system, operating at 60 kHz, produced a positive response in four pacemakers. One unipolar pacemaker was affected when passed though the center of the detection field when programmed to maximum sensitivity (frontal plane) and when programmed to nominal sensitivity (lateral plane). Inhibition and noise reversion were observed in four pacemakers (unipolar and bipolar) when placed in close proximity to the EAS transmitter. A single nonreproducible episode of close-coupled (400 msec) artifact resulting in ventricular capture was observed in one unipolar pacemaker at a distance of eighteen inches from the EAS transmitter coil.

Lucas et al. (1994) concluded that:

> UHF (915 MHz), RF (3.25 MHz), high frequency and dual frequency magnetic EAS (systems) produced few effects during *in vitro* testing. Except with the MA (magnetoacoustic, 60 kHz) and low-frequency magnetic devices, positive results occurred only in WC (worst case) conditions. Additional *in vitro* and *in vivo* testing is required to evaluate the interaction between pacemaker patients and EAS devices. Careful evaluation of EAS systems with a wide variety of PMs (pacemakers) is indicated to rule out RF induction through the lead system of the pacemaker.

Wilke et al. (1998), in Germany, studied the effect of two security systems (both emitting pulses of 120 kHz) on fifty-two pacemaker patients (twenty-seven single chamber, twenty-five dual chamber). The patients were requested to stand before, then pass through the security gate while ECG recordings were obtained. The pacemaker systems were first measured in their basic programmed modes, then the intervention frequency was changed to 100/min and, thereafter, the maximum sensitivity without T-wave oversensing was added. In the security system with the highest field strength, a pacemaker malfunction could be observed in 13 percent of the monitored patients. In one case, a pacemaker (VVIR) switched to ventricular fixed-rate pacing (VOO mode). In the security system with the lower field strength a pacemaker malfunctioned in 4 percent of the tested patients. With the antitheft device, in the electromagnetic access device and in pacemaker systems with bipolar sensing, none of these dysfunctions were observed. Reprogramming did not occur in any pacemaker. They found that bipolar pacemakers were less susceptible to interference from the security systems.

McIvor et al. (1998) investigated the response of pacemakers in fifty volunteers exposed to six different EAS systems that used three different modes of operation: (1) magnetic audiofrequency which operates in the 200–900 Hz range with continuous emission of electromagnetic energy, (2) swept radio frequency operating in the 2- to 10-MHz range, and (3) acoustomagnetic energy which operates in the 65 kHz frequency range using pulses. The study also involved ICD patients; the results of this latter study are discussed later.

The pacemaker patients first walked through the center of the EAS field; then they stood in the center of the field and rotated 360 degrees for five minutes. Finally they leaned against the EAS system generator (coil) facing perpendicular and then parallel to it. Summarizing the results of their extensive study, McIvor et al. (1998) stated that their pacemakers interacted variably depending on the type of EAS system. Swept radio frequency systems produced no interaction with any implanted pacemaker. One magnetic audiofrequency system interacted with two of fifty pacemakers. The acoustomagnetic system interacted with forty-eight of fifty pacemakers. Interactions included asynchronous pacing, atrial oversensing (producing "EAS induced tachycardia" in the ventricle), ventricular oversensing (with pacemaker inhibition), and paced beats resulting from the direct induction of current in the pacemaker. These interactions produced symptoms in some patients (palpitations, presyncope) only while patients were in the EAS field. No pacemaker was reprogrammed. They concluded that high energy, pulsed low-frequency EAS systems such as acoustomagnetic systems interfere with most pacemakers and pacemaker patients should be advised to minimize exposure to the fields of such systems to prevent the possibility of serious clinical events.

The most recent study of the interaction between two EAS systems and implanted cardiac pacemakers was reported from France by Mugica et al. (2000). Two EAS systems were used: the acoustomagnetic (which emits bursts of 58 kHz) and the magnetic audiofrequency system (which emits a continous 73 kHz, according to the investigators). However, this designation is used to describe a system that emits a continuous 200–900 Hz field. Whatever the system produced, they obtained data from 408 patient exposures and they tested 120 DDD, seventy-one VVI and four VDD pacemakers from several manufacturers. ECGs were obtained while the patients were in the fields of the EAS systems for thirty seconds. Complete interrogation of the pacemakers were obtained before and after EAS system exposure. EAS interference was observed in twenty-six (20 percent) of 129 patients with DDD, seven (10 percent) of seventy-one patients with VVI, and two (50 percent) of four patients with VDD pacemakers. Over twice as many instances of interference were observed with the acoustomagnetic system as were with the magnetic audiofrequency system. Among pacemakers programmed in the DDD mode, a considerably greater prevalence of interference was observed at the atrial versus ventricular level, despite the same programmed sensing polarity in both chambers in all but one case. Sensing abnormalities were the most common EAS-induced disturbance which typically lasted for the duration of exposure. In a few instances of pacing inhibition, the phenomenon was limited to one cycle at the onset of EAS exposure. No changes occurred in the programming of the pacemakers, and a single patient experienced palpitation during EAS which induced rapid pacing. During exposure to EAS mimicking the normal use of the systems, interference with a variety of pacemakers was relatively common. However, the abnormalities observed were transient and caused no symptoms or device reprogramming. In conclusion, the authors recommended that patients should not stand in the proximity of an EAS system.

b. Conclusions about pacemaker-EAS interactions. From the foregoing review of pacemaker interactions with the various EAS systems, it is difficult to make definite conclusions because new and old monopolar and bipolar pacemakers produced by many different manufacturers (foreign and domestic) were used and pacemakers vary in their ability to reject EMI. Nonetheless, it appears that the UHF (900 MHz) systems cause the least trouble. However the EAS systems that produce a pulsed electromagnetic field (magnetoacoustic), appear to be the most troublesome. Nonetheless interaction can be minimized by walking through the center of the field and not lingering in it.

Of the types of pacemakers, the monopolar appears to be more susceptible to EMI than the bipolar type. Also of considerable importance is the sensing sensitivity; a high-sensitivity setting favors detection of environmental electromagnetic fields. Interestingly, reprogramming a pacemaker by an EAS system appears not to be a problem. Any interaction that is investigated should identify the type of EAS system, the malfunction response type and should ascertain if the security gate exhibited a warning to subjects with implanted electronic devices.

Some of the pacemaker tests were performed with electromagnetic fields that are not standard. For this reason, it is essential to specify the type of electromagnetic field that it emits.

c. Pain-suppression stimulators. It is possible to reduce and often abolish pain by stimulating nerves that carry information to the central nervous system. When such stimuli are applied to skin-surface electrodes, the technique is called transcutaneous electrical nerve stimulation (TENS); when applied to peripheral nerves, the term PNS is used. In addition, such stimuli can be applied to the spinal cord; the technique is known as spinal cord stimulation (SCS) or dorsal column stimulation (DCS), see Chapter 7 for details. Such techniques are used to alleviate chronic intractable pain.

An interesting case of an antitheft device, operating in the 7.2–9 MHz range, interfering with the operation of a spinal cord stimulator, was reported by Eisenberg et al (1998) who described a sixty-nine-year-old man who had left upper-extremity pain that had persisted for two years. The pain was described as intense, constant and stabbing; it involved the posterolateral aspect of the arm, forearm and hand, and was aggravated by cold weather. Previous treatments with nonsteroid anti-inflammatory agents and physical therapy were ineffective.

Examination revealed purplish discoloration of the hand and the radial aspect of the forearm and incomplete finger flexion. Pain was increased by palpation of the hand; however, no true allodynia or temperature or trophic changes could be detected. Electromyography showed normal ulnar and median motor and sensory conduction velocities. The F responses were delayed bilaterally. Vibration and quantitative thermal thresholds were within the normal range. A computerized tomography (CT) scan of the cervical spine showed diffusely bulging of the C4–5 and C5–6 discs.

A spinal cord stimulator (SCS) was implanted subcutaneously at the C5–6 level on the left side and at the C6–7 level on the right. The patient reported significant pain relief, required no pain medication and did well for the following six months. Shortly thereafter the patient went shopping in a department store that was protected by an antitheft device. Being well informed and aware of how to act under such circumstances, he requested the doorkeeper to deactivate the antitheft system. Once a clearance signal had been given by the doorkeeper, the patient passed through the antitheft device into the store. He recalls feeling an intense "shocklike" sensation at the back of his skull immediately before losing consciousness. He was rushed to an emergency department, where he gradually regained consciousness.

Neurological examination revealed moderate confusion, impaired speech, gait ataxia, bilateral upper extremity intentional tremor and weakness of the left upper extremity. Brain CT scanning and electroencephalography performed several days later yielded normal results. Cranial magnetic resonance imaging was not obtained because of the implanted SCS device. Followup neurological examination conducted six months later showed some improvement, although mild dysarthria, impaired memory, tremor of the right hand and gait ataxia (for which a cane was required during walking) were still notable. Repeated brain CT scanning performed two months later showed an old infarction in the left basal ganglia.

In discussing the case Eisenberg et al. stated the following:

> To the best of our knowledge, this is the first report of long-term neurological impairments due to CNS injury caused by an SCS device. Permanent neurological deficits as a result of electrical injury are well documented in the literature. In most cases however, they are caused by exposure to more than 25 V. In contrast, the SCS device used in this patient was operated by a low-voltage battery that produced a maximum amplitude of 10.5 V. It is assumed that a sudden burst of electrical current (see following paragraph) was induced by the antitheft device that the doorkeeper failed to disarm and was conducted by the SCS electrodes directly to the cervical spinal cord and brainstem. The relatively low voltage was strong enough to cause injury because of the proximity of the electrodes to neural tissues and the minimum electrical resistance of the meninges [in contrast to the relatively high skin resistance that can reduce the severity of electrical injuries caused by external electrocution].
>
> The mechanism of the SCS activation by the antitheft device is probably one of radio frequency (RF) transmission. The SCS device used in this patient, consisted of an external transmitter and an implanted receiver. The transmitter turns the electrical current generated by a battery into RF waves that are transmitted transcutaneously and activate the implanted receiver. The receiver turns those RF waves back into electrical current. [See Chapter 7, Figure 7.2.]. The antitheft device was also operated by transmission of RF waves. It is possible that the SCS receiver was activated by the antitheft transmitter in an uncontrolled fashion and, consequently, generated a burst of electrical current at a level of duration sufficient to cause neurological injury.

d. Implanted cardioverter defibrillators (ICDs). There have been quite a few reports of EAS surveillance systems reacting with ICDs since the mid-1990s. Inasmuch as the number of ICDs implanted annually is on the increase and these patients are free to move more in society, the number of EAS incidents involving ICDs will likely increase. The following review of the literature will demonstrate the type of response and the scenarios that can produce interaction.

McIvor (1995) reported an EAS system incident in an elderly male who had atrial fibrillation and bouts of ventricular tachycardia. His A-V node was ablated and an ICD with a pacemaker was implanted, tested for function and the patient was discharged. Eighteen months after implantation, the patient had his only ICD firing. In a grocery store, after passing uneventfully though an EAS system gate, the patient leaned against the EAS device while chatting with the cashier. While in such close proximity to the EAS device for a ten- to fifteen-minute conversation, the ICD fired without any clinical prodrome. Later interrogation of the ICD suggested a tachyarrhythmia. To ascertain if the EAS device was the cause of the ICD firing, the patient was taken back to the store, with monitoring via the beeper tone feature of the device. When the ICD was brought within 2–3 inches of the device (where the electromagnetic field of the EAS device is maximal), or when leaning the patient against the EAS device, the ICD audibly detected high-frequency noise, although the ICD did not fire during this second monitored visit. Nonetheless, it is clear that the ICD was susceptible to the field produced by the EAS system.

Three years later, McIvor et al. (1998) reported on the effect of EAS systems on twenty-five adult volunteers with ICDs. Three EAS systems were used: low audiofrequency, swept radio frequency and acoustomagnetic technology (pulsed) low frequency. All patients had ECG monitoring during the tests and their implants were interrogated before and after each test protocol. The ICDs were inhibited from firing during each test. Four test protocols were used: (1) walking through, (2) placing the subject midway between the gate and rotating 360° for five minutes, (3) moving 50 percent closer to the transmitter coil and repeating #2, and (4) leaning against the transmitter coil with the subject's body parallel and perpendicular to the coil.

From this extensive test protocol with the three EAS systems, McIvor et al. reported that there was no reprogramming of any ICD by EAS fields, and no events were detected by the sensing amplifiers. Both transvenous and epicardial ICD lead systems were immune to interference from EAS fields. Only the potential for ICDs to oversense EAS fields as "phantom" tachyarrhythmias were tested. They did not have any patients in ventricular tachycardia (VT) or ventricular fibrillation (VF) during testing, so they could not comment on whether an ICD in an EAS field would be able to properly sense true arrhythmias. In the summary they stated that no ICD exhibited interference mimicking sensing of tachyarrhythmias with any EAS system that they used.

A case of ICD interaction with an EAS system was described by Matthew et al. (1997). The patient was a sixty-year-old male who was implanted with an ICD and returned six months later for a routine followup; the ICD was interrogated and revealed no spontaneous events. The report stated:

> A few hours later while entering a hardware store, the patient stopped by an EAS device and inadvertently touched the security gate. He received a shock without any preceding symptoms. The patient returned immediately to the clinic where device interrogation was performed. The electrogram and R-R intervals suggested oversensing in normal sinus rhythm as the cause of the shock. The stored intracardiac electrogram showed normal sinus rhythm with irregular noise signals and R-R intervals in the ventricular fibrillation zone. Pacing and high-voltage lead impedance remained unchanged. Pocket manipulation with the programming head over the device revealed no oversensing via the electrogram and the marker channel. A chest radiograph showed no lead fracture and blood electrolytes were within normal limits.

The authors further commented that with modern ICDs (fourth generation), review of the episode log contained in the unit can show the sensed R-R intervals and can serve to confirm the evidence of interference with the ICD function. They also stressed the need for patient education.

An interesting and near-fatal case of ICD interaction with an EAS system was reported by Santucci et al. (1998), who stated that a seventy-two-year-old male was implanted with an ICD that contained a dual-chamber pacemaker, both of which functioned normally and the patient was discharged. Four months later, while standing in a bookstore, he received a shock from his defibrillator. Presyncope developed and a second shock was delivered. Shortly thereafter, third and fourth shocks were delivered. A quick-thinking bystander, who was a registered nurse, noticed that he was standing next to the store's electronic antitheft surveillance equipment and pulled him away. No further shocks were delivered and he soon recovered.

The reason for the inappropriate shock was investigated by Santucci et al. (1998) who stated:

> To confirm that the surveillance equipment was the cause of the electromagnetic interference (and to assess the effect of changing the detection threshold to the least sensitive setting), a "rechallenge" was performed under controlled circumstances. Another antitheft device of the same model was set up, and a manufacturer's representative confirmed that it was functioning properly. At a distance of about 0.3 m, electromagnetic interference from the antitheft device affected the defibrillator on three separate occasions, resulting in an abrupt inhibition of ventricular pacing and asystole (the mechanism for delivering shocks was disabled). Presyncope occurred, and the antitheft device was disabled rapidly to prevent syncope. The fact that the interference was reproduced with a surveillance unit exactly like the one in the bookstore was not caused by a malfunction of the particular unit. Intracardiac electrograms confirmed the presence of oversensing in both chambers (which was interpreted as sustained ventricular fibrillation), and the defibrillator would have delivered shocks if the mechanism for doing so had not been deactivated. Reducing the ventricular detection threshold to the least sensitive setting did not eliminate the interference, although it occurred only when the patient was in closer proximity to the electronic surveillance device.

Groh et al. (1999) investigated the effect of three EAS systems on 170 subjects with ICDs. The three systems were made by the same manufacturer; one produced a continuous low frequency electromagnetic field at 535.7 Hz, and the other two produced a pulsed field of 58 kHz. With ECG monitoring and a standby defibrillator, three test protocols were used: (1) routine exposure: subjects would walk through the middle of the gate over a ten- to fifteen-second period. This very slow transit was intended to replicate the exposure that the absolute slowest person might experience normally, (2) extreme exposure: subjects stood in the surveillance system within six inches of the gate transmitter for two minutes. Subjects slowly rotated near (or leaning on) the gate transmitter to assure exposure despite directional field effects, and (3) extreme exposure with pacing. They tested exposure during pacing because in many ICDs, the maximal sensitivity for detecting cardiac events (or noise) occurs during pacing.

Groh et al. (1999 stated:

In sixty-nine subjects, no evidence of any ICD interference was seen during a ten-to-fifteen-second walk-through of the surveillance systems. During a protracted exposure of two minutes within six inches of the gate transmitter, nineteen subjects had evidence of defibrillator-surveillance system interference. In twelve of these subjects, this interference was not clinically relevant, with evidence of only minor oversensing. In seven of the subjects, the interference was clinically relevant, with three interactions likely to produce inappropriate ICD shocks and four possibly producing inappropriate ICD shocks. These seven subjects also had complete or prolonged inhibition of pacing during extreme exposure. Only one subject was pacing via his defibrillator before testing, and he remained asymptomatic during pacing inhibition."

Groh et al. (1999) concluded by stating that:

On the basis of our study, it does not appear that electronic article surveillance systems pose a threat to patients with ICDs if exposure is kept to ten- to fifteen-second (i.e., very slow) walk-through. More intense exposure in both time and proximity may lead to inappropriate shocks. The already minimal risk of an interaction should diminish even more as older and abdominal ICDs are replaced with newer pectoral defibrillators.

The conclusions following the preceding review of EAS system interaction with implanted pacemakers are applicable to ICDs.

4. Metal detectors

Metal detectors are used in high-security areas such as airports, courthouses, banks, government buildings, etc. In these institutions a person is required to walk through a sensing gate (sometimes called an arch), or be screened by a guard with a handheld metal detector. Both types emit low-frequency electromagnetic radiation in the 30-Hz to 3-kHz (low frequency) range. When a metal object enters the field of a coil excited by low-frequency current, eddy currents are induced in the object that produces a secondary magnetic field which changes the inductance of the exciting coil; the inductance change is detected and an alarm is sounded. The sensitivity can be set high enough to detect small coins in a pocket or purse.

a. Background. As a result of many incidents traceable to the ability of criminals to conceal weapons and use them to commit illegal acts, in 1968 the US Congress mandated that there be created new and improved techniques to strengthen law enforcement and criminal justice. Accordingly, in 1974, the

National Institute of Law Enforcement and Criminal Justice (NILECJ) established a Law Enforcement Standards Laboratory (LESL) at the National Bureau of Standards. One of the accomplishments of LESL was to develop a law-enforcement equipment standard entitled NILECJ-STD-0601.00 Walk-Through Metal Detectors for Use in Weapons Detection. This standard is a technical document that consists of performance requirements and test methods to help manufacturers of law enforcement equipment meet NILECJ requirements.

The need for metal detectors also derives from the hijacking of aircraft. Beginning in the late 1950s, such incidents began to increase and the author was unfortunate enough to be involved in a hijacked flight scheduled from Panama to New Orleans. The flight was hijacked to Havana where I was detained and finally released after about six hours. According to Hood et al (1972), "As of July 26, 1971 there have been 118 separate hijackings, 100 of commercial air carriers." To combat such events that could be life threatening to passengers and crew, many different approaches were used. Hood stated:

> The use of intelligence data, hijacker profiles, passive magnetometers and physical search have been employed to prevent hijackers from boarding aircraft. Sky marshals have been established to aid in aborting a hijacking under way.

Under the aegis of the FAA, the first metal-detector was developed by Westinghouse, and was designed for preboard screening. In parallel, research was undertaken to identify the potential risk to pacemaker patients. Accordingly, *in vitro* tests were performed with three pacemakers, made by the leading manufacturers at that time, to determine if the metal detector affected pacemaker function. Hood et al. (1972) reported:

> The tests showed as expected, that triggered or demand pacemakers are more affected than fixed-rate pacemakers, and that the unipolar pacing systems are more effected than bipolar systems. In no case did any of the pacers slow down or stop. In a few there was a small increase in rate at field strengths of 1.35 gauss and above.

A search of the literature failed to uncover quantitative data on the effect of metal detector device fields on pacemakers and the FAA decided to conduct such studies.

b. Cardiac pacemaker interaction. Hood et al. (1972) reported that:

Under contract with the Potomac Fund for Cardiovascular Research, with participation by members and consultants of the Office of Aviation Medicine, fifty-three volunteer pacemaker patients were evaluated while exposed to the FAA unit in a manner identical to the exposure they would receive as an airline passenger being screened for weapons. Eight different types of pacemakers were involved in this group of patients.

Considerable detail was given about the field through which the subjects passed. Hood et al. (1972) stated:

The Westinghouse Weapon and Metal Detector produces a three-axis, two-frequency time-varying electromagnetic field within a space through which individuals pass while being screened for excess metal and weapons. The zero-to-peak electromagnetic field in the center of the pass way is on the order of 0.5 gauss. The electromagnetic field is purposely kept low to minimize interaction with materials and devices such as magnetic tapes, hearing aids, and other devices which may be sensitive to electromagnetic fields. The field reaches maximum intensity near the top of one end of the pass way, normally the end where the passenger leaves the unit. The highest field accessible to the implanted pacer is about 1.35 G. (0-peak). As each individual passes through, measurements are made of eddy-current loss and magnetic effect (change in inductance) caused by the metal carried on the person. By making measurements of these two quantities at both a low and high frequency in the audio range, it is possible to discriminate between thick and thin metals, ferrous and nonferrous materials and to sense the presence of metal in excess of the amount normally present. From these measurements, signatures for various materials can be obtained.

After reviewing results of this extensive study, Hood et al. (1972) stated:

An external electromagnetic field used in a weapon detector system (WD-4) may produce minor changes in the rate of certain pacemakers, especially the sensitive unipolar atrial or the atrial or atrio-ventricular pacing systems. These changes were clinically insignificant to the patient and to the pacing system. Other systems, such as unipolar fixed rate, and unipolar and bipolar ventricular pacemakers were totally unaffected. The weapons detector studied (WD-4) was determined to be safe for use in the public environment of an airport.

The same study was reported by Smyth et al. (1972) in the JAMA for the general medical audience. They stated:

> Certain sensitive unipolar atrial and atrioventricular pacemakers showed minor temporary rate changes that were clinically insignificant. We believe that the weapons detector [WD-4] can be safely employed with patients who have any of the pacemakers tested.

Copperman et al. (1988), in Israel, investigated the effect of airport security gates on 103 pacemaker patients. During the test, which required the patient to walk through the metal detector gate in both directions at least three times as an ECG telemetry system recorded any responses. Pacemaker pulse rate and duration were measured immediately before and after the test. They stated, "No ill effect was seen on any of the units tested, pacemaker inhibition was not observed, and programmability was not affected. Metal detector security gates have no effect on implanted permanent pacemakers."

5. Dynamic cardiomyoplasty stimulator

Dynamic cardiomyoplasty uses an implanted stimulator that delivers periodic bursts of pulses to contract a skeletal muscle that is configured to assist the heart to pump blood. Typically in dynamic cardiomyoplasty, the latissimus dorsi muscle is brought from its normal position on the upper back into the chest and wrapped around the ventricles. An implanted stimulator, triggered by the R wave of the ECG, stimulates the muscle tetanically during ventricular systole to augment the stroke volume of a failing heart. To be effective, the proper timing is essential. Usually the muscle is stimulated for a submultiple of ventricular contractions.

Peteiro et al. (1996), in Spain, reported the reprogramming of an implanted dynamic cardiomyoplasty stimulator in a thirty-three-year-old male. The device was appropriately timed when implanted and improved the patient's cardiac condition. Ten months after implantation, during a routine followup, the stimulator was operating asynchronously. The device was reprogrammed and operated normally. In commenting on the reason for reprogramming, they stated: "The only significant event in the patient's recent medical history had been exposure to metal detection equipment some three months earlier at an airport security gate. Therefore, moderate to severe EMI may have been responsible for this programming change." Unfortunately, the author did not identify the type of metal detector or the types of electromagnetic energy it emits. Therefore, this case remains unexplained.

6. Electromagnetic field strength of metal detectors

Moss (1998), of the National Institute of Occupational Safety and Health (NIOSH), reported a study in which field strengths were measured in metal detector gates (sometimes called arches) in courthouses in fifteen states over a seventeen-day period. The security devices were similar and were manufactured by five different companies. Measurements were made at the head, chest, waist, knee and floor levels for the following frequencies: ELF = 30–300 Hz and VLF = 3–30 kHz. Table 2.7 presents the results. It is important to note that this study was undertaken to evaluate the hazards to attendants constantly exposed to these fields. It did not address subjects with implanted electronic devices.

Moss concluded, "Based on the data collected in this evaluation, security personnel who work with metal detectors are not exposed to magnetic fields in excess of applicable occupational guidelines."

Table 2.7
Range of Magnetic Field Strength Levels (in Milligauss) at Various Distances from Unit by Manufacturer

	No. of	Contact		30 cm		61 cm	
MFGs	Units	ELF	VLF	ELF	VLF	ELF	VLF
A	9	7-1264	1-120	4-140	0-107	0-33	0-12
B	18	7-1690	5-70	2-64	2-14	1-25	1-4
C	2	2-1800	0-220	1-58	0-10	1-10	0
D	16	0-2440	0-350	0-115	0-40	0-15	0-10
E	7	0-1100	0-270	4-107	0-20	0-33	0-10
Total	52	0-2440	0-1200	0-140	0-107	0-33	0-12

ELF = 30-300 Hz; VLF = 3-30 kHz
Data from Moss, E. 1998; 10,000 gauss – 1 Tesla

7. Conclusion

Like EAS systems, metal detectors pose minimal, but not negligible risk, to patients with implanted electronic devices. The same considerations for subjects exposed to EAS systems can be applied to metal detectors. If a patient refuses to pass through the metal-detector field, he/she can be scanned by a handheld detector. This practice is often used when all detected metal objects have been removed from a subject and the detector still alarms. This happened to the author when the metal handheld detector identified the metal frame on his reading glasses in his shirt pocket.

2.9 Electrostatic Discharge

A. Introduction

Electrostatic discharge (ESD) pertains to the transfer of electric charge from a body at one potential to a body at a different potential. The most familiar example is the charge that is accumulated on a subject after walking on a carpet in a dry room and a spark discharge occurs when another person or object is touched. Other examples are the sparks drawn when combing the hair or removing clothing made of synthetic fabric. Although the voltages can be high, the discharge lasts only microseconds. Dash and Straus (1995) stated that the capacitance of a standing subject is typically 150 pF. Parenthetically, the dielectric breakdown (arcing voltage) for dry air is about 25,000 V/cm for a point source. The breakdown is slightly higher for spherical bodies. It is to be noted that the relative humidity is an important factor in ESD; a low relative humidity favors the genesis of electrostatic charge buildup.

B. ESD testing

In the U.S., professional groups are developing procedures for ESD testing. However, in Europe, there is a protocol for testing the susceptibility of devices to ESD; it is contained in the International Electrotechnical Commission document 1000-4-2 (1995). Briefly, the method exposes the device under test to a graded high-voltage discharge to determine the voltage for malfunction. The method employs a capacitor (150 pF) connected to a ground plane (grounded metal sheet) on which the device rests. The other (positive) side of the capacitor is connected to a resistor (330 ohms), which is connected to a spherical electrode at the tip of a wand. The test starts with 2 kV on the capacitor. As the charged sphere is brought toward the device the intervening air becomes ionized and a current starts to flow and evidence of device malfunction is sought. The test is repeated ten times at each selected site on the device under test. The procedure is repeated by incrementing the voltage in 2-kV steps until 8 kV is reached. The voltage for device malfunction is identified.

Three modes of testing are employed: (1) the charged sphere on the wand is brought toward the ground plane on which the device rests, (2) the charged sphere is advanced toward the chassis of the device, and (3) the charged sphere is advanced toward connector shells, displays, keyboards, switches, etc. on the device. During these three modes of testing, the lowest voltage for malfunction is identified. Ideally, malfunction should not occur at 8 kV.

C. Mechanism of action of ESD

ESD can affect medical devices in many ways, ranging from a transient event to permanent malfunction. Because many medical devices contain electronic circuitry with solid-state components (analog and digital), ESD can reveal itself in bizarre ways. Proving that ESD was the cause of a malfunction is not always easy because an on-site test for reproducibility is not always possible. However, witnessing an arc in association with a device malfunction confirms the diagnosis of ESD as the culprit.

When no arc is witnessed it is difficult to establish that the malfunction or failure is due to ESD. However, the static discharge produced when a subject is touched while a bioelectric event is being recorded can produce a spike in the recording; such an event is reproducible. Of course, a higher intensity ESD can enter an amplifier input via a disconnected electrode lead and damage the input stage, rendering the amplifier permanently inoperative unless protective circuitry has been provided. The same type of fault can occur with both electrodes connected to the patient. In this case the discharge follows the common-mode path.

ESDs of even moderate intensity can reprogram a microprocessor that may be controlling a ventilator, drug-infusion pump, a wheelchair, etc., resulting in disastrous consequences. In some cases, it may only be necessary to reprogram the microprocessor.

D. ESD incidents

The most complete listing of ESD incidents can be found in a paper by Silberberg (1993), who reported the following items:

1. The loose-lead alarm failed to sound and the respiration sensitivity was reduced in apnea monitors due to component damage from ESD.
2. The respiratory or heart-rate alarms of apnea monitors failed to sound due to electrostatic discharges to the screws on the setting knobs.
3. Electrostatic interference influenced the normal operation of the synchronization unit of a ventilator in a hospital in Europe. Customers were informed not to use the synchronization unit.
4. ESD caused "system check" alarms or failure of an infusion pump.

5. Ventilators stopped cycling while on patients in a hospital. The ventilators were found to be susceptible to ESD.
6. ESD caused CMOS components to latch up, disabling apnea monitors without an alarm until power was turned first off and then on.
7. ESD caused unintended movement of a gamma camera, which could potentially cause a patient to be crushed.
8. ESD caused infusion pumps to shut down, sometimes without activating an alarm.
9. In radiation therapy devices, ESD caused the source to turn on, the display to blank, unintended gantry movement, or timer failures which resulted in possible patient overdose. Recovery required first switching the device off. In one instance a discharge from an operator to the timer of a radiation therapy system caused the timer's display to blank just as the treatment had begun. The treatment was terminated by opening the treatment room door.
10. ESD from an operator to the membrane switch of an internal feeding pump resulted in continuous alarm and destructive failure of the firmware EPROM.
11. ESD affected infant radiant warmers, causing the heater to turn on or off, alarm failure, and the display to become blank or corrupted.

An unusual incident of roller-pump failure in a heart-lung machine was reported by Leahy et al. (1993). During an operation, the pump indicator signaled a failure. The pump was restarted and the machine was checked and functioned normally. Several weeks later, multiple failures occurred with the same and other machines. It was found that an electrostatic discharge near the machine could stop the pump.

During the operation, the perfusionist made notes on a plastic-backed clipboard. Leahy et al. stated, "When the clipboard was placed on the front of the pump module, its electrostatic charge was released onto the pump case, causing the pump to fail."

Pursuing the matter further, Leahy et al. reported, "The clipboard is made of plastic with a metal clip. When it was rubbed against the operating room uniform, it built up and stored an electrical charge."

They continued:

> At our institution, preventive measures have been adopted to reduce the incidence of pump failure from static discharge. These include discontinuing the

> practice of placing the clipboard on the pump module and maintaining the relative humidity at the required levels.

A good example of susceptibility to ESD was reported by Martin (1993), who tested a laboratory blood sampler having an LCD display. He stated:

> The product consisted of a totally plastic case with conductive coating applied on the interior surfaces. A tongue-and-groove joint was used to affix the front and back half of the seams of the chassis. The failures experienced included resets of the processor or initiation of unexpected mechanical movements.

Careful examination of the device revealed that inadequate contact existed between the conductive coatings on the front and back of the device. This lack of contact caused a high field to exist at the seam where discharges occurred. In addition, there was inadequate grounding of the circuit card and LCD frame to the chassis. When these improvements were made, Martin stated that the device was immune to the 8-kV test specified by IEC 801-2 (now 1000-4-2).

E. Effect of ESD on human subjects

Everyone has perceived ESD as a mild, often surprising shock. The issue of whether such a shock can do harm is less well known. McCarty and Glasser (1977) noted that an ad hoc commission stated that static electric discharges could induce fatal cardiac arrhythmias. Because of this it was recommended that a carpet not be placed in critical care areas. After searching the literature, McCarty and Glasser could find no basis for this recommendation and initiated a dog study to evaluate this hazard.

Using seven anesthetized dogs, they placed a #5 bipolar pacing catheter in the right ventricle and confirmed its proximity to the endocardium by recording the cardiac electrogram and testing the pacing threshold. Static-electricity discharges were generated by, they reported:

> Shuffling our shod feet over synthetic or wool carpet. Static charges were discharged from the fingertips and measured through a 50.1-megaohm resistor into a Tektronix storage scope. More than one spike, i.e., double static discharge, was induced occasionally by incomplete initial contact with the catheter tip. Similar static charges were then applied directly on the external end of the pacemaker wire leading in the distal electrode within the right ventricle.

They reported that:

> The voltage of static charges reached 22,000 volts. The charges varied with the shoes worn, type of rug, duration of shuffling, and the day—presumably related to temperature, humidity, etc. The perceptible level of shock to the finger was established at two to three thousand volts. The energy delivered, as measured through the 50.1-megohm resistor, was calculated at 4.3 millijoules (4300 microjoules) for an 8,000 volt discharge.

They continued:

> Static discharges exceeding 2,000 volts uniformly resulted in paced beats, unless delivered in the absolute refractory period. Ventricular beats were often initiated by discharges below the level of perceptible shock. In fact, a single gliding movement of one's foot across the rug generated a sufficient charge to pace the heart. This allowed repetitive pacing at rates nearing 60/min. Powerful shocks delivered in the vulnerable period of the cardiac cycle did not produce repetitive tachyarrhythmias.

Although ventricular fibrillation was not produced in normal dog hearts, the creation of myocardial infarction by coronary ligation (three dogs) allowed the induction of ventricular fibrillation. They reported on one dog:

> A discharge approximating 6,000 volts clearly initiated ventricular fibrillation. This appears to have resulted from a double discharge in which current was repetitively delivered after the initial discharge had produced a ventricular premature beat (VPB). This secondary shock occurred within the vulnerable period of the VPB and initiated VF, electrical countershock returned the rhythm to sinus.

McCarty and Glasser emphasized that a single shuffle of one foot provided enough ESD to evoke a ventricular beat. They stated that the type of shoe was an important factor; those that produced measurable friction generated enough ESD. Shoe coverings, such as booties used in operating rooms, are not effective generators of static electricity.

References

AAMI Association for the Advancement of Medical Instrumentation. 3330 Washington Blvd., Arlington, VA 22201-4598.

Aggarwal A, Farber NE, Kotter GS et al. Electrosurgery-induced fibrillation during pacemaker replacement. J. Clin. Mon. 1996, 12:339–342.

Bassen HI, Ruggera PS and Casamento J. Changes in susceptibility of a medical device resulting from connection to full-size model of a human. Proc. 14th Annual Int. Conf. of the IEEE Engineering in Medicine and Biology Society, 1992. pp. 2832–2833.

Beaugeard D, Kacet S, Bricout M and Gamblin J. Interferences entre les stimulateurs cardiaque et les detecteurs de vol dans les magasins. Arch. Mal de Coeur. 1992, 82:1457–1461.

Bellott PH, Snads S and Warren J. Resetting of DDD pacemakers due to EMI. PACE. 1984, 7:169–172.

Birnbaum MR and Stasz P. Apnea monitoring system. U.S. Patent 4,580,575, April 8, 1986.

Bonnet CA, Elson JJ, Fogoros RN et al. Accidental deactivation of the automatic implantable cardioverter defibrillator. PACE. 1990, 13:546.

Bostrom U. Interference from mobile telephones. Newsl. Clin. Eng. Div. IFMBE 1991, 10 (November).

Bren SPA. Revealing the RF safety issue in cellular telephones. IEEE Eng. Med. Biol. 1996, May–June.

Butros GS, Mate JC, Webber RS et al. The effect of power frequency high intensity electric fields on implanted cardiac pacemakers. PACE. 1983, 6:1282–1291.

Calkins H, Brinker J and Veltri EP. Clinical interactions between pacemakers and automatic implanted cardioverter defibrillators. J. Am. Coll. Cardiol. 1990, 16(3): 666–673.

Canadian Standards Association, 235 Montreal Road, Ottawa, Ontario, Canada.

Carleton RA, Sessions RW and Graettinger JS. Environmental influence on implantable cardiac pacemakers. JAMA. 1964, 190:160–162.

Ching Man K, Davidson T, Langberg JJ et al. Interference from a hand-held radiofrequency remote control causing discharge of an implantable defibrillator. PACE. 1993, 16:1756–1758.

Clifford KJ, Joyner KH, Stroud DB et al. Mobile telephones interfere with medical electrical equipment. Austral. Phys. Eng. Sci. Med. 1994, 17(1):23–27.

Cohen AL, Wish MH, Fletcher RD et al. The use and interaction of permanent pacemakers and the automatic implantable cardioverter defibrillator. PACE. 1988, 11:704–711.

Copperman Y, Zarjati D and Laniado S. The effect of metal detector gates on implanted permanent pacemakers. PACE. 1988, 11:1386–1387.

Dash G and Straus I. Testing for ESD immunity. Compliance Eng. 1995, B5-B11.

DeBarros Moraes JCT. Effects of electronic autodefense devices on cardiac pacemakers. Artif. Organs. 1995, 19(3):238-240.

Dodinot B, Godenis JP and Cista AB. Electronic article surveillance: A possible danger for pacemaker patients. PACE. 1993, 19, part 1:48–53.

Domino K and Smith TC. Electrocautery-induced reprogramming of a pacemaker using a precordial magnet. Anesth. Analg. 1983, 62 609–612.

Duru F, Lauber P, Klaus G et al. Hospital pager systems may cause interference with pacemaker telemetry. PACE. 1998, 21 (11 Pt 2):2353–2359.

Echt DS. Potential hazards of implanted devices for the electrical control of tachyarrhythmias. PACE. 1984, 7:580–587.

Eisenberg E. Spinal cord stimulator activation by an antitheft device. Case report, published erratum appears in Journal Neurosurg. 1998, April, 88(4):491.

Embil JM, Geddes JS, Foster D et al. Return to arc welding following defibrillator implantation. PACE. 1993, 16:2313–2316.

Erlebacher JA, Cahill PT, Pannizzo F et al. Effect of magnetic resonance imaging on DDD pacemakers. Am. J. Cardiol. 1986, 57:437–440.

Ferrick KJ, Johnston D, Kim SG et al. Inadvertent AICD inactivation while playing bingo. Am. Heart J. 1991, 121:206–207.

Fetter JG, Benditt DG, Stanton MS et al. Electromagnetic interference from welding and motors on implantable cardioverter-defibrillators tested in the electrically hostile work site. J. Am. Coll. Cardiol. 1996, 28(2): 423–427.

Food and Drug Administration (FDA). Center for Devices and Radiological Health, Manufacturer and User Facility Device Experience (MAUDE) Database (online), Rockville, MD: FDA, July 22, 1998.

Foster K. Interference from cellular phones. Sci. Eng. Biomed. 1994, December.

Furman S. Electromagnetic interference. PACE. 1982, 1–3.

Geddes LA. Technical note: Observations of intermittent electromagnetic interference on impedance respiration monitors. J. Clin. Eng. 1995, 20(2):151–155.

Geddes LA, Hoff HE, Hickman DM and Moore AG. The impedance pneumograph. Aerospace Med. 1962, 33:28–33.

Geddes LA, Hoff HE, Hickman DM et al. Recording respiration and the electrocardiogram with common electrodes. Aerospace Med. 1962, 33:791–793.

Geddes LA and Valentinuzzi ME. Temporal changes in electrode impedance while recording the electrocardiogram with dry electrodes. Ann. Biomed. Eng. 1973, 1(3):356–367.

Giedwoyn JO. Pacemaker failure following external defibrillation. Circulation. 1971, 44: 293.

Greene LF and Meredith J. Transurethral operations employing high-frequency currents in patients with demand cardiac pacemakers. J.Urol. 1972, 108:446–448.

Groh WJ, Boschee SA, Engelstein ED et al. Interactions between electronic article surveillance systems and implantable cardioverter-defibrillator systems. Circulation. 1999, 100:387–392

Hauser RC. Status report: Interference in modern pacemakers. Medtronic News. 1994, 22(1):12–20.

Hayes DL, Carrillo RG, Findlay GK et al. State of the science: Pacemaker and defibrillator interference from wireless communication devices. PACE. 1996, 19:1419–1430.

Hayes DL, Wang PJ, Reynolds DW et al. Interference with cardiac pacemakers with cellular telephones. N. Engl. J. Med. 1997, 336(21):1473–1479.

Health Devices, ECRI. Interference between telemetry transmitters programmed to the same frequency. Health Devices. 1999 Jan–Feb; 28(1-2):82–83. ECRI = Emergency Care Research Institute, Plymouth Meeting, PA.

Hood OC, Keshishian NP, Smyth PD et al. Anti-hijacking effort and cardiac pacemakers—Report of a clinical study. Aerosp. Med. 1972, 43(3):314–322.

Hunn RH, Ashbaugh TJ, Calderini M et al. Multiple inappropriate shocks precipitated by interrogation of an implantable cardioverter defibrillator. PACE. 1998, 21:1329–1330.

International Electrotechnical Commission, Geneva, Switzerland. Documents available from Global Engineering Documents, Clayton, MO 63105.

International Electrical Commission (Commision ElectroTechnique Internationals), 1211 Geneva, 20 Switzerland, P.O. Box 131.

Jenkins JM and Woody JA. Cardiac pacemaker responses to power frequency signals. IEEE Int. Symp. on Electromagnetic Compatibility. IEEE. 1978:273–277.

Jenkins JM and Caswell SA. Detection algorithms in implantable cardioverter defibrillation. Proc. IEEE. 1996, 84(3):428–445.

Karson TH, Grace K and Denes F. Stereo speaker silences automatic implanted cardioverter defibrillator. N. Engl. J. Med. 1989, 320(24):1628–1629.

Kaye GC, Butros GS, Allen A et al. The effect of external electrical interference on implanted cardiac pacemakers. PACE. 1988, 11:999–1008.

Khastgir T, Aarons D and Veltri E. Sudden bradyarrhythmic death in patients with the implanted cardioverter defibrillator: report of two cases. PACE. 1991, 14:395–398.

Kim SG, Furman SG, Matos JA et al. Automatic implantable cardioverter defibrillator inadvertent discharges during permanent pacemaker magnet tests. PACE. 1987, 10(Part 1):579–582.

Kim SG, Furman S, Waspe L et al. Pacer artifacts induced failure of an automatic implanted cardioverter defibrillator to detect ventricular fibrillation. Am. J. Cardiol. 1986, 57:880–881.

Knutson T and Bulkeley WM. Stray Signals. Wall Street Journal. June 15,1994.

Lau FYK, Billiteh M and Wintroub HJ. Protection of implanted pacemakers from excessive electrical energy of defibrillation shock. Am. J. Cardiol. 1969, 23:244–249.

Leahy WR, Messimino RJ and Wohlfert WJ. Intermittent failure of a Stockert/Shiley multiflow roller pump. J. Extracoporeal Technol. 1993, 25(1):74–77.

Lerner SM. Suppression of a demand pacemaker by transurethral electrocautery. Anesth. Analg. Current Res. 1973, 52(5):703–706.

Levine PA, Barrold SS, Fletcher RD et al. Adverse acute and chronic effects of electrical defibrillation and cardioversion on implanted unipolar cardiac pacing systems. J. Am. Coll. Cardiol. 1983, 1(6):1413–1422.

Lichter L and Borrie J. Radio-frequency hazards with cardiac pacemakers. Br. Med. J. 1965,1:1513–1518.

Lilly JC, Hughes JR, Alvord EC et al. Noninjurious electrical waveform for stimulation of the brain. Science. 1955, 121(1144)468–469.

Lucas EH, Johnson D and McElroy BP. The effects of electronic article surveillance on permanent cardiac pacemakers. PACE. 1994, 17 (part 2):2021–2026.

Madrid A, Sanches A, Bosch E et al. Dysfunction of implantable defibrillators caused by slot machines. PACE. 1997, 20 (part 2):212–214.

Marco D, Eisinger G and Hayes DL. Testing a work environment for electromagnetic interference. PACE. 1992, 15:2016–2022.

Martin R. Designing for compliance: immunity to ESD. Compliance Eng. 1993, 10: 1321.

Matthew P, Lucas C, Neglia J and Drol RB. Interaction between electronic article surveillance systems and implantable defibrillators. PACE. 1997, 20 2857–2859.

MAUDE Reports. U.S. Food and Drug Administration.

McCarty RJ and Glasser SP. The arrhythmogenic effect of static electricity on the dog heart. Am. Heart J. 1977, 93(4):496–500.

McIvor ME. Environmental electromagnetic interference from electronic article survelliance devices interaction with an ICD. PACE. 1995, 18:2229–2230.

McIvor ME, Reddinger J, Floden E et al. Study of pacemaker and implantable cardioverter defibrillator triggering by electronic article surveillance devices. PACE. 1998, 21:1847–1861.

Mehdirad A, Love C, Nelson S et al. Alternating current electrocution and termination by one implanted cardioverter defibrillator. PACE. 1997, 20:1885–1886.

Mirowski M et al. The development of the transvenous automatic defibrillator. Arch. Intern. Med. 1972, 129:773–779.

Mirowski M et al. Feasibility and effectiveness of low-energy catheter defibrillation in man. Circulation. 1973, 47:79–85.

Moss E. Exposure to electromagnetic fields while operating walk-through and hand-held metal detectors. Appl. Occup. Env. Hyg. 1998, July: 501–504.

Mugica J, Henry L and Podeur H. Study of interactions between permanent pacemakers and electronic antitheft surveillance systems. PACE. 2000, 23:333–337.

Naegeli B and Burkart F. Intermittent pacemaker malfunction caused by digital mobile telephones. J. Am. Coll. Cardiol. 1996, 27:1471–1477.

National Fire Protection Association, 470 Atlantic Avenue, Boston, MA 07210. National Electrical Code (NFPA #70), Essential Electrical Systems for Hospitals (NFPA #76).

Nowak B, Roscona S, Noff C et al. Is there risk for interaction between mobile phones and single-lead VDD pacemakers? Abstracts 45th Ann. Sci. Session ACC. J. Am. Coll. Cardiol. 1996, 27(2):236A.

Ochetta A, Plebani L, Bootnik M et al. Implantable cardioverter defibrillators and cellular telephones: is there any interference? PACE. 1999, 22:983–989.

O'Donoghue JK. Inhibition of a demand pacemaker by electrosurgery. Chest. 1973, 64(5):664-665.

Office of Science and Technology. U.S. Food and Drug Administration CDRH Annual Report. Oct 1 to Sept. 30, 1996.

O'Handley RC. Magnetic materials for EAS sensors. Journ. Mats. Eng. Performance. 1993, 2(2):211–218.

Peteiro J, Struble C, Vasquez N and Castro-Beiras A. Spontaneous reversion of a cardiomyostimulator to asynchronous mode. PACE. 1996, 19:367–369.

Pride HB and McKinley DE. Third-degree burns from the use of an external cardiac pacing device. Crit. Care Med. 1990, 18:572–573.

Ruggera P and O'Bryan ER. Studies of apnea monitor radiofrequency electromagnetic interference. Int Conf. IEEE EMBS. 1991, 13(4):1641–1643.

Ruggera PS, O'Bryan R and Casamiento JP. Automated radiofrequency electromagnetic interference testing on apnea monitors using an open area test site. Proc. IEEE EMBS Conf. 1992, 2839–2840.

Rustan PL, Hunt WD and Mitchell JC. Microwave oven interference with cardiac pacemakers. Med. Instr. 1973, 7:185–188.

Santucci PA, Haw J, Trohman RC and Pinski SL. Interference with an implantable defibrillator by an electronic antitheft surveillance device. New Engl. Journ. Med. 1998, 339(19):1371–1373.

Schmitt C, Brachmann J, Waldecker B et al. Implantable cardioverter defibrillator: possible hazards of electromagnetic interference. PACE. 1991, 14:982–984.

Silberberg JL. Performance degradation of electronic medical devices due to electromagnetic interference. Compliance Eng. 1993, Fall:1–8.

Silbert PL, Roth PA, Kanz BS et al. Interference from cellular telephones in the electroencephalogram. J. Polysomnog. Technol. 1994, December: 20–22.

Smith RB and Wise WS. Pacemaker malfunction from urethral electrocautery. JAMA. 1971, 218:256.

Smyth NPD, Keshishan JM, Hood OC et al. Effect of an active magnetometer on permanently implanted pacemakers. JAMA. 1972, 221(2):162–166.

Spotnitz HM, Ott GY, Begger JT et al. Methods of implantable cardioverter-defibrillator pacemaker insertion to avoid interactions. Ann. Thor. Surg. 1992, 53:253–257.

Titel JH and El Etr AA. Fibrillation resulting from pacemaker electrodes and electrocautery during surgery. Anesthesiology. 1968, 29(4):845–846.

Valentinuzzi ME, Geddes LA and Baker LE. The law of impedance pneumography. Med. Biol. Eng. 1971, 9:157–163.

Wajsczuk W, Mowry FM and Dugan NL. Deactivation of a demand pacemaker by transurethral electrosurgery. N. Engl. J. Med. 1969, 280(1):34–35.

Wilke A, Kruse T, Hesse H et al. Interactions between pacemakers and security systems. PACE. 1998, 21:1784–1788.

Witters D. Medical device EMI: the CDRH perspective. AAMI Conf. on Electromagnetic Compatibility for Medical Devices 1995, AAMI Conf. Rep. pp. 7–23.

Zoll PM, Zoll RH and Belgard AH. External noninvasive electrical stimulation of the heart. Crit. Care Med. 1981, 9(5):393–394.

Zoll PM. Resuscitation of the heart in ventricular standstill by external electric stimulation. N. Engl. J. Med. 1952, 247:768–771.

Chapter 3

Electrosurgery, Electrocautery and Laser Surgery

Synopsis

3.1 Introduction

Electrosurgery employs 0.5 to 2 MHz (alternating) radio frequency current applied to a small-area (active) electrode to produce desiccation, coagulation, and cutting in living tissue. Although Cushing and Bovie (1928) are usually credited with popularizing electrosurgery, it was in use much earlier. In 1911, Clark, in the U.S. developed a spark-gap generator and used its alternating current to remove skin blemishes. However, Doyen (1909), in France, had used a similar unit to excise skin blemishes. By 1930, the advantages of electrosurgical techniques were recognized; among these are the saving of time, assurance of asepsis, absence of bleeding, and elimination of the transfer of infection from diseased to normal tissue that sometimes occurred with a scalpel. Wound healing with electrodissection is almost the same as with scalpel cuts. These features were testified to by a panel of eminent surgeons who were convened on the occasion of the Conference on Electrosurgery at the Clinical Congress of the American College of Surgeons (1931). The enthusiasm in these reports, which cover a wide range of surgical procedures, shows how quickly surgeons embraced the new techniques. At this conference there was a report on wound healing (Ellis, 1931), in which it was shown that, except for skin incisions, there is little difference between scalpel and electrosurgical cutting methods. Shortly thereafter, the first American textbook on electrosurgery was published by Kelly and Ward (1932). In it there is a good review of the histologic changes in tissue in response to electrosurgical currents. Earlier Doyen (1917) outlined his experience with the spark-gap electrosurgical unit.

The electrosurgical instrument is a generator of controlled radio frequency (rf) current that is applied to an active point, blade, ball, or loop electrode to produce the desired thermal tissue response. Bipolar electrodes are also used.

The terminology associated with electrosurgery is not always precise. Terms such as cautery, electrocautery, surgical diathermy, and Bovie are in common use. The following definitions of these terms will serve as a guide to use the correct term. A cautery is a heated rod (like a poker) used to cut and coagulate tissue; its origin is in Arabic medicine. An electrocautery is an electrically heated rod, not unlike a soldering iron, which can indeed be used to cut and coagulate tissue. Surgical diathermy is an older term that is used in the U.K. to designate the use of high-frequency current in surgery. The term "Bovie" is used almost interchangeably with an electrosurgical unit because it was W. T. Bovie who built the first practical (spark-gap) electrosurgical unit that was introduced to medicine in 1928 by Cushing and Bovie (see Geddes et al., 1977, for the history of electrosurgery). Because modern electrosurgical units no longer contain spark gaps or vacuum tubes to generate the cutting and coagulating currents, the correct term for the generator of high-frequency current for surgery is an electrosurgical unit (ESU).

Figure 3.1 is a sketch of the three components of an electrosurgical system: (1) the handheld probe (active electrode), (2) the dispersive electrode and (3) the electrosurgical unit (ESU). It is at the probe tip, which may or may not be in contact with the tissue, where the three processes (desiccation, coagulation, and cutting) occur.

Figure 3.1 depicts the use of a monopolar active electrode which has a small area; consequently, the current density is high and heating occurs thereunder. Note that the dispersive electrode is very large so that the current is dispersed widely to avoid skin heating. In normal operation the current (Ia) leaving the ESU passes through the active electrode and enters the body. The return current (Id) from the dispersive electrode is equal to Ia and returns to the ESU. The subject of alternate current paths and the bipolar electrode will be discussed subsequently. The ESU is under the control of the surgeon either by buttons on the active electrode or by a double foot switch.

It is important to note that the large-area dispersive electrode provides a safe return path for the electrosurgical current. It is useful to recognize that heating depends on current density (mA/cm^2) squared and the duration of current flow. Therefore, the maximum heating occurs under the tip of the small-

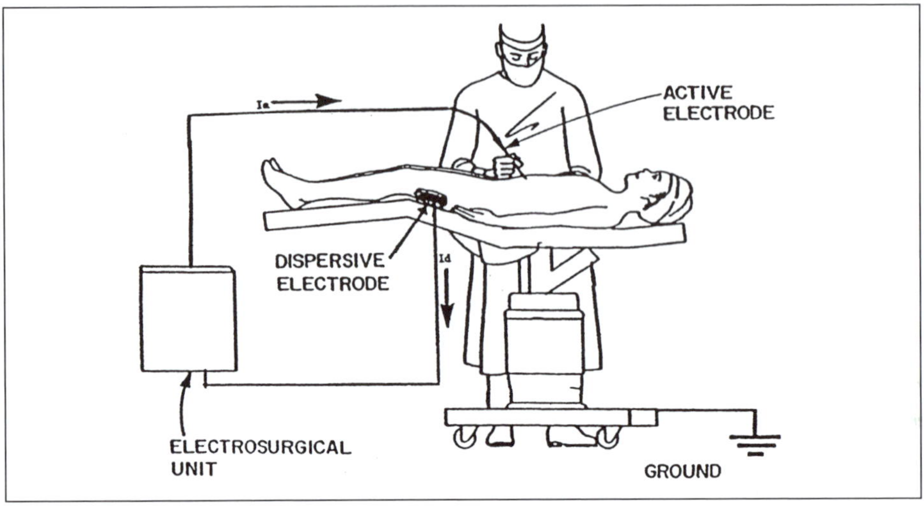

Figure 3.1 *The three components of an electrosurgical system: (1) the active electrode, (2) the dispersive electrode, and (3) the electrosurgical unit (ESU)*

area, handheld probe electrode. The dispersive electrode is designed so that negligible skin heating occurs thereunder. There is a performance standard for dispersive electrodes.

3.2 Electrodes

A. Active (monopolar) electrodes

Both monopolar and bipolar electrodes are used. The monopolar electrode will be discussed first. A variety of electrode tips are used to deliver desiccating, coagulating, and cutting current. These tips are plugged into the pencil-like holder held by the surgeon. Figure 3.2a illustrates the standard blade (scalpel) tip which is flat, smooth, and not sharp like a scalpel blade. Smooth cutting is produced by vaporization of the cells in contact with the tip as it is advanced through tissue. The speed of cutting is determined by the intensity of the cutting current. The needle electrode, shown in Figure 3.2b, is inserted into the tissue and is used for desiccation and coagulation. The cutting loop (Figure 3.2c) is used to excise warts, polyps and tumors. The ball electrode (Figure 3.2d) is used to provide a broad area of fulguration (i.e., sparking; fulgur = lightning), as is often used in treating skin blemishes.

In Figure 3.2e is shown an active electrode with two push buttons; one allows delivery of cutting current and the other permits delivery of coagulating current. Such handheld probes come packaged and sterilized and are dispos-

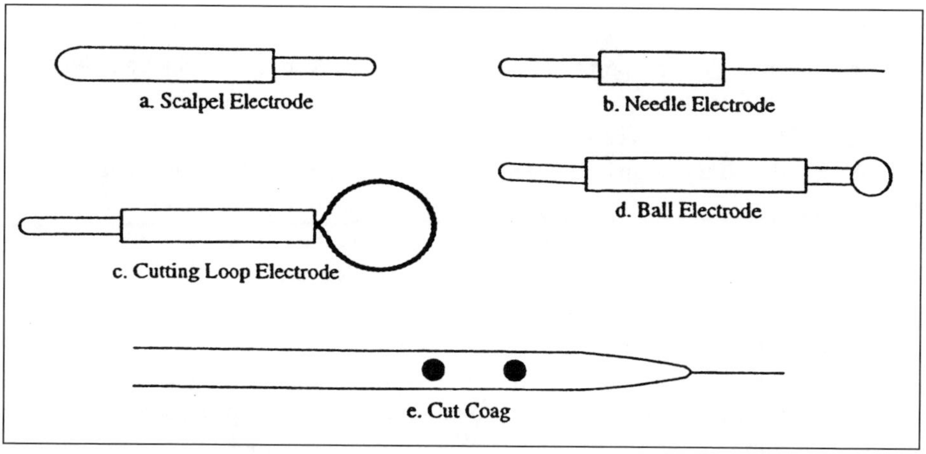

Figure 3.2 *Monopolar electrodes*

able items. With most ESU units, a dual foot switch allows delivery of these currents to the handheld active electrode.

Some ESUs have more than one monopolar outlet to which, for example, a cutting electrode and a coagulating electrode can be connected simultaneously. In such ESUs, these outlets are connected in parallel and activation of one activates both; therefore there exists a hazard if the unused instrument is in contact with the subject. Most ESU manuals warn about this situation and the hazard can be avoided if holsters, made of insulating material, are provided for each electrode.

B. Electrode holster

For all of the electrode types shown in Figure 3.2, good practice provides an electrode holster in the sterile field when the electrode is not in use. Such a device prevents an incident if the ESU is accidentally activated. The use of a holster prevents the electrode from falling to the floor and becoming unsterile.

Likewise a holster is advisable for the probe with cut and coagulation buttons (Figure 3.2e, cut/coag). Accidental activation by laying something on the probe will be avoided.

C. Incidents with cut-coag electrodes

Several incidents have been reported with use of the cut/coag electrode, shown in Figure 3.2e. Such an event was reported in the MAUDE (formerly MDR) report of March 11, 1998, which stated:

> The customer had reported that the cautery side of the electrosurgical control had stayed on during a procedure. Upon initial observation, the handpiece had been rinsed/cleaned by the hospital staff prior to shipment to [the manufacturer]. The device was carefully disassembled and tested for electrical continuity with no indication of failure. A closer review of the PCB/clamshell subassembly revealed that the coag. side of the stamped dome switch was lower than the cut side. It's possible that the dome could have oil-canned following activation by the customer. There is no indication on the CCR to indicate when the fault occurred. Upon review of the dome switch component detail drawing, it was learned that the component was modified in mid to late 1997. A search of where else the component is used indicated that the PCB subassembly is used in various [manufacturer's] electrosurgical pencil lines. A review of the ratio of electrosurgical pencil customer complaints to products produced has been steadily decreasing. The [manufacturer] might review this trend to ensure the effectiveness of this modifications made to the dome switch.

Another incident involving a handheld electrode with cut/coag buttons was described in the *ECRI Health Alert* (1999) as follows:

> The doctor reported two occurrences of the activation buttons being super sensitive, and is afraid to lay the pencils down for fear that the pressure will activate them.
>
> Two MDR's were filed based on the information provided that no injuries occurred; however reoccurrence of these events may cause or contribute to a serious injury. The devices were not returned for evaluation. [Previous units] tested with reported sensitive activations and initially they would operate normally with no self activation of the switches observed. When the pencil was flexed upward a small amount by pressing on the tip of electrode area, the pencil would self activate in the coag mode. When that pencil configuration was examined in the switch core area, there was visual evidence that the coag switch wire was misaligned low during the mfg. process, thus the switch could become stuck on or remain active with a small movement of the pencil tip. The importance of the switch wire form positioning has been reinforced with the operators to ensure the proper alignment is achieved. Although the device has always been tested 100 percent during production and other reports of sticking are very rare, this increased awareness has improved the mfg. test pass rate. [Manufacturer] regrets that the incidents occurred, although the self activation identified with these pencils has occurred with other devices of this configuration on a very infrequent basis. Changes to the

> switch core configuration implemented in mid Q98 and the increased awareness with the operators should further reduce the possibility of reoccurrence. The user is reminded that to prevent injury from accidental activations, good electrosurgery practice requires that active accessories be stored in the safety holster provided, when not in use.

Previous information on the excessive sensitivity of the cut/coag buttons on the ES handpiece was reported by the CDRH of the FDA on May 22, 1998. Another report provided the following: "The customer stated that the cautery pencil in open heart packs has on one occasion been extremely sensitive and turned on without being engaged. There was not any pt. injury." The report continued:

> The investigation of the referenced complaint has been completed. The complaint on the device stating that "pencil is extremely sensitive and was turned on without being engaged" was received 5/22/1998 and a malfunction MDR was filed based on the info provided that no injuries occurred; however reoccurrence may cause or contribute to a serious injury. The device was not returned for evaluation by [manufacturer]. Previous like devices have been tested which had reported "sensitive activations," and initially they would operate normally with no self activation of the switches observed.

D. Bipolar electrodes

Figure 3.3a illustrates a bipolar electrode. No dispersive electrode is required because the tissue to be coagulated is grasped between the tips of two active electrodes. The arms of the older bipolar electrodes were uninsulated; modern bipolar electrodes carry insulation down to near the tip. Activation of the bipolar electrode is via depressing the foot pedal controller. Note that the current is confined to the region between the electrode tips.

With the advent of minimally invasive surgery many new types of ES electrodes have appeared. One of these is a bipolar scissor. Later in this chapter a bipolar forceps is described.

An interesting type of catheter bipolar electrode that is used in arthroscopic surgery is shown in Figure 3.3b. The active electrode at the tip of the catheter consists of many pointed projections and the return electrode is on the shaft of the catheter. The electrode is used in a conducting (saline) environment which fills the expanded joint space and irrigates it simultaneously. Fluid pressure in the range of 100 mmHg is used. When the ESU is activated using cutting cur-

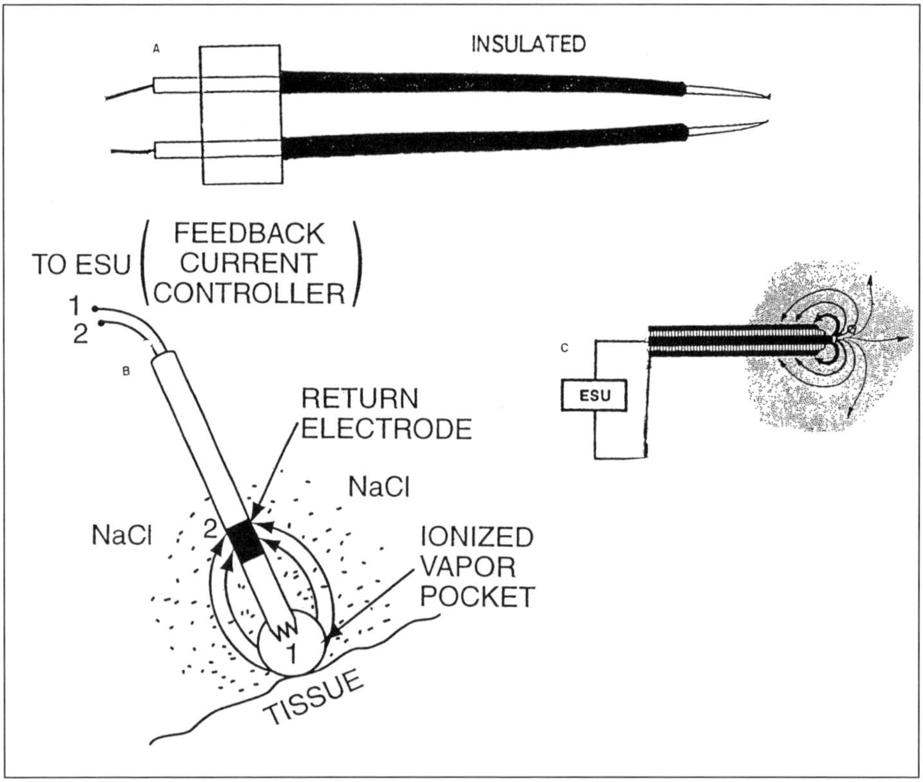

Figure 3.3 *Bipolar electrodes: (a) forceps type, (b) catheter type for use in a conducting-fluid medium and (c) coaxial bipolar electrode*

rent, the high current density at the electrode points creates a vapor pocket that contains ionized gas. The output circuit of the ESU is responsive to the electrode-vapor pocket impedance in such a way as to maintain the ionized vapor pocket. Although the intimate details of the tissue ablation process are not fully understood, this type of electrode allows controlled smooth removal of tissue in the joint space. The electrode can also be used in body cavities that can be saline filled, e.g. the uterus.

Although the arthroscopic bipolar catheter electrode has allowed great advances to be made in arthroscopic surgery, the procedure is not without risks. The high joint-distending pressure (70–100 mmHg) fills and irrigates the joint space, allows viewing and provides the conducting fluid (saline) environment needed for the electrode. A typical procedure may last thirty or more minutes and this combination of pressure and time leads to extravasation, i.e. fluid being forced into the adjacent soft tissues. If this fluid shift is large it can lead to what is known as the compartment syndrome, i.e. local tissue (including nerve) damage. According to a *Health Devices* (1999) review, extravasation occurs in 1.4 percent of all knee procedures. The amount of fluid driven out depends on the particular joint, the pressure and how long it is maintained.

3.3 Dispersive Electrodes

In the early days of electrosurgery no dispersive electrodes were used. The distributed capacitance to ground from the patient provided the return path for the electrosurgical current. This practice invited the risk of burn if the patient came into contact with a grounded object, such as an operating table. It was to eliminate this hazard that a large indifferent (dispersive) electrode was used under the patient.

The dispersive (sometimes called the Bovie pad, patient plate, ground, or indifferent) electrode provides a safe return path for the electrosurgical current. The electrode area is large enough so that there is negligible heating of the skin thereunder. Typically the dispersive electrode is placed over a fleshy part of the body; it is never placed over a bony prominence because there is the risk of uneven current distribution which could produce a hot spot or a burn.

There are two types of dispersive electrode: (1) conductive and (2) capacitive. The conductive type establishes ohmic (resistive) contact with the subject; the capacitive type does not. The capacitive electrode consists of a metal plate covered by insulating film (dielectric). In this way one "plate" of the capacitor is the subject, the other is the metal within the electrode.

A. Conductive dispersive electrodes

The first dispersive electrodes consisted of a large-area, bare, dry metal plate on which the patient lay. Variable contact area led to the use of flexible metal foil, insulated on the back and surrounded by an adhesive perimeter which allowed placement of the electrode at any convenient body site. The temperature distribution under a dry metal-plate electrode on human skin was reported by Pearce et al. (1978) and Geddes et al. (1980). Such dry electrodes are rarely used nowadays.

To improve contact with the skin, an electrolytic gel is used with metal-foil dispersive electrodes. A peel-off cover protects the electrode during storage. The skin-temperature distribution of a typical gelled metal-foil electrode was reported by Pearce et al. (1978) and Geddes et al. (1979).

In some dispersive electrodes, the electrolytic gel is incorporated into a foam pad that bridges the gap between the metal foil and skin; Figure 3.4a il-

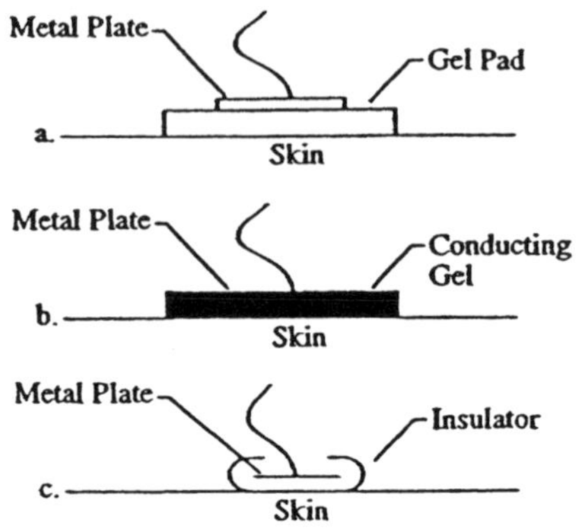

Figure 3.4 *Dispersive electrodes*

lustrates the essential components. A peel-off cover protects the electrode in storage. The temperature distribution is similar to that for the gelled metal-foil electrode.

Advances in adhesive technology resulted in the ability to include an electrolyte and thereby create a conducting adhesive dispersive electrode. Such an electrode is shown in Figure 3.4b and consists of a metal foil, backed by an insulator with an adhesive perimeter. The conducting adhesive sticks to the metal foil and a peel-off cover exposes the conducting adhesive which embraces the skin well.

Irrespective of design, the conductive dispersive electrode makes ohmic (resistive) contact with the subject. The current distribution under such an electrode is not uniform, the current density under the perimeter being several times higher than under the center of the electrode (Caruso et al., 1979; Overmeyer et al., 1979). Because heating depends on current-density squared, the skin under the perimeter of a conducting electrode is warmer than the skin under the center of the electrode; Figure 3.5 illustrates this point.

B. Uniform current-density electrode

Many strategies are available to provide a more uniform current-density electrode. Such an electrode is desirable to eliminate the red rings seen under paddle defibrillating electrodes. Such an electrode would be less painful when closed-chest pacing is applied and its use in electrosurgery would be advantageous, but not as much as in the two foregoing applications.

A nearly uniform current-density distribution electrode was developed by Ferrari (1996) and is available from Contour Medical (LaVergne TN). The

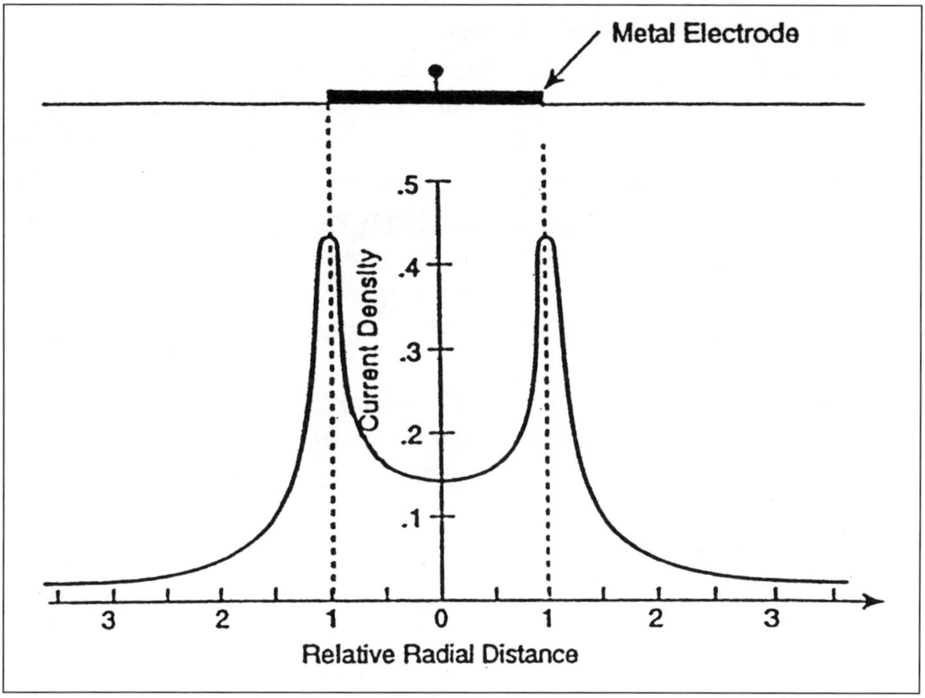

Figure 3.5 *Current density on the skin under a conducting dispersive electrode (Redrawn from Caruso P, Pearce JA and DeWitt DP.* Proc. 7th N. Engl. Bioeng. Conf. 1979, *373–374; and Overmeyer K, Pearce JA and DeWitt DP.* Trans. ASME *1979, 191: 66–72)*

electrode is disposable, self-adhering, x-ray transparent and can be used for applying current and recording the ECG. These features are achieved by a carbon-loaded polymer with multilayered coating of silver/silver chloride producing an increased surface perimeter impedance. A current-distributing mat within the electrode is connected to an x-ray transparent conducting fiber cable which carries the current to the electrode.

The temperature distribution under the Contour Medical electrode was reported by Bourland et al. (1998) who measured the temperature rise on electrodes applied to the skin of live pigs at four sites with fiberoptic thermal probes. Three anesthetized pigs, ranging in weight from seventy-nine to ninety-two pounds, were used. Temperature-time curves were obtained and the maximum temperature was identified. For seventeen measurements at each site, the maximum rise for a 360-joule shock was 317.3 ± 53.0 millidegrees Celsius.

C. Capacitive dispersive electrode

Because the frequency (f) of electrosurgical current is high, it is possible to cover the metal foil with a thin insulating (dielectric) film; Figure 3.4c illustrates the principle. The capacitance (C) depends on the electrode area (A), dielectric constant (k), and inversely with the thickness (t) of the dielectric film. $C = kA/t$. The size (area) of the electrode is chosen so that the reactance ($1/2\pi fC$) of the capacitance is sufficiently small that an adequate return path is established with the subject. As with the other dispersive electrodes, an insulating back and adhesive perimeter are provided and a peel-off cover protects the dielectric surface during storage.

Two features distinguish the capacitive electrode from all other types: (1) there is no ohmic (resistive) contact with the subject, and (2) the skin-temperature distribution is more uniform than that for conductive dispersive electrodes, this being the nature of a capacitive interface (Pearce, 1986). The skin-temperature distribution for capacitive dispersive electrodes was reported by Pearce et al. (1980).

D. Reuse of disposable dispersive electrodes

Reuse of disposable dispersive electrodes is another cause for burns under electrosurgical electrodes. *Health Devices* (July 23, 1999) reported:

> The Ministry of Health of France has received reports of incidents and serious hazards associated with the use of electrosurgical units (ESUs) with reusable return electrodes (REs). The Ministry of Health states that reported incidents include cases of insufficient patient/RE contact, alarm failure, unjustified RE alarm, improper use of REs, abusive reuse of REs, and lack of systematic control of REs. The Ministry of Health also states that such incidents may result in superficial, deep-warming, or third-degree burns, mostly in the area of contact with the RE and sometimes in surrounding areas of the RE. Burns can occur as a result of leakage current conducted by tabletops, electrocardiogram electrodes, or other conductive parts. The Ministry of Health provides the following recommendations: (1) Systematically use disposable and "dual contact" REs, as well as ESUs in which the monopolar mode provides control of RE/patient contact impedance. (2) Whenever possible, apply CE-marked, dual-contact REs. REs should be checked to verify that they are in good condition before each use. (3) Be aware of various factors that need to be considered when applying REs to patients, including contact site and size and the possibility of poor contact to the patient. Poor areas for RE placement include areas with antiseptics, urine, hair, fat, bone, scars, bad skin vascularization,

and close proximity to metallic prostheses. The proximity of the RE and the active electrode and other types of ECG electrodes must also be considered. For further information, contact the Ministry of Employment and Solidarity, Direction des Hôpitaux, Bureau des Dispossitifs Medicaux (EM1), by fax at 01 40 56 50 89.

E. Dispersive electrode monitors

Because of the hazard of alternate-current path burns if a dispersive electrode is not connected to the ESU or becomes partially or totally dislodged, three types of dispersive electrode monitors have been developed: (1) patient sentry, (2) current comparator, and (3) patient-return monitor.

1. Patient sentry

With the patient sentry the dispersive electrode (Figure 3.6) is connected to the ESU by two conductors (1, 2). A circuit within the ESU prevents delivery of current unless there is continuity between conductors 1 and 2. In the earlier ESUs, a relay was held closed by the continuity measured between conductors 1 and 2. The patient sentry was first incorporated into the Bovie CSV units. Newer ESUs use an SCR (silicon-controlled rectifier) to allow delivery of electrosurgical current only when continuity is verified. An alarm is sounded if it is not.

Although a useful safety method, such dispersive electrodes with two conductors can only be connected to an ESU with the patient sentry feature. Such a patient sentry provides no information on whether or not the dispersive electrode is applied to the subject; it only informs that the electrode is connected to the ESU.

2. Current comparator

Referring to Figure 3.1, it is obvious that the magnitude of the current (Ia)

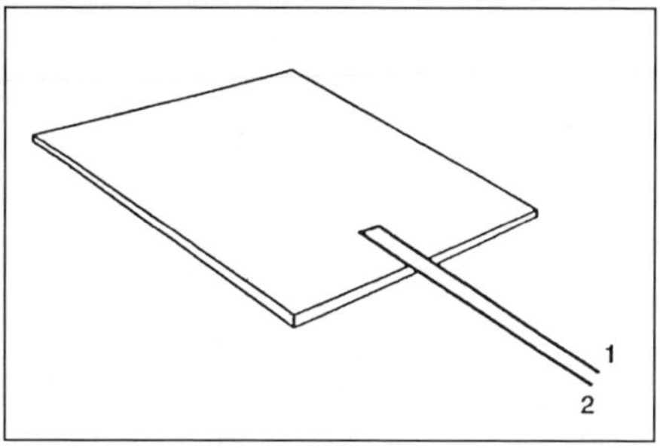

Figure 3.6 *Patient sentry*

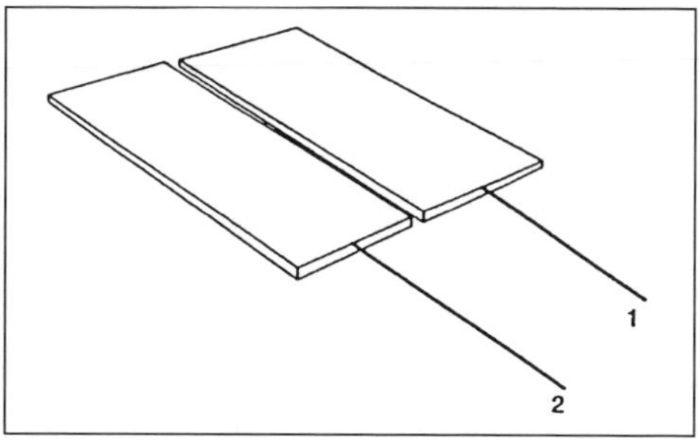

Figure 3.7 *Split dispersive electrode*

flowing through the active electrode is the same as the current (Id) flowing through the dispersive electrode. If the dispersive electrode becomes dislodged and an alternate current path to ground is established by the patient, Ia will be larger than Id. Therefore, by comparing the magnitudes of Ia and Id, it is possible to identify the existence of an alternate current path and automatically disable the output of an ESU and sound an alarm. This type of current comparator is embodied in some ESUs.

3. Patient-return monitor

A different type of electrode monitor was developed by Valleylab, Inc. and uses a split dispersive electrode, as shown schematically in Figure 3.7. When the electrode is applied to the patient, a circuit in the ESU monitors the impedance between conductors 1 and 2. When the split electrode is on the patient, the impedance between electrodes 1 and 2 is low. If the ESU senses a high impedance between conductors 1 and 2, it means that the dispersive electrode has not been applied properly, or has not been applied to the patient; therefore, the ESU is inhibited from delivering current and an alarm is sounded. Note that this type of monitor identifies (1) connection of the electrode to the ESU, (2) proper application of the electrode to the patient, and (3) continuity of the two conductors leading to the ESU. To obtain the advantages of the split dispersive electrode requires the use of an ESU designed for use of such an electrode.

4. Performance standards

As stated previously, the function of a dispersive electrode is to provide a safe return path for the electrosurgical current. The area of the electrode must be large enough so that excessive skin heating does not occur. There is a performance standard (AAMI HF 18-R-2/93) being developed. Briefly, it states that the skin-temperature rise must not exceed 6°C for a 700-mA (rms) current applied for sixty seconds. The latest standard should be consulted for the methods for testing.

3.4 Types of Current

Two types of radiofrequency current (unmodulated and modulated) are used to induce the three types of tissue response (desiccation, coagulation, and cutting). Moreover, there are two techniques for applying the handheld probe, also called the active electrode or pencil: one brings the tip of the probe in contact with the tissue, then the ESU is activated. The other technique brings the tip of the probe in close proximity to the tissue; then the ESU is activated and an arc carries the current to the tissue. Which technique is used depends on the desired tissue response.

Figure 3.8 illustrates the current waveforms for cutting and coagulation. In general, cutting is achieved with continuous, i.e., unmodulated current. Figures 3.8a and 3.8b illustrate the type of current used for cutting. The waveform in Figure 3.8a is produced by the older push-pull type of vacuum-tube units. The radio frequency cutting current is delivered in 1/120 half-sinusoidal bursts. In the newer solid-state units the current is more constant, as shown in Figure 3.8b.

The coagulating current waveforms are shown in Figures 3.8c and 3.8d. Note that in both cases the duty cycle is short. Figure 3.8c illustrates the coagulating waveform provided by the older spark-gap (Bovie) generators and the bursts of radiofrequency current are delivered at 120/sec. Figure 3.8d illustrates the coagulating waveform provided by the newer solid-state units which

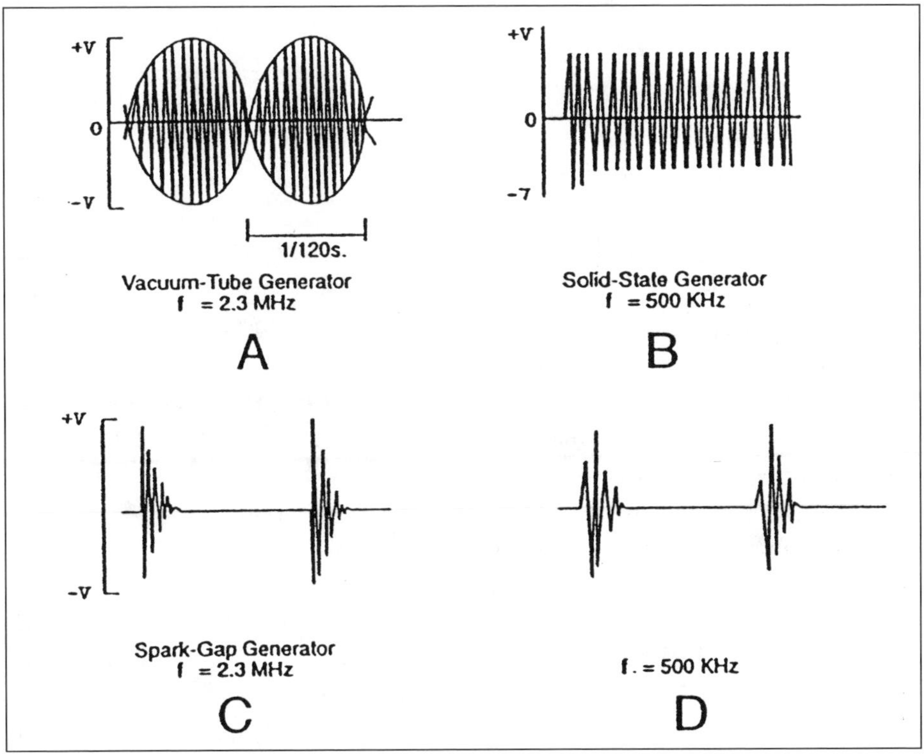

Figure 3.8 *Electrosurgical current waveforms*

Table 3.1
Current Used in Electrosurgical Procedures

Procedure	Current[a] (mA)			Duration of activation[a] (sec)		
	Min	**Max**	**Avg**	**Min**	**Max**	**Avg**
Transurethral resection						
Cut	239 (162)	407 (297)	297 (200)	1.6 (0.68)	3.8 (2.3)	2.1 (0.69)
Coag	179 (78)	419 (400)	256 (88)	1.4 (0.5)	5 (7.6)	1.9 (0.7)
Laparoscopic tubal ligation						
Cut	126 (120)	430 (290)	239 (135)	1.7 (0.58)	5.4 (4.9)	2.6 (3.2)
Coag	61 (57)	118 (80)	86 (70)	3.2 (0.31)	26 (20)	10 (7.4)
General surgery[b]						
Cut	238 (188)	340 (101)	281 (147)	2 (2)	7.6 (11)	2.2 (1.8)
Coag	146 (94)	267 (157)	198 (114)	4.7 (5.2)	11 (7.8)	6.5 (5.2)

[a] Numbers in parentheses are standard deviations.

[b] General surgical procedures include prostatectimy, laparotomy, thoracotomy, hip pinning, hysterectomy, nephrectomy, and D&C.

Courtesy of J. DeRosa, NDM Co., Dayton, OH.

deliver the bursts at typically 20,000/sec. Table 3.1 presents the current levels and activation times used for different surgical procedures.

Electrosurgical current is low in frequency when one considers the "skin effect", which describes the manner in which high-frequency current crowds to the periphery of a conductor. Skin effect for tissues is discussed in the chapter on electromagnetic interference (EMI); it is unimportant for ES current frequencies.

3.5 Isolated-output Electrosurgical Unit

An isolated-output circuit is defined as one with no ohmic contact and low leakage capacitance to ground. This is achieved with a transformer, the secondary winding providing the isolated voltage source. Figure 3.9a illustrates this scheme and Figure 3.9b shows the equivalent circuit in which the distributed capacitance (C) has been gathered and represented as C_1 and C_2. Note that although there is no ohmic connection to ground on the isolated output, there is

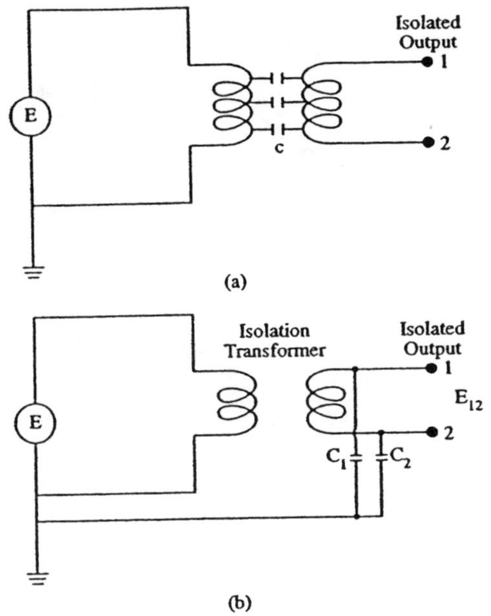

Figure 3.9 *Isolated-output circuit*

distributed capacitance (C_1, C_2) to ground and therefore the degree of isolation from ground depends on the magnitude of these capacitances, the less the capacitance, the better the isolation.

Many modern electrosurgical units have an isolating transformer that delivers the electrosurgical current to the active and dispersive electrodes. Theoretically contact with any grounded object and one side of the isolated output should cause little current to flow. However, electrosurgical current has a frequency ranging from 0.5 to 2 MHz; therefore, the effect of the distributed capacitance (C_1, C_2) is not negligible and some current will flow in a conductor connected between one side of the isolated output and ground; the conductor could be a subject.

To demonstrate that current can flow through a conductor connected to one side of the output of an isolated ESU and ground, Finlay et al. (1974) measured the current for different values of resistance (R) connected between ground and one side of the output of an isolated-output ESU. The current was measured for different ESU output settings using cutting current; Figure 3.10 presents his results. Note that a substantial current can flow to ground.

Many manufacturers specify the quality of isolation in teams of a power ratio (P_2/P_1), where P_1 is the output power delivered to a 1000-ohm noninduc-

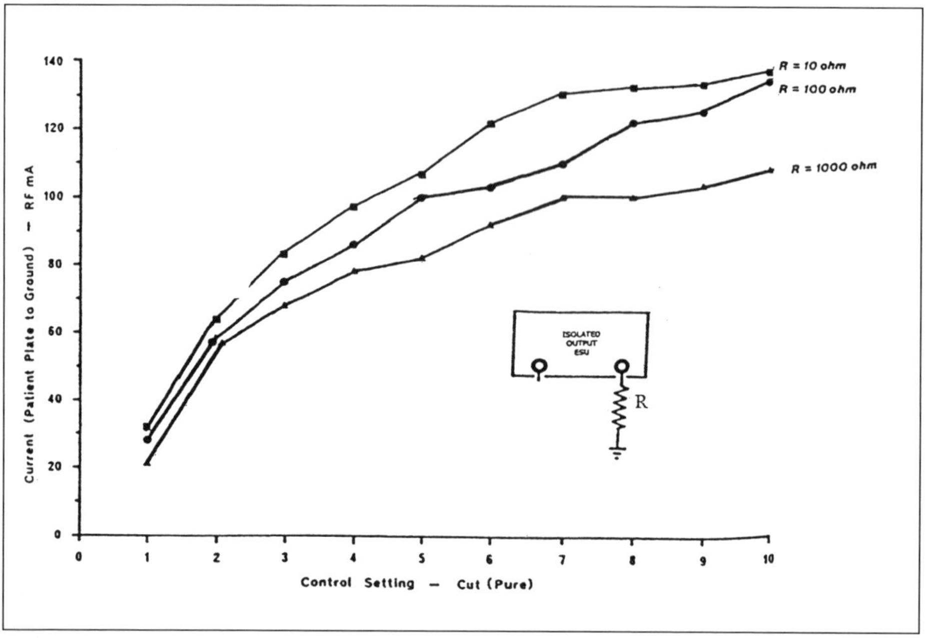

Figure 3.10 *Current to ground through R versus output setting for an isolated output ESU. (Redrawn from Finlay B, Couchie D, Boyce L et al.* Anesthesiology *1974, 41(3): 263–269.)*

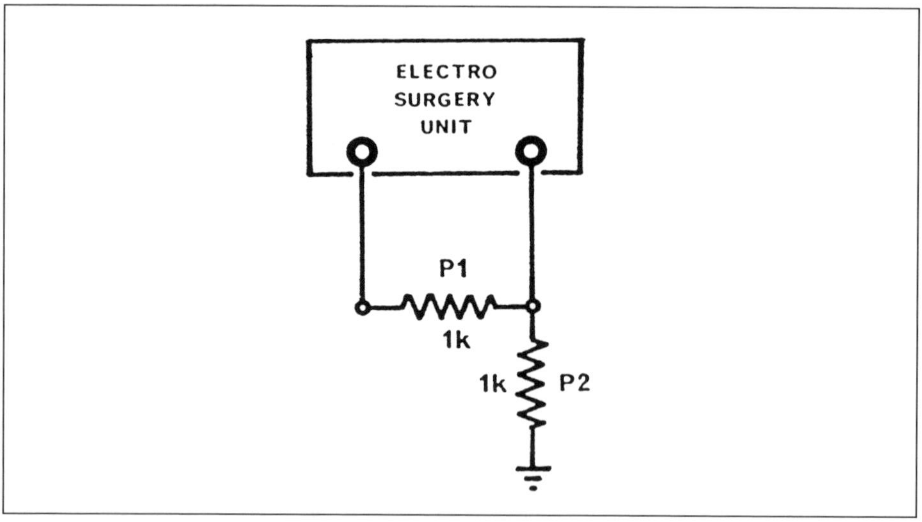

Figure 3.11 *Method of measuring leakage power (P2) and output power (P1) for an isolated-output ESU. (Redrawn from Finlay B, Couchie D, Boyce L et al.* Anesthesiology *1974, 41(3): 263–269.)*

tive resistor connected across the output terminals of the isolated ESU and P_2 is the leakage power delivered to a 1000-ohm resistor connected between ground and one side of the isolated output of the ESU; Figure 3.11 illustrates the test circuit and measurements are usually made with the ESU delivering cutting current at half maximum output setting. According to Finlay et al. (1974), a typical value for P_2 / P_1 is about 0.5 percent. Note that this test describes the performance of the ESU with a dummy load (lK) and without patient cables attached.

The importance of this leakage current with an isolated-output ESU was demonstrated by Finlay et al. (1974), who described a burn under an ECG electrode on a small child undergoing electrosurgery for a neurosurgical procedure. The effective electrode skin-contact area was 5 mm^2, resulting in a current density of 9.1 mA/mm^2, a current density above burn threshold, as Finlay et al. demonstrated by a dog study.

Although the isolated output ESU reduces the hazards associated with electrosurgery, there are still situations that arise in which patient injury occurs. Figure 3.12a shows the equivalent circuit when an isolated-output ESU is connected to a monopolar active and a dispersive electrode on a patient (tissue); C_1 and C_2 are the leakage capacitances to ground. In this normal situation, ES current flows from the active electrode, through the patient to the dispersive electrode back to the ESU.

A fairly common situation is one in which the dispersive electrode is on the patient, but not plugged into the ESU, or is not applied to the patient; Figures 3.12b1–2 illustrate the equivalent circuits. When the active electrode is applied and the ESU is activated, ES current will flow, the amount depends on the capacitance C of the subject to ground and/or any resistive R contact between the subject and ground. Figure 3.12b1 illustrates the case in which the patient is not contacting a grounded object and Figure 3.12b2 illustrates the situation when the patient is in contact with a grounded object via R. This return current flows through C_2. If the contact area of the subject and a grounded object is small, the current density is high and a burn will result at that site. This situation reveals itself by the surgeon calling for a higher output setting on the ESU. It should be noted that capacitance (C) and resistance (R) to ground can coexist.

A potentially dangerous situation arises if the ESU is activated when the active electrode is in contact with a grounded object and a dispersive electrode has been applied to the patient and connected to the ESU; Figures 3.12c1 and 2 illustrate the equivalent circuits. In this case the patient is exposed to the full

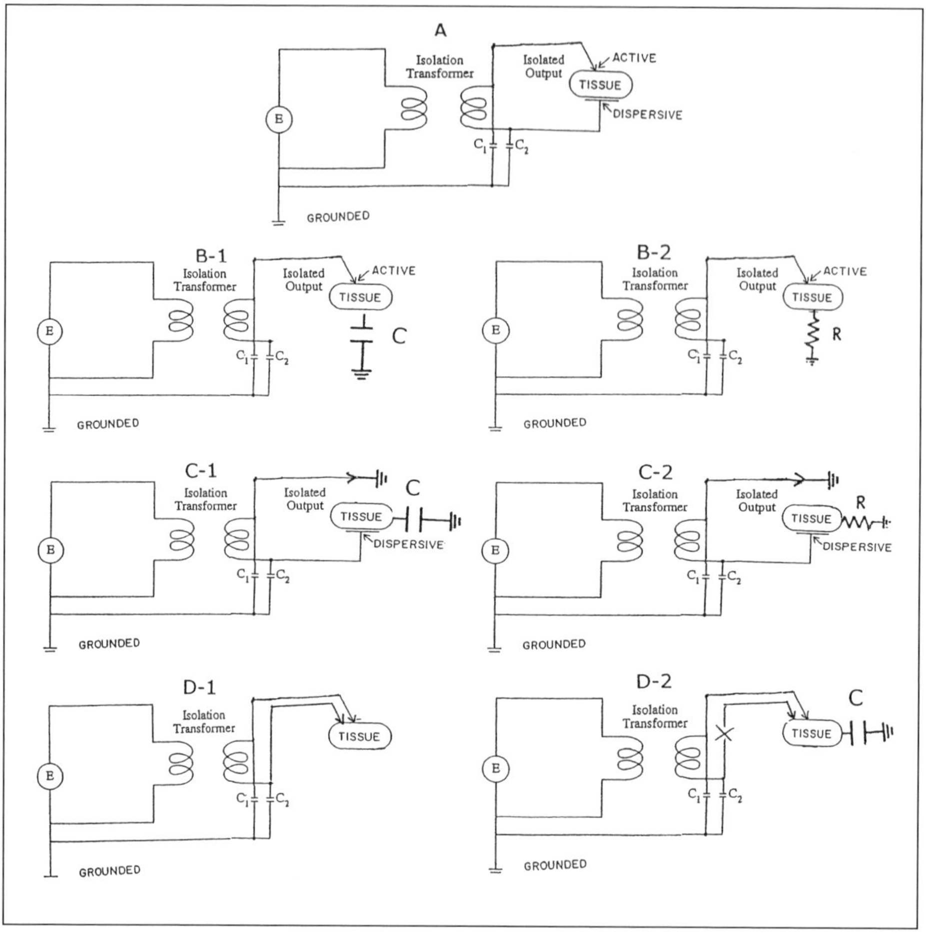

Figure 3.12 *Isolated output circuit: (a) normal operation, (b) return electrode disconnected, (c) active electrode grounded and (d) bipolar broken at X, D-2*

open-circuit voltage of the ESU and current will flow through the capacitance C of the patient to ground (Fig. 3.12c1) and, if the patient comes in contact with a grounded object, through the ground resistance R contact with the patient. In such a case (Figure 3.12c2), a burn will result at the ground contact site.

It would appear that the safest situation is when a bipolar active electrode is connected to an isolated-output ESU, as shown in Figure 3.12d1. However, if one of the bipolar electrodes becomes disconnected at X (Figure 3.12d2), current will flow through the subject and to ground via the capacitance (C) to ground and return to the ESU via C_2. In such a case, the bipolar electrode is operating as a monopolar electrode.

3.6 Tissue Responses

A. Cutting

Surgical cutting (Figure 3.13a) employs unmodulated radiofrequency current of the type shown in Figures 3.8a and 3.8b. The tip of the probe is brought into contact with the tissue surface and the ESU is activated. An arc is struck and the tissue vaporizes, producing a scalpel-like cut. The permissible speed of cutting depends on the current intensity. However, the lips of the incision usually bleed and coagulation current is used to arrest the bleeding. In many ESUs it is possible to combine (blend) cutting and coagulating current electrically so that coagulation accompanies cutting.

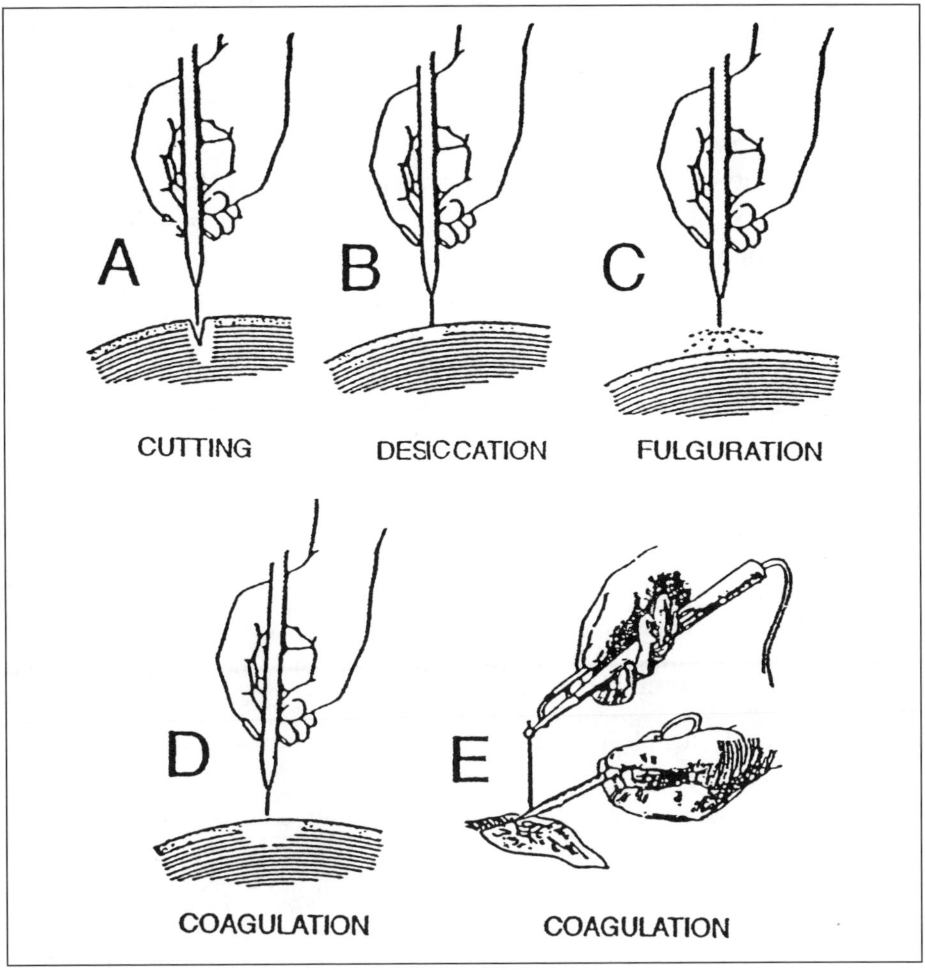

Figure 3.13 Tissue effects

Honig (1975) has shown that the temperature at the tip of the electrode is high enough to boil tissue fluid, which causes the cells to burst. The arc represents a very localized source of heat so that the cutting is highly localized. In addition, the arc represents ionized gas (plasma), which has a low resistance. Therefore, as the cutting electrode is advanced, it is surrounded by steam and hot ionized gas which emits light.

B. Desiccation

Desiccation (Figure 3.13b), i.e., drying, is produced by placing the tip of the probe in contact with the tissue and activating the ESU. Low current of either type can be used; no arc is formed and the fluid is driven from the tissue surrounding the probe tip.

C. Coagulation

Coagulation employs modulated current (Figures 3.8c and 3.8d) and several different techniques are employed with the active electrode. With spray coagulation (Figure 3.13c), sometimes called fulguration (fulgur = lightning), the active electrode is brought close to the tissue and the ESU is activated. Arcs travel from the tip of the probe to the tissue, each arc striking a different site, the result being a more or less circular area of coagulation. This technique is used to remove skin blemishes and sometimes to close very small bleeding vessels. Alternately, the active electrode is placed in contact with the bleeder (Figure 3.13d) and the ESU is activated; no arcing occurs and the tissue temperature rises to above 45°C. White coagulation is the term used when lower current and longer times are used. The tissue is dehydrated slowly and becomes whitish.

Another technique for closing larger blood vessels was developed by Ward (1925) and is shown in Figure 3.13e. The bleeder is grasped with a hemostat or forceps to arrest bleeding; then the tip of the active electrode is touched to the hemostat and the ESU is activated. No arc is formed and either type of current can be used to seal the bleeder. The surgeon's gloves provide insulation for the hands.

The ESU must never be activated while holding a hemostat (or metal instrument) which is in contact with the active electrode while the instrument is not in contact with the tissue, because the open-circuit voltage of an ESU is high and could break down the insulation of the glove and burn or shock the surgeon. The breakdown voltage for rubber is 300 V/1000th in. (mil). The breakdown for a typical plastic is 300 to 1000 V/mil of thickness.

D. Argon-enhanced coagulation

McGreevy and Bertrand (1988) found that the forcible passage of argon gas through a hollow electrode during coagulation not only cleared the field, but the gas became ionized and produced a flexible eschar with uniform depth and absence of charring. The ionized gas at the electrode tip is very uniform in extent, easy to manipulate, and coagulates very well on highly vascularized tissue, such as the liver. Other than the special hollow electrode and means for controlling the flow of argon, standard electrosurgical fulgurating current is used. The hazards associated with this technology are no different than those with conventional open electrosurgery.

3.7 Current Crowding

A. Introduction

Even with everything operating properly, there are situations in which there is a risk of injury resulting from electrosurgical current crowding, i.e., a condition in which the return-path current is forced to flow through tissue with a small cross-sectional area. Mitchell and Lumb (1966) use the term "channeling" for this situation. Perhaps the best way to illustrate current crowding is to consider first a no current-crowding example. Figure 3.14a illustrates an active electrode delivering electrosurgical current to a tissue. Note that the current spreads radially from the small-area entry site (active electrode); therefore, all of the heating is at this site. The bulk of the tissue and blood flow constitute a heat sink.

Figure 3.14b illustrates the application of electrosurgical current to an organ connected to the body by a slender stalk, which might be a duct, nerve, artery, and/or vein. Observe that the electrosurgical current spreads radially from the active electrode tip. All of this current is forced to reach the dispersive electrode via the tissue stalk, which has a small cross-sectional area and therefore a high electrical resistance. Because the heating is proportional to the current density (amps/cm^2) squared, the resistance and the duration of current flow, the opportunity for coagulating the stalk is high. Mitchell and Lumb (1966) and Schellhammer (1974) recognized this hazard. Mitchell and Lumb stated:

> The example of this condition (channeling) most commonly occurring is in operations on the testis and scrotum (e.g., hydrocele), when the spermatic cord and its vessels channel the whole of the operating current. In these circumstances the narrow pedicle formed by the cord may concentrate sufficient heat to thrombose all the blood-vessels, resulting in necrosis of the organ.

Figure 3.14c illustrates a disastrous case of current crowding in which the surgeon used electrosurgery as an aid in circumcision. The penis was coagulated and lost. Other current-crowding accidents are described elsewhere in this chapter.

B. Temperature rise due to current crowding

Using the penis as an example of current crowding, it is possible to calculate the temperature rise. In Figure 3.14c, note that all of the current flows through the penis and heating is produced in the entire organ. The temperature rise ($\Delta T°C$) can be calculated from the current (I amps), its duration of flow (t sec), along with the length (L cm), cross-sectional area (A cm^2) and resistivity (ρ ohm-cm) of the tissue.

In the case of the penis, Schonfeld (1943) published graphs showing the length (L) and circumference (C) of the penis of subjects from birth to twenty-four years. The study involved 1500 normal subjects. Figure 3.15 presents his data.

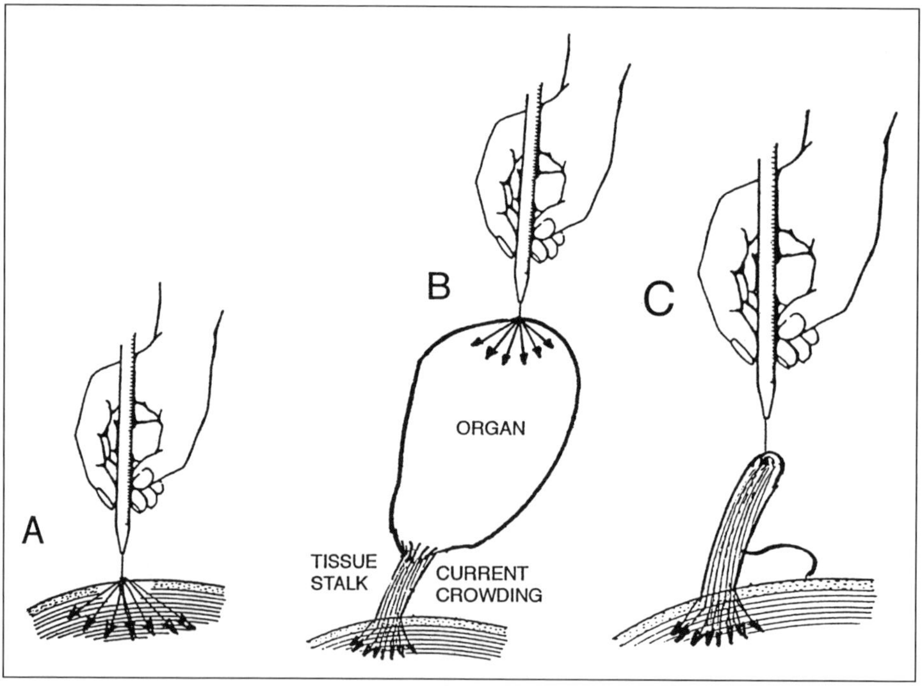

Figure 3.14 *(a) No current crowding; (b) current crowding by a slender tissue stalk and (c) current crowding due to use of electrosurgical current applied to the penis*

The number of calories produced by the electrosurgical current is $0.24I^2Rt$, where I is the rms current in amps, R is the resistance of the flaccid penis in ohms and t is the duration of current flow in seconds. This calorie input equals the product of the mass (M) heated, the specific heat (s) and the temperature rise (ΔT); therefore:

$$0.24I^2Rt = Ms\Delta T$$

The mass of the penis is equal to its density (D) multiplied by its volume which is equal to the cross-sectional area (A) multiplied by its length (L). Therefore:

$$0.24I^2Rt = DsAL\Delta T$$

The resistance (R) of a cylindrical conductor is $\rho L/A$, where ρ is its resistivity in ohm-cm; therefore:

$$0.24I^2t\left(\frac{\rho L}{A}\right) = DsAL\Delta T$$

which yields:

$$\frac{0.24I^2\rho t}{A^2} = Ds\Delta T$$

For typical biological tissues, $D = 1$ and $s = 1$; therefore the temperature rise is:

$$\Delta T = \frac{0.24I^2\rho t}{A^2}$$

To use Schonfeld's data it is necessary to convert the area A to circumference. This yields:

$$A = C^2/4\pi$$

Entering this into the foregoing equation and collecting terms provides the following equation for ΔT:

$$\Delta T = \frac{37.9I^2\rho t}{C^4}$$

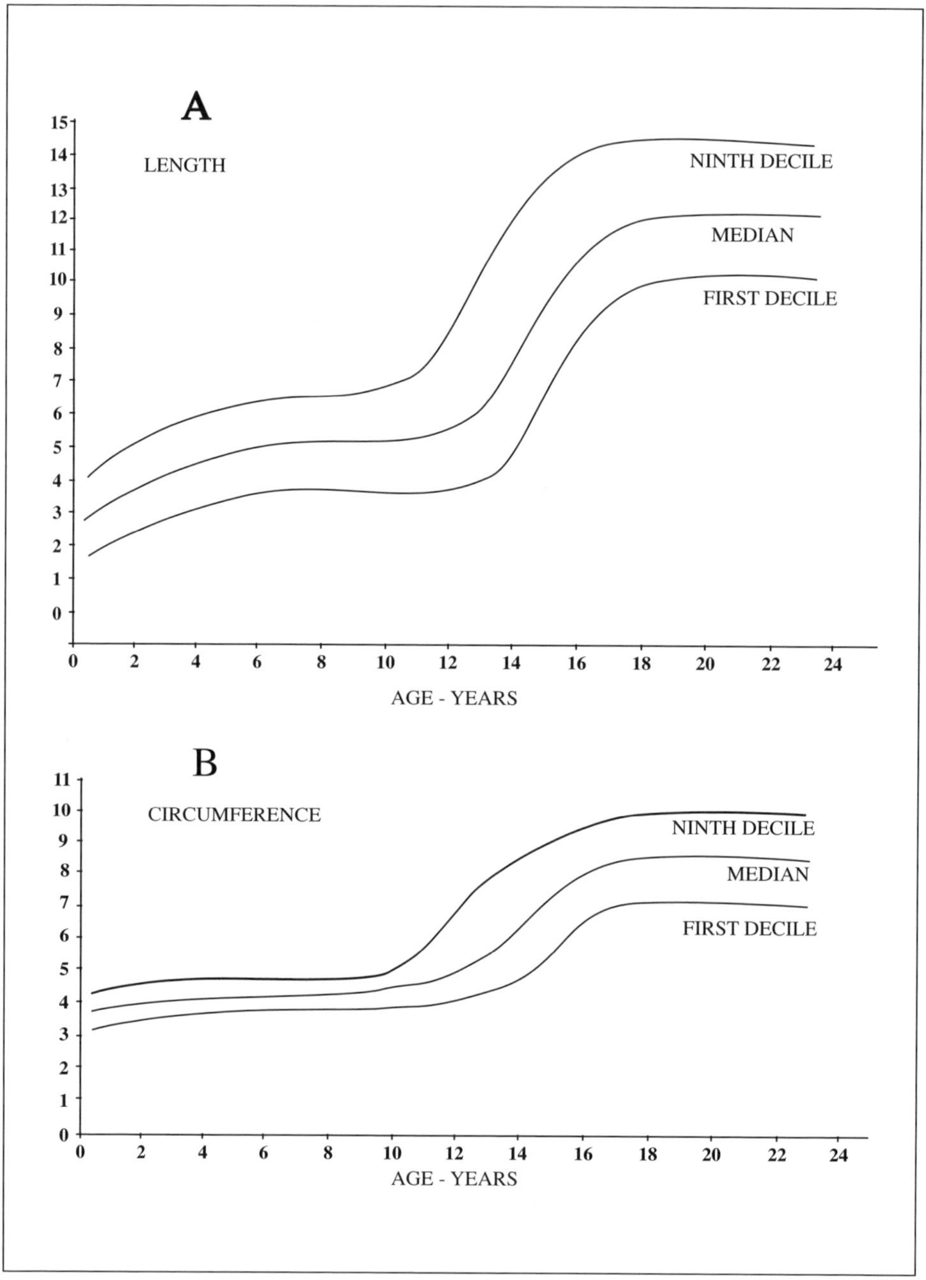

Figure 3.15 *In (a) is shown the length of the penis of normal subjects from birth to twenty-four years of age; (b) illustrates the penile circumference for the same age range. (Redrawn from Schonfeld 1943)*

Observe that the temperature rise (ΔT°C) varies inversely with the fourth power of the circumference. Because $C = \pi d$, the temperature rise varies inversely with the fourth power of the diameter, therefore the hazard is greater the smaller the girth of the penis.

It is now appropriate to determine the time (t sec) for the current flow to produce a 10°C rise in penile temperature using a typical coagulating current (0.24 amps, Geddes and Baker 1989). A 10°C temperature rise will bring the penis to 47°C, which is above the temperature for protein coagulation in a few seconds (Gendron 1988). However the missing quantity is ρ, the resistivity of the penile tissue. There are no published data, but a reasonable estimate of 200 ohm-cm is based on the resistivity of skin, muscle and blood.

From Schonfeld (1943), the mean circumference of a newborn's penis is 3.75 cm. Entering the value into the foregoing equation reveals that a current flow of 4.5 sec will produce a temperature rise of 10°C. A total coagulation time of 4.5 sec is well within the time used for circumcision.

Schonfeld (1943) provided maximum and minimum values for the circumference of the newborn penis of 4.2 and 3.1 cm respectively. Entering these values into the foregoing equation provides times of 7.12 sec and 2.11 sec. for the largest and smallest newborn penis for an increase of 10°C in temperature. These times are well within those used for tissue coagulation.

3.8 Complications with Electrosurgical Current

Electrosurgical current can be a source of electromagnetic interference (EMI) and can cause environmental and implanted devices to malfunction. These cases are discussed in the chapter on EMI. Muscle stimulation is by no means rare with electrosurgery; these cases are discussed in this chapter. Accidental burns are all too common; these will also be discussed in this chapter. Finally, the inappropriate use of electrosurgery in the presence of a flammable material and oxygen constitutes a fire hazard; these accidents are discussed in the chapter on anesthesia and in this chapter.

Since 1928 when Cushing popularized the use of ES, considerable experience has accrued on the efficacy and safety of the use of electrosurgery and guidelines, regulations and warnings have been published by many; the following will describe the most important of these.

1. AAMI/ANSI Standard HF18, 1993
2. NFPA-99, Annex 2

3. JCAHO Accreditation Manual for Hospitals
4. Warnings in ES manuals

Among the warnings found in various manuals that accompany electrosurgical units are the following:

- Accidental and unintended burn injury has occurred during procedures in small surgical fields and on small appendages. Catastrophic results have been reported in the context of neonatal and pediatric circumcisions. In those cases of confirmed thermal injury during neonatal and pediatric circumcisions, the mechanism of injury appears to have been associated with contact between a metal clasp (such as a Gomco clamp or a Kocher clamp) in the surgical field and the active electrode, which greatly increased current flow.
- Use electrosurgery with caution in the presence of internal or external pacemakers. Interference produced with the use of electrosurgical devices can cause devices such as a pacemaker to enter an asynchronous mode or can block the pacemaker entirely.
- Manufacturers recommend against the use of laparoscopic surgery on pregnant patients.
- Do not use electrosurgical equipment unless properly trained to use it in the specific procedure being undertaken.
- This equipment is for use only by trained, licensed physicians. Always use the lowest output setting necessary that achieves the desired surgical effect. The active electrode should be utilized only for the minimum time necessary to lessen the possibility of unintended burn injury.
- Pediatric applications or procedures performed on the small anatomic structures may require reduced power settings.
- The higher the current flow and the longer the current is applied, the greater the possibility of unintended thermal damage to tissue, especially during use in small appendages.
- This equipment is capable of producing a physiological effect. Read the instructions, cautions, and warnings provided with electrosurgical accessories before using.

A. Muscle contraction

Skeletal-muscle contraction is not uncommon during electrosurgery and can present a hazard in some circumstances. For example, Prentiss et al. (1965), referring to transurethral resection, stated:

> It is estimated that the adductor contraction occurs in one of five patients with large intraurethral prostatic adenomas or laterally placed vesical neoplasms.
>
> The obturator nerve stimulation occurs when the prostatic capsule or deeper muscular layers of the bladder are approached. The adductor muscle contraction develops so suddenly that perforation may be unavoidable and leads to extravasation. It always deters the completion of the operation and dissemination of tumor cells is a distinct possibility.

To avoid adductor muscle contraction during transurethral resection, Prentiss et al. (1965) recommended the use of nerve block or myoneural-junction block. Interestingly, they noted that the cutting current provided by their ESU was modulated at 120/sec (Figure 3.8a). They developed an unmodulated ESU operating at 3.601 MHz, but still encountered muscle contraction and concluded that the presence of a cutting arc generated low-frequency currents that produced the stimulation, a fact that was proved much later.

Foster and Geddes (1986) devised a simple experiment designed to test the ability of electrosurgical current to stimulate the dog sciatic nerve with and without an arc at the tip of the electrosurgical probe, which was remote from the nerve, as shown in Figure 3.16. The active electrosurgical electrode was placed over a saline-soaked sponge in a metal dish which was connected to a gauze-covered, saline-soaked electrode applied to the exposed sciatic nerve of an anesthetized dog. A conventional dispersive electrosurgical electrode provided the return path to the ESU. Thus, the electrosurgical current could be applied with or without an arc by selecting the position of the tip of the active electrode (e.g., above the sponge or advanced into it), as shown in Figure 3.16.

Stimulation of the sciatic nerve causes contraction of the gastrocnemius muscle and rotates the foot (downward) around the ankle joint. Therefore, if any pulsating current flowed in the circuit, the sciatic nerve would be stimulated, thereby contracting the gastrocnemius muscle.

Two types of experiment were performed. One consisted of applying electrosurgical current with no arc, i.e., the tip of the active electrode was

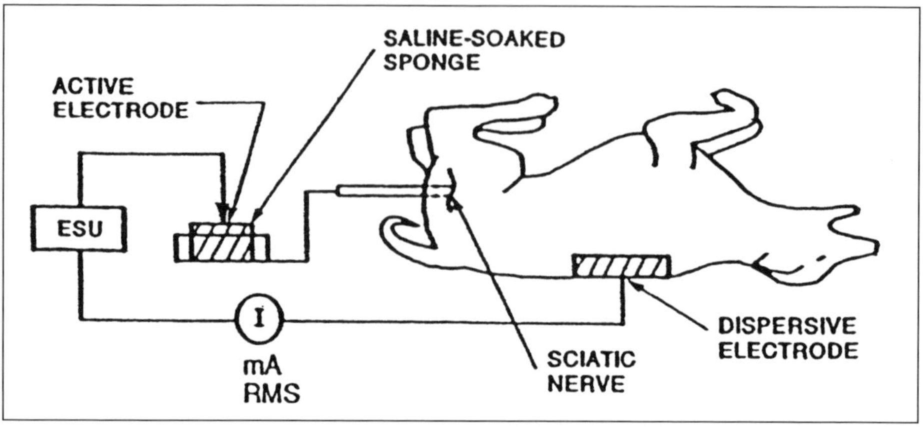

Figure 3.16 *Method of demonstrating muscle stimulation with electrosurgical current (Redrawn from Foster KS and Geddes LA. Med. Instrum. 1986, 20(6): 335–336.)*

plunged into the sponge before the ESU was activated; the other employed activation of the ESU with the tip of the active electrode just above the sponge and slowly advancing it until an arc was struck. Thus, the current that flowed represented the no-arc and arc conditions. The rms current (I) was measured in both cases with a thermocouple-type ammeter. Table 3.2 summarizes the results and shows that with no arc, in only one case was there a trace of muscle contraction. In all cases with an arc, muscle contraction occurred.

It has been shown by Pearce et al. (1986) and Tucker et al. (1984) that the presence of an arc in the path of electrosurgical current produces low-frequency components capable of stimulation. That the cause of muscle contraction during electrosurgery is due mainly to stimulation of motor nerves comes from two sources: (1) the muscle contraction can be distant from the site of the active electrosurgical electrode and (2) nerve blockade and myoneural blocking agents block muscle contraction.

In addition to adductor muscle contraction during transurethral resection, other muscles have been observed to contract during electrosurgery. The following is an example.

Geddes and Moore (1990) reported the following accident that resulted from muscle contractions during electrosurgery:

> A thirty-two-year-old white male with tender enlarged lymph nodes in the left posterior cervical triangle presented to the office of a general surgeon. There was also a twenty-five to thirty-pound weight loss over a two to three-month

period. He was hospitalized for diagnostic studies which were negative. Suspecting possible Hodgkin's disease, he was taken to the operating room for removal of the largest node. When the surgeon encountered a small bleeder in the subcutaneous fat, he used a standard, solid-state electrosurgical unit in the monopolar mode with coagulation at a setting between three or four to stop the bleeding. As the bleeder was approached with the active electrode to perform coagulation, the patient experienced a severe jolt which he likened to being shocked by an electric outlet. The operative report made no reference to the incident or the electrosurgical unit, stating only that, "A nerve, presumably of the cervical plexus was anesthetized and retracted posteriorly and the subjacent node was dissected out."

The discharge summary, however, noted:

During this operation, while in the subcutaneous tissue under local anesthesia, a standard ESU was used to coagulate a small bleeding blood vessel and this caused a rather violent jerk in the patient's left leg and left arm. The ESU was used no further during the operation. As the operation continued, the ac-

Table 3.2
The Stimulating Capabilities of Cutting and Coagulating Current

Instrument		Current	Contraction	
No.	**Mode**	**[mA rms)]**	**Arc**	**No Arc**
1	Coag.	200	Yes	No
	Cut	500	Yes	No
2	Pure cut	200	Yes	No
	Spark gap coag.	600	—	No
	(mod. hemo.)	200	Yes	—
	Spark gap coag.	500	_	No
	(marked hemo.)	100	Yes	_
	Spark gap coag.	250	_	Trace
	(max. hemo.)	<100	Yes	

cessory nerve was noted to be near the area and it was presumed that the stimulation of a nerve is what caused this violent spasm.

The surgeon was concerned that the ESU had malfunctioned. Although the machine used in the procedure was not identified, all machines were checked approximately two months after the operation and all were reported to be functioning normally. The disposable active electrode and grounding pad were not retained.

Subsequent to the operation, the patient complained of pain in the neck, left arm, and shoulder. When seen in the physician's office three days later, he was unable to completely abduct his left arm. An electromyographic study eighteen days after surgery revealed "moderately severe denervation of the rhomboids, levator scapulae, supra-spinatus, infra-spinatus, and trapezius muscles," prompting the neurologist to note that the results "may provide evidence of involvement of the nerve to the trapezius, dorsal scapular nerve, and supra-scapular nerve. This may be secondary to partial injury to the upper brachial plexus on the left."

Approximately one month after surgery, the surgeon was concerned that the patient exhibited diffuse atrophy of his deltoids and other shoulder girdle muscles. Subsequent orthopedic treatment resulted in a conclusion of a dual lesion: brachial plexus injury and cervical disc degeneration at C5–6, the latter resulting in anterior intervertebral disc excisions and fusion from C4 through 7. The orthopedic surgeon felt that the patient suffered an electrical injury to the brachial plexus from direct spread of current. In addition, he doubtless had degenerative disease in his cervical spine which was not symptomatic until the violent jerking of his neck occurred. After that, the symptoms persisted until the surgery was performed on the cervical disc.

From the foregoing, it appears that the active electrosurgical electrode was near a motor nerve or plexus and that the presence of the arc produced low-frequency components that resulted in stimulation. Of the two types of electrosurgical current, the coagulating current, which is delivered in bursts, is the most likely to stimulate if an arc is struck. However, cutting (unmodulated) radiofrequency current has the potential for stimulation if an arc is struck.

B. Pacemaker accidents

Since introduction of implanted cardiac pacemakers in the early 1960s, there have been many accidents in which electrosurgical current has caused pacemaker malfunction. Many such accidents and the principles underlying pacemaker operation have been described in the previous chapter. However, the following pacemaker accident investigated by the author serves to illustrate how complex an accident can become and how careful investigation is needed to explain it.

The following case illustrates several important points about the function of a monopolar pacing system. In 1991, a child underwent surgical repair of the great arteries of the heart and experienced total A-V block and required a pacemaker. Because the conventional venous approach for inserting the pacing lead was not practical, a monopolar lead was screwed into the right ventricular surface. The pacemaker was implanted in the left abdomen, the pacemaker case being the indifferent pacing electrode. In the fall of 1995, a routine check showed that the pacemaker battery was nearing the end of its life and elective pacemaker replacement was scheduled for September 28, 1995, when the boy was nine years old. An incision was made in the skin superior to the pacemaker to remove it from its pocket and electrosurgery (ES) was used to control bleeding at the skin incision. The ES dispersive electrode was on the right anterior thigh. The pacemaker was removed from its pocket and the monopolar lead was disconnected and connected to a pacemaker analyzer to test the lead and determine the threshold pacing voltage and impedance. A clip lead, affixed to the skin incision served as the indifferent pacing lead. Cardiac pacing was not possible and the wires to the analyzer were replaced without being able to pace the heart. The spontaneous ventricular rate was 30/min, indicative of total A-V block. Closed-chest pacing was applied and although the chest muscles and diaphragm twitched, the heart could not be paced. By this time, the patient was becoming cyanotic (blue) and CPR was applied. Electrosurgery was used to open the left chest, the heart was exposed and a screw-in lead was applied to what appeared to be the right ventricle, but pacing could not be achieved with this electrode which appeared to be in fat and another pacing lead was placed, but pacing was not possible. The thoracotomy was enlarged so that direct cardiac compression could be applied, which was effective in producing low pulsatile pressure. Cessation of cardiac compression revealed no spontaneous cardiac activity and atropine and epinephrine were administered with resumption of rhythmic cardiac compression. Cessaton of compression revealed pulsatile pressure lasting for a short time. Another pacing electrode was applied and pacing was possible and a new pacemaker was implanted in the right upper quadrant. The skin incisions were closed and the original pacing lead was left *in situ*. The patient was transferred to the intensive care unit in critical condition. The patient died a few days later. A review of the operating room record showed a mean arterial pressure of 30 mmHg for one-half hour and a mean pressure of 40 mmHg for two hours, indicative of poor tissue perfusion.

It is now appropriate to examine the proximal cause of failure to pace. Figure 3.17a shows the monopolar pacemaker implanted in the left abdominal region with the monopolar pacing lead attached to the right ventricle; the case (can) of the pacemaker was the indifferent pacing electrode. Figure 3.17b shows the ES electrode (arrow tip) placed on the skin above the implanted pacemaker. There are two return paths for the electrosurgical current: (1) from the active ES electrode, through the metal case of the pacemaker and through the conducting body tissues to the dispersive electrode on the right thigh, and (2) from the active ES electrode (arrow) to the metal case of the pacemaker, up the pacing lead to the right ventricle and back through the conducting tissues to the dispersive electrode on the right thigh. Note that the area of the pacing electrode in the heart is very small; therefore the current density for ES current is high, thereby raising the issue of local myocardial thermal damage. Now recall that when the pacing lead was disconnected from the pacemaker and connected to the pacemaker analyzer, pacing could not be achieved. This raises the issue of a broken pacer lead, which is very unlikely because it functioned up to the

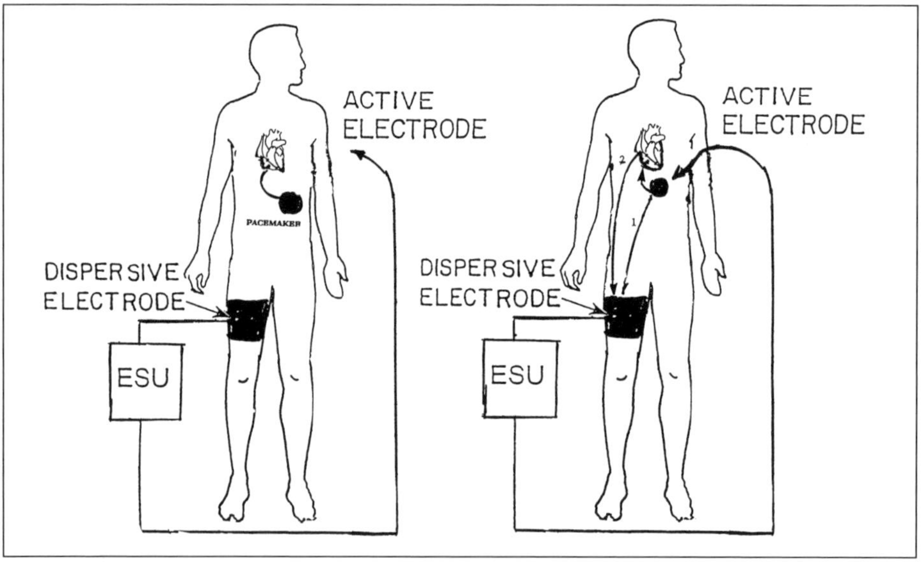

Figure 3.17 *In (a) is shown a monopolar pacemaker implanted in the abdomen and the ES dispersive electrode on the right thigh. In (b) is shown application of the active ES electrode to the tissue adjacent to the pacemaker. The arrows 1 and 2 show the two paths for the ES current.*

time that the pacemaker was removed. That breakage occurred during surgery cannot be the case because during postmortem the lead was removed and tested, revealing a resistance of 25 ohms, which is typical for such a lead according to the manufacturer. Therefore we are left with explaining why the myocardium could not be paced. The only plausible explanation is damage to the myocardium at the tip of the pacing lead. Damaged myocardium is inexcitable.

The manufacturer's instruction manual addresses the issue of the effect of ES current on pacemakers. In this particular case, the manual states:

> Electrosurgical units should never be used in the vicinity of [i.e., six inches/15 cm or closer] to a pulse generator/lead system. Currents generated from electrosurgical units may cause a permanent loss of output, setting low battery voltage status, or a resetting of mode and pacing rate in these units. Where alternatives to electrocautery are available, these should be used. However, if an electrocautery unit must be used, the physician should take the following steps to minimize the potential for complications:
>
> 1. To avoid malignant tachyarrhythmias and/or fibrillation, program the device to the VOO mode beforehand and avoid direct contact with the pulse generator or lead,
> 2. Position the ground plate so that the current pathway does not pass through or near the pacemaker system, e.g., under the patient's buttocks or legs during abdominal surgery,
> 3. Use short, intermittent, and irregular bursts, at the lowest feasible energy levels,
> 4. Where possible, use a bipolar electrocautery system,
> 5. Have temporary pacing equipment available, and
> 6. Defibrillation equipment should be available.

When interrogated during deposition, the physician said that the ES electrode tip was about two mm from the pacemaker. Note that the manufacturer recommends no closer than six inches (152 mm). In other words the active electrode was about seventy-five times closer than recommended.

However, there are other aspects to this case that need explanation. For example, why was pacing not possible with the lead inserted into "what appeared to be myocardium?" It is likely that this electrode was in the fat pad on the heart. That the myocardium was excitable is demonstrated by the last lead that was applied and connected to the new pacemaker that was implanted.

Another issue relates to the inability to pace with the transdermal (transchest) pacemaker, in view of the fact that it was delivering output, as evidenced by chest-muscle and diaphragm twitching. This was testified to by the manufacturer's representative who was in the operating room to use the pacemaker analyzer.

Successful transchest pacing requires placing the electrodes on the chest at the correct location and increasing the output until capture is achieved using a pacing rate higher than any spontaneous rate. Recall that the patient was a nine-year-old child and the transdermal pacer is designed to provide enough output to pace a large adult. In this case, either the electrodes were improperly located or the output was not set sufficiently high, or both. If the electrodes were too far headward, little current could reach the ventricles, the target for pacing. However, in this situation, the chest muscles and the diaphragm would twitch because the phrenic nerves that innervate the diaphragm descend in the neck and travel midline in the chest, passing the heart on their way to the diaphragm. Therefore, electrodes too far headward can fail to deliver adequate pacing current, yet still stimulate the chest muscles and the diaphragm.

The case was settled for a confidential amount after many depositions were taken from the physician, the manufacturer's representatives and the author. Reports from physician consultants also provided information about the inappropriate conduct of the physician.

3.9 The Skin

A. Anatomy

Histologically the skin is divided into three layers; the outermost is the epidermis, and below it is the dermis or corium, which rests on subcutaneous tissue. The epidermis and the dermis are in turn characterized by cells, tissues, and organs that endow the skin with its properties. Figure 3.18 illustrates a typical section of skin. However, skin anatomy varies over the body surface.

About three-quarters of the outermost layer of the epidermis, the stratum corneum, consists of a sheet of cells; the outer horny layers are dead and are continually cast off. These cells are replaced from below. The thickness of the stratum corneum varies considerably; on the palm and sole it is 0.4 to 0.7 mm.

Below the stratum corneum, in the skin of the palm and sole is the stratum lucidum, a clear zone consisting of several rows of flattened nonnucleated cells amounting to about 10μ in thickness. The time taken for the cells of the stratum corneum and the stratum lucidum to be shed is about two days. Immediately

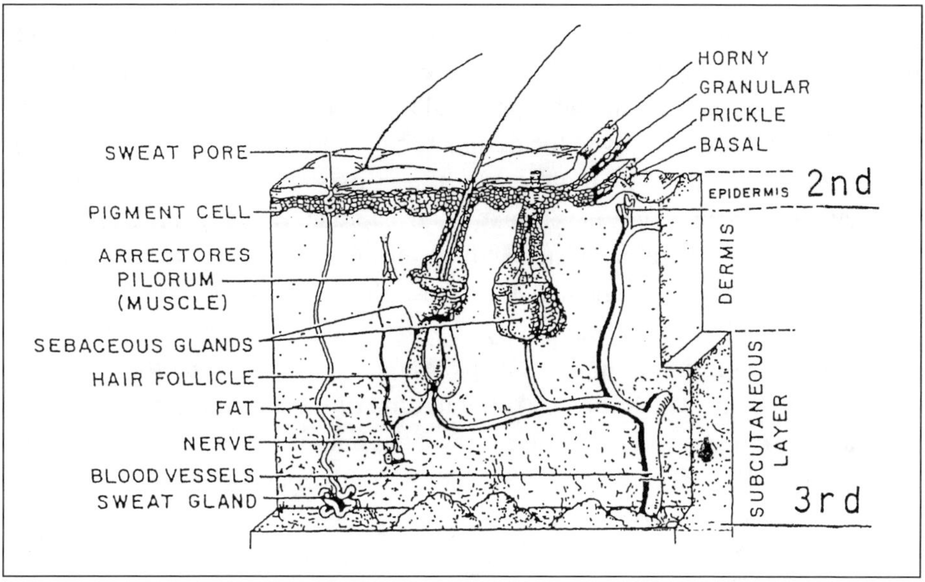

Figure 3.18 *Cross-sectional view of a typical skin site, showing depth of injury for second- and third-degree burns*

below the stratum lucidum is a layer composed of granular, prickle, and basal (germinative) cells. From two to five layers of spindle-shaped cells arranged with their long axes parallel to the surface of the skin constitute the granular layer. The cytoplasm of these cells contains pigment (melanin) granules. The prickle and basal cell layers—the latter believed to be the main source of the overlying cells – are indented by the papillae of the dermis. In the white race, melanin is found mainly in the granular layer; in dark-skinned races, most of the cells in the basal layer contain melanin. The origin of the melanin-producing cells is still an unsettled matter. Exposure to ultraviolet light increases the amount of melanin in the basal cell layer; this response is a protective mechanism because melanin absorbs ultraviolet light.

While the epidermis is characterized by dead cells on top of pigmented dying and living cells, the dermis is a structure of connective and elastic tissue and living cells, nourished by a rich vascular supply that penetrates to its most superficial layers, where numerous papillae containing capillary networks are located. Also within the dermis are numerous nerve fibers, sense organs, smooth muscle fibers, and glands.

The vascular supply of the dermis consists of arteries and a venous plexus that is located in the lowest part of the dermis. A richly branching arterial network springs upward to nourish the papillae and other structures. In addition to this return path to the venous plexus, there is an arterialvenous shunt which, if open, can divert blood from the superficial layers and reduce heat loss from the skin. Thus the blood supply to the dermis serves a double role—nutrition of the cells within it and regulation of heat loss from the surface of the skin. Associated with the vascular system is an extensive capillary network and a lymphatic drainage system. There is a transfer of water and electrolytes throughout this region which, because of the nature of these fluids, would be expected to be a region of high electrical conductivity.

In hairy skin, the basal cell layer (stratum germinativum) folds into the dermis to form the hair follicles. At the bottom of the hair follicle is a bulbous cellular matrix from which the hair grows; the bulb is nourished by a vascular papilla. Near the root of the hair, the shaft is continuous with the follicle wall. The hair shaft is composed of kerantinized cells. Opening into the hair follicle is a duct leading to a sebaceous gland composed of cells whose central axes are filled with vacuoles. The secretion of a sebaceous gland is accompanied by breaking down of the central cells, and the contents of these cells is poured into the follicle and passes up the hair on to the surface of the skin as an oily protective deposit. When the hair is made to stand erect by contraction of the piloerector muscles, it is believed that a small quantity of sebum is expelled; both processes are believed to be heat conserving.

Located deep within the dermis are the eccrine sweat glands, which deliver their secretion (mainly a dilute saline solution) via a duct to a pore on the surface of the skin. Sweat glands are distributed over most of the surface of the human body; they are simple, convoluted tubules composed of cells containing secretory granules. The ducts are lined with a double layer of cells; one layer which is longitudinal, is believed to be muscular and functions to expel the sweat, which is the most dilute of all animal fluids. It is about 99 percent water, but the remaining 1 percent contains a rich variety of other substances.

B. Skin burns

The severity of a skin burn is described by a three-stage scale. A first-degree burn is skin reddening (erythema), like a sunburn; there is no permanent skin damage. A second-degree or partial-thickness burn is characterized by blisters, vesication, and hemorrhage. A third-degree, or full-thickness burn, is characterized by zones of coagulum, denatured collagen, and brown leathery tissue called an eschar; often carbonized tissue is present if the burn is due to electrical current. All full-thickness burns and some partial-thickness burns require skin grafting. Figure 3.18 illustrates the depth of skin damage described by second and third degree burns. In trauma studies, a fourth degree is identified when the injury extends to the muscle and bone.

C. Diagnostic difficulties

In assessing skin injuries in the operating room, it is necessary to distinguish between burns due to electrosurgical current, burns due to heated objects in contact with the skin, burns due to chemicals and "burns", i.e. skin injury due to mechanical force which produces tissue damage due to ischemia, i.e. inadequate blood perfusion of tissues.

Electrosurgical burns result from a high current density acting over a time. There are two situations that produce this condition: (1) inadequate contact between the patient at the dispersive electrode site and (2) an alternate current site, which produces the same result. In both cases the injury is visible immediately following the operation. The tissue damage is proportional to the current density (squared) and the duration of current flow. If the return path for the electrosurgical current is via a dispersive electrode that makes inadequate contact with the subject, the area of injury is always less than the area of the dispersive electrode.

If the injury is due to an alternate current path, the injury is apparent at the end of the operation. The site of the injury is the site of the alternate current path.

Burns due to contact with a heated object are not very apparent at the end of surgery; at best a reddening of the skin is evident. However such lesions become much more prominent many hours or days later as tissue necrosis develops. The burn site is consistent with the location and shape of the heated object. The critical factors are the temperature of the heated object and the duration of its application to the skin.

Skin lesions due to chemical agents are fairly uncommon in the operating room. A discussion of these can be found in Chapter 8.

Skin lesions due to pressure necrosis, i.e. due to poor tissue perfusion are not apparent immediately post-surgery. The injury appears in several hours and becomes increasingly evident with the passage of time as tissues die. The location of pressure sores is typically over bony prominences (occiput, shoulder blades, sacrum, calf and heels for a supine subject). Critical factors are the subject's weight and duration in that position. Pressure sores are more likely to appear in subjects with vascular disease (hypertension, diabetes, etc.) and older subjects. Cross clamping the aorta for vascular replacement surgery arrests the circulation in the lower body for the clamp time, consequently the distal tissues are unperfused and the normal heat dissipation due to blood flow is absent. Additional information on pressure necrosis can be found in Chapter 8.

It should be obvious that thermal injury and pressure injury can coexist. For example, if a part of the body is supported by a hot pack that is above about 45ºC (114.8ºF), the poor tissue perfusion due to the pressure exerted by the hot pack will impair tissue perfusion and the full heat of the hot pack can produce a burn readily.

If an electrosurgical dispersive electrode is placed over a bony prominence (which is contraindicated) and the patient lies on it, an interesting situation arises. For example, if there is a skin lesion that is first noticed on the following day, it may be argued that this is an electrosurgical burn. However, electrosurgical burns are evident at the end of the operation and the circulating nurse would have seen it when the dispersive electrode was removed. Obviously this evidence is needed. However, it can be argued quite correctly that a dispersive electrode placed over a bony prominence can produce a pressure sore with no activation of the electrosurgical unit. The critical factors in this situation are how soon the lesion was observed and for how long the electrode supported the body.

3.10 Experimental Burn Studies

The most important factors in producing skin burns are contained in the temperature exposure-time curve, originally presented by Moritz and Henriques (1947). This study showed that for complete transepidermal necrosis, there is a hyperbolic relationship between temperature and exposure time. Moritz and Henriques showed that the shorter the duration of exposure, the higher the temperature required to produce irreversible dermal injury in porcine skin, which is an excellent analog for human skin; Figure 3.19 presents their data. It is generally believed that a skin temperature of 44°C can cause a burn if it persists for a long time.

To identify the factors that produce an increase in skin temperature with electrosurgical current, Pearce et al. (1983) carried out controlled burn studies on pigs using 500 kHz electrosurgical current delivered to circular disk electrodes 1, 2, 4, and 8 cm applied to the backs of pigs. The skin temperature and burn severity were determined for different currents (300 to 700 mA) and times (30 to 60 sec). The skin temperature, determined thermographically, was plot-

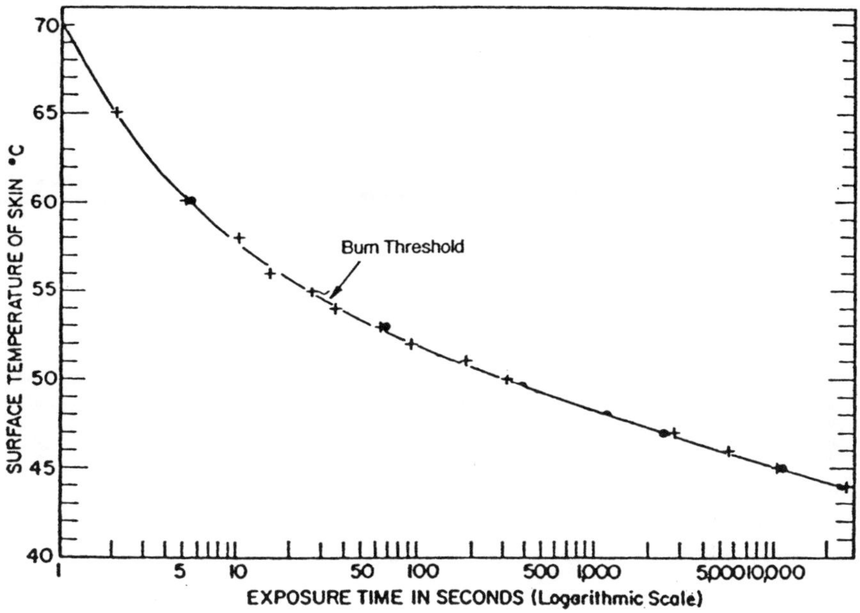

Figure 3.19 *Skin temperature versus exposure time for complete transdermal necrosis (burn threshold). Redrawn from Moritz and Henriques 1947.*

ted versus the energy density factor (seconds multiplied by the square of the current density in amps/cm^2 of electrode area). Figure 3.20 illustrates the result; the numbers (1, 2, 3) along the abscissa identify the burn degree.

The Pearce et al. study (1983), in general, with an energy-density factor in the range of 0.7 to 1.6 the maximum skin temperature below the electrodes was between 49 and 55°C, with single or multiple rings of second-degree burns located just inside or beyond the rim of the electrode. At all sites exposed to higher energy density (1.60 to 7.50), the maximum skin temperature beneath the electrodes was 55 to 81°C, and severe burns were produced with white to brownish, dry, firm, third-degree burns surrounded by peripheral rings of second-degree burns. No significant skin damage was produced with a skin temperature less than 45°C, representing an energy density factor of about 0.75.

DeRosa and Gadsby (1979) conducted electrosurgical burn studies with ECG electrodes and obtained data that allowed relating the skin-temperature rise to the energy density factor (seconds multiplied by current density squared). Figure 3.21 shows this relationship, which is in agreement with the data reported by Pearce et al. (1983) and shown in Figure 3.20.

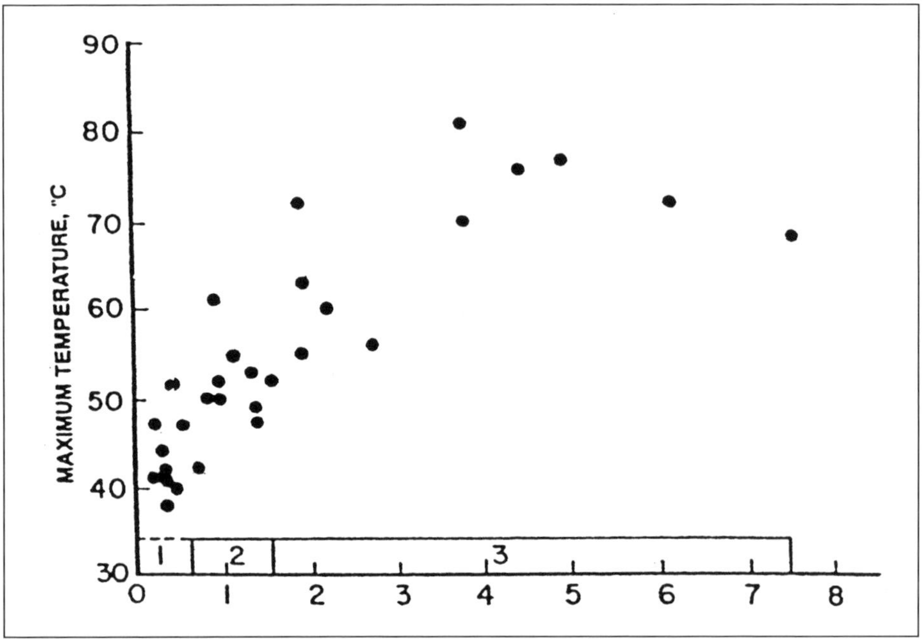

Figure 3.20 *Skin temperature versus energy density factor (Redrawn from Pearce JA, Geddes LA, Van Vleet J, Foster K and Allen J.* Med. Instrum. *1983, 17: 225–231.)*

3.11 Accidental Burns

A very common cause of skin burn results from inadequate contact area between a dispersive electrode and the patient. Such a situation can arise after the electrode has been applied properly and the patient is repositioned, which can put a strain on the cable and partially remove the electrode. Repositioning a patient may cause the electrode to buckle, a situation known as "tenting". The author has investigated several cases in which there was inadequate contact with the patient after initial correct application of the dispersive electrode, followed by placing the legs in stirrups as is used in obstetrics and gynecology. In these cases, burns occurred at the dispersive electrode site.

Another burn site can be the contact between the body and a grounded object when a dispersive electrode makes inadequate contact with a patient, or if the dispersive electrode is not on the patient, or if the patient cable is broken, thereby creating an alternate current path, as will be described now. (also see Fig. 3.12b2).

As stated previously, the heating at an electrode site depends on the current density squared and the duration of current flow. It is useful to identify the

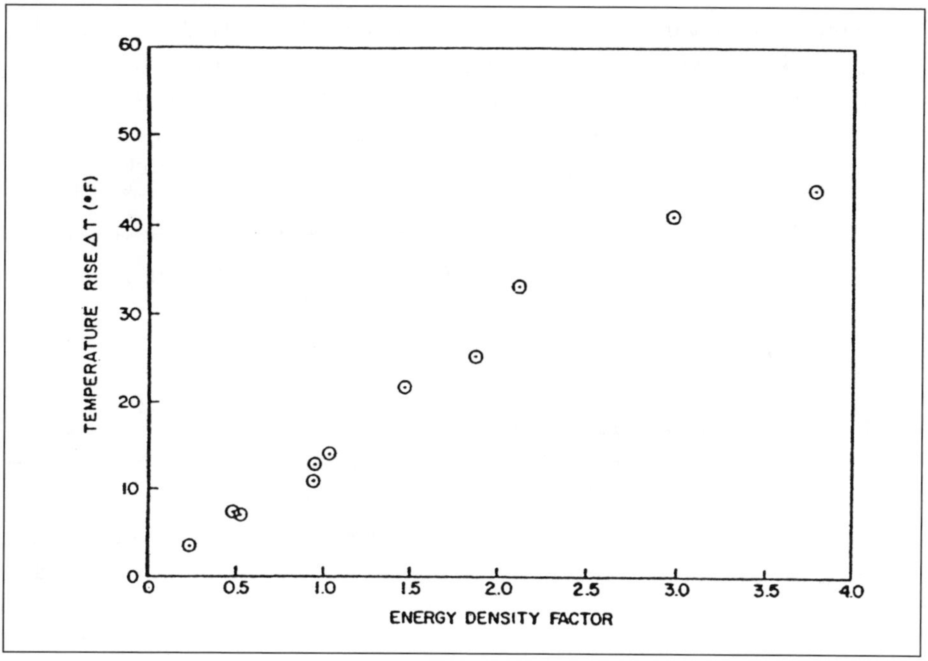

Figure 3.21 *Skin-temperature rise under ECG-monitoring electrodes for different energy density factors. Calculated from DeRosa and Gadsby (1979)*

events that occur in the absence of a satisfactory dispersive-electrode contact with the patient. In this case, the return path for the electrosurgical current will be any grounded object that the patient contacts. An example in which the dispersive electrode cable is broken at X is shown in Figure 3.22. Note that the return path is via the ECG monitoring electrodes, causing current to flow into the monitor and to any other contact between the patient and the grounded operating table, as shown by R at the patient's heel. Because these areas of contact are not large, the current density will be high and burns can result at these sites. Such alternate-path currents are by no means uncommon in accident cases.

A. Burns under ECG electrodes

As just shown, if one or more of the ECG electrodes become part (or all) of the electrosurgical current path, skin burns can result. Wald (1971) reported such an incident; he stated:

> Throughout the surgical procedure the ECG trace on the cardioscope appeared normal, without excessive interference. At the end of the procedure when the ECG electrodes were removed, second-degree burns, approximately 0.5 × 0.5 cm in size, were noted under the right and left shoulder electrodes. Inspection of the cautery showed that one of the wires connecting the patient plate to the cautery was broken.

Similar incidents were reported by Becker et al. (1974) when the ground electrode of the ECG acted as the return path for electrosurgical current because the wire to the dispersive electrode was broken.

1. Temperature-probe accidents

Body temperature is measured frequently during anesthesia because anesthetic agents depress the body's temperature-regulating system. Therefore, the temperature of a patient in a cool operating room will decrease with the passage of time. Two sites, (1) rectum and (2) esophagus, are often used for place-

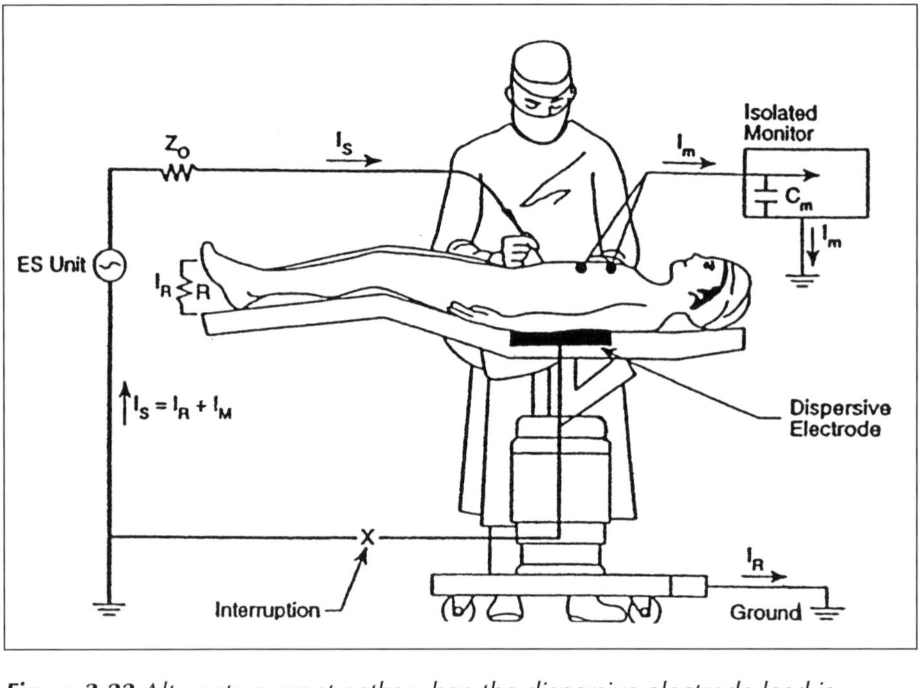

Figure 3.22 Alternate current paths when the dispersive electrode lead is interrupted. Leakage current (IR) can flow from the body to the operating table and current (Im) can flow into a patient monitor

ment of an electrical temperature probe. Injuries at these sites have been reported in association with the use of electrosurgery.

Wald (1971) reported a case of burn in the rectum of a patient in whom a battery-operated temperature probe had been installed. In describing the temperature-sensing system, Wald stated:

> It is a battery-operated portable device consisting of a case which contains the electronic components and battery, and a probe which contains the temperature-sensing element at its tip. The telethermo-meter case is metal, but is finished all around with insulated surfaces. In addition, on the bottom surface of the case there are four short (0.5 mm) cork legs which are intended to keep the case electrically isolated from the surface on which it rests. Thus, in design, battery operation and case construction completely isolate the case from ground or any other electronic equipment. However, in practice, examination of several telethermometer cases has shown the insulated surfaces scratched in various areas, exposing the metal. Also, the cork feet can be worn or fall off, which brings the exposed surface of the case in contact with its support. In operating room use, the telethermometer case normally rests on a well-grounded pedestal.

The foregoing clearly shows that the temperature probe formed part of the return path for the electrosurgical current.

An esophageal burn at the site of a temperature probe was reported by Parker (1984). The patient underwent knee surgery and the electrosurgical dispersive electrode was placed on the left thigh. Parker reported:

> The operation, lasting slightly over four hours, was devoid of any unusual anesthetic or surgical events. There were no arrhythmias, and the esophageal temperature ranged between 35.5 and 35.9°C. However, the temperature probe, after removal, was noted to have several smooth dark brown and black areas of discoloration on the white surface not noted prior to its insertion. After a routine emergence and extubation of the trachea in the operating room, the patient was admitted to the recovery room in a drowsy, easily arousable, stable condition, with blood pressure 130/80 mmHg, heart rate 84 beats/min, and respiratory rate 20 breaths/min while receiving 40 percent humidified oxygen via face mask.
>
> In recovery room, approximately one hour after admission, the patient began spitting up copious amounts of blood-tinged saliva. Auscultation of the lungs revealed generalized congestion. An immediate chest radiograph revealed right hilar opacification. Vital signs remained stable with blood pres-

sure 150/80 mmHg, heart rate 90 beats/min, and respiratory rate 20 breaths/min, without dyspnea or ectopy. An elective awake left nasotracheal intubation was performed because of increasing hemoptysis. Approximately two hours later, copious amounts of frothy red sputum were suctioned. The patient breathed 10 1/min oxygen via a T-tube, arterial blood gases revealing a pH 7.27, PaO_2 302 mmHg, $PaCO_2$ 50.7 mmHg, and BE -4.4 mEq/l. A general surgeon then performed esophagoscopy and flexible bronchoscopy. Bronchoscopy revealed frothy, bloody fluid from the right main stem bronchus with the posterior tracheal wall blistered and red. Esophagoscopy revealed the probable site of primary burn as the middle of esophagus with whitened (linear) burns. The patient then was sedated, treated with steroids and antibiotics, and ventilation controlled. He made a rapid and uneventful recovery with no apparent permanent adverse sequelae.

It was later found that the temperature probe was grounded. Despite its distance from the dispersive electrode on the left thigh, the temperature probe carried enough return-path electrosurgical current during the four-hour operation to produce the burn. The instruction manual for the temperature probe cautioned, "In medical use, remove the probe from patient contact before activating electrosurgical apparatus or other direct-coupled RF energy source."

2. Airway fires

The presence of a combustible endotracheal tube containing oxygen sets the stage for a fire; all that is needed is a source of ignition, namely a spark from an electrosurgical electrode. Such accidents due to electrosurgery are described in Chapter 4 (Anesthesia); those due to laser energy are described later in this chapter.

3.12 Endoscopic Electrosurgery

New surgical techniques with endoscopes have introduced "minimally invasive surgery" and shortened in-hospital stays considerably. However, endoscopic electrosurgical techniques merit scrutiny for potential hazards because such endoscopes operate in cramped, electrically hostile environments. Although there are many types of endoscopic techniques, they may be classified as single-entry site or multiple-entry site techniques. The cystoscope or resectoscope (Figure 3.23) is an example of the former. Laparoscopy (Figure 3.24) uses two instruments and often two additional entry sites for holding instruments. The laparoscope is passed through a trocar into a body cavity. The tro-

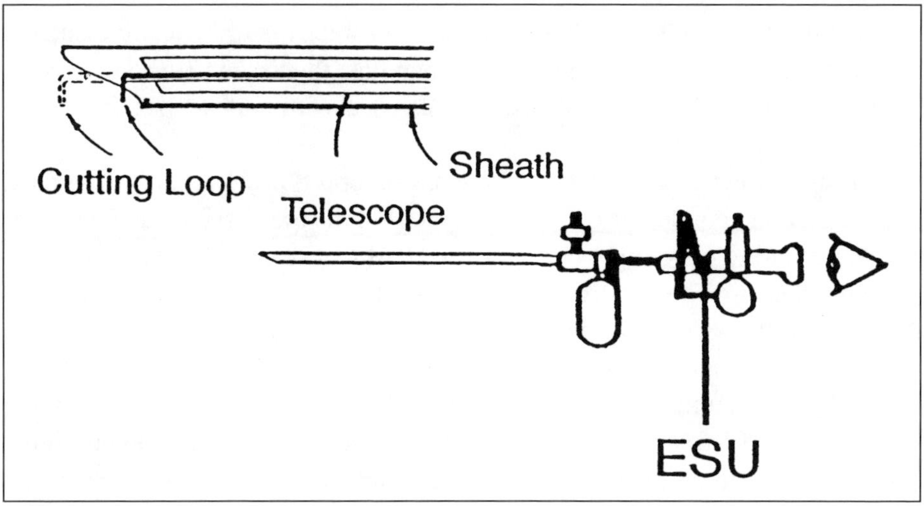

Figure 3.23 *Resectoscope showing the cutting loop*

car may be of metal or plastic. The endocsope may have many lumens; the model shown in Figure 3.24 contains a lumen for inflating the body cavity with a nonflammable gas, e.g. carbon dioxide. There is a lumen for a fiberoptic bundle which illuminates the cavity, and a lumen for a telescope for viewing the operating site; sometimes a video camera is mounted to the eyepiece and a video monitor displays the body cavity. Two additional trocars may be used for the passage of grasping tools. Figure 3.24 also shows a grasping forceps that is

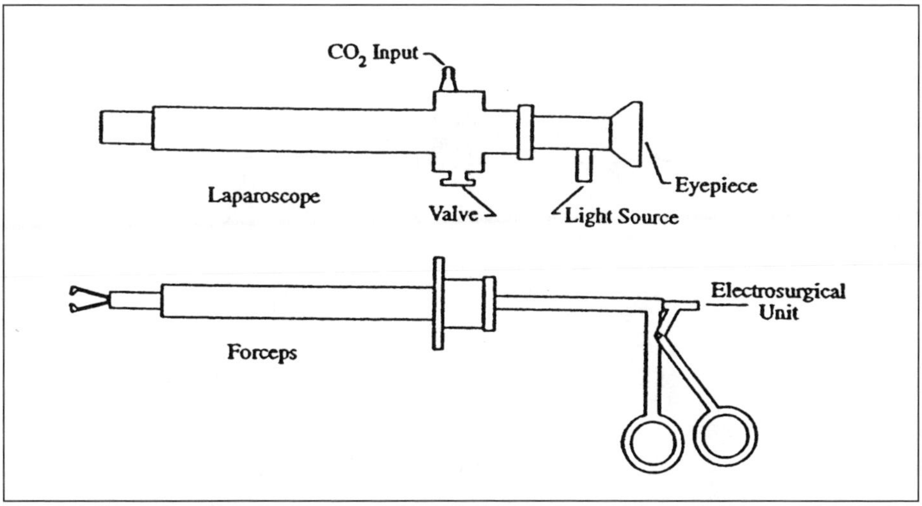

Figure 3.24 *Endoscope and grasping forceps*

passed into the body cavity. The shaft of the forceps is electrically insulated and electrosurgical current is applied to coagulate the tissue between the jaws. There are many other types of instruments used with endoscopes (e.g., scissors, loops, snares, etc.).

From an electrical viewpoint, there are several types of endoinstruments; one has an inner conductor that is insulated from the metal sheath and the other has an insulating covering over the metal shaft that carries the electrosurgical current. There are older instruments in which the metal shaft is uninsulated and the surgical gloves afford the only protection for the operator.

Figure 3.25 characterizes the situation when a sterilized forceps is inserted into a body opening or one made with a trocar. The metal sheath of the endoinstrument is insulated. A sterilized cable connects the instrument to the ESU. With the tip of the active electrode in contact with tissue, the ESU is activated and the solid arrow in Figure 3.25 identifies the principal current path. Because of the insulation there is a distributed capacitance between the metal sheath of the forceps and the patient. Consequently, there is a current path to the surrounding tissue (via region L) to the dispersive electrode; this alternate current path is shown by the dashed arrow in Figure 3.25. If the distributed capacitance C = 100 pF, the reactance of C at 0.5 and 2 MHz is 3185 and 796 ohms, respectively. This means that in normal operation, the current in the alternate path is small. However, Hayes (1979) reported that with some instruments this alternate current amounts to one-third to one-half of the total current. If the forceps is uninsulated and passed through a plastic trocar, the cur-

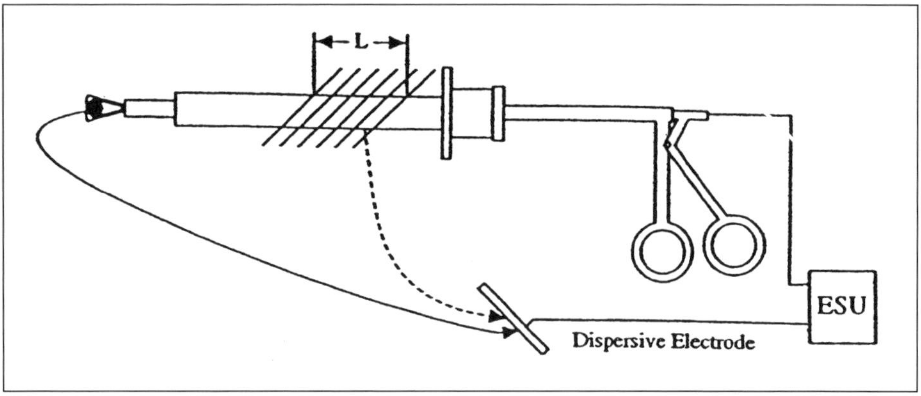

Figure 3.25 *Monopolar grasping forceps with electrical insulation covering the metal parts and principal current path (solid arrow) and alternate current path (dashed arrow)*

rent in the alternate path would be less. If the forceps were uninsulated and in contact with the body wall, the alternate current would be a substantial fraction of the total current.

Figure 3.26a illustrates schematically an endoinstrument in which a central current-carrying conductor is insulated from the metal sheath and the active electrode is not in contact with tissue and the ESU is activated. The dashed arrow identifies the current path. In this case the ESU (open-circuit) voltage would be high and the current due to the distributed capacitance (C) would be the major current path. Table 3.3 lists the open-circuit peak-to-peak voltage of typical ESUs for the different modes of use.

If the ESU output setting is high and the active electrode is not in contact with tissue, an arc could form between the active electrode and the metal sheath of the endoinstrument, as shown in Figure 3.26b, and a high current could flow from the sheath to the dispersive electrode. Such a situation could occur if the tip of the instrument is in a gas-filled cavity. Consequently, the instrument sheath resembles an active electrode and the patient and/or the operator could be burned. The burn will be severe if the area of contact of an uninsulated sheath with the patient is small.

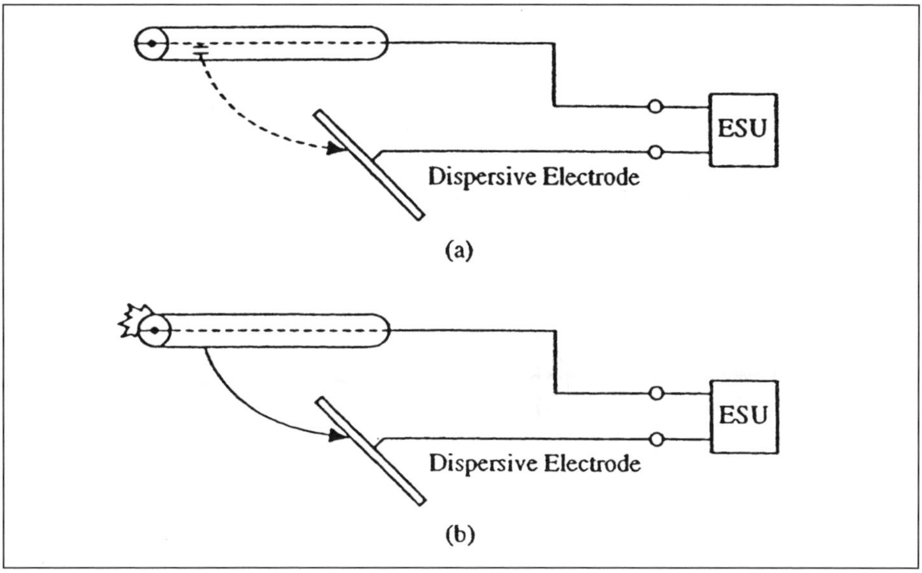

Figure 3.26 *In (a) is shown an endoinstrument in which the current-carrying conductor is insulated from the metal sheath and the ESU is activated with the active electrode not in contact with the tissue. In (b) is shown an arc between the current-carrying conductor and metal sheath of the endoinstrument.*

The situation illustrated in Figure 3.26b is hazardous to the surgeon who is holding the endoscope with gloved hands. Because the voltage on the endoscope is high, there is the likelihood of breakdown of the insulation on the instrument and the gloves, resulting in a burn sustained by the patient and surgeon, a situation that is not unknown. The breakdown voltage for gloves was discussed earlier in this chapter.

A. Urological Applications

Electrosurgery is used extensively in urology; for example, it is used to increase the diameter of the urethra that has been narrowed by prostatic enlargement, the operation being known as transurethral resection (TUR). Other uses include the removal of tumors or polyps in the bladder. The current levels are the highest and the activation times are the longest in all of electrosurgery (see Table 3.1).

In bladder electrosurgery, the resectoscope is passed into the bladder via the urethra as shown in Figure 3.27. The bladder is first evacuated of its highly conducting urine and filled with a poorly conducting isotonic fluid, such as 5 percent dextrose in water. In this process, the operating area is usually quite wet, contributing to electrical hazard.

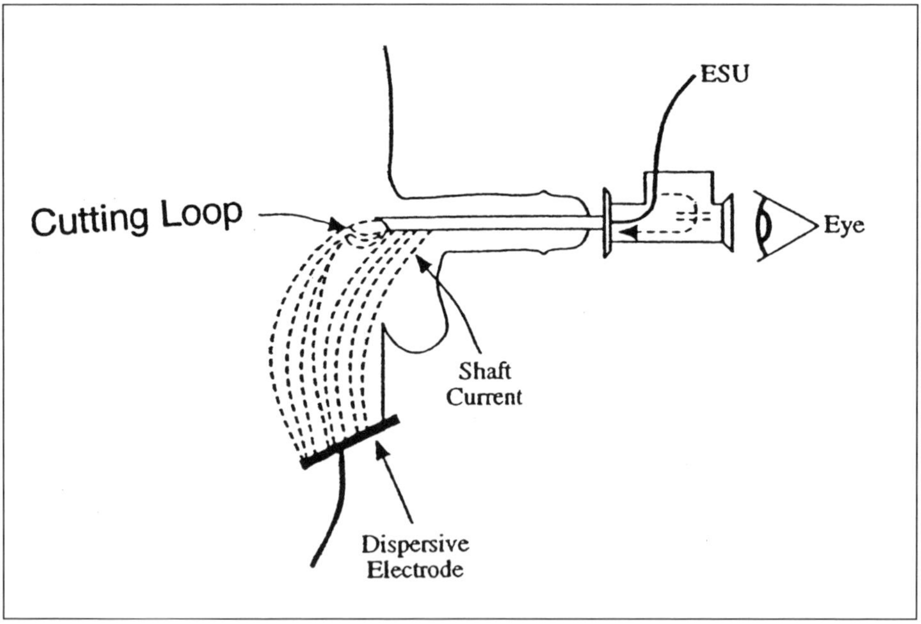

Figure 3.27 *Current flow from the tip electrode and shaft of a cystoscope*

Table 3.3
Output Characteristics of Electrosurgical Units

	Output Voltage Range Open Circuit, $V_{peak\text{-}peak}$	Output Power Range, W
Monopolar Modes		
Cut	200–5,000	1–400
Blend	1,500–5,800	1–300
Desiccate	400–6,500	1–200
Fulgurate/spray	6,000–12,000	1–200
Bipolar Mode		
Coagulate/desiccate	400–100	1–70

Data from von Maltzahn and Eggelston. *Biomedical Engineering Handbook,* Bronzino, J., Ed. 1995. CRC Press, Boca Raton, FL.

The shafts of some resectoscopes are bare metal; others are covered with a thin layer of electrical insulation. To improve current distribution Flachenecker and Fastenmeier (1979) recommended the use of a conducting lubricant if the resectoscope sheath is uninsulated and a poorly conducting lubricant if the resectoscope sheath is insulated.

In transurethral resection the cutting loop of the resectoscope (Figure 3.23) is advanced and withdrawn to ablate tissue to enlarge the urethra. Owing to the capacitance between the conductor carrying current to the loop and the metal sheath of the resectoscope there is current flow from the shaft to the patient, as shown in Figure 3.27.

Cutting loops can be bent or broken and come into contact with the metal sheath of the resectoscope, thereby making it an active electrode and presenting a hazard to the urologist and patient. Careful inspection of the resectoscope prior to sterilization is essential. The cable from the resectoscope to the ESU must be inspected carefully for continuity and insulation cracks before each sterilization. Cracks in insulation favor the genesis of a spark which could produce injury or be a source of ignition. Although steam sterilization is the best, it is hard on cables and insulation. Manufacturers of resectoscopes (and other endoinstruments) and cables provide recommendations for sterilization that must be followed to insure patient and operator safety.

In summary, among the hazards associated with urologic electrosurgery are burns due to accidental contact with tissues other than those intended, as well as those due to alternate current paths, muscle contraction, and interference with patient monitoring equipment and implanted electronic devices, such as cardiac pacemakers and implanted cardioverter defibrillators (ICDs). The use of a temporary cardiac pacing lead with an external pacemaker in the vicinity of an ESU is hazardous and may result in ventricular fibrillation; these cases are discussed in the chapter on EMI. Because urologic electrosurgery uses the highest current levels and the longest activation times, the opportunity for accidents is high.

As discussed previously, leg muscle contraction frequently accompanies TUR procedures and arises from stimulation of the obturator nerve which courses near the prostate. Stimulation of this nerve by electrosurgical current causes the leg to move toward the midline. Hodika and Clarke (1961) advocated the use of myoneural blocking agents to abolish muscle contraction. However, the use of such agents also paralyzes the muscles of respiration and positive-pressure breathing must be applied.

B. Injury to the urologist

Whereas most resectoscopic injuries are suffered by the patient, urologists have been injured while performing a transurethral resection. For example, Thomas (1975) reported that he was using:

> An Iglesias resectoscope element with a telescope fitted with the photographic type eyepiece. The current supplying the resectoscope came from an electrosurgical unit of the spark-gap variety. During the operation the entire instrument heated and warmth emanated to the surgeon's hands. Various parts of the instrument were exchanged but the final instrument was as described. While cutting a piece of tissue the author experienced sudden severe pain in the right eye. The pain was so intense that the operation had to be completed by another surgeon. Examination by an ophthalmologist revealed a burn and laceration to the cornea. The eye was treated symptomatically and conservatively with the resulting residual effects of myopia and uniocular diplopia producing four images in the injured eye.

After investigating the accident, Thomas reported:

> Analysis of this accident revealed the photographic eyepiece as being responsible for allowing arcing to occur to the surgeon's eye. More specifically, the metal resectoscope post protruding through the center of the eyepiece allowed the arcing to occur. The investigation of this accident confined itself to the instrument being used. However, many eyepieces (in daily use) have metal exposed around the plano lens of the telescope ocular and are, in the opinion of this author, unsafe for use with electrosurgical units inasmuch as unrelated electrical problems or system breakdown exposes the surgeon's eyes to a risk of serious injury.

An accident investigated by the author resulted in a serious back injury to the urologist. The bladder had been emptied of urine and filled with D5W. The resectoscope was in place ready to perform a transurethral resection. The urologist was looking through the eyepiece and activated the electrosurgical unit. Immediately he fell off his stool, bending the bracket on the operating table that held the drainage basin, and landed on the floor in extreme pain such that he could not get up. The anesthesiologist deadened the dorsal nerve roots to abolish the pain. The urologist suffered so much injury to the spine that he could no longer perform many of the duties of a urologist.

On examination of the resectoscope and its cable, it was found that there was a break in the cable at the connector. On interrogating the urologist, he reported that an arc struck his nose when the ESU was activated and this shock caused him to lose his balance and fall. Note that with a broken cable, the ESU is operating under an open-circuit condition and the voltage is very high, favoring the production of an arc.

C. Polypectomy

A polyp is a pedunculated growth arising from the mucosa and extending into the lumen of an organ. A polyp can be removed with the aid of a cystoscope, colonoscope, sigmoidoscope, or proctoscope. The procedure often employs a wire snare to which electrosurgical current is applied. Figure 3.28a illustrates the snare around the stalk and Figure 3.28b shows the direction of current flow down the stalk which is coagulated, then cut by the current. Alternately, the coagulated stalk can be cut mechanically by tightening the snare. Some surgeons use blended current to coagulate and cut the stalk.

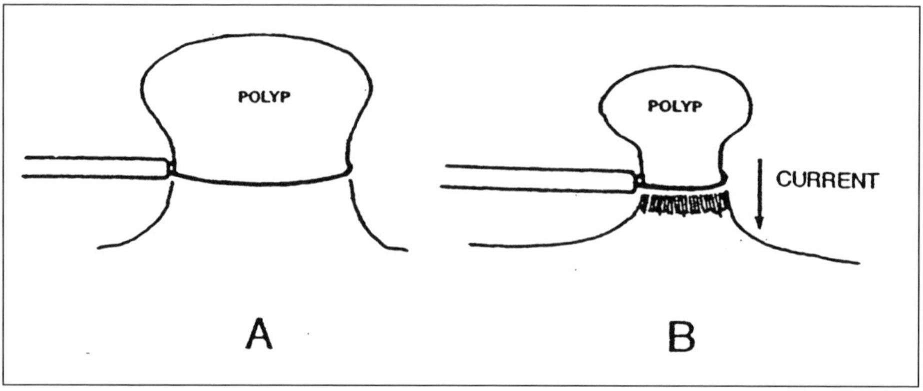

Figure 3.28 *(a) Snare around the stalk of a polyp and (b) electrosurgical current direction*

In Figure 3.28b, the electrosurgical current flows down the stalk to the cavity wall. This situation will occur only if the top of the polyp is not contacting any other conducting tissue. If the top of the polyp is in contact with tissue, current will flow up the stalk and a burn may occur at the top contact site.

D. Explosions in the gastrointestinal tract

It should be remembered that the gastrointestinal tract contains flammable gases: methane, hydrogen, and a small quantity of hydrogen sulfide; Table 3.4 shows the maximum and minimum values reported by Levy (1954). The average values should be noted in which there is 7.2 percent methane and 20.9 percent hydrogen with 3.9 percent oxygen. In his paper Levy discussed the proportions for combustion.

Table 3.4
Composition of Intestinal Gas

Intestinal Gas Found (%)	CO_2	O_2	CH_4	H_2	N_2
Highest	25.4	20.0	44.0	43.9	87.0
Lowest	00.0	00.0	00.0	00.0	24.7
Average	9.0	3.9	7.2	20.9	9.0
Volume of flatus average 1.48 ml/min					

Data from Levy EI. *Am. J. Surg.* 1954, 88: 754–758.

The composition of bowel gas is influenced by the amount of milk and legumes ingested (Table 3.5). On the average diet, the bowel content for hydrogen is about 21 percent and for methane it is about 7 percent.

Table 3.5
Bowel Gas Composition

Diet	H_2 (%)	Methane (%)
Average	21	7
Milk	44	
Legume		44

On a milk diet, gut hydrogen increases to about 44 percent, and on a legume diet, methane also increases to about 44 percent. It should be recognized that the bowel contains oxygen from swallowed air. Therefore, an explosive mixture can be present. Ignition of these gases is easily accomplished by a spark from an active electrosurgical electrode. The ensuing explosion can produce a disastrous accident; the following are a few examples from the published literature which reveals a preexisting knowledge of the hazard.

Arnous (1945) described an anoscope with which flowing carbon dioxide (2L/min) could be used during electrosurgery to avoid the hazard of bowel-gas explosion. Becker (1953) also advocated purging the bowel with carbon dioxide to prevent bowel-gas explosion. Woodward (1961) advocated passing carbon dioxide down the suction lumen of the endoscope. Hussey and Pois (1970) recommended "the use of a cold knife technique to open the bowel" before using electrosurgery. Apparently, these recommendations went unheeded because many bowel-gas explosions appeared in the subsequent literature.

Carter (1952) scheduled a patient for polypectomy and reported:

> The patient was prepared with cleansing tap water enemas for sigmoidoscopic biopsy and electrodesiccation of the polyps. Without anesthesia the highest polyp was biopsied and its base destroyed by a desiccating current using a Birtcher Hyfrecator. The accumulated smoke was removed by suction and the sigmoidoscope was readjusted to bring the lower polyp into view. It was also biopsied and after the resulting blood in the bowel was evacuated with suction and the desiccating current was applied to the base. An accumulation of smoke was removed from the bowel and the sigmoidoscope readjusted. It was noted that a small portion of the base of the polyp remained and

> the desiccating current was again applied to that area. When the current was turned on this last time, there was a sudden violent explosion within the bowel causing a blue flame to shoot out the end of the sigmoidoscope for a distance of one or two feet. A loud muffled sound that was audible into the adjoining room accompanied the explosion. The patient immediately screamed and started to climb off the examining table.

The patient was taken to the operating room for laparotomy. Carter continued:

> There were numerous areas in the sigmoid colon which showed separation of the serosal coats of the bowel but with the mucous membrane intact. These areas were closed with interrupted sutures of No. 7-0 cotton. As the bowel was further examined it was found that the proximal one-half of the descending colon near the splenic flexure had been lacerated in many places and was actively bleeding. The lacerations measured up to 10 cm in length and involved all coats of the bowel. It was necessary to resect the distal end of the transverse colon, the splenic flexure and the proximal one-half of the descending colon in order to remove the lacerated portions of the bowel and to control bleeding. The ends of the colon were exteriorized at the superior and the inferior portions of the abdominal incision and two Penrose drains were placed in the peritoneal cavity.
>
> During his convalescent period he continued to complain of burning epigastric discomfort which had been present before the operation and on two or three occasions mild symptoms of partial intestinal obstruction developed which subsided with conservative management. Approximately three months following the accident the abdomen was reopened and after freeing numerous intestinal adhesions the two ends of the colon were anastomosed. Following the operation the patient's course was uneventful and he began to have normal bowel movements through his rectum on the fourth postoperative day.

The term "detonation" was used by Zimmerman (1959) to describe a bowel-gas explosion in a seventy-nine-year-old, eighty-two-pound lady admitted for occasional bleeding at the stool. Zimmerman stated:

> A proctoscopic examination showed moderate sized internal hemorrhoids and a sessile adenoma 0.5 cm in diameter on the anterior wall of the rectum at the four-inch level. The patient complained so much during the examination that no treatment was attempted and no biopsy taken.

> Five days later she consented to have the polyp removed. A plain water enema was given the night before, and repeated at 11 a.m. on the morning of the anticipated removal. There is no definite record of what she ate during the twenty-four hours previous to this incident, but she had little appetite and had only picked at her food since her admission to the hospital.
>
> At 2:30 p.m. she was placed in the invert position and a seven-eighths-by-eight-inch sigmoidoscope inserted into her bowel. The adenoma was located without difficulty. A ten-inch electropoint, connected to the single pole of a Hyfrecator which was adjusted to its highest setting, was touched to the lesion. As the current was turned on by the foot-switch, there was a muffled but loud explosion. This noise was loud enough to be heard in the hall outside the room even though the door was closed.
>
> The sigmoidoscope and electropoint were withdrawn reflexively at the time of the explosion, and the patient jumped up and screamed, "You tore me apart!" After a minute or two she was persuaded to lie back on the table, and the sigmoidoscope was reinserted. The rectum seemed a little pale, but otherwise showed no sign of damage. The mucous membrane of the sigmoid colon was torn in irregular ragged lines as might be expected from overstretching, and was bleeding. No perforations were seen. No pictures were taken at this time as a camera was not available. Examination of the abdomen showed it to be tense and tender. There was no discernible distention, and an occasional peristaltic gurgle could be heard. The pulse rate was 100. She was given 50 mg of meperidine (Demerol) intramuscularly. The blood was typed and cross-matched. She was sent for a plain x-ray film of the abdomen; this showed no free air in the abdominal cavity.

Careful medical management was applied and Zimmerman stated:

> One week after the incident, another proctosigmoidoscopy was performed. The rectum appeared normal, while the sigmoid still contained some small white irregular areas of healing. The membrane between these patches was normal. Since discharge from the hospital, the patient has had no abdominal complaints. Her bowels are moving regularly without cathartics, but she refuses to come to the office for any further examination or treatment.

Zimmerman was aware that methane and hydrogen could be in the intestinal tract and that both were explosive. To eliminate the hazard, he recommended: "(1) to place the end of the instrument tightly against the mucous membrane surrounding the polyp, thereby isolating it; and (2) to force carbon dioxide across the area being treated."

A colostomy explosion was described by Bellemore (1962) in a patient who had a colonic lavage for three days prior to surgery and who was on a low-residue diet. After removing a tumor, a loop of transverse colon was brought to the abdominal wall to fashion a colostomy. Bellemore wrote:

> After the paramedian incision was sealed, it was decided to open the colostomy with the (surgical) diathermy. A violent explosion occurred, a blast of air shot past my face and I thought that the patient had succumbed. However, the patient's condition was unchanged, but where the colon had been incised there was an irregular opening the size of a two-shilling piece. After some deliberation it was decided not to reopen the abdomen although it was realized that the caecum probably had borne the brunt of the explosion. I regretted this decision later and in retrospect it was an error of judgment.
>
> Her condition remained unchanged for some four to six hours and then it was apparent that the blast had produced serious damage. There was profuse sero-sanguinous discharge from the drainage tube and the patient's systolic blood pressure fluctuated between 70 and 90 mm of mercury. Blood and later several bottles of serum albumen were administered as the profuse serous drainage continued. Within forty-right hours fluid feces were draining through the tube and gradually the patient's general condition improved.

It is obvious that there were explosive gases in the colon and that entry into it to open the colostomy using an active electrosurgical electrode provided the igniting spark.

An explosion associated with cauterization of a large polyp in the rectum was reported by Ross (1961), who wrote:

> The first, second, and third cauterizations were administered without incident. However, during the fourth session, with the patient in the genupectoral position and the proctoscope inserted about 5 cm, cauterization was begun. After about three minutes there was an explosion within the bowel. The impact of the explosion was so violent that the proctoscope and the cautery were blown out of the rectum, landing a considerable distance from the operating table.
>
> Two linear perforations were discovered on the border of the sigmoid flexure opposite the mesenteric attachment. Each perforation was 2 cm long, loops of small intestine were dilated and a small quantity of dark fluid had accumulated in the cul-de-sac of Douglas. The splits in the intestine were closed in two layers and a provisional colostomy was established. The postoperative period was uneventful.

In the foregoing case, the intestinal tract was not purged of gases, probably because the polyp was so near the anus. It is likely that the explosion resulted from propulsion of intestinal gas by peristalsis during the surgical procedure.

Another explosion was reported by Bigard et al. (1979). The patient was admitted for the removal of a cecal polyp. The patient preparation included a two-day, nonresidue diet and an intestinal lavage (5 l of isotonic solution) the evening before the operation. They reported:

> After locating the polyp, it was snared with an Olympus diathermy snare connected to the Olympus PSD electrosurgical source. No inert gas was insufflated. A coagulating current was used, the control being on setting 4. After 8–10 sec of current passage, there was an explosion which was audible in the endoscopy room, the patient jerked upwards off the endoscopy table, and the colonoscope was completely ejected. The diathermy snare contained only a small portion of the polyp.
>
> The patient immediately showed clinical signs of shock and complained of generalized abdominal pain. Examination showed evidence of massive pneumoperitoneum with a distended abdomen and loss of hepatic dullness to percussion. Needle puncture of the abdomen released a large quantity of gas and slightly reduced the abdominal pain. The patient was immediately transferred to the operating theater, and laparotomy was carried out 15 min after explosion. Immediately on opening the abdomen a hemoperitoneum was visible. There was no fecal matter in the abdomen. Examination of the colon showed numerous full-thickness lacerations in the right colon and the transverse colon as far as the splenic flexure. There were multiple bleeding points around these perforations. In addition the spleen was found to have numerous capsular lacerations. An extended right hemicolectomy was carried out to include the right colon, the transverse colon, and the splenic flexure. Massive blood transfusion was continued during the whole procedure; the patient received 45 units of blood. Multiple bleeding points occurred in all areas of dissection (right flank, left hypochondrium, and the pancreatic region), and it proved impossible to achieve hemostasis. There was presumably a serious coagulation defect as a result of the multiple transfusions, and the surgeon closed the abdomen after packing the abdomen. Death occurred a few minutes later.

Barkman (1965) reported another bowel-gas explosion in a patient who was admitted for resection of a carcinoma of the rectosigmoid colon. He wrote:

The caecum was then opened, using the cutting [surgical] diathermy. Some sparking took place at the point of the diathermy needle on cutting through the caecal wall, and immediately the point entered the lumen of the bowel a loud explosion took place with a forcible upward rush of gas and a small amount of feces. The noise of the explosion was considerable, but no flash or burning was noted by any of the attendants at the operation. A few seconds later, however, a small puff of white smoke was noted coming from the drainage tube in the left iliac fossa.

The report was followed by an immediate fall in the patient's blood-pressure to 110/60 mm Hg from 140/100 mm Hg, which was the level during the operation, and the pulse rate dropped to 65, with poor volume. The operating table was tipped into the Trendelenburg position, and within 15 minutes the blood-pressure settled back at the level it had maintained during the operation. The pulse rate became steady at 70, with good volume. No signs of burning were noted at the site of the explosion or the surrounding skin. No inflammatory gases were in use by the anesthetist at the time of the explosion, nor, indeed, had any been used at any time throughout the operation.

The patient's abdomen was carefully examined after the explosion by several people and nothing untoward could be detected clinically, but the problem of deciding, at that time, whether there had been any visceral damage was a difficult one. As her general condition had recovered so well in a short time it was decided that no good purpose would be served by immediate re-exploration of the abdomen. The cecostomy was therefore sutured to the skin and a catheter inserted into the bowel lumen through the cecostomy.

After a further period of observation in the theatre with maintenance of her satisfactory general condition, she was returned to the ward and kept under close observation.

Her general condition started to deteriorate in the late afternoon of the day of operation, as evidenced by a progressive fall in blood pressure and rise in pulse rate, and it became increasingly difficult to maintain her blood pressure by various resuscitative measures.

In spite of vigorous resuscitative measures it was found impossible to maintain her blood pressure, and she died some thirty hours after operation.

Commenting on the postmortem findings, Barkman wrote:

The caecum and ascending colon were comparatively normal in appearance, which is interesting, as the explosion initiated in the caecum. Several large perforations were present in the colon, particularly in the hepatic and splenic flexures. There was evidence of early abscess formation in the region of the hepatic flexure. The small bowel and the other viscera appeared to be unaffected by the blast.

A stomach explosion was reported by Carroll (1964):

There was a hard mass 2 in. (5 cm) in diameter obstructing the duodenum. It was decided to open the stomach and empty it and then perform a gastrojejunostomy. Diathermy was used and an opening made in the stomach wall; as soon as the mucosa was incised a loud explosion occurred which was heard outside the operating theatre. The escaping gases had ignited and were burning with an intense blue flame, but with no odor. An attempt was made to extinguish the flame with swabs, but after about 10 seconds it had ceased. At the same time the anaesthetist, thinking that the explosion might have been due to anaesthetic gases, quickly wheeled his trolley out of the theatre. In retrospect, the explosion could not have been caused by the gases he was using (oxygen, nitrous oxide, and halothane, with intermittent suxamethonium chloride). The stomach was then emptied and a gastrojejunostomy performed. The patient made an uneventful recovery.

E. Laparoscopic sterilization

Since the early 1970s, the laparoscope has been used in conjunction with electrosurgery for sterilization by coagulating the Fallopian tubes. Typically, a monopolar grasping forceps is used to which electrosurgical current is applied. Sometimes the more preferable and safer bipolar forceps is employed.

With the monopolar technique (Figure 3.29), the grasping forceps fitted with a biopsy sleeve is used. A Fallopian tube is grasped and fulguration current is applied to the forceps to coagulate the tube. When a sufficient length of tube is coagulated, the rotary biopsy sleeve is advanced to cut off the coagulated tissue. The biopsy sleeve may not be used by some operators.

Basically, two types of injury have been reported with the endoscope: (1) injury at the site of entry when a metal trocar is used and (2) perforation of the bowel due to sparking. The following cases illustrate these injuries.

Referring to Figure 3.29, note that the principal current path (solid arrow) is from the monopolar forceps, along the Fallopian tube to the uterus, and thence through the body to the dispersive electrode. However, there is an alternate current path (dashed arrow) along the Fallopian tube to the ovary and thence to the ileum. Sparking and small-bowel perforation have been reported. A potentially hazardous situation arises if multiple regions of the Fallopian tube are coagulated; the hazard depends on the order in which the coagulated

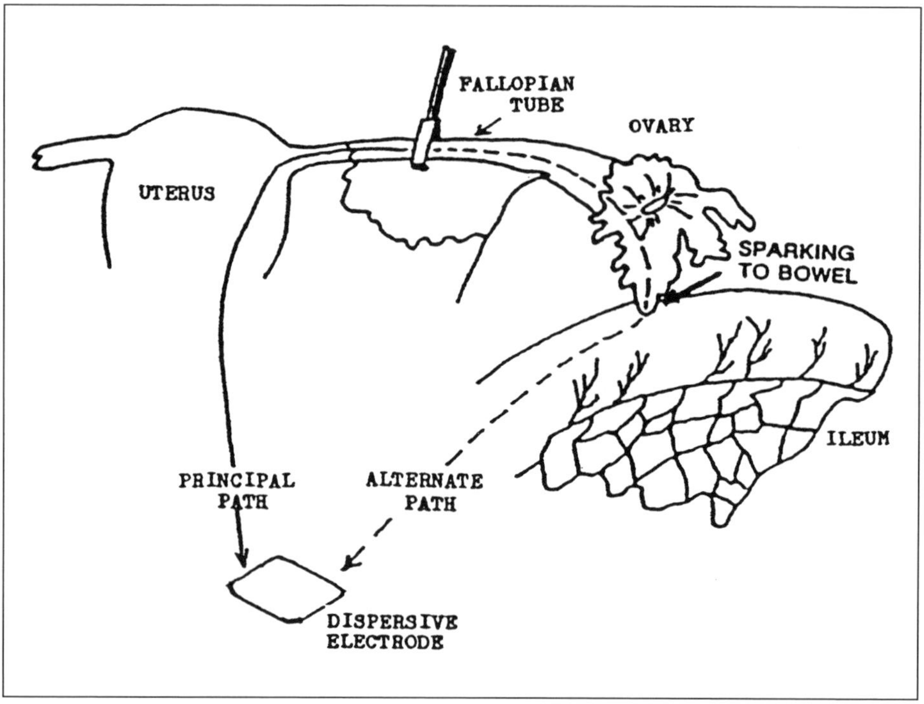

Figure 3.29 *Tubal sterilization with electrosurgical current applied to a grasping forceps*

regions are created. Coagulated tissue becomes a poor conductor of electric current; therefore, to minimize current flow to the ovary and sparking to the ileum, the first coagulation should be made closer to the ovary; the second and subsequent coagulations should be made advancing toward the uterus along the Fallopian tube. In this way after the first coagulation, the principal current path is along the tube toward the uterus.

F. Tubal coagulation accidents

A variety of unusual accidents have accompanied tubal coagulation. For example, Esposito (1973) reported an abdominal wall burn due to a metal trocar used in conjunction with a grasping forceps. He reported on a thirty-year-old female who was transferred from the emergency room because of pain in the lower abdomen:

> She had laparoscopy and tubal cautery on March 23, 1972. At the time of tubal cautery, an area of hyperemia, approximately 3 cm, had been noted around

> the lateral trocar sleeve. Her postoperative course was, however, unremarkable and she was discharged on March 24, 1972.
>
> She presented in the Emergency Room on March 27, 1972, complaining of pain in the lower abdomen of one-day duration. Temperature, 102.4°; blood pressure, 110/70; pulse, 104. Physical examination was unremarkable except for the abdominal findings: an area of necrosis approximately 4 cm with a silk stitch in the center was noted. This was surrounded by a zone of hyperemia of approximately 2 cm. This portion of the abdomen was markedly tender. The rest of the abdomen was tender but soft. Bowel sounds were hypoactive. She was allowed nothing by mouth and Ampicillin was administered intravenously.
>
> The patient was taken to the Operating Room on March 28, 1972, at 3:30 p.m. Exploration was performed through a midline incision and the intestines were found intact. The peritoneal surface under the burn was examined and did not appear to have been damaged. The abdomen was closed, the burnt skin and subcutaneous tissue were excised down to the fascia, and a culture was taken. The fascia was intact and did not show signs of thermal damage.
>
> Postoperatively, the antibiotic was changed to Keflin, by mouth, and her temperature returned to normal on March 30, 1972. The wound was healing well when the patient was discharged on April 2, 1972. She was followed in the Surgical Clinic until complete healing.
>
> In the case under discussion, we believe that the metal trocar sleeve must have come in contact with the conductive portion of the coagulating forceps. The trocar then conducted current from the tip of the forceps to the peritoneum, muscle fascia, subcutaneous tissue, and skin. The depth of the injury must have been directly proportional to the amount of current, the sensitivity of the tissues involved, and the time of exposure. [See Figure 3.25.]

To assist future users of laparoscopic electrosurgery for sterilization, Esposito made three recommendations: (1) use a nonconducting trocar, (2) use minimal electrosurgical current, and (3) if a conductive sleeve is used, it must not contact the grasping forceps.

Levinson et al. (1973) reported that a twenty-four-year-old female patient underwent bilateral tubal coagulation on October 5, 1971 without incident. She later reported that:

> On Oct. 8, 1971 the patient was readmitted to the hospital after a sudden onset of lower abdominal pain that became increasingly severe within thirty minutes. In the lower abdomen, there was marked guarding, marked tenderness

> on palpation and rebound tenderness. No definitive pelvic masses were determined, but there was marked paracervical tenderness.
>
> The patient was taken to surgery the evening of October 8, 1971, with a differential diagnosis of small-bowel perforation secondary to cautery vs. pelvic inflammatory disease. There was no evidence of acute inflammatory disease and the site of the tubal cauterization appeared to be normal for this stage of postoperative recovery. In the proximal ileum, an area of perforation with localized coagulation necrosis was identified. An area of approximately 2 cm surrounding the perforation appeared to represent burned tissue. Therefore, it was elected to resect a three- to four-inch segment of small intestine.

Levinson et al. (1973) reported a second case of a twenty-three-year-old female who underwent laparoscopic tubal coagulation on December 3, 1971, with the patient experiencing an uneventful recovery:

> She was readmitted to the hospital after she developed sudden lower abdominal pain. Diffuse abdominal tenderness with moderate distention of the lower abdomen was noted. The tenderness was most marked in the right lower quadrant. On pelvic examination, no abnormalities were noted. A culdocentesis revealed 10 ml straw-colored fluid. The patient was treated conservatively for several days. On December 13, 1971, exploratory laparotomy revealed perforation of the distal ileum with a localized area of necrosis. Approximately six inches of ileum was resected.

In discussing the cases, they stated that the ESU had not been inadvertently activated. They stated that "there was no evidence of direct coagulation, sparking probably occurred with a focal point of injury to the adjacent viscera."

Schwimmer (1974) reported three cases of small-bowel burn associated with laparoscopic tubal coagulation. One additional case provides evidence of a burn at the site of the trocar:

> When the instruments were removed, a burn was seen at the trocar site involving the skin, subcutaneous fat, fascia, muscle, and peritoneum. The central area was firm and white, and surrounded by a thin margin of pink tissue. A 3 × 5-cm ellipse of skin was excised together with all of the subcutaneous tissue and fascia that appeared nonviable, but the coagulated muscle was not removed. On the second postoperative day, the wound was slightly tender. By the fourth postoperative day it was no longer tender but there was a serosanguineous discharge. The patient had remained afebrile and was discharged to

be followed as an outpatient. One week later, the area became erythematous and mild fever developed, which promptly subsided in response to a ten-day course of ampicillin. Complete healing required six to seven weeks.

An unusual peritoneal explosion occurred during laparoscopic sterilization using electrosurgical current was reported by El Kady and Abd-El-Razek (1976):

Pneumoperitoneum was created using nitrous oxide gas introduced from a Boyle's anesthetic machine for ten minutes (from induction of pneumoperitoneum to completion of electrocoagulation of both tubes at two sites). A final check via the laparoscope showed no bleeding nor any apparent damage to adjacent internal organs.

Immediately before withdrawing the Palmer forceps and the laparoscope, a loud explosion was heard. The laparoscope was broken into two parts. The upper part, nearly one-third of its length, was separated and blown away from the patient. The lower part of the laparoscope, still in the trocar, remained in the peritoneal cavity. The Palmer biopsy forceps was blown out of the peritoneal cavity. The puncture site was a ragged opening 2–3 cm in diameter. An immediate laparotomy was performed. All abdominal viscera were intact. The abdominal blood vessels appeared uninjured, and there was no intraperitoneal bleeding. A large tear at the center of the diaphragm, wide enough to admit a closed fist, was noted. A thoracotomy revealed that the heart was ruptured. The patient had died immediately.

The foregoing event occurred early in the development of this technique. Note that nitrous oxide, which is a noninflammable gas at room temperature, was used to inflate the peritoneal cavity. There was considerable speculation about its role in the accident. It is useful to note that above 300°C, nitrous oxide becomes a strong oxidizing agent. Many possible reasons for the accident were postulated, perhaps an unrecognized bowel perforation occurred with leakage of explosive gases into the peritoneal cavity.

Small-bowel perforation was reported by Stewart et al. (1973) in a patient ten days after laparoscopic sterilization. They stated:

At laparotomy, two areas of ulceration were seen on the anti-mesenteric surface of the ileum, 15 and 30 cm proximal to the ileocecal junction, which measured 1.5 by 2.5 cm. One of these had perforated. The lesions were excised, and the ileal wall was reconstituted, the patient thereafter making an

> uneventful postoperative recovery. Histologic examination of the excised tissue showed full-thickness necrosis of both lesions.
>
> There being no evidence of other disease, the bowel wall injuries were considered to date from the time of sterilization. The cause of the damage however was not clear. Direct [surgical] diathermy burn due to contact of the diathermy forceps or forceps cannula against the bowel wall had not been suspected at operation. It was suggested that thermal injury to the bowel might have resulted from direct contact with the hot Fallopian tube closely following diathermy.

Several temperature-measurement experiments were carried out subsequently to determine if contact with the hot Fallopian tube could be implicated. Commenting on the experiments Stewart et al. stated:

> The evidence derived from the above observations establishes that, although the tubal temperature of the point of diathermy is high, cooling occurs rapidly. Furthermore, attempts to produce damage to both parietal peritoneum and appendix wall when these structures were held against the hot Fallopian tube resulted in only trivial lesions.

They concluded:

> It would appear, therefore, that the lesions described in the introductory case were unlikely to have been caused as a result of contact with the recently diathermized Fallopian tubes. [The issue of possible sparking to the bowel was not discussed.]

Peterson et al. (1981) reported another case of bowel injury associated with laparoscopic tubal sterilization:

> A healthy, forty-one-year-old woman, gravida 6, para 5, abortus 1, underwent laparoscopic tubal sterilization via electrocoagulation with a segment of each tube performed without apparent incident. The patient was discharged the day after operation.
>
> Twenty-three days later, she returned to the hospital with abdominal pain and evidence of peritonitis. She gave a history of having been constipated for several days prior to admission but of otherwise doing well until shortly before entering the hospital, when she had begun to vomit and experience severe abdominal pain. When seen in the emergency room, the patient was found to be in septic shock.

The following morning, she underwent laparotomy. Purulent material was noted throughout the peritoneal cavity. Although the upper gastrointestinal tract was normal, the small and large bowels were covered by a large fibrinous exudate. Multiple adhesions were present and a perforation was noted on the anterior wall of the midportion of the sigmoid colon. A colectomy and diverting colostomy were performed. Histologic review of the 5 cm colectomy specimen revealed that the perforation had occurred at the site of a thermal injury. The patient's condition deteriorated and she died forty-one days after laparotomy. Autopsy revealed a right-sided subdiaphragmatic abscess, peritonitis, and a small bowel perforation communicating with a subcutaneous abscess and fistula tract to the skin.

Peterson (1981) reported a second case as follows:

A healthy, twenty-two-year-old woman, gravida 4, para 4, underwent dilatation and curettage followed by laparoscopic coagulation tubal sterilization with a unipolar device. The curettage proceeded without incident and yielded a scant amount of normal-appearing tissue. Electrocoagulation with resection and division of each Fallopian tube was performed without apparent difficulty. The woman was discharged on the following day.

Seven days after the operation, the patient was hospitalized because of abdominal pain. She was febrile and had evidence of intestinal obstruction. Antibiotics were initiated, and an emergency laparotomy was performed. Findings included diffuse peritonitis. Although the surgeon believed preoperatively that bowel perforation had occurred, an attempt to identify the perforation site was unsuccessful. The effort was hampered because the bowel was covered with purulent material. No gastroduodenal perforation could be identified and the pelvis appeared entirely normal. Material from the abdominal cavity was cultured, the cavity was irrigated, and then the wound was closed.

After operation, the patient's condition deteriorated and she died two days later of septic shock. An autopsy was performed the following day. There were no new findings from those identified at surgery, i.e., no source of the peritonitis could be determined. Cultures of the abdominal cavity material grew Enteribacter cloacae, Citrobacter freundii, Escherichia coli, Klebsiella pneumoniae, Clostridium perfringens, and Bacteroides spp.

In commenting on these two cases, Peterson et al. concluded that thermal injury was sustained by the bowel in the first case and that perforation of the bowel occurred in the second case. This view was supported by the profuse purulent discharge covering the bowel and the growth of fecal flora in the cultures from the peritoneal cavity. They speculated on accidental contact of the bowel by the forceps and sparking. The foregoing injuries are not inconsistent with the alternate current path shown in Figure 3.29. Peterson et al. recommended the use of bipolar forceps.

The incidence of small-bowel perforations associated with laparoscopic tubal coagulation is small. For example, Thompson and Wheeless (1973) reported ten such incidents in 3,600 cases, providing an incidence of 0.28 percent. In a series of 7,466 cases, Maudsley and Quizilbash (1979) reported only four small-bowel perforations, providing an incidence of 0.05 percent. In these four patients, symptoms of abdominal pain and tenderness appeared between four and eleven days. In all cases the lesions were sutured with the aid of the laparoscope and all patients survived.

An unusual incident involving the use of bipolar forceps to effect coagulation of the Fallopian tubes was investigated by the author; the following is a description of the events.

On Friday November 3, 1995, Dr. X performed a laparoscopic electrosurgical sterilization procedure on Mrs. Y using bipolar forceps connected to an electrosurgical unit (ESU) having an isolated output circuit. By Monday November 6, 1995, it was discovered that there were complications and Mrs. Y underwent an emergency laparotomy performed by Dr. Z who found three small-bowel lesions; two of which had perforated and one was about to perforate.

Dr. Z stated in his deposition: "I have a note here saying the tubes appear to be sufficiently cauterized."

In his operation note of November 3, 1995, Dr. X stated that he cauterized the left and right Fallopian tubes three times.

Dr. A, a hired biomedical engineer expert, tested the bipolar forceps used by Dr. X and stated, "I have tested the continuity of the forceps and determined that one side was still intact and the other side was open circuited."

Dr. A believed that the bipolar forceps had been incorrectly connected to the monopolar outlet of the ESU. However, the circulating nurse, in her deposition, stated that the bipolar forceps was plugged into the bipolar outlet of the ESU. The nurse further stated that no grounding pad was applied to Mrs. Y and wrote in the operating room record NA (not applicable), which is correct when a bipolar forcep is used.

In her report on hospital policies and procedures, a hired consultant, stated: "Hospital did not establish policies and procedures to proactively maintain the

ESU and forceps. The Hospital did not establish policies and procedures to check equipment for proper functioning prior to a surgical procedure."

The foregoing clearly points to a defective bipolar forceps that was used by Dr. X, yet the tubes were "sufficiently cauterized" as Dr. Z testified. Therefore, it is necessary to explain the mechanism of injury in this case which involved the use of electrosurgical current.

Figure 3.30a illustrates the connections when a properly functioning bipolar forceps is used to effect coagulation of the Fallopian tubes. In this case, all of the electrosurgical current flows between the jaws of the forceps, thereby coagulating the embraced Fallopian tube.

Figure 3.30b illustrates the circuit when the connection to one of the jaws of a bipolar forceps is interrupted, as in this case. The return path for the electrosurgical current (dashed line) is from the intact jaw of the forceps, along the Fallopian tube to the ovary, then sparking(s) to the ileum, causing the perforation, then through the internal organs to the body surface which has a distributed capacitance (Cd) to ground. The circuit is completed by the distributed

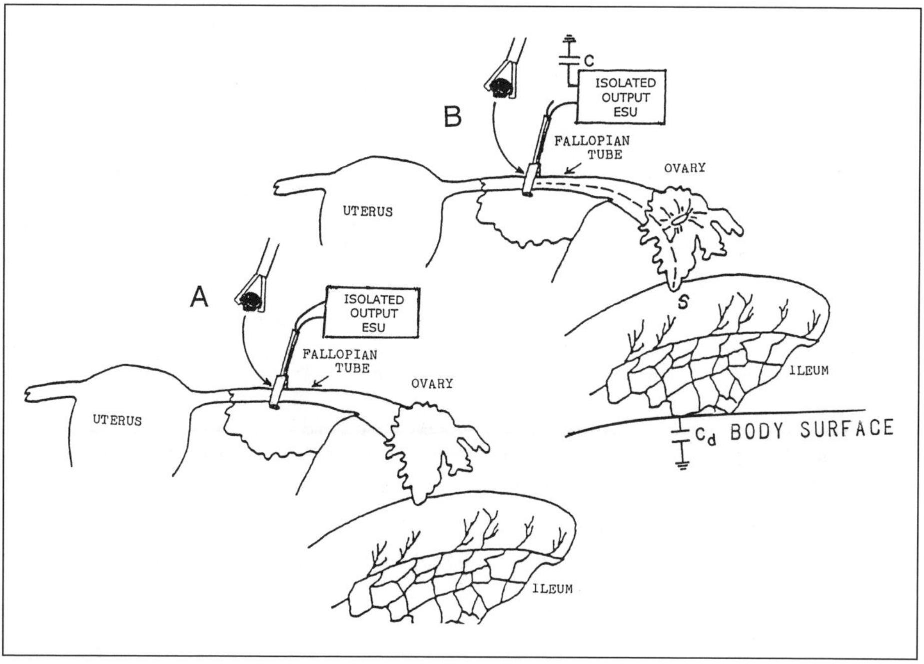

Figure 3.30 *In (a) is shown the use of a bipolar forceps electrode to coagulate a Fallopian tube. In (b) is shown the current path when the connection to one jaw of the forceps is interrupted; S = sparking to the ileum.*

capacitance (C) in the output of the ESU. It is clear that this circuit provided enough current to coagulate the Fallopian tubes, as testified by Dr. Z. Figure 3.12d further analyzes this situation.

The manufacturer's ESU manual deals with the distributed capacitance and identifies its effect in terms of leakage current by stating "The isolated bipolar output of the ESU has less than 150 milliamperes RMS leakage [current] to ground." This is more than enough current to cauterize a Fallopian tube, which requires 61–118 milliamperes (Geddes, *Medical Device Accidents*, first edition, Table 3.1, p. 99). Therefore, the defective bipolar forceps functioned as a monopolar forceps and at least six activations of the ESU were used by Dr. X to cauterize both tubes successfully.

The manufacturer's ESU manual includes an illustration that shows sparking to the small bowel as the ESU current seeks a return path (via ground) to the ESU when a monopolar electrode is used. Note again that no grounding pad was applied to Mrs. Y.

During Dr. Z's deposition, the issue of mechanical trauma from the trocar or Verres needle used to puncture the abdomen for entry of the surgical instruments was raised. His deposition discussed the three small-bowel injuries:

> Well, it could have been due to a trocar perforation. But that only answers two out of the three areas. That doesn't give my third dead area, if you will. I have the two that were perforated and the third one that looked as bad except it hadn't broken through, and that wouldn't occur with a trocar injury. And I have seen trocar injuries of my own and other people's, and it just, it just did not look like, if you will, a trocar injury.

Dr. Z's deposition continued:

> Question: All right. I'm going to come to the pathology report in a second, but before we get off this November 6th procedure I would like to ask just a few additional questions. You have already indicated to us, I think, that it was at least your impression based upon what you had seen during the November 6th procedure that this was an electrosurgical injury as opposed to some other type of injury; is that right?
>
> Answer: Yes.

Regarding the pathology report (addendum 11/7/99), Dr. B stated:

> I have reviewed multiple additional levels on the slides that were designated as coming from the perforation sites in the small bowel of the above patient. The findings are the same as previously. While no evidence of cautery artifact was present in the slides I examined, neither was histologic evidence of a perforation. The material reviewed may represent an area that was away from the actual perforation sites, either through the choice of tissue placed in the cassette at the time, or through the orientation of the tissue as it was processed. It is my opinion, within a reasonable degree of medical certainty, the lack of finding cautery artifact in these slides does not exclude injury in [this] case.

Earlier in his testimony, Dr. Z stated that "The two perforations appeared to be very similar to the area that was blackened and gangrenous, just that they had perforated and it hadn't." This response indicates that the three lesions were due to the same insult, namely electrosurgical current.

The foregoing account clearly indicates that the surgeon. Dr. X, who was given a bipolar forceps to effect tubular coagulation in the most efficient and safe way, had no knowledge, during the procedure, that the bipolar forceps was not functioning properly. Furthermore, he had the right to expect that any instrument furnished to him would be in proper working order. Indeed, if it were not for the small-bowel perforation, the defective bipolar forceps may not have been discovered and it may have been used previously and probably would be used in the future if this incident had not occurred because the Hospital had no checking protocol in place.

The incidence of major complications associated with gynecologic laparoscopic procedures in Finland in 1995–1999 was reported by Harkki-Siren et al. (1999). During this period, 32,205 gynecologic laparoscopic procedures were performed and a total of 130 major complications were encountered. They stated:

> The incidence of major complications was 0.6 per 1,000 diagnostic procedures, 0.5 per 1,000 sterilization procedures, and 12.6 per operative procedures. Of the complications that were associated with operative procedures, 28 percent were ureteral injuries, 19 percent were bladder injuries, 13 percent were intestinal injuries, 7 percent were incisional hernias, 2 percent were large-vessel injuries, and 11 percent were other injuries. 75 percent of the major complications in operative laparoscopy occurred during laparoscopic hysterectomies. Twenty-four bowel injuries, most commonly to the small intestine, were caused by electrocoagulation in thirteen cases, during Veres needle or trocar placement in ten cases, and by grasping forceps in one case.

> Four of twenty-four bowel injuries were recognized during the primary procedure. Eight incisional hernias were reported. Twenty-two bladder injuries and fifty-seven ureteral injuries occurred. Fifty-one ureteral injuries and all ten vesicovaginal fistulae that were reported occurred during laparoscopic hysterectomies. Electrocoagulation in forty-four cases, scissors in three cases, clips with electrocoagulation in three cases, and a stapler in one case caused the ureteral injuries. There were three iliac vessel injuries and one aortic injury; these injuries were caused by a trocar in two patients, electrocoagulation in one patient, and scissors in one patient. Hemorrhage from smaller vessels occurred in eight cases. Two patients developed abdominal abscesses, one patient developed deep venous thrombosis, and one patient receiving no anticoagulant experienced pulmonary embolism and died. The authors conclude that use of a laparoscope to perform hysterectomies is associated with a stable 1 percent risk of ureteral injury.

G. Circumcision accidents

Circumcision, the removal of all or part of the foreskin, is an ancient custom. Genesis 17:10 states, "Every male among you shall be circumcised." According to Gendron (1988), although circumcision is common in the U.S., it is uncommon in Great Britain and Australia. According to Gee and Ansell (1976), circumcision in the neonate is the second most frequently performed surgical procedure on the male in the U.S. They stated that controlling the small amount of bleeding presents no problem and the use of electrosurgery for this purpose is not recommended, especially when a metal clamp is used. Bloom et al. (1992) described circumcision as follows:

> The skin is incised by knife or scissor (never with electrocautery when a metallic clamp is adjacent to the glans) and the clamp is left in place a full 10 min. The clamp is removed and the result is assessed to assure complete disruption of the adhesions and adequacy of the circumcision.

The use of electrosurgery for circumcision raises the issue of current crowding (channeling) in which all of the return current must be carried by the small-diameter penis which becomes heated. The expected temperature rise is discussed earlier in this chapter and Figure 3.14b, c illustrates the situation. The following case reports clearly show the inadvisability of the use of electrosurgery in circumcision.

That a disastrous consequence can result when monopolar electrosurgery was used in association with circumcision in which a metal clamp was used was reported by Gee and Ansell (1976).

> Slough of the penis following Gomco circumcision in conjunction with the electrosurgical unit occurred at another hospital and is included because of the devastating result. A four-month-old was circumcised electively in the operating room under anesthesia; a Gomco device was used, and the surgeon employed the cutting current of an electrosurgical unit to excise the foreskin. Within five days, the glans and most of the shaft of the penis had sloughed. The patient was referred to this institution. Suprapubic cystostomy was done, and the patient underwent a number of staged procedures over two years to reconstruct the penis. These were unsuccessful, and the patient was surgically changed to a female.

An explanation for this tragic event is that the return path for all of the electrosurgical current was through the small-diameter, high-resistance penile shaft, resulting in current crowding (Figure 3.14c) and thermal injury to this organ. When a monopolar electrode is used conventionally, the current spreads radially from the tip of the active electrode and tissue heating is confined to the tip area (see Figure 3.14a).

Another circumcision accident was reported by Strimling (1996), who used a Mogen clamp which fits over the glans. The case report stated:

> This 3450-g term infant underwent circumcision with a Mogen clamp on his first day of life at his parent's request. His genital anatomy was notable only in that he had a relatively small penis, a scrotum that inserted about halfway up the penile shaft, and a considerable but not abnormal amount of redundancy of his foreskin.

The procedure was performed by a pediatrician who had extensive experience with this operation. The report continued:

> Following a dorsal penile nerve block, the Mogen clamp was applied in the usual manner. When the clamp was removed it was obvious that the distal 2 mm (or tip) of the penis, including the urethral opening, had been amputated. This was immediately retrieved along with the foreskin remnant and placed in a medicine cup containing 10 ml of saline, which was then placed on ice.

With assistance of a plastic surgeon, the severed tip was reattached using microsurgical techniques. Two years later, there was minimal cosmetic defect and normal urethral function. In discussing the case, Strimling stated:

> Although circumcision with a Mogen clamp has been reported as easy, quick, and safe and is being taught in a number of centers, it may be that some children, particularly those with smaller organs or those with redundant foreskin, should not be considered as candidates for the use of this device. Although this may be an isolated event, as there is a reluctance to report adverse occurrences, the true risks of this device are not known.

H. Spermatic cord coagulation

The author investigated an accident in which the spermatic cord of a neonate was coagulated. While performing the surgical repair of a hernia, the surgeon lifted a testis from the body and proceeded to trim tissue from the testis with a monopolar electrode. When he looked down, the spermatic cord was coagulated and brownish in color. In this case, all of the electrosurgical current was carried by the slender cord, being an excellent example of current crowding or channeling, as shown in Figure 3.14b.

Another accident investigated by the author is as follows:

> The patient, approximately five weeks old, had an operation performed for an undescended right testicle. The patient had bilateral inguinal hernias repaired. At the time of the procedure, the right testicle was lost due to injury to the testicular vessels and vas deferens. The procedure was performed as an outpatient and he went home that day.

During the surgery, the nurse, writing in the surgery report, stated that they used a (manufacturer) ESU with settings of 15 cut/15 coagulation, which worked properly at the beginning of the case. The output was increased to 20 cut/20 coagulation because of a decrease in effectiveness. Then it was increased to 30 cut/30 coagulation; the results remained unsatisfactory.

The operating-room report showed the following:

> There was necrosis of the right vas deferens and right testicular artery and vein for at least a 6-cm length beginning just at the testicle and ending all the way up at the inguinal ring with complete disintegration and necrosis, turning black of all of the tissue with no viable tissue left. This injury occurred shortly after an episode using the Bovie at which time the testicle was held in the left hand and the Bovie in the right and a small amount of tissue adjacent to the testicle on its end was Bovied with the testicle stretched straight out and well away from the skin and the patient. There was also a gauze moistened and wrapped completely around the vas deferens, artery and vein protecting this

> area. There were no signs of the Bovie touching anything besides the tissue on the edge at the testicle and it, at no point, touched any of the cord structures, the patient or any metal retractors or other objects; however, at the end of the Bovie episode, which was set on 15 and then increased to 20, the area was completely necrosed. This necessitated an orchiectomy as there was no way that there was any viable tissue to be repaired.

The Medical Device Report (MDR) sent by the hospital to the FDA three days later stated:

> A thirty-two-day-old baby underwent an inguinal hernia repair and during the procedure the right testicle was destroyed. The generator was originally set at 15 watts in coag and turned up to 20 watts and the power was still insufficient. The generator was turned up to 30 watts. The small vessels were tied off and ligation of the right testicle resulted in "blackened veins."

There was no malfunction of the (manufacturer) electrosurgical unit when it was checked. The fact that the nurse described the need to increase the output from 15 cut/15 coagulation to 30 cut/30 coagulation confirms that the return path for the electrosurgical current (the spermatic cord and vessels) was becoming a high-resistance path. It is clear that this incident is an example of current crowding shown in Figure 3.14b.

Mitchell and Lumb (1966) and Schellhammer (1966) commented on such accidents. Schellhammer stated, "Similar vessel damage may occur to penile vessels during circumcision or hypospadias repair. Only later may testicular atrophy or distal penile necrosis be recognized." The report continued:

> If a saline-soaked sponge is placed under the cord and testes or penis, wide area contact with the thigh will prevent current channeling. Low generator voltage settings are advisable as well. The fact that heat concentration depends on the tissue volume interposed between electrodes makes it mandatory to reduce generator power for use in children because of the reduced size and volume of their structures.

3.13 Summary and Conclusions about Electosurgery

Electrosurgery achieves its goal by the controlled delivery of thermal energy at a desired site. With a monopolar electrode, the desired site is at the tip of the active electrode and nowhere else in the electrosurgical circuit. With a bipolar electrode, the desired site is between the tips of the bipolar electrode. The amount of thermal energy, and hence the heating, depends on the current density (squared) and the duration of activation (energy density factor). The heating is therefore maximum at the small-area electrode. The foregoing are the basic facts of electrosurgery and should be recognized by all who use it.

Patients are burned when a dispersive electrode makes partial contact or when a dispersive electrode is not applied or applied and not plugged into the ESU and an alternate current path is formed by patient contact with a grounded object. Such burns are obvious immediately following electrosurgery. In contrast, pressure injuries, due to prolonged lying in the same position for an excess of more than three hours, are not readily apparent following surgery and take days to manifest themselves. Moreover, burns from a poorly applied electrode or one that has been dislodged are always smaller in size than the dispersive electrode.

Particularly lacking by most in this field is an appreciation for the nature of radio frequency (rf) current as it is used in electrosurgery. Such information can be found in the instruction manuals that accompany every ESU. Not only do these manuals discuss the various types of electrosurgical current, they also describe good electrosurgical technique and even illustrate hazardous situations. All who use electrosurgery should be required to prove that they have read the manual. There can be no doubt that the accident incidence can be decreased with better training and education. A starting point is to read the instruction manual.

It is useful to recognize that both old and new electrosurgical instruments are in daily use. The old spark-gap and vacuum-tube units have a long life and, for this reason, still see service. Therefore, when investigating an accident, the characteristics of the ESU must be determined.

Because of the nature of electrosurgical current, it is likely that it will continue to interfere with implanted electronic devices and environmental monitoring and therapeutic devices unless they are designed for immunity (hardened). Implanted devices, such as cardiac pacemakers and automatic defibrillators, can be adversely affected by the ESU, particularly if the electrosurgical current traverses electrodes connected to them. Care must be exercised in placing the dispersive electrode so that the return current path avoids such implants. Environmental monitoring devices can be improved to reduce their susceptibility to the ESU, or at least to recover quickly after cessation of electrosurgical current. It should be possible to render such external environmental devices as ventilators, drug-infusion pumps, etc. virtually immune from ESU current; however, such immunity has not been achieved yet.

Despite all of the hazards and accidents described in this chapter, their incidence is very small in comparison to the huge number of electrosurgeries performed annually. Perhaps the best method of reducing the number of accidents is via education programs for nurses and surgeons. All should be required to prove that they have read the instruction manual and should receive hazard training from the clinical engineer.

3.14 Electrocautery

An electrocautery is an electrically heated probe used to cauterize tissues for the purpose of cutting or arresting bleeding. Recently disposable, battery-operated, handheld electrocauteries have been introduced. However, cauterization appears in the Egyptian papyri and became an accepted practice in Arabic medicine. It was used to control bleeding in amputations in the 15th century and beyond, being replaced by electrosurgery at the dawn of the 20th century.

According to Axelrod et al. (1993), there are 1.5-volt and 3-volt electrocauteries available. The former provides a filament temperature of 680°C and the latter 1200°C. The former uses a single AA battery and the latter uses two AA batteries in the handheld probe. Although electrocauteries eliminate an electrical hazard, they do not eliminate a fire hazard.

A. Electrocautery accidents

Apparently, the first to report a fire due to a heated filament cautery was Lederman (1986). During ophthalmic surgery, Lederman encountered a flash fire while using a disposable electrocautery. The case involved a sixty-year-old woman who was scheduled for intracapsular cateract extraction. A nasal catheter with an oxygen flow rate of 5 liters per minute was placed in position at the nostrils. The patient was prepped using hexachlorophene and a local anesthestic was injected. After the eye was massaged, a sterile disposable sheet and plastic adhesive drape were used to cover the patient. The drape was incised, and an open wire lid speculum was inserted to retract the drape and lids. An operating microscope was used for visualization. A cellulose sponge and disposable cautery were used to obtain hemostatis. While using the cautery, the surgeon felt a "sting" and the assistant noticed a small flame on the drape against the upper lid. The flame, which appeared to originate at the site where the cautery touched the cellulose sponge, was extinguished with saline and by smothering the flame using the gloved fingers. The patient sustained mild first-degree burns which resolved without treatment. The postoperative course was uncomplicated and three months following surgery the visual acuity was correctable to 20/25.

Three cases of intraoperative flash fire caused by a disposable electrocautery were reported by Chestler et al. (1989). The first case occurred during excision of a 1-cm dermoid from the anterior superotemporal orbit in a three-year-old child. The cautery unit was being used within an upper lid crease incision when a flash occurred, causing a nearby (approximately 0.5 cm away) cotton-tipped applicator to burst into flames and burned off the lateral one-third of both upper and lower eye lashes. The child was intubated at the time, and although the endotracheal tube was uncuffed, the anesthesiologist believed there was not a significant leak of oxygen.

The second fire occurred during a bilateral levator repair in a sixty-six-year-old woman. During cauterization a flash occurred with immediate burning of the central two-thirds of the right upper and lower eyelashes. Nasal canulae were in place, providing oxygen at a rate of 3 L/min. The patient was draped below the chin, and therefore oxygen theoretically could have pooled at the operative site.

The third fire occurred during a full-thickness upper eyelid wedge resection for a large keratoacanthoma. A flash occurred as the heated cautery tip was being brought toward the operative site. Fortunately, the patient was not burned. In this case, oxygen was given at a rate of 1 L/min by mask to a tracheostomy, and was at least 20 cm from the surgical field, in addition to being under cloth drapes.

Accompanying the Chestler et al. paper was a note from the journal editor who wrote:

> There have been fire incidents associated with all kinds of cautery, i.e., hand-held disposable, bipolar, and Bovie types in the presence of oxygen of any concentration over that of ambient air. Turning oxygen on and off when using cautery means that cautery is still being used in the presence of oxygen because O_2 doesn't regain ambient air concentration that fast. An oxygen source 20 cm (8 in) away is still not far enough away from the cautery to be considered a safe distance.

Curtin (1989) reported three cases of fire associated with the use of a disposable electrocautery. He stated that on two separate occasions one of our general surgeons had a fire on the Mayo stand that was caused by the cautery button sticking in the depressed position and igniting the gauze 4 × 4's. On another day a large fire in the disposable linen room was put out by fire extinguisher safely, although the fire department was called. The reason for this fire was again the cautery button on the disposable ophthalmic cautery sticking in the depressed position and igniting the disposed linen in the storage area.

A solution to the button-sticking problem was offered by Curtin who stated: At the end of each operation when the ophthalmic cautery is used, the nurse in charge covers the end of the cautery with the appropriate lid and then disposes that cautery unit in a metal container that is basically used for sharp objects.

Axelrod et al. (1993) reported the following cases of fire associated with use of the hotwire cautery. To help explain the fires, they conducted flammability studies on typical materials found at a surgical site. The cases are as follows:

1. A healthy eleven-year-old, forty-kilogram boy was brought to the operating room for excision of two 3-mm lesions superomedial to the right orbit. Local anesthesia with intravenous sedation was used for the surgery. Oxygen at a flow rate of 3 L/m was administered *via* a nasal cannula. The surgical site was prepared with povidone-iodine and allowed to dry. The face was draped with a fire-resistant drape (manufacturer). After incremental intravenous administration of fentanyl (50 mcg), midazolam (1.5 mg), and droperidol (0.625 mg), the surgeon injected 1 percent lidocaine containing 1:200,000 epinephrine around the lesion and made the initial incision without incident. Shortly thereafter, the surgeon requested a battery-operated 3-volt, hot-wire cautery to control bleeding. His first use of the cautery caused an ignition of a dry gauze sponge held in his other hand near the glowing cautery filament. A brisk fire ensued, but the team rapidly extinguished the fire by smothering it with a dry towel. Nevertheless, the boy suffered mixed first and second-degree burns of a 12–15 cm^2 area of his nose, cheeks, upper lip and anterior nares. There was no respiratory or eye involvement. A thorough search revealed the charred sponge and no other burned material. The boy made an uneventful recovery and was discharged on the fourth postoperative day. For several months, a small area of his face remained unusually prone to sunburn.

2. A healthy six-year-old, twenty-five-kilogram boy presented for bilateral otoplasty. After being premedicated with 10 mg midazolam and 0.6 mg atropine given orally in 20 cc apple juice, he was brought to the operating room where anesthesia was induced with halothane and nitrous oxide in oxygen. The trachea was intubated without muscle relaxant using a 6.0 mm uncuffed

(manufacturer) tube, brought out over the center of the lower lip. A very slight leak occurred between the uncuffed tube and the trachea with positive pressure ventilation. Anesthesia was maintained with 1.0–1.5 percent halothane and 50 percent N_2O in oxygen. The right ear was prepared with providone-iodine and draped with a plastic drape (manufacturer). Approximately thirty minutes after making the initial incision, the surgeon asked for a 3-volt hot-wire cautery (manufacturer) for hemostasis. Initial use of the cautery led to a brisk flame originating in a dry gauze sponge held in the surgeon's hand and some melting of the plastic drape. Although promptly extinguished, the fire caused a 2.5 cm × 2.5 cm second-degree burn of the preauricular area. After the burn was treated with silver sulfadiazine cream (manufacturer), the surgery was completed on both ears without further use of cautery. The burn healed uneventfully.

3. A twenty-three-year-old, fifty-one-kilogram healthy woman came to the operating room for excision of two nevi from her right upper arm. Premedication consisted of intravenous midazolam (1.5 mg) and oral ibuprofen (800 mg). Intravenous sedation consisting of alfentanil (250 mcg), lidocaine (50 mg), and propofol (30 mg) was administered while the surgeon injected 0.25 percent bupivacaine around the nevi. Oxygen was administered via the nasal cannula at a rate of 3 L/min behind a full drape that separated the patient's face and neck from the operating field. After excision of the lesions, the surgeon used a 3-volt, hot-wire cautery (manufacturer) to achieve hemostasis. There followed a sudden ignition of a dry gauze sponge held in his other hand; but the fire was extinguished without injury to the patient. An observer noted an "arc between the hot wire and the nearby gauze."

4. A healthy forty-three-year-old, 68-kg man was brought to the operating room for bilateral upper and lower lid blepharoplasties. He was anesthetized with intravenous sedation and local anesthesia. Oxygen was administered at a rate of 3 L/min via the nasal cannula, but was discontinued before use of the cautery began. A wet gauze sponge was draped over the patient's nose. While a 3-volt, hand-held hot-wire cautery (manufacturer) was being used, there was a sudden yellow flash and both the upper and lower eyelashes of one of the patient's eyes were singed off.

The fires in these four cases occurred because the three ingredients needed were present (1) flammable material, (2) oxygen, and (3) a source of ignition, namely the hot-wire cautery. In cases 1, 3, and 4, the oxygen flow was 3 L/min which is much in excess of the consumption by an adult subject, which is about

0.3L/min. We don't know the oxygen flow in the second case, but there was a leak around the tracheal tube which contributed to an accumulation of oxygen in the environment.

The flammability studies performed by Axelrod et al (1993) tested several materials (plastic tubing, operating-room cap, paper tape, paper gown, cotton towel, plastic drape and sponges). Specimens 2.5 × 2.5 cm of each material were prepared. Two hot-wire cauteries (1.5 and 3 volts) were used. The procedure consisted of activating the hot-wire cautery, then touching the tip to the material. Five trials were preformed on each specimen in the absence of supplemental oxygen. With the 1.5-volt cautery, the materials either melted or charred. With the 3-volt (hotter) cautery, three charred and five flamed.

They concluded: "the present work shows that the combination of a 3-volt hot-wire cautery and cotton gauze, paper tape, cotton towels, or Weck-Cels are inherently dangerous without supplemental oxygen. In acknowledgment of this danger, the cautery manufacturer has inscribed the words, "Do not use in the presence of flammable materials," prominently on the plastic casing of the cauteries.

The authors continued:

> Despite the inherent danger of the combination of the danger described above, it is common to see a disposable cautery in a surgeon's one hand and a dry cotton gauze in the other. Contact of the gauze with the cautery tip is liable to produce a fire, the intensity of which would be increased by the presence of supplemental oxygen or nitrous oxide. Should a surgeon need to use the hot-wire cautery, we recommend that the gauze sponges be first soaked in saline and wrung out, so that they will not ignite in room air. In addition, to minimize any remaining danger of fire, we recommend that a supplemental air-oxygen mixture, the oxygen concentration of which is increased as little as possible above 21 percent, should be employed (as guided by oxygen saturation monitoring), and where possible that the oxygen flow should be turned off before each possible use of the cautery.

Another fire involving a hot-wire cautery was reported by Martin et al. (1999) who stated:

> A fifteen-year-old female was scheduled for a levator sling procedure for congenital ptosis of the eye. An oxygen mask was placed on the patient's face with 5 L·min-1 flow. The area was prepared with proviodine solution and allowed to dry completely and then infiltrated with lidocaine. A disposable, bat-

> tery-powered, electrocautery unit (manufacturer's name) was used to control bleeding in the incision above the eyebrow. This ignited the eyebrow hair resulting in a brisk flame which was immediately extinguished by hand. The patient sustained a 2 × 0.5 cm first-degree burn above the left eyebrow and singed eyebrow hairs. Subsequently, the oxygen was turned off and allowed to dissipate prior to use of the cautery and the procedure was completed without further event. The burn had healed within three days and the brow hairs returned within four weeks.

An explanation of this incident is simple because all three ingredients for a fire were present: (1) combustible material (hair), (2) ignition source (hot wire), and (3) oxygen. Note that this patient was a fifteen-year-old female who would consume about 200 mL of oxygen per minute. Observe that the oxygen flow was 5,000 mL/min, i.e. twenty-five times the patient's oxygen consumption, the excess being discharged to the environment of the face mask.

3.15 Laser Surgery

Lasers provide high-intensity radiation in the spectrum ranging from the ultraviolet to the far infrared. Their use has invaded virtually every specialty in medicine and biology. The term laser is an acronym for light amplification by stimulated emission of radiation. Laser radiation is monochromatic and coherent, i.e., the waves are all in phase across the beam. Laser radiation can be absorbed, refracted, reflected, polarized, converged, diverged and split. The monochromatic and coherent character of laser radiation makes it possible to focus the beam to a very small spot and hence the power density can be extremely high. These characteristics make it possible to create many novel and useful devices.

The laser principle was first proposed by Schawlow and Townes (1958), who suggested the use of a gas of alkali metal excited by strong ultraviolet light. The first practical laser was described by Maiman (1960), who used a synthetic ruby (aluminum oxide containing a small amount of chromium). The ruby rod was excited by a discharge lamp. Since then, numerous other types of lasers have been created and are widely used in industry; their use in medicine is increasing rapidly. By 1966, the CO_2 (infrared) laser became available and thereafter many other gas-based lasers appeared commercially. By 1981, approximately 15 percent of all surgical procedures employed lasers. With the advent of minimally invasive surgery and the availability of new optical fibers, the use of lasers has increased dramatically.

A. Laser system components

To convert the input electrical energy to laser radiation, the following four components are required:

1. an excitation medium (gas, liquid, solid, or semiconductor) to produce the desired radiation
2. a power supply with sufficient energy to create and sustain a population of excited atoms within the active medium
3. an optical feedback mechanism which returns laser energy to the active medium, increasing the likelihood of collisions with other atoms within the active medium. The feedback means consists of at least two reflecting surfaces that are parallel to each other and perpendicular to the optical axis to sustain standing optical waves
4. an output coupler to allow the energy to exit the laser as a collimated beam

The wavelength of radiation produced depends on the excitation medium and the nomenclature identifies this fact. Table 3.6 lists some of the more commonly used lasers and the wavelengths emitted.

Observation of Table 3.6 reveals that lasers are available for emission in the ultraviolet (<300 nm), visible (300–700 nm) and infrared (>700 nm) spectra. Choice of a particular laser depends on the tissue type and the result de-

Table 3.6
Laser Types and Emitted Wavelengths

Laser Type	Wavelength nm
Helium-neon (HeNe)	632.3
Ruby	694.3
Argon	476.5–514.5
Krypton ion	476.1–647
Neodymium (Nd)	1060
Neodymium and yttrium aluminum garnet (YAG)	1060
Carbon dioxide (CO_2)	10.600
Helium cadmium	235–441.6
Nitrogen	337
Excimer	157, 193, 248, 308, 351 depending on excitation medium
KTP (Nd:YAG)	1064 amd 532

sired.

It is important to recognize that for any type of radiation to have a tissue effect, it must be absorbed by the molecules and/or atoms of the tissue that is irradiated. In general, laser energy can produce two main responses in biological tissue (1) thermal and (2) photochemical. To produce thermal effects (cutting, coagulation and vaporization), long-wavelength infrared lasers are used. Photochemical effects (breaking chemical bonds) are produced by short-wavelength lasers with much less heat production. Sometimes the process is called cold ablation. However, high-intensity ultraviolet lasers can produce heat. Because the absorption of short-wavelength energy is high, the beam penetration is very small, which is an asset when it is desired to produce only superficial ablation of a tissue layer.

The intensity of the effect depends on (1) the tissue type, (2) wavelength of the radiation, (3) the intensity of the beam (watts/cm^2 or joules/pulse) and (4) the duration of exposure to the radiation.

B. Laser hazards

Because of the wide variety of lasers, they are grouped into classes according to their propensity to produce injury. The classes are as follows.

Class 1. Exempt lasers, or laser systems that cannot, under normal operating conditions, create a hazard

Class 2. Low-power visible-light lasers, or laser systems that, because of the normal human aversion response, do not usually present a hazard, but may present some potential for hazard if viewed directly for extended periods

Class 3a. Lasers or laser systems that normally would not create a hazard if viewed for only momentary periods with the unprotected eye. They may present a hazard if viewed with collecting objects.

Class 3b. Lasers or laser systems that can produce a hazard if viewed directly. This includes intrabeam viewing and specular reflections. Except for the higher-power Class 3 lasers, this class of laser will not produce a hazardous diffuse reflection.

Class 4. Lasers and laser systems that can produce a hazard not only from direct or specular reflections, but also from a diffuse reflection. In addition, such lasers may produce fire and skin hazards.

Because they produce substantial energy, medical lasers fall into class 4.

The American National Standards Institute (ANSI) published a standard (1986) relating to lasers (ANSI Z136.1). Briefly, this document contains a wealth of information ranging from definitions (engineering and medical), the most important of which is MPE, maximum permissible exposure to laser radiation. There are numerous tables that provide information on MPE for the eye and skin for the various wavelengths emitted by typical lasers. In addition the hazards (electrical shock and laser-irradiation) are identified, along with warning (labels) and the protective measures that should be taken by personnel in the laser environment. A tabulation of wavelengths emitted by the various laser types is included, along with a bibliography of references pertinent to the safe use of lasers. This standard is a very useful document for those investigating laser-associated accidents.

A laser beam can hit its intended target and perform its intended task. It can miss its target and cause injury to the patient or operating-room personnel. It can also ignite flammable materials. It can be reflected from surgical instruments and other objects and the reflected beam can strike the eyes of environmental personnel. Even if the beam strikes its intended target, tissue damage can occur if the energy in the beam is excessive; the damage can be behind the laser target. The term overlasing is used when excessive energy is used for a particular task.

The type of damage will depend on the tissue type, wavelength, intensity and duration of exposure. The most common injury is a burn, which is a hazard to the patient and operating team. Ocular damage, i.e. to the lens or retina are serious hazards and the eyes should be protected by wavelength-specific eyewear. Chronic exposure of the lens to some types of laser irradiation can cause opacification. Again the wavelength of the laser beam is very important in determining the tissue effect.

Laser burns, like electrosurgical burns, are painful and slow to heal, especially if the tissue is charred. Laser irradiation of charred (carbonized) tissue produces considerable heat and a deep injury. Carlson (1987) reported that lasering of charred tissue can produce a temperature of 4000°C and the site can emit ultraviolet radiation which is injurious to the eye.

C. Fire

Fire results from the combination of a flammable material, oxygen and a source of ignition. All three are present during laser surgery and the laser beam provides the ignition source. During surgery, oxygen is delivered via the anesthesia machine connected to a tracheal tube or face mask. Often oxygen is delivered by nasal prongs. Typically the oxygen flow rate is far in excess of the metabolic uptake, which is about 0.3L/min for an adult. The excess accumulates in the environment of the patient, thereby setting the stage for a fire ignited by the laser beam.

Among the flammable materials in the operating site are drapes, surgical clothing, 4×4 swabs and plastic (tracheal tube, nasal prongs and face mask) as well as the patient's hair and surgeon's gloves.

Although drapes may be treated with a flame retardant, they can still ignite in an oxygen-rich atmosphere. At present, laser-safe drapes are under development, but every precaution should be taken to prevent a laser beam from striking all cloth materials. Moistening the 4×4 swabs and towels used at the surgical site is a good preventative measure. The ready availability of saline or sterile water to quench a fire is highly desirable.

D. Laser accidents

As with any emerging technology, accidents occur with its use. The accidents can cause harm, injury or even death and can be due to device misuse or failure. According to an editorial in *Minimally Invasive Surgical Nursing* (1995) the number of laser-related reports received by the Food and Drug Administration (from January 1993 to September 1994) was about 400. This was about three times the number received over the past several years. The high number does not necessarily mean that more laser-related incidents have occurred in the operating room, although that is distinctly possible. Most likely, according to the FDA, the increase reflects a growing awareness among practitioners of the FDA's incident reporting requirements, (MDR and MAUDE reports), plus the advent of MEDWatch.

A previous issue of *Minimally Invasive Surgical Nursing* (1995) published the text of 100 FDA reports covering the period from 1/5/93 to 3/15/94. As stated previously, these reports included many device malfunctions, but relatively few serious patient injuries.

1. Airway fires

Airway fires due to a laser beam igniting a flammable material in the airway can be found in Chapter 4 (Anesthesia). Other airway fires due to electrosurgery can be found in this chapter.

2. Laser-induced circumcision accident

Circumcision accidents are not confined to electrosurgery; the following report of a lawsuit involved a laser-induced injury. The *Journal of Medical Malpractice* (1999) reported:

> A legal case is described in which it was alleged that the defendant improperly used a Nd:YAG laser during circumcision, causing damage to a thirteen-month-old child's penis. The plaintiff claimed that the defendant was not properly trained to use the laser and did not know the extent of damage possible with use of the device. The plaintiff further claimed that the hospital had direct corporate liability since hospital policies did not require the doctor to be trained on the laser used. He also claimed that the laser nurse was liable, because she was not aware that the laser tip needed to be conditioned before cutting. The hospital maintained that the doctor was fully responsible for the damage to the patient's penis. A $2.3 million verdict was returned for the plaintiff.

3. Bowel perforation

The *Medical Malpractice Journal* of October 1999 reported a case of bowel perforation following laser surgery for endometriosis that required additional surgery with the loss of one ovary:

> The plaintiff, age nineteen, underwent surgery in July 1994 to remove endometriosis. She underwent surgery two days later for bowel perforation. The plaintiff claimed that the endometriosis should have been vaporized rather than excised and that the laser used to excise the tissue caused heat damage to the bowel, which later perforated when bowel movements resumed after surgery. The defendant claimed that excising endometriosis was the standard of care and that the perforation was caused by an inflating needle and was a known risk of the procedure. The plaintiff claimed that the perforation caused scar tissue in her abdomen and she required surgery for removal of a large abdominal cyst four years later. An ovary and Fallopian tube were removed at this time. The plaintiff claimed that the ovary and Fallopian tube would not have needed removal if the scar tissue had not been present. The defendant maintained that removal of the cyst would have required removal of the ovary even without the scar tissue. The plaintiff alleged fertility problems as a result of the surgery, which the defendant disputed.

3.16 Laser Transmyocardial Revascularization

Transmyocardial revasularization is a technique in which tiny channels are made in the left ventricular wall with the goal of increasing blood flow to ischemic areas. Alas, the small holes remain patent for only a short period of time. However, by an unknown mechanism, some patients with angina obtain relief of their chest pain. Some believe the relief is due to destruction of pain fibers in the myocardium.

The CO_2 laser was first used to create the tiny channels by the procedure designated laser transmyocardial revascularization (LTMR). The laser beam is applied directly to the ventricular myocardium. Mirhoseni et al. (1982) reported that when the laser beam strikes the myocardium, it acts as a stimulus and evokes a contraction.

In a dog study with 100 msec laser pulses, ventricular fibrillation occurred during application of laser pulses. Allen et al. (1999), using an unsynchronized Ho:YAG laser with a power of 6–8 watts/pulse, reported an incidence of 7.1 percent ventricular arrhythmias and 4.7 percent atrial arrhythmias. To reduce the arrhythmias, the authors advocated making the channels slowly.

To circumvent the occurrence of arrhythmias Kadipasaoglu et al. (1999) synchronized the laser beam with the R wave of the ECG. They studied the arrhythmogenic side effects of the CO_2, Ho:YAG, and Xe:Cl lasers to make transmyocardial channels in pig ventricles. They used a continuous-wave, chopped CO_2 laser (20 J/pulse) synchronized with the R wave; unsynchronized Ho:YAG laser (2 J/pulse, 250 μs/pulse, 5 Hz) and an unsynchronized excimer Xe:Cl laser (35 mJ/pulse, 20 ns/pulse, 30 Hz). Each laser was used thirty times as the sole modality in four consecutive pigs to produce 120 channels. They found that the average number of pulses needed to create a channel was 1, 11 ± 4, and 37 ± 8 for the CO_2, Ho:YAG, and Xe:Cl lasers, respectively. All Ho:YAG and Xe:Cl laser-produced channels were associated with premature ventricular contractions. Ventricular tachycardia occurred in 70 percent with the Xe:Cl and 60 percent with the Ho:YAG lasers. Only 36 percent of the CO_2 channels were associated with premature ventricular contractions, and only 3 percent of the channels made with the CO_2 laser produced ventricular tachycardia ($p < 0.001$ versus Ho:YAG and Xe:Cl). In their conclusion, they stated that the way to minimize these reactions is to synchronize the laser energy with the R wave of the ECG. During the R wave the ventricles are refractory to all stimuli.

Although the foregoing study was designed to create tiny channels in the myocardium, it clearly demonstrates the ability of a laser beam to stimulate the ventricles. As stated in the chapter on catheter accidents, a single stimulus delivered during the ventricular vulnerable period can precipitate ventricular tachycardia and fibrillation. The vulnerable period is associated with the T wave of the ECG. Therefore, if a stimulus (electrical, thermal, mechanical etc) is delivered during this period, ventricular fibrillation can occur. Although the study just described did not report ventricular fibrillation, ventricular tachycardia was produced. However, the earlier study by Mirhoseini et al. encountered ventricular fibrillation during delivery of the laser pulses. The messages here are: (1) if a laser beam is used and is likely to strike the ventricles, there is the hazard of precipitating ventricular tachycardia and fibrillation, and (2) if these side effects are to be avoided, the laser beam should be delivered when the ventricles are inexcitable, namely during the QRS wave. It is for this reason that the CO_2 laser in the foregoing study ws synchronized with the QRS wave.

References

AAMI (Association for the Advancement of Medical Instrumentation). 3330 Washington Blvd., Arlington, VA 22201–4598. AAMI Order Code HF18–R–2/93. Proposed 2nd edition of the American National Standard for Electrosurgical Devices.

Allen KB, Dowling RD, Heimansohn DA et al. Transmyocardial revascularization utilizing a Ho: YAG laser. European Journ. Cardio-Thor. Surg. 1999, 14 (supp 1): S100–104.

American College of Surgeons. Conference on Electrosurgery. Surg. Gynecol. Obstet. 1931, 52: 502–520.

American National Standards Institute ANSI. Standard for the safe use of lasers, Z136.1, 1986. Laser Inst. Amer. Toledo OH 43623.

Arnous MJ. Anuscope permettant les electro-coagulations intra-rectales sous une atmosphere de gaz inerte. Arch. d. mal. de l'app. digestif. 1945, 34:277–279.

Australia. Thereapeutic Goods Administration, Aust. Ther. Devices Bull., 1998 May, No. 35-1/98:6.

Axelrod EH, Kusnetz, AB and Rozenberg MK. Operating room fires initiated by a hotwire cautery. Anesthesiology. 1993, 295(5):1123–1126.

Biley MK, Bromley HR, Allison JG et al. Electrocautery induced airway fire during tracheostomy. Anesth & Analg. 1990, 71:702–704.

Barkman MF. Intestinal explosion after opening a cecostomy with diathermy. Br. Med. J. 1965, June: 1594–1595.

Becker CM, Malhotra IV and Hedley-White J. The distribution of radio frequency current and burns. Anesthesiology. 1974, 38(2):106–122.

Becker GL. Prevention of gas explosions in the large bowel during electrosurgery. Surg. Gynecd. Obst. 1953, 97:463–467.

Bellemore C. Colostomy explosion. Austral. New Zealand J. Surg. 1962, 31:325–326.

Bigard MA, Gaucher P and Lassalle C. Fatal colonic explosion during colonoscopic polypectomy. Gastroenterology. 1979, 77:1307–1310.

Bloom DA, Wan J and Key D. Diseases of the male external genitalia and inguinal canal. In Clinical Pediatric Urology. Vol. 2, 3rd ed. 1992. W.B. Saunders, Philadelphia.

Bourland JD, Graber GP, Geddes LA, Foster KS and Schoenlein WE. Skin-temperature distribution under a new type of defibrillating electrode. Biomed. Instr. Technol. 1998, 32:164–168.

Burgess CE and LeJeune FE. Endotracheal tube ignition during laser surgery of the larynx, Arch. Otolaryngeal. 1979, 105:561–562.

Carlson BA. Complictions associated with laser surgery. Clin. Podiatric Med. Surg. 1987, 4(4):823–824.

Carroll KJ. Unusual explosion during electrosurgery. Br. Med. J. 1964, November: 78.

Carter HG. Explosion in the colon during electrodesiccation of polyps. Am. J. Surg. 1952, November: 514–517.

Caruso P, Pearce JA and DeWitt DP. Temperature and current density distributions at electrosurgical dispersive electrode sites. Proc. 7th N. Engl. Bioeng. Conf. 1979, 373–374.

CDRH: Center for Devices and Radiological Health. U.S. Food and Drug Administration, Manufacturer and User Facility Device Experience Database, 1998 Apr 23.

CDRH: Center for Devices and Radiological Health. U.S. Food and Drug Administration, Manufacturer and User Facility Device Experience Database, 1998 Apr 23.

Chestler RJ and Lemke BN. Intraoperative flash fires associated with disposable electrocautery. Ophthal. Plastic & Reconstru. Surg. 1989, 5(8):194–195.

Clark WL. Oscillatory desiccation in the treatment of accessible growths and minor surgical conditions. J. Adv. Ther. 1911, 29:169–183.

Curtin JH. The disposable cautery: a fire hazard. Plastic & Reconstr. Surg. 1989, 84:853.

Cushing H and Bovie WT. Electro-surgery as an aid to the removal of intracranial tumors. Surg. Gynec. Obst. 1928, 47:751–784.

DeRosa J and Gadsby PD. Radio frequency heating under ECG electrodes. Med. Instrum. 1979, 13:273–276.

Doyen E. Sur la destruction des tumeurs cancereuses accessible. Arch. Elect. Med. Physiol. 1909, 17:791–795.

Doyen E. Surgical Therapeutics and Operative Techniques. Vol. 1. 1917. William Wood, New York, 439–52.

ECRI Health Devices, 1990, Plymouth Meeting, PA.

ECRI. Laser Resistant Endotracheal Tube and Wraps. 1990 (April), 19(4):112–139.

ECRI Health Devices Alert. April 23, 1999 (23R4).

El Kady A A. and Abd-El-Razek M. Intraperitoneal explosion during female sterilization by laparoscopic electrocoagulation. Int. J. Gynecol. Obst. 1976, 14:487–488.

Ellis JD. The rate of healing of electrosurgical wounds. JAMA 1931, 96: (1):16–18.

Esposito JM. Electrical burn of the abdominal wall as a complication of Fallopian tube cautery. Fertility Sterility. 1973, 24(2):158–161.

Ferrari RK. X-ray transmissive transcutaneous stimulating electrode. U.S. Patent 5,571,165, Nov. 5, 1996.

Finlay B, Couchie D, Boyce L et al. Electrosurgery burns resulting from use of miniature ECG electrodes. Anesthesiology. 1974, 41(3):263–269.

Flachenecker G and Fastenmeier K. High frequency current effects during transurethral resection. J. Urol. 1979, 122:336–347.

Food and Drug Administration (DFA). Center for Devices and Radiological Health, Manufacturer and User Facility Device Experience Database, Rockville, MD: FDA, 1998 May 22.

Foster KS and Geddes LA. The cause of stimulation with electrosurgical current. Med. Instrum. 1986, 20(6):335–336.

Geddes LA. Medical Device Accidents, 1st ed. Boca Raton, FL, CRC Press 19.

Geddes LA, Silva LF, DeWitt DP and Pearce JA. What's new in electrosurgical instrumentation. Med. Instr. 1977, 11(6):355–359.

Geddes LA, Pearce JA, Bourland JD et al. The thermal properties of gelled and metal-foil electrosurgical dispersive electrodes. Proc. 14th AAMI Conf., 1979, 14:90.

Geddes LA, Pearce JA, Bourland JD and Silva LF. Thermal properties of dry metal-foil dispersive electrodes. Clin. Eng. 1980, 5:13–18.

Geddes LA and Baker LE. Principles of Applied Biomedical Instrumentation, 3rd ed. New York 1989, Wiley Interscience.

Geddes LA and Moore C. Stimulation with electrosurgical current. Physics Eng. Sci. Med. 1990, 13(2):63–66 (Australia).

Gee WF and Ansell JS. Neonatal circumcision. Pediatrics. 1976, 58(6):824–827.

Gendron FG. Unexplained Patient Burns. Brea Ca 1988. Quest Publishing Co.

Harkki-Siren P, Sjoberg J and Kurki T. Major complications of laparoscopy: a follow up study. Obstet. Gynecol. 1999 July, 94(1):94–8.

Hayes C. Making laparoscopy electrically safer. J. Reproductive Med. 1979, 23(2):92–93.

Health Devices: See ECRI.

Hirschberg CA and Smith J. Indirect ignition of the endotracheal tube during carbon dioxide laser surgery. Arch. Otolaryngol. 1980, 106:639–641.

Hodika JH and Clarke G. Use of neuromuscular blocking drugs to counteract thigh adductor spasm induced by electrical shocks of obturator nerve during transurethral resection of bladder tumors. J. Urol. 1961, 85(3):295–296.

Honig WM. The mechanism of cutting in electrosurgery. IEEE Trans. BME. 1975, January: 60–62.

Hussey GL and Pois AJ. Bowel-gas explosion. Am. J. Surg. 1970, 120:103–105.

Kadipsaoglu KA, Sartori M and Masai T. Intraoperative arrhythmias and tissue damage during transmyocardical laser revascularization, Ann Thor Surg. 1999, 67:423–431.

Kelly HA and Ward GE. Electrosurgery. 1932. W.B. Saunders, Philadelphia, 305.

Lederman IR. Fire hazard during ophthalmic surgery. Ophthal. Surg. 1986, 16:577–578.

Levinson CJ, Schwartz SF and Saltzstein ED. Complication of laparoscopic cauterization small bowel perforation. Obst. Gynecol. 1973, 41(2):253–256.

Levy EI. Explosions during lower bowel electrosurgery. Am. J. Surg. 1954, 88:754–758.

Maiman TH. Stimulated optical radiation in ruby, Nature. 1960, 187:493–494.

Martin L and Dolman P. Fire. Canadian Journ. Anesthiol. 1999, 46(9):909.

MAUDE: see CDRH, FDA.

Maudsley RF and Quizilbash AH. Thermal injury to the bowel as a complication of laparoscopic sterilization. Can. J. Surg. 1979, 22(3):232–234.

McGreevy FT and Bertrand C. Electrosurgical Conductive Gas Stream Technique of Achieving Improved Eschar for Coagulation. U.S. Patent 4,781,175, November 1, 1988.

Medical Malpractice Verdicts, Settlements and Experts. 1999, Feb: 15(2):48–9.

Medical Malpractice Verdicts, Settlements and Experts. 1999, 15(10):15.

Minimally Invasive Surgical Nursing. 1995, 9(1):9–22.

Minimally Invasive Surgical Nursing. 1996, 10(3):

Ministry of Employment and Solidarity, Direction des Hôpitaux, Bureau des Dispossitifs Medicaux (EM1), by fax at 01 40 56 50 89, (France).

Mirhoseini M, Muckerhelde M and Cayton MM. Transventricular revascularization by laser. Lasers in Surg. Med. 1982, 2:187–198.

Mitchell JP and Lumb GW. A Handbook of Surgical Diathermy. 1966. John Wright & Sons, Bristol, England.

Moritz AR and Henriques FC. The relative importance of time and surface temperature in the causation of skin burns. Am. J. Pathol. 1947, 23:605–720.

Norton ML and De Vos P. New endotracheal tube for laser surgery of the larynx. Ann Otolaryngol. 1978, 87:554–557.

Overmeyer K, Pearce JA and DeWitt DP. Measurements of temperature distribution at electrosurgical dispersive electrode sites. Trans. ASME. 1979, 101:66–72.

Parker EO. Esophageal burn at the site of an esophageal temperature probe. Anesthesiology. 1984, 61(1):93–95.

Pashayan AG and Gravenstein JS. Helium retards endotracheal tube fires from carbon dioxide lasers. Anesthesiology. 1985, 62:274–277.

Pearce JA. Electrosurgery. 1986. Chapman and Hall, London, 258.

Pearce JA, Geddes LA, Smith J et al. The performance of dry and gelled electro-surgical electrodes. Proc. 31st ACEMB, paper 25.2. 1978. Atlanta.

Pearce JA and Geddes LA. The characteristics of capacitive electrosurgical dispersive electrodes. Proc. 15th AAMI Conf., 1980, 15:162.

Pearce JA, Geddes LA, Bourland JD and Silva LF. The thermal behavior of electrolyte-coated metal-foil electrodes. Med. Instrum. 1979, 3(5):298–300.

Pearce JA, Geddes LA, VanVleet J et al. Skin burns from electrosurgical electrodes. Med. Instrum. 1983, 17: 225–231.

Peterson HB, Ory HW, Greenspan JR et al. Deaths associated with laparoscopic sterilization by unipolar electrocoagulation devices. Am. J. Obst. Gyn. 1981, January: 141–143.

Prentiss GWH, Bethard WF, Boatwright DE and Pennington RD. Massive adductor muscle contraction in transurethral surgery. J. Urol. 1965, 93: 263–271.

Rita L and Sellny F. Endotracheal tube ignition during laryngeal surgery with resectoscope. Anesthesiol. 1982, 56:60–64.

Ross JV. Explosion during electrocauterization of a rectal polyp. Dis. Colon Rectum. 1961, 6: 364–366.

Schellhammer PF. Electrosurgery. Urology. 1974, 3(3):261–268.

Schawlow AL and Townes CH. Infrared and optical masers. Phys. Rev. 1958, 112:1940–1949.

Schonfeld WA. Primary and secondary sexual characteristics. Amer. Dis. Childn. 1943, 65:535:549.

Schwimmer WB. Electrosurgical burn injuries during laparoscopy sterilization. Obst. Gynecol. 1974, 24(4):526.

Simpson JI and Wolf GL. Endotracheal tube fire ignited by pharyngeal electrocautery. Anesthesiol. 1986,m 65:76–77.

Snow JC, Kripke BJ, Strong MS et al. Anesthesia for carbon dioxide laser microsurgery on the larynx and trachea. Anesth & Analg. 1974, 53:507–512.

Snow JC, Norton ML, Saluja TA and Estanislao AF: Fire hazard during CO2 laser microsurgery on the larynx and trachea. Anesth. Analg. 1979, 55:146–147.

Stewart KS, Pearson JF, Docker MF et al. A possible hazard of laparoscopic sterilization. Am. J. Obst. Gynecol. 1973, 115(8):1154–1157.

Strimling BS. Partial amputation of glans penis during Mogen clamp circumcision. Pediatrics. 1996, 87(8) Part 1:906–907.

Thomas SD. Eye injury during transurethral surgery. J. Urol. 1975, 114:584–585.

Thompson BH and Wheeless CP. Gastrointestinal complications of laparoscopy sterilization. Obst. Gynecol. 1973, 41 669.

Tucker RD, Schmitt OH, Silvert CE and Silvis SE. Demodulated low frequency currents from electrosurgical procedures. Surg. Gynecol. Obst. 1984, 159:39–43.

United States Food and Drug Administration (FDA). Center for Devices and Radiological Health, Manufacturer and User Facility Device Experience Database (online), Rockville, MD, FDA, 1998 May 22.

Wald AS, Mazzia VDB and Spencer FC. Accidental burns. JAMA. 1971, 217(7):916–921.

Ward GE. An efficient method of hemostasis without suture. Med. J. Record. 1925, 121:470.

Wegrzynowicz E, Jensen NF, Pearson K et al. Airway fire during jet ventrilation for laser excision of vocal cord papilloma. Anesthesiology. 1992, 76:468–469.

Wolf GL, Simpson JI. Flammability of endotracheal tubes in oxygen and nitrous oxide enriched atmospheres. Anesthesiology. 1987, 67:236–239.

Woodward NW, Prevention of explosion while fulgurating polyps of the colon. Dis. Colon and Rectum. 1961, 4:32.

Zimmerman K. Detonation of intestinal gas by an electrosurgical unit. Southern Med. J. 1959, 52:605–608.

Chapter 4

Anesthesia

Synopsis

4.1 Introduction

At present in the U.S. there are about 20 million anesthetic procedures performed annually, and it is estimated that there are 5,000 cases of brain damage associated with them. Most anesthesiologists believe that appropriate instrumental aids could reduce this number by about 85 percent and would allow better management of all anesthetic procedures. In fact, use of the pulse oximeter, which measures oxygen saturation, has dramatically improved assessment of the adequacy of respiratory function. The number of anesthetic mishaps that result in neurological deficit is unknown. During anesthesia, the anesthesiologist is the custodian of the patient's life and vigilance is the essential ingredient. As one experienced anesthesiologist put it, managing the depth of anesthesia is like flying an airplane; the pilot responds to all the cues that permit a smooth flight, but an unexpected storm can occur, and the pilot must rely on instrumental aids and good judgment to ensure a safe flight and smooth landing.

4.2 Anesthesia Machine

The anesthesia machine provides a metered amount of the anesthetic gases and oxygen, removes the expired carbon dioxide and includes a low-resistance path to a collapsible reservoir to permit easy breathing of the gas mixture. Because most modern anesthetics are volatile liquids, a vaporizer is used to evaporate the liquid. The collapsible bag can be compressed manually to apply artificial respiration. Valves are included in the circuit to ensure unidirectional flow of the gas mixture. There are two types of anesthetic circuit (circle): (1) the vaporizer is in the circle and (2) the vaporizer is outside of the circle.

A. In-circuit vaporizer anesthesia machine

Figure 4.1 illustrates the anesthetic circuit in which the vaporizer (Vap) is in the breathing circuit. Oxygen and sometimes another gas, such as nitrous oxide (N_2O), are delivered, being metered by flowmeters. Note that part of the inspired gas passes over the liquid anesthetic, which evaporates, and part of the inspired gas bypasses the liquid. The ratio of these two components determines the concentration of the anesthetic in the breathing circuit. Inspiratory (I) and expiratory (EX) check valves guarantee unidirectional gas flow. The carbon-

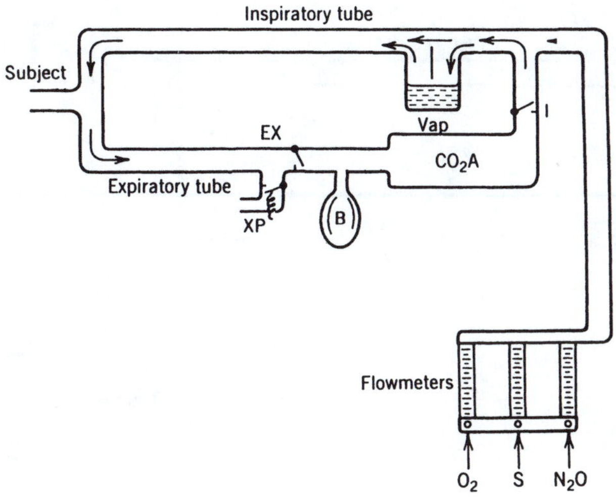

Figure 4.1 *Anesthesia machine in which the vaporizer (Vap) is outside of the breathing circuit. S: supplemental gas for special studies.*

dioxide absorber (CO_2A) removes the exhaled CO_2 from the breathing circuit. The absorber is soda lime with an indicator that changes color when the absorber is exhausted. XP is an excess-pressure valve.

B. Out-of-circuit vaporizer anesthesia machine

Figure 4.2 illustrates the out-of-circuit vaporizer anesthesia machine, which has the same components except that the vaporized anesthetic is delivered into the breathing circuit by first passing oxygen (and sometimes N_2O) through the vaporizer (Vap). Again, the concentration of the anesthetic gas in the breathing circuit is determined by the proportion of gas that passes over the anesthetic liquid.

The breathing bag (B) serves several important functions. Because the system is closed, the flow of oxygen and other gases into the system must equal the amount absorbed by the subject plus the amount due to any leak. The inflow of gases is constant and occurs slowly. Inspiration requires a relatively large volume of gas in a short time. With excessive gas inflow, the pressure in the circuit will rise and the excess pressure valve (XP) will automatically open to reduce the pressure. For an adult, the uptake of oxygen is about 300 ml/min, and the inflow above that accommodates any leakage from the circuit.

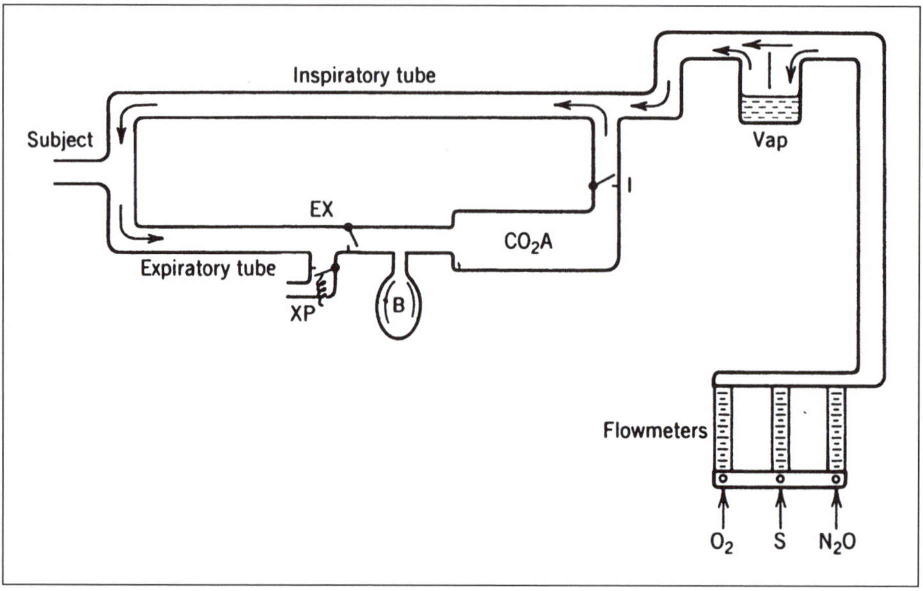

Figure 4.2 *Anesthesia machine in which the vaporizer (Vap) is outside of the breathing circuit*

The breathing bag also acts as an indicator of spontaneous respiration, decreasing in size during inspiration. Even more important, it affords a means for assisting respiration. Squeezing the bag forces gas into the lungs; releasing the bag allows the elastic recoil of the lungs and rib cage to effect expiration. The resistance offered to lung inflation informs the anesthetist about the airway compliance.

4.3 Endotracheal Tube

An endotracheal tube is placed in the trachea via the mouth to maintain an open airway. The tube may be cuffed or uncuffed; the inflatable cuff at the tip provides a leakproof seal; Figure 4.3 illustrates a typical example. Such tubes are used with anesthesia machines and ventilators. Since the 1960s, sterilized, packaged, plastic disposable endotracheal tubes have been used. Prior to then, red rubber tubes were popular. There is an American Society for Testing Materials Standard (ASTM F1242–89) for endotracheal tubes.

Most modern disposable endotracheal tubes are of polyvinyl chloride (PVC); some are of silastic, which can be sterilized and reused. There are special endotracheal tubes for use with the laser, which produces a thermal pulse to cauterize tissue.

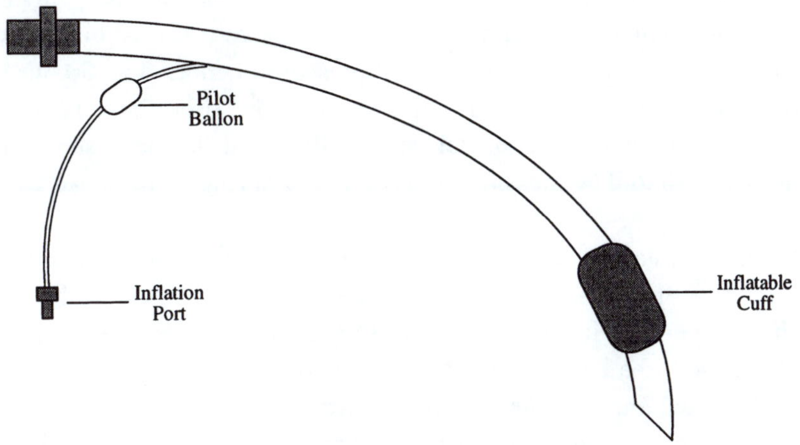

Figure 4.3 *A typical disposable cuffed endotracheal tube with a pilot balloon to identify cuff inflation. The radius of curvature is 14 cm.*

There are two scales for endotracheal tubes, the French (F) and the internal diameter in millimeters. The F scale identifies the outer diameter in millimeters and is this dimension multiplied by three; i.e., a 10-mm-diameter endotracheal tube would be designated 30F.

As stated previously, the cuff at the tip of the endotracheal tube is inflated to provide a seal. Inflation with air (or sometimes saline) is via a port at the end of a tube in the wall of the endotracheal tube. A pilot balloon at the external (mouth) end of the tube allows identification that the cuff is inflated. The inflation pressure is important. A pressure of 25 to 35 cm H_2O is typical.

As innocent looking as it may be, the cuffed endotracheal tube is associated with many different hazards and accidents. For example it can be passed into the esophagus and not only be ineffective in providing a patent airway, but can actually obstruct the airway. When properly placed in the trachea, pressing on the chest will expel air from the tracheal tube. Conversely, blowing air into the tracheal tube will cause the chest to rise, which confirms proper placement.

It is to be noted that the endotracheal tube can be pushed too far into the trachea and enter one of the bronchi, thereby obstructing airflow into one lung while permitting flow into the other. Usually this condition can be recognized by listening to the breath sounds on both sides of the chest with a stethoscope.

When in the trachea, the cuff is inflated to provide a seal so that positive-pressure ventilation can be applied to inflate the lungs. The pilot balloon identifies inflation of the cuff and manual squeezing of the pilot balloon provides evidence of adequate inflation. However, excessive pressure in the cuff will compress the surrounding capillaries; a pressure of more than 30mm Hg (41 cm H_2O) will collapse them and shut off blood flow. If prolonged excess pressure is maintained, environmental tissue will die. It has been suggested that cuff pressure should be measured intermittently during a prolonged anesthetic procedure.

Obviously, an inflated cuff can only be tolerated by an anesthetized subject. If the subject starts to regain consciousness, he or she will attempt to cough it out because it is perceived as a foreign body in the airway, which it is. This happened to a friend of mine who pulled out the endotracheal tube with the cuff inflated and damaged his vocal cords.

Fire and explosion are other hazards associated with endotracheal tubes which are usually made of PVC, silicone or rubber. The conditions for a fire and explosion are (1) a flammable material (in this case the endotracheal tube), (2) oxygen, which is always present during anesthesia in the tube in concentrations of 80–95 percent, and (3) a source of ignition, for example, a spark from the use of electrosurgery or the thermal energy in a laser pulse. These hazards are discussed elsewhere in this chapter.

4.4 Auxiliary Equipment

Associated with an anesthesia procedure are a variety of supporting devices, such as a ventilator and humidifier (which may or may not be a part of the anesthesia machine), a warming blanket, a warming cabinet to heat intravenous fluid containers, and ECG and a defibrillator for terminating cardiac arrhythmias. A typical ventilator consists of a flexible cylindrical bellows in a transparent chamber to which intermittent gas pressure is applied. There are hazards associated with use of these devices and the hazards will be described later.

4.5 Monitoring Equipment

During anesthesia, both the anesthesia machine and the patient are monitored. Although the monitoring devices mounted on the anesthesia machine may sound an out-of-range alarm, those that are connected to the patient may or may not. Before describing the various monitoring systems, it is appropriate to recognize a recommendation by Satwicz and Shagrin (1981) who stated:

> The most useful monitoring is still done by sight, sound, smell, and touch, which requires physical proximity of the anesthesiologist to the patient.

> Ever-increasing amounts of electrical and mechanical devices are being marketed. These must be regarded as an extension of the anesthesiologist's discriminatory powers and not as a substitute for his decision-making processes. They must not detract from his direct observation of the patient.

A. Anesthesia-machine monitoring

Because anesthesia machines have a very long life, it is difficult to characterize the type of monitoring on a typical machine. Out-of-range alarms can be provided for the pressure in the breathing circuit, the concentration of oxygen and carbon dioxide in the circuit, oxygen/nitrous oxide ratio, and low oxygen pressure (after the regulator and before the flowmeters). Many of the monitoring devices are power-line operated and in case of a power failure, there is usually a backup battery supply. There is a trend to create pneumatically driven alarms. However, it is important to recognize that no electric power is needed to operate the basic anesthesia machines shown in Figures 4.1 and 4.2.

B. Patient monitoring

The physiological events monitored during anesthesia depend, in part, on the nature and length of the procedure and the anesthesiologist's preference and experience. Typically the electrocardiogram (ECG) is monitored from chest electrodes. The ECG provides heart rate and can identify any abnormality in rhythm, as well as myocardial ischemia, revealed by a change of the S-T segment. Blood pressure is often obtained directly from an arterial line and often indirectly with a blood-pressure cuff. Systolic, mean, and diastolic pressure are obtained after the cuff has undergone an inflation and deflation cycle to seat the cuff. Central venous pressure (CVP) is often measured with a catheter advanced into a jugular vein. The oxygen saturation (redness of the blood) is measured noninvasively with a pulse oximeter applied to a fingertip. Some anesthesiologists place a tube in the esophagus and connect it to the stethoscope to monitor heart and breath sounds. Sometimes the stethoscope is taped to the upper chest over the trachea. Body temperature is also measured because anesthesia depresses the temperature-regulating capability of the body. Often an electronic thermometer is placed in the rectum or esophagus. If the procedure is long, blood gases (pH, pO_2, and pCO_2) will be determined from drawn blood samples, usually from the radial artery at the wrist. Airway carbon dioxide concentration is measured with an infrared analyzer; this technique is known as capnometry (capnos = smoke). The end-expiratory CO_2 reflects arterial pCO_2, which is a useful indicator of the metabolic state of the patient.

Some anesthesiologists monitor cardiac output noninvasively with the impedance cardiograph (see below), which employs passage of a low-intensity, high-frequency current through the chest by electrodes on the neck and thorax. Cardiac output is sometimes measured invasively with the thermodilution method, in which a bolus of chilled 5 percent dextrose in water (D5W) is injected into the right atrium and the transient decrease in blood temperature is measured in the pulmonary artery. Usually several injections are used to obtain a reliable value for assessing cardiac output.

C. Alarms

By definition, an alarm is any sound, outcry, or information intended to give notice of approaching danger. Clearly, alarms are highly desirable during anesthesia. However, the most desirable alarm types (audible and/or visual) are the subject of considerable debate. Samuels (1986) pointed out that many of the audible alarms on different monitoring devices are similar, making it difficult to identify which physiological event or machine parameter is out of range.

There is an interesting background to alarms. For example, aviation cockpit alarms were standardized in civil aviation in the U.K. following the recommendation by Patterson (1982). According to Weinger (1991), these alarm tones were modified for the medical environment and consist of:

> Well-defined, complex sequences of tones producing distinctive auditory signatures. There are three "general" alarm sounds of increasing complexity for advisory, caution, and warning. Six "specialized" alarm categories have been defined (ventilation, oxygenation, cardiovascular, perfusion, drug administration, and temperature), each with its own unique auditory signature. For each category, both a caution alarm and a warning alarm are specified.

In 1986 the American Society of Anesthesiologists published recommended standards for monitoring, which included arterial blood pressure, electrocardiography, an oxygen analyzer, and a ventilator disconnection alarm. Alarms are now included in pulse oximeters and capnographs.

The American Society for Testing Materials published alarm standards for anesthesia and respiratory care. The standard requires that alarm sounds have a fundamental frequency between 150 and 1000 Hz based on standard musical pitches. There must be at least four frequency components ranging from 300 to 4000 Hz and these must be related so that they form a distinct sound. Adjustable alarms must have an intensity between 45 and 85 dB. Those with fixed intensity must be between 70 and 85 dB.

Despite the fact that there are recommended standards for alarm signatures, not all anesthesia machines carry the same monitoring equipment; often what is installed reflects the preference and experience of the anesthesiologist. Moreover, all alarms are not equal; some represent a life-threatening emergency, while others may indicate a relatively benign condition. Therefore, prioritization and integration of alarms is an important consideration. The technology of alarming is evolving toward development of the "smart alarm" which, according to Dorsch and Dorsch (1994), "will identify the source of the alarm, analyze the data, provide the operator with a list of possible conditions that could have triggered the alarm, and may present information that will aid in determining the correct way to deal with the condition that triggered the alarm." Parenthetically, modern aircraft cockpit audible and visible alarms are converted to speech commands that are heard by the pilot in his or her headset. Feldman et al. (1985) advocated the use of synthetic speech as an alarm signal in anesthesia. Although there are recommendations for alarm standards, Weinger (1991) stated that the AAMI committee developing human factors guidelines for medical devices opposes rigidly defined alarm standards for medical equipment until more input is obtained from clinicians. Note that in the case of anesthesia alarms, three fields of instrumentation are involved: cardiovascular, respiratory, and anesthesia. In the meantime, the alarms on these three types of equipment sound separately.

The kinds of events that sound alarms were reviewed by McIntyre (1982), who surveyed members of the Canadian Anesthetists Society and reported that over half of the 852 respondents had deliberately deactivated audible alarms at the start of the anesthetic procedure and 314 (37 percent) stated that they did so because there were too many false alarms. Fifty-three respondents (6 percent) believed that the confusion between different audible signals made the alarm useless, while forty-five (5 percent) believed that an audible alarm hindered patient care. In a study by Kestin et al. (1988) involving fifty patients undergoing pediatric anesthesia, a mean of ten alarms sounded during each procedure and 75 percent of these were spurious; only 3 percent indicated risk to the patient. Of all alarms, 99 percent were from the pulse oximeter, electrocardiogram, or blood-pressure monitors, although the alarm limits were set at values that most anesthetists would consider entirely appropriate for patients in this age group.

Another survey of alarm incidence was presented by Schaaf and Black (1989), who reported:

> The number of alarms averaged three per case, with a mean frequency of one every thirty-four minutes. Spurious alarms (those caused by electrocautery, accidental patient movement, or other nonphysiologic reasons) represented only 24 percent of all alarms. Those alarms sounding that were outside the limits occurred at a rate of 53 percent and those that were considered patient risks occurred at a rate of 22 percent. Of the alarms, 67 percent occurred at the beginning and end of anesthesia. The end-tidal carbon dioxide reading accounted for 42 percent of the alarms, mostly during intubation and extubation. The other alarm percentages were as follows: inspired oxygen fraction, 2 percent; ECG heart rate, 5 percent; noninvasive blood pressure, 30 percent; and pulse oximeter, 20 percent.

As sources of artifact, Kestin et al. (1988) reported interference from the electrosurgery or operating room lights; both of these were causes of spurious alarms.

The status of alarms on the three types of monitoring equipment remains unsettled. It is hoped that the evolutionary path does not result in alarms that harm. For example, there is a loud cockpit horn that sounds when the throttle and wing flaps have a certain setting for landing and the landing gear is not extended. On one occasion the airport tower radio was calling the pilot to tell him that his landing gear was not down. The pilot could not hear the tower because the alarm horn was so loud.

While an ideal alarm system is being developed, it should be recognized that if artifacts cause alarms to sound repeatedly when there is no danger to the patient, the alarm is usually turned off. While this practice is common, the alarm may not be turned on again, which could be hazardous.

4.6 Anesthesia Machine Mishaps

Despite the fact that monitoring equipment and alarms have been added to the anesthetic procedure, mishaps still occur. Arens (1996) analyzed the American Society of Anesthesiologists' (ASA) closed-claim files and reported:

> That 79 percent of claims related to equipment were due to misuse and 19 percent were due to equipment failure. In addition, modern anesthesia machines powered by electricity can immediately become a major problem in times of weather disasters and power outages, when backup generators may fail.

Arens went on to argue that over reliance on monitoring equipment leads to a reduction in vigilance and stated that "the anesthesiologist is the patient's most important monitor" and that the anesthesiologist should be in close contact with the patient at all times.

A. Carbon-dioxide absorber failure

Exhaled carbon dioxide (CO_2) is absorbed chemically by soda lime that contains an indicator (e.g., ethyl violet) which turns purple when the absorber is exhausted. Carbon dioxide is a potent respiratory stimulus, causing the breathing rate and depth to increase. An increase in the concentration of CO_2 in the blood is known as hypercarbia. If this occurs when a spontaneously breathing patient is connected to an anesthesia machine, several undesirable consequences could occur, not the least of which is the inhalation of more anesthetic, thereby deepening the level of anesthesia.

Detmer et al. (1980) reported a case of hypercarbia due to carbon-dioxide absorber failure because of absence of the color indicator (ethyl violet) which signals exhaustion of the absorber. The hypercarbia was discovered by blood-gas analysis. The event was not due to an oversight on the part of the manufacturer of the soda lime; the hospital had purchased industrial-grade soda lime which has no color indicator.

Andrews et al. (1990) reported a case of CO_2 absorber failure due to deactivation of the color indicator by radiation from room fluorescent lights (which emit a small amount of ultraviolet radiation). They carried out a series of carefully controlled experiments and reported that:

> After twenty-four hours of fluorescent light exposure with a received flux density of 46 mwatts/cm^2 at 254 nm, the concentration of functional ethyl violet remaining in pulverized Sodasorb was 16 percent of the baseline value. Furthermore, using multiple light sources of various intensities, the greater the intensity of light, the more rapid the rate of decline of the ethyl violet concentration.

Finally, they pointed out:

> Photodeactivation is more likely to occur in operating rooms (OR) that are brightly lighted or in those that utilize UV germicidal bulbs. Intensely lighted OR is the trend, and many existing OR contain germicidal UV bulbs. End-tidal CO_2 monitoring may be more beneficial than color change of absorbent to diagnose rebreathing in those operating rooms.

B. Valve malfunction

The function of the check valves is to guarantee unidirectional gas flow in the breathing circuit. If the valves do not close properly, rebreathing of CO_2 will result. Expiratory-valve failure was reported by Nunn and Rosewarne (1990), who observed an increase in airway CO_2 identified by the capnometer. The importance of incompetent valves was reported by Podraza et al. (1991), who examined the effect of removing the inspiratory and expiratory valves. Removal of the expiratory valve resulted in the greatest rebreathing of CO_2.

Hypercarbia can be detected by blood-gas analysis (pCO_2) and by capnometry. With continuous rebreathing, the end-tidal CO_2 will increase, alerting the anesthesiologists to the problem. Sticking valves were described by Parry et al. (1991) as a source of CO_2 buildup.

C. Leaks and disconnections

Leaks can occur anywhere in the breathing circuit and in the oxygen line. Leaks can be identified with the application of soapy water to the suspected leak site.

Although disconnections can occur anywhere in the breathing circuit, the most common site is between the endotracheal tube and the anesthesia machine. Typically, the tubing in the anesthetic circuit is held together by friction at the joints which may be plastic-to-plastic or metal-to-plastic. Some clamping devices, as well as adhesive tape are used to secure these joints, the latter not being recommended because it makes reconnection more difficult. In many cases it is desirable to have an easy way of disconnecting the anesthesia machine from the tracheal tube to permit suction of mucous.

Accidental disconnection of the anesthesia machine at the tracheal tube is a serious mishap. Either of two events can occur: if the patient is breathing spontaneously, he/she will breathe room air and blow off the anesthesia gas, resulting in a lessening depth of anesthesia. If the patient was treated with a muscle relaxant, as occurs frequently, the respiratory muscles may be paralyzed and breathing will cease. The use of a muscle relaxant during anesthesia is quite common.

4.7 Pulse Oximeter

The pulse oximeter is well established in clinical medicine as an indicator of the oxygen saturation (SaO_2) of the blood in the tissue bed encompassed by the photoelectric detecting means. Used since the mid-1980s, it provides a continuous, noninvasive reading of SaO_2, as well as pulse rate. It is especially valuable as a cardiorespiratory monitor. At present, more than one half-dozen manufacturers provide pulse oximeters, most of which indicate pulse rate continuously. The term SpO_2 is used when SaO_2 is measured with a pulse oximeter.

Noninvasive oximetry dates from the 1930s (see Geddes 1997) and became very popular in the 1940s and 1950s. However, two difficulties prevented widespread use of these devices: (1) the need to calibrate them and (2) the need to render the optical path bloodless by an inflated pressure capsule. Typically the optical absorption of tissues other than blood is substantial and this is why rendering of the optical path bloodless was necessary to obtain an initial setting of the instrument. The pulse oximeter eliminated this requirement by measuring transmission during the pulse.

A. Principle of operation

The pulse oximeter determines the oxygen saturation by measuring the optical transmission at two wavelengths (650 and 805 nm) of light passing through a tissue bed, usually the fingertip. Figure 4.4a illustrates the method by which one fiberoptic bundle transmits broadband radiation from a halogen lamp through the fingertip. A second fiberoptic bundle carries the transmitted light back to two optical filters which allow measurement of the transmission at 650 and 805 nm. The unique feature of the pulse oximeter is that the optical transmission measurement is made during each pulse and special electronic circuitry is used to make this beat-by-beat measurement, which is averaged. The oxygen saturation ($Sp\ O_2$) is proportional to the ratio of the optical density (Y) at 650 and 805 nm. The readout is in percent oxygen saturation. The optical density is equal to the logarithm of the reciprocal of transmissittance.

The pulse oximeter shown in Figure 4.4a employs fiberoptic bundles to make the two-wavelength measurement of the tissue bed. This design provides excellent electrical isolation for the patient. However, there are alternative methods available to make the two-wavelength measurement. For example, the light source and detectors can straddle the tissue bed, as shown in Figure 4.4b. In this application, a red light-emitting diode (LED), paired with a red-sensitive photodiode (R) can be used to make the red-transmission measurement. Similarly, an infrared LED, paired with an infrared (IR) sensitive photodiode can be used to measure the infrared transmission. Figure 4.4b shows a practical embodiment in which the two LEDs are side by side on one side of the tissue bed and the two photodetectors are side by side on the opposite side of the tis-

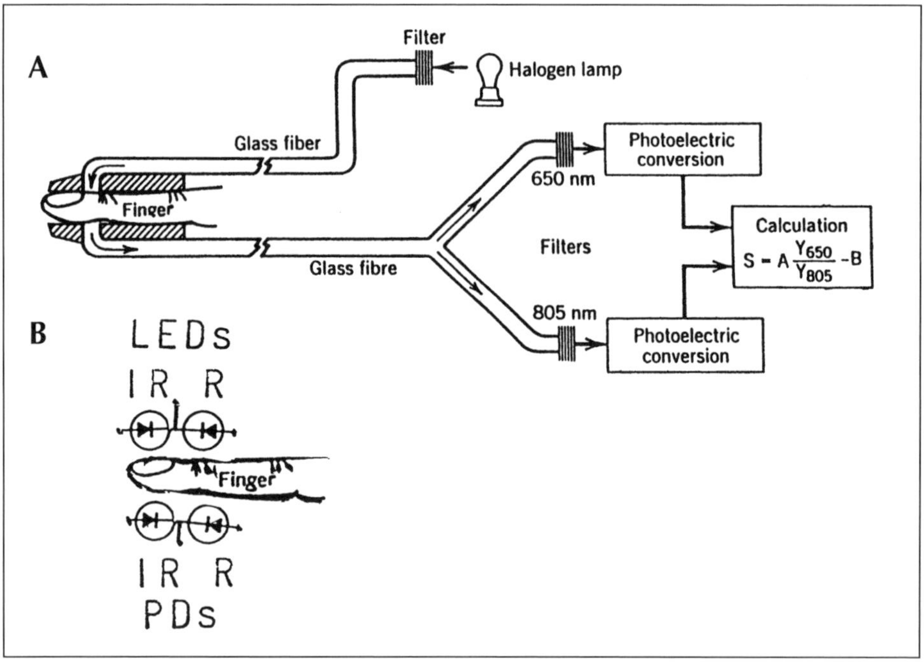

Figure 4.4 *In (a) is shown the fiberoptic pulse oximeter described by Yoshiya et al. (1980) and in (b) is shown the model in which two light-emitting diodes (LEDs) and two photoelectric detectors (PDs) straddle the tissue bed.*

sue bed. With this arrangement, the tissue bed is slightly different for the red and infrared channels, depending on the size and spacing of the detecting system. Probably, due to light scattering, this difference is unimportant. However, with the two LEDs at the tissue bed, there is the possibility of warming the bed, which can produce local vasodilatation, a desirable situation. Heating can be excessive if the designer fails to provide a method of dissipating the heat. Another feature of such a design must address the issue of electrical isolation for the patient, which is an important consideration when electrical devices contact the patient, as for example an electrosurgical unit.

The use of fiberoptic bundles to make the optical measurement has two advantages: (1) the same tissue bed is seen by both red and infrared channels and (2) the patient is electrically isolated from the oximeter. This latter feature is of considerable importance when other electrical devices come into contact with the patient, intentionally as in the case of electrosurgery, or unintentionally, as in the case of excessive leakage current from a malfunctioning power-line driven device comes in contact with the patient.

B. Oxygen saturation

Oxygen saturation is defined as the ratio of oxygenated hemoglobin (HbO_2) to the total hemoglobin ($Hb + HbO_2$). The former is measured at 650 nm and the latter at 805 nm. In a normal subject the hemoglobin concentration is 15 g/100 ml blood. One gram of hemoglobin combines with 1.34 ml of oxygen; therefore, the oxygen content for 100% saturation is $15 \times 1.34 = 20.1$ ml O_2/100 ml blood. There is, in addition, a small amount of oxygen dissolved in the plasma. Note that if the hemoglobin concentration is less than normal, 100 percent saturation represents less than 20.1 ml O_2/100 ml blood.

C. Oxygen dissociation curve

Oxygen saturation depends on the partial pressure of oxygen to which the blood is exposed. The concept of partial pressure is readily understood by the following example. If the barometric pressure is 760 mmHg, then 100 percent oxygen would have a partial pressure of 760 mmHg. If the gas sample has 20 percent oxygen, the partial pressure for a barometric pressure of 760 mmHg is 20 percent of 760 = 152 mmHg.

Figure 4.5 illustrates how the oxygen saturation increases with the partial pressure of oxygen (pO_2). The different curves are for blood pH of 7.2, 7.4, and 7.6. Note that with a normal pH = 7.40, 95 percent saturation is achieved with a $pO_2 = 80$ mmHg, i.e., $100 \times 80/760 = 10.5$ percent oxygen. Twenty percent oxygen ($pO_2 = 152$) provides an oxygen saturation of about 98 percent for a normal subject at 760 mmHg barometric pressure.

D. Hazards and accidents with pulse oximetry

It would appear that there are few hazards associated with pulse oximetry; however, there have been a few disastrous fires, not due to the pulse oximeter, but associated with its use during anesthesia in the operating room. For example, a high concentration of oxygen (more than 80 percent) is typically used with anesthetic gases, and the oxygen flow for an adult is often one L/minute or more. This high flow and partial pressure guarantee high oxygen saturation, as predicted by Figure 4.5. Anesthesiologists like to keep the SaO_2 as high as possible and use high oxygen flow to the anesthetic circuit. However, this practice is not without a fire hazard. An adult human consumes about one quarter liter of oxygen per minute. The oxygen flow rate into an anesthetic machine is often four to ten times this amount and the excess leaks into the environment if an open system is used and if the exhaled gases are not scavenged. The drapes

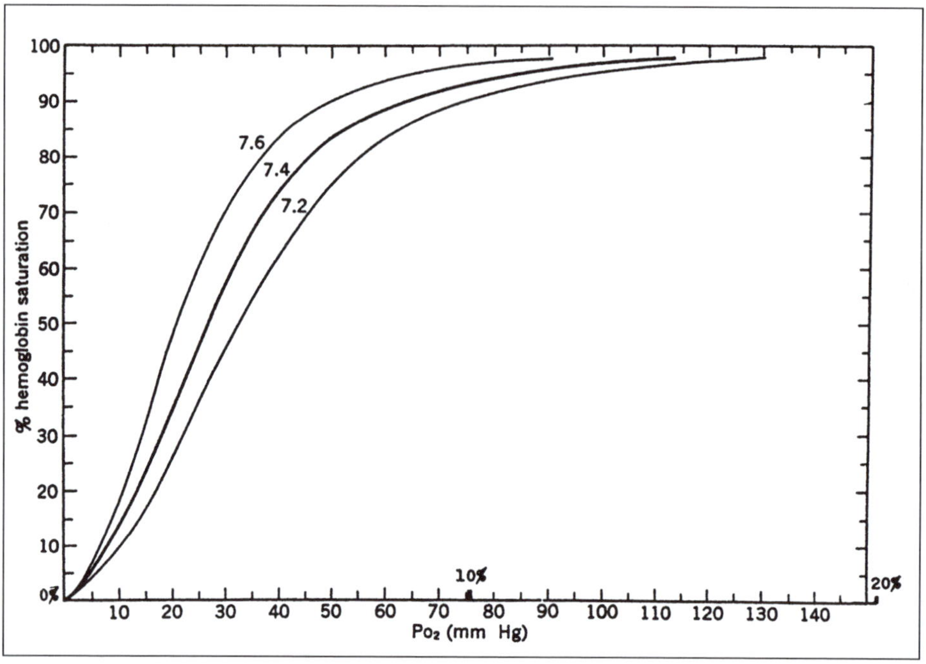

Figure 4.5 *The relationship between oxygen saturation and partial pressure of oxygen (and percent oxygen) for different pH values (7.2, 7.4, 7.6)*

over the patient can constitute an oxygen-filled tent. Despite the fact that drapes are treated with a flame retardant, there have been instances of the drapes catching fire when a small spark occurred. In one case, investigated by the author, under a poorly applied defibrillating electrode, a spark to the patient's skin caused the drapes to catch fire. Another instance of a fire was due to the leakage of oxygen around a plastic facemask and an electrosurgical spark ignited the drapes, and burned the patient, the facemask, and the surgeon's fingers. These and other cases will be described elsewhere in this chapter.

Artifacts and alarm sounding can occur with pulse oximeters. For example, if the finger probe is on the same arm as is used to measure blood pressure with a cuff, the pulse signal will disappear during cuff inflation and deflation. Motion artifacts sometimes occur due to shivering during light anesthesia. A poorly applied probe is also a source of artifact. The use of electrosurgery nearby also disrupts normal operation of the pulse oximeter. Any or all of the foregoing may signal an alarm, which may or may not represent a threat to the patient.

The following case is of interest. A thirty-one-year-old male patient died due to an oximeter not sounding an alarm. The patient underwent surgery at the hospital to remove a cyst at the base of his brain. The decedent was alert post-operatively, and the surgery was successful. The defendant administered O_2, using an oximeter to measure O_2 saturation of the blood. The oximeter alarm was allegedly left "off" and failed to sound when the decedent's O_2 saturation dropped to dangerous levels, causing his death. The plaintiff claimed that the defendant was negligent for using a defective oximeter and for failing to monitor the decedent. The defendant stated that the oximeter defect was not the cause of its failure but agreed to a breach in standard of care.

According to *Medical Malpractice* (1999) the case was settled for $750,000 in favor of the plaintiff.

Three thermal injuries due to a malfunctioning pulse oximeter were reported by Sloan (1988) . Three patients were monitored with a pulse oximeter applied to a finger for 3.5, 6 and 10.5 hours. The finger injuries (blisters) were not noted until three to five days postoperatively by the nursing staff, and not visible at the end of the procedure. The type of oximeter had a light-emitting diode (LED) in the probe and its casing was warped and cracked. When returned to the manufacturer, it was found that there were two puncture areas in the probe cable that caused excessive current to be delivered to the LED, causing it to overheat. The manufacturer has redesigned the probe to eliminate this problem.

A skin burn due to an oximeter probe was reported by Murphy (1990) who described an unusual act on the part of the operator. He stated:

> A 4.4-kg full-term infant was born by vaginal delivery with the aid of a vacuum extraction. A subcapsular occipital hematoma developed and the patient was transferred to the newborn nursery. All the nursery's pulse oximeters (manufacturer A) were in use and one [probe] (manufacturer B) was borrowed from the Anesthesia Department. The nursery personnel connected the infant to the A machine. Initially, a wraparound finger sensor was applied to the right ring finger, but no saturation (SaO_2) reading was obtained. The problem was assumed to be a faulty sensor. This sensor was removed after approximately one minute and noted to be "a little warm." A second type of sensor (clip-on type) was then applied to the superior aspect of the right ear pinna. After approximately three minutes without obtaining any SaO_2 or pulse rate readings, the tip of the ear was noted to be acquiring a red color. The sensor was removed and further attempts to monitor SaO_2 were abandoned. Over

> the next several hours, it became apparent that the infant had been burned in two locations suffering from a second-degree burn to the right ring (and adjacent middle) finger and a third-degree burn to the tip of the right ear. The infant subsequently recovered uneventfully from the occipital hematoma. The burns were initially treated with topical therapy and the patient was seen in consultation by a surgeon prior to discharge. Reconstructive surgery will likely be required at sometime in the future for repair of the right ear.
>
> Subsequently, the temperature at the tip of the clip-on sensor was measured while connected to the machine used in this incident. Within two minutes, the temperature at the tip of the sensor was 200°F. This information was reported to the manufacturer and to the Food and Drug Administration.

The surprising thing about the foregoing incident is that the connector for the probe of one manufacturer's probe could engage the receptacle on the other manufacturer's instrument. No mention was made of any warnings that may have appeared in the manuals of A and B manufacturers.

Vasoconstriction, for whatever reason (cold, drugs, shock or excess pressure on the tissue by the probe), reduces tissue-bed blood flow and a typical oximeter will not indicate oxygen saturation. Reduced blood flow due to misapplication of the probe or placing something on the probe site can lead to reduced tissue blood flow. Reduced blood flow will impair the dissipation of any heat produced by an oximeter probe.

Pettersen et al. (1992) provided the following account of skin injury at the site of an oximeter probe; they stated:

> An eleven-month-old girl received twenty-three propofol anaesthetics for radiation treatment of a retinoblastoma. After the first two anaesthetics, a skin injury appeared on the pulp of the toes, where the light source of a pulse oximeter probe had been placed. During the remaining twenty-one anaesthetics the light source of the probe was placed over the nail, and no other skin lesions occurred. Examination of the equipment revealed no malfunction.

It is important to note that the injury occurred in only two of twenty-three applications of the probe and that there was no equipment malfunction. They first called attention to the fact that the same nurse applied the oximeter probe in the same way on each occasion. They further stated:

> No skin lesion occurred during the twenty-one procedures for which the light source of the probe was facing the nail, indicating that the nail probably damps out potential thermal effect of the probe on soft tissue. It thus seems important that the nail side of the oximeter probes is marked clearly to avoid the risk of this kind of injury.

The foregoing indicates that the authors believed that the skin injury was due to heating by the LED. It is noteworthy that Petterson's suggestion was accepted by at least one manufacturer who now labels the finger probe "palm side."

The following case of a pulse-oximeter burn reported by Mills and Ralph (1992) has several interesting features. They stated that a four-month-old baby, whose lungs were ventilated for fourteen days for ventilatory failure secondary to bronchiolitis, suffered burns to his big toe related to the site of application of a pulse oximeter probe. Prior to discovery of the burn, the patient had no periods of poor peripheral perfusion and there had been no problems with the pulse oximeter trace. On the thirteenth day he was noted to have blistering beneath the pulse oximeter probe on two-thirds of the circumference of his left big toe, and a similar, but smaller lesion on the right big toe. These had not been present during examination earlier in the day and had not been noticed during routine rotation of the position of the probe. This consists of movement of the probe to another limb every three hours and is standard practice for the nurses in the intensive care unit. The pulse oximeter probe was removed and the light source felt to be hotter than usual. The pulse oximeter probe was returned to the manufacturer for assessment.

Suspecting environmental factors as a possible cause of the burn, they conducted the following experiments. The heat production from a number of similar probes was tested. Six pulse oximeter probes were suspended in an incubator maintained at 37.0°C. Temperature probes were attached to the light source and the sensor of the pulse oximeter probe and recorded for three hours using the temperature monitor. The temperature of the incubator remained constant between 36.9 and 37.0°C. The pulse oximeter probes warmed rapidly when brought in from room temperature to the incubator environment. The light sources quickly reached their working temperature, after which their temperature remained remarkably constant over the three hour period. The working temperature varied between the individual probes (range 39.1 to 39.7°C). The light remained very close to the ambient temperature. The sixth probe was monitored for twenty-four hours. The temperature of the light source remained constant, ± 0.1°C, once it had reached to within its working level for the whole twenty-four hours.

They stated that the baby suffered burns due to short circuiting between the wires in the pulse oximeter probe lead. There was also some damage to the protective film over the light source. These defects were the result of the repeated use of a disposable probe, an unfortunate practice that had arisen due to the need to curb expenditure.

In concluding their report, Mills and Ralph provided the following excellent advice:

> We would suggest that pulse oximeter probes and connecting wires should be inspected frequently and although not seen in this case, any freezing of the pulse oximeter display should be investigated to aid the detection of short circuits in the wiring within the leads. We would also suggest that the point of application should be regularly inspected and the position of the probe varied at regular intervals, especially during conditions of decreased skin perfusion. Finally, we would strongly recommend that disposable pulse oximeter probes are reused only in strict compliance with the manufacturer's recommendation.

4.8 Capnograph

The capnograph (*capnos* means "smoke') is a device for measuring the concentration of carbon dioxide (CO_2) in the airway. It is especially valuable during anesthesia and its sensor is placed between the anesthesia machine and the patient, as shown in Figure 4.6a in which it is connected to an endotracheal tube. It can also be used with a facemask. The CO_2 concentration is displayed in terms of partial pressure of CO_2, i.e. pCO_2. Because the end-tidal pCO_2 reflects arterial pCO_2, it is a useful indicator of ventilation. An exhausted CO_2 absorber in the anesthesia machine will reveal itself by an increase in end-tidal pCO_2.

The principle underlying operation of the capnograph is shown in Figure 4.6a, and employs measurement of the transmission of infrared (IR) energy in the airway. CO_2 absorbs infrared (IR) energy strongly at 4.26 microns, as shown in Figure 4.6b. Water vapor (H_2O) also absorbs energy in the infrared spectrum, but minimally at 4.26 microns. The other gases (N_2 and O_2) do not absorb IR. However nitrous oxide (N_2O), which is used in anesthesia, has some absorption in the IR spectrum.

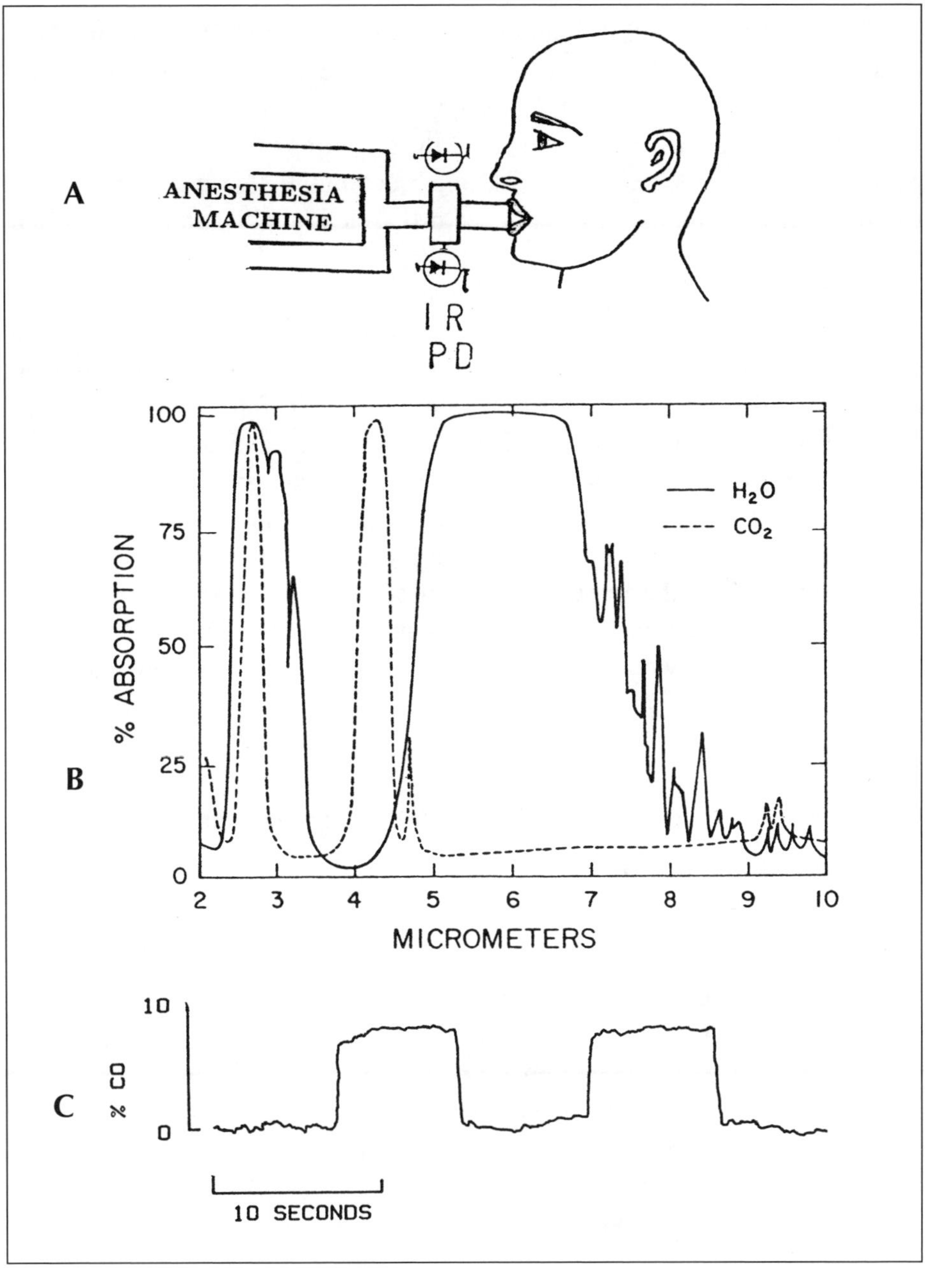

Figure 4.6 *The components of the capnograph. (a) illustrates the infrared (IR) emitter and photodetector (PD) that measures the absorption of* CO_2 *in the airway. (b) illustrates the spectral absorption of* CO_2 *and water vapor. In (c) is shown a record of* CO_2 *concentration in the airway during breathing.*

Figure 4.6a illustrates the method used to measure the CO_2 in the airway, in which an infrared (IR) emitter is placed on one side of the breathing tube and a matched IR photodetector (PD) is placed on the opposite side to detect the IR radiation after passing through the gas in the breathing tube. Figure 4.6c shows a typical record of the percent CO_2 during breathing. In this case, the end-tidal CO_2 was 8.1 percent, i.e. pCO_2 = 61.6 mmHg, clearly indicating hypercarbia.

4.9 Burns from Warming Devices

During general anesthesia, the body's temperature-regulating mechanism is depressed and body temperature decreases. Contributing to this decline is the relatively cool environment of the operating room. Therefore, a variety of devices, such as warmed mattresses, hot-water bottles and bags, heat lamps, heated humidifiers, forced-air warming blankets, etc. are employed. Burns have been associated with the use of some of these warming devices.

Cheney et al. (1994) reviewed the Closed Claims Database of the American Society of Anesthesiologists which lists a total of 3,000 claims (1985–1994) of which fifty-four were burn cases, and of these, twenty-eight resulted from materials or devices used to warm patients; Table 4.1 presents their results.

Table 4.1
Source of Burns from Warming Devices

	N	% of 28
Heated material	20	71
IV bag/bottle	18	64
Hot packs/compresses	2	7
Warming equipment	8	29
Circulating water blanket	5	18
Warming light	1	4
Heated humidifier	1	4
Heating pad	1	4

From Cheney FW, Posner KL, Caplan RA et al. *Anesthesiology* 1994, 80: 806–810.

Cheney et al. stated that:

> Among the eighteen burns caused by a heated i.v. bag or bottle, fifteen involved an i.v. bag or bottle being used to warm the patient (fourteen directly and one by warming an i.v. blood transfusion). In the other three claims, a warmed i.v. bag or bottle was placed on the patient's skin in order to provide local heat. In five of the eighteen burns caused by i.v. bags or bottles, the reviewer explicitly stated that the burn was of second or third-degree severity.
>
> Burns from electrically powered warming equipment represent only 29 percent of the total burns from warming devices. More than half of the burns in this category were from circulating water mattresses. In only one of the burns caused by circulating-water mattresses did the reviewer explicitly state that the device was defective.

Of more than passing interest are the circumstances surrounding the incidents. According to Cheney et al. (1994):

> One burn resulted from a warming light that was being used to treat hypothermia in a two-day-old infant. The anesthesiologist had removed the diffusing lens from the lamp and placed the lamp 3 m from the patient. The infant sustained third-degree burns despite constant vigilance over skin temperature.
>
> One burn was caused by a heated humidifier. The tubing was padded but came in contact with the arm and a permanent disfiguring scar resulted. The one heating pad burn resulted from treatment of an i.v. infiltration. The patient sustained scars and underwent multiple surgical procedures.

It is of more than passing interest to scrutinize the circumstances surrounding some of the burn cases identified in Table 4.1. The following cases are presented to identify two types of skin injury (1) that due to a heating device and (2) that due to prolonged pressure against the skin; both can coexist, making it difficult to dissect the components. Additional information on skin injury can be found in Chapter 8.

A heating pad is frequently used to keep a patient from excessive cooling during a long surgical procedure. Such a device contains warmed water, which circulates through tubes or channels in a plastic pad. The temperature of the water can be set to any temperature below 105°F (40.5°C). Sometimes heated intravenous fluid (IVF) bags are used as an aid in posturing a patient. Such bags are stored in thermostatically controlled cabinet at 131°F (55°C) according to Pamaar et al. (1992). This temperature was chosen to accommodate the cooling that occurs prior to use.

Although skin lesions have been attributed to such heated objects, it is not always possible to be certain of the culprit device, because, in many cases, the patient is supported, in part, by the warmed object, which raises the issue of pressure necrosis, particularly if the procedure lasts more than a few hours. If the peripheral circulation is impaired due to age, hypertension, diabetes, etc. or the aorta is cross clamped for vascular replacement surgery, the susceptibility to pressure necrosis is increased. The following cases are cited to make the point.

Scott (1967) reported three cases of skin injury on patients on warming pads undergoing long surgical procedures. The first case was a forty-year-old white man weighing 90 kg (198.5 1b) who had aortic insufficiency. The procedure was uncomplicated and the patient remained on the operating table and on the thermal blanket for less than four hours. The blanket was at room temperature except when heated to a temperature of 42°C for an estimated period of one hour. Following surgery, three linear areas of ischemia corresponding to ridges of the thermal pad were present over the patient's sacrum. Although the injury remained superficial, the patient experienced considerable discomfort throughout his postoperative course.

The second case was a thirty-five-year-old white man who had a prosthetic mitral valve replacement for mitral stenosis. Following extracorporeal circulation the patient developed ventricular fibrillation. Two and one half hours of pump support were required and the operation was prolonged to almost ten hours. The patient was in a lateral position on the thermal pad during most of this time. The pad was kept at room temperature for the first six hours and at 40 to 42°C for approximately six hours. An area of ischemia developed over the left greater trochanter, which progressed to full-thickness necrosis of the skin. Hospital stay was prolonged because of this lesion, although healing occurred without the aid of a skin graft.

The third case was a fifty-four-year-old white man with refractory congestive heart failure due to aortic stenosis and insufficiency. He was on extracorporeal circulation for two hours during which time the aortic valve was replaced with a prosthesis and the mitral valve was explored. Because of the bleeding diathesis, the patient remained in surgery on the operating table and the thermal pad for eight hours. For approximately the first four hours the pad was at room temperature. It was then heated to 42°C for the remaining four hours. A 6-cm area of full-thickness necrosis developed over the patient's sacrum.

In discussing the three cases, Scott stated that all three injuries occurred at sites of maximum pressure over a bony prominence. Surgery was prolonged in two patients and one patient was very heavy. A Bovie plate was observed to have been in contact with the skin at the site of injury in one patient (case 2). It was postulated that perhaps the metal plate, acting as a heat conductor, contributed to the injury.

Whether the injuries are burns in the true sense or areas of pressure necrosis or partly both is not clear. The thermal pad is very firm and is corrugated by the rubber circulating coils. Such a hard, irregular surface predisposes to localized pressure necrosis. The result is an injury which may prolong hospital stay and increase patient discomfort.

Chino and Nagel (1968) reported two cases in which skin injury occurred in patients on warming blankets undergoing long surgical procedures. The first case was a sixty-three-year-old white man weighing 187 lbs who was admitted with the diagnosis of bilateral iliac artery occlusion, arteriosclerotic heart disease and diabetes mellitus. A warming pad was placed on the operating room table, under the patient's hips and lower back, because of the anticipated prolonged surgical time. This pad was covered by a double layer of drape sheet and the pad's temperature regulator was set at 100°F (37.8°C). The patient underwent an aorta-bifemoral bypass with Dacron graft placement and uneventful general anesthesia. The total time for the procedure was six hours and fifteen minutes. After several hours in the recovery area, the patient was returned to the operating room for further surgery. This procedure required an additional hour and forty-five minutes. The postoperative course was then uncomplicated until the second postoperative day when the patient began to complain of severe discomfort in the sacral area. On examination he was found to have an area of burn over the sacrum estimated to be 40 percent third-degree, 60 percent second-degree, with strips of second-degree burn extending over the buttocks. The area of burn corresponded to the location of the warming pad used during surgery and the pattern of burn to the fluid channels in the coils of the warming pad.

The second case was a sixty-seven-year-old white woman weighing about 150 pounds who was admitted with gangrene of the right great toe and diabetes mellitus. After attempts to control the diabetes, she underwent an aortofemoral bypass graft under general anesthesia. A warming pad covered by a sheet was placed under the patient's shoulders and mid-back. The total operating time was seven hours and fifteen minutes. On the second postoperative day the patient complained of soreness over her upper back. Examination revealed several areas of second-degree burn in a symmetrical pattern over the midthoracic area. Lenear areas of erythema extended along the back and corresponded in spacing to the fluid channels in the warming pad.

In discussing these two cases, Chino and Nagel stated that the most severe injury occurred in areas of greatest pressure, namely over a bony prominence. Both patients were diabetic, moderately obese, and had some degree of vascular insufficiency. Preparative solutions used for skin cleansing may have predisposed to this injury. The pattern of burn in each case corresponded exactly to the area of contact and to the fluid channel spacing in the warming pad.

Following these incidents Chino and Nagel had four thermal pads checked. All four units were found to be within manufacturer's tolerances which allow approximately 9 degrees F differential between the control unit reservoir and the pad surface temperature.

In their discussion, Chino and Nagel correctly pointed out the importance of patient weight, the presence of vascular disease, and duration of procedure.

Parmaar et al. (1992) reported a case of burn from a heated IVF bag. Under general anesthesia, the patient was positioned supine with both arms tucked by the sides. The neck was hyperextended by placing a one liter bag of intravenous fluid between the scapulae. The IVF bag was placed on the top of a heating pad warmed to 39°C. Two layers of cotton sheets were between the patient and the IVF bag. Surgery proceeded for thirty minutes and after uneventful extubation and emergence, the patient was brought to the recovery room. Fifteen minutes later, the patient complained of pain and burning sensations across the upper back. Examination at this time revealed a 10 × 30 cm area of second-degree burn with blistering, transversely across the upper back. The outline of the injury corresponded to the position and shape of the IVF bag.

They then simulated the incident with a conscious volunteer and a heated IVF bag from the same warmer as was used to support the patient's shoulder. Although only warm to the touch, the IVF bag was uncomfortably hot when laid upon, and the pain was intolerable after ten minutes. The temperature of this IVF bag was 48°C at the outset and decreased only 3.2°C during thirty minutes of exposure to the warming pad, which apparently limited the dissipation of heat from the IVF bag.

From the forgoing it appears that the IVF bag temperature was 48 to 44.8°C and the duration of exposure was thirty minutes; the combination produced a second-degree burn. Note that the IVF bag was under the scapulae providing support for the patient, thereby compromising tissue perfusion at this site, predisposing the tissue to thermal damage from the 48–44.8°C temperature of the IV bag.

Additional information on skin temperature for first-, second- and third-degree burns can be found in Chapters 3 and 8.

4.10 Fire

A. Introduction

For a fire to occur, three ingredients must be present: (1) a source of flammable material, (2) oxygen, and (3) a source of ignition (i.e., a spark or high temperature as produced by an electrocautery or electrosurgery or laser beam). In the operating room all three ingredients can be present and circumstances can conspire to cause a fire or explosion.

Typically during anesthesia, 80 to 95 percent oxygen is used with the anesthetic agent applied to the airway via a plastic endotracheal tube. Occasionally, there may be a leak in the anesthetic circuit and thus oxygen may accumulate around the patient, who is covered with sterile paper or cloth drapes which are usually treated with a flame retardant. As stated previously, it is not uncommon for the flow of oxygen to be one L/min or more. An adult subject consumes about 0.25 to 0.3 L/min; therefore, the excess oxygen can accumulate in the environment providing the opportunity for a fire. The following cases are examples of fires in which all three ingredients were present.

B. Defibrillator-induced fire

The author investigated a case in which a defibrillation shock was delivered to two, handheld chest electrodes, one of which was not well applied and there was an arc under this electrode; the result was a flash that ignited the drapes, even though they were treated with a flame retardant. There is no arc under properly applied defibrillating electrodes.

C. Electrosurgically induced fires

1. Facial injury

An FDA MAUDE report (6/19/90) describes a drapery fire associated with the use of electrosurgery. The report stated: “a physician was removing a large benign lipoma from the left forehead when a flash fire occurred. There was oxygen being delivered by nasal cannula and an electrocautery in use at the time. The patient sustained first- and second-degree burns around her eyelids, nose, and mouth. A product code or lot number was not provided.” The manufacturer’s comments were as follows:

There was no sample available for analysis nor was a lot number provided. The fabric used in this product has been extensively tested and has been repeatedly shown to meet the Class 1 requirements of the federal flammability standards 16 CFR 1610. The federal standards establish requirements for maximum allowable rate of flame spread over a fabric. These federal standards do not imply that a material meeting the standards will not discolor, char, melt or ignite when exposed to a sufficiently intense heat source. Graphics for this line of products depict a caution statement that states the following. "The contents of this package, as with any linen or single-use drape and gown material, may ignite/burn if exposed to an open flame or high intensity heat source."

2. Airway fires

The use of a urethral resectoscope to eliminate obstructions in the airway was introduced by Johnson and Stewart (1975). Resection is achieved with electrosurgical current and when used in urological practice, only tissue and fluid surround the cutting loop. When used in the airway, tissue and oxygen surround the cutting loop.

Downing and Johnson (1979) reported successful use of an infant urethral resectoscope to excise subglottic stenoses in twenty-two infants. They described the resectoscope as follows:

> The instrument we use is an infant urethral resectoscope with a size 13 insulated sheath (3.5 × 4.2 mm O.D.) and a 0° rod lens telescope with fiberoptic illumination. Ventilation can be achieved for a limited period of time when working without a tracheostomy by using a semi-closed system attached to the irrigating channel of the resectoscope sheath. Under such conditions, the endoscopic manipulations must be performed rapidly and at several short intervals. We have used intra-operative blood-gas monitoring with computer automated rapid analysis when working under these conditions without a tracheostomy.

Commenting on the results, Downing and Johnson stated:

> Twenty patients have had a successful clinical result with no evidence of recurrent airway stenosis. The result was unsuccessful in two patients, one of whom re-stenosed and has subsequently been retreated and decannulated successfully. The second patient re-stenosed and still has a tracheostomy. There were no deaths directly related to the resection procedure.

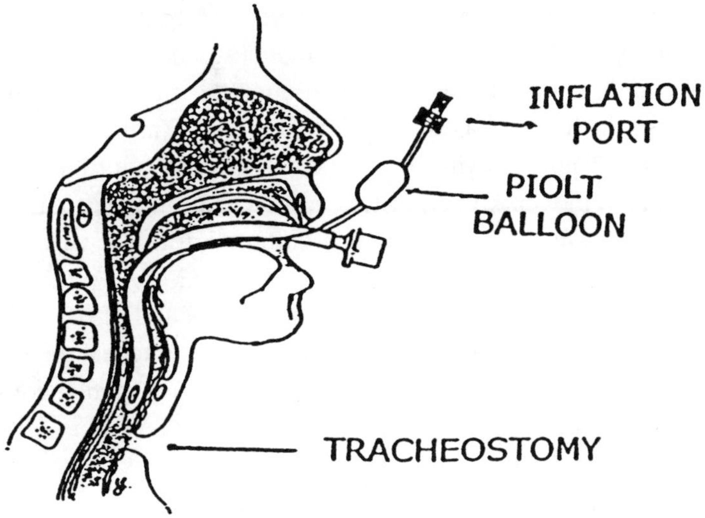

Figure 4.7 Endotracheal tube in the airway of a patient with a tracheostomy (opening in the neck). Note that the tip of the endotracheal tube is just headward to the tracheostomy.

It is of more than passing interest to note that Downing and Johnson did not encounter a fire or explosion, which was reported by subsequent clinicians using the same technique (see below). The lack of fire or explosion may have been due to the absence of combustible material in the operating field. Although they reported using a suction cannula, they did not identify its construction. Because no fire was encountered, it is likely that the cannula was made of metal. As discovered by subsequent clinicians, the combination of oxygen, a plastic catheter, and an electrosurgical spark constitute the ingredients for a fire.

Rita and Seleny (1982) reported an electrosurgically-induced endotracheal tube fire when they used a urethral resectoscope to remove granulous tissue in the trachea of a twelve-year-old child. They reported: "bronchoscopy and tracheal dilatations had been done periodically under general anesthesia. The same technique has always been employed without complications, namely, passing an endotracheal tube through the tracheostomy. Anesthesia was induced and maintained by inhalation of halothane and 50 percent nitrous oxide and oxygen. The last four procedures included removal of granulation tissue found at the tracheostomy site which was resected with the urethral resectoscope. No complications had occurred." Figure 4.7 illustrates the operative site.

This time, the same procedure was followed. Atropine 0.2 mg, was administered intramuscularly one hour before inducing anesthesia with halothane and 50 percent nitrous oxide and oxygen through the tracheostomy tube. When adequate anesthetic depth was achieved, the epiglottis, arytenoids, vocal cords and trachea were sprayed with a 1 percent lidocaine solution. The tracheostomy tube was removed and a plastic endotracheal tube was passed through the tracheostomy. During bronchoscopy, granulation tissue was found at the tracheostomy site in the area above the endotracheal tube. While resecting it with the urethral resectoscope, smoke suddenly came out of the child's mouth and a flash occurred at the tracheostomy site. The endotracheal tube was immediately withdrawn. It was on fire, which rapidly ceased spontaneously. Bronchoscopy showed burns on the lower trachea and right bronchus, with minimal involvement of the left bronchus.

Interestingly, the authors commented as follows.

> In the past year, we have done sixty-seven cases under general anesthesia without complications using halothane, 50 percent nitrous oxide, and an endotracheal tube inserted through the tracheostomy. This time, ignition of an endotracheal tube occurred during resection of tracheal granuloma using a urethral resectoscope.

Another electrosurgically-induced tracheal tube fire was reported by Simpson and Wolf (1986), who stated:

> A four-year-old boy was admitted for elective adenoidectomy and tonsillectomy. His past medical history was negative except for recurrent tonsillitis, the last episode having occurred three to four weeks prior to surgery. He weighed 17 kg and his physical examination was normal except for large, opposed tonsils touching at the midline.
>
> Anesthesia was induced by inhalation of O_2, N_2O, and halothane and was uneventful. An IV infusion was then started. The trachea was automatically intubated with a 4.5 mm ID polyvinyl chloride (PVC) endotracheal tube. Lubricant was not used on the endotracheal tube. Breath sounds were equal bilaterally in all four quadrants. The endotracheal tube was fixed with the aid of a David-Crow mouth gag. Endotracheal tube position was again confirmed by equal breath sounds bilaterally. The eyes were protected with tape. The patient breathed N_2O 3L/min, O_2 3L/min, and 1 percent halothane, by con-

trolled ventilation. A moderate retrograde leak of gases was noted around the tube at the larynx.

The surgeons performed the adenoidectomy and right tonsillectomy without incident, then began to use a suction and electrocautery to control the bleeding in the right tonsillar fossa. The electrocautery was set at 35-watts coagulation in the "spray" mode. After approximately twenty seconds of cautery, a fire erupted in the pharynx that "blow-torched" toward the lips. Breath sounds were immediately lost and increased airway pressure was noted. The fire was extinguished with saline, the pharynx was suctioned, and the endotracheal tube was immediately removed. The tube was noted to be melted and charred externally for 2 cm, midway between the distal tip and the adaptor, and fused for 1 cm at that point with 100 percent occlusion. From the point of fusion distally, the tube was blackened internally. The trachea was immediately reintubated with a 5.0 mm ID PVC, uncuffed, endotracheal tube. With a fractional inspired O_2 concentration (FiO^i_2) of 0.99 and 1 percent halothane, pH was 7.43, $PaCO_2$ 28 mmHg, and PaO_2 575 mmHg. On direct examination the mucosa of the posterior tongue, uvula, and hypopharynx was noted to be erythematous and charred. Rigid bronchoscopy using a 4.0 mm × 30 cm bronchoscope was performed. The cords were not burned, but were edematous. The mucosa of the anterior trachea, carina, and left mainstem bronchus was erythematous and charred in some areas. This was probably caused by a "blow-torching" of thc firc downward. The burns were mostly anterior and not circumferential. After bronchoscopy, the trachea was reintubated orally with a 5.0 mm ID PVC, uncuffed, endotracheal tube under direct vision. Breath sounds were again equal and clear bilaterally. The patient was given dexamethasone 2 mg IV. Ours is the first reported case of an endotracheal tube fire ignited by "spray-type" coagulation cautery.

An airway fire, during a tracheostomy, was reported by Bailey et al. (1990). The title of the paper stated "electrocautery induced airway fire." An electrocautery is an electrically heated probe which would lead one to believe that such a device was used. However, the authors recommended the "use of bipolar rather than unipolar electrocautery for prevention of current leakage;" this clearly shows that conventional electrosurgical current was used with a monopolar electrode.

The accident was described as follows:

The neck was cleansed with povidone iodine; surgical drapes were put in place and surgery was started. After the neck incision was made, an electro-

> cautery device was used to secure hemostasis. After approximately fifteen minutes as the electrocautery device was being used, a loud pop was heard, followed by a fire in the surgical field. Moist towels were used to extinguish the flames, and the charred endotracheal tube was removed.

The report continued:

> Flexible bronchoscopy and direct laryngoscopy revealed a thermal injury to the posterior midtrachea involving approximately a 3-cm area extending 50 percent around the tracheal circumference. The patient tolerated the remainder of the procedure well and was taken back to the intensive care unit in stable condition.

Although advertised as an electrocautery fire, there is little doubt that this was an electrosurgically induced fire, caused by the presence of flammable material (the tracheal tube), oxygen and a source of ignition (electrosurgical current).

Recently, the author investigated a case involving an anesthetized subject with a plastic endotracheal tube in place and the surgeon entered the trachea with an electrosurgical probe via a tracheostomy which resulted in an explosion, melting the anesthetic-machine hoses and burning the patient.

D. Laser-induced fires

After performing 700 endotracheal and laryngeal procedures over a three-year period, Snow et al. (1976) reported two cases of laser-induced tracheal tube fire using a red-rubber endotracheal tube. The first case was a twelve-month-old girl. They stated:

> The larynx was exposed with a pediatric laryngoscope and placed on the suspension apparatus. A Zeiss operating microscope with laser attachment was brought into position.
>
> When the laser beam was continuously discharged, the papillomas obstructing the larynx were vaporized, so that the laser beam impacted on the tube within the trachea at the tracheotomy level. A fire started, which was brought under control immediately by removal of the burning tube. Examination of the endotracheal tube revealed a superficial burned area, 1×0.5 cm in size, 4 cm from the distal end. Bronchoscopy revealed a small superficial burn of the tracheal mucosa, which later healed.

The second case was a twelve-year-old boy with laryngeal papillomas. The red-rubber endotracheal tube was covered with aluminum foil, except for the tip. They stated:

During the operation, laser beam repeatedly hit the unprotected distal end of the tube. A fire started, which was brought under control immediately by removal of the burning tube. Examination of the tube showed a superficial burned area, 1.2 × 0.5 cm in size, including the aperture opposite the beveled end of the endotracheal tube. Bronchoscopy revealed a small superficial burn of the tracheal mucosa, 1 cm below the vocal cords, which healed uneventfully.

In commenting on their experience, they stated:

> During CO_2 laser microsurgery on the larynx and trachea, we have observed that if the laser beam repeatedly hits the red-rubber endotracheal tube (four or five times) in the same area, there is the risk of fire. The laser beam must be carefully focused to avoid impact with the tube.

Despite the aluminum foil used to protect the rubber tracheal tube, the unprotected tip was struck and the combustible rubber, in the presence of oxygen, caused a fire.

By 1979, it was recognized that a plastic tracheal tube in the airway could be ignited by a laser beam. Desirous of preventing such an event, Burgess and LeJune (1979) wrapped a polyvinyl tracheal tube with aluminum foil tape to within 1 cm of its tip. Despite this precaution, a laser-induced endotracheal tube fire occurred in a six-year-old girl admitted for resection of papillomas on the left and right vocal cords. After induction of anesthesia and placement of the tracheal tube, Burgess and LeJune stated:

> When the papillomas that extended into the subglottic region were excised, however, heat from the laser beam melted and then ignited the endotracheal tube tip, which had become exposed below the area that was protected by tape. The tube was immediately withdrawn.
>
> Careful inspection of the trachea with a 5-mm bronchoscope showed no significant thermal injury in the subglottic area. Indeed, the area appeared to be notably improved by the surgery. The patient's trachea was reintubated, and the oropharynx was inspected and found to be uninjured. To prevent inflammation, dexamethasone, 8 mg IV, was given intraoperatively and continued for two days postoperatively in a dose of 2 mg IV. every six hours. The

> three loose teeth were carefully extracted to prevent their being aspirated into the tracheobronchial tree. The trachea was extubated and the patient was given cool mist oxygen (40 percent) for the next forty-eight hours. Arterial blood gases remained satisfactory. Ampicillin sodium, 250 mg four times daily, was administered for the next ten days. The patient's voice continued to improve over the next three weeks.

Another laser-induced endotracheal tube fire was reported by Hirshman and Smith (1980). The patient was a fourteen-year-old-boy with a tracheostomy who had 110 previous operations for tracheal and laryngeal papillomas (fingerlike tumors). After sedation, they stated:

> The trachea was intubated via the larynx with a 6-mm-cuffed vinyl plastic endotracheal tube that was positioned just below the vocal cords to allow laser removal of the tracheal papillomas via the tracheal stoma. After spontaneous ventilation returned, the patient was allowed to breathe oxygen (O_2), nitrous oxide (N_2O) (50:50), and 2 percent halothane. Using a nasal speculum in the tracheal stoma, the CO_2 laser was used in 0.2-s bursts to remove several papillomas in the tracheal stoma entrance. After the papillomas in the stoma were removed, several large pedunculated papillomas were removed with cup forceps, and the bases were treated with the CO_2 laser, set at 0.5 s. All papillomas were removed from the right lateral wall. This took approximately ten minutes and, during this time, it was noted that the carbon/eschar from previously lasered areas produced sparks. Attention was then focused on the left lateral wall. After half of the first papilloma was removed, a hissing and then a small explosion were heard. The hoses from the anesthesia machine were immediately disconnected, the endotracheal tube was removed, the tracheostomy site was intubated with another tube, and 100 percent O_2 was administered.
>
> Vital signs were stable. A bronchoscope was used to inspect the larynx, which was free of damage. The trachea, however, showed a burn of the anterior wall, approximately 0.5 cm wide, beginning below the vocal cords to just above the tracheostomy site. There was also a small burned area 2.5 cm long and 1.2 cm wide above the tracheostomy on the posterior wall.

With careful medical management, the patient was discharged from the hospital on the following day. In explaining the accident, Hirshman and Smith stated:

> We are postulating that the vinyl plastic endotracheal tube was ignited by flaming tissue either in close proximity to or inhaled into the tip of the endot-

racheal tube during spontaneous ventilation with gases that support combustion.

An editorial comment by Strong (1980), which followed the Hirshman and Smith paper, states:

> Fortunately, the problem can now be avoided by using a bronchoscope with a laser attachment or a stainless steel flexible endotracheal tube, both of which are now commercially available. These steel instruments are, of course, noncombustible in air or 100 percent oxygen (O_2) when impacted with laser energy currently in use in surgery.

The flexible, stainless-steel endotracheal tube referred to by Strong was described by Norton and DeVos (1978). The device was made from strip wound hose using stainless steel or, as an alternative, wire-wound square spring. The tube was wire brushed or matte finished to diminish light reflection into the surgeon's field of vision. Dorsch and Dorsch (1994) pointed out that many airway tubes designed for use with lasers are not entirely metal; some have plastic tips and cuffs. A laser strike on these parts, in the presence of oxygen, could ignite a fire. Moreover, such tubes are not as easy to manipulate and are not as smooth as conventional, all-plastic tubes.

A fire associated with the use of a laryngoscope was reported by Wegrzynowicz et al. (1992), who stated:

> A twenty-five-year-old man presented for laser ablation of recurrent laryngeal papillomata. History and physical examination were unremarkable other than a 20-pack/yr smoking history, a bushy mustache, and a weight of 129 kg. Anesthesia was induced with thiopental and Fentanyl. Ventilation via mask with oxygen, nitrous oxide, and isoflurane was without difficulty. Vecuronium was given to provide relaxation. The surgeon inserted an adult Dedo laryngoscope, and jet ventilation was instituted with oxygen via a 13-G cannula inserted in the left light-carrier channel of the Dedo laryngoscope. A thumb-controlled valve and 50-psi oxygen powered the jet.
>
> The patient's face and the perioral area were covered with soaking wet towels such that only the barrel of the Dedo laryngoscope was visible. Anesthesia was maintained with thiopental and Fentanyl during jet ventilation. There were no intraoperative problems except for brief periods of decreased hemoglobin oxygen saturation measured by pulse oximetry (S) during some

episodes of apnea that were requested by the surgeon to eliminate movement of the vocal cords.

Near the end of the surgical procedure, the surgeon suddenly yelled "fire", and bright blue and orange flames accompanied by a muffled roar were observed coming up through and around the laryngoscope. Jet ventilation was stopped; the towels were removed and the patient's blazing mustache was extinguished with the wet towels. The surgeon, who was in a great deal of pain, noted that the latex glove had been burned away from two of the fingertips of his right hand. The Dedo laryngoscope was removed, and bag-and-mask ventilation was commenced. Subsequent rigid bronchoscopy revealed no carbonaceous material in the trachea, and except for evidence of lasering, the glottis was normal. Muscle relaxation was reversed and the patient was awakened. Recovery from anesthesia was otherwise unremarkable.

The patient suffered second-degree burns to his right upper lip and nasal rim. These were treated with 1 percent silver sulfadiazine (Silvadine) and healed over the next two weeks without further incident. The only other evidence of airway fire was burned nasal hair. The surgeon suffered second-degree burns to the right index and middle fingers that were severe enough to prevent him from operating for a week.

This patient experienced an unusual complication. An errant laser strike on the surgeon's latex glove ignited the glove, producing hot volatile fuel that was entrained by the jet ventilator. Combustion of the vaporized latex accelerated dramatically in the oxygen-enriched atmosphere of the airway. The gaseous products of combustion escaped through either the patient's nose or mouth and in turn ignited his mustache, despite the "protective" wet drapes. It would be impossible to determine to what degree the patient's mustache contributed to his facial burns, or whether combustion alone under the drapes would have been adequate to cause the degree of injury sustained.

4.11 ECRI Alert

The Emergency Care Research Institute (ECRI) brought the hazards of endotracheal tube fires to the attention of the medical community in 1990 by publishing the results of tests on four types of tracheal tubes exposed to oxygen and laser irradiation. The two types that were found acceptable were constructed of (1) stainless steel and (2) aluminum and silicone rubber. Those types that were found to be unacceptable were made of polyvinylchloride (PVC) and aluminum and silicone rubber. The criterion for unacceptability was ignition by the laser beam under typical surgical operating conditions. It is interesting to observe that the aluminum/silicone rubber tube made by one manufacturer passed the test while that made with the same material produced by another manufacturer did not, clearly indicating a design difference. In the investigation of such accidents the indications and contraindications in the package insert should be consulted.

Because of the incidence of tracheal tube fires induced by electrosurgical sparks or a laser beam, a variety of fire-resistant endotracheal tubes have been developed, ranging from flexible metal tubes, metal oxide dispersed in the tubing, to tubes wrapped with overlapping, adhesive-backed aluminum foil ribbon. The flexible, stainless-steel endotracheal tube was described by Norton and DeVos (1978). The device was made from strip wound hose using stainless steel or, as an alternative, wire-wound square spring. The tube was wire brushed or matte finished to diminish laser-light reflection into the surgeon's field of vision.

It should be noted that the term fire resistant does not mean fireproof. Whereas, an all metal flexible endotracheal tube may be fireproof and it will not burn; however, it can still cause injury if it carries electrosurgical current. Likewise, if an intense laser beam strikes repeatedly, it will become heated and can cause thermal injury to adjacent tissues.

Flexible metal endotracheal tubes are more difficult to insert than plastic or rubber tubes. For this reason, plastic or rubber tubes have been spirally wrapped with an overlapping layer of aluminum foil to make them fire resistant. Endotracheal tubes are made of silicone rubber, polyvinylchloride (PVC) or rubber. If wrapping is to be applied, ECRI (1990) recommended the following procedure: Wrap only rubber tubes; avoid silicone tubes, which lose their structural integrity if burned. Also, do not use PVC tubes, which are slightly more ignitable, soften with the heat of a fire, and produce gases that are more toxic than those produced by burning red rubber. Select a tube suitable for the patient, accounting for the increased diameter due to the tape. Wrap the tape in an overlapping spiral, starting from just above the cuff and proceeding toward the machine end. Overlap the spirals by one-third to one-half of the tape width to provide good protection and still allow for some flexure of the tube. This wrapping pattern presents a relatively smooth surface for intubation, but an abrasive surface can damage the mucosa during extubation. The tube should be allowed to retain its manufactured shape.

ECRI correctly points out that adhesive-backed aluminum-foil tape is not a medical product because it has not been approved by the FDA. Although, most metal wrapping affords fire resistance, it also adulterates the product, making it not what the manufacturer intended. If an accident occurs and a lawsuit is filed, the manufacturer can argue that his product was misused and adulterated. In such a case, the hospital or physician may be liable, despite performing an act designed to improve patient safety. Fortunately, fire-resistant endotracheal tubes are becoming more available. However, each type is designed with a view to use with a certain type of surgical instrument. As yet there is no laser-resistant tube for use with all laser types.

It should be noted that the inflatable cuff and usually the tip beyond it are unprotected. Laser-beam puncture of the cuff is not uncommon. Some protection is afforded by inflating the cuff with saline.

4.12 Anesthesia Gas Mixtures for Use with Lasers

A. General

To reduce the laser-induced fire hazard, yet retain the use of a polyvinylchloride (PVC) cuffed endotracheal tube, Pashayan et al. (1988) developed an anesthesia protocol using helium and oxygen, without nitrous oxide. The protocol was designed for airway surgery using the CO_2 laser. In addition to the nonflammable anesthetic gas, the inspired oxygen was equal to or less than 40 percent and the helium concentration was equal to or greater than 60 percent. Careful monitoring of the oxygen concentration with an analyzer was required.

During a five-year period when this protocol was used, 148 patients underwent 523 laryngotracheal procedures according to the helium protocol for CO_2 laser resection of tissue, the number of procedures per year increasing from six in 1982 to 149 in 1986. Of the 523 procedures, the tracheas of 233 patients were intubated through tracheostomy stomas, and 290 patients had orotracheal intubation. The majority of the procedures were performed on patients younger than fifteen years of age (n = 360), all but twelve of whom suffered from juvenile papillomatosis or subglottic stenosis. Although thirteen records indicated that the tracheal tube had been exposed to the laser beam and had to be changed due to leaking cuffs, there were no reports of tracheal tube fires or tracheal burns. There were no cases in which the surgeon requested that the laser power density be raised above the limits set in the protocol.

Regarding the laser-power density and manner of delivery, Pashayan et al. recommended:

> The helium protocol for laryngotracheal surgery requires that carbon dioxide laser output be limited to 10 W and that a beam spot size of 0.8mm (power density less than 1,992 W/cm^2) be used; also, the surgical technique must al-

low tissue to cool by delivering the beam in a series of repeated, brief bursts. The power density we specify is adequate to resect most tracheal pathologic tissue; in fact, power density of 1,000–2,000 W/cm^2 is considered advisable in laryngeal microsurgery to increase precision, promote hemostasis, and prevent burns to normal tissue adjacent to the pathologic tissue.

B. Flammability index

To enable comparison of the combustibility of endotracheal tubes (ETT) on the one hand and anesthetic gas mixtures on the other, Wolf and Simpson (1987) conducted tests which resulted in the creation of a flammability index. Three types of ETT (polyvinyl chloride, red rubber and silicone rubber) were tested. Each ETT was mounted in a glass chamber (7.5 cm diameter × 60 cm high) containing glass beads (3–10 mm diam.) at the bottom where the gasses were admitted; the beads constituted a mixing bed. Also in the chamber was a propane torch used to ignite the tracheal tube, after which the torch was extinguished. Contact time with the ETT was 3–5 seconds and the flame was 3–5 mm. Starting with oxygen, the diluent gas flow was increased by 1 percent increments until the flame was extinguished. The flammability index was defined as O_2 flow/(O_2 flow plus diluent gas flow). The combustibility tests used nitrogen and helium in oxygen and nitrous oxide in nitrogen; nitrogen and helium do not support combustion. Table 4.2 presents the results.

The data in Table 4.2 show that helium and nitrogen are equally effective as diluents. In their 1989 paper, Simpson and Wolf stated that the flammability of ETTs in nitrogen is the same as that for helium in an oxygen mixture. Fur-

Table 4.2
Flammability Indices*

ETT	O_2/N_2 Index	O_2/He Index	N_2O/N_2 Index
PVC	0.263	0.263	0.450
RR	0.176	0.194	0.374
SI	0.189	0.194	0.414

PVC = polyvinyl chloride
RR = red rubber
SI = silicone rubber

*Data from Wolf and Simpson (1987) and Simpson and Wolf (1989) ther they showed that the flammability of the three types of ETT tubes in a nitrous oxide-oxygen atmosphere decreased linearly with a decrease in the concentration of nitrous oxide and that for all such mixtures, the red-rubber ETT was more flammable than the silicone rubber ETT, which was more flammable than the ETT made of PVC. They also stated that a mixture of 50 percent oxygen and 50 percent nitrous oxide will render all three types of ETT flammable, whereas a mixture of 23 percent oxygen and 5 percent nitrous oxide in nitrogen will render PVC ETTs nonflammable and the red-rubber and silicone-rubber ETTs flammable.

Simpson and Wolf (1986) investigated the flammability of presently used esophageal stethoscopes, nasogastric tubes, feeding tubes and nasopharyngeal airways in oxygen and nitrous-oxide atmospheres with nitrogen as the diluent. The method used to determine the flammability index was that described above. They found that the oxidant O_2 index of flammability (in nitrogen) for esophageal stethoscopes was 0.218, for sump nasogastric tubes 0.229, for enteric feeding tubes 0.192, for plastic nasopharyngeal airways 0.196, and for rubber nasopharyngeal airways 0.172. The oxidant N_2O index of flammability (in nitrogen) for esophageal stethoscopes was 0.430, for sump nasogastric tubes 0.430, for enteric feeding tubes 0.375, for plastic nasopharyngeal airways 0.415, and for rubber nasopharyngeal airways 0.366. These data show that all of these tubes are flammable in oxygen and nitrous oxide.

4.13 Blood-Pressure Monitoring Incidents

In a large study of patients undergoing general anesthesia in Australia, Cockings et al. (1993) analyzed failures in blood-pressure monitoring in 1,256 incident reports. Blood-pressure monitoring incidents ranked fourth after pulse oximetry, capnography and low-pressure alarms. Of the 1,256 incident reports, twenty were associated with blood-pressure monitoring; Table 4.3 summarizes the results.

A review of Table 4.3 reveals that there were twenty-three incidents of failure, which amounts to 1.6 percent; of these only three were due to device failure. However, a falsely low or high reading can cause the anesthesiologist to make an incorrect decision or no decision.

An unusual oscillatory signal, appearing on a pulmonary-artery pressure record was reported by Kleinman and Frey (1998). They stated that a fifty-seven-year-old patient underwent a routine anesthesia for elective coronary artery bypass surgery. Prior to induction of anesthesia, a 7.5 F, five-lumen ther-

Table 4.3
Incidents of Misleading Readings from Blood-Pressure Monitors

Type	Number
Manual	
Overestimation	1
Non-invasive Measurement	
Delayed failure due to profound hypotension	4
Falsely high readings	4
Falsely low readings	4
Invasive Methods	
Loss of power supply	3
Incorrect calibration	3
Broken transducer	2
Incorrect use of display	1
artery pressure (due to subclavian artery stenosis)	1

*Data from Cockings et al. 1993

modilution pulmonary artery catheter was passed without difficulty. After the catheter was positioned into the pulmonary artery, an oscillatory signal was noted on the pulmonary artery trace as well as on the central venous trace and ascribed to 60-cycle AC electrical interference. However, the signal was not present in the ECG trace. The anesthesia and surgery proceeded uneventfully.

Postoperatively the grounding and the equipment were checked and found to be normal. This careful checking was performed because of the risk of current being carried by the fluid in the catheter. Careful review of the pressure recordings revealed that the frequency of the oscillations was 20Hz, not 60Hz, the frequency of the power line. Further investigation revealed that the operating room table, to which the transducer holders were attached, was vibrating. Directly under the operating room floor (which formed the ceiling of the hospital's sub-basement) and positioned directly under the operating table ran a large metal duct, that is part of the airhandling system for the operating room. Large volumes of air enter the duct when called for by the operating room thermostat. During these periods of air exchange the duct vibrates quite noticeably. The duct itself is attached to the bottom of the cement operating room floor by metal straps screwed directly into the floor. No rubber or plastic washers are used to dampen any vibrations. The frequency of these vibrations recorded directly at the transducer holder, which is attached to the operating room table by a transducer (not attached to a patient), showed that the frequency matched the frequencies recorded on the central venous pressure trace and pulmonary artery tracing. Therefore in this case, there was no hazard to the patient.

4.14 Impedance Cardiography Incidents

Stroke volume and cardiac output are measured noninvasively by injecting a low-intensity, high-frequency current via neck and abdomen electrodes. Two sensing electrodes, placed between the current-injecting electrodes, detect a cardiac-induced, pulsatile impedance change that can be processed to obtain stroke volume and cardiac output when blood resistivity is known. Without knowing blood resistivity, impedance cardiography is useful for tracking changes in cardiac output.

Using impedance cardiography to monitor a patient with an implanted pacemaker during surgery, Aldrete et al. (1995) reported that the patient's heart rate increased to 120/min. Drug therapy failed to reduce it and the ECG showed pacemaker spikes at 120/min. When the impedance cardiograph was disconnected, the heart rate returned to 72/min. The event occurred a second time.

Worthy of note is the fact that the 2.5 mA, 70-kHz current applied for impedance cardiography gained access to the pacemaker via the pacing electrodes, which are virtually in line with the 70-kHz current path. The pacemaker was of the programmable type and had been operating properly for eleven months prior to the event. It is clear that the 70-kHz current caused the pacemaker rate to increase from 72 to 120 beats/min. Neither the instruction manual for the pacemaker, nor that for the impedance cardiograph identified this hazard.

4.15 Muscle Relaxant Monitoring Incidents

Frequently a muscle relaxant is administered during general anesthesia to facilitate surgery. Anesthesiologists can monitor the degree of muscle relaxation by stimulating a motor nerve with skin-surface electrodes and monitor the ensuing muscle contraction visually. Typically a few stimuli per sec are used and the motion of the twitching muscle is observed. Usually the ulnar nerve at the elbow is stimulated and finger twitching is monitored visually.

With the scenario just described, an incident occurred with a normally functioning pulse oximeter. Block and Stahl (1995) were monitoring oxygen saturation in an anesthetized patient. The control values were 96 percent saturation and 80 heartbeats/min. The efficacy of a muscle relaxant was assessed by applying electrical stimuli at 1/sec to a pair of electrodes placed across the elbow to cause the fingers of the hand to twitch. Immediately the pulse oximeter showed a saturation of 73 percent. The stimulator was turned off and the saturation returned to 98 percent. In explaining this incorrect indication of saturation, the authors stated:

> The technology of pulse oximetry depends upon the assumption that blood is the only substance that pulsates between the emitter and the detector of the oximeter. In the case presented here, the muscular contractions evoked by the nerve stimulator simulated a "pulse" at a frequency of sixty "beats"/min. These contractions caused obvious motion of the finger, which probably resulted in blood volume shifts larger than those caused by the small pulsations of the heartbeat in the finger. Alternatively, the contractions may have produced small motions of slippage between the oximeter probe and the finger.

In the foregoing case, had the authors not been so vigilant they might have increased the oxygen flow in an attempt to raise the saturation from its incorrectly indicated value of 73 percent. The result would have been more oxygen in the environment of the patient with an increase in the risk of fire or explosion. The obvious solution to this problem is to place the oximeter on a finger on the opposite hand.

4.16 Peripheral Nerve Stimulator Incidents

An interesting case of skin burn associated with the use of a peripheral nerve neuromuscular stimulator (NMS) to assess the degree of neuromuscular blockade was reported by Cooper et al. (1990) who stated:

> As each of twelve new anesthesia machines was being prepared for service, a new constant-current peripheral nerve stimulator was installed in the instrumentation pod. Soon after introduction of these anesthesia machines, it was noted by the biomedical technicians that frequent battery changes were required. This was relatively time-consuming because it involved disassembly of the instrument. To simplify this task a biomedical technician installed a battery holder for the two 9-V batteries on the back of the case of the instrument. Following the modification the device was replaced in the anesthesia machine instrument panel and tested for performance and safety, including DC voltage between the output terminals.

> Several weeks after the first NMS was modified, a sixty-eight-year-old man arrived in the operating room for elective coronary revascularization. Following routine preanesthetic medication and hemodynamic assessment, general anesthesia was induced with fentanyl 100 μg/kg and enflurane 0.5 percent in oxygen. Neuromuscular blockade was established initially with vecuronium 0.2 mg/kg and subsequently maintained with metocurine 0.2 mg/kg in the prebypass period, and then d-tubocurarine 0.3 mg/kg during the rewarming phase of cardiopulmonary bypass.
>
> A disposable, electrosurgical dispersive electrode with conductive adhesive was placed on the left side of the lower back. During the surgical procedure a Bovie electrosurgical unit (ESU) was used intermittently. Prior to initiation of cardiopulmonary bypass, the NMS was applied over the right ulnar nerve proximal to the first volar crease of the wrist via a disposable dual-element foam electrode. The monitor was turned on five times during the operation [for brief determinations of blockade] via train-of-four measurements (a series of four 0.20-ms pulses at 500-ms intervals).
>
> Following an uneventful procedure and prior to moving the patient from the operating table, the stimulating electrode was removed. A 1 cm^2 full-thickness burn was noted to be present under the negative electrode, with a slight reddening of the skin under the positive electrode. The skin under the ESU dispersive electrode appeared normal. The skin burn was treated with debridement of eschar on two occasions and seven days of Silvadene dressings followed by ten days of b.i.d. wet-to-dry dressings at home. This treatment resulted in complete healing without requirement for skin grafting.

The incident was thoroughly investigated and electrosurgical current was eliminated as a cause of the skin injury. The ESU and the NMS unit were tested and found to be functioning normally. They continued by stating:

> The NMS was then reinstalled in the anesthesia machine and safety and functional testing were repeated. Although the NMS functioned correctly, under some conditions of tightening of the mounting bolt, a voltage equal to the battery voltage appeared between the negative output terminal and the chassis of the anesthesia machine. Close inspection suggested that the positive battery terminal was contacting the inside of the rear panel of the anesthesia machine.

Additional extensive tests with a chicken carcass revealed that the injury was due to direct current.

4.17 Somatosensory Evoked Potentials (SSEP) Monitoring Incidents

During anesthesia, it is useful to monitor the integrity of the central nervous system (brain and spinal cord). To do so, requires the application of an electrical stimulus to skin-surface electrodes and to record the brain response with appropriately placed scalp electrodes on the opposite side of the head. Because the evoked signal is small and is time-locked to the stimulus, computer averaging is used to enhance the response. Figure 4.8 illustrates use of the method with stimulating electrodes applied to the wrist and recording electrodes applied to the scalp over the area representing the hand on the brain surface (cortex). The stimulus frequency is low (a few/sec) and a typical evoked response is shown in Figure 4.8, along with the nerve pathways to the brain. A reduction in the amplitude, or disappearance of the response, indicates impaired function of the central nervous system.

The following accident reported by Merritt et al. (1988) is typical. The stated:

> The patient was a seventy-eight-year-old lady who was medicated for Parkinson's disease and suffered a fall, requiring surgery to stabilize the first two cervical vertebrae. One and one-half years earlier, she received a dual-chamber monopolar pacemaker (DDD). SSEP recording was instituted with electrodes at the ankle to stimulate the left posterior tibial nerve at 3.3 stimuli per sec. Increasing the stimulator output up to 300 volts produced no SSEP, but did produce a tachycardia of 100/min, which disappeared when the stimulator was turned off. SSEP recording was attempted using the upper extremity with the same result. The SSEP equipment was checked and found to be functional, except that the stimulus frequency was 5/sec (i.e., 300/min). In both cases, SSEP recordings could not be made and recording was abandoned and the operation was continued.

Fortunately, ECG and arterial pressure were monitored throughout the procedure and allowed explanation of the incident. They stated that the mechanism:

> Resides with the mistaken interpretation by the pacemaker of the SSEP stimulus once the energy delivered by the latter exceeds the sensitivity threshold of the atrial channel. Although the transcutaneous stimuli occur at the rate of 300/min, the rate of ventricular pacing is only 100/min.

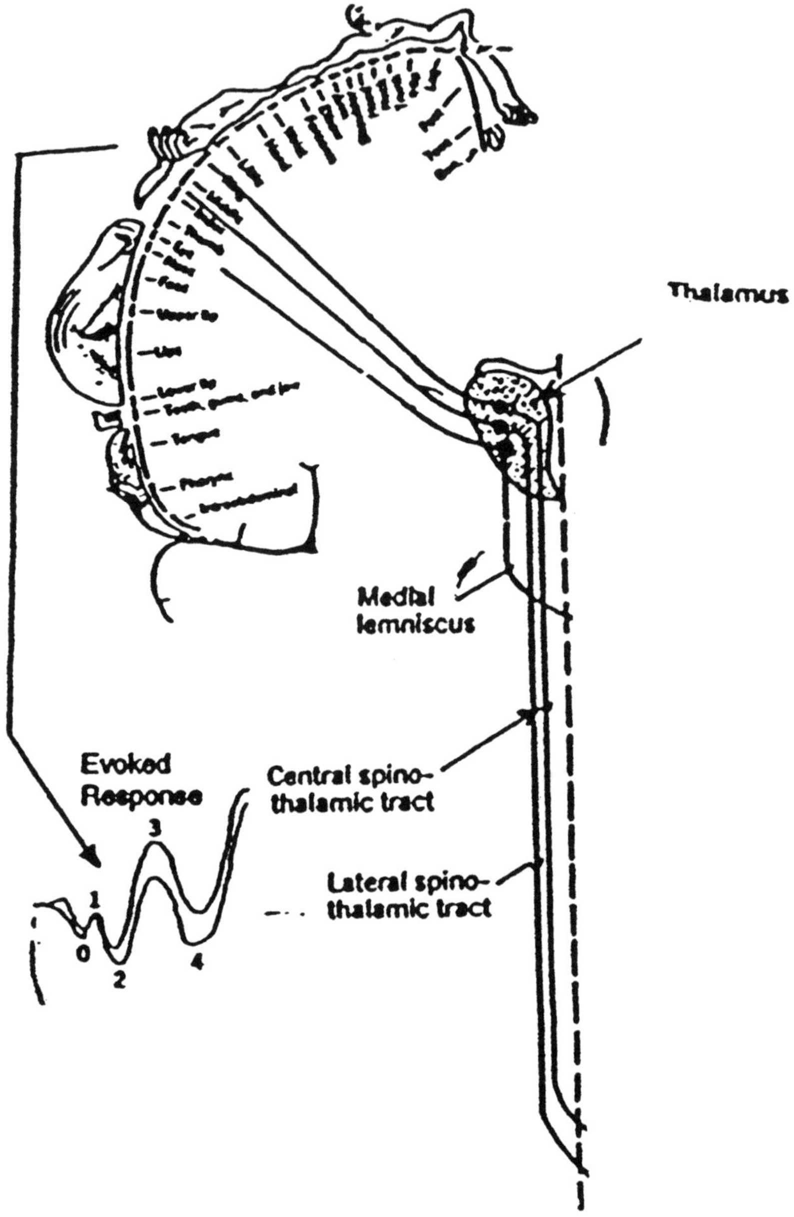

Figure 4.8 *Pathways from the peripheral sense organs to the cortex and the topographical distribution of sensation along the cortex with Penfield's homunculus. Also shown are the stimulating electrodes on the wrist and the SSEPs recorded.*

They explained that it was the refractory period setting in the pacemaker that allowed it to pace for every third SSEP stimulus. The authors could find no reason for failure to obtain SSEPs and correctly pointed out that monopolar pacemakers are the most sensitive to interference due to the large separation between the active (intracardiac) electrode and the return electrode (pacemaker case).

A different type of incident associated with SSEP recording was investigated by the author. An anesthetized patient was prepared for surgery with two stimulating electrodes behind the knee and recording electrodes on the scalp to detect somatosensory-evoked potentials (SSEPs) during surgery. The patient was draped and the equipment was connected to the electrodes. During early surgery, the equipment functioned normally. However, somehow the stimulating electrode cable became disconnected from the stimulator. The electrodes were reconnected, not to the stimulus output, but to the battery-test jacks which were connected to an internal 90-V battery. The SSEPs were no longer recordable and at the end of the operation, when the patient was being prepared for transport to the ward, a very large electrochemical "burn" was found at the site of the two stimulating electrodes.

Tests carried out later with the stimulating electrodes placed on a thick slice of steak and connected to the battery-test jacks confirmed the possibility that the injury could have occurred this way. It was also argued that the injury was due to electrosurgical current, but this was not proven.

The foregoing case raises several important questions. For example, was the accident due to a lack of training of the technician who reconnected the stimulating electrodes? Did the stimulator have a design defect that allowed this inappropriate connection to be made? Finally, could this accident have been foreseen in terms of the possibility of connecting the stimulating electrodes to the battery-test jacks? The answers are obvious.

References

AAMI—Association for the Advancement of Medical Instrumentation. 3330 Washington Boulevard, Arlington, VA 22201-4598.

Aldrete A, Brown C, Daily J et al. Pacemaker malfunction due to microcurrent injection from abioimpedance noninvasive cardiac output monitor. J. Clin. Mon. 1995, 1(2):131–133.

American National Standards Institute ANSI Standard for the safe use of lasers Z136.1. 1986, Laser Inst. Amer. Toledo OH 43623.

American Society of Anesthesiologists. Newsletter. 1986, 50:12, 12,. 520 N. Northwest Highway, Park Ridge, IL 60068-2573.

American Society for Testing and Materials. Standard specification for cuffed and uncuffed tracheal tubes (ASTM F1242-89) Philadelphia.

Andrews JJ, Johnston RV, Bee DE and Arens JF. Photodeactivation of ethyl violet. A potential hazard of sodasorb. Anesthesiology. 1990, 72:59–64.

Arens JF. Pro: there is nothing wrong with old anesthesia machines and equipment. J. Clin. Mon. 1996, 12:37–38.

Australia: Therapeutic Goods Administration, PO Box 100, Woden, ACT 2606, Australia.

Bailey MK, Bromley HR, Allison JG et al. Electrocautery induced airway fire during tracheostomy. Anesth. & Analg. 1990, 71:702–704.

Block FE and Stahl D. Interference in a pulse oximeter from a nerve stimulator. J. Clin Mon. 1995, 11:392–393.

Burgess CG and LeJune FE. Endotracheal tube ignition during laser surgery of the larynx. Arch. Otolaryngol. 1979, 105:561–562.

Cheney FW, Posner KL, Caplan RA et al. Burns from warming devices in anesthesia. Anesthesiology. 1994, 80:806–810.

Chino MH and Nagel EL. Thermal burns caused by warming blankets in the operating room. Anesthesiol. 1968. 29(1):149–150.

Cockings JGL, Webb RK, Klepper ID et al. Blood-pressure monitoring-applications and limitations. Anesth. Int. Care. 1993, 21:565–569.

Cooper JB, DeCesare R and D'Ambra M. An engineering critical incident: direct-current burn from a neuromuscular stimulator. Anesthesiology. 1990, 73:168–172.

Detmer MD, Chandra P and Cohen PJ. Occurrence of hypercarbia due to an unusual failure of anesthetic equipment. Anesthesiology. 1980, 52:278–279.

Dorsch JA and Dorsch SE. Understanding Anesthesia Equipment. 3rd ed. 1994. Williams & Wilkins, Baltimore.

Downing TP and Johnson DG. Excision of subglottic stenoses with the urethral resectoscope. J. Pediatr. Surg. 1979, 14(3):252–257.

ECRI Health Devices Alert. Apr. 23, 1999 (34R4).

ECRI-Health Devices 1990, Plymouth Meeting, PA.

ECRI. Laser Resistant Endotracheal Tube and Wraps. 1990 (April), 19(4):112–139.

FDA. Center for Devices and Radiological Health. Manufacturer and User Facility Device Experience Database [online]. Rockville (MD): FDA; 1998 May 22.

FDA. MAUDE report 19 June 1990. US Food and Drug Administration CDRH.

Feldman JM, Pugh G, Gravenstein JS et al. Automated data presentation using synthetic voice. J. Clin. Mon. 1985, 1:283.

Geddes LA. Heritage of the tissue bed oximeter. IEEE. Eng. Med. Biol. 1997, Mar-Apr. 87–91.

Hirshman CA and Smith J. Indirect ignition of the endotracheal tube during carbon dioxide laser surgery. Arch. Otolaryngol. 1980, 106:639–641.

Johnson DG and Stewart DR. Management of acquired tracheal obstructions in infancy. J. Pediatr. Surg. 1975, 10:709–719.

Kestin IG, Miller BR and Lockhart CH. Auditing alarms during anesthesia monitoring. Anesthesiology. 1988, 69(1):106–109.

Kleinman B and Frey K. Artifact mistaken for electrical interference recorded from a pulmonary artery catheter. J Clinical Monitoring and Computing. 1998 14(5): 361–363.

McIntyre JWR. Ergonomics: anesthetists' use of auditory a larms in the operating room. J. Clin. Mon. Comput. 1982, 2:47–55.

Medical Malpractice Verdicts, Settlements and Experts. 1999, Feb: 15(2):48–9.

Medical Malpractice Verdicts, Settlements and Experts. 1999, 15(10):15.

Merritt WT, Brinker JA and Beattie C. Pacemaker mediated tachycardia induced by intraoperative somatosensory evoked potential stimuli. Anesthesiol. 1988, 69:766–768.

Mills GH and Ralph SJ. Burns due to pulse oximetry. Anesthesial. 1992. 47(3):275–276.

Murphy KG, Secunda JA and Rockoff MA. Severe burns from a pulse oximeter. Anesthesiology. 1990. 73(2):350–352.

Norton ML and DeVos P. Endotracheal tube for laser surgery of the larynx. Ann. Otol. 1978, 87:554–557.

Nunn BJ and Rosewarne FA. Expiratory valve failure. Anaesth. Intensive Care. 1990, 18:273–274.

Pamaar CG, Ahmad I and Marsh NJ. Accidental burn during tonsillectomy. Anesthesiology. 1992, 76:869–870.

Panday CK, Rani A, Soivastave K et al. Thermal injury with pulse oximeter probe in hypothermic patient. Pulse oximeter probe burn in hypothermia. Carodian Journ. Anesth. 1999, 46(9):908–909.

Pashayan AG and Gravenstein JS. Helium retards endotracheal tube fires from carbon dioxide lasers. Anesthesiology. 1985. 62:274–277.

Pashayan AG, Gravenstein JS, Gassisi NJ et al. The helium protocol for laryngotracheal operations with CO_2 laser. Anesthesiol. 1988, 68:801–804.

Parry TM, Jewkes DA and Smith M. A sticking flutter valve. Anaesthesia (American Society of Anesthesiologists [ASA]. 1991, 46:229.

Patterson RD. Guidelines for auditory warning systems in civil aircraft. Paper 82017. Aviation Authority. London, England. 1982.

Pettersen B, Kongsgurd U and Aune H. Skin injury in an infant with pulse oximeter. Brit. Journ. Anesthesia. 1992, 69:204–205.

Podraza AG, Salem MR, Joseph NJ and Brenchley JL. Rebreathing due to incompetent unidirectional valves in the circle absorber system. Anesthesiology 1991, 75: A422.

Rita L and Seleny F. Endotracheal tube ignition during laryngeal surgery with resectoscope. Anesthesiology. 1982, 56:60–61.

Samuels SJ. Letter to the editor. Anesthesiol. 1986, 64:128.

Satwicz PR and Shagrin JM. The selection of anesthetic equipment. Int. Anesthesiol. Clin. 1981, 19(2):97–111.

Schaaf C and Black FE. Evaluation of alarm sounds in the operating room. J. Clin. Mon. 1989, 5(4):300–301.

Scott SM. Thermal blanket injury in the operating room. Ach. Surg. 1967, 94:181.

Simpson J and Wolf GL. Endotracheal tube fire ignited by pharyngeal electrocautery. Anethesiology. 1986, 63:76–77.

Simpson JI and Wolf GL. Helium does not reduce endotracheal tube flammability. Anesth. & Analg. 1989, 68:S1–S231.

Simpson JI and Wolf GL. Flammability of esophageal stethoscopes, nasogastric tubes, feeding tubes and nasophargngeal airways in oxygen and nitrous oxide-enriched atmospheres. Anesth. & Analg. 1988, 67:1093–1095.

Sloan TB. Finger injury by an oxygen saturation monitor probe. Anesthesiology. 1988 Jun, 68(6):936–938.

Snow JC, Kripke BJ, Strong MS et al. Anesthesia for carbon dioxide laser microsurgery on the larynx and trachea. Anesth & Analg. 1974, 53:507–512.

Snow JC, Norton ML, Tejinder SS et al. Fire hazard during CO_2 laser microsurgery on the larynx and trachea. Anesth. Analg. 1976, 55(1):146–147.

Snow JC, Norton ML, Saluja TS and Estanislao A. F. Fire hazard during CO_2 laser microsurgery on the larynx and trachea. Anesth Analg. 1979, 55:146–147.

Strong MS. Editorial comment. Arch. Otolaryngol. 1980, 106:641.

Weinger MB. Proposed new alarm standards may make a bad situation worse. Anesthesiology. 1991, 74:791.

Wegrzynowicz E, Jensen NF, Pearson K et al. Airway fire during jet ventrilation for laser excision of vocal cord papilloma. Anesthesiology. 1992, 76:468–469.

Wolf GL and Simpson JI. Flammability of endotracheal tubes in oxygen and nitrous oxide enriched atmosphere. Anesthesiology. 1987, 67:236–239.

Yoshiya I, Shimada Y and Tanaha K. Spectrophotometric monitoring of arterial oxygen saturation in the fingertip. Mod. Biol. Eng. and Comput. 1980, 18(1):27–32).

Chapter 5

Catheters and Catheter Electrodes

Synopsis

5.1 Introduction

Catheters have been used in medicine for therapy and diagnosis since Egyptian medicine in the time of the Pharaohs (see Geddes and Geddes 1993). Modern sterilized disposable catheters appeared in the 1950s. Catheter electrodes appeared with the evolution of the cardiac pacemaker in the early 1960s. Catheters are placed in every body opening, as well as through surgically made openings. Blood vessels, ducts, and body cavities are all catheterized for sampling fluids, pressures, or to inject substances. Catheters are also used to remove materials such as stones. Electric current can gain access to internal body sites via the conductivity of the fluid in a catheter. Catheters can induce clots and emboli; they can fracture, break, and migrate. Catheters are also used to deploy stents, devices for holding open dilated blood vessels and ducts.

5.2 The F Scale for Catheter Diameter

The F (French) scale for specifying the outer diameter of a catheter derives from the use of catheters in urology. Widening of urethral strictures was well established by the mid-1800s. Not surprisingly, it was desirable to identify the outer diameter of catheters so that successively larger diameter catheters could be passed into the urethra. With some national pride, there arose three diameter scales: the French devised by Charriere (1803–1876), the English and the Scottish, all being created by manufacturers in these countries. The three scales were quite different; Charriere's was based on the one-third millimeter, (i.e. a size-one Charriere catheter had a diameter of one-third millimeter). The English scale was based on one sixty-fourth inch (i.e. 0.397 mm, or slightly larger than one-third millimeter). The Scottish scale was coarser, being one and one half times larger than the English scale. Because the Charriere (F) scale provided uniform one-third millimeter diameter increments, it survived and the outer diameter of a catheter in mm is its F-number divided by 3.

The lumen diameters of thick and thin-walled catheters appear in Table 5.2 elsewhere in this chapter.

5.3 Intravascular Catheter Incidents

A. Catheter whip

When recording pressure with a fluid-filled catheter connected to a pressure transducer, occasionally spurious oscillations appear on the blood-pressure recording. Figure 5.1A illustrates a typical arterial pressure record from a normal subject and Figure 5.1B is a record showing spurious waves. Such a recording

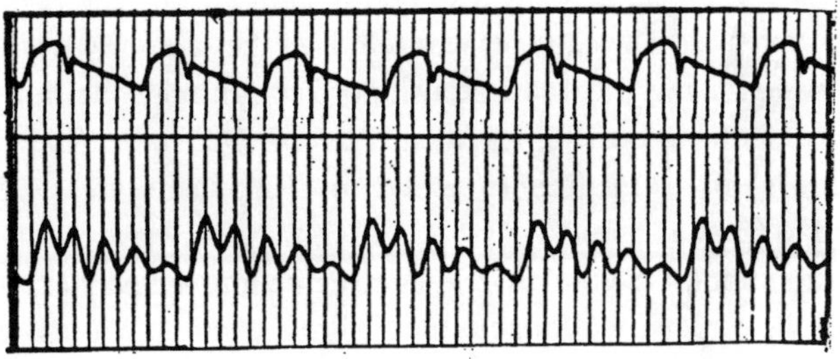

Figure 5.1 *In (a) is shown a normal arterial pressure record made with a fluid-filled catheter connected to a pressure transducer. In (b) is shown the same recording made with a long fluid-filled catheter that was flailing in the artery, thereby producing spurious oscillations known as "catheter whip."*

could lead to considerable confusion and could make the observer think that there is something wrong with the patient—or the equipment.

The phenomenon shown in Figure 5.1B is known as "catheter whip" and can arise when a long, fluid-filled catheter flails in an artery. The bending and flailing of the fluid-filled catheter produces accelerative forces in the fluid therein which manifests itself as low-frequency oscillations. In this case, there is nothing wrong with the patient or the equipment.

B. Catheter pinchoff or clavicular crush

Accompanying the use of venous-access catheters for chronic delivery of medications are a variety of hazards such as blockage, breakage, embolization, and infection. Careful catheter management has minimized such events; however, a few still occur. Fracture of a venous-access catheter was reported by Prager and Hintzberg (1987):

> On May 23, 1984, a subcutaneous venous access device (manufacturer name) was implanted over the left anterior chest wall. No sutures were used to stabilize the catheter to the subclavian vein. The implantation site was overlying the second left rib laterally and inferior to the lateral one-third of the left clavicle. Subsequently, the patient received multidrug chemotherapy and had a documented complete response to the drug treatment program. On March 7, 1985, ten months after port placement, the patient experienced the sudden onset of bilaterial chest pain. Physical examination revealed a patient in evident pain with an unremarkable subcutaneous disc access noted over the left

> anterior chest wall. Chest x-ray revealed an embolized catheter in the left pulmonary artery area. The catheter was removed the same day from the left pulmonary artery, using a percutaneous approach through the right subclavian vein. The embolized catheter fragment was retrieved under fluoroscopy guidance, using a No. 8.3 medium [manufacturer] catheter with a 0.25 guide wire fashioned to form a snare.
>
> Examination of the broken catheter segment revealed that the embolized portion of the catheter was not circular in cross-section, but instead was elliptical in configuration. When one of the catheter pieces was rotated 90° relative to the mating half, the difference in cross-section shape was readily apparent.

Later, this type of compression fracture became known as "pinchoff" or "clavicular crush" and it was attributed to compression of the catheter by the clavicle and first rib. Figure 5.2 shows the anatomic details of the clavicle, first rib, and associated veins. The region where pinchoff can be avoided is identified, along with the recommended catheter-entry region.

This author investigated a similar catheter accident that occurred to a thirty-five-year-old lady who was receiving chronic intravenous drug therapy for cancer through a Groshong-valved catheter, the tip of which had been placed in the superior vena cava. The insertion was made through the left subclavian vein. A venogram showed that the catheter was patent. Sometime later, the patient complained of chest pain, shortness of breath, rapid irregular heart rate, and she was diaphoretic when admitted to the emergency room. Her symptoms were strikingly similar to those of a heart attack. Radiological examination revealed a four-inch segment of broken catheter in the right ventricle. The report stated:

> The patient was brought to the cardiac catheterization laboratory and prepped and draped in sterile fashion. Local anesthesia was obtained over the right femoral vein with 1 percent plain Lidocaine after which a 8 French hemostatis sheath was placed into the right femoral vein by modified Seldinger technique. Next, a four-prong grasping forcep was used to retrieve the catheter fragment under fluoroscopic guidance. The catheter fragment forcep and hemostasis sheath were all removed as one piece. Fluoroscopy demonstrated no residual catheter fragment. Complete hemostasis was achieved by direct pressure over the site for ten minutes. The patient was returned to her room in stable condition.

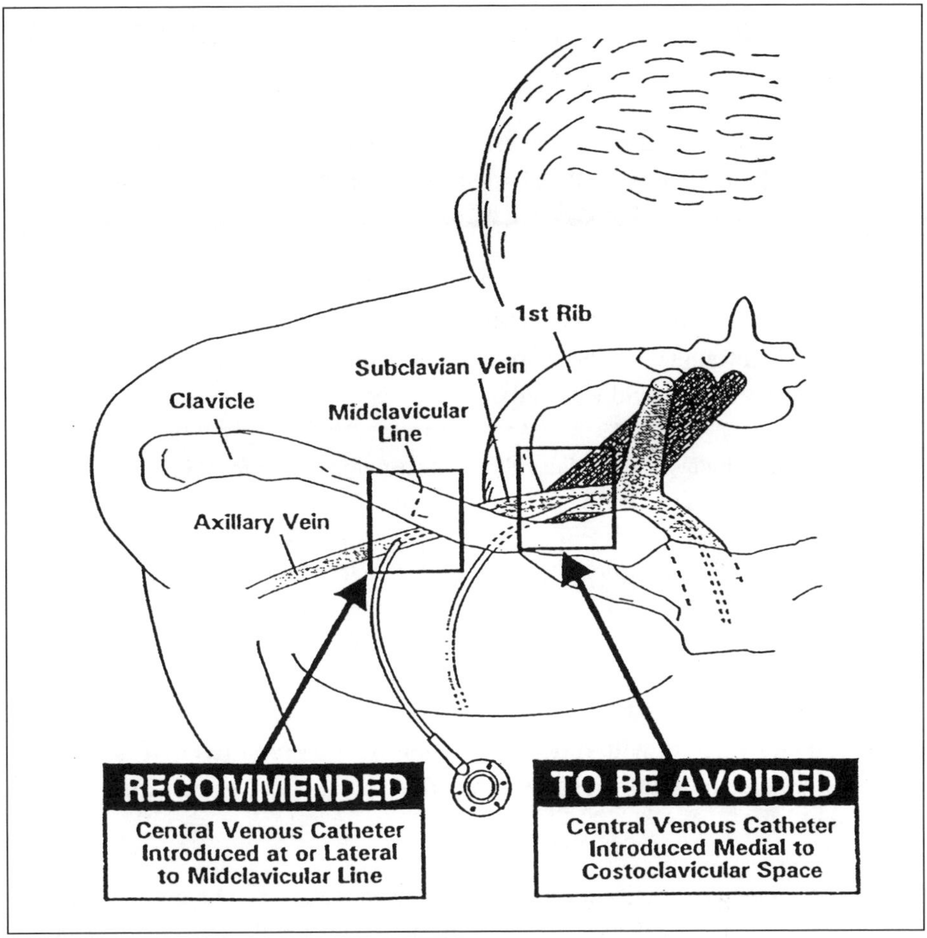

Figure 5.2 *Anatomical details of the clavicle, first rib, and associated veins, identifying recommended catheter entry site and region to be avoided. (Courtesy of Cook Endovascular Leechburg, PA 15656)*

The author had the opportunity to examine the explanted catheter fragment. The piece that broke off was 12.2 cm long and exhibited a pinched or flattened region where it broke. The tip having been originally placed in the superior vena cava, a breakage would cause blood flow to carry the broken segment into the right ventricle. With the continued beating of the heart, the broken segment acted as a mechanical stimulus and produced ectopic beats and runs of tachycardia, which reduced cardiac output leading to reduced coronary perfusion, hence the chest pain.

The manufacturer's instructions carry a warning that identifies catheter pinchoff:

> When placing the catheter in the axillary-subclavian vein, insert the catheter into the vein at a point lateral to the angle between the clavicle and the first rib to avoid pinchoff of the catheter which may cause occlusion, damage, or breakage.

In the manufacturer's instructions, reference was made to a report by Aitken and Minton (1984), who studied forty-eight patients undergoing intravenous chemotherapy, and it stated:

> Four of the patients had partial catheter obstruction owing to a pincher action of the clavicle and first rib. The roentgenographic presence of the pinchoff sign indicates serious potential problems with the central venous Silastic catheter and is an indication for immediate catheter removal and replacement at another site or position. The other catheter entry sites recommended were a more lateral site or entry into the subclavian, cephalic, or internal jugular vein.

A catheter fracture with moderate symptoms was reported by Franey et al. (1988), who stated that thirteen months after subclavian catheter implantation the patient:

> Noted a mild acute discomfort in the subclavian area while playing golf. Saline infusion into the device created pain and swelling in the same region and blood drawing was impossible. Chest x-ray revealed the device in place with one end of the catheter tip in the region of the subclavian vein and a separate segment of the catheter in the right atrium and ventricle. A nuclear medicine study using technetium-99 showed the proximal segment to be outside the vein. The catheter fragment was retrieved via a percutaneous right femoral vein approach using a snare. Examination of the 13.5 cm segment revealed a fish-mouth appearance at the point of fracture.

The report continued:

> As described earlier it is the pinching force between the clavicle and first rib with any shoulder and pectoral girdle movement which causes the catheter to fracture. The patient involved in this case report is an avid golfer. Golf re-

quires a great deal of shoulder and pectoral girdle motion to swing the club. It is this exact motion which is implicated in catheter failure.

Hinke et al. (1990) created a grading scale for the pinchoff syndrome (POS); grade 0 was used to designate no catheter narrowing. If the catheter exhibits bending from a smooth curve, grade 1 is used. Grade 2 identifies narrowing and grade 3 is used for transection and embolization. In a six-year study of 987 implants using Silastic catheters, eleven met the foregoing criteria for the pinchoff syndrome within three weeks of catheter implantation. One patient exhibited grade 3 (fracturing and embolization); the others exhibited grade 1 or 2. The pinchoff incidence in this study was therefore 1.1 percent.

Bach et al. (1991) reported catheter fracture and extravasation:

> A forty-seven-year-old woman had acute myeloid leukemia diagnosed in March 1988. The patient had a Port-A-Cath catheter [manu-facturer's name] implanted medially in the left infraclavicular region before chemotherapy. We inserted the catheter in the space between the clavicle and the first rib and passed it through the subclavian vein and vena cava superior to the entry of the right atrium.

The report continued:

> Ten months later, during infusion of chemotherapy, the patient had paresthesia and severe pains in the left infraclavicular region and paresis of the left upper limb. The infusion was stopped immediately, but clinical evaluation showed no neurologic or cardiovascular deficits, and the symptoms disappeared within a few minutes. Radiography showed the catheter *in sutu*, but contrast injection confirmed our suspicion of catheter damage with leak of contrast in the area of the left costoclavicular ligament. We removed the catheter, and subsequent close examination demonstrated a weak, thin area with a large irregular fissure (incompatible with a cut during its original placement).

A similar catheter fracture was reported by Lafreniere (1991), who stated that, in November 1988:

> A Port-A-Cath was also inserted in the right subclavian vein using a percutaneous technique. A chest x-ray obtained post-operatively confirmed proper positioning of the catheter. Postoperatively, she was placed on high-dose folinic acid and 5-fluorouracil (5-FU) given at monthly intervals until October

1989 when an attempt at flushing her Port-A-Cath created intense pain along the course of the subcutaneous catheter. A chest x-ray done at that time revealed that the catheter had fractured at the junction of the first rib and clavicle and that the distal segment had embolized into the right atrium. The embolized segment was easily removed percutaneously through the right femoral vein; two weeks later a new Port-A-Cath was inserted in the left subclavian vein and removal of the right venous access was also carried out. Examination of the tip of the catheter disclosed pattern consistent with a fracture secondary to mechanical shearing forces associated with a compressed fish-mouth appearance at the fracture site.

Lafreniere (1991) reviewed the literature and uncovered thirteen additional cases of subclavian catheter fracture; all catheters were used for chemotherapy. On viewing these cases and his own experience, he provided the following recommendations.

1. The subclavian puncture should be made at the mid-clavicular location rather than more medially;
2. fluoroscopic assessment at the time of insertion and a chest x-ray in the upright position should be done to look for catheter kinking;
3. if kinking is identified then a chest x-ray at two-monthly intervals should be done to identify progression of kinking;
4. if any evidence of kinking is seen on follow-up chest x-rays, the catheter should probably be removed before six months has elapsed, as the mean time to fracture in this review was 6.5 months, and then replaced if necessary with another catheter.

The foregoing cases illustrate several types of catheter pinchoff mishaps, identifying the symptoms and offering an explanation for their occurrence. It is to be pointed out that catheter electrodes are also subject to pinchoff and can be fractured and embolized. Such incidents are described elsewhere in this chapter.

C. Swan-Ganz catheter

1. Operation and use

The Swan-Ganz, balloon-tipped catheter shown in Figure 5.3A, is used to measure pulmonary artery (PA) and pulmonary capillary wedge (PCW) pressure and cardiac output by the thermodilution method. The catheter contains

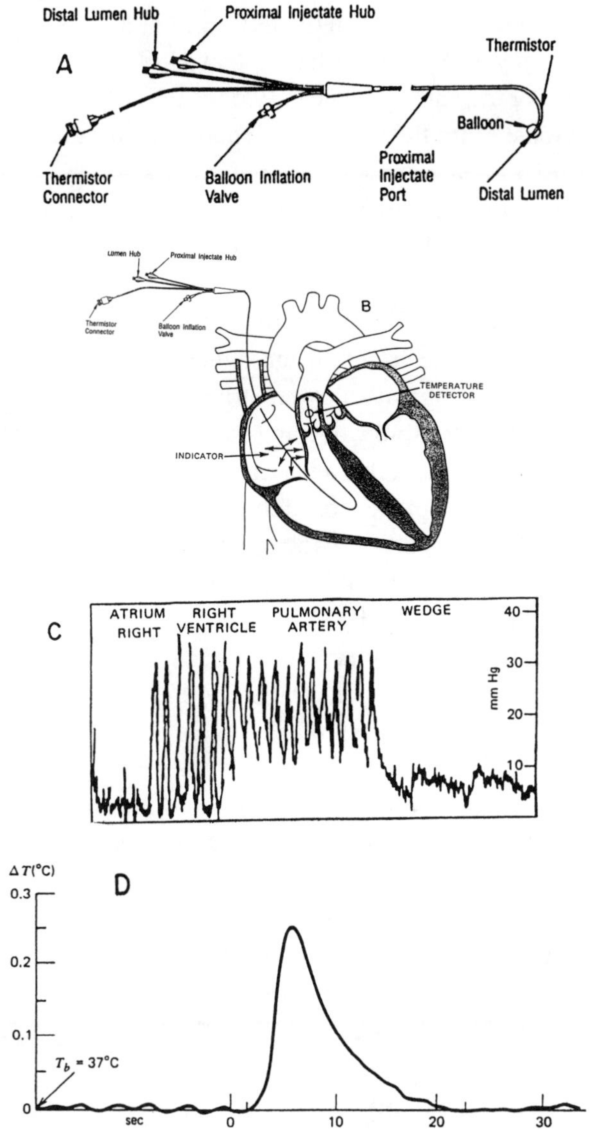

Figure 5.3 *(a) shows the components of the Swan-Ganz catheter, (b) illustrates the tip of the catheter in the pulmonary artery, (c) shows the pressures that are encountered as the catheter tip advances from the right atrium to the pulmonary artery to record wedge pressure, and (d) shows a typical thermodilution curve from which cardiac output is calculated. (Courtesy Baxter Healthcare Corp. Irvine CA, 92714)*

four lumens: (1) a distal lumen for measuring pressure, (2) a proximal lumen for injecting the indicator (a chilled solution), (3) a lumen for the wires connected to the temperature sensor (thermister) and (4) a lumen for inflating the balloon at the tip of the catheter. The balloon is deflated when the catheter tip is inserted pervenously into the right atrium and then inflated and the blood flow carries the tip of the catheter into the pulmonary artery, entry into which is identified by pressure recording from the tip lumen. A special volume-limited syringe is used to inflate the balloon. Figure 5.3B shows the tip of the catheter in the pulmonary artery.

Figure 5.3C illustrates the pressures recorded from the distal tip of the catheter as it passes into the right atrium; when therein the pressure pulsations amounting to a few mmHg with slower variations due to respiration. When the tip passes through the tricuspid valve and enters the right ventricle, the pressure pulsations increase dramatically; a typical pressure being 30/0 mmHg. As the tip is advanced further, it passes through the pulmonic valve to reveal pulmonary artery pressure, typically 30/15 mmHg. Advancing the catheter further into the smaller branches of the pulmonary circuit causes the pressure pulses to fall dramatically as the tip is wedged in a small branch of the pulmonary artery; this pressure is pulmonary capillary wedge (PCW) pressure which reflects left-ventricular, end-diastolic pressure, a quantity that is of clinical value in identifying the pumping capability of the left ventricle. This entire sequence is shown in Figure 5.3C.

Cardiac output is measured with the thermodilution method in which a few mL of chilled 5 percent dextrose in water (D5W) is injected into the proximal injectate hub which delivers the D5W into the right atrium where it mixes with flowing blood which passes through the right ventricle and into the pulmonary artery where the thermistor (on the catheter) is located. A record of the temperature change is the dilution curve, shown in Figure 5.3D.

Cardiac output (CO) is calculated using the following equation:

$$CO = \frac{V(T_B - T_i)\,53.46}{A}$$

Where:

T_B is the temperature of the blood (°C) in the PA (prior to injection)

T_i is the temperature of the injected indicator (D5W) in °C

V is the volume injected in mL

A is the area of the dilution curve in °C × sec

CO is the result in mL/min.

The thermodilution method is widely used in clinical medicine. Its value lies in the fact that multiple determinations can be made using an inert indicator (D5W). Although room temperature D5W can be used, chilled (0°C) D5W is preferred.

2. Accidents

According to the *Medical Malpractice Journal* (July 1999), the following accident occurred associated with the use of a Swan-Ganz catheter. The report is summarized as follows:

> A seventy-five-year-old lady was admitted to a hospital for a hysterectomy because of sporadic vaginal bleeding for a number of months which had not been resolved with conservative treatment. The day before the surgery a Swan-Ganz catheter was inserted by a cardiologist to monitor her fluid volume. This was reportedly performed without difficulty. According to family members at her bedside, the patient appeared pale, uncomfortable and complained she was not eating well. Readings from the transducer at the catheter tip indicated hypovolemia and her pulmonary artery pressures had also dropped. At a regularly scheduled vital sign check early that evening, a nurse lowered the head of the bed to take an updated pressure reading by inflating the balloon at the tip of the catheter, which must be done with the patient lying down. When the bed was lowered, the patient complained of difficulty breathing and began spitting up blood, which rapidly progressed to a massive hemorrhage which led to the patient's death.

A lawsuit was filed naming the cardiologist and the hospital codefendants. The plaintiff argued that the nurse had improperly inflated the balloon and had failed to recognize that the tip of the catheter had migrated to a distal position in the pulmonary artery, which was too narrow, causing it to rupture. The plaintiff also claimed that a chest x-ray taken after the catheter was inserted showed that the tip was improperly located too far from the main branch of the pulmonary artery. The nurse denied that she had inflated the balloon and maintained that there was no evidence to indicate that the catheter tip was not in an appropriate position.

An autopsy revealed that the pulmonary artery had been ruptured by the tip of the catheter fourteen centimeters from the main branch of the pulmonary artery. All medical witnesses agreed that this site was an improper location for the tip of the catheter. The defendant claimed that the initial insertion of the catheter was properly performed and that it went out of position shortly before the massive bleeding started, which is a recognized risk of use of the catheter. A defense verdict was returned.

An FDA MAUDE report of 1/2/98 described the following catheter accident:

> A triple lumen vascular catheter separated on removal. The internal lumen migrated and became dislodged within the PT's [patient] vascular system before it could be found and removed, the PT coded and expired after insertion of a [manufacturer] catheter and development of a pneumothorax.

D. Cardiac catheterization aneurysm accident

The *Medical Malpractice Journal* of December 1988 reported the following accident:

> A legal case is described in which a forty-seven-year-old woman underwent cardiac catheterization for aortic insufficiency. An ascending aortic aneurysm discovered during the procedure prohibited the use of standard angiography catheters. The aneurysm ruptured during attempted angiography, resulting in the patient's death. The plaintiff contended that a computed tomography scan should have been performed when the aneurysm was discovered and that additional catheters should not have been used. The defendant argued that catheterization is generally performed in the presence of an aneurysm and that angiography is necessary to repair the aorta and aortic valve. The jury returned a defense verdict.

E. Balloon angioplasty

1. General characteristics

Balloon angioplasty uses a catheter-borne, expandable, stiff-walled balloon to enlarge the lumen of a blood vessel. With advancing age, arteries become narrowed locally (stenosed) and develop plaques on the inner walls, thereby reducing blood flow. An appreciation of the effect of a diameter reduction can be established by recalling Poiseuille's law, which relates flow to the driving pressure, fluid viscosity and vessel geometry. The resistance to flow, identified by this law, is inversely proportional to the fourth power of the diameter. A reduction in diameter of one half increases the resistance to flow sixteen fold.

Many different terms are associated with balloon angioplasty. For example, percutaneous transluminal coronary angioplasty (PTCA) is the term used for dilation of coronary arteries. However, PTA is a more generic term. Although enlargement of blood vessels by a variety of intravascular devices had been practiced for some time, it was introduction of the specially designed stiff balloon by Gruentzig in 1977 for coronary-artery dilation, that brought the technique to the attention of clinicians. The method is now widely used for enlarging blood vessels, valve openings, ducts, etc. and wherever a catheter can be placed.

Gruentzig's own words provide the best description of the technique of balloon dilation. After locating the catheter-borne balloon centrally over the narrowed region, he stated:

> The distensible segment is inflated with fluid (50 percent contrast medium, 50 percent water) to a maximum diameter of 3.0–3.8 mm by a pump-controlled pressure of 5 atmospheres (about 500 kPa). This pressure compresses the arteriosclerotic material in a direction perpendicular to the wall of the vessel thereby dilating the lumen.

Note the high pressure (5 atmospheres = 3800 mm Hg) needed to distend the balloon, which reflects the stiffness of the balloon material. A soft-walled balloon will not perform the task because it will conform to the narrowed region and only expand axially.

Balloon dilation traumatizes the vessel wall and healing starts. Platelets are attracted to the site, clotting takes place, smooth muscle and collagen are deposited. The healing can be gradual or rapid and may progress to produce stenosis or occlusion. Various pharmacologic agents are used in an attempt to control the healing rate, but restenosis occurs in a non-negligible percentage of cases. In this situation, a stent is placed (see below).

2. Technique

Contrast agent (preferably non-ionic) is mixed with saline and used to inflate the balloon. The appropriate size balloon is centered over the region to be dilated and pressure is applied (10–20 atmospheres, depending on the balloon), for about thirty seconds under fluoroscopic visualization. To facilitate placement of the balloon centrally over the region to be dilated, radio-opaque markers are on the catheter to identify the ends of the balloon.

There are surprisingly few accidents with PTA. The major complications are related to over expansion of the balloon, creating a dissection, aneurysm or blood leakage. Although technological advances have been made involving balloon material and adhesives to secure the balloon to the catheter, balloons do leak occasionally and the diluted contrast agent leaks into the vessel. However, the amount of fluid filling the balloon is relatively small (a few mL) and it is compatible with blood, unless it is hypertonic, in which case it will shrink blood cells. If it is hypotonic, it will cause the red cells to swell and burst, liberating hemoglobin.

F. Stents

1. Description and use

One of the several dictionary definitions for a stent is "a device or mold of any suitable material used to hold a graft in place or to provide support for tubular structures that are being anastomosed." In the early days of surgery, a percutaneous thread, which kept a wound open for drainage, was called a stent. Perhaps the simplest definition is a device to hold something open.

Stents are used in association with balloon angioplasty to prevent the dilated vessel from narrowing after dilation. A wide variety of stents are in use; Figure 5.4 presents a few of the more popular types, some of which are coated to prevent restenosis. They fall into two categories: (1) self-expanding and (2) balloon-expanded. The self-expanding stent is contained inside the tip of the delivery catheter. It is deployed by force applied to a smaller-diameter catheter within the stent-carrying catheter. Some are made from Nitinol, an alloy that expands to its preformed shape with heat.

The balloon-expandable stents are mounted on a carefully matched balloon and inserted so that the stent is centrally located over the stenosis. Then the balloon is inflated with contrast medium. Pressures ranging from 8 to 12 atm are used and when expanded, the stent shortens from 5 to about 20 percent, depending on the type of stent.

There are some hazards associated with the use of stents; among these are underexpansion (with the danger of migration) and overexpansion (with the risk of excessive wall damage and dissection). Misplacement and dislodgment from the balloon can occur. As with any invasive procedure there is the risk of infection. The following describes a few stent mishaps.

2. Accidents

The Center for Devices and Radiological Health (CDRH) of the FDA (1998) reported that:

While advancing the endovascular stent with delivery system to the target lesion site located in the PT's renal osteo [ostium] of the right renal artery, it was reported that the stent was observed to be located on the shaft of the balloon catheter. In response, the stent delivery system was withdrawn from the PT without complication. Subsequently, the stent was removed from the de-

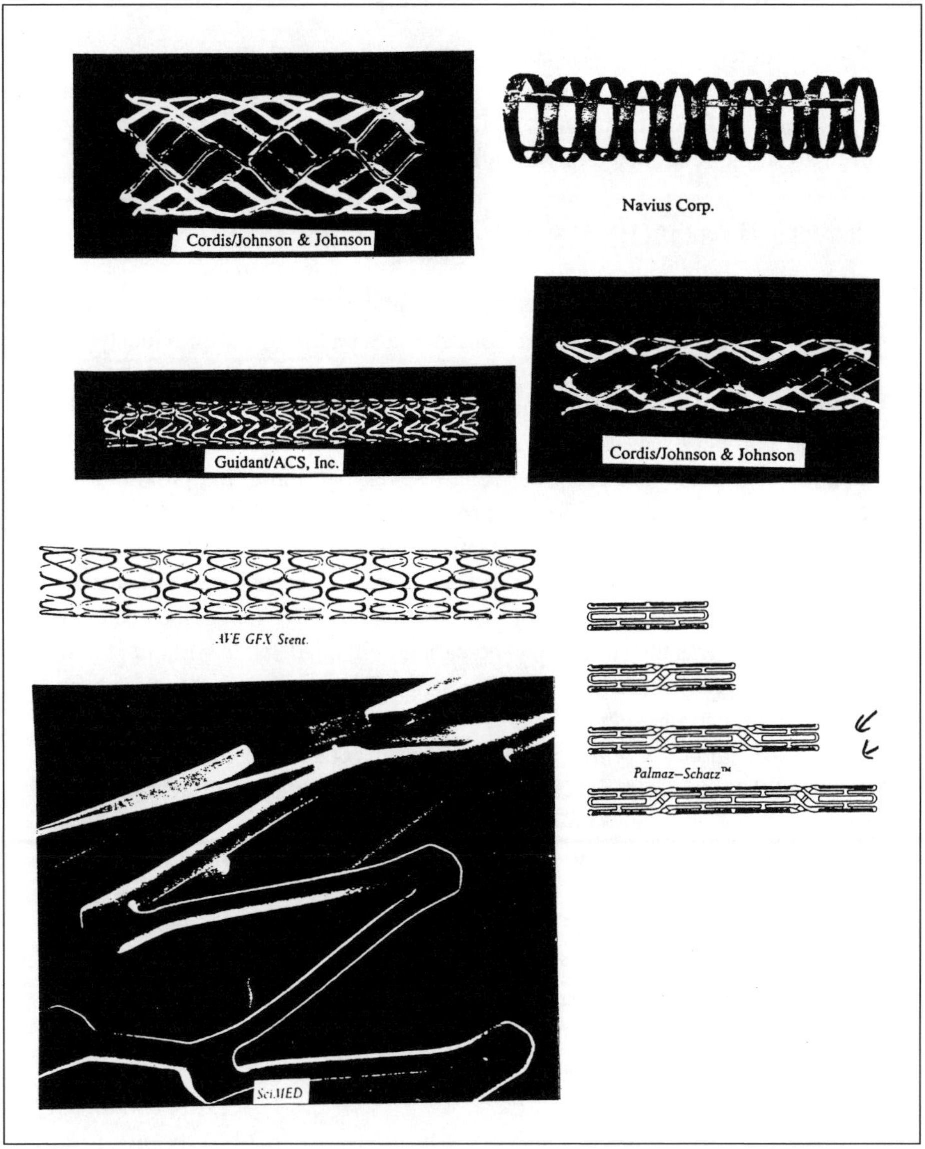

Figure 5.4 *Balloon-expandable stents*

> livery system and placed onto another balloon catheter. While advancing the modified stent delivery system to the target lesion site, the stent became dislodged from the balloon catheter and was not retrieved. There were no additional complications reported relative to this event.

The manufacturer was quick to respond:

> The manufacturer does not support the removal and remounting of the [manufacturer's] balloon expandable stent onto another balloon catheter. This modification of CO [company] device is not FDA approved and there have been no studies conducted on the safety and efficacy of this modification.

Another CDRH report (1998) stated:

> A 3.0 mm diameter × 18 mm length ave. [manufacturer] stent was inserted into the left anterior descending coronary artery through a previously deployed [manufacturer] stent. It was not possible to inflate the stent delivery system balloon; therefore the stent and delivery system were pulled back from the coronary artery. Upon retraction of the stent and stent delivery system, the stent dislodged from the stent delivery system at the proximal left anterior descending artery and was protruding into the left main artery. A 3.0 mm diameter percutaneous trans-luminal coronary artery balloon was inserted to reposition and deploy the dislodged stent at the proximal left anterior descending artery. Another attempt was made to place a stent at the distal target lesion, but was unsuccessful. The patient remained stable without pain or electrocardiograph changes. There was no additional clinical sequelae reported relative to the event.
>
> Manufacturer's Comments: The returned goods investigation revealed that the 3.0 mm diameter × 18 mm length ave. [manufacturer] stent delivery system was returned without the stent. There were no kinks or damage noted to the outside of the catheter and the balloon had slight evidence of inflation. It was not possible to inflate the balloon when positive pressure was applied to the inflation port with an inflation device. However, [when] the proximal section of the stent delivery system was separated from the distal section, it was possible to inflate the balloon and hold pressure at 8 atm. The proximal portion of the stent delivery system was dissected just distal to the luer nipple and it was noted that the inflation lumen was collapsed at that area.

The Australian Therapeutic Goods Administration (TGA) reported an incident in which the balloon of an angioplasty catheter burst during deployment of a second stent distal to the first deployed stent. The manufacturer of the catheter observed a pinhole leak at the proximal edge of the distal marker band, which may have been caused by the stent itself. The catheter was promoted as being suitable for deployment of more than one stent in the same procedure, although neither the manufacturer or supplier provided any documentation to support such an allegation. Supplied product information states that the device is to be used one time only.

5.4 Conducting Properties of Fluid-Filled Catheters

Modern catheters are made of plastic, which is a good electrical insulator. Such catheters are usually fluid filled, often with 0.9 percent saline. Radio-opaque solutions and intravenous fluid, such as whole blood, plasma, 5 percent dextrose in water (D5W), urine, and bile, may also be transported by catheters. Most of these fluids, except D5W, are fairly good conductors of electric current. The electrical resistance (R) of a fluid-filled catheter depends on the length (L), inversely on the crosssectional area (A) of the catheter, and directly with the resistivity (ρ) of the fluid therein. The resistance $R = \rho L/A$, where R is in ohms, L and A are in centimeter units, and ρ in ohm-cm; Table 5.1 lists the resistivity values for several body fluids and those often carried by catheters. Radio-opaque (contrast) medium may be a good or poor conductor and is available in two types, ionic and nonionic, the latter having a higher resistivity than the former. The nonionic types were developed to minimize the sensation felt when injected intravascularly.

Monsees and McQuarrie (1971) investigated the resistance of fluid-filled catheters with a view toward identifying whether they constituted a low- or high- resistance path into the body. Using resistivity values of 80 and 130 ohm-cm for physiological saline and blood, respectively, the resistance of a typical cardiac catheter can be calculated. For example, an 8F catheter has an internal diameter of 1.42 mm; for a 100-cm length, the resistances when filled with saline and blood are 0.5 and 0.8 MΩ, respectively. These two examples illustrate that the resistance is quite high.

It should be noted that if the tip of a fluid-filled catheter is in contact with the myocardium, it is possible to calculate the 60 Hz voltage required to induce ventricular fibrillation. For example, many studies have shown (see Geddes and Baker 1989) that 50 μA rms of 60 Hz applied for a few seconds will induce ventricular fibrillation. The voltage needed to obtain this current is the product of this current and the resistance. For the 0.5- and 0.8-MΩ fluid-filled catheters, the rms voltages are 25 and 40. If the catheter tip is not against the endocardium, a higher voltage would be needed to produce fibrillation. It should be noted that the voltage would be much lower for a catheter electrode with 1000-ohm impedance. In this case, ventricular fibrillation would be produced by 50 mV. Calculations can be made for fluid-filled catheters of other diameters and lengths using the data in Tables 5.1 and 5.2, the latter providing the internal diameters of catheters. Note that for the French (F) scale, the outer diameter in millimeters is the F size divided by three.

Table 5.1
Resistivity of Fluids

Fluid Type	Temperature (°C)	Resistivity (ohm-cm)
Blood (40% Hct)	37	130
Plasma	37	53
Saline (0.9%)[a]	37	60
Saline (0.9%)[a]	25	80
CSF	25	65
Bile	37	60
Amniotic fluid	37	50
Urine	37	30
Whole milk (cow)	35	170
D5W	Room	67,000
Radio-opaque fluids		
Potassium iodide		
5%	Room	30
10%	Room	15
Hypaque (50%)[b]	Room	70
Omnipaque (180 mg/ml)[b]	Room	1,857
Ioxilanc (300 mg/ml)[c]	Room	4,500

a. Resistivity decreases with increasing temperature, typically 2%/°C.
b. Sanofi-Winthrop
c. Cook Imaging

Table 5.2
Catheter Dimensions

	Thick-Walled Catheter		Thin-Walled Catheter	
Catheter size "F"	**Outer diameter (mm)**	**Lumen diameter (mm)**	**Outer diameter (mm)**	**Lumen diameter (mm)**
3F	1.00	0.36	—	—
4F	1.33	0.46	1.33	0.58
5F	1.67	0.66	1.67	0.86
6F	2.00	0.91	2.00	1.17
7F	2.33	1.17	2.33	1.47
8F	2.67	1.42	2.67	1.73
9F	3.00	1.63	3.00	1.98
10F	3.33	1.83	3.33	2.24
11F	3.67	2.11	3.67	2.49
12F	4.00	2.39	4.00	2.74
14F	4.67	2.90	4.67	3.25

From catalog of the U.S. Catheter & Instrument Company, Glens Falls, NY.

A. Current sinks and sources

A medical device connected to a patient can function as a return path (sink) or as a provider (source) of current that can do harm. When a catheter or electrodes are applied to a subject, there is the opportunity for undesired current flow and whether or not it does harm depends on the type of current, local current density, duration of current flow and site.

An example of a medical device acting as a current sink is shown in Figure 5.5. A patient is connected to a grounded (G) medical device via an intravascular catheter, the fluid in which is in contact with ground via the device. An electrosurgical unit (ESU) is used to cut and/or coagulate tissue of the patient via an active electrode. However, the return conductor from the dispersive electrode to the ESU is interrupted at X. Therefore, on activating the ESU, the return path for the electrosurgical current is through the distributed capacitance (C) of the ESU to ground and through the intravascular catheter to ground (G) through the medical device. If, instead of a catheter, recording electrodes were

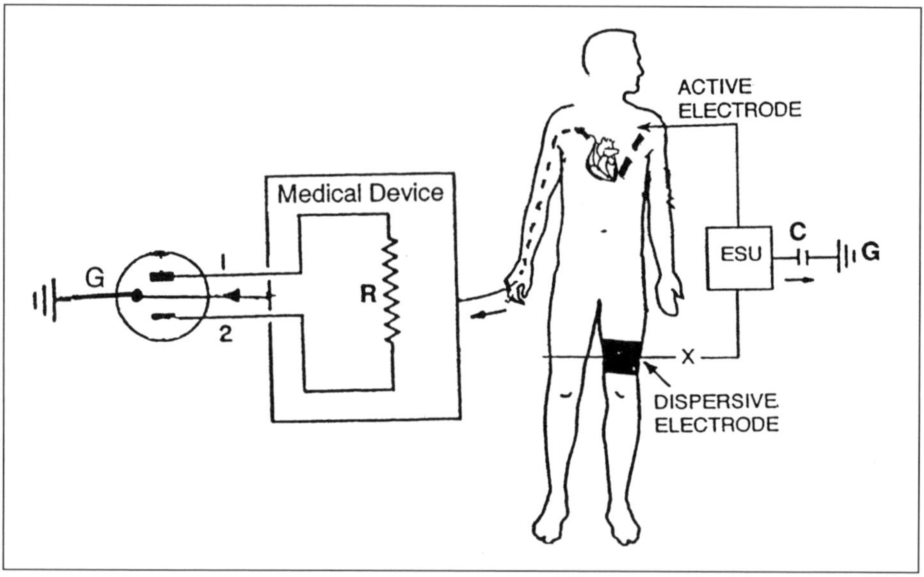

Figure 5.5 *Current flow through a catheterized, grounded (G) subject as a result of interruption (X) of the return path to the electrosurgical unit (ESU)*

on the patient, they could constitute the return path for the electrosurgical current. These undesired current routes are known as alternate current paths and if adequate ESU current flows, thermal injury can result at the point of contact with the patient. Ventricular fibrillation can also occur.

Figure 5.6 illustrates the situation in which the medical device acts as a source of current flowing through an intravascular catheter to a grounded (G) patient. The source of the leakage current is from the hot side of the power line (1), through the distributed capacitance (C) in the medical device. This current is present because the conductor that grounds the medical device is interrupted at X. If the leakage current is large enough, ventricular fibrillation can result. However, if the connection to ground were not interrupted at X, no leakage current would flow through the subject.

B. Electrosurgically induced ventricular fibrillation with fluid-filled catheters

Electrosurgical current can stimulate nerve, skeletal and cardiac muscle. It follows that it can produce ventricular fibrillation. The first report of such an event in man was presented by Hungerbuhler and Swope (1974):

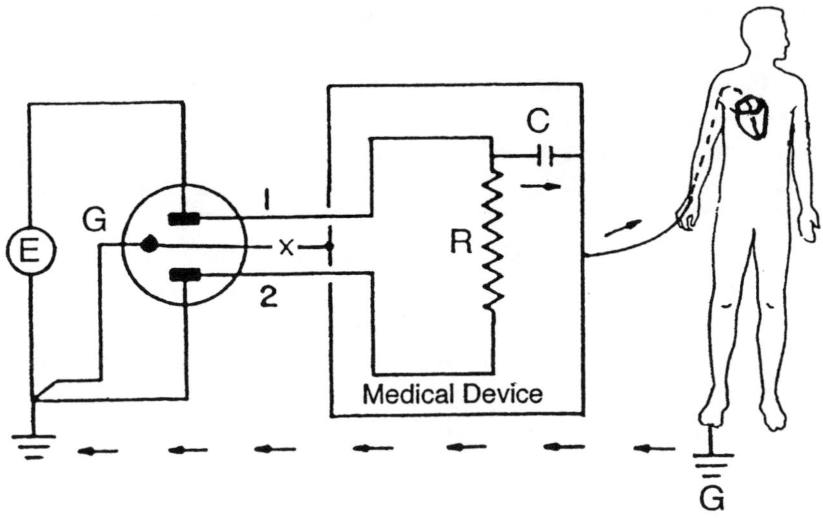

Figure 5.6 *Leakage current caused to flow through a grounded subject through an intravascular catheter by interrupting (X) the conductor that grounds (G) the metal case of the device*

A twenty-four-year-old woman was scheduled for elective surgical correction of an asymptomatic secondum-type atrial septal defect. Preoperatively, a central venous catheter and two intravenous catheters were inserted percutaneously. A left radial arterial catheter connected to an electronic pressure transducer [manufacturer] was also inserted. An electrocardiographic oscilloscope, with an electrocardiographic pad placed under the back, was used. An additional electrocardiogram was monitored with extremity leads connected to a system designed for amplification of low-level electronic signals originating within the body. A patient grounding plate was placed under the right buttock; the ground clip was attached and then plugged into the electrosurgical unit.

During the initial part of the surgery, the electrocautery was used to cauterize bleeding vessels in the subcutaneous fat, which resulted in the usual amount of high-frequency interference on the oscilloscope. The auscultatory esophageal rhythm remained regular.

However, five to ten seconds after application of the electro-surgical knife in the cutting mode to the sternal periosteum, the auscultatory rhythm was noted to be irregular and then absent. Simultaneously, an increased electrical high-frequency interference appeared on the electrocardiographic oscilloscope. When the high-frequency interference cleared, the patient was noted to be in ventricular fibrillation, and had a blood pressure of less than 50 mmHg systolic.

The patient was immediately resuscitated over the next seventy seconds with external cardiac massage, lidocaine (150 mg total intravenous dose), phenylephrine (Neosynephrine hydrochloride 2 mg given intravenously), and direct-current electroshock (200 watt-seconds) with paddles applied to the thorax.

The patient recovered and later it was found that the ground clip to the ground plate was disconnected and examined. A paper remnant torn from a previously used disposable ground plate was discovered wedged into the clip, but contact appeared adequate. Further, the male ground plug to the unit itself was noted to be loose. The unit was replaced with another electrosurgical unit (the same model) with the same ground plate and a new clip.

Electrosurgically induced ventricular fibrillation had been reported on the dog by Becker et al. (1974). Geddes et al. (1975) and Geddes (1979) produced ventricular fibrillation in the dog in which a saline-filled catheter in the right ventricle was connected to a blood-pressure transducer. A dispersive electrode was placed under the dog in dorsal recumbency. The active electrode was used to cut the skin prior to a thoracotomy and no cardiac arrhythmia occurred. The dispersive electrode was then disconnected and ESU current was delivered to the active electrode applied to the chest, and ventricular fibrillation occurred.

In the foregoing cases, the subject and the associated recording devices were a sink for the electrosurgical current. The arrows in Figures 5.5 and 5.6 illustrate the current paths.

An explanation for the induction of ventricular fibrillation with electrosurgical current was presented by Foster and Geddes (1986). It was shown that the presence of an arc at the active electrode/tissue interface produces pulsating current that causes stimulation. It had been shown by Tucker et al. (1984) and Pearce (1986) that the presence of an arc in the path of electrosurgical current alters the frequency spectrum markedly, producing low-frequency components capable of stimulation.

C. 60-Hz leakage current-induced ventricular fibrillation

Leakage current is an undesired current passing through a subject connected to a power-line-operated medical device. In this case the device is the current source. The effect of leakage current depends on its magnitude, pathway, and the duration of flow. Safe 60-Hz current limits and different types of patient contact have been established by AAMI (1978), along with the methods of testing devices for leakage current.

By far the most hazardous leakage current is that borne by intravascular catheters. Figure 5.6 illustrates how leakage current due to distributed capacitance (C) within an ungrounded medical device allows power-line (60-Hz) current to flow through a cardiac catheterized subject who is grounded (G). The current is caused to flow by an interruption (X) in the connection that grounds the case of the device by its connection to the grounding pin (G) of the three-prong plug (1, 2). Note that one side (2) of the 117-V (E) power line is grounded. This is typically done where the power line enters into the building.

An important factor in the foregoing scenario is the catheter type and its location. If it is a catheter electrode, the situation is hazardous. If the catheter is connected to an isolated pressure transducer or another type of isolated device, the situation is far less hazardous.

Medical devices can malfunction and send enough current through a patient to do harm. The following examples illustrate this point. Such events were very common in the 1960s; they are less common today because of the performance requirements imposed by the FDA and compliance with applicable AAMI/ANSI standards.

Ventricular fibrillation due to leakage current from a densitometer connected to a cardiac catheter was reported by Mody et al. (1962). With the catheter tip at different sites, blood was drawn into the densitometer to measure oxygen saturation. Mody et al. reported:

> Pressures and blood-oxygen saturations were obtained from the right pulmonary artery, the main pulmonary artery, the outflow tract, and the cavity of the right ventricle. The tip of the catheter was then withdrawn into the right atrium so that its blood-oxygen saturation could be estimated. At precisely that instant the technician operating the instrument received an electric shock, and the patient began to show convulsive movements of the body and limbs. The catheter was immediately disconnected from the densitometer and withdrawn until the tip was in the superior vena cava. The electrocardiograph showed ventricular fibrillation, and the patient had become unconscious and was not breathing.

The patient was ultimately resuscitated and Mody et al. investigated the accident, stating that:

> Our patient suffered the effects of direct electrical stimulation of the myocardium through the saline contents of a cardiac catheter connected to a [manufacturer] densitometer. The densitometer had previously been used without ill effects and in precisely the same manner for blood-oxygen sampling from the pulmonary artery and right ventricle. At the time of sampling from the right atrium, movement of the apparatus may have resulted in loss of contact of the earth (ground) lead from the densitometer, thereby allowing a current to flow from the chassis of the apparatus through the catheter into the patient.

Clearly this is a case in which the densitometer was the source of the current, as illustrated in Figure 5.6.

A case of ventricular fibrillation due to catheter-borne leakage current was reported by Bousvaros et al. (1962) at a time when many medical devices exhibited a relatively high leakage current:

> A No. 8 N.I.H. catheter was introduced into the right ventricle for cineangiographic studies of the right ventricular outflow tract and pulmonary valve.
>
> When, by the use of the fluoroscope, the tip of the catheter was seen to lie in the region of the apex of the right ventricle, the catheter was connected to a [manufacturer[high-power injection syringe. At the moment of connection, considerable interference developed in the electrocardiographic tracing on the oscilloscope, implying a change in the electrical environment of the patient. Owing to this interference, it was not possible to read the electrocardiogram, but within a few seconds it was noted that the patient had become rigid, and on the fluoroscope the heart was seen to be fibrillating. The injector was disconnected; immediately the interference stopped and the ventricular fibrillation was noted on the electrocardiogram. Open-heart cardiac massage was performed immediately, and after three shocks were applied to the surface of the heart with an internal defibrillator, normal rhythm was restored.

Subsequent investigation of this accident revealed that the patient was grounded through the ECG electrodes and that the electrically driven power injector was inadequately grounded. They stated that it was the contrast agent in the catheter that carried the current to the heart. Commenting on the conductivity of the contrast agent, they stated, "Furthermore, it was found that 50 percent diatrizoate solution was a somewhat better conductor than either saline or blood." In this accident, the injector was the source of the current.

In addition to ventricular fibrillation due to leakage current flowing through a contrast medium filled cardiac catheter, Viamonte and Hobbs (1967) pointed out that the same event can be induced by the sudden injection of contrast agent into a ventricle. They stated, "Ventricular fibrillation may be triggered by the injection of contrast material against the surface of the heart during the vulnerable period of ventricular repolarization."

The vulnerable period is that time during recovery of the ventricles when a single stimulus will precipitate ventricular fibrillation. The center of this period is associated with the T wave of the ECG (Jones and Geddes, 1977).

Rowe and Zarnstorff (1965) commented on the possibility of ventricular fibrillation resulting from contrast agent striking the endocardium during the vulnerable period:

> The endocardial stimulation provided by forcible ejection of contrast material against its surface is enough to provoke ventricular premature contractions in most subjects during intraventricular injection. Presumably this stimulus could occur in the vulnerable period of ventricular repolarization.

Rowe and Zarnstorff (1965) reported seven episodes of ventricular fibrillation in patients undergoing cineangiocardiography. These episodes were unrelated to grounding of the electromechanical injector or to contrast agent striking the endocardium. A solenoid-driven injector was used. It was noted that the onset of fibrillation was associated with opening of the injector switch. They documented the source of the electrical transient that induced fibrillation and stated:

> It was demonstrated that each time the injector switch was released [opened], an electrical discharge of 40 V was delivered for 1 to 2 msec to the syringe in the injector. A smaller and more variable transient occurred when the circuit was closed. Furthermore, during opening and closing of the injector switch, transients could be demonstrated on the oscilloscopic tracing of the ECG of a dog attached to the injector by a cardiac catheter filled with contrast substance. A similar injector from another hospital produced the same type of electrical discharge, as did an injector manufactured by another company. [Their paper describes a simple circuit for eliminating this transient.]

5.5 Catheter Electrodes

Catheter-borne electrodes are placed in the heart via a venous route for pacing, cardioversion, and defibrillation. A catheter may carry a single electrode and a single conductor (monopolar) or it may carry two conductors connected to two electrodes (bipolar). Some catheters carry electrodes to defibrillate the atria or the ventricles as well as pace them. In such a case there are multiple conductors in the catheter. Damage to such electrode catheters could allow the entry of tissue fluids leading to current escape and shunting, as well as corrosion. In such a case, sensing, pacing and/or defibrillation can be impaired. Malfunction could consist of conductor breakage or short circuit. Breakage of a conductor that serves as a sensing lead can result in detecting noise or muscle-action potentials, informing the device to which it is connected that a rapid electrical activity exists and is therefore an inappropriate device response.

A six-center study of the fate of 7,311 implanted polyurethane (atrial and ventricular) pacing leads provided by three manufacturers was reported by Furman et al. (1990). The ten-year cumulative survival percentage rates for the three manufacturers were 96.6 ± 0.4, 99.9 ± 0.1 and 97.7 ± 0.9. The types of failures found were (1) insulation break, (2) conductor break and (3) both. It was stated that "All failures occurred early and few failures occurred after the fifth year following implantation," a fact that is not evident from the results. Similar data can be found in the product liability chapter (Chapter 1).

A. Catheter (clavicular) crush

Catheter crush or pinchoff resulting from force applied to a catheter in the subclavian vein between the clavicle and first rib has been known since 1984, when Aitken and Minton described this phenomenon associated with chronically implanted catheters for chemotherapy for cancer. The phenomenon was rediscovered for pacing leads by Stokes and McVenes (1987). It is therefore not at all surprising that implanted cardioverter defibrillator (ICD) leads can succumb to the same fate. Obviously the insertion site for a catheter or catheter electrode should avoid passage at this site.

Stokes et al. (1987) reported that since 1980, nearly 5,000 explanted pacemakers were examined, and of them, 1.8 percent exhibited fractured leads, the fracture being located 25 ± 5 cm from the terminal pin. Stokes et al. stated that lead failure occurred due to crushing and that the fracture was located at the point "where the lead crosses the first rib in very close approximation to the sternoclavicure joint." In a subsequent paper, Stokes and McVenes (1988) stated that "The fracture could be attributed to clamping between the first rib and clavicle."

Stokes and McVenes (1988) reported that pacing catheter damage can manifest itself in many ways, stating that:

> Silicone rubber leads with parallel bipolar conductors can have the insulation between coils cut through due to external pressure. Some coaxial leads have outer coils fractured by a crushing mechanism. Some unipolar leads have exhibited flattened spots on the conductors, coil fracture due to fatigue and/or insulation failure.

Jacobs et al. (1993) called attention to the difference between flexural and compression (pinchoff) fracture in pacemaker leads. They found that the compression fracture was located 27.5 ± 5.2 cm distal to the connector pin on a 58-cm lead. The average time to failure was 11.1 months, with a range of one day to fifty-three months. They estimated the average incidence of such fractures was 1 to 2 percent. In addition to these studies they performed an experiment on a cadaver in which pressure in a balloon catheter in the subclavian vein was measured for different arm positions and different balloon sites. They reported that:

> It was demonstrated fluoroscopically that in some instances kinking of the balloon catheter with these (arm) motions was causing pressure changes. There was little evidence fluoroscopically of any compressive effect at the costoclavicular angle from these motions. With caudal traction; however, there was compression that could be identified fluoroscopically with medially and laterally placed catheters. Significantly higher pressures were generated with caudal traction in the medially placed catheters with a mean of 126 ± 26 mmHg change from baseline compared to 63 ± 15 mmHg change for laterally placed catheters and 38 ± 13 mmHg change for catheters placed through the cephalic vein ($P < 0.01$).

From the studies on the explanted leads and those on the cadavers, they concluded:

> Our data suggest that it would be preferable to avoid the costoclavicular angle completely, either by placing the lead percutaneously into the axillary vein lateral to the costoclavicular ligamentous complex or by insertion through the cephalic vein. Most described techniques of subclavian venipuncture in the literature use landmarks that directly traverse the medial costoclavicular angle. Laterally the vein is more difficult to cannulate and injury to the subclavian artery and brachial plexus is potentially more problematic.

A different view of the cause of catheter-lead fracture was presented by Magney et al. (1993), who performed catheter implant studies on cadavers. Careful dissections were then used to determine the path taken by the catheter electrode. They reported:

> While blood vessels can be compressed by movements of the clavicle, our research suggests that lead and catheter damage in that region is caused by soft tissue entrapment rather than bony contact.

Magney et al. (1993) concluded that:

> The placement of the lead should be checked by multiview cineradiography during movements of the ipsilateral upper extremity to ensure that leads or catheters have not been entrapped by the subclavius muscle or the costoclavicular ligament. If cineradiography is not available, posteroanterior chest x-rays (as described) should be used to confirm that newly placed leads are free of soft tissue entrapment.

The author investigated the case of a twenty-four-year-old lady who had right ventricular dysplasia and recurrent ventricular tachycardia for which she received medication. Because her ventricular tachycardia was difficult to control with drugs, she received an implanted cardioverter defibrillator (ICD) which contained a pacemaker. While at work one day, she collapsed. Fortunately, bystanders applied cardiopulmonary resuscitation (CPR) until the paramedics arrived in about ten minutes. Ventricular fibrillation was found and transchest defibrillation was attempted several times. Although each shock was successful, ventricular fibrillation recurred. She was transported to the emergency room (ER), all the while CPR was continued for about thirty-five minutes. In the ER, she was defibrillated and given medication for her arrhythmia and was then transferred to the coronary care unit for observation and further treatment.

At the hospital, the ICD was interrogated and it was found that the charge time was prolonged. The interrogation also revealed that the high-voltage (defibrillating) lead impedance was 20 ohms, indicating a short circuit which caused damage to the output circuit of the ICD. A radiograph showed crushed leads (coils) in the catheter at the first rib-clavicle intersection. A new ICD and lead were implanted. This case is clearly one of clavicular crush. The short-circuit was due to the clavicle and first rib crushing the catheter conductors in the subclavian vein.

Another ICD accident that the author investigated involved a thirty-five-year-old male who had right ventricular dysplasia with recurrent ventricular tachycardia (VT). Several prior myocardial ablations with high-frequency current were unsuccessful in controlling his VT. Drug therapy for the VT was moderately successful and he was implanted with an ICD on Dec. 8, 1997. The ICD was in the left pectoral region and its case (can) was the negative electrode. A monopolar electrode in the right ventricle was the anode. A pacemaker was implanted at the same time. To test the device, ventricular fibrillation was induced and the ICD defibrillated the heart with a 500-volt shock and the lead impedance was 38 ohms. The pacemaker was also checked and captured the heart with a 1 volt pulse of 0.5 msec duration; the impedance of the pacing lead was 500 ohms. The sensed R wave was 9 mV. All of these parameters were in the normal range and the patient was discharged.

At follow-up one month later, the defibrillating lead impedance was 43 ohms, the slight increase probably being due to encapsulation of the electrodes by fibrous tissue. On 4/14/98 and 6/9/98 follow-up checks revealed everything normal.

On 9/29/98, slightly less than a year following ICD implantation, the patient felt poorly and called his physician; during the call he collapsed and became unconscious and his wife called the paramedics who arrived in about ten minutes to find that his heart was in ventricular fibrillation. He was defibrillated several times with transchest electrodes; but fibrillation recurred. CPR was applied for about forty-five minutes during transport to the emergency room where his heart was defibrillated with transchest electrodes and he was given antiarrhythmetic medication, then transferred to the critical-care unit. Interrogation of his ICD on Sept. 30, 1998 revealed that to date thirty-six shocks had been delivered. The interrogation showed that the defibrillating lead impedance was in excess of 200 ohms, the highest resistance that the ICD could measure. Clearly the continuity of the lead from the ICD to the right ventricle had been interrupted, that is, open circuited. Soon thereafter (Oct. 5, 1998) the patient died in the hospital. The autopsy report indicated that his wife authorized donation of only his bones.

An interrogation of the FDA Medical Device Reports (MDRs) provided additional information on this accident. The physician sent the report to the FDA, which stated:

> On 9/29/98, the PT telephoned the physician's office to report that he was not feeling well. During this telephone conversation, the PT became unresponsive. The paramedics were called. When the paramedics arrived the PT was reportedly in ventricular fibrillation and was externally defibrillated six times. The PT was transported to the hosp. The PT became comatose, neurologically unresponsive and placed on a ventilator. The PT was admitted to the hosp. and the device was turned off. Further info rec'd by the clinical engineer on 9/30/98 reported that she had viewed the x-rays that had been taken of the device which appeared to show a fracture of the defibrillation lead in the area of the proximal defibrillation coil at the subclavian and an indentation of the pace/sense lead at the same point. Since admission to the hospital, the device has been manipulated in the pocket, an act which produces noise on the EGM [electrocardiogram]. On 10/9/98, the physician's office informed the hospital that the PT had died on 10/5/98.

Figure 5.7 is a print made from the radiograph, showing the fracture (arrow) identified in the MDR.

A further search of the FDA MDR files by the author revealed more reports of subclavian crush. The terms used to describe the damage to the catheter conductors were as follows.

July 23, 1997	The lead was removed due to clavicular crush
Oct. 24, 1997	The morphology of the abrasion provides evidence of mechanical damage indicative of clavicular crush
Feb. 5, 1998	An x-ray showed that the lead had been crushed between the clavicle and the rib, resulting in noise and inappropriate shock
Feb. 11, 1998	An x-ray showed that the coils were cut in two locations. This damage is indicative of a condition known as clavicular crush
May 4, 1998	The x-ray showed stretched wires. This damage is indicative of a condition known as clavicular crush.
Sept. 12, 1998	This lead is the second replacement on this PT reported on MDR report #2938836-1998-00051 where clavicular crush damage was observed. The user manual advises that this type of lead damage may be decreased with leads placed by cephalic vein cutdown or a subclavian puncture site as lateral as possible.

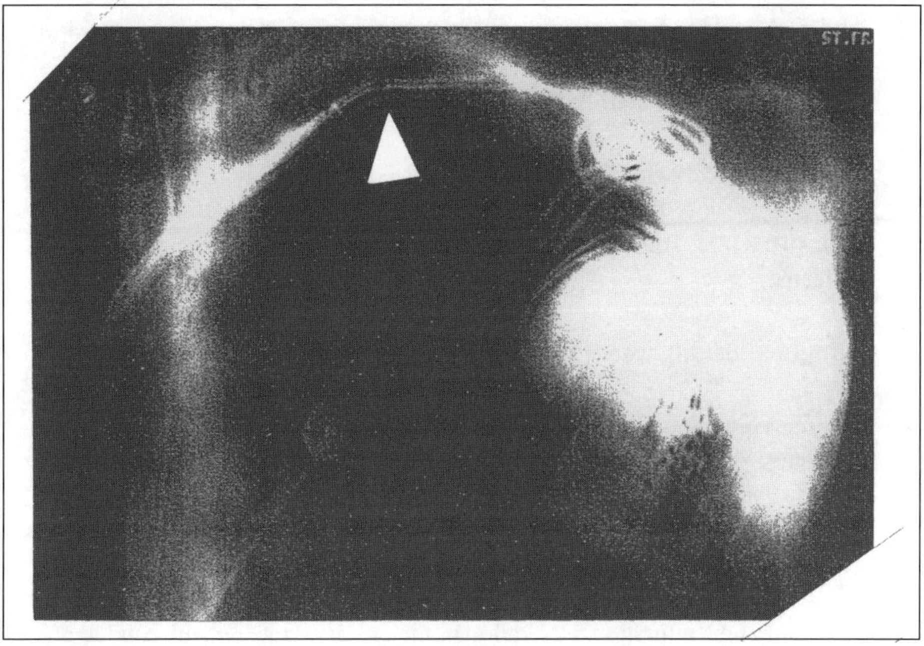

Figure 5.7 *Photograph of a radiograph showing clavicular crush (arrow) of a defibrillating catheter electrode in the subclavian vein*

Catheter crush or pinchoff results from force applied to a catheter in the subclavian vein between the clavicle and first rib. Obviously the insertion site for a catheter or catheter electrode should avoid passage at this site.

B. The twiddler's syndrome

The dictionary definition of twiddle is to turn around and around, especially with the fingers. This being so, the syndrome is well named as it applies to the implanted cardioverter defibrillator (ICD). It seems that some patients twiddle their ICDs, as shown by the following MDRs derived from one manufacturer's experience.

The 7/10/95 report stated:

> An invasive procedure was performed to investigate a possible lead failure. When the pocket was opened the physician noted that this device had been twisted approx. 50 times and the lead had "broken." When the remaining portion of the lead was removed from the subclavian area, it was noted to be twisted an add'l 100 times. The cause of the lead twisting is thought to be "twiddler syndrome." Lead implanted 6/17/95. Explanted approx. 7/7/97. Total implant time 24 mo."

The lead was replaced.

The 1/26/96 MDR stated that:

This PT, who had twiddler's syndrome, twisted this lead multiple times causing a lead fracture. The lead was replaced, implanted 3/31/95. Removed from service 10/31/95. Total implant time 7 mo. The lead was capped and remains implanted.

Additional details were provided by a second report of the same date:

This transvenous defibrillation lead was explanted because of "twiddler's syndrome." Implant date—1/17/94. Explant—8/24/94. Total implant time 7 months. Visual inspection noted that the lead had been twisted excessively in one direction. The trilumen insulation has fold marks from the distal end to the proximal and distal high voltage DBS cables in multiple regions. Damage consistent with lead manipulation during explant includes the following: yoke crimp tube migration, elongation of the proximal rate sensing conductor coil and a breakdown of the distal porous tip to tined insulation bond. The stylet insertion test failed 620 mm from the bifurcated terminal pin due to the twisted nature of the lead. The pressure test failed at the distal porous tip to tined insulation junction. The hipot test passed. Device history records and x-rays indicate conformance to the device specification at the time of shipment from Mfr.

An MDR of 4/26/96 cited another case as follows:

An invasive procedure was performed to replace this transvenous defibrillation lead after being "completely broken as a result of twiddler's syndrome" Implant date: 10/26/94. Explant date: 1/31/96. Total implant time: 15 months. The lead has been returned and is being analyzed.

A 12/12/96 MDR stated:

The company received information that this patient had twiddler's syndrome, and as a result of the patient's constant manipulation of the [company] transvenous defibrillation lead it was "broken." The lead was explanted and a new [company] lead was implanted.

The foregoing incidents should alert the investigator to patient-induced device failures, rather than accidental failures. A relevant issue is whether the implanting physician should warn the patient of the twiddler's syndrome, and if so, this information should be in the instruction manual. These incidents also raise the issue of creating a twiddler-proof system.

C. Inappropriate ICD shocks due to electrode failures

One of the major complaints associated with an automatic implanted cardioverter defibrillator (ICD) is the delivery of a shock when not needed. Shock delivery requires the sensing circuit of the ICD to receive an electrical signal having a frequency equal to or higher than the programmed frequency for shock delivery. Such signals can be of cardiac or noncardiac origin; the following will discuss both.

A study of 241 ICD patients who received inappropriate shocks was reported by Grimm et al. (1993). During follow-up, fifty-four of the 241 patients received 132 inappropriate shocks. The rhythms preceding the shocks were atrial fibrillation (thirty patients), sinus or supraventricular tachycardia (eleven patients), antitachycardia pacing resulting in ventricular tachycardia (three patients) and normal sinus or pacemaker rhythm (ten patients).

A similar study was reported by Peters et al. (1995) in which four patients received inappropriate ICD shocks more than six months after implantation due to sensing-lead insulation failures. In the first patient the insulation defect caused the pacing threshold to be in excess of 10 volts, indicative of current shunting. In the second case, spurious shocks were attributed to a 1-mm transverse insulation defect, which when repaired, eliminated the spurious shocks. The third case experienced shocks after thirty months of implantation. An interrogation of the ICD revealed 100 ICD activations. Surgical examination revealed fluid in the insulation near the pin of the proximal lead and manipulation of the lead reproduced the oversensing. The lead was capped and replaced. The fourth patient had no spurious shocks for fourteen months. Some time after he received two shocks when he lifted his hand over his head. One week later, he received multiple spurious shocks and was taken to the hospital where a large insulation defect was found in the sensing lead. Manipulation of the lead confirmed the oversensing and the lead was replaced.

Among the noncardiac reasons for spurious ICD discharges are (1) fracture of the sensing lead and (2) insulation failure of the lead. A search of the FDA files (MDR and MAUDE) revealed that both produced spurious ICD shocks. Table 5.3 summarizes the data obtained that represent one manufacturer's experience.

Table 5.3
Incidence and Causes of Inappropriate Shocks from ICDs*

FDA Report Dates for			
Lead Fracture		**Insulation Fracture**	
3/11/94	1/26/96 (2)	1/11/94	3/16/97
5/5/94	4/26/96 (2)	3/16/94	5/8/97 (4)
6/17/94	5/3/96	5/19/94	7/8/97 (4)
9/9/94	1/9/97 (2)	5/26/94	
10/25/94	1/16/97 (2)	7/8/94	
1/6/95	1/20/97	7/12/94	
2/6/95	3/6/97 (3)	8/19/94	
2/16/95	5/8/97 (4)	8/30/94	
2/20/95	5/15/97	10/26/94	
3/3/95 (2)	7/8/97 (6)	2/27/95	
4/25/95	9/8/97	5/8/95	
5/8/95		5/19/95	
6/1/95		6/12/95	
6/5/95		8/7/95	
6/12/95 (2)		8/25/95	
6/19/95		9/1/95	
7/20/95		4/26/96 (2)	
9/21/95		1/9/97	
		1/16/97	

*Derived from FDA MDR and MAUDE reports from one manufacturer.

A fracture, that is, a break in the conductor in the sensing lead means that the ventricular electrogram is not detected and opens the sensing circuit to any 60 Hz or other interference in the environment, as well as the electrical activity of nearby contracting muscles. An insulation break in the sensing lead will reduce the amplitude of the ventricular electrogram by shunting part of its signal through body fluids. However, depending on where the insulation break occurs, the electrical activity of nearby contracting muscles can be detected. The frequency of these signals can be from a few to 30/sec and easily mimic ventricular tachycardia and fibrillation. Supportive evidence can be found in MDR dated 10/25/94 which is summarized as follows:

> A patient with an ICD received a shock while lifting an object. Interrogation of the lead showed an increase in impedance since the last follow-up. An invasive procedure was performed to identify the cause and it was found that

the sense lead was fractured and had a hole in the insulation; both factors favor the detection of muscle-action potentials while lifting an object.

Another example of exercise-induced shocking of an ICD patient can be found in an MDR dated 2/16/93. In brief, it states that "lead insulation break, inappropriate shocks and occasional shock without symptoms while bending or crouching. Chest x-ray shows possible lead fracture. Beepo-gram with magnet and myopotential testing positive for noise."

It should be noted that the ventricular sense lead in an ICD is frequently a pacing lead, and failure to pace is often indicative of a fractured or a dislodged pacing-sensing lead.

5.6 Implant-Site Infection

Infection at an implant site is a serious complication. It can result from the implantation of an unsterile device or, if the device is sterile, infection can be the result of infection at the time of surgical implantation. In either case, the use of antibiotics is usually ineffective because the blood circulation at an implant site is usually poor and the blood-borne antibiotic is inadequate. Therefore, the solution to the problem is surgical explantation and cleanup of the implant site. The replacement implant is made at a different site if possible.

A case of infection associated with an implanted cardioverter defibrillator (ICD) and a case of infection associated with a pacemaker were reported by Almassi et al. (1999). In the first case, a computed tomography scan revealed thickening and a large volume of questionable fluid under the epicardial defibrillating patch leads of a fifty-four-year-old man with an ICD. Operative findings included a thick fibrous ball encasing the ICD patch electrodes. Cultures of the explanted ICD leads grew colonies of *Staphylococcus epidermidis*. Two weeks later, a transvenous ICD system was implanted.

The second case was a seventy-seven-year-old man with a transvenous pacemaker who developed swelling and pain sensitivity in the skin over the generator. Operative findings included a thick fibrous capsule surrounding the pacemaker without evidence of purulent material in the pocket. Sonication of the explanted leads grew colonies of *S. epidermidis*. The patient responded to intravenous vancomycin therapy and subsequently underwent placement of a new pacemaker.

The authors conclude that chronic infection of an ICD or implantable cardiac pacemaker with *S. epidermidis* can cause exuberant fibrous tissue formation encasing the implanted device without systemic inflammatory response.

The authors add that the presence of these findings indicates an ongoing infectious process necessitating removal of the entire implant.

The author investigated a case of ICD failure due to a programming flaw in the ICD which caused the ICD not to function. It was removed and a new ICD was implanted, which became infected. It was removed and a third ICD was implanted. The patient suffered from failure of the first ICD and infection of the second; the third is functional at this time and the manufacturer settled for an undisclosed amount.

5.7 Removal of Intracardiac Leads

A. General

Intracardiac leads are used for pacing and with the implanted cardioverter defibrillator (ICD), and it is essential that such leads do not migrate after implantation. To assure this, a variety of fixation devices (tines, hooks, barbs, screws, etc.) have been incorporated into the catheter. With the passage of a few months, fibrous tissue encapsulates the catheter and anchors it securely. For this reason, when a pacemaker (or ICD) is replaced, it is highly desirable to use the previously implanted lead. However, when the lead becomes infected or damaged due to fracture, short circuit or insulation breakdown, the clinician is faced with the decision of removing the lead or leaving it in place and inserting a new lead. If the damaged lead is left in place, it is cut off and capped; such a lead is called an abandoned lead. There is reason to be concerned if there are several abandoned leads passing through the tricuspid valve because they can impair valve function. Such leads can also constitute an electrical hazard when the patient is exposed to an electromagnetic field.

Before describing the methods of lead extraction, it is useful to know about the construction of such leads, which may have one or more electrodes and contain one or more conductors. Because such leads flex with each heart beat, the conductors are made of spring-like metal wound in the shape of a coil and embedded in the insulation that forms the catheter. Typically, silicone rubber or polyurethane are used as the catheter material.

Occasionally it is possible to dislodge a lead and remove it by gentle turning and pulling. However this procedure is fraught with danger because the myocardium can be lacerated or punctured and blood will leak into the pericardial sac and impair the ability of the ventricles to fill, which is designated cardiac tamponade, thereby progressively reducing stroke volume and cardiac output. Correction requires emergency surgery. A report of such an accident associated with removal of a pacemaker lead appeared in *Medical Malpractice* (July 1999). The report described the incident as follows:

An eighty-five-year-old lady was admitted for a pacemaker replacement. She already had two pacing leads in situ. The cardiologist put in a third lead and then attempted to remove one of the two old leads. During the trial, the cardiologist testified that the patient "suffered a ventricular rupture of her heart during a pacemaker procedure." Subsequently the patient went into respiratory arrest and had to undergo chest surgery to evacuate the hematoma. As a result of the procedure the patient suffered "a massive loss of blood and became brain dead."

Plaintiffs alleged unnecessary removal and negligence in the removal of the lead and contended that if removal of the lead was in order, it should have been done by an electrophysiologist. Furthermore, the plaintiffs argued that if insertion of a third lead was a concern, there were two other places in the decedent's body where the lead could have been placed. Additionally, the plaintiffs also claimed that the defendant failed to adequately inform the decedent of the kind of procedures and the risks involved.

The defendant cardiologist "contended that the patient was adequately informed of the risks inherent in the procedure and disputed whether the decedent suffered any brain damage because of the surgery. Rather he contended that her condition was a normal progression of dementia."

A judgment for the defendants (cardiologist and hospital) was returned. It is useful to remember in such cases, failure to warn of the risks is essential. Evidently the court believed that the risks were adequately identified to the patient prior to the procedure.

A. Lead-extraction devices

1. Mechanical devices

Several different types of lead-extraction instruments are in use; virtually all use countertraction, the principle of which is shown in Figure 5.8. A typical monopolar lead is shown in Figure 5.8A, in which the lead has been cut. The simplest type of lead is mechanical in which a grasping stylet is passed down the lumen of the lead, as shown in Figure 5.8B, so that the grasping mechanism is located at the tip of the catheter, as shown in Figure 5.8C. Then the grasping mechanism is caused to engage the catheter tip. Many different engaging mechanisms have been patented, the simplest of which is a coil of wire that is uncurled by rotating the handle of the grasping stylet in a counterclockwise direction. Next a coring sheath is passed over the flattened loop handle of the grasping stylet, as shown in Figure 5.8D, and advanced over the catheter electrode. While advancing the coring sheath, the loop is grasped to apply countertraction. The coring sheath is carefully advanced, freeing the catheter from the

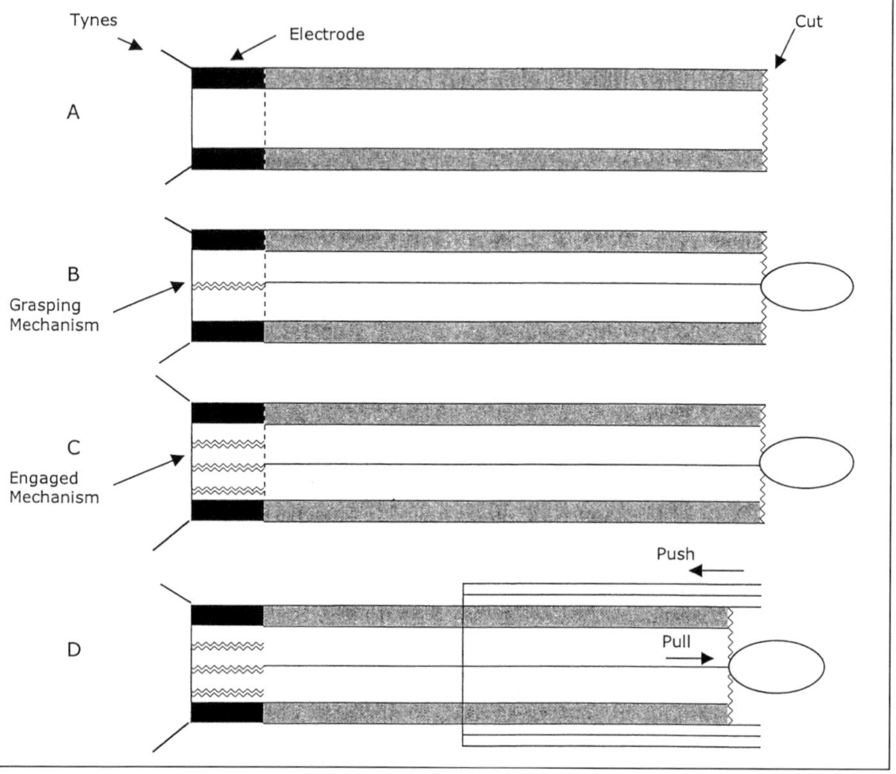

Figure 5.8 *Countertraction principle used with lead-extraction devices*

fibrous tissue that embeds it. Sometimes a second dilator sheath is passed over the coring sheath to facilitate advancement of the coring sheath. During the procedure application of the correct amount of countertraction is essential. Fluoroscopic observation is often used. Such a device is available from Cook Endovascular, Leechburg, PA.

Sometimes it is not possible to gain access to the catheter electrode in the pectoral region and in such a case the femoral vein approach is used. The cut end of the catheter electrode must be grasped with a catheter-deployed snare or basket; this is a much more difficult approach that is less frequently used.

2. Laser-assisted extractor

Laser energy is delivered by a fiber-optic bundle in the coring sheath. Ultraviolet radiation at 308 nanometers is delivered in 135 nanosecond pulses at

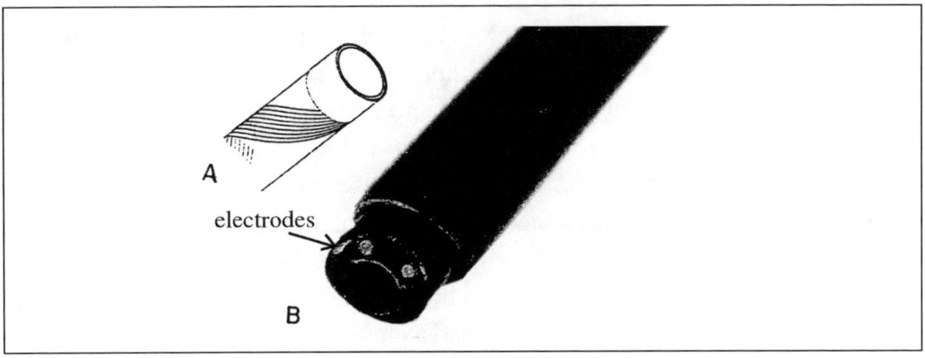

Figure 5.9 (a) *Spectranetics fiberoptic laser-energy dissection sheath and (b) Cook vascular electrosurgical dissecting sheath*

25 to 40/sec; the energy density is 3060 millijoules/cm^2. The fiber-optic bundle is spirally wound in the sheath that is passed over the catheter to be extracted. Thus a band of ultraviolet energy appears at the end of the sheath for ablating the encapsulating tissue; Figure 5.9A illustrates the principle. The use of ultraviolet energy results in strong tissue absorption and the ablated particles are less than 5 microns. It is stated that the depth of energy penetration is less than 100 microns, thereby assuring a localized effect. This device is available from Spetranetics in the Netherlands.

3. Electrosurgical-assisted extractor

Electrosurgical energy is applied by bipolar tungsten (radiopaque) electrodes embedded in the coring sheath, as shown in Figure 5.9B. The electrosurgical current flows through the tissue between the two closely spaced electrodes and dissects it. Rotation of the sheath allows circumferential dissection. This device, produced by Cook Endovascular, Leechburg, PA, is now in clinical trials as an investigational device,

4. Complications with lead extractors

Implanted catheter electrode removal is associated with some risks about which the patient must be informed. One risk is the inability to remove the electrode, in which case it is capped and abandoned and another catheter electrode is implanted. Multiple abandoned leads can impair tricuspid valve function. Other hazards are avulsion (tearing) of the myocardium, causing bleeding into the pericardial sac which produces tamponade and reduced cardiac output. Perforation leading to air entering the thorax (pneumothorax) can cause one or both lungs to collapse. Dislodged clots (emboli) can enter and block pulmonary artery branches, as can broken catheter segments. Mechanical manipulation of the lead can produce ventricular ectopic beats and/or tachycardia. All interventional procedures carry the risk of infection.

a. Mechanical extractors. Two unusual cases of partial rupture of the tricuspid valve, associated with a mechanical pacemaker-lead extractor, were reported by Assayag et al. (1999) in which countertraction was used. Both cases were confirmed by transesophageal echocardiography (TEE). The first case was a seventy-one-year-old male who had a pacemaker implanted twenty years earlier. Five months prior to admission to hospital for heart failure, he had a lead extraction by countertraction. The procedure was uneventful and apparently the lead was replaced. The TEE revealed multiple ruptured chordae and with a prolapse of the anterior leaflet. The patient was treated medically but had recurrent bouts of heart failure during a five-year follow-up.

The second patient was a sixty-five-year-old man who had a pacemaker implanted three years earlier and was admitted for nosocomial (hospital) infection related to prostate surgery. He was discharged and readmitted five months later for a lead extraction and replacement because of infection. TEE revealed rupture of the head of a papillary muscle and severed chordae with prolapse of the anterior leaflet of the tricuspid valve. The patient was stable during a one-year follow-up.

In discussing the two cases, Assayag et al. stated that lesions to the tricuspid valve due to lead extraction are rare. However, they stated that the complications that they reported were unrecognized at the time of lead extraction and reimplantation but they were well revealed by TEE.

A failed lead-extraction accident was reported by Walters and Kay (1999), which involved a twenty-six-year-old woman who was admitted for an elective ventricular pacemaker lead extraction and replacement. A commercially available lead extractor was used and they stated that the procedure was complicated by lead fracture, partial lead retrieval, and embolization of the distal electrode fragment into the pulmonary vascular bed. Despite this complication, the patient remained asymptomatic and in consequence no attempt was made to retrieve the fragment. A new ventricular lead was inserted and the generator upgraded. The patient was discharged and readmitted two years later with an episode of sudden onset right-sided pleuritic chest pain, dyspnea, and hemoptysis. Investigations included a chest x-ray which confirmed the presence of a pacing electrode fragment in the pulmonary vasculature. A radioisotope ventilation/

perfusion scan demonstrated a small mismatched wedge-shaped perfusion defect in the right basal lung. It could not be ascertained whether this was old or new, but on the basis of her presentation it was assumed that the x-ray represented an acute arterial occlusion, most likely secondary to thrombosis in situ consequent to the intravascular electrode fragment. The report stated:

> The patient's subsequent management included full anticoagulation with warfarin, and to date, she remains well. Although radiographically accessible, a decision was made not to retrieve the fragment because of concerns about the degree of localized fibrosis that may have rendered it adherent to the pulmonary arterial wall.

The discussion stated that:

> In consequence, and particularly in the absence of an absolute indication such as lead infection, extraction should only occur where the risks of serious morbidity and mortality have been considered and discussed.

Smith et al. (1994) reported on a five-year retrospective study involving extraction of 2,195 pacemaker leads from 1,299 patients in 193 healthcare centers. The leads were implanted for 0.2 months to twenty-four years. The results revealed that 86.8 percent of the leads were completely removed; 7.5 percent were partially removed and 5.7 percent were not removed. Both implant vein sites and femoral removal (18 percent) sites were used. Backup pacing and intrathoracic surgery were available. Table 5.4 summarizes the potentially life-threatening complications and their incidence. Commenting on their experience, Smith et al. stated that:

> Intravascular lead extraction techniques offer a low-morbidity alternative to open-chest removal of chronic pacemaker leads, but no lead-extraction procedure is without risk of complications. The indication for extraction should be balanced against the risk of complications. Patient selection is important in the preparation for extraction, and experienced operators are conscious of the need to be fully equipped and prepared for every eventuality before undertaking a lead extraction.

Another analysis of complications with lead extractors was reported by Wilkoff et al. (1999) and covered the years from 1988 to 1997. Table 5.5 summarizes the results.

Table 5.4
Potentially Life-Threatening Complications*

	Number	Percent
Hemopericardium/tamponade (2 caused by temporary pacing lead; 3 deaths)	16	1.2%
Hemothorax (includes 1 subacute, 1 hemopneumothorax, 1 death)	6	0.5%
Pulmonary embolism (3 deaths)	3	0.2%
Migrating lead fragment	4	0.3%
Bacteremia after failed extraction	1	<0.1%
Stroke, post-op (death)	1	<0.1%
Ventricular tachycardia during extraction	1	<0.1%
Total	32	2.5%

*Data from Smith, H. et al. PACE 1994, 17(Pt11): 2016–2020.

Table 5.5
Experience with Lead Extraction*

Analysis Group	Number of Cases	Years Implanted	Removal Outcome			Major Complications
			complete	partial	failed	
(1) 1988-1993 Early Cases	1251 Patients 2110 Leads	4.7 ± 3.8	86%	8%	6%	2.0%
(2) 1994-1995 Accufix	985 Patients 1237 Leads	3.1 ± 2.0	94%	4%	2%	1.4%
(3) 1994-1995 Non-Accufix	1011 Patients 1743 Leads	4.5 ± 4.1	91%	6%	2%	1.5%
(4) 1996-1997 Mechanical	1456 Patients 2279 Leads	4.2 ± 3.8	93%	5%	2%	1.4%
(5) 1996-1997 Laser	636 Patients 1155 Leads	5.8 ± 4.0	94%	4%	1%	2.7%

In viewing the data in Tables 5.4 and 5.5, two facts should be borne in mind: (1) experience gained and (2) technology improvement. The last entry in Table 5.5 refers to laser extraction.

b. Laser-assisted lead extraction experience. The first European experience with the ultraviolet (excimer) laser sheath lead extractor was reported by

Kennergren (1998). Using a locking stylet to permit the application of countertraction, he extracted fifty leads (thirty-eight atrial, twelve ventricular) from forty-five patients (twenty-two females, twenty-three males, mean age 65.1 years, range 32–94). Mean lead implantation time was 47.7 months (range 10.5–351.7). Indications for extraction were suspected J-wire fracture in sixteen leads, prophylactic in eight leads, infection in twelve leads, exit block in four leads and other reasons in ten leads. Mean extraction time, excluding reimplantation, was ten minutes (range 1–50). Complete lead extraction was accomplished in all cases but three. All intended lead replacements were successful. No complications occurred and all patients left the hospital in good condition, although one patient died within thirty days due to progressive heart failure.

In using the laser sheath, Bracke et al. (1998) found evidence of a learning curve in association with nineteen patients. Forty-two leads were removed: five leads were removed by traction alone, five required a femoral approach as a primary procedure and a laser sheath was used in thirty-two lead extraction attempts. Primary laser success was achieved in twenty-six attempts (81 percent). A femoral approach was successfully applied as a backup procedure in five of the failures. Overall, 26 percent of the leads were removed by the femoral approach. The overall success rate was 98 percent (forty-one of forty-two leads).

Bracke et al. (1998) concluded:

> Given the unpredictability of the occurrence of complications and the possible need for immediate reparative surgery, we believe that laser-sheath extractions should be performed in an operating room or a catheterization laboratory prepared for cardiovascular surgery. Under these conditions, laser sheath-assisted extraction of pacing leads is highly successful even in less experienced centers. Extraction of pacing leads without the availability of a laser sheath is discouraged.

A new type of complication associated with use of the laser sheath lead extractor was reported by Bracke et al. (1999), who described a single case of arteriovenous fistula in a forty-year-old woman referred for laser-assisted pacemaker lead extraction. She had a subcutaneously implanted dual chamber pacemaker in the left pectoral area connected with bipolar leads in the right ventricle and in the right atrium. The ventricular electrode was extracted first. Entrance from the pacemaker pocket into the subclavian vein was easily established with the laser sheath. Both laser sheath and outer sheath were advanced to the distal electrode, and the tip of the pacing lead was freed with countertraction. A guidewire was left in place for subsequent implantation of a new pacemaker lead. After removal of the outer sheath, leakage from the vein persisted. The atrial lead was extracted. A 14F laser sheath and outer sheath were again easily introduced into the subclavian vein. The tip of the lead was freed with traction. The lead was completely removed although it disintegrated during extraction. An 8F sheath was introduced over the guidewire and a bipolar lead was positioned in the right atrium. The bleeding from the entrance site of the subclavian vein was controlled with a suture. A single-chamber pacemaker (AAI-R) was connected to the lead and the pocket closed. During and after the procedure, the patient was hemodynamically stable. However, after the procedure there was a significant drop in hemoglobin. A chest x-ray showed widening of the superior mediastinum. Computer tomography revealed an aneurysmatic structure at the level of the left subclavian artery. Angiography then revealed a severed left mammary artery as it crossed the subclavian vein. The mammary artery emptied into a newly formed cavity which emptied into the left subclavian vein along the route of the pacemaker lead. Phlebography showed no damage to the subclavian vein. Treatment consisted of embolization of the proximal part of the mammary artery with a coil. Because the cavity still filled from the distal end of the mammary artery, it was clipped surgically through a small intercostal incision. During followup, the aneurysm gradually disappeared. The patient recovered without sequellae.

Wilkoff et al. (1999) studied the safety and efficacy of pacemaker lead extraction with the laser sheath and compared the results with those of other extraction methods. The randomized trial was conducted in 301 patients with 465 chronically implanted pacemaker leads. The laser group and the nonlaser group had the leads removed with identical instruments, with the exception that the inner telescoping sheath was replaced with a 12F laser sheath. Success for both groups was defined as complete lead removal with randomized therapy without complications. Complete lead removal rate was 94 percent in the laser group and 64 percent in the nonlaser group ($p = 0.001$). Failed nonlaser extraction was completed with the laser sheath 88 percent of the time. The mean time to achieve a successful lead extraction was significantly less for laser patients—10.1 ± 11.5 min compared with 12.9 ± 19.2 min for nonlaser patients. Potentially life-threatening complications occurred in none of the nonlaser patients. Three of the laser patients had complications, including one death. A summary of the types of leads and their locations is shown in Table 5.6.

Table 5.6
Comparison of Nonlaser and Laser Lead Extraction Experience*

	Nonlaser	Laser	P
Randomized leads	221	244	
Leads/patient	1.49 ± 0.69	1.59 ± 0.67	
Atrial	119 (54%)	125 (51%)	
Ventricular	101 (46%)	118 (48%)	
Coronary sinus	1	1	
Fixation			
Active	99 (45%)	106 (43%)	0.84
Passive	117 (53%)	134 (55%)	0.74
Other/unknown	5 (2%)	4 (2%)	0.88
Lead age (mo)	69 ± 46	65 ± 42	0.16

*Data from Wilkoff et al. Journ. Amer. Coll. Cardiol. 1999, 33:1671–1676.

Wilkoff et al. (1999) concluded:

> Not only were 94 percent of the leads completely removed with this technique, the mean procedure duration was 10.1 min. When the initial approach was nonlaser with the willingness to crossover to the laser techniques, 95.9 percent of these patients achieved a clinical success with an additional mean extraction time of 14.1 min. When the nonlaser technique was used, 34 percent of the leads required this additional intervention which made the total extraction time an average of 23.7 min. The frequently time-consuming use of femoral extraction tools was uncommon (<1 percent of leads) in the trial. The combination of improved complete success rates and reduced extraction times makes the laser approach attractive.

c. Electrosurgical lead extractor experience. The first animal studies with the Cook vascular electrosurgical dissecting sheath were conducted by Byrd et al. (1997). In this study the focus was on safety and efficacy, ventricular fibrillation being a suspected complication. The active region of the bipolar dissecting sheath electrode was placed on the external surface of the ventricle of an anesthetized sheep. A power of 65 to 110 watts was used. Adequate tissue cutting was seen at 65 watts and no fibrillation occurred at any of the settings. In another sheep, the sheath was used intravascularly to remove an atrial lead implanted six months earlier. Scar tissue was freed by electrosurgical dissection in the superior vena cava and atrium. In a third sheep, scar tissue along a coronary sinus lead, implanted twelve months earlier, was freed by electrosurgical dissection in combination with sheath rotation within the coronary sinus. Injection of a contrast agent confirmed the integrity of the vessel after extraction. No complications arose from use of the device. The technique involved maintaining traction on the lead using a locking stylet. The sheath set was advanced over the lead and its scar tissue. The sheath was activated when mechanical resistance was encountered. When activated, bipolar electrosurgical current passing between the electrodes at the tip of the sheath caused an arc which produced dissection of fibrotic tissue. Because tungsten is radiopaque, the electrodes could be visualized fluoroscopically for directed localized dissection. Of the nine leads, seven were completely removed and two were partially removed, leaving the distal electrodes. Because the size of the custom device as configured was not adequate to allow its advancement to the tip of one lead, an additional device was used to complete removal of that lead. There were no complications.

The most recent efficacy and safety study with the Cook electrosurgical dissecting sheath was reported by Byrd et al. (1999) who attempted removal of chronic cardiac leads from ten sheep. The twenty-two leads were implanted 14 ± 5 months (9–19); twelve were atrial active fixation leads (two pacing, ten atrial defibrillation) and ten were ventricular pacing leads with tines. Of twenty-two leads, seven were easily removed with only mechanical traction. The remaining fifteen leads were removed using a combination of electrosurgical dissection and mechanical dilation of scar tissue. In combination with a conventional outer sheath, the electrosurgical sheath was advanced over the lead for mechanical dilation of scar tissue. When needed for localized dissection, radiofrequency energy was delivered to the tungsten electrodes, at the tip of the Teflon sheath, from an electrosurgical generator (40–50 watts) connected through a custom interface unit.

Two sheep exhibited PVCs (total of six single events and one run of three PVC complexes), all of which were of short duration and self-limiting, similar to those experienced during manipulation of conventional extraction sheaths. No sheep experienced complications related to removal of these leads.

The first clinical experience with the Cook electrosurgical dissecting sheath was reported by Byrd et al. (1999). The study involved four patients (ages 33–77, two males, two females) and the attempted removal of nine chronic leads (implanted 9 ± 3 years). All leads had been implanted through left subclavian approach. Two leads had active fixation, including one Accufix; seven leads had passive fixation, including one Encor lead with a fractured J wire. The bipolar sheath was connected to an electrosurgical generator through a custom interface unit. Used in combination with a conventional outer sheath, the device allowed conventional mechanical dilation of scar tissue. While maintaining traction on the lead using a locking stylet, the sheath set was advanced over the lead and its scar tissue. The sheath was activated when mechanical resistance was encountered.

At this time, the Cook electrosurgical dissecting sheath is an investigational device which continues to be evaluated clinically. It is used with a locking stylet and often with a dilating sheath. The bipolar dissecting sheath is a disposable item that can be used with a conventional electrosurgical unit (ESU) through a custom interface which reduces the output of an ESU to the power needed for tissue dissection. It is to be noted that cutting (unmodulated) electrosurgical current is used.

References

AAMI—Association for the Advancement of Medical Instrumentation. Safe current limits for electromedical apparatus (1978). AAMI. 330 Washington Blvd., Arlington, VA 22201-4598.

Aitken DR and Minton JP. The pinch-off sign. Am. J. Surg. 1984, 148:633–636.

Almassi GH, Edmiston CE and Oblinger GN. Fibrous Ball. Ann. Thor. Surg. 1999, 67(6):1782–1783.

Assayag P, Thuaire C, Benamer H et al. Partial rupture of the tricuspid valve after extraction of permanent pacemaker leads. PACE. 1999, 22 (pt. 1):971–974.

Australian Therapeutic Goods Administration. P.O. Box 100, Woden A ACT. 2606 Australia.

Bach F, Videbaek C, Holst-Christensen J et al. Cystostatic extravasation. Cancer. 1991, 68:538–539.

Becker CM, Malhotra IV and Hedley-White J. The distribution of radio-frequency current and burns. Anesthesiology. 1974, 38(2):106–122.

Bousvaros GA, Dan C and Hopps JA. An electrical hazard of selective angiography. Can. Med. Assn. J. 1962, 87:286–288.

Bracke FA, Meijer A and van Gelder B. Learning curve characteristics of pacing lead extraction with a laser sheath. PACE. 1998, 21 (pt 1):2309–2313.

Bracke FA, Van Gelder B and Meijer A. Arteriovenous fistula after injury of the left internal mammary artery during extraction of pacemaker leads with a laser sheath. PACE. 1999, 22:833–834.

Byrd CL, Bood L, Lowser L et al. Bipolar electrosurgical dissection sheath for lead extraction: Design and initial feasibility. PACE 1997, 20:1129. NASPE New Orleans May 1997.

Byrd CL, Wilkoff BL, Niebauer MJ et al. Localized dissection of scar tissue using a bipolar eletrosurgical sheath for lead extraction. PACE. 1999, 22:758.

Byrd CL. Extraction of chronic cardiac leads using a bipolar electrosurgical dissection sheath: First clinical experience. PACE. 1999, 22:A208. XIth World Symy. Berlin June 1999.

CDRH—See Food and Drug Administration.

Food and Drug Administration, Center for Devices and Radiological Health. 12720 Twinbrook Parkway, Rockville MD, 20857.

Foster KS and Geddes LA. The cause of stimulation with electrosurgical current. Med. Instrum. 1986, 20(6):335–336.

Frager C and Hertzberg R. Spontaneous intravenous catheter fracture and embolization from an implanted venous access port and analyses by seaming electron microscopy. Cancer. 1987, 60: 270–273.

Franey T, De Marco LC, Geiss AC et al. Catheter fracture and embolization in a totally implanted venousaccess catheter. J. Paren. Enteral Nutrition. 1988, 12(5): 528–530.

Furman S and Beneded ZM. Survival of implantable pacemaker leads. PACE. 1990, 13 (12 pt 2): 1910–1014.

Geddes LA and Baker LE. Principles of Applied Biomedical Instrumentation. 1989. Wiley Interscience, New York.

Geddes LA, Tacker WA and Cabler P.A new electrical hazard associated with the electrocautery. Med. Instrum. 1975, 9(2):112–113.

Geddes LA. Ventricular fibrillation due to low and high frequency electrical current. Proc. 14th AAMI Conf., 1979, 14:88.

Geddes LA and LE. The Catheter Introducers. Chicago, IL 1993, Mobium Press (1993).

Grimm W, Flores BF, and Manhlinski FE. Complications of implanted cardioverter defibrillator therapy: follow-up of 241 patients. PACE. 1993, 16 (part 2):218–222.

Groshong LE and Brown RJ. Valved Two-Way Catheter. U.S. Patent 4,549,879 (October 29, 1985) and 4,671,796 (June 9, 1987).

Gruentzig A. Letter to the Editor. Transluminal dilation of coronary-artery stenosis. Lancet 1978, Feb. 4: 263.

Hinke DH, Zandt-Stastny DA, Goodman LR et al. Pinch-off syndrome. Radiology 1990, 177: 353–356

Hungerbuhler RF and Swope JP. Ventricular fibrillation associated with the use of electrocautery. JAMA. 1974, 230(3):431–435.

Jacobs DM, Fink AS, Miller RP, et al. Anatomical and morphological evaluation of pacemaker lead compression. PACE. 1993, 16:434–444.

Jones M and Geddes LA. Strength-duration curves for acardiac pacemaking and ventricular fibrillation. Cardiovascular Res. Center Bull. 1977, 15:101–112.

Kennergren G. First European experience using excimer laser for the extraction of permanent pacemaker leads. PACE. 1998, 21 (pt 2):268–270.

Lafreniere R. Indwelling subclavian catheter and a visit with the pinchedoff sign. J. Surg. Oncol. 1991, 47:261–264.

MAUDE—See Food and Drug Administration

MDR—See Food and Drug Administration.

Magney JE, Flynn DM, Parsons J A et al. Anatomical mechanisms explaining damage to pacemaker leads. PACE. 1993, 16:445–451.

Medical Malpractice Verdicts, Settlements and Experts. 901 Church St. Nashville, TN 37203-3411.

Mody SM, Foona MB and Richings M. Ventricular fibrillation resulting from electrocution during cardiac catheterization. Lancet. 1962, 2:698–699.

Monsees LR and McQuarrie DG. Is an intravascular catheter a conductor? Med. Electron. Data. 1971, 12:26–27.

Pearce JA. Electrosurgery. 1986. Chapman & Hall, London.

Peters RW, Foster AH, Shorofsky et al. Spurious discharges due to late insulation break in endocardial sensory leads for cardioverter defibrillators. PACE. 1995, 18 (pt 1): 478–481.

Prager D and Hertzberg RW. Spontaneous intravenous catheter fracture and embolization. Bancer. 1987, 60:270–272.

Rowe GG and Zarnstorff WG. Ventricular fibrillation during selective angiocardiography. JAMA. 1965, 192(11): 105–108.

Smith HJ, Fearnot NE, Byrd CL et al. Five-years experience with intravascular lead extraction. PACE. 1994, 17(pt11):2016–2020.

Stokes K and McVenes R. Pacing lead fracture, a previously unknown complication of subclavian stick. Cardiostim 88,265 P/755. PACE. 1988, 11:855.

Stokes K, Staffenson D, Lesser J et al. A possible new complications of subclavian stick: conductor fracture. PACE. 1987, Part II 10:748.

Tucker RD, Schmitt, OH, Silvert CE, and Silvis SE. Demodulated low frequency currents from electrosurgical procedures. Surg. Gynecol. Obst. 1984, 159:39–43.

Viamonte M and Hobbs J. Automatic electric injector. Invest. Radiol. 1967, July–August: 262–265.

Walters M and Kaye GC. Pulmonary embolization of a pacing electrode fragment complicating lead extraction. PACE. 1999, 22:823–8.

Wilkoff BL, Byrd CL, Love CL et al. Pacemaker lead extraction with the laser sheath. Journ. Amer. Coll.Cardiol. 1999, 33:1671–1676.

Wilkoff BL, Bryd CL, Love CL et al. Trends in intravacular lead extraction. PACE 1999, 22:A207, XIth World Symp. Berlin, June 1999.

Chapter 6

Transdermal Drug Transport

Synopsis

6.1 Introduction

It is becoming increasingly common to deliver drugs by their application to the skin via an adhesive patch. Analgesics and a variety of drugs such as nicotine and methacholine are but a few examples. The transport rate per unit area is governed by Fick's law of diffusion which states that the rate of transport is proportional to the concentration difference between that on the skin and that below the skin. When a drug is first applied, the skin-surface concentration is high and that below the skin is low. With the passage of time, the drug diffuses and the subdermal concentration increases and the rate of transport decreases. Then capillary blood flow carries away the drug and the ultimate rate of transport is determined by these mechanisms. The amount transported per unit time can be increased by increasing the drug concentration, the area for transport and by warming the area, which increases capillary blood flow. The amount transported can be increased by dissolving the drug in an organic solvent such as dimethylsulfoxide (DMS0). Drug transport can be facilitated by the application of an electric field if the drug molecule is electrically charged; this technique is called iontophoresis. Ultrasound is also used to enhance transport; this technique is called sonophoresis or phonophoresis. Ultrasound can facilitate the transport of neutrally charged drugs. Recently, electroporation, the application of a high-voltage pulse to break down cell membranes to create pores, has been introduced to facilitate transdermal drug delivery. These techniques will be described later.

6.2 Accident with Skin-Patch Drug Delivery

The *Medical Malpractice Journal* (1999) reported a fatal case:

> The plaintiff's decedent, age thirty-six, was taking the drug Fentanyl through a transdermal patch, (brand name). The patch was being used while the man was convalescing from a back injury. He was using the patch along with a heating pad and heating blanket to alleviate his back pain. The plaintiff claimed that the man overdosed on the drug due to the heat from the pad and blanket, increasing the amount of the drug being released into his system. The plaintiff claimed that the manufacturer, (name) failed to warn of the potential to overdose if the patch became heated. According to published accounts a jury awarded $1 million for lost earnings and $4 million for the decedent's mother's emotional distress claim.

The explanation as stated is correct. Heat applied to the skin dilates arterioles, increases capillary blood flow, thereby transporting more drug per unit time through the skin.

6.3 Iontophoresis

Iontophoresis is the term used when a direct current is applied to facilitate delivery of a charged molecule through the skin. In the late 1800s it was discovered that the application of direct current to an electrode placed over a drug-coated skin site facilitated the transdermal transport of the drug. The method of applying iontophoresis is shown in Figure 6.1, in which the charged drug molecule to be transported is contained in a skin-surface structure (A) within which is an inert metal electrode that establishes electrolytic contact with the drug solution. The other inert (dispersive) electrode (B) is much larger in area and at a convenient distant site. Between the two electrodes is connected a con-

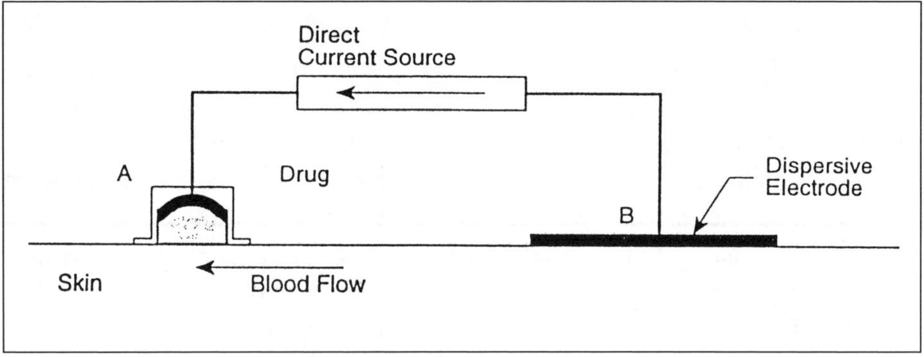

Figure 6.1 *Principle of iontophoresis in which a constant direct current is used to transport drug molecules in an electrode chamber (a) into the skin. The return path for the current is via a large-area dispersive electrode (b).*

stant direct-current source. The polarity is selected on the basis of the polarity of the charge on the drug molecule. For example, if the drug carries a positive charge, the active electrode is made positive. The opposite polarity is used if the charge on the drug molecule is negative. The pH of the solution in the active electrode chamber is important for efficient drug transport. For this reason, a buffer is usually added to the drug solution. Small drug molecules are transported best. It should be noted that other ions having the same charge polarity as the drug will also he transported.

To avoid producing an unpleasant sensation, the current density (mA/cm^2) under the active electrode is kept low, about 0.5 mA/cm^2 or less. The current is increased slowly to its selected value to avoid sensation. Likewise, when the treatment is to he terminated, the current is slowly reduced to zero before the electrodes are removed. If the current is turned on or off suddenly, the subject may feel a sensation like a pin prick, or stronger if the current density is high.

The amount of drug transported through the skin by iontophoresis depends on the type of drug, the current density and its duration of flow, and the concentration of the drug in the active electrode chamber, as well as pH. Treatment times usually last from ten to thirty minutes. The treatment is quantitated in terms of charge, i.e., the product of milliamperes and minutes. The current density is preferably less than 1 mA/cm^2 . High current density will produce an unpleasant pricking sensation and erythema. Iontophoresis should not be applied to sites where there is skin damage.

A. Side effects

Apart from the use of excessive current which can produce an unpleasant skin sensation and injury, there can be side effects due to the species of metal used for the active electrode. Many different metals have been used for the active electrode which can be either positive or negative, depending on the charge on the drug molecule. Silver, tin, zinc, stainless steel, copper and carbon-loaded silicone rubber have all been used. Because direct current is used, a wide variety of electrolytic products can be produced at the active electrode site. For example, if silver is used and made positive, it is chlorided; if it is made negative, silver ions are transported into the skin producing a black spot. The presence of silver in the skin is called argyria. Copper ions have been intentionally deposited in the skin for their germicidal effect. Such heavy metal ions combine with proteins. For iontophoresis, it is wise to use an inert electrode material such as stainless steel, platinum, gold, or carbon, and keep the current below the sensation threshold to avoid pain, erythema or skin sloughing.

B. Iontophoresis accidents

An injury that accompanied the use of iontophoresis was reported as follows: The U.K. Medical Devices Agency (MDA) issued a safety notice stating that it has received several reports of patients being burned by iontophoresis equipment and that the most recent incidents were caused by the use of inadequately maintained iontophoresis electrodes that had corroded and buckled. Buckling of flexible disposable skin-surface electrodes is not unknown in electrosurgery where the phenomenon is known as "tenting" which causes local regions of high current density, resulting in localized burns.

Reinauer et al. (1993) reported an accidental skin lesion during application of iontophoresis to the palm. They stated that an electrical skin burn occurred when iontophoresis current was conducted by a ring on a finger.

At present, iontophoresis is approved for the delivery of only a few drugs. However, its use will increase as it is found to be useful for new drugs. It is well suited for the transdermal transport of small charged molecules.

6.4 Ultrasonic Facilitation of Transdermal Drug Delivery

It has been found that the application of low-frequency (20 kHz to about 1 MHz) ultrasound facilitates transdermal drug delivery. Because the attenuation of ultrasound in tissues increases with increasing frequency, low frequencies are used. The procedure is called sonophoresis or phonophoresis and involves several different mechanisms. It is used to transport local anesthetics, anti-inflammatory drugs, nicotine and nitroglycerin. Small molecules are transported more efficiently than large molecules.

A. Coupling agent

The application of ultrasound requires the use of a coupling agent (gel) placed between the transducer and the skin. The drug can be placed on the skin first and then the coupling agent is applied. The drug can be incorporated into the coupling agent. which may be a cream or a hydrogel. Unlike iontophoresis, which requires that the drug molecule be charged, sonophoresis can transport uncharged molecules.

B. Mechanisms of action

Several different mechanisms are believed to underlie the facilitation of transdermal drug transport by ultrasound: thermal, cavitation (which depends on frequency and power density), microstreaming and mechanical effects. Cavitation is the development of vapor bubbles in a liquid due to the creation of local steep pressure gradients. A thermal effect can result from absorption of ultrasonic energy by tissues. Microstreaming is the production of local eddy current flow, probably due to thermal and cavitation effects. Mechanical effects of ultrasound on the skin are believed to alter permeability. Studies by Mitragotri et al. (1995) showed that cavitation was the dominant factor in a study using human cadaver skin through which the transport of several drugs was measured using 1- or 3-MHz ultrasound with a power density of 0–2 W/cm^2. Cavitation disorganized the lipid layer of the stratum corneum cells and thereby facilitated transport.

Another sonophoresis study by Johnson et al. (1996) used 1 MHz ultrasound at a power density of 1.4 W/cm^2 to facilitate drug transport across human cadaver skin. A similar study by Ueda et al. (1996) using rat skin required 0.111 W/cm^2 of 150 kHz ultrasound to facilitate drug transport. Finally, Mitragotri et al. (2000) established the threshold energy density as 222J.cm^2 for 20 kHz ultrasound to transport drugs through full-thickness pig skin (which is a good analog for human skin). They stated that above this threshold, the transport was proportioned to the intensity and duration of the 20-kHz ultrasound and believed that cavitation is the principal mechanism of transport.

C. Side effects

Transdermally delivered ultrasound typically encounters fat, muscle and bone. At each interface there is a reflection and scattering of the energy resulting in a temperature rise at the fat/muscle and muscle/bone interface. The temperature rise depends on the intensity of the ultrasound, the absorption coefficients of the tissues and the duration of application of the ultrasound. In a typical case, the temperature rise at the fat/tissue interface is less than that at the muscle/bone interface. If the duration of application is longer, a substantial temperature rise can result at the muscle/bone interface with considerable periosteal pain. If this occurs treatment is stopped or continued at another site. There are, as yet, no data on the thermal response when ultrasound encounters a metal implant, such as a cardiac pacemaker or bone pin or screw. At these sites, it is expected that there may be considerable heating.

D. Ultrasound experiences in physical medicine

Ultrasound has been used in physical medicine since the late 1940s to relieve aches, pains and reduce edema. It is not uncommon to add a vasodilating drug to the coupling gel to enhance capillary blood flow (Summer and Patrick 1964). It is still used for this purpose and undoubtedly it will be used to facilitate the transport of analgesic drugs. When properly employed, the hazard is low.

The power density (W/cm^2) levels used in sonophoresis are similar to those used in physical therapy and the side effects encountered merit attention. Summer and Patrick (1964) provided the following power densities for 1 MHz ultrasound therapy; low <1, medium 1–2 and strong 2–4 W/cm^2. They pointed out that:

> A patient with normal sensory reaction to pain will complain of a burning sensation or pain when the upper limits of insonation are being reached. These sensations are usually first felt over bony tissues as there is an extra buildup of heat owing to the reflection of the beam on striking the bone and a lack of blood supply in the periosteum.

It is important to note that the periosteum is richly endowed with nerve endings. Bogner (1994) stated that ultrasound should not be applied near bony prominences because of the hazard of periosteal burns. She also stated that sonophoresis should never be applied prior to iontophoresis.

6.5 Electroporation

Plant and animal cells are enveloped by a living insulating (dielectric) membrane. Electroporation is the technique by which a pulse of high-intensity electric field (volts/cm) is applied to create a tiny hole (pore) in the cell membrane. By this means large molecules can enter the cell. However, unlike physical dielectrics (rubber, plastic, etc.) in which the breakdown hole persists, cell membranes heal, i.e., the pore closes in a short time and the molecules that entered the cell are trapped therein. The pore diameter depends on the cell type and electrical field strength; typical pores range from 20 to 120 nm in diameter. The pore density (pores/area) depends on the orientation of the cell with respect to the direction and the strength of the electrical field, as well as the cell type. Electroporation is used in genetic research to deliver foreign DNA into a cell so that it responds to the injected DNA in a desired way to alter the cell's reproductive capability. Electroporation is now beginning to be used to deliver drugs into cells.

Electroporation is also used to join cells together; this process is called electrofusion. Cells in a medium are placed in contact under the influence of an electric field, then a pulse of electroporation current is applied and a pore is made in each cell's membrane when they are in contact. Then the cells fuse into a single cell. As stated earlier, the dielectric breakdown of cell membranes is self healing and the pores close in a short time. Coster and Zimmerman (1975) used transmembrane electrodes to study the breakdown of membranes of the plant cell valonia with 0.5–1 msec pulses. They found that the breakdown was local and recovery occurred in less than four seconds. Gauger and Bentrup (1979) investigated membrane breakdown in brown alga using pulses of 1–1760 μsec in duration and field strength of 50–400 V/cm. They, too, found that the breakdown was local and recovery occurred in less than three seconds. The pore lifetime of excised pig skin was found to be about one second by Gallo et al. (1997). To maintain pores for longer periods, pulses are delivered at a slow rate (e.g. 1/sec).

A. Electrical parameters for electroporation

To cause dielectric breakdown of cell membranes to create pores, single capacitor-discharge or rectangular-wave pulses are employed. There are typically two methods: (1) short-duration (≈ 1 msec), high voltage (0 to a few kV) and (2) long duration (≈100 msec), low voltage (0 to hundreds of volts). In both cases the pulse causes current to flow through the medium to achieve a gradient (volts/cm) sufficient to cause breakdown of the cell membranes to create pores. The voltage required depends on electrode geometry, the tissue resistivity and location of the cells between the electrodes. If the cells are in a small chamber between the electrodes, less applied voltage is required than if the electrodes are on the skin surface or encompass a large cell mass. The essential factors are the intensity of the voltage and the duration of the pulse.

B. Transdermal drug delivery by electroporation

Unlike iontophoresis, which requires a charged molecule and sonophoresis, which uses ultrasound to increase permeability of the stratum corneum (for small uncharged molecules), electroporation creates pores through which fairly large molecules can enter cells.

That electroporation enhances drug delivery through the skin has been proven by in-vitro studies using hairless rat skin, pig skin and human cadaver skin placed between two chambers containing electrodes. The concentration of the drug in the donor and recipient chambers has been measured as a function of the electrical parameters (voltage and pulse duration). Such studies reveal that electroporation facilitates drug transport by about four orders of magnitude over passive diffusion.

Okino et al. (1992) employed electroporation to drive the anticancer drug bleomycin into rat tumor cells using subcutaneous electrodes 2.5 cm long and separated by 2.5 cm so that they straddled the 1–2 cm tumors in a rat study. They applied a single voltage pulse to each of the seventy-two rats (150–200 gm); the pulses were synchronized with the QRS wave of the ECG to eliminate the risk of producing cardiac arrhythmias (ventricular tachycardia and fibrillation). They studied the effect of voltage (0–5 kV) and pulse duration of (2.5–8.5 msec) on the effectiveness of drug delivery and found that the tumoricidal effect was proportional to the voltage squared multiplied by the pulse duration, namely the energy delivered. They concluded:

> Our maximal tumoricidal effect was achieved at a field strength of 5 kV/2.5 cm (2 kV/cm) or greater for 3 ms. Since we expect that any adverse effects on surrounding normal tissues will also be in proportion to electric energy, it may be possible to minimize adverse effects while maximizing the tumoricidal effect by using an electric pulse of 2 kV/cm for 3 ms.

Although the Okino et al. study showed that the effectiveness of drug delivery was proportional to the product of the voltage squared (V^2) and the duration (d); it should be recognized that this study examined the effect of duration over a narrow duration range (2.5 to 8.5 msec) and that it is unlikely that the product (V^2d) may be varied over a wide voltage range to achieve an effective

V^2d because it requires above a threshold voltage to effect a dielectric breakdown. This was found to be the case by Cemezar et al. (1995) who studied different cell types using 100 μsec pulses. They also found that the critical breakdown voltage depended on cell type. A similar result was obtained by Gallo et al. (1997) who applied electrodes to the surface of excised pig skin.

The first clinical trial using electroporation pulses to treat cancer patients was reported by Belehradek et al. (1993). They treated eight patients with forty permeation nodules of head and neck squamous cell carcinomas with 10 mg/m^2 bleomycin intravenous bolus, followed by four to eight short (10 μsec) and intense (1300 V/cm) pulses administered through two external electrodes (10 mm, separated by 6 mm) located on each side of the treated nodule. They reported that a clear local antitumor efficacy was found: twenty-three (57 percent) nodules were in clinical complete response within a few days. They also stated that the peak current was 1.9 to 8 amps delivery at 1/sec and that a muscle contraction accompanied each electroporation pulse. In addition, the patients reported "a local shock or punch at the level of the treated area." There were no cardiovascular responses, nor were there any long-lasting sequelae.

Heller et al. (1996) conducted a clinical study to determine if electroporation would be effective in the use of bleomycin to treat cutaneous malignant tumors. A group of patients, three with malignant melanoma, two with basal cell carcinoma and one with metastatic adenocarcinoma, were enrolled in the study. The treatment was administered in a two-step procedure. Each patient received a 10-unit/m^2 dose of bleomycin administered intravenously at one to fifteen units/minute. This was followed by eight 99 μsec pulses at 1/sec with an amplitude of 1.3 kV/cm administered directly to the tumors five to fifteen minutes after the bleomycin was completely infused. Pulses were administered after the administration of 1 percent lidocaine solution around the treatment site (lidocaine has anesthetic properties). The electrodes were of stainless steel 2×2 cm and mounted on a caliper so that they straddled the tumor. ECG electrode paste was used as the conductive coupling agent. Each pulse was a square voltage wave.

The results of Heller's study were encouraging. Two of three melanoma patients had objective responses. In these two patients, five of six treated tumors decreased in size, and three completely responded. Untreated tumors displayed continued growth. Objective responses were observed in both basal cell carcinoma patients. One patient had partial responses in both treated tumors. The other patient had one of four primary basal cell carcinomas that responded completely, and the remaining three responded partially. Patients with metastatic breast adenocarcinoma showed complete responses in both treated nodules after electroporation treatment.

All patients tolerated the treatment with no residual effects from the electric pulses. However, during the treatments, all patients except one, reported mild pain at the treatment site. Muscle twitches followed each pulse. The patients were interviewed twenty-four and forty-eight hours after treatment and none complained of any residual pain or discomfort from the electric pulses. Slight burning of the skin was observed at various sites on four of the six patients which healed within two to four weeks. Following delivery of the pulses to an arm or leg, muscle fatigue was reported in that particular limb for twenty-four to forty-eight hours after treatment. Two of the six patients reported that they had nausea, fever, chills, and general malaise for twenty-four to forty-eight hours after treatment, perhaps related to the systemic administration of the bleomycin.

C. Stimulation of excitable tissue

Because electroporation uses substantial voltage pulses, stimulation of excitable tissue is expected when applied transdermally. For this reason it is desirable to understand the factors that govern stimulation so that an electroporation pulse can be optimized to minimize an unpleasant sensation or muscle twitch.

The law of stimulation is embodied in the strength-duration (S-D) curve, which is a plot of the threshold peak current (I) required to evoke a response versus the duration (*d*) of the pulse, Figure 6.2 illustrates strength-duration curves for heart muscle, skin sensation and a typical motor nerve for rectangular (square) and capacitor-discharge (exponentially decaying) waves. The duration (*d*) of the capacitator-discharge wave is defined as the time for the current to fall to 37 percent of its initial peak value. With this definition the charge $Q = Id$ is equal for the two waveforms.

Several important concepts are evident in Figure 6.2 in which, for all excitable tissues there is a long-duration asymptote that is designated the rheobase (b). For all excitable tissues, as the duration (d) is decreased more current (and voltage) is required to evoke a response. Note that the curves for the various excitable tissues differ only in location; but they have the same shape.

The rheobase (b), the duration-independent quantity, depends on the distance that the excitable tissue is from the stimulating electrodes on or in the tissue. For example, the heart is further from skin-surface electrodes and the

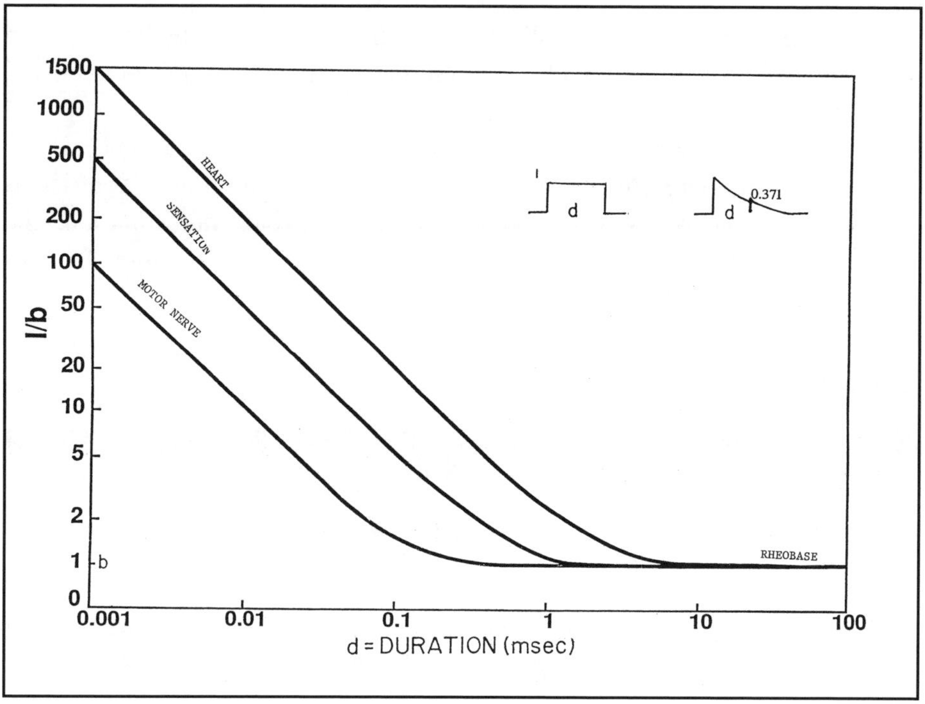

Figure 6.2 *Normalized strength-duration curves for cardiac-muscle stimulation, sensation and motor-nerve stimulation. The current (I) is expressed as I/b, where b is the rheobasic current.*

rheobase (b) will be higher, therefore its strength-duration curve will be above that for the skin-sensation stimulation curve. In such a case, the lowest current for heart stimulation would favor choice of a long-duration pulse, e.g. 10 msec or more. The price paid is sensory stimulation. A different example can be selected to illustrate the opposite situation, namely one in which a motor nerve is superficial and close to skin sensation receptors. Observe in Figure 6.2 that the strength-duration curve for motor-nerve stimulation lies to the left of that for sensation. If the two excitable tissues are equidistant from the stimulating electrodes, their rheobases will be the same and if one wants to avoid stimulating sensory receptors, the choice of pulse duration would be when the ratio of sensation to motor nerve is greatest, which is in the region of 0.01 msec or less.

From the viewpoint of minimizing stimulating excitable tissue with electroporation pulses, Figure 6.2 indicates that a pulse duration shorter than 1 msec would be preferable to a longer duration pulse to avoid the risk of cardiac stimulation. However, it may be that the character of the pore may be better with a longer duration, low-amplitude pulse. Such a comparison has not been made in view of the ability of electroporation pulses to stimulate excitable tissue.

However, it should be noted that if electroporation current pulses gain access to the heart, there is the danger of serious cardiac arrhythmias (ventricular ectopic beats, tachycardia and fibrillation). To avoid this situation, the electroporation pulse must be synchronized with the QRS wave of the ECG as described by Okino et al. (1992).

References

Belehradek M, Domenge C, Lubionski B et al. Electrochemotherapy, a new antitumor treatment. Cancer. 1993, 72(12):3694–3700.

Bogner RH and Bagna AK. Iontophoresis and sonophoresis. US Pharmacist. 1994, 19: H14–16, 20, 22, 24–26.

Cemazar J, Shan I, Jarm T et al. Determination of optimal electric pulse amplitude for electropermeabilization of different tumor cell lines in-vitro. Int. Mtgs. Life Sci. 1995, p77.

Coster HGL, Zimmerman U. The mechanism of electric breakdown in the membranes of valoria utriculars. J. Membr. Biol. 1975, 22:73.

Coster HGL, Zimmerman U. Dielectric breakdown in the membranes of valonia utricularis. Biochim. Biophys. Acta. 1975, 382:410.

Heller R, Jaroszeki JJ, Glass LF et al. Phase 1/11 trial for the treatment of cutaneous and subcutaneous tumor using electrothermotherapy. Cancer. 1996, 77:964–971.

Gallo SA, Oserfoo AR, Johnson PG et al., Characterization of electric-pulse permeabilization of porcine skin using surface electrodes. Biophys. Journ. 1997, 72:2805–2811.

Gauger B and Bentrup FW. A study of dielectric membrane breakdown in the focus egg. Journ. Membr. Biol. 1979, 48:249–264.

Johnson ME, Mitragotri S, Patel A et al. Synergistic effects of chemical enhancers and therapeutic ultrasound on transdermal drug delivery. Journ. Pharm. Sci., 1996, 86:670–679.

Medical Malpractice Verdicts, Settlements and Experts. 1999, 15(12):9.

Meidan VM, Docker M, Walmsley D et al. Low intensity ultrasound as a probe to elucidate the relative follicular contribution to total transdermal absorption. Pharm. Res. 1998, 15(l):85–92.

Mitragotri S, Edwards DA, Blankschtein et al. A melhanistic study of ultrasonically enhanced transdermal drug delivery. Journ. Pharm. Sci. 1995, 84:697–706.

Mitragotri S, Farrell J, Tang H et al. Determination of threshold energy dose for ultrasoundinduced transdermal drug transport. Journ. Controlled Release. 2000, 63:41–52.

Okino M, Tomic H, Kanesada H et al. Optimal electrical conditions in electrical impulse chemotherapy. Japan Journ. Cancer Res. 1992, 83:1095–1101.

Reinauer S, Neusser A, Schaupf G et al. Iontophoresis with alternating current and direct current offset. Brit. Journ. Dermatol. 1993, 129:166–169.

Summer W and Patrick MK. Ultrasonic Therapy. Amsterdam, 1964, Elsevier. 163pp.

Ueda H, Ogihora M, Sugiba K et al. Difference in the enhancement effects of ultrasound on the skin penetration of polar and non-polar drugs. Chem. Pharm. Bull. 1996, 44(10):1973–76.

U.K. Medical Devices Agency (MDA) 1999. http//www.medical-devices.gov.uk/.

Chapter 7

Pain Suppression by Electrical Stimulation

Synopsis

7.1 Introduction

It is possible to reduce or abolish pain by applying electrical stimuli to strategically placed electrodes. When such stimuli are applied to skin-surface electrodes, the technique is known as transcutaneous electrical nerve stimulation (TENS); when applied to peripheral nerve, the method is known as peripheral nerve stimulation (PNS). When the stimuli are applied to electrodes on the spinal cord, the technique is called dorsal column stimulation (DCS; sometimes the term spinal cord stimulation (SCS) is used. Occasionally stimuli are applied to electrodes on the acupuncture sites; this method is known as electroacupuncture. Finally, high-voltage, low-current stimuli are applied to body-surface electrodes to stun or restrain a subject; such techniques are described in this chapter.

7.2 Transcutaneous Electrical Nerve Stimulation (TENS)

A. Introduction

Transcutaneous electrical nerve stimulation (TENS) employs mild, short-duration, repetitive electrical stimuli, applied to skin-surface electrodes to reduce or abolish acute or chronic pain, the latter being loosely defined as pain lasting more than six months. A TENS unit is prescribed by a physician and is operated by the patient. Because electrical stimuli are applied to the body, there is the possibility of such signals interfering with the operation of implanted electronic therapeutic devices.

TENS is used widely to relieve the pain associated with athletic injuries, trauma, surgical procedures, cancer, and childbirth. Among other conditions now treated are migraine, bursitis, tennis elbow, tendonitis, rheumatoid arthritis, tinnitus, diabetic neuropathy, radiculopathies, carpal tunnel syndrome, shoulder-hand syndrome, osteoarthritis, sciatica, sinus headache, reflex sympathetic dystrophy and hemiplegic pain.

Pain intensity is graded on a scale of zero (no pain) to ten (incapacitating pain). Although pain from any cause is amenable to TENS treatment, not all subjects experience complete relief. The zero-to-ten pain scale is used to identify the relief, i.e., by a reduction in the scale number. Adequate relief is obtained by about 50 percent of the subjects. There are many who believe that the use of TENS plus an analgesic reduces the amount of drug needed to suppress pain.

There are a few contraindications for the use of TENS; for example, in patients with demand cardiac pacemakers, the pacemaker could be inhibited if it detects the TENS pulses. This controversial situation will be discussed later in this chapter. TENS should not be used for undiagnosed pain; nor should it be used if the current flowing between the electrodes is transcranial. The effect of transcranial current is discussed elsewhere in this chapter. TENS should not be used with electrodes around the eyes because phosphenes (light flashes in the visual field) may be perceived. Another contraindication is the placement of electrodes on the neck over the carotid sinuses, vagus, or laryngeal nerves, stimulation of which could produce cardiac arrhythmias.

B. Mechanisms of pain inhibition

Wall and Sweet (1967) discovered that pain could be suppressed by electrical stimulation of large-diameter sensory nerve (A) fibers which verified the gate theory of Melzack and Wall (1965). Wall and Sweet carried out studies on eight patients using direct-nerve and transcutaneous electrical stimulation. They applied 0.1-msec rectangular wave stimuli with a frequency of 100/sec. Superficial nerves were stimulated using needle or wire electrodes—a needle or wire paired with a skin-surface electrode or two skin-surface electrodes. In each case, the stimulus intensity was increased until a tingling sensation was perceived by the patient. In general, two minutes of stimulation provided about thirty minutes of pain relief.

A second mechanism of pain suppression by TENS involves the endogenous secretion of morphine-like substances (endorphins) from the periaqueductal region in the brain. Sjolund and Eriksson (1976, 1979) advanced this theory on the basis of blockade of pain suppression by naloxone, a drug that inhibits the analgesic effect of morphine, the most potent pain killer.

The goal of TENS is to stimulate large-diameter, sensory afferent nerve fibers only; therefore, short-duration pulses of current are used because the chronaxie of these nerve fibers is shorter than that for pain fibers. Figure 7.1 shows strength-duration curves for sensory (A) and pain (C) nerve fibers. Note that the current required for stimulating pain fibers starts to rise for a pulse duration shorter than about 2 msec; whereas the threshold for sensory fibers rises for a pulse duration shorter than about 0.05 msec. Therefore, the use of a

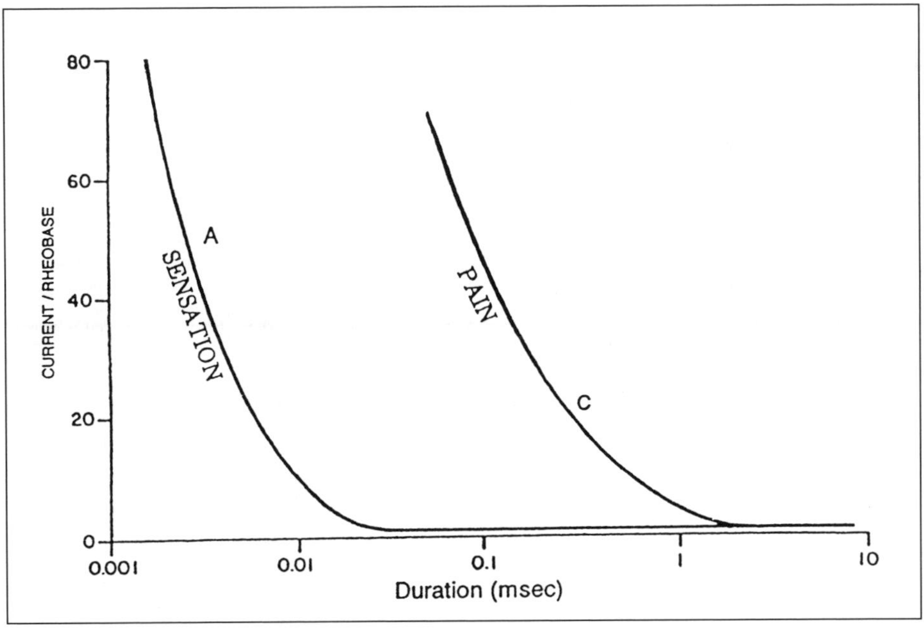

Figure 7.1 *Strength-duration curves for pain and sensation*

stimulus of this duration will minimally stimulate pain and maximally stimulate sensory fibers.

C. Current-pulse characteristics

Although repetitive short-duration pulses are employed with TENS, there are many ways of delivering these pulses. Low-frequency TENS employs 2 to 5/sec pulses and high-frequency TENS uses 80 to 140/sec pulses. Some TENS units deliver short bursts twice/second, while another mode employs rhythmic modulation of the pulse width. Finally, some TENS units employ a positive/negative (bidirectional) wave. All modalities seek to produce a mild tingling sensation. Table 7.1 presents a compilation of output characteristics of 18 TENS units. Note that pulse rates available range from less than 1 to 285/sec and the pulse widths available range from 16 to 720 μsec.

D. Electrode placement

At present, there are no standard sites for TENS electrodes. Mannheimer (1978) and Mannheimer et al. (1978) recommended that the best sites were motor, acupuncture, and/or trigger points. A motor point is a skin site where the lowest stimulus intensity will evoke muscular contraction. A trigger point is a site where gentle pressure evokes a specific sensation, usually pain. In general, one electrode is placed over, or just proximal to the site of pain and over a superficial nerve. The other electrode is placed distally at a convenient site. Uniform contact with the skin is essential to prevent the development of localized regions of high current density. Sometimes four electrodes are used with a two-channel TENS unit. Diagonal lines joining the electrodes form an X, the center of which is the pain site.

E. Electrode types

Two types of electrodes are used; one employs metal foil with a conductive gel and the other is black rubber or carbon-loaded silicone rubber. Usually any hair on the skin site is clipped and the skin is washed with mild soap. After the electrodes are applied, the output of the TENS unit is increased very slowly until a mild tingling sensation is perceived. The relief of pain occurs slowly; often it requires more than thirty minutes to start to be perceived. Pain relief far outlasts cessation of stimulation.

Table 7.1
Output Characteristics of Typical TENS Units

	Pulse Characteristics			
Manufacturer	Rate/Sec	Amplitude mA PK-PK	Width μSEC	Charge μC Max/Pulse
A	7.1	41	200	3
B	2.9–131.6	130	60–140	19
C	2.3–106.4	480	200	100
D	0.9–87.7	110m	100–160	42
E	3.7–113.6	52	40–300	14
F	0.7–27.8	200	200	150
G	2.2–106.4	80	40–230	24
H	40.8–104	130	720	57
I	2–104.1	135	40–270	34
J	3.3–100	170	400	71
K	94.3b	120	150	59
L	2.1–192.3	78	50–600	41
M	14.300–14.3	8	34	0.14
N	1.8–119	160	45–120	23
O	4.2–151.5	70	50–250	16
P	2.2–50	230	350	71
Q	10.4–270	120	16–280	29
R	2.9–285	86	30–220	11

Note: b = bursts, m = modulated.
Data from *Health Devices*, June 1981. ECRI Plymouth Meeting, PA 19462.

F. Standards of performance

There is an AAMI/ANSI standard for the performance of TENS units. It sets performance requirements when the TENS unit is connected to a resistive load and specifies the maximum charge per pulse. The standard can be obtained from AAMI and is designated ANSI/AAMI-NS4-1985.

G. Complications with TENS units

A TENS unit is a mild electrical stimulator, the output of which is set by the patient. For this reason only fully conscious, responsible patients should use a TENS unit. The patient must have been instructed on the proper use by a knowledgeable therapist.

Skin irritation accompanying the use of TENS has been reported by Zugerman (1982), who described a case of allergic contact dermatitis. It was found that the conductive coupling agent used with the electrodes contained propylene glycol, to which the patient was allergic, verified by a patch test. Patch tests with other coupling agents revealed one that produced no irritation, and with it the patient was able to resume TENS treatments.

Bolton (1983) suggested that the skin reaction that Zugerman reported could be due to electrochemical decomposition of the conducting coupling medium at the electrode-skin surfaces where hydrogen and hydroxyl ions are liberated. While this can occur with unidirectional current pulses, the positive patch test with propylene glycol indicates that the patient was allergic to this chemical constituent of the electrode coupling medium.

To avoid skin reaction under TENS electrodes, Bolton (1983) recommended the use of a 1- to 2-mm-thick gauze pad, moistened thoroughly with physiological saline (0.9 percent) or weak buffer as the electrode coupling agent. She also recommended the use of a waveform consisting of a short train of positive-going pulses followed immediately by an identical train of negative-going pulses. In this way there is no net charge delivered and, hence, no net electrochemical decomposition of the coupling agent.

There has been some concern about the safety of TENS in obstetrics because the electrodes are close to the fetus *in utero*. Typically, the electrodes are placed on the lower back (T-10, 11, S-2, 4) or the suprapubic region. Bundsen and Ericson (1982) reported that in over 500 obstetric patients undergoing TENS, no harmful effects have been observed in the mother or child.

The ability of a TENS unit to interfere with an implanted demand cardiac pacemaker is a controversial issue. Such a device senses the electrical activity of the heart and, if present, is inhibited. Such a pacemaker could sense low-frequency TENS pulses and be inhibited. There is also the possibility of reprogramming of the pacemaker by TENS pulses. Whether or not these events occur depends on the type of pacemaker, the type of electrodes (monopolar or bipolar), the distance and orientation of the TENS electrodes with respect to the pacing lead, and the intensity and type of pulses delivered by the TENS unit. It should also be noted that implantable nerve and muscle stimulators are used for a variety of purposes and the output of such devices could be detected by a demand pacemaker or implanted cardioverter defibrillator. Whether there are few such incidents or whether many are unreported is not known.

Shade (1985) reported on her experience with a seventy-four-year-old, 200-lb man with a cardiac pacemaker who had metastatic cancer and was using TENS to control pain. The TENS electrodes were placed on the left lateral chest, two slightly anteriorly and two posteriorly at the 5th and 10th intercostal areas. The amplitude range for this unit was 0 to 130 V, the frequency range 12 to 100/sec, and the pulse width range was 120 to 330 μsec. A stimulation pulse width of 20 μsec was used. The rate and amplitude were set at 5 to give a frequency of 35 pulses per second (pps). At this setting, the patient's pain was rated 2 as opposed to a maximal rating of 10 at pretreatment. This decrease in pain occurred within one hour after TENS application. The patient used the TENS unit 24 h/day. Shade stated that "an ECG readout was taken before the TENS unit was applied that showed strong, sufficient cardiac rhythm. Once the TENS unit was applied, the settings were slowly increased to the level of pain relief. This increase was achieved with a rate of thirty-five pulses per second. During this adjustment period, continuous ECG readouts were taken for approximately two minutes." No cardiac arrhythmia was observed. She concluded by stating "with close monitoring, some patients may be able to wear a TENS unit simultaneously with cardiac pacemakers." Shade recommended recording the ECG while increasing the output of the TENS unit with pacemaker patients.

Rasmussen et al. (1988) applied TENS at four sites to fifty patients with twenty models of cardiac pacemakers. The sites were on the same side of the body as the pacemaker and included the lumbar, neck, left leg, and lower arm. The TENS frequency was 24.7/sec and no episodes of interference or reprogramming were encountered. They stated:

> We believe that most patients with permanent cardiac pacemakers can safely undergo TENS. We suggest that the TENS electrodes not be placed parallel to the pacemaker electrode vector until studies have verified the safety of this positioning.

This admonition is very relevant because if the TENS electrodes are on the chest in a line parallel to the pacemaker electrode axis, there will be the maximum likelihood of the pacemaker sensing the TENS pulses.

When considering the possibility of a TENS unit interfering with a demand cardiac pacemaker, it is important to distinguish between low-frequency and high-frequency TENS. The former employs 2 to 5 pulses/sec, which is equivalent to 120 to 300/min, which is in the heart-rate range. Because the sensing circuits in demand pacemakers are band-pass limited, high-frequency TENS may not be so easily detected as low-frequency TENS.

7.3 Peripheral Nerve Stimulation (PNS)

Two techniques are used with PNS: (1) electrodes are inserted percutaneously and connected to an external pulse generator and (2) an implanted pulse generator is connected to implanted electrodes. In the latter case, the pulse generator can be an active, battery-operated device that is programmed externally or a passive receiver that is excited by a skin-surface transmitter. Often prior to implanting a pulse generator and its electrodes, tests are carried out with percutaneous electrodes connected to an external stimulator that the patient controls to assess the efficacy and any side effects of PNS. Later, stimulating electrodes, connected to an implanted receiver (or pulse generator) are placed surgically. Local anesthesia can be used to implant the electrodes and receiver which is located in a nearby subcutaneous pocket. Thus, the implantation procedure is associated with a low risk and few complications.

For success in pain relief, the patient must be selected carefully. Patients in a disturbed emotional state (e.g. anxiety), are not good candidates for PNS. Unfortunately, there are few criteria for optimal patient selection and it is difficult, at present, to predict those who will obtain significant pain relief. It is important to recognize that among those who obtain relief, it usually lasts for some time after cessation of stimulation.

The patient can control the intensity, and with some units, the frequency of the stimuli. A typical frequency range is 10–100/sec which was advocated by Wall and Sweet (1967). There are those who claim that a lower frequency (1–10/sec) is more effective and the results seem to resemble, in part, those obtained with TENS and acupuncture. However, there is often objectionable muscle twitching with the lower frequency current. Regardless of the frequency or intensity range provided by the pulse generator, it is important to note that the patient decides when and for how long the stimulus is to be applied and how intense it should be. It appears that a mild paresthesia (tingling or burning) sensation is usually required for maximum benefit.

External peripheral nerve stimulators are small battery-operated, modulated radio frequency oscillators that deliver energy to the passive implanted receiver. The principle is illustrated in Figure 7.2. The implant consists of a coil (L) and capacitor (C) which are resonant at the frequency of the external pulse generator. Connected to the L-C resonant circuit is a diode (D) to rectify (demodulate) the pulsed radio frequency carrier. A capacitor (C’) integrates the unidirectional pulses provided by the diode and thereby recovers the stimulus, which appears across R. Often a third capacitor (C”) is used to block the direct-current component in the recovered stimulus.

The external pulse generator contains a stimulus waveform generator and a radio frequency oscillator. The stimulus generator amplitude modulates the oscillator which transmits bursts of radio-frequency energy with the stimulus rate and duration.

The current that is required for PNS depends partly on the electrode area and location and the stimulus duration. In general, peak currents ranging from 1–10 mA are effective. Assuming a typical value of 1000 ohms for the interelectrode impedance, the peak voltages used varies from 1 to 10.

The difficulties encountered with PNS are few. Within a few weeks, the electrodes become encapsulated with a thin fibrous tissue capsule; consequently, the threshold for stimulation increases slightly. This effect is common to all implanted stimulating electrodes. The implanted PNS is like a cardiac pacemaker in that it contains an externally programmable, battery-operated stimulator. Not only can the stimulus parameters be programmed, but the battery voltage and electrode impedance can be interrogated. The complications with the PNS will be discussed after the description of the DCS, which follows.

7.4 Dorsal Column Stimulation (DCS)

Information ascending to the brain travels mainly along nerve fibers in the dorsal (posterior) and lateral columns of the spinal cord. Pain relief can be obtained by stimulation of these ascending nerve fibers. However, the mechanism of pain relief may involve more than that attributable to afferent nerve-fiber stimulation. Sjolund (1979) has shown that there is an endorphin (morphine-like) substance secreted from the periaqueductal region of the brain that may participate in the pain relief. When originated by Shealy (1969), the technique was called dorsal-column stimulation (DCS); sometimes the term spinal cord

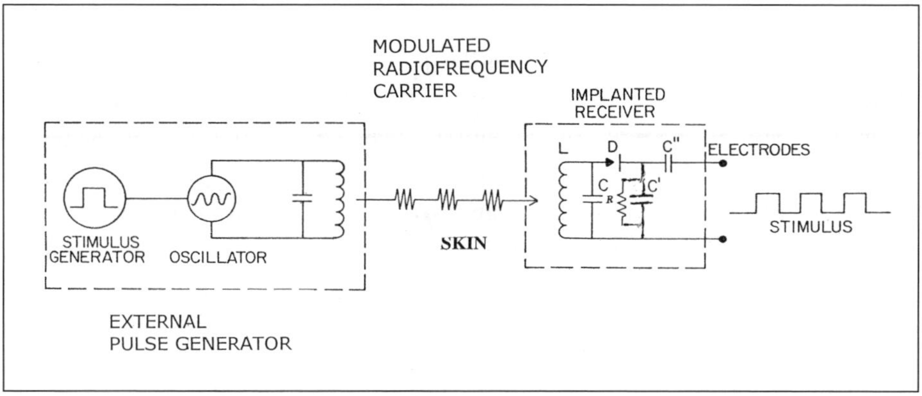

Figure 7.2 *External pulse generator used to energize an implanted receiver that delivers stimuli to electrodes applied to executable tissue.*

stimulation (SCS) is used. Because it ultimately requires a surgical procedure to apply this technique, patient selection becomes very important.

With DCS, typically two electrodes are placed dorsally against the thick membrane that covers the spinal cord; sometimes the electrodes are placed below this membrane. The site of the electrodes depends on the site of pain. Sometimes several electrodes are connected in parallel to increase the spread of current. However, there is not universal agreement on the optimum electrode site for the various types of pain. In general, the electrode sites are cervical (C), thoracic (T), lumbar (L) or sacral (S). A numerical suffix identifies the vertebral position.

To evaluate the efficacy of DCS, often wire electrodes are inserted percutaneously under fluoroscopic control. The acronym used to describe this technique is PISCES or percutaneously inserted spinal-cord electrode system. This technique allows evaluation of the suitability of the patient and identification of the stimulus parameters and any side effects. Urban and Nashold (1978) advocated a two-week period of stimulation with percutaneously implanted electrodes to evaluate the patient for an implanted pulse generator.

When electrodes are implanted surgically, general anesthesia may be required. The electrodes are connected to an implanted receiver or pulse generator that is the same type as is used for peripheral nerve stimulation.

The duration of the stimulus pulse ranges between 0.1–1 msec, with the shorter durations being preferred. The frequency employed ranges from 10–100/sec. The current intensity varies with electrode size and location, duration and frequency. Jobling et al. (1980), who employed 0.2 msec duration pulses with a frequency of 33/sec, provided data on typical stimulus intensities; Table 7.2 presents his data.

As with the other nerve-stimulation techniques used to relieve pain, the results with DCS and PISCES are variable. When Shealy (1969) introduced the technique, he reported a 50 to 200 percent increase in pain threshold as determined by stimulation of the skin surface. Shealy reported good to excellent pain relief in four patients. Sweet and Wall (1974) reported similar results. Loeser (1978) reviewed the literature up to the time and presented the results in summary form; Table 7.3 presents the data. If the eight peripheral-nerve stimulation (PNS) subjects are excluded, there was an average 52.7 percent successful relief of pain due to cancer in fourteen subjects.

Electrode positions were established by x-ray, and the figures indicate the thoracic vertebral body at the level of the electrode. Symbols S and U denote

Table 7.2
Pulse Current and Energy Requirements and Electrode Location for Patients Receiving Spinal Cord Stimulation

Patient	Date	Pulse Current	Pulse Energy	Electrode anode	Positions cathode	Response
		mA	μJ			
SE	21/09/76	9	12.7	T5	T7	S
SE	12/07/78	7	7.8	T4	T8/9	S
SE	06/10/78	7	9.1	T3/4	T5	S
SE	06/10/78	7	10.5	T3/4	T4	S
SE	11/10/78	6	8.2	T4	T6/7	S
SE	23/10/78	8	11.2	?	?	S
SE	29/11/78	7	6.4	T4	T5/6	S
CF	11/10/77	9	10.2	T4/5	T6/7	S
CF	20/10/77	8	6.4	T5	T7/8	S
CF	17/02/78	12	18.7	T7/8	T8/9	S
CF	22/02/78	13	19.5	T4/5	T5/6	S
CP	14/10/76	6	3.8	?	T3	S
CP	02/11/77	13	23.4	T9	T10	S
SB	02/12/77	9	16.2	T4	T6	S
SB	06/12/77	10	20.0	T4	T6/7	S
DS	10/11/76	8	7.6	T3	T5	S
SBT	15/11/78	5	8.3	T2/3	T4/5	S
SBT	24/11/78	6	7.2	T5/6	T4/5	S
MS	06/10/78	8	12.8	?	?	S
MS	11/10/78	10	17.0	T3/4	T4/5	S
MS	24/10/78	6	7.2	T5	T6	S
JL	15/11/78	8	12.2	T4/5	T5	S
JL	24/11/78	6	6.6	T5	T5/6	S
MR	20/12/77	9	15.3	?	?	S
MR	05/01/78	14	46	T1/2	T2/3	U
MR	20/06/78	15	60	T1	T5	U
(MW)	14/03/78	4	2.5	T1/2	T5/6	U
GM	19/04/78	11	20.0	T3/4	T4/5	U
GM	28/04/78	10	17.0	T2/3	T4/5	U
AM	03/02/78	19	48	T8	T8/9	U
JM	03/08/77	20	44	T4/5	T5	U
JM	17/08/77	8	19.2	T6/7	T9	U
OB	24/08/77	10	14.0	T5	T7	U
OB	21/09/77	11	14.3	T8	T9/10	U
NP	14/09/77	30	144	T3	T4	U

Electrode positions were established by x-ray, and the figures indicate the thoracis vertebral body at the level of the electrode. Symbols S and U denote successful and unsuccessful responses, respectively. Where reliable information on electrode position is not available, this is indicated by? Patient MW was not a reliable reporter and is shown in brackets.

Data from Jobling DT. Et al. Med. Biol. Eng. & Comput. 1980, 18:48-56.

Table 7.3
DCS and PNS for Pain Relief in Cancer*

Investigator	Year	Type	No. of Patients	% Success
Burton	1975	DCS	1	1
Campbell	1976	PNS	3	0
Clark	1975	DCS	3	67
Freidberg	1975	DCS	1	100
Hunt	1975	DCS	1	0
Long	1975	DCS	6	50
Medtronic	1975	PISCES	9	44
Miles	1974	DCS	2	100
Nashold	1972	DCS	1	0
Nielson	1975	DCS	18	61
North	1977	PISCES	2	50
Picaza	1975	PNS	5	60
Pineda	1975	DCS	4	50
Shealy	1969	DCS	2	100
Sheldon	1975	DCS	17	47
Sweet	1974	DCS	3	67

*Data from Loeser 1978

successful and unsuccessful responses, respectively. Where reliable information on electrode position is not available, this is indicated by? Patient MW was not a reliable reporter and is shown in brackets in the paper.

Whereas, the traditional DCS employs posterior electrodes, Shealy (1969) postulated that pain relief can be obtained by stimulation of the lateral or anterior columns of the spinal cord. It was found by Larson et al. (1975) that stimulating electrodes placed over the anterior surface of the spinal cord provided pain relief with less paresthesia than with dorsal stimulation. Sances et al. (1975) reported that better relief from cancer-related pain was obtained by applying the stimuli to anterior (negative) and posterior (positive) electrodes.

7.5 Complications and Hazards with PNS and DCS Systems

Even with properly functioning PNS and DCS systems, not all patients obtain relief; in some there is little and some obtain considerable relief. Implanted PNS and DCS systems share the same complications as with cardiac pacemakers and implanted cardioverter defibrillators. These are (1) electrode lead fracture, (2) insulation fracture, (3) lead migration, in addition to pulse generator failure due to battery depletion or exposure to excessive electromagnetic interference or defibrillating current, and (4) infection.

Electrode-lead fracture interrupts the flow of current from the pulse generator to the electrodes which results in a loss of stimulation. Insulation fracture causes current to leak to tissues surrounding the fracture and decreases the current delivered to the electrodes. Lead migration can result from normal bodily movements which can cause electrode dislodgement. Infection is a hazard associated with any implanted device. It can result from a lack of adequate device sterilization or improper surgical technique.

With the passive implanted stimulator (Figure 7.2), any electromagnetic interference having frequency components in the range of the resonant frequency of the implanted receiver will be indistinguishable from those produced by the external pulse generator. Moreover, the pulse generator can produce unwanted signals that can interfere with bioelectric recorders. High-level electromagnetic interference (EMI), acting on implanted PNS or DCS systems, can inhibit or change the programming of such devices. It is to be noted that PNS and DCS systems can produce pulses that can be detected by the sensing circuits of pacemakers and ICDs and cause malfunction.

7.6 Complications with Dorsal Column Stimulators

Racz et al. (1989) reported the use of percutaneously inserted leads for DCS in twenty-six patients with intractable pain who used the stimulators for periods of twelve to 42.7 months. Seventeen patients rated their pain relief as good to excellent. Two-thirds reported improved ability to do daily tasks. However, the authors stated, "There are still many technical problems that plague this procedure, as evidence by a very high technical complication of lead migration and lead breakage." Recall, however, that these leads were percutaneously inserted for long periods.

A ninety-two-patient study was reported by Pineda (1978) who used an implanted dorsal column stimulator and electrodes. Difficult-to-correct complications occurred in twenty-six patients. Late stimulation failure occurred in thirty-two implants that had provided excellent pain relief for months to years. Davis and Gray (1981) reported the results of DCS on 101 patients over a $5^1/_2$-year period. Both passive implanted receivers (Figure 7.2) and implanted pulse generators were used; sixty-five patients had the former type and thirty-six had the latter type. Twenty percent failures occurred with the passive implant (Figure 7.2) and no failures, other than battery depletion, occurred with the fully implanted units. Electrode displacements occurred in twenty-seven patients and breakage in six patients.

That there was the possibility of a DCS to interfere with the operation of an implanted cardioverter defibrillator (ICD) was investigated by Monahan et al. (1998). The case involved a patient with a previously implanted spinal cord stimulator (DCS) who presented for an implantable cardioverter defibrillator (ICD). The DCS device was located in the left lower abdominal quadrant with a stimulation electrode array placed on the dorsal aspect of the spinal cord at the T-11 lower thoracic level. Interaction testing demonstrated that the bipolar sensing transvenous ICD system (manufacture) did not detect the DCS output at burst rates ranging from 20–130 pulses/s., even with the ICD set to its maximum sensitivity of 0.15 mV and the stimulator programmed to the highest patient tolerated output combinations of 5 V. 0.45 ms in the bipolar configuration and 3 V. 0.45 ms in the unipolar, i.e., worst case-electrode configuration.

It is to the credit of the authors that they tested the interference susceptibility of the ICD to the DCS. This should be recommended practice with all types of pain-suppression stimulators.

7.7 Electroacupuncture

Electroacupuncture employs needle electrodes to which short-duration, low-frequency pulses of current are applied to produce analgesia and often local anesthesia to permit some surgical procedures. The mechanism of action is not fully understood, but it probably shares the mechanism underlying TENS.

Fujiwara et al. (1980) reported the use of electroacupuncture as the anesthesia for removal of the thyroid gland in a forty-one-year old female who had multiple medical problems, including bradycardia. To assure cardiac pumping, a temporary, bipolar demand cardiac pacemaker was used. The acupuncture needle electrodes were applied to the ears, lateral neck, right leg and arm; the indifferent electrode was on the upper abdomen. The stimulus pulse frequency was 3/sec. and the pulse duration was 1 msec. The output was gradually increased to a maximum of 20 volts. ECG recordings were obtained throughout the surgery and revealed periods of pacemaker inhibition when the output voltage exceeded a certain level. The acupuncture spikes could be identified in the ECG limb leads and the intracardiac lead used for sensing and pacing. No pacing occurred when the authors estimated the acupuncture stimulus to be 3mA.

Fujwara et al. concluded that electroacupuncture is contraindicated for patients who have a ventricular rate of less than 50/min and those who are pacemaker dependent. They also recommended locating the acupuncture electrodes so that the current is directed away from the heart.

7.8 Stunning Devices

There are several high-voltage, low-current stimulators that are used to control the behavior of animals and man. The most familiar is probably the cattle prod which provides a strong sensory stimulus via a pair of protruding electrodes that causes an avoidance response, thereby making it possible to cause an animal to go in a desired direction. Typically the peak voltage is high (kilovolts) and the current is low (microamperes); the pulse duration is short (tens of microseconds) and the frequency ranges from 50–200/sec. The sensation is certainly attention getting.

The Stun Gun (Nova Technologies, Austin, TX 78758) is similar to the cattle prod. It is a handheld device that delivers a localized stimulus that is strong enough to stun a person, thereby facilitating capture. When the probe electrodes are placed close to the skin, preferably over a muscle, a strong surprise sensation is produced with minor muscle contractions. Only about a few seconds of application is needed and the subject usually loses balance. The presence of clothing does not diminish the effectiveness because the high voltage pulses penetrate clothing easily. The victim falls to the ground and he/she is weakened and dazed. Two red spots, resembling insect bites, may appear on the skin and disappear in a few days. It is not advisable to apply the shock to the head. The Stun Gun delivers a high peak voltage (90,000) train (17–22/sec) of short-duration pulses. According to tests conducted by Bernstein (1993), the XR 5000 unit delivers a train of damped sinusoidal stimuli (70kHz). The energy in each pulse depends on the subject resistance. In bench tests into a resistive load, the energy ranges from 52 mJ for a 200-ohm load to 19 mJ for a 1,000-ohm load.

Although the Stun Gun is effective, there have been reports that some subjects under the influence of drugs become enraged and even more violent when shocked. However, such cases are by no means common.

The Taser (Tasertron, Newport Beach, CA 92658) is a handheld, nonlethal stimulator that ejects two dart electrodes from a cassette. Two slender fifteen-foot wires follow the electrodes, which engage a victim's clothing. The dart separation is one foot for each five feet of range.

The output of the Taser is 50,000 volts. The frequency of the short-duration pulses ranges from 8 to 22/sec; the energy per pulse is approximately 0.5 joule, the peak current being 100 μA. It is not necessary for the dart electrodes (1.4 gm) to penetrate the skin because the high voltage will cause the current to be carried by the tiny arc that forms. About three seconds of current flow will incapacitate a subject who falls to the ground and is dazed and confused for a few minutes. However, when downed, the subject is able to obey commands.

Many safety tests have been conducted with human volunteers and animals. The shock delivered by the Taser encompasses a fairly wide region that stimulates both sensory nerves and muscles. When the subject is struck and the Taser is activated, there is a complete loss of balance and the subject falls to the ground because all voluntary muscle control is temporarily lost. For this reason, the response is not affected by prior use of drugs. The subject is dazed and confused for minutes depending on the activation time of the shock.

De Barros Moraes (1995) called the foregoing stunning devices "autodefense systems" and investigated the effect of two such devices on explanted pacemakers and one external pacemaker. Both personal defense devices had the same electronic circuit; however, one was in the shape of a truncheon and the other was shaped similar to a TV remote control. The pacemaker from (manufacturer) was studied for ventricular and atrial sensing; the pacemakers from (manufacturer) and (manufacturer) were studied only for ventricular stimulation. All pacemakers were tested to ensure that they were functioning properly before exposure to interference; the sensitivity was adjusted according to the implanted conditions. Each pacemaker was positioned on a wooden table and the autodefense device was placed at different distances on the right, the left bottom, the top, and above the pacemaker. The autodefense device was turned on for five seconds. This duration was established because of the warning appearing in the manuals of the autodefense devices. The behavior of each pacemaker was monitored and evaluated with a two-channel oscilloscope. Every test was repeated three times for each position. There was no other known source of interference in the room and all the pacemakers functioned properly before the autodefense devices were activated.

There was no effect on the pacemakers when operating in the fixed-rate mode. The effects of both autodefense devices on the pacemakers were the same when operated in the VVI mode. All the pacemakers were severely affected by the interference generated by the devices, but with a duration of no more than five seconds. The effects were not permanent and the pacemakers returned to the correct operation as soon as the interference ceased. The effects on the implantable pacemakers were random pulse generation and reversion to fixed-rate mode. The maximum distance to cause interference with one unit was 7 to 12 cm.

The effects exhibited on the external pacemaker were change of frequency and reversal of working condition (inhibited to not inhibited or vice versa). The greatest distance to cause interference was 3 cm.

In viewing the foregoing bench tests, it should be noted that they may not truly represent an in-vivo situation. The authors concluded, "It should also be emphasized that the duration of five seconds was established due to a warning written in the manual of the autodefense devices with installation and handling instructions. It is not certain, however, that the user will operate the device within this limitation which is not imposed by the equipment itself."

Stunning devices are becoming of much more interest to law enforcement personnel because they are nonlethal and enable capture of lawbreakers. in these days of terrorist attacks, it is highly desirable to capture the perpetrator for interrogration purposes. A review of recent experience with stunning devices used for capture was presented by Fish and Geddes (2001).

References

AAMI NSA-1985. Standard for TENS. (American Association for the Advancement of Medical Instrumentation), 1901 Fort Meyer Dr., Suite 602, Arlington, VA 22209.

Berstein T. Personal communication, 1993.

Bolton L. TENS electrode irritation. J. Am. Acad. Dermatol. 1983, 8:134–135.

Bundesen P and Ericson L. Pain relief in labor by TENS. Acta Obst. Gynecol. Scand. 1982, 61: 1–5.

Davis R and Gray E. Technical factors important to dorsal column stimulation. Appl. Neurophysiol. 1981, 44(1–3):160–170.

De Barros-Moraes JCT. Effects of electronic autodefense devices on cardiac pacemakers. Aritf. Organs. 1995, 19(3):238–240.

ECRI, Health Devices. Evaluation: Transcutaneous electrical nerve stimulator (TENS) units. 1981, 10(8):179–195. Plymouth Meeting. PA 19462.

Fujiwara H, Taniguchi K, Takeuchi J and Ikezono E. The Influence of low frequency acupuncture on a demand pacemaker. Chest. 1980, 78(1):96–7.

Fish RM and Geddes LA. Stun guns and Tasers. Lancet. 2001, 358:687–689.

Jobling DT, Tallis RC, Sedgwick EM and Illis LS. Electronic aspects of spinal-cord stimulation in multiple sclerosis. Med. Biol. Eng. & Comput. 1980, 18:48–56.

Larson SJ, Sances A, Cusick JE et al. A comparison between anterior and posterior spinal implant systems. Surg. Neurol. 1975, 4(1):180–186.

Loeser JD. Dorsal column and peripheral nerve stimulation. In Bonica J et al. Adv. in Pain Res. and Therapy. 1978, 2:499–507. New York, Raven Press.

Mannheimer GS. Electrode placements for transcutaneous electrical nerve stimulation. Phys. Therap. 1978, 58(12):1455–1462.

Mannheimer GS et al. Clinical Transcutaneous Electrical Nerve Stimulation. 1978. Davis, Philadelphia.

Melzack R and Wall PD. Pain mechanism: A new theory. Science. 1965, 150:971–979.

Monahan K, Casavant D and Rassmussen C. Combined use of a true-bipolar sensing implantable cardioverter defibrillator in a patient having a prior implantable spinal cord stimulator for pain. PACE. 1998, 21:2669–2672.

Pineda A. Complications of dorsal column stimulation. Journ. Neurosurg. 1978, 48(1):64–68.

Racz GB, McCarron RF and Talboys P. Percutaneous dorsal column stimulator for chronic pain control. Spine. 1989, 14(1):1–4.

Rasmusse MJ, Hayes DL and Vlietstra RE. Can transcutaneous electrical nerve stimulation be safely used in patients with permanent cardiac pacemakers? Proc. Mayo Clin. 1988, 63(5):443–445.

Sances A, Swointek TJ, Larson SJ et al. Innovations in neurologic implant systems. Med Instrum. 1975. 9(5):213–216

Shade SK. Transcutaneous electrical nerve stimulation for a patient with a cardiac pacemaker. Phys. Therapy. 1985, 65(2):206–208.

Shealy CN. Dorsal-column electro-hypalgesia. Headache. 1969, 9:99–102

Sjolund B and Eriksson M. Electro-acupuncture and endogenous morphines. Lancet. 1976, 11:1085.

Sjolund B and Ericksson,MB. Endorphins and analgesia produced by peripheral conditioning stimulation. Advances In Pain Research and Therapy. Bonica JJ, Ed. 1979. Raven Press, New York.

Sweet WH and Wepsic JD. Stimulation of the posterior columns of the spinal cord for pain control. Clin. Neurosurg. 1974, 21:273–311

Urban BJ and Nashold BS. Percutaneous epidural stimulation of the spinal cord for relief of pain. Journ. Neurosurg. 1978, 48(3):323–328.

Wall PD and Sweet WH. Temporary abolition of pain in man. Science. 1967, January 6:108–109.

Zugerman C. Dermatitis from transcutaneous electric nerve stimulation. J. Am. Acad. Dermatol. 1982, 6:935–939.

Chapter 8

Tissue Injury

Synopsis

8.1 Introduction

There are many ways that tissue can be injured. For example, thermal injury can be caused by coming into contact with hot solids, liquids, gases, or by being exposed to radiant energy (from microwaves, heat lamps, etc.). Likewise, tissues can be injured thermally by electric current; such accidents are described in the chapter on electrosurgery (Chapter 3). Similarly, thermal injury can result from laser energy; such incidents are also described in Chapter 3. Thermal injury from contact with heated objects is described in the chapter on anesthesia (Chapter 4) and in this chapter. Thermal damage due to hot solutions are described in this chapter, along with the more fundamental aspects of skin injuries.

Burn specialists distinguish between a thermal contact burn and an electrical burn. With the former, the heat is conducted from the heated object on the skin surface to the underlying tissue. The damage depends on the temperature of the heated object, its size, and how long it is in contact. The blanch test (see below) is often used to assess the subcutaneous capillary circulation which, if compromised, will cause the burn to become more prominent over a period of days.

With an electrical burn, the skin is actively heated by the current flow. The skin damage is usually apparent immediately. However, the subcutaneous tissues are also actively heated by the current and the damage depends on the current density (squared), the duration of current flow, and the resistivity of the tissues carrying the current. Electrosurgical burns are common when the dispersive electrode makes only partial contact with the skin. Although an electrosurgical burn is usually evident immediately, if the subcutaneous capillaries are damaged, the lesion will become more evident with the passage of time.

Laser burns are also visible at the time of the incident and become more apparent with the passage of time. Electrosurgery and laser energy can produce high temperatures capable of carbonizing tissues.

8.2 Burn Treachery and the Blanch Test

With tissue injury, the term "burn treachery" is often used and refers to the difficulty in predicting the future course of tissue damage. When skin is injured by coming into contact with a heated object, the superficial circulation is assessed by the blanch test, i.e., thumb pressure is applied for many seconds, then removed. If neither blanching, nor reddening occurs when pressure is released, this is evidence that there is little or no local circulation and the underlying tissues will die, and the injury will become more apparent with the passage of time.

Prolonged lying or sitting in one position compresses capillaries and produces tissue ischemia and injury; such pressure sores are rarely evident at the time and become more and more obvious after a few hours to days. Pressure sores (ulcers) will be described in this chapter.

Finally, tissues can be injured by chemical compounds; in such cases it is necessary to distinguish between injury due to the species of chemical and injury due to an allergic response. Both types are discussed in this chapter. Parenthetically, in describing allergic injuries, the burn scale is used frequently.

8.3 Experimental Burn Studies

The classical studies of Moritz and Henriques (1947) established the relationship between burn severity and the skin temperature and exposure time. Using pigs, they determined the reciprocal relationship between temperature and exposure time to create complete transepidermal necrosis. The experiments consisted of applying a cup-shaped chamber to the skin and circulating water, at a measured temperature, through it for a measured time. In this way they were able to show that the shorter the exposure time, the hotter the water had to be to produce complete transepidermal necrosis. Figure 2.19 in Chapter 2 and Figure 8.1 in this chapter presents their data.

Figure 8.2 shows a cross-sectional view of a typical skin site. As stated earlier in this book, burn severity is classified into four categories:

first degree: reddening of the skin (erythema)
second degree: partial thickness injury (blistering and hemorrhage)

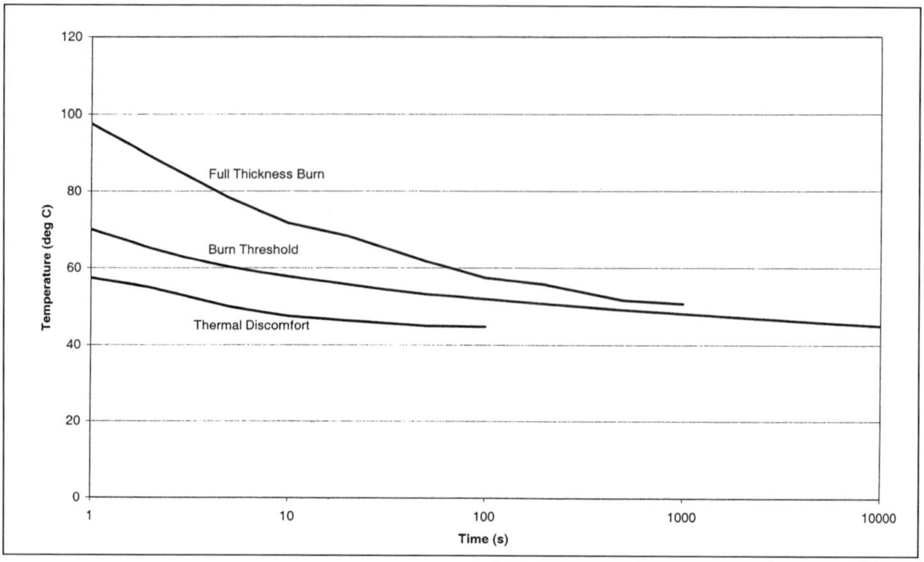

Figure 8.1 *Thermal burn threshold temperature (complete transepidermal necrosis) (Moritz & Henriques 1947), full thickness burn and thermal discomfort (Bull and Lawrence 1979) versus time curves*

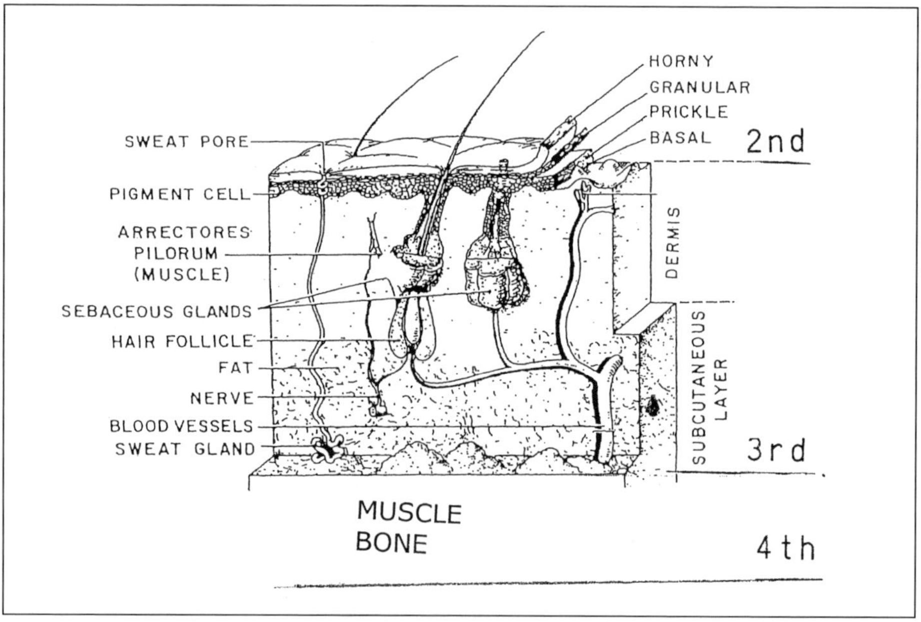

Figure 8.2 *Cross section of a typical skin site showing second-, third- and fourth-degree injury.*

third degree: full dermal thickness injury extending down to the fat layer and no response to pin prick

fourth degree: injury down to the muscles and bone

It should be obvious that no burn or injury fits into a single burn category. For example, with a full-thickness burn, there will also exist second and first-degree burns in the perimeter. A complete burn description requires defining the degree and extent of the injury.

For obvious reasons, there is a paucity of data relative to temperature and exposure time that allows construction of a temperature versus exposure time curve for a full-thickness burn on human skin. However, there are data that describe the thermal discomfort temperature versus exposure time for human skin. Lawrence and Bull (1975) carried out studies with human subjects to determine the thermal discomfort curve. The subjects held on to a metal pipe through which hot water (at a controlled temperature) was circulated and they measured the contact skin temperature with microthermo-couples. The data they obtained are shown in Figure 8.1; the shape of the curve resembles that obtained by Moritz and Henriques (1947) for complete transepidermal necrosis.

Bull and Lawrence (1979) published data on the relationship between the temperature and exposure time required for a full dermal thickness injury. Their data are shown in Figure 8.1.

8.4 Radiant Heater Burns

Bull and Lawrence (1979) processed data obtained by Perkins et al. (1952) which relates the power density (watts/cm^2) and exposure time for an erythema threshold burn and a full-thickness injury. These data are shown in Figure 8.3. Observe the similarity of the power-density versus exposure-time curves to those shown in Figure 8.1.

8.5 Skin Temperature

Skin temperature ranges from 27 to 32°C (80.6–89.6°F), which is well below body temperature of 37°C (98.6°F). However, skin temperature varies considerably over the surface of the body and what feels hot or cold is subjective and depends on the prevailing skin temperature as the following simple experiment demonstrates. Take three basins of water, a, b, and c: a contains cold water, b tepid water, and c hot water. The left hand is immersed in the cold water and the

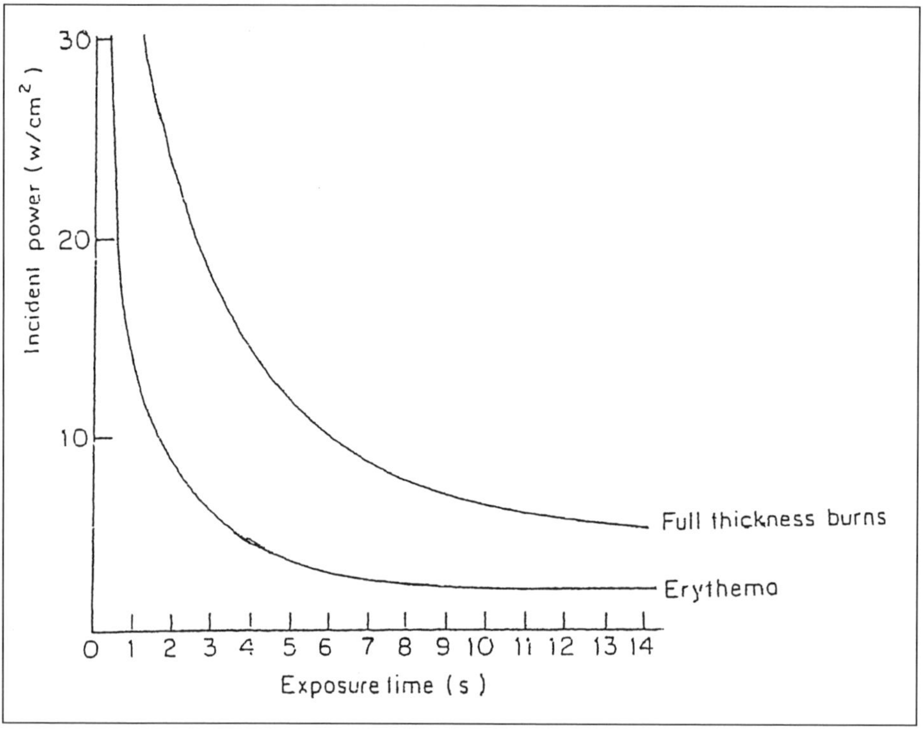

Figure 8.3 *Relationship between incident radiant power density and exposure time for full dermal thickness burn and erythema (Redrawn from Bull and Lawrence 1979)*

right hand in the hot water for a few minutes. Now place both hands in the basin of tepid water; it feels hot to the left hand and cold to the right hand.

Another interesting fact about temperature sensitivity relates to the wide range of temperature receptors. The thermal sense is most marked in the nipples, chest, nose, anterior surface of the upper arm and the anterior surface of the forearm and the surface of the abdomen. It is much less marked on the exposed parts of the body, such as the face and hands; it is even less in the mucous membranes. Thus, it is possible to drink hot fluid at a temperature that is painful to the hand and still more to other parts of the body.

The acuteness of the thermal sense varies considerably with the condition of the skin and with the previous stimulation of the sense organs. The sense is most acute at about ordinary skin temperature, i.e. between 27° and 32°C (80.6° and 89.6°F). At this temperature the skin can appreciate a difference of 0.2°C. When the skin is very cold or very hot, the thermal sense is not nearly so delicate. Restaurants keep soups at about 140°F (60°C) to 160°F (71°C) and coffee at 160°F (71°C). Clearly these potable liquids can burn the skin if present for a sufficient time.

8.6 Hand-Washing Water Temperature

The tolerance temperatures for hand washing was investigated by the author who selected fifteen subjects, ranging in age from twenty-one to seventy-eight (nine males, six females) who were asked to adjust water temperature to that each used for hand washing. In each case the water temperature was measured when the hand-washer decided that this was the temperature that he/she used. The average temperature was 41.9°C (133°F). The maximum and minimum temperatures were 38.4 to 45.4°C (127–139°F). Clearly these temperatures were not injurious for the brief time it required to wash the hands and emphasizes the importance of exposure time in injury assessment. There was no significant difference between age or sex nor health; three of the subjects were type II diabetics.

The foregoing results are complemented by a study reported by Gendron (1988) who stated that too hot for human skin is 43–45°C (109–113°F) which is the threshold for pain. He further stated that 46°C (114.8°F) is intolerably painful. At this temperature, protein is denatured in minutes.

8.7 Tap-Water Burns

Scalds from tap water are by no means rare and it is of interest to examine the temperature of the water that issues from the domestic faucet. Tap-water temperature varies throughout the country and depends, in part, on local codes. For example, if there is an automatic dishwasher or washing machine in the home, a certain temperature is required by a local ordinance. Some households set the temperature of their water heaters to suit themselves. Nonetheless, the temperature of the tap water is known to be hot enough to produce a scald burn as reported by Feldman et al. (1978) and Erdmann et al. (1991). Fedlman et al. stated that tap water scald burns account for 7 percent to 17 percent of all childhood scald burns that require hospitalization. Often the burns are severe and disabling. Toddlers and preschool children are the most frequent victims. In 45 percent of the injuries, the unsupervised victim or a peer turned on the tap water; in 28 percent, the cause was abuse. In Seattle, eighty percent of the homes tested had unsafe bathtub water temperatures of 54°C (130°F) or greater, exposing the occupants to the risk of full-thickness scalds with a thirty-second exposure to hot water.

Erdmann et al. (1991) stated that, in 1988, Washington State law required new water heaters to be preset at 49°C (120°F); 77 percent of homes (84 percent of homes with postlaw and 70 percent of homes with prelaw water heaters) had tap water temperatures of less than 54°C. In 1977, 80 percent of the homes had tap-water temperatures greater than 54°C. Mean temperature in 1988 was 50°C compared with 61°C in 1977. Both changes were significant compared with 1977 temperatures. Few people increased their heater temperature after installation. Eighteen burn victims were identified from July 1979 through May 1988, for an average admission rate of 2.4 per year. Compared with the 1970s, total body surface area burned, mortality, grafting, scarring, and length of hospital stay were all reduced, while the likelihood that scald burns were the result of child abuse increased to 50 percent.

It is obvious that reducing the temperature of tap water will reduce the incidence of scald burns. However, this is only one of the two factors; the other is exposure time. If we select 50°C (122°F) as the temperature for hot water, from the Moritz and Henriques (1947) data (Figure 8.1), it requires 300 seconds for complete transepidermal necrosis.

8.8 Injury from Hot Packs

As described in the chapter on anesthesia (Chapter 4), intravenous fluid bags are kept in a warming cabinet until used for infusion. They are also used for warming or posturing a subject, sometimes resulting in skin damage.

Gel packs are also used for posturing a patient; such packs can be heated or cooled. A skin-burn accident associated with the use of such a pack that was heated in a microwave oven was described by Dave (1993); he reported as follows:

> A three-year-old, developmentally delayed girl was admitted for treatment of a grand mal seizure. Intravenous fluids were administered through a catheter on the dorsum of the right foot. Swelling of the foot, secondary to extravasation of the IV fluid, was observed. The infusion was discontinued and the site was wrapped in a thin layer of wet gauze. Subsequently, heat was applied by placing a microwave-heated commercially available, Cryogel pack on the IV site. The child became combative and irritable during this procedure and was restrained. At a later time, the gauze dressing was removed to check the progress of the extravasation. The site showed an extensive area of necrosis clearly demarcated by surrounding healthy skin. No drugs had been administered through the IV at that site. The injured area required debridement and

subsequent skin grafting. There were no long-term complications as far as the function of the foot was concerned.

Dave investigated the cause of this accident by heating gel packs in the same microwave oven for different times and measured the surface temperature of the pack following three, two, and one minute of heating in the microwave oven; Figure 8.4 presents his results. Note that the emergence temperatures (time equal to zero minutes) were 178, 146, and 135°F (81, 63.3 and 57.2°C) respectively. In commenting on these results Dave stated that:

> One second is sufficient to acquire a third-degree, full-thickness burn at 158°F, whereas sixty seconds is necessary when the temperature is 127°F. At the time of the accident, no safety instructions were available with the microwave-heated Cryogel pack. Currently, a wrapper is included to be used when microwaving the pack, but lack of sufficient warning on the pack itself is a potential hazard.

A similar skin burn due to an IV bag being warmed in a microwave oven was reported in *Medical Malpractice* (2000); the account follows:

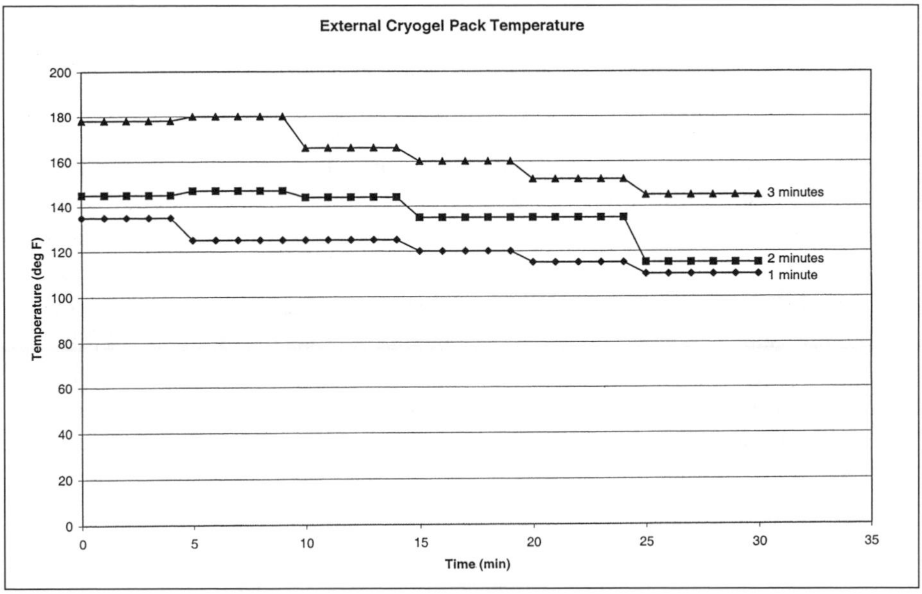

Figure 8.4 *Surface temperature-time curves for Cryogel packs heated in a standard microwave oven for one, two, and three minutes (Composed from data reported, by Dave 1993)*

The plaintiff mother had been pregnant for twenty-seven weeks and three days with an unremarkable pregnancy. In January 1996 the woman began having contractions and went to the hospital in the early morning. During labor the mother suffered placental abruption. A cesarean section was performed without complications. The plaintiff child was born weighing only two and one-half pounds, but was healthy, crying and breathing on her own. She had apgars of 8 and 8. Almost immediately after birth she was placed on top of plastic bags filled with intravenous saline liquid which the nurses had heated in a staff-lounge microwave oven. The hospital did have the child in NICU, which was equipped with warming devices for premature newborns. The child sustained first, second, and third-degree, full-thickness burns over large areas of her back and buttocks due to the bags being overheated. She suffered intracranial bleeding, which progressed to Grade IV intraventricular hemorrhage and hydrocephalus, which required shunting. The burn cultured positive for serratia marcescens, a bacteria which eventually entered her bloodstream and cerebral spinal fluid, causing meningitis. The child was neurologically devastated by the incident. The hospital eventually conceded that its employees were negligent and that such negligence caused the severe burns to the child, but maintained that the intracranial bleeding and meningitis were merely coincidental. During the initial stages of discovery the hospital answered an interrogatory regarding how the bags came to be heated and who had been involved in the newborn's care relative to the bags. When the plaintiff took the deposition of the nurse who was listed in the medical records as present in the NICU during the relevant time, some of the facts surrounding the heating of the bags became known, but not much was revealed about the identities of the nurses involved. After this deposition, additional written discovery was requested from the hospital. More than a month later a memo was produced, which was written by one of the nurses involved on the day of the incident. This memo described the incident in detail and identified those involved. The plaintiff's motion for amending the complaint alleged a claim for punitive damages was granted. The defendant ultimately admitted liability. The defendant disputed the plaintiff's assertions that the child could live into adulthood and possibly have a near-normal life span. A $9 million present-value settlement was reached after mediation.

8.9 Ischemic Injury

Ischemia pertains to a deficiency of capillary blood flow, the consequence of which depends on the particular tissue bed that is compromised and for how long. Tissue ischemia can result from the manner in which the body is supported, e.g., lying on an operating table or a bed or sitting in a chair for a prolonged period without moving.

There are two types of mechanical force that can produce injury to tissues (1) a force that is applied at right angles to the tissue and (2) a force that acts parallel to the tissue surface. The former impairs the circulation by compressing the capillaries, thereby compromising blood flow; this is the force that produces pressure ulcers, often called bedsores. The second type is produced when a patient is pulled or slides on a surface, thereby stretching the skin; shear is the medical term used to describe this force. Examples of these two forces will be given in the following paragraphs.

A. Pressure injury

For a lesion to develop there is a reciprocal relationship between pressure applied to a body region and the duration of its application; this was reported by Brooks (1940). However, this relationship has not been quantitated despite the considerable evidence. From experimental animal studies, Dinsdale (1974) showed that 70 mm Hg applied for more than two hours produced irreversible skin damage. However, if pressure was intermittently relieved, minimal tissue change was noted, even with pressures as high as 240 mm Hg. Dinsdale (1974) showed that the higher the pressure the less time is needed to produce tissue necrosis. In animal studies, Kosiak (1961) also reported that a pressure of only 70 mm Hg applied for two hours produced irreversible damage. However, if pressure was alternated every five minutes, minimal changes were noted. There was no difference between rats with injured and uninjured spinal cords using this model. The results of these experimental studies suggest that the critical period of pressure application is within the one-to-two-hour time period. Beyond this time, irreversible changes occur. It is from such studies that good nursing practice evolved for bedridden patients, who are typically turned every two hours to prevent the development of bedsores.

According to Pearce (1986), it takes only one hour to initiate tissue breakdown with local ischemia which produces tissue anoxia. The longer the period of anoxia, the greater the tissue damage. With pressure-induced anoxia, the damage is usually not apparent immediately, although some skin blanching may be seen when the site is examined carefully. It usually takes many hours to days before the tissue damage has fully matured.

An interesting commentary on pressure sores was presented by Gendron (1988), who stated that:

> No device on the market claims to be a complete substitute for routine relief of pressure. If routine turning of all patients is required every two hours, and they rest on seven-inch-thick hospital mattresses, it's obvious the standard 1.5" foam pads on a steel table offer no real protection against pressure sores. The author observed the exact detailed outline of a tabletop machine screw head on a patient's side after a 3.5-hour procedure even though a 1.5" pad was between the patient and the screw.

It is useful to note how a 10,000-pound elephant handles the high pressure on the four feet. Assuming an even distribution of load, each foot supports 2,500 lbs. and if we assume a ten-inch-diameter foot, the pressure sustained is 31.8 pounds per square inch. Now 1 psi is equal to about 52 mm Hg; therefore the pressure on the foot capillaries is 1654 mm Hg. When standing, elephants sway their trunks and shift the load from foot to foot; walking achieves the same goal.

Remarkably clear examples of contact pressure necrosis, which produced hair loss (alopecia) were given by Lawson et al. (1976), who stated that postoperative alopecia is a minor complication of surgery, but a cosmetic disaster to the patient. Over a three-year period, sixty cases of occipital alopecia were discovered in patients following open-heart surgery and five cases on the other surgical services. In contrast to previous reports, twenty patients had alopecia one year later, presumed to be permanent. Extensive operations, with prolonged recovery and elective overnight mechanical ventilation, were common to all. Retrospective analysis and prospective studies clearly demonstrated that localized scalp pressure was the cause of the alopecia and that the duration of the pressure determined the extent of the damage. Moving the patient's head at regular intervals during operation and recovery eliminated alopecia. The type of head rest used did not modify the development of alopecia. Electrical injury and the use of heparin, hypothermia, electrocautery, or hypotension were eliminated as possible causes. Conclusive evidence correlating perioperative events with the formation of pressure sores in man has not been previously reported. However Figure 8.5 shows that the back of the head experiences a high localized pressure in a supine subject.

The pressures under a typical male and female lying on a hard surface and a regular bed were derived from Pearce 1971.

Figure 8.5 (right) shows the isopressure contours for a supine subject; the smaller the loops, the higher the pressure. Note that the pressure is highest under the back of the head (occiput), the shoulder blades, the sacrum, the buttocks, the calf muscles and the heels. Pearce (1971) measured the pressure distribution under a typical male and female lying on a hard surface and a regular bed; these pressures are shown on the right and left of the isopressure contour map, and show the effect of the type of surface on which a subject is lying.

B. Incidence of pressure sores

It is difficult to quantitate the incidence of pressure sores because of the many different environments that patients may occupy, e.g. in a hospital, nursing

Average Male Data
Weight: 173 lbs.
Height: 71"
Width: 14"

	CONTACT PRESSURE mm. Hg	
	Hard Surface	Regular Bed
Head	109	106
R. Shoulder	26	2
R. Shoulder Blade	60	20
R. Elbow	51	124
L. Shoulder	20	3
L. Shoulder Blade	50	20
L. Elbow	75	30
C. of Spine	283	20
R. Buttock	24	32
R. Thigh	–	4
R. Calf	21	16
R. Heel	158	100
L. Buttock	28	42
L. Thigh	–	3
L. Calf	25	12
L. Heel	91	130

Average Female Data
Weight: 124 lbs.
Height: 69"
Width: 11"

	CONTACT PRESSURE mm. Hg	
	Hard Surface	Regular Bed
Head	87	236
R. Shoulder	21	8
R. Shoulder Blade	9	36
R. Elbow	–	34
L. Shoulder	47	–
L. Shoulder Blade	25	28
L. Elbow	–	30
C. of Spine	20	–
R. Buttock	24	28
R. Thigh	0	6
R. Calf	28	8
R. Heel	63	120
L. Buttock	20	28
L. Thigh	0	2
L. Calf	40	16
L. Heel	62	110

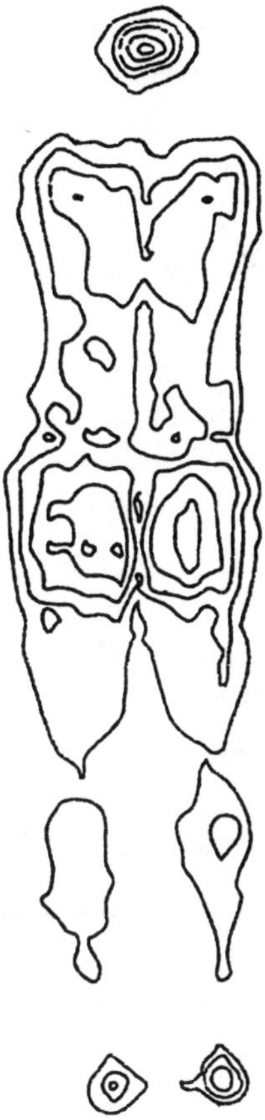

Figure 8.5 *Isopressure contour map of a supine adult subject lying on a sleep surface. Higher pressures are under the head, shoulders, sacrum, thighs, calves and heels—the regions that support the body. (From Geddes LA.* Handbook of Electrical Hazards and Accidents. *1995, CRC Press, Boca Raton FL. 1995. By permission)*

home or at home. Another factor relates to the health of the patient. Diseases that impair skin circulation (hypertension, diabetes), the age and the nutritional state of a patient are all important factors. Despite these many factors, estimates are available on the incidence of pressure ulcers, often called bedsores or decubitus (lying-down) ulcers. The National Pressure Ulcer Advisory Panel (1989) reported that:

> Conservative estimates indicate that well over a million persons in hospitals and nursing homes suffer from pressure ulcers. One large study found that one in four Americans who died in 1987 had a dermal ulcer. The prevalence of pressure ulcers is almost certain to grow due to increasing numbers of fragile elderly and survivors of serious trauma.

When pressure ulcers appear, the question of adequate nursing care arises. However, any inquiry into the cause must recognize the patient's age, health, any disease and nutritional state. Pressure sores can become infected and thereby are difficult to heal and requires the attention of one specialized in this field.

It is to be noted that we all sleep many hours each night. However, we do not remain in the same position for very long. Gendron (1988) reported that many normal people make as many as 400 movements in an eight-hour period. Elderly patients who made twenty-five to 225 movements during sleep did not develop bedsores. However, all who made less than twenty-five movements developed bedsores.

C. Pressure lesions from electrodes

A relatively rare complication of the use of ECG electrodes applied to the heads of premature infants to measure cerebral blood volume by impedance plethysmography was reported by Golditz et al. (1999). This technique was used to detect intracranial hemorrhage. Sixteen gel ECG electrodes measuring approximately 7×10 mm were equally spaced around the maximal occipito-frontal head circumference and secured with an elastic adhesive tape. At the completion of monitoring, a swab moistened with cottonseed oil was used to soften the tape adhesive for removal. The electrodes were removed and did not stick strongly to the skin. Warm water was then used to remove any traces of oil or adhesive that remained. On removal of the electrodes all infants showed very mild reddening of the forehead skin under the electrodes that faded rapidly, as commonly seen at the time of removal of any ECG or EEG electrode. The impedance recorder uses a 5 mA peak-to-peak, 50-kHz current applied through standard gel ECG electrodes. The monitoring was carried out during the first forty-eight hours of life in fifty infants. The current was applied for only a few seconds each hour. In two infants (both female; gestational age, twenty-seven weeks; birth weights, 630 and 520 grams) the parents noticed 5-mm diameter, slightly raised and firm papules on the infants' foreheads at approximately three months of age. The papules were hypopigmented and corresponded to the sites of electrode placement. Over the next four years the papules remained similar in appearance, became softer, and increased in size proportional to childhood growth. No differences were noted in the ease of electrode application and removal in these two infants. After investigation of chemical and allergic causes for these lesions. Golditz et al. stated that:

> The electrodes and adhesive tape were not applied tightly. However, the resolution of head molding during forty-eight hours after birth may have increased pressure on the electrodes. We postulate that pressure from the electrodes may have caused a local hypoxemia leading to skin damage.

D. Bedsore classification

Shea (1975) divided bedsores into four classes; Table 8.1 presents his summary. His classification resembles that for skin burns, namely first, second and

Table 8.1
Classification of Pressure Sores*

Stage 1

Acute inflammatory response in all layers with an irregular, ill-defined area of soft tissue swelling, induration and heat. This is limited to the epidermis, resembles an abrasion, and is reversible.

Stage 2

An inflammatory and fibroblastic response extending through the dermis to the subcutaneous fat and is also reversible.

Stage 3

Extension into the subcutaneous fat with extensive undermining, essentially a fullthickness skin defect

Stage 4

Penetration into the deep fascia with involvement of muscle and bone.

* From Shea JD, 1975.

third-degree, the latter being a full skin thickness injury. Table 8.1 presents Shea's classification scale.

E. Pressure-sore sites

Examination of Figure 8.5 allows identification of the high-pressure sites on a supine subject and consequently where sores are most likely to develop. According to Reuler and Cooney (1981), 96 percent of pressure-sores are located in the lower part of the body with the sacral and coccygeal areas, ischial tuberosities, and greater trochanter accounting for the majority of pressure-sore sites. Other areas that are frequently involved include the medial condyle of the tibia, the fibular head, the malleolus and the heel. Prominences such as those caused by hypertrophic bone formation by fixation pins may serve as foci for pressure-sore development.

F. Shear-force injury

According to Maklebust (1991) a shear injury can occur when the head of a bed is raised more than 30 degrees. In this position the patient's skeletal frame tends to slide down and the skin tends to stick to the sheet because of friction. This situation applies a shear force between the skin and underlying tissues, thereby reducing capillary blood flow; the longer the shear force persists, the more likely an ulcer will develop. Sliding a patient over bed linen is another way of producing shear force.

8.10 Neuropathy Following Anesthesia

In addition to the prolonged application of mechanical force to the skin, injury can result to nerves due to improper positioning of a patient on the operating table. A nerve can be compressed or stretched which can result in numbness, pain, muscle weakness and paralysis. Autonomic nerves can be involved. One of the mechanisms underlying these events is compromised circulation (ischemia) of the nerve fibers. The symptoms can appear following recovery from anesthesia or over a period of weeks. There is little or no evidence of skin damage in these cases.

Britt and Gordon (1964) reviewed the literature on the nerves that can be damaged during anesthesia. In their survey they included nerves that could be damaged due to intravenous injection as well as those relevant to obstretical procedures. Excluding these, they listed the following that could sustain injury and by what means: (1) brachial plexus (stretch), (2) radial nerve (compression), (3) ulnar nerve (compression), (4) peroneal nerve (compression), (5) saphenous nerve (compression) and (6) sciatic nerve (compression). They stated that symptoms of injury appeared as soon as recovery from anesthesia to a few weeks postanesthesia and reported that the longer the time spent in the abnormal position, the poorer the prognosis.

Kroll et al. (1990) reviewed the ASA closed claims file to 1989 and found 1,541 cases of nerve injury and discovered that only 227 (15 percent) were due to anesthesia procedures. Ulnar neuropathy represented one third of the cases; less prominent were brachial plexus and lumbosacral nerve injuries. The author concluded that the mechanisms underlying these injuries were not always clear.

8.11 Reflex Sympathetic Dystrophy (RSD)

Reflex sympathetic dystrophy is a syndrome that can follow tissue injury of many types. It is characterized by unexplained diffuse pain with patchy colored skin regions (mottling) with a difference in skin color and temperature relative to the opposite limb. A skin rash is not uncommon, accompanied by itching and diffuse edema (swelling due to the accumulation of subcutaneous tissue fluid). Often headache, sweating, muscle weakness and limited range of motion are present. Frequently, numbness and burning pain are reported. The symptoms appear later than the event that precipitated RSD, from hours to months.

RSD is a dysfunction of the sympathetic nervous system which controls the caliber of the small blood vessels, among other things. A sympathetic blocking agent usually relieves the symptoms. RSD is also known as complex regional pain syndrome (CRPS).

The symptoms associated with RSD can be initiated with many different types of injury, e.g. direct or altering current shock, lightning strike, or a burn. Fish (2000) summarized several cases of RSD initiated by electric shock that appeared in the published literature; he stated that:

> A nineteen-year-old man received a "jolt" when he touched a phone booth with his right leg and left hand. He reported pain on the palm of his left hand. Electromyography (EMG) studies done two and twenty-one days after the trauma were normal, despite continued pain. Four months after the incident, he was seen because of persistent burning, numbness and difficulty in moving his fingers. His left hand was edematous. He improved with stellate ganglion block (injection of anesthetic to block sympathetic nerve fibers).

A thirty-seven-year-old female touched a 120-volt ac appliance. She "immediately" released her grip when she felt the shock. During the next five days, she noted a progressive onset of numbness and tingling and swelling of her right hand. There was no burn injury. Over the next two months, there was progression of the burning sensation and swelling of her right hand.

A twenty-nine-year-old man received an electrical shock, but no skin burns from a 110-volt ac power line. He was diagnosed as having reflex sympathetic dystrophy with problems including pain and edema of the hand. Nerve conduction studies were normal.

A forty-seven-year-old man was injured on his left arm by contact with a 380-volt switch. A few hours later, he had burning pain, dysesthesia, weakness and motor impairment of the arm. During subsequent months the symptoms did not change except for the appearance of signs of autonomic nervous system dysfunction, including hyperhidrosis, edema, atrophy of the skin and nails, and excessive sweating. One year later, he improved with sympathetic nerve blockade.

Two telephone operators developed severe burning pain after being struck by lightning while wearing telephone headsets. They were sitting next to each other when they were struck. Both women felt a shock going through their bodies, most of which seemed to pass from their heads to their right arms. They felt as if they had been hit with a baseball bat. Their right arms turned purple and developed a painful burning sensation immediately after the injury. Treatments for arm swelling and pain included pain medications, antidepressants, physical therapy and transcutaneous electrical nerve stimulation. Six months later, their arms were still swollen. There was persistent burning, aching, tightness, throbbing and numbness. Pain was worsened with exposure to heat or cold. Generalized symptoms included psychological problems, dizziness and headaches. The arms and forearms were swollen, cold, and tender to the touch.

Both women had excessive sensitivity to painful stimuli, the sensation remaining after the pain stimulus was removed with abnormal sensory responses and abnormal constriction or dilation of the small blood vessels. Their heads were slightly tilted to the right. Sympathetic blocks brought relief. Interpleural (nerve) blocks were done at the right fourth intercostal space about 6 cm from the spinous process. These were repeated and accompanied by physical and occupational therapy, psychotherapy and biofeedback. Symptoms were 90 percent relieved after one week of daily injections and both women were able to return to work.

The author investigated a case of RSD which was initiated by an electrosurgical burn. The case involved a surgical nurse who was assisting with a laparoscopic procedure. During the operation she rested the laparoscope which was connected to an electrosurgical unit, (ESU) on the bend of her elbow while using her other hand to pass an instrument to the surgeon. During this time, the ESU was activated accidentally and the nurse received a small burn on the bend of her elbow where it touched the laparoscope. Several weeks later, she exhibited the signs of RSD and could not continue her work as a surgical assistant. The case was settled and the details were not made public.

RSD presents diagnostic difficulties in that it shows some of the characteristics of infection and allergy. However, there is no skin infection. The delayed response shares the characteristics of an allergy; however there is no allergen.

8.12 Chemical Injury

A. Introduction

When considering tissue injury due to chemical compounds, it is necessary to distinguish two types of response: (1) true chemical injury and (2) allergic response. With the former, it is the nature of the chemical compound that produces the injury and with the latter, the host exhibits hypersensitivity to a substance (allergen); the response is typically unexpected and vigorous to the presence of very little allergen, which may be a very ordinary environmental substance. The correct term for the second type of response when it occurs on the skin is allergic contact dermatitis; all too often the term allergic is dropped. An allergic response is due to a prior exposure to a substance that endows the subject with an acquired hypersensitivity. Allergic responses will be described later in this chapter.

B. Chemical toxicity

Valuable information about the effects of chemicals can be found in the Materials Safety Data Sheets (MSDS), the package insert and the *Physician's Desk Reference* (PDR); the contents of these sources are described in the chapter on product liability. The Occupational Safety and Health Administration (OSHA) requires that all personnel who handle chemical substances must have a copy of the MSDS and read it. Briefly, the MSDS identifies the name of the compound, its composition, brand name, physical and chemical properties, fire, explosion and health hazard, first aid, antidote and storage and disposal of the substance. The package insert and the PDR identify indications, contraindications, dose, side effects, toxicity and antidotes. The availability of such information often allows evaluation of the forseeability of an accident.

C. Ethylene oxide sterilization

Ethylene oxide (ETO), which is a gas at atmospheric pressure and completely soluble in water, has been used as a sterilizant since the early 1960s. Its value lies in the fact that the item to be sterilized can be placed in a sealed thermoplastic container which is then placed in the ETO sterilizing chamber. The first step in the process involves evacuating and warming the sterilizing chamber. Then ETO with a carrier gas (carbon dioxide or nitrogen) is admitted under controlled vacuum and humidity. The sealed container is bathed in the gas mixture for a prolonged period. Then the chamber is evacuated and the chamber (containing the item in the plastic container) is air washed several times with vacuum cycling to remove the ETO residue. This final step is necessary because ETO is a potent skin irritant (Sexton and Henson, 1950). There are standards that specify the maximum amount of ETO that can be present after sterilization. For example, the Health Industries Manufacturers Association (HIMA) and the New York Mt. Sinai Z-79 Committee have promulgated standards. There is an AAMI (1986) and an AAMI/ANSI standard (1988) that pertain to this issue.

A wide variety of medical items are sterilized with ETO. For example, all items that cannot withstand the heat of steam sterilization are candidates. In fact, it was development of the ETO sterilizer that gave birth to the disposable medical products industry. Familiar examples of items sterilized by ETO are medical instruments, hospital bedding, drapes, gowns, sheets, catheters, catheter electrodes, anesthesia equipment etc.

1. Accidents with ETO-sterilized items

The following accidents occurred in the early days of ETO sterilization when residue controls were not so strict. However, the cases are presented to illustrate the kinds of mishaps that can occur when ETO residue is present.

Randell-Baker and Roberts (1969) called attention to the numerous reports of tissue reactions to plastics and rubber items after ETO sterilization. They stated:

> Reactions have included hemolysis, either in pump oxygenators or blood administration sets, burns to surgeons' hands from ETO-sterilized rubber

gloves, tracheal inflammation and necrosis during prolonged intubation or tracheostomy and possible thrombophlebitis following the use of intravenous tubing. Toxic stabilizers leeching out of polyvinyl chloride (PVC) plastics may be one cause of tissue reaction.

No references were cited for these responses, but Randall-Baker and Roberts made the following recommendations to avoid such difficulties:

1. Adequate aeration of gas-sterilized materials for a minimum of five to seven days at 50ºC or six to eight hours in a properly designed aerator with bacterial filters

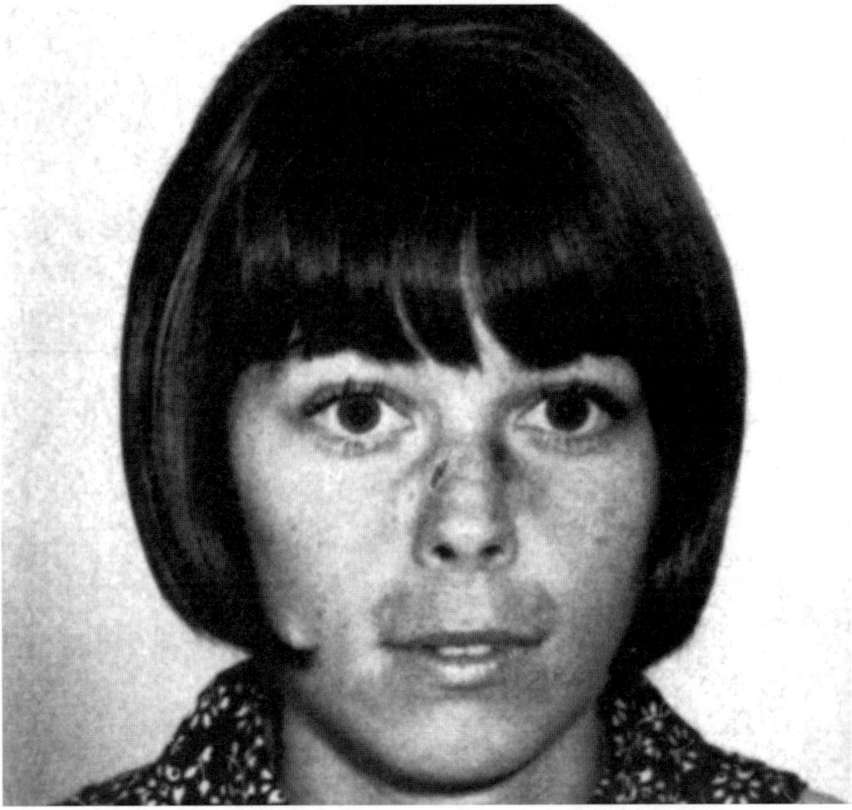

Figure 8.6 *Facial injury due to a facemask sterilized with ETO. (From LaDage LH. Plastic Reconstr. Surg. 1970, 45(2):179 By permission)*

2. Avoidance of the use of 3-ml polythene wrap plastics containing acid phthalic ester plasticizers which absorb ETO selectively and any previously gamma-ray-sterilized items
3. Avoid increased use of disposable items

White (1970), who was then chairman of the ASA Subcommittee on Standardization, was concerned about the need to provide a sterile tracheal tube and anesthesia breathing circuit for each patient. He made the following seven recommendations:

1. Polyvinylchloride or rubber materials sterilized with ethylene oxide should not be used within *seven days* following sterilization, if stored at room temperature.
2. A properly designed aerator heated to 50° C may be used to reduce safe aeration time to twelve to eighteen hours
3. Polyethylene (3–5 mil) and paper wrap are the best packaging materials. Nylon and polyvinilidine chloride (e.g., Saran Wrap) are less permeable to ethylene oxide; polyvinylchloride delays elution).
4. Polyvinylchloride objects which have been gamma-irradiated should not be resterilized with ethylene oxide because significant amounts of ethylenechlorohydrin will be formed.
5. Disposable items should be discarded after use because the by-products of later ethylene oxide sterilization may be injurious, because of ethylene chlorohydrin in particular.
6. Water droplets should be removed from material to be sterilized in order to prevent the formation of ethylene glycol.
7. Biological indicators should be used as a frequent check on the effectiveness of sterilization.

LaDage (1970) reported a case of facial skin irritation due to a face mask that had been sterilized with ETO; he stated:

> The patient is a twenty-one-year-old lady who underwent lengthy surgery under general anesthesia, which was administered with a mask. Apparently, the mask had been sterilized with ethylene oxide gas. She incurred severe burns of the facio-labial areas and on each side of her nose. What pressure and moisture had to do in aggravating the toxicity to produce this severity, I do not know.

An editor's note to La Dage's paper stated:

> In some reports on this subject it would appear that the gas may be absorbed on the surface of impermeable materials (such as metals and glass) for a short time, but is actually absorbed into such permeable materials as rubber and some plastics (particularly, polyvinyl chloride). In the latter, it is said that forced ventilation for long periods (or exposure to room air for days, weeks, or months) may be necessary before use is free from risk.

Nineteen cases of skin irritation due to ETO-sterilized reusable gowns were reported by Biro et al. (1974); they stated:

> Nineteen hospitalized women postoperatively suffered from severe burns of the buttocks and back from contact with reusable surgical gowns and drapes that had been sterilized with ethylene oxide and had not been properly aerated.
>
> The lesions were described as erythematous, edematous with bullae (blisters) 1 to 5 cm in diameter. The bullae ultimately ulcerated in some cases and healed with scarring and hyperpigmentation.

Tests were performed to determine the amount of ETO residue on the gowns; Biro et al. (1974) reported:

> Testing samples of reusable gowns that had been worn by the patients showed that the amount of ethylene oxide residue varied from 3,600 ppm ethylene oxide to 10,800 ppm ethylene oxide. The safe level for ethylene oxide gas recommended by both Health Industries Association (HIA) and Z-79 Committee of New York Mt. Sinai Hospital is 200 ppm (maximum). The levels of residual ethylene oxide in the implicated gowns were thus determined to be sixteen to fifty times the safe level for skin contact. (ppm = parts per million)

2. Summary

The foregoing cases indicate the need for removing residual ETO from the sterilized item; failure to do so can result in tissue damage. Removing ETO residue requires appreciable time; therefore, the turn-around time for ETO sterilization can be days.

D. Glutaraldehyde sterilization

Glutaraldehyde is a powerful, water-soluble, biocidal agent that kills most microbial life, such as bacterial and fungal spores, tubercle bacilli, and viruses (Scott and Gorman, 1991). The biocidal action is enhanced by alkalization. Glutaraldehyde is available in concentrations up to 50 percent; however, a 2 percent solution is typically used to sterilize instruments and items that cannot withstand the heat of steam sterilization. Common preparations are Cidex, Glutarol, and Verucasep.

The device to be sterilized is first cleaned of debris and washed. It is then soaked in the glutaraldehyde solution. The biocidal efficacy depends on the concentration of the glutaraldehyde, the pH, the temperature, and the duration of soaking. It is advisable to use a nonmetallic container when sterilizing metallic devices, such as endoscopes, to avoid corrosion due to bimetallic contact because the glutaraldehyde solution can conduct electric current. Manufacturers of surgical instruments provide concentration and time recommendations for sterilization.

As with other chemical sterilizants, after the exposure phase, it is necessary to remove the glutaraldehyde residue adhering to the device. Soaking and repeated washing with sterile saline solution or sterile water removes the residue. Drying (if used) must occur in a germfree environment.

Various authors have recommended different soaking times for sterilization. Corson et al. (1979) recommended that for routine laparoscope use between cases, a fifteen-minute soak in Cidex is adequate, followed by a rinse in sterile water. A longer soak time (ten hours) is necessary following use of an instrument in a patient with suspected infection. Shyu et al. (1992) recommended that transesophageal echocardiograph probes should be soaked in a gluaraldehyde solution for at least twenty minutes. Scott and Gorman (1991) reviewed the literature and recommend a thirty-minute immersion following use of an endoscope on a patient or carrier of hepatitis B or AIDS and a one-hour immersion following use in tuberculosis patients.

Scott and Gorman (1991) stated:

> More recently, the interim report of the Working Party of the British Society of Gastroenterology recommended glutaraldehyde as a first-line disinfectant and proposed a four-minute soak as sufficient for inactivation of vegetative bacteria and viruses, including HIV and HBV. Many additional references have been made to the use of glutaraldehyde for rapid and safe disinfection of gastrointestinal endoscopy equipment.

1. Toxicity

The use of glutaraldehyde for chemical sterilization is now widespread and brings with it possible risks of toxic reactions to the individual handling the equipment during the sterilizing process and to the patient exposed to equipment treated with glutaraldehyde. In some cases this may bring a device in contact with the bloodstream.

The Materials Safety Data Sheet (MSDS) identifies the hazards of handling glutaraldehyde. For example, its vapors are irritating to the eyes; therefore, goggles or an eye shield should be worn. Vapor from a glutaraldehyde solution, if breathed, is irritating and will cause stinging sensations in the nose and throat, coughing, chest discomfort and tightness, breathing difficulty and headache. Brief skin contact may cause mild to moderate local redness and possibly swelling. Prolonged contact may result in severe inflammation. Therefore, protective impermeable gloves should be worn.

2. Accidents with glutaraldehyde sterilization

Glutaraldehyde sterilization is now a mature procedure and there are few patient-related incidents. Numerous studies have been carried out on the microorganism level remaining on instruments and devices sterilized with glutaraldehyde preparations. Also, the absorption and rate of elution of glutaraldehyde from rubber and plastic goods have been documented. These issues were reviewed by Scott and Gorman (1991).

There have been a few incidents resulting from exposure to glutaraldehyde sterilizing solutions, which are typically 2 percent in strength. Using the results of a questionnaire, Axon et al. (1981) analyzed the responses from fifty-two centers in the UK, each of which conducted about 500 endoscopic examinations annually. The analyses showed that 37 percent of the endoscopic units using glutaraldehyde solution as a disinfectant reported health problems among their staff attributable to glutaraldehyde use. Axon et al. stated:

> Sixteen (37 percent) of those centers using glutaraldehyde had experienced problems with staff becoming sensitive to the disinfecting agent. A further questionnaire was sent to these centers and replies were received from all sixteen. These showed that thirty-six individuals had complained of forty-six symptom complexes thought attributable to glutaraldehyde sensitivity. In thirty-two, dermatitis had developed; these included twelve with symptoms in skin remote from the hands in addition to local dermatitis; eight complained

> of conjunctivitis and in six nasal irritation developed; four described this as sinusitis. (Information on allergic testing was not provided.)

Corrado et al. (1986) used provocative testing to determine allergic reactions in nurses who reported respiratory symptoms that they attributed to exposure to glutaraldehyde. Two of the four patients investigated had a confirmed reaction to glutaraldehyde.

E. Antiseptic solutions

In the late 1800s, Lister, a surgeon in Scotland, found that cleansing the skin with carbolic acid solution eliminated the infection associated with surgery. Then surgeons began to soak their hands in dilute carbolic acid to prevent bringing infectious agents into the surgical site. The use of rubber gloves arose from hand soaking in dilute carbolic acid. According to Haagensen and Lloyd (1946), it was Charles Goodyear, in collaboration with William Halstead, a surgeon at the Johns Hopkins Hospital, who introduced the use of rubber gloves to surgery in 1889. It is reported that Halstead's nurse developed lesions on her hands from carbolic-acid soaking. Halstead sought the aid of Goodyear to create rubber gloves, which were fabricated for the nurse. Others began to wear rubber gloves, which are now an essential component in asepsis.

1. Skin preparation

Preoperative skin preparation is not a standardized procedure and uses many different antiseptic agents. Prior to the application of such agents, the skin may be washed with soap, shaved, or the hair removed by clipping or by the use of a depilatory. These pretreatments may affect the susceptibility of the skin to infection (Craig, 1986). However, irrespective of which antiseptic agent is used, it is essential to avoid its pooling because many of such agents can injure the skin if the pooling period is prolonged. Referring to skin injuries due to skin preparation solutions, Health Devices (1980) reported:

> Preventing chemical injury to the skin requires care on the part of the surgeon and the operating room staff. All prepping agents should be applied with great care and should not be allowed to pool beneath the patient or beneath a tourniquet.

A similar recommendation appeared in the FDA Drug Bulletin (1985) referring to an iodine tincture and stated:

> The warning section of the labeling states that Hibitane Tincture must not be allowed to pool around the patient. Before the surgical procedure and electrosurgery are begun, the skin must be completely dry. Excess liquid should be removed with a sterile towel.

2. Iodine compounds

Tincture of iodine, i.e., iodine in ethyl alcohol, supplanted carbolic acid as an antiseptic skin preparation and was used for some time until more recently, being supplanted by iodophors, i.e., organic substance-containing iodine. Several manufacturers provide such compounds under different trade names.

The toxicity of tincture of iodine and the iodophors is very low. Nonetheless, accidents have been reported. Llorens (1972) described two cases of skin injury due to povidone-iodine (Betadine). In cancer patients he described the first case as follows:

> The night prior to the operation, the patient's abdomen was scrubbed with povidone-iodine, and again at the time of operation a ten-minute scrub with the same agent was done. A vaginal preparation with the same agent was also done. The surgical skin cleanser was used initially for approximately ten minutes, followed by application of the povidone-iodine solution which was painted on with a gauze sponge. The patient had been previously placed on a water-circulating heating mattress. The surgical procedure lasted four hours and thirty minutes. On the day following the operation, a reddened area over the sacrum was noted. This area became darkened and eventually the superficial layer of epidermis desquamated.

Regarding the second patient, Llorens reported:

> This patient had the same preparation as the previous patient, and a water-circulating heating mattress was also used. On the second postoperative day, a darkened area was noted over the lower back and sacral area. This measured approximately 20 by 20 cm, and was quite painful to the touch. As in the previous patient, this area also desquamated and with conservative measures healed spontaneously. She, too, was discharged on the fourteenth postoperative day.

A later statement in Llorens' paper offers a possible explanation for the injury. He stated, "Steps have been taken to prevent seepage of the scrub solution under the patient and in subsequent operations of this type, no further difficulty has been encountered."

Referring to the *PDR*, the following is stated for this antiseptic (Betadine): "Prolonged exposure to unabsorbed wet solutions may cause irritation." The fact that sacral contact pressure was probably high and heat was used may likely have exacerbated the injury reported by Llorens.

Feldtman et al. (1979) reported skin irritation due to Betadine; they stated:

> We have noted eleven patients who have had their surgical wounds covered with a dressing containing 10 percent povidone iodine (Betadine). The wounds showed cutaneous erythema, induration, and also papulation which conformed to the configuration of the dressing. All eleven patients who demonstrated this also showed a similar reaction to a 2 × 2 cm cotton pledget saturated with 10 percent povidone iodine. Diagnosis on ten of the eleven patients was suspect for altered immune state.

Note that the skin was exposed to liquid Betadine on a pledget which simulates pooling, a situation to be avoided according to the manufacturer. Later in the paper, the authors stated that they did not test for an immune response.

Another report recommending that wet iodine solutions should not be covered was presented by Howes et al. (1979), who stated:

> Clinically, it is well known that solutions of iodine applied to the skin should not be covered with an occlusive dressing, a view supported by Dr. Morgan-Hughes's observations that erythema occurred in all areas painted with tincture of iodine and covered by Sleek (an occlusive dressing).

Another similar incident was reported by Duffy (1981), who stated:

> After successfully cannulating the epidural space in a pregnant patient the anesthetic registrar covered the site with a gauze swab soaked in Betadine Antiseptic Solution (povidone iodine), as was his usual habit. At the suggestion of the assisting midwife this swab was then sprayed with a proprietary plastic skin and the whole area covered with a waterproof dressing.

At the opposite end of the spectrum of using an iodophor for wound-infection control is a report by Glick et al. (1985), who stated:

> Continuous povidone-iodine irrigation is frequently used to treat mediastinitis after median sternotomy and has been considered safe and effective. We describe a thirty-four-month-old patient with mediastinitis after median sternotomy who was treated with continuous povidone-iodine irrigation and who absorbed toxic quantities of iodine (total serum iodine, 9,375 μg/dl; normal range, 4.5 to 9.0 μg/dl). An unexplained metabolic acidosis developed, along with changes in mental status, and the patient died.

They concluded by stating:

> Based on our clinical experience, experimental investigation, and critical review of the available literature, we believe that the routine use of povidone-iodine mediastinal irrigation is contraindicated. Whenever possible, antimicrobial irritants should be picked based on specific bacterial sensitivities from cultures obtained at the time the irrigation tubes are placed. If this is not possible, or if microbial resistance occurs, then a highly dilute solution (1:1000) of povidone-iodine should be used. Administration of a highly dilute solution reduces the steady state serum iodine concentration but not the antiseptic efficacy of povidone-iodine. In addition, if povidone-iodine is used, frequent serum iodine levels should be obtained to prevent excessive accumulation of iodine.

Response to Glick's paper by Rothwell (1986), on behalf of the manufacturer of Betadine, stated that the cause of the child's death was not established. Rothwell stated:

> In my view, this isolated case report should not be extrapolated in absolute terms as stated in the article. Other prominent cardiovascular surgeons have found povidone-iodine to be highly effective when used preoperatively to prevent infection and postoperatively when infections have occurred as a result of operation. The intent of this letter is to bring some balance to the article by presenting reports in which povidone-iodine was used successfully when administered at appropriate dosage.

3. Mercury compounds

Hodgkinson et al. (1978) commented on the effect of a mercury-containing antiseptic (thimerosal) and the exacerbating effect of pressure; they stated:

If the thimerosal has not been allowed to dry and has been trapped under the body of the patient in a pooled dependent position, like the buttocks for a patient in the stirrups, or under a tourniquet, the solvent may irritate the skin and result in a skin burn. Freon and alcohol as well as thimerosal usually evaporate after application. If these agents do not evaporate on contact with the skin and are trapped under a tourniquet or the buttocks of the patient or under drapes or dressings, they may irritate the skin. This irritation, coupled with pressure, leads to a situation analogous to that seen in the development of an acute accelerated decubitus ulcer, irritation, maceration and pressure compounding each other to result in a skin burn or superficial ulcer in the skin. Friction from the underlying sheets has a variable role, as may the underlying heating blankets on the operating table.

4. Mercury poisoning

Rennie et al. (1999) reported a case of mercury poisoning in a nine-year-old boy. Three months before presentation, he had dismantled and spilled the mercury from a mercury sphygmomanometer provided for home use. The patient presented with a three-week history of abdominal pain, constipation, lethargy, limb pain and unsteadiness. Because features of encephalopathy and peripheral neuropathy were present, heavy metal poisoning was suspected. Blood testing confirmed mercury poisoning and the patient was treated with an intravenous or oral administration of a chelating agent for eighteen days. The patient developed hypertension, requiring drug treatment, but was eventually successfully weaned from medication. Other family members demonstrated increased serum mercury concentrations, but did not require treatment. Very high concentrations of mercury were discovered in the patient's bedroom.

Spilled mercury is difficult to collect and its collection can be dangerous. Mercury thermometers can break and cause a health hazard. Ondeck et al. (1999) discussed the safe collection of spilled mercury and stated that protective gloves and masks should be worn while picking up the mercury spill with sand or another absorbent material. The material should be disposed of properly and that spills of greater than one pound should be reported to local emergency authorities. To reach toxic levels of exposure, individuals must come in contact with 30 mg of mercury, which is far more than the average thermometer contains. She stated that mercury thermometer breakages occur in the home-care setting and home-care nurses should be prepared to clean mercury spills properly when they occur.

F. Allergic responses

An allergic response reflects a hypersensitive state acquired through prior exposure to a particular substance (allergen) and re-exposure produces an enhanced capability of the immune system to react. An allergen is any substance capable of producing a specific type of susceptibility. One may view an allergic response as an exaggeration of the body's defensive mechanisms. The allergic response may result from simple skin contact or inhalation, injection, ingestion, or implantation of a substance. The response can be in the respiratory, gastrointestinal, or nervous system, but cutaneous responses are perhaps the most frequently encountered allergic reactions. The respiratory responses are rhinitis and bronchial asthma. Among the gastrointestinal responses are vomiting, abdominal pain, and edema of the mouth, lips, and esophagus. Nervous-system responses include persistent headache, vomiting and disturbances in the autonomic nervous system. A bewildering array of terms is used to describe allergic skin lesions; Table 8.2 presents a list of the terms along with simplified definitions.

Table 8.2
Terms Used to Describe Allergic Skin Lesions

Term	Brief definition
Bulla	Blister
Cyst	Fluid-filled sac
Dermatitis	Skin inflammation
Dermatographia	A condition in which tracing on the skin produces an elevated reddened track
Ecchymosis	Blood seen under the skin due to capillary damage
Eczema	Skin inflammation with vesication
Edema	Fluid accumulation in intercellular spaces
Erythema	Skin reddening
Induration	Hardening
Papule	Solid, skin elevation
Petechiae	Small round, purplish-red spots
Pruritus	Intense itching of the skin
Purpura	Purple
Stigmata	A spot or mark on the skin
Ulceration	Tissue disintegration and necrosis
Urticaria	Itchy, smooth, elevated skin patches of a different color
Vesicle	Small, fluid-filled sac
Wheal	Discolored, smooth, elevated skin region

Two interesting aspects of an allergic response are its unpredictability and recurrence in response to the allergen, despite a long dormant period when no allergen was present. The paragraphs that follow provide many examples of allergic response in association with the use of medical devices. The responses were not foreseen, nor could they be, unless (1) the subject knew of his or her allergy and (2) the material contacted contained the allergen. Although it is customary to inquire of allergies before administering drugs, the issue is usually not raised when using ordinary, frequently used, medical devices. However, the issue of forseeability of an allergic response can always be raised.

1. Allergic contact dermatitis

The prevalence of allergic contact dermatitis varies widely because its incidence is related to previous allergen exposure. Patch testing is used to identify persons suspected of being allergic to a substance. According to Larsen and Maibach (1992), surveys of normal subjects have shown that in a group of 1,200 patch tests, sensitivity to the following was revealed: nickel 5.8 percent, neomycin 1.1 percent, ethylenediamine 0.43 percent, and benzocaine 0.17 percent. Among the common metallic sensitizers are nickel and chromium; some women cannot wear jewelry containing these elements. Larsen and Maibach tabulated many allergens; among the common items are benzocaine, black rubber, epoxy resin, formaldehyde, lanolin-alcohol, tetracycline and thimerosal (a mercury-containing antiseptic).

2. The patch test

The patch test is used to identify an allergen. Although the techniques used in patch testing vary widely, the following is a simplified version. The test substance is applied to a piece of cloth or soft paper that is placed on intact skin and covered with an impermeable substance which acts as a backing and is affixed to the skin with tape. Often different concentrations of test substance are used to identify any threshold effect. After forty-eight hours the patches are removed and the condition of the underlying skin is examined. A rash is evidence of a positive test. It must be recognized that the test is applied with each component of a substance that was suspected of producing an allergic response. The test can be designed to reveal the threshold concentration of the allergen.

3. Alcohol allergy

Ethyl and isopropyl alcohols are used widely to disinfect the skin prior to its puncture by a needle. These alcohols are also used as a preservative in some skin preparations, as well as in electrode pastes to inhibit bacterial growth. Other compounds are added to prolong shelf life and there is remarkably little adverse reaction to these compounds. However, a small percentage of subjects are allergic to such preparations.

Two cases of allergic response to ethyl (potable) alcohol were reported by Drevets and Seebohm (1961) as follows:

> Case 1. A sixty-seven-year-old white widow was referred to the University Hospitals on Nov. 3, 1958 because of congestive heart failure. She had dyspnea on exertion, orthopnea and progressively more distressing right upper quadrant abdominal pain intermittently for several months. She had noted itching and redness of the hands and fingers on the morning after drinking small amounts of alcoholic beverages the previous evening. She had first observed this sixteen years previously. She drank alcoholic beverages, such as beer and wine, only on rare social occasions or for "medicinal" purposes. Because of the distressing symptoms following the ingestion of only two or three ounces, she had refrained from drinking alcoholic beverages during the previous year. There was no other history of clinical allergy.
>
> Case 2. A twenty-five-year-old medical student, who lived in Hong Kong until he came to Iowa when eighteen years old, was seen in the Allergy Clinic in January 1960, with complaints of rhinorrhea and nasal stuffiness which he had had for twelve years. These symptoms had occurred during the period from mid August to early October for seven years. He had not had eczema or asthma, but had experienced frequent respiratory infections during childhood. In addition to his respiratory complaints, he had noted a diffuse erythematous, pruritic rash over his hands, wrists, elbows and feet after drinking one to two ounces of one or another of several alcoholic beverages. This was first noted after the third or fourth time he ingested alcohol. Almost immediately after drinking, he had a diffuse erythema of the face which lasted for about one hour. The rash appeared the next day and lasted twelve to eighteen hours. He rarely drank such beverages because of this reaction.

Patch tests were used to identify the allergens in these two cases; the authors reported:

> In the study of the first patient, we applied patches with various dilutions of ethyl alcohol ranging from 5 to 70 percent. Two millimeter cubes of cotton soaked with the test solution and then squeezed free of excess fluid were put

> under the patches. These were applied to the arm or back for twenty-four hours. Other tests with 70 percent methyl alcohol, 70 percent isopropyl alcohol, 35 percent butyl alcohol, 35 percent amyl alcohol, 50 percent acetone, 5 percent acetaldehyde, 5 percent formaldehyde, 1 percent formic acid, 1 percent phenol food coloring, and 1 percent glycerol were made. There were marked inflammatory reactions to the alcohols, but no response to the aldehydes, acetone, formic acid, glycerol, phenol, or food coloring. Patch tests with these same solutions caused no reaction on a control subject.

The patch test was followed by an interesting experiment described as follows:

> We then gave the patient 60 ml of 90-proof whiskey through a nasogastric tube while she was fasting. In thirty minutes she began to appear giddy and in two hours she complained of itching of the palms. Three hours later we noted minimal redness of the palms and backs of her hands. After five hours, both surfaces of the patient's hands were moderately erythematous and pruritic. Eleven hours later intense pruritus developed over the arms, hands, anterior chest, neck and thighs. These areas were markedly erythematous. Because of the intense pruritus and erythema of the skin, diphenhydramine hydrochloride and prednisone were given orally and calamine with 1 percent phenol lotion was applied topically. These reactions were not as intense as those after the patch tests. At no time did she experience pain or any other systemic symptoms. The skin reaction gradually subsided. After seventy-two hours there was no pruritus and only minimal erythema which disappeared completely by the fifth day.

The response of the second patient was described as follows:

> The second patient had a dermatitis to ingested alcoholic beverages, but the lesions could not be reproduced with topical application of alcohol.

The possibility that contaminants in ethanol could be responsible for dermatitis was considered by Fregert et al. (1965). They stated:

> The patient was a sixty-two-year-old housewife; heredity—inquiry into her familial history revealed nothing of interest; previous illnesses—for six years she had had ulcerative colitis for which she had undergone gastroenterostomy; present illness—for the previous twelve years she had had a postthrombotic leg ulcer with periodic dermatitis. During an exacerbation of the dermatitis of the lower leg, epicutaneous tests were performed with the

agents used for local treatment and routine test substances. The patient gave positive eczematous reactions to all test substances dissolved in ethanol. She also reacted positively to a patch test with ethanol.

After extensive patch testing, they concluded:

An eczematous contact dermatitis is described in a woman after application of low aliphatic primary alcohols, including methanol and ethanol. She reacted positively to ethanol but negatively to methanol. The corresponding acids gave negative reactions. Secondary and tertiary alcohols and ketones gave negative reactions.

Gas chromatography showed commercially available alcohols to contain contaminants, including aldehydes. However, even chromatographically pure ethanol produced dermatitis. Ethanol thus seems to possess allergenic properties in this patient, but the possibility of a metabolite of ethanol, i.e., ethanol, being the allergen responsible cannot be excluded.

Fregert et al. (1969) pursued the allergic response to ethanol that was free of impurities. They summarized their results in four patients as follows:

Four female patients with eczematous reactions to lower aliphatic alcohols are described. One of them had skin symptoms also after consumption of alcohol and three had severe symptoms of the oral mucosa. Testing with gas-chromatographically pure methanol, ethanol, and 1-propanol showed positive reactions in all four. They also reacted positively to unpurified 1-butanol. Of the secondary alcohols, two patients had reactions to 2-propanol and one to 2-butanol. None of the patients reacted to tertiary alcohol and only one patient reacted to croton aldehyde, which was one of the five aldehydes tested. All four reacted positively to patch test with beer and red wine.

Van Ketel and Tan-Lim (1975) described another case of allergy to ethyl alcohol; the reported:

A fifty-two-year-old female patient was seen in a surgical ward after an operation for gallstones. Within forty-eight hours after the operation an itching eruption developed on her abdomen underneath the gauze bandage which had been fixed with adhesive tape. The eruption had spread within two days beyond the bandage on the abdomen and thighs; rather ill-defined patches of erythema, papules, vesicles, and erosions were observed. It was diagnosed as

> contact eczema with an i.d. reaction. This patient was patch-tested also with Leukosilk (Beiersdorf), which showed no reaction. Patch tests with salts of iodine, chlorhexidene, ethanol 60 percent ketonated with oil of lavender and non-ketonated ethanol 60 percent showed a strong positive allergic reaction after forty-eight hours which proved that in this case an allergy to ethanol itself was present.

The cases just described demonstrate that some subjects are allergic to alcohols. Alcohols are found in many substances that contact the skin and it follows that such subjects will exhibit an allergic response to alcohol-containing compounds.

4. Skin rashes associated with recording bioelectric events

When bioelectric events, such as the electrocardiogram (ECG), electroencephalogram (EEG), electromyogram (EMG), electronystagmogram (ENG) etc., are recorded, an electrolytic preparation is placed between the metal electrode and the skin to make ohmic contact with the subject. Such preparations contain an electrolyte, usually sodium chloride, a gel and a bacteriostatic agent. Sometimes the skin is first cleaned with alcohol; occasionally the skin is lightly abraded prior to placing the electrodes. In the early days of bioelectric recording, metal-plate electrodes were retained with rubber straps. Appearance of the self-adhering, disposable electrode has largely displaced the bare metal electrode for many applications. Nonetheless, in the disposable electrodes there is typically a metal electrode, a coupling gel containing the electrolyte, and a preservative; therefore, there exists the opportunity for one or more of these components to produce an allergic reaction in some subjects.

a. Electrocardiography (ECG). Richardson et al. (1969) reported several cases of allergic contact dermatitis associated with routine electrocardiography; they stated:

> In a five-month period during 1969 and 1968, three individuals were seen at the University of Virginia Hospital with peculiar, discrete, rectangular areas of erythema and microvesiculation on the distal aspect of all four extremities. The areas of dermatitis in each patient corresponded to sites of electrocardiogram (ECG) electrode placement on the skin.
>
> Inquiry revealed that a prepackaged alcohol sponge had been utilized as a conductor between the patient's skin and the metal ECG electrodes. It was

> learned that it had become customary to substitute this same type of prepackaged alcohol sponge for electrode paste on the medical service.

A second observation of the nursing personnel was reported as follows:

> A few months later a nurse was seen who developed a hemorrhagic, vesiculobullous dermatitis on the tips of the fingers of the left hand, which cleared when she was on vacation and recurred when she returned to work. Upon questioning, it was learned that she frequently held the alcohol sponge in her left hand to cleanse a patient's arm prior to giving an injection with her right hand. Subsequently, another nurse with a similar history, who had an eczematoid eruption of her hands for many weeks, was brought to our attention. She had found that "alcohol sponges" were the cause of her eruption, and her dermatitis promptly cleared when she discontinued all contact with alcohol.

Patch tests were performed to confirm that the alcohol was the allergen. A similar case was reported by Schick (1981), who stated:

> ECG electrodes were placed using isopropyl alcohol swabs (Webcol Alcohol Prep, 70 percent alcohol, Kendall Co, Chicago) for conduction. Immediately following resuscitation, erythema in the areas of the ECG leads were noted on both arms and legs. This progressed to blister formation and skin sloughing, followed by eschar development.

Para-chloro-meta-xylenol (PCMX) is an antibacterial agent that is used as a preservative in some electrode pastes. It is known that it is an allergen to some subjects and Storrs (1975) reported several cases of allergic contact dermatitis caused by this agent. The first case was a young man who treated himself with several skin preparations some years earlier; Storrs reported:

> When he became an intern and surgery resident, he began to develop a vesicular eruption on several fingers of his right hand. He quite rightly suspected that Redux, electrocardiogram paste, was the culprit. When he was patch-tested to this paste, he developed a 3+ reaction within twelve hours. Subsequently, he was tested to 0.5 percent PCMX in petrolatum and also had a 3+ reaction. He is now enlightened and his skin is clear as long as he avoids products which contain PCMX.

Storrs reported on other cases as follows:

> Two of our other patients also developed their dermatitis after exposure to Redux paste. Five patients were troubled by Carbolated Vaseline. One of these patients had trouble initially with Carbolated Vaseline and then developed dermatitis at the sites of the application of the electrodes with Redux paste when she received an electrocardiogram while hospitalized for treatment of her Carbolated Vaseline dermatitis.

In his paper, Storrs listed thirty-five familiar products that contain PCMX. Many of these products are widely used skin preparations, including Vaseline.

Coskey (1977) reported a case of allergic contact dermatitis due to one component in an electrode paste used for recording the ECG. He stated:

> A four-year-old boy was seen on March 23, 1976 because of persistent dermatitis on his chest and extremities. He had developed the eruption two months previously, shortly after an ECG had been taken. The eruption was confined to the areas where the electrode jelly had been used for contact between the skin and the electrodes.

Patch testing revealed that the subject was sensitive to tragacanth, a gum that was used as a binder in the electrode paste.

Over a two-year period, Fisher (1977) encountered nine patients who developed allergic contact dermatitis associated with ECG recording. Five patients reacted to gels and/or pastes containing parabens, FD&C yellow #5, propylene glycol, PCMX and pine oil. Two patients were allergic to the rubber straps that contained mercaptobenzothiazole. He described the reaction in these two patients as follows:

> Two patients were studied who acquired band-like, erythematous, vesicular dermatitis at the sites of contact with the rubber straps used to fasten the ECG electrodes. Both patients showed a positive reaction to a piece of the rubber strap and to mercaptobenzothiazole. One patient gave a history of shoe dermatitis with previous hypersensitivity to mercaptobenzothiazole, which continues to be the most common cause of rubber sensitivity.

Fisher continued by reporting on a patient who acquired allergic contact dermatitis due to the nickel in the ECG electrodes; he stated:

A twenty-six-year-old nurse at University Hospital acquired dermatitis at the sites where electrodes had been applied. It was at first suspected that she was allergic to the ECG paste, but patch testing with the paste, which was performed elsewhere, gave negative results.

The history revealed that she could not wear costume jewelry without acquiring dermatitis. A strongly positive patch test reaction to nickel sulfate was obtained and the metal electrodes gave a strongly positive reaction to dimethylglyoxime, indicating the presence of "available" nickel in the metal electrode.

At that time, nickel-plated electrodes and German-silver electrodes were used for ECG. The latter alloy contains nickel, copper, and zinc, but no silver.

Fisher described his final case in which the patient was allergic to alcohol; he reported:

A thirty-eight-year-old male had a sharp localized rectangular patch of vesicular dermatitis corresponding to the sites of the ECG cotton sponges which were used as conductors instead of ECG paste. This patient was found allergic, on patch testing, to the isopropyl alcohol used in the gauze pad and to ethyl alcohol. However, there was no systemic reaction from drinking alcoholic beverages.

b. Electroencephalography (EEG). To record the EEG it is customary to adhere silver-disk electrodes to the scalp with collodion; alternatively, bentonite paste is used. Silver (1950) reported a case of allergic contact dermatitis when bentonite paste was used as the coupling agent. He reported:

A fourteen-year-old white male with petit mal and grand mal attacks since three months of age was admitted for surgical consideration because of the focal nature of his attacks.

Previous electroencephalograms had been made using collodion as the adhesive agent for scalp electrodes. Nine days following the use of Bentonite paste as the adhesive agent in electroencephalography, small annular, slightly elevated skin lesions were noted on the scalp; these had erythamatous centers and yellow borders.

The site of the lesions corresponded to the points of application of the scalp electrodes. Patch testing proved that the patient was sensitive to Bentonite powder and not to the $CaCl_2$ or glycerin which comprise the paste.

c. Electronystagmography (ENG). Nystagmus is a rapid movement of the eyeball which can be recorded by placing electrodes just lateral to the inner and outer canthis of the eye to obtain lateral eyeball movements. Electrodes can be placed supraorbitally and infraorbitally to record vertical motion of the eyeball. Such recordings are possible because there is a standing potential across the eyeball, the cornea being positive with respect to the back of the eyeball. For a discussion of recording methods, see Geddes and Baker (1989).

Strahan and Simmons (1968) reported two cases of skin lesions in an ENG study involving 600 patients. Placement of the electrodes was described as follows:

> The flat areas lateral to the lateral canthi are cleaned with an alcohol sponge and rubbed briskly with a wooden tongue blade after a standard electroencephalogram (EEG) electrode paste composed of bentonite, calcium chloride and glycerin, has been applied. The 9-mm silver electrodes are placed against the paste (not the skin) and secured with paper tape. A ground electrode is similarly placed on the forehead. In one of these patients (and in many others) a sodium chloride electrocardiogram ECG paste was used instead.

Strahan and Simmons described the two cases as follows:

> Case 1. A forty-three-year-old psychiatrist had an electronystagmogram as part of a workup for an unilateral sensorineural hearing loss. The patient and the technician who performed the test reported nothing unusual. Approximately four days later the patient noted raised, plaque-like red skin lesions bilaterally in the region of the electrode application. These lesions did not enlarge during the next week; however, several crusts were removed from their surfaces. By the third week the patient had bilateral, well circumscribed, erythematous bulky lesions which gradually calcified during the next two months. Since this time these lesions have diminished somewhat in size, but still remain as firm white blemishes.
>
> Case 2. A forty-five-year-old housewife underwent electronystag-mography as a part of a workup for dizziness. The following day she noted a serous transudate from a flat, but reddened 1-cm skin area in the region of electrode application on the left side. In the next two weeks this area crusted several times resulting in a raised erythematous plateau. By the end of three weeks, a hard, C-shaped white area appeared within the confines of this 1-cm raised

> erythematous lesion. This did not change in the next four weeks and surgical excision was performed for cosmetic reasons.

In analyzing their results, Strahan and Simmons ruled out electrical injury by testing their equipment and correctly pointing out that the skin lesions occurred in only two out of more than 600 patients. They concluded by stating:

> Though possible etiologies of these skin lesions include electrical burns, sensitivity to the electrode paste and overzealous preparation of the skin, the lesions were probably caused by a problem specifically related to the silver electrode and the individual's sensitivity.

Patch testing was not performed by Strahan and Simmons; therefore, the reason for the skin lesions is unknown. However much earlier, Silver (1950) had reported allergic contact dermatitis due to benetonite paste.

d. Electrosurgical electrodes. Sidhu and Shaw (1999) reported two cases of allergic contact dermatitis associated with the use of electrosurgical dispersive electrodes. Both patients had prior acrylate sensitization due to the use of sculptured fingernails. Describing the two cases, the authors stated:

> A forty-two-year-old woman underwent surgery for a ruptured Achilles tendon and experienced itching at the site of a disposable blue dispersive electrode after six hours and developed erythema, scaling, and fissuring after seven days that took five weeks to resolve.
>
> A fifty-three-year-old woman underwent surgery for varicose vein stripping and developed erythema conforming to the shape of a disposable dispersive electrode, twenty-four hours after the procedure and removal of the pad. Dermatitis in the area continued for six weeks.
>
> Both women had a past history of dermatitis from the use of artificial sculptured acrylic nails. The manufacturer of the disposable blue dispersive electrode stated that 2-hydroxyethylacrylate and 2-hydroxyethylmethacrylate were contained in the conducting gel and blue polyurethane foam were in the dispersive electrodes. The authors conclude that review of an occupational history, including a history of hand dermatitis, can be used to screen individuals at a high risk of acrylate sensitization and that nondisposable electro-surgical electrodes that do not contain acrylates are an alternative in such patients.
>
> [Author's note: In the U.K., electrosurgery is called surgical diathermy.]

5. Allergenic metals

Many of the commonly encountered metals and alloys produce allergic responses in some people. Among these metals are nickel, chromium, beryllium, mercury, copper, gold, silver, and cobalt. Many people exhibit an allergic contact dermatitis when wearing items fabricated from these metals or their alloys. Of considerable importance are the allergic responses associated with implants made from these metals or alloys. Implants can be prosthetic devices, such as pins, plates, tooth fillings, dentures, and even bullets, shrapnel, or material deposited by tattooing. A few illustrative examples will be presented in the following paragraphs.

Table 8.3 lists a few of the commonly encountered alloys. An alloy is a uniform mixture of two or more elements, usually created by fusion, to obtain a material with desirable properties which are usually different from those of the components. Nonmetals are also used in alloys. Some believe that many pure metals are not allergens and it is the additives used to create the alloy that produce the allergic capability. For example, Gaul (1967) demonstrated this point by using controlled patch testing. Some of his patients had negative patch tests to pure gold, pure silver, and copper, but positive patch tests to nickel, 14-karat

Table 8.3
Composition of Common Alloys

Alloy Name	Ingredients
Gold (14 kt)	gold, copper, silver
Gold (white)	gold, copper, nickel
Steel	Carbon, iron +
Stainless steel (316)	manganese, carbon, phosphorus, sulfur, chromium, nickel, molybdenum
Monel	copper, nickel
Sterling silver	silver, copper +
German silver	copper, zinc, nickel
Dental amalgam	mercury, silver, tin, copper, zinc+
Brass	copper, zinc
Vitallium	chromium, molybdenum, iron, carbon, nickel, silicon manganese, cobalt

Note: + = plus other ingredients

gold rings, and sterling silver rings. Although this may be true, it is surprising that an allergy can result from exposure to a single component in an alloy and this component can be a metallic element, as for example nickel in stainless steel.

There is some controversy about the allergic properties of the salt of a metal and the pure metal. For example, in a case reported by Comaish (1969), patch testing to metallic gold was negative, although 2 percent gold chloride produced a positive test reaction. From the foregoing examples, it appears that an allergic response can result from exposure to a pure metal, as well as its salt or an element in an alloy.

a. Nickel. Five cases of allergic contact dermatitis subsequent to earlobe piercing were reported by McKenzie (1967). All subjects were young ladies (sixteen to twenty years) who had their earlobes pierced to wear ornamental earrings. Sterling silver and 14-kt gold contacted the pierced sites and patch testing for nickel gave positive results in four of five subjects; the no-response in one case was not explained.

Because ladies will continue to have their ears pierced, Gaul (1967) provided the following recommendations:

> Ear lobes should be pierced by approved techniques. Channel patency should be maintained with gold or silver wires of known composition, or black silk thread. Earrings should not be worn until the channels are completely epithelialized. The person piercing the ear should follow through with his subjects and direct them to a source of earrings which are known to be nonirritating and nonsensitizing.

Over a twelve-month period, Watt and Baumann (1968) encountered seventeen female patients who developed an allergic contact dermatitis to nickel as a result of earlobe piercing; they reported their cases as follows:

> The ages of our patients ranged from fifteen to twenty-three years. The time interval between the earlobe piercing and the onset of a draining earlobe dermatitis was between two and four weeks. In one patient the reaction occurred many years after piercing, but shortly after the use of some "cheap" earrings. In approximately one half of the cases the dermatitis spread to involve other areas where metal was in contact with the skin. In two patients a generalized dermatitis of auto-eczematization ensued. All seventeen of the women developed strongly positive eczematous reactions to nickel patch tests.

To prevent such an occurrence, they recommended: “A history of nickel allergy is an absolute contraindication to earlobe piercing procedures.”

Barranco and Soloman (1972) reported a case of nickel dermatitis in a twenty-year-old lady who had her ears pierced prior to a surgical implant; they reported:

> A twenty-year-old white woman had her ears pierced in 1967. In July 1968, a Hauser procedure was done on the left knee for a chronically dislocated patella. A stainless steel screw was used to secure a transferred tendon in its new location. The patient experienced no difficulty with this procedure. The same procedure was done on the right knee in June 1969; again, a stainless steel screw was used to reattach the transferred tendon. This time the procedure was complicated by a wound dehiscence and secondary closure.

In October 1969:

> An extensive eruption on the chest and back developed. This was a subacute eczematous dermatitis involving the skin of the shoulders, midback, buttocks, abdomen and breast. She was treated with both topical and systemic corticosteroids with only minimal improvement. She then disappeared from follow-up until November 1970. At this time the dermatitis was noted to be widespread as before, but also in areas of contact with jewelry such as the earlobes, neck and ring fingers. It was thought that she had a contact dermatitis most likely to nickel.

Patch testing with nickel sulfate gave a 4+ result and, Barranco continued:

> Out of sheer desperation, the stainless steel screws were considered a possible cause of the dermatitis and the orthopedic surgeon begrudgingly removed them. The day following removal of the screws, the erythema had markedly subsided with very little itching present. Seventy-two hours later, she was essentially clear of her dermatitis, with no itching. Her treatment continued to be only topical corticosteriods.
>
> Five days following removal of the screws, closed patch testing was done with pure nickel, nickel sulfate, pieces of the stainless steel screw recently removed from the patient, and a current routine chemical patch-testing tray. All tests were negative except for a 4+ reaction to nickel, nickel sulfate, and the stainless steel screw.

Barranco continued, stating that:

> The orthopedist still doubted that the stainless steel screw could be the cause of her dermatitis and reapplied the screw to the skin of the back. In a period of four hours, generalized pruritus and erythema again developed.

A case of allergic contact dermatitis due to the nickel in a chromium-cobalt alloy in a partial dental plate was reported by Brendlinger and Tarsitario (1970), who stated:

> A twenty-five-year-old mother of three was first seen by a dermatologist on January 30, 1968. She had generalized pruritic eczematous eruptions on the trunk, arms, and legs. Treatment with topical corticosteriod preparations gave her some relief. She was released from treatment after one month.
>
> On August 29, she returned with a dermatitis on her ring finger. Just before this time she began working for an electronics firm. It was thought that the dermatitis was due to the metal in her gold ring. In spite of repeated topical corticosteroid and hydration treatments the dermatitis became worse. By October she had eczematous dermatitis over her entire body. It was particularly severe wherever metal touched her skin: ear, fingers, wrist, waist, and so on. Her hands were becoming fissured and erythematous. Neither topical nor systemic corticosteroids helped.

Numerous laboratory tests were performed without resolving the problem. Treatment consisted of corticosteroids and avoidance of metal contact by wearing gloves. The report continued:

> In November she began to complain of soreness in her mouth. She was referred to the oral surgery clinic where it was discovered that she was wearing an all-cast chrome cobalt-type removable partial denture to replace her maxillary right central incisor. This had not been observed or considered during her previous treatment. The mucosa under the metal was denuded of epithelium and she still had generalized eczematous lesions over most of her body. Although the probability was low, the possibility of sensitivity to the partial dentures was pursued. The patient was referred to the prosthodontic section of the dental clinic for further evaluation.
>
> An all-acrylic resin treatment partial denture was made to replace the metal denture. The acrylic resin was heat cured for twelve hours. A gold-fixed prosthesis was temporarily ruled out until more specific allergens could be

> identified. The day after the insertion of the acrylic resin denture the patient began to improve. The itching stopped and the skin lesions healed. All cortisone and antibiotics were stopped. Within three days she became completely clear of symptoms and signs.
>
> The dermatology clinic confirmed the patient's sensitivity to chrome and nickel by skin testing pure samples of these metals provided by a manufacturer of a chrome-cobalt alloy and the metallurgy department of the University of Illinois. All chrome cobalt alloys contain enough nickel to produce allergic reactions in sensitive individuals.
>
> Of her own volition, the patient inserted the metal partial denture one evening and by the next morning she began to break out with lesions again. She came into the oral surgery clinic that morning. After pictures were taken she removed the metal denture and reinserted the acrylic resin treatment denture. The next day she was clear of lesions.

McKenzie (1967) reported an allergic response to the implantation of a Vitallium nail used to repair a fracture of the neck of the femur, he stated:

> On 11 January 1965 a woman of sixty-five sustained a fracture of the right femoral neck. The next day a Smith-Petersen Vitallium nail was inserted under halothane anesthesia. On the day after operation, pruritus and generalized urticaria developed, and these symptoms persisted for the next ten months. During this time there was radiological healing of her fracture, but there was little weight-bearing on the limb on account of anginal congestive cardiac failure and three episodes of cerebral thrombosis. A right-sided hemiplegia followed one of these strokes.
>
> On 8 December she was admitted to the Norfolk and Norwich Hospital for investigation of urticaria. Her major physical findings were right-sided flaccid hemiplegia, generalized urticaria, and dermographism.

After considerable laboratory work, patch testing was performed which revealed:

> An eczematous response to a solution of 2 percent nickel sulfate at 48 h. A similar response was produced by a Vitallium nail strapped to the thigh for 48 h. During patch testing there was no increase in severity of urticaria, but severe non-eczematous periorbital oedema developed at 48 h and resolved within the following 12 h. A scratch test with 2 percent nickel sulfate solution resulted in an itching wheal (3 cm) at 10 minutes and was associated with patchy erythema and swelling of the same forearm for 1 h.

> Since the patient was bedfast and her fracture had healed clinically, the nail was removed on 10 January 1966 under local anesthesia. Within 24 h spontaneous urticaria resolved but dermographism persisted. Exquisite and troublesome dermographism was still present one year after removal of the nail.

Note that Table 8.3 identifies the ingredients of Vitallium, one of which is nickel.

An interesting case of nickel allergy was described by Pegum (1974) in which the time between allergy identification and an allergic response was more than one quarter century. He stated:

> A thirty-eight-year-old woman had reacted to white metal since the age of twelve. At the age of thirty-five an osteotomy of the left hip was performed and a Wainwright stainless-steel plate was inserted (nickel 8–12 percent, chromium 17–20 percent, manganese 2 percent, molybdenum 2.5-3.5 percent). All went well for some three years, and then dermatitis of various parts of the skin and sterile suppuration around the plate developed. The suppuration and the dermatitis resolved after the plate was removed. Patch tests to nickel and chrome, as well as to the central plate, were positive. It will be evident that not only did dermatitis develop in our patient, but also "rejection of the implant."

b. Mercury. Mercury is found in the amalgam used to fill cavities in teeth. Foussereau and Laugier (1966) reviewed the literature on allergic responses to such dental fillings. From 1934 to 1951 four cases of allergy to the mercury in the amalgam were reported; the allergy was confirmed by patch testing.

Allergic responses to the deposition of mercury salts in tattoo procedures were reported by Foussereau and Laugier (1966). The red pigment is mercury sulfide; the blue is cobalt aluminate and the green is chromium oxide. In addition to mercury, potassium bichromate was shown to be an allergen associated with tattoos.

c. Gold. Pure gold (24-kt) is a soft malleable element that is rarely used in this form. It is alloyed with a variety of elements such as copper and silver to harden it.

Forster and Dickey (1949) described an unusual case of gold allergy; they stated:

> On admission here, the visual acuity of the right eye was to hand movements; of the left eye, no light perception. The diagnosis was bilateral congenital dislocated lenses with uveitis and secondary glaucoma. The left eye was blind and painful. Enucleation was performed and a 14-karat gold ball, 14 mm in diameter, of the standard variety used at that time, was implanted into Tenon's capsule. Recovery was uneventful. A glass prosthetic shell was procured.

After a stormy time dealing with apparent infection, it was ultimately suspected that allergic contact dermatitis to gold may be present. It was determined that 14-kt gold is composed of 60 percent fine gold, 35 percent copper, and 5 percent silver and tin. Standard, closed-patch tests were made with 1 percent copper sulfate, gold sodium thiosulfate, silver, copper, tin, and gold leaf, the 14-kt ball, and the plastic prosthetic eye. The gold salt, gold leaf, gold ball all gave 4+ responses.

The report concluded by stating:

> At the time of this report two years have elapsed since removal of the gold ball and the patient has had no recurrence of her disfiguring orbital discharge, which for three years prior to removal of the gold ball, had made her life miserable.

An unusual dental case was reported by Elgart and Higdon (1971), who summarized it as follows:

> Gold sensitivity (the eighth reported case, the seventh proved case) occurred in a twenty-seven-year-old woman. This is the first instance where a dental appliance was involved. The gingival mucosa sloughed following contact with a gold crown and previous sites of contact dermatitis to jewelry flared.

Reporting on the case, Elgart stated:

> A twenty-seven-year-old woman had no allergic problems until 1967, when her ears were pierced. Following this, she developed an eczematous reaction to gold earrings and had to stop wearing them. She then found that she could no longer wear her gold rings or wristwatch. In each instance, the reaction was characterized by an erythematous, scaly and weeping dermatitis. It was noted to subside a few days after she stopped wearing the offending jewelry. The problem seemed more severe during the summer months.
>
> In October 1969, a gold crown was placed on a left lower bicuspid. Within a few days, there was irritation of the gingival mucosa around it and an

> eczematous dermatitis again appeared under her ring. When she removed the ring, the erythema did not subside.
>
> The lesions were treated with ointment with little success. Extensive patch testing was performed with gold (auric) tricholoide, 0.5 percent aqueous. A positive response was noted within twenty-four hours, with vesicules, severe erythema and edema. Exacerbation of previous locations of her dermatitis again occurred.
>
> In July 1970, because of repeated episodes of difficulty with her gums and hand dermatitis, the gold crown was removed. Within a week, the oral lesions had improved and at the end of a month, all traces of irritation of the gingival mucosa and of the hands disappeared.

d. Metals in military missiles. Metals can be implanted by bullets and shrapnel. Foussereau and Laugier (1966) reported that grenade and mortar shell cast iron and American shell steel contain nickel and chromium. They reported the interesting case of:

> Mr. O., aged forty-three, a former bricklayer, had been working as a chromium and nickel plater since 1960. In December 1960 an eczema broke out, for the first time, under his watch on his left wrist and was aggravated through his work. Metal allergy was proved by the strong positivity of the skin tests (+++ to chromium, nickel, and cobalt). The patient changed his occupation, becoming a warehouseman in a spinning factory. His condition remained satisfactory up to 1963, when a swelling occurred on his left forearm, becoming fistulas within a few weeks and accompanied by an outbreak of eczema on the upper limbs, particularly on the left side. As confirmed by x-ray, the fistula was due to a piece of grenade shrapnel which had embedded itself in the patient's left elbow in 1942. On March 14th, 1963, because of the fistulization and the metal allergy, the shrapnel was removed. Since then the eczema has ceased to develop in the form of acute episodes.

e. Cobalt allergy. An interesting case of an allergic response, in which the authors disagreed about the causative agent, was reported by McFadden et al. (1999). Their paper stated:

> A thirty-six year-old woman experienced a cell-mediated allergy to a cobalt alloy cerebral aneurysm clip used to treat a subarachnoid hemorrhage. The bone flap had been fixed in place with a stainless steel wire made of a nickel alloy. Symptoms resolved after removal of the nickel and cobalt-containing implants. The first author (1) stated that the implication of a cobalt-containing

> clip as a stimulus for a hypersensitive reaction is based on assumptive evidence and that the author (2) replied that it is possible that the stainless steel wires used in the case may have been the major cause of the clinical manifestation of the allergic reaction. . . . They add, however, that the patient had a severe allergy to nickel and cobalt, that the symptoms of pruritus disappeared after removal of all recently implanted material containing these elements, and that there was histologic evidence of both the cranium and the aneurysm clip.

8.13 Allergic Response to Bed Linens

These days there are few allergic responses to bed linens owing to the considerable improvements in hospital laundries and the reduced time patients remain in hospitals. Nonetheless, there is some concern that antibacterial and softener residues from the washing cycle are not totally removed by the rinse cycles. Parenthetically, washing is carried out at a highly alkaline pH and acid correction (souring) is used later to make the pH neutral (e.g., about 7.0).

A case of severe asthma and urticaria induced by an antibacterial agent (phenylmercuric proprionate, PMP), used in laundering bedclothes, was reported by Matthews and Pan (1968). The subject was described as follows:

> A thirty-four-year-old male resident physician was first seen on March 30, 1962, complaining chiefly of asthma and urticaria. His mother has asthma. As a child, in Europe, the patient had urticaria which occurred only after eating pork, green beans or strawberries. He had experienced reactions, probably of an allergic nature, to tetanus antitoxin, penicillin, erythromycin and perhaps sulfaguanidine. After coming to this country (Cincinnati) in the summer of 1960, he had symptoms typical of allergic rhinitis. This difficulty subsided in late September but recurred the following June. He moved to Ann Arbor in July 1961. During the summer his rhinitis became progressively worse, and for the first time he experienced mild asthma. All symptoms promptly subsided on a trip to Europe in September with no recurrence of his rhinitis upon returning to Ann Arbor in October.
>
> During the fall of 1961, he began to have nocturnal attacks of asthma. These progressed in severity and occurred almost exclusively while in his bed in the Interns' and Residents' Quarters (night or day) and would subside within an hour or two after leaving his room. He was free of symptoms in his room if he did not lie on the bed. However, while assigned to the Tuberculosis Service in February 1962 he noticed that he would have asthma at work if he wore a gauze mask but no asthma if he wore a paper mask. At this time he also

> started to have urticaria and angioedema. These lesions usually broke out at night or in areas of contact with his white uniforms.

The report continued with a detailed account of subsequent attacks and describes the extensive testing that identified PMP as the allergen. The report concluded by stating:

> The patient was exceptional in giving a passively transferable immediate wheal and erythema skin test reaction to relatively low molecular weight compounds. Other immunologic studies were negative except for in vitro histamine release from leukocytes by the allergen. The patient also gave skin test reactions to other phenylmercuric compounds. In high concentrations these compounds are irritants. They are widely employed as antibacterial and antifungal agents in agriculture, industry and medicinals and are used in washing the linens of many hospitals.

Rycroft (1976) reported on nine cases of dermatitis associated with sheets and pillow cases; he stated:

> Since April 1975 we have seen nine patients with widespread dermatitis who had recently purchased cheap Canadian bed sheets. Three days to two weeks after starting to use the sheets they had developed severe itching and burning sensations, especially at night. When pillow cases had also been purchased, redness of the ears and puffy eyelids were early complaints. In some cases several members of one family were affected, and in others one bed partner was spared.

The report continued:

> Patch tests with the patients' own sheets produced negative results in five out of eight cases tested, and there were no positive patch test results with formaldehyde. Only one patient reacted to a standard formaldehyde clothing resin patch test. Laundering the sheets helped in only one case, in which tolerance was reported after three washes. Once the patients stopped using the sheets the rash usually resolved in three to four weeks.

Curran (1988), a hospital laundry manager, recommended a procedure to minimize skin irritation from sheets. He stated:

> In our operation, all of our wash persons sign a policy statement that they must test each and every load of linen before they take it out of the washer. The test is simple and easy. Just put one drop of pH indicator on a piece of linen in that load, if it turns orange-red, the load is at a pH level of 5 or 6, the pH of normal skin. If it turns green, then you have alkali left in the linen. This could cause skin irritation. If this happens, the load of linen must be put back through the sour and softener cycle to insure the linen comes out at the proper pH level. (The term "sour" means acidification.)

8.14 Allergic Response to Rubber and Plastics

Rubber is known to be an allergen, as described in a preceding paragraph relating to the use of rubber bands to secure ECG electrodes to the extremities. According to Larsen and Maibach (1992) it is some of the additives, notably, mercaptobenzothiazole, tetramethyl-thiuram, and others that endow rubber with its allergenic properties.

We live in a world in which we are surrounded by objects made of plastics or covered by plastic and the incidence of allergic reaction is small, but finite. For example, Mather et al. (1993), after encountering skin reactions due to nylon catheters in nine patients, sought to determine the incidence of such an event. They reported, "After computer searches and direct inquires to eleven manufacturers, we can find no reports of any similar reaction to any epidural catheter."

The responses of the six patients who received epidural catheters were similar; one case is presented as follows:

> A healthy sixty-six-year-old woman was admitted for total abdominal hysterectomy and bilateral salpingo-oophorectomy. She gave a history of allergy to rubber, horse serum, adhesive bandages and several types of tapes.
>
> Before induction of general anesthesia, an epidural catheter was inserted at the L3-L4 interspace and established using 2 percent lidocaine with epinephrine (2 percent w lidocaine). Following the Acute Pain Service protocol, 5 percent providone-iodine (Betadine) spray was used prior to catheter placement. Thereafter, tincture of benzoin and a Tegaderm dressing (10×30 cm) were used to secure and cover the catheter.
>
> For postoperative analgesia she received an epidural dose of 2 mg morphine (one hour before the end of surgery) and was subsequently prescribed 2 mg epidural morphine every six hours as needed. On the second morning after surgery (forty hours after epidural catheter insertion) she complained of "soreness" only at the point of entry of the catheter, where there was also a

> "circle of inflammation and a small amount of swelling." It was decided that the best course of action would be to remove the catheter and extend the course of perioperative antibiotics (cephalexin). Upon removal there was a small amount of serous discharge, but it also became evident that there was an inflammatory "trail", which traced the exact course of the epidural catheter from her lower back, up to and over her shoulder. The "trail" was about 5 to 6 mm wide and persisted, albeit faded, until her discharge on postoperative day six.
>
> Clinically, each of the cutaneous reactions appeared identical. All six patients had a reddened, non-raised trail, which began at the site of catheter insertion and coursed along the back. Each trail appeared simultaneously and faded simultaneously over the length of catheter-skin contact. The observed time to onset ranged from forty hours to several days with resolution over one to three days. Additionally only case 4 had associated blistering; only cases 1 and 3 had palpable swelling at the site of catheter entry; and only cases 1 and 3 complained of localized itching. Clinically, the course and dimensions of the inflammatory "trails" in our patients corresponded exactly with the epidural catheters. However, other local factors may have caused this reaction.

They summarized by stating:

> Since an allergic reaction to an epidural catheter has not been reported, it can be presumed to be a rare event. This makes the likelihood of six cases of allergy in a matter of weeks improbable. We, therefore, considered any other recent changes in our practice that might coincide with these occurrences. However, nothing has been changed in six years. We are using the same antiseptic, catheters, dressings, and drugs. The manufacturer states that there have been no recent changes to the manufacturing process of their catheter.

8.15 Conclusion

Although allergic responses are quite uncommon, they require good detective work to identify the allergen. Fortunately, patch testing or disappearance of the allergic response when the allergen is removed is all that is required to identify the allergen.

References

AAMI. Recommended Practice for Determining Residual Ethylene Oxide in Medical Devices. 1986. Association for the Advancement of Medical Instrumentation, 3330 Washington Blvd., Suite 400, Arlington, VA 22201-4598.

AAMI/ANSI. Guideline for Industrial Ethylene Oxide Sterilization of Medical Devices. 1988. Association for the Advancement of Medical Instrumentation, 3330 Washington Blvd., Suite 400, Arlington, VA 22201-4598.

American Society of Anesthesiologists. 520 N. Northwest Highway, Park Ridge, IL 60068-2573.

Axon ATR, Banks J, Corket R et al. Disinfection in upper digestive tract endoscopy in Britain. Lancet. 1981, May 16: 1093–1094.

Barranco VP and Soloman H. Eczematous dermatitis in nickel. JAMA. 1972, 110:1244.

Biro L, Fisher AA and Price E. Ethylene oxide burns. Arch. Dermatol. 1974, 110:924–925.

Brendlinger DL and Tarsitario JJ. Generalized dermatitis due to sensitivity to a chrome cobalt removable partial denture. JADA. 1970, 81:392–394.

Britt BA and Gordon RA. Peripheral nerve injuries associated with anesthesia. Can. Anaesth. J. 1964, 11(5):514–536.

Brooks B and Duncan GW. Effects of pressure on tissues. Arch Surg. 1940, 40:696–709.

Bull JP and Lawrence JC. Thermal conditions to produce skin burns. Fire and Materials. 1979, 3(2):100–105.

Chino MJ and Nagel EL. Thermal burns caused by warming blankets in the operating room. Anesthesiology. 1968, 29(1):149–150.

Comaish S. A case of contact hypersensitivity to metallic gold. Arch. Derm. 99:720–1969.

Corrado OJ, Osman J and Davies RJ. Asthma and rhinitis after exposure to glutaraldehyde in endoscopy units. Hum. Toxicol. 1986, 5:325–327.

Corson SL, Block S, Mintz C et al. Sterilization of laparoscopes. J. Reprod. Med. 1979, 23:49.

Corson SL, Dole M, Kraus R et al. Studies in sterilization of the laparoscope. J. Reprod. Med. 1979, 23:57.

Coskey RJ. Contact dermatitis caused by electrode jelly. Arch. Dermatol. 1977, 113:839–840.

Craig CP. Preparation of the skin for surgery. Today's OR Nurse. 1986, 8(5):17–21.

Curran CC. Laundry plays roll(e) in pressure sore prevention. Health Care Systems. 1988, 25(a):September.

Dave AL. Third-degree burn following use of microwave-heated cryogel pack. Clin. Pediat. 1993, 32:191–192.

Dinsdale SM. Decubitus ulcers: role of pressure and friction in causation. Arch Phys Med Rehabil. 1974, 55:147–152.

Drevets CC and Seebohm PM. Dermatitis from alcohol. J. Allergy. 1961, 32(4):277–282.

Duffy BL. Betadine burn. Anesth. Intensive Care. 1981, 9(4): Correspondence.

Elgart ML and Higdon RS. Allergic contact dermatitis to gold. Arch. Dermatol. 1971, 103:649–653.

Erdmann TC, Feldman KW, Rivara FP et al. Tap-water burn prevention. Pediatrics. 1991, 88(3):572–577.

Feldman KW, Schaller RT and Feldman JA. Tap-water scald burns in children. Pediatrics. 1978, 52(1):1–5.

Feldtman RW, Andrassy RJ, Page CD et al., Providone-iodine skin-sensitivity observed with possibly altered immune status. JAMA. 1979, February: 487.

Fish RM. In Electrical Injuries: Engineering, Medical and Legal Aspects. 2000. Lawyers & Judges Publ. Co., Tucson, AZ.

Fisher AA. Dermatologic hazards of electrocardiography. Cutis. 1977, 20:686.

Fisher AA. Safety of stainless steel in nickel sensitivity. JAMA. 1972, 221:1232.

Forster HW and Dickey RF. A case of sensitivity to gold ball orbital implant. Am. J. Ophthal. 1949, 32: 659–662.

Food and Drug Administration. FDA Drug Bull. (Washington, D.C.) 1985, 15(1):9.

Foussereau J and Laugier P. Allergic eczemas from metallic foreign bodies. Trans. St. John's Hosp. Dermatol. Soc. (London). 1966, 57:220–225.

Fregert S, Hakanson R, Rossman H et al. Dermatitis from alcohols. J. Allergy. 1965, 34:404–408.

Fregert S, Groth O, Hjorth N et al. Alcohol dermatitis. Acta. Derm. Venerol. 1969, 49:493–498.

Gaul LE. Development of allergic nickel dermatitis from earrings. JAMA. 1967, 200:186–188.

Geddes LA and Baker LE. Principles of Applied Biomedical Instrumentation. 3rd ed. 1989. John Wiley & Sons, New York.

Geddes LA. Handbook of Electrical Hazards and Accidents. 1995, CRC Press, Boca Raton, FL.

Gendron FC. Unexplained Patient Burns. 1988. Quest Publishing (now Lippincott-Raven Press), Brea, CA.

Glick PL, Gugielmo BJ, Tranbaugh RF et al. Iodine toxicity in a patient treated by continuous providone-iodine mediastinal irrigation. Ann. Thoracic Surg. 1985, 39(5):478–480.

Golditz PB, Dunster KR, Joy GJ et al. Anetoderma of prematurity in association with electrocardiographic electrodes. J. Amer. Acad. Dermatol. 1999, 41(3):479–481.

Haagensen CD and Lloyd WEB. Anesthesia and antisepsis. In New Worlds in Medicine. Wood HB, Ed., 1946, R.M. McBride, New York.

Health Devices. Hazard: Skin injury in the OR and elsewhere. Health Devices. 1980, 9(12):312. Emergency Care Research Institute. 5200 Butler Pike, Plymouth Meeting, PA 19462

Hicks DJ. An incidence of pressure sores following surgery. In ANA Clinical Sessions (1970). 1971, Appleton-Century-Crofts, New York.

HIMA. Guidelines for the Analysis of Ethylene Oxide Residues in Medical Devices. Document No. 1, Vol. 1. 1980. Health Industries Manufacturers Association, 1200 G St NW, STE 4000, Washington, D.C. 20005.

HIMA. Ethylene Oxide Residues on Sterilized Medical Devices. Report 88–6. 1988. Health Industry Manufacturers Association, 1200 G St NW, STE 4000, Washington, D.C. 20005.

HIMA. Sterilization in the 1990s. Report 89-1. 1989. Health Industry Manufacturers Association, 1200 G St NW, STE 4000, Washington, D.C. 20005.

Hodgkinson DJ, Irons GB and Williams TJ. Chemical burns and skin preparation solutions. Surg. Gynecol. Obst. 1978, 147:534–536.

Howes JG, Baud C and Kirwan P. Iodine and acetone-containing plastic spray dressing. Br. Med. J. 1979, February:487.

Kosiak M. Etiology of decubitus ulcers. Phys. Med. Rehabil. 1961, 42:19–29.

Kroll DA, Kaplan RA, Posnerk et al. Nerve injury associated with anesthesia. Anesth. Esiol. 1990, 73:99–101.

LaDage LG. Facial irritation from ethylene oxide sterilization of anesthesia mask? Plastic Reconstructive Surg. 1970, 45(3):179.

Larsen WG and Maibach HI. Allergic contact dermatitis. In Dermatology. 3rd ed. 1992, Moschella SL. and Hurley HJ Eds. W.B. Saunders, Philadelphia.

Lawrence JC and Bull JP. Thermal conditions which cause skin burns. Inst. Mech. Eng. 1975, 5(3):61–62.

Lawson NW, Mills NL and Ochser JL. Occipital alopecia following cardiopulmonary bypass. J. Thor. Cardiovasc. Surg. 1976, 71:342–347.

Llorens AS. Reaction to providone-iodine surgical scrub associated with radical pelvic operations. Am. J. Obst. Surg. 1972, November 15:834–835.

Maklebust J. Pressure ulcer updates. RN. 1991, 54(12):57–63.

Mather CMP, Anaes, FC and Neuman M. Inflammatory cutaneous reactions to epidural catheters. Anesthesiology. 1993, 78(1):200–204.

Matthews KP and Pan PM. Immediate type hypersensitivity to phenylmercuric compounds. Am. J. Med. 1968, 44:310–318.

McFadden JT. (1) Ross IB (2) Warrington RJ and Halliday WC. Cell-mediated allergy to a cerebral aneurysm clip: Case Report [letter and reply]. Neurosurgery. 1999, 45(1):200–202.

McKenzie AW. Urticaria after insertion of Smith-Peterson vitallium nail. Br. Med. J. 1967, 4:36.

Medical Malpractice Verdicts, Settlements and Experts. 2000, 16(8):25–26.

Moritz AR and Henriques FC. The relative importance of time and surface temperature in the causation of skin burns. Am. J. Pathol. 1947, 23:605.

Nabours RE, Fish RM and Hill PF. Electrical Injuries: Engineering, Medical and Legal Aspects. 2000. Lawyers & Judges Publ. Co., Tucson, AZ.

National Pressure Ulcer Advisory Panel. Decubitus. 1989, 2(2):24–28.

Ondeck DA. The right to know: mercury thermometer breakage: hazardous or not? Home Care Manage Prac. 1999, 11(4):63–4.

OSHA. Occupational Safety and Health Administration, 200 Constitution Ave. NW, Room N2439, Washington, D.C. 20402.

Pearce JA. Skin pressure distributions on three methods of patient support. In Air-Fluidized Bed Clinical and Research Symposium. 1971. Artz C, Ed. Med. University of South Carolina Press, 85–9.

Pearce JA. Electrosurgery. 1986. Chapman & Hall, London.

Pegum JS. Nickel allergy. Lancet. 1974, April 13:674.

Perkins JB, Pearse HE and Kingsley HD. Atomic Energy Project UR217. Univ. Rochester, NY, 1952.

Randell-Baker L and Roberts RB. Hazards of ethylene oxide sterilization. Anesthesiology. 1969:349–350.

Rennie AC, McGregor-Schuerman M, Dale IM et al. Poisoning after spillage at home from a sphygmomanometer on loan from hospital. Brit Med J. 1999, 319(7):366–7.

Reuler JB and Cooney TC. The pressure sore pathophysology and principles of management. Ann Int Med. 1981, 94:661–666.

Richardson DR, Caravati CM and Weary PE. Allergic contact dermatitis to alcohol swabs. Cutis. 1969, 5:1115–1118.

Rothwell KG. Iodine toxicity. Ann. Thoracic Surg. 1986, 42(4):481.

Rycroft RJG. Canadian sheet dermatitis. Br. Med. J. 1976, November 13:1175.

Schick JF. Burn hazard of isopropyl alcohol in the neonate. Pediatrics. 1981, 68(4):587–588.

Scott EM and Gorman SP. Glutaraldehyde. In Disinfection, Sterilization and Preservation. 4th ed. 1991. Block SS, Ed. Lea & Febiger, Philadelphia.

Sexton RJ and Henson RV. Experimental ethylene oxide human skin injuries. Arch. Ind. Hygiene. 1950, 25:549–564.

Shea JD. Pressure sores-classification and management. Clin Orthop. 1975, 112:89–100.

Shyu K, Hwang J, Lin S et al. Prospective study of blood cultures during transesophageal echocardiography. Am. Heart J. 1992, 124(6):1541–1544.

Sidhu SK and Shaw S. Allergic contact dermatitis to acrylates in disposable blue diathermy pads. Royal College of Surgeons of England. 1999, 81(3):187–90.

Silver ML. Sensitivity to bentonite. EEG. Clin. Neurophysiol. 1950, 2:115.

Strahan RW and Simmons B. Electronystagmographic electrode skin lesions. Arch. Otolaryngol. 1968, 88:152–155.

Storrs FJ. Para-choloro-meta-xylenol allergic contact dermatitis in seven individuals. Contact Dermatitis. 1975, 1:211–213.

Van Ketel G and Tan-Lim KN. Contact dermatitis from alcohol. Contact Dermatitis. 1975, 1:7–10.

Watt TL and Baumann RR. Nickel earlobe dermatitis. Arch. Derm. 1968, 98:155–158.

White CW. Ethylene oxide sterilization of anesthesia equipment. Anesthesiology. 1970, 33:120.

Chapter 9

Important Information for the Technical Expert

Synopsis

9.1 Introduction

During the last decade and a half, I have served as an expert witness in lawsuits related to patent infringement and invalidation, libel, trade secrets, medical device accidents and industrial accidents. These cases brought me into contact with a large number of attorneys and quite a few judges. I learned a lot about the legal process and lawyers and hereby share some experiences that may help other technical experts. Most of my experience has been in two areas: (1) medical device accidents and (2) patent infringement and invalidation. After discussing these topics, I will dwell on various items of interest to a technical expert.

9.2 Medical Device Accidents

An accident is defined as an undesirable or unfortunate happening or anything that occurs unexpectedly. Medical devices embrace a very broad range of technologies and therefore accidents occur in many medical specialties, such as surgery, radiology, obstetrics, gynecology, neonatology, cardiology, respiratory therapy, orthopedics etc. Although most of the accidents associated with these medical specialties occur in the hospital or clinic, out-of-hospital accidents are associated with implanted devices, such as cardiac pacemakers, defibrillators, heart valves, orthopedic implants, silicone implants etc. It is anticipated that with the increase in home health care, accidents in the home and nursing home will increase. Special knowledge, investigative skills and tact are required to identify the causes of accidents in these various areas. Therefore, it is essential to become aware of the device technology, its proper use, accepted procedures, as well as the environment in which the device is used.

9.3 Accident Investigation

The goal of an accident investigation is to determine what happened, how it happened and why it happened. The primary goal is not to establish blame; this comes later. A secondary goal is to make recommendations so that the risk of a subsequent accident is minimized. The sooner the investigation after the accident, the more likely it is to obtain reliable information; memory dims with the passage of time.

An accident investigation is a search for the truth. There are two aspects to an accident investigation: (1) examination and testing of the accused device or faulty procedure and (2) seeking relevant information about the accident. Soon after the accident, an Incident Report and a Medical Device Report (now called a Manufacturer and User Device Experience, or MAUDE) are filed. The accused device and its accessories are impounded and time starts to pass as litigation commences with filing of the complaint.

It is important to collect critical pieces of information as soon as possible. For example, if the accident site is visited, it is necessary to identify the date, obtain the address and room number in the organization and the names, occupations and telephone numbers of those present and interviewed. Sketches of the scene and photographs are very useful in reconstructing the accident. If a piece of equipment is involved, note its type, serial number and manufacturer before examining the device. Then compose a short narrative that describes the state of the device when you received it. Sketches, measurements and photographs are useful if there is visible damage. Identify the name and telephone number of the person who sent you the device, the date that it was sent, and the means of conveyance to you. Many useful suggestions on accident investigations are given in a book by Shepard (1992) and in a chapter by Bruley (1996).

It is always necessary to determine if the accused device malfunctioned and nondestructive testing is instituted. Obviously, the plaintiff, the defendant(s) and the manufacturer are involved. It is common for the testing to be performed in the presence of the representatives (e.g. expert witnesses) for the plaintiff and defendant. Sometimes a third party (e.g. a testing laboratory) is used for the tests. Occasionally one of the expert witnesses will perform the testing in the presence of the other party. Sometimes the manufacturer is sent the device for testing to determine if it performs according to manufacturer's specifications and existing standards. Reports generated from these activities can be made available.

Medical device accidents occur long before litigation begins; a delay of one to two years is not uncommon before the expert witness becomes involved. However, there exist documents that were composed at the time of the accident. For example, it is mandatory that a dated Incident Report and a MDR (now MAUDE) report be completed; all of these contain valuable information relative to an accident. The institutional Incident Report may or may not be made available; often legal steps can be taken to obtain it. It is possible to obtain a file of MAUDE reports on the accused device from the FDA. Additional information can be obtained from medical records, including operative, anesthesia, and recovery-room records when applicable. The patient's admission and discharge record and nurse's progress notes often contain useful information. Most medical procedures require the patient to read, understand and sign a consent form. Such a document often plays a crucial role if a complication arises. Depositions taken from those present at the time of the accident are especially useful in putting together the events that led to the accident, as well as providing additional information on the accident.

From this inventory of information, you must identify all of the possible causes of the accident; then you choose the most likely cause and provide enough evidence to support your conclusion. At this point a conference with the hiring attorney is necessary before committing your decision to writing. At deposition, or in court, you will be asked to prove why you excluded any other causes of the accident.

9.4 Time of Death

In a fatal accident investigation, establishing the time of death often becomes important in determining the culpability of one accused of causing the death or determining if a life-support device failed or a monitor failed to alarm. Forensic pathologists use many indicators to establish the time of death; the four that are most prominent are body temperature, lividity, rigor and decomposition. All have different onset times and durations; Figure 9.1 summarizes the temporal aspects of these events.

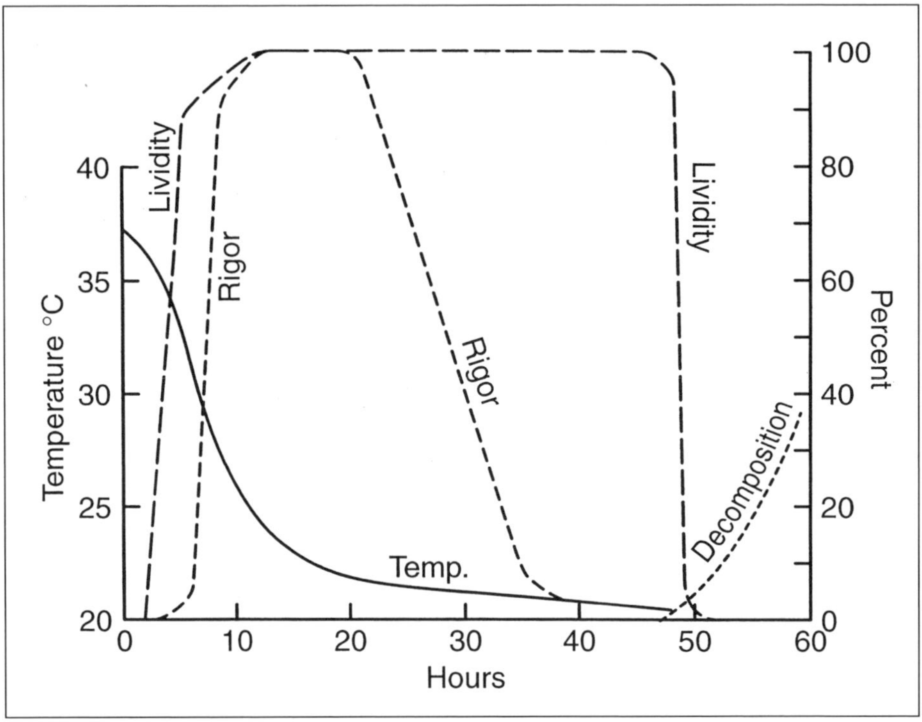

__Figure 9.1__ Onset and duration times for postmortem temperature fall, lividity, rigor mortis and decomposition

When the circulation ceases, cell metabolism decreases and body temperature falls slowly, then more rapidly. The rate of cooling is affected by environmental temperature. Clothed or covered bodies cool more slowly than naked ones. Ventilation also affects the rate of cooling. Large obese subjects cool more slowly than smaller subjects. Persons with elevated temperature due to fever or vigorous muscular exercise prior to death take longer to cool. According to Simpson (1974), body temperature falls about one degree C during the first hour, after which it falls more rapidly at a rate of about 1.5 to 2 degree C/hour for the next six hours, after which the cooling curve resembles an exponential decay. At about twelve hours, the body feels cold. By forty-eight hours the body temperature has fallen to almost room temperature. The temperature during the first eighteen hours is the most useful in estimating the time of death.

Lividity, sometimes called livor or hypostasis, results from the red blood cells settling in the dependent parts of the body. Because the red cells have lost so much of their oxyhemoglobin, the skin takes on a purplish blue color. Lividity can appear in one half hour to many hours. It may not be prominent in some subjects, especially if they are anemic. According to Simpson (1974), lividity reaches a maximum in about twelve hours, and persists until about 48 hours. Lividity is not an accurate indicator of the time of death. A change in body position confounds the situation.

Rigor is a stiffening of all muscle fibers due to their shortening. It appears first in the facial muscles at about five to seven hours. During the next two or three hours, rigor progresses to the shoulders and arms, then to the trunk and legs. By twelve hours, full rigor is present and it lasts typically twelve hours. It takes twelve more hours to subside completely. Environmental temperature is an important factor. Rigor mortis is not an accurate indicator of the time of death.

Decomposition of the body starts to manifest itself at about forty-eight hours postmortem. The abdominal skin appears greenish and the superficial veins take on a reddish hue, appear branching and this pattern extends to the groin. The veins are filled with hemolyzed blood and gas bubbles appear due to microorganisms from the intestines entering the circulatory system. The skin develops blebs and the subject becomes bloated. Soon maggots, flies and other insects invade the skin and further decomposition occurs.

According to Simpson (1974), there is a temporal hierarchy of decomposition that starts with the intestines, stomach, liver blood, heart blood, circulation and heart muscle. The next to decompose are the air passages, then the lungs and liver, followed by the brain and spinal cord. Next to decompose are the kidneys, bladder and testes, followed by the voluntary muscles. Finally the uterus and prostate are the last to decompose. This decay hierarchy provides a time scale for the experienced forensic pathologist.

9.5 The Technical Expert

We live in a time when technology abounds and litigation requires a clear understanding of technological issues. For this reason, expert witnesses are needed to explain such issues. Federal Rule of Evidence 702 provides for this need and specifies the qualifications for such expert testimony by stating:

If scientific, technical, or other specialized knowledge will assist the trier of fact to understand the evidence or to determine a fact in issue, a witness qualified as an expert by knowledge, skill, experience, training, or education, may testify thereto in the form of an opinion or otherwise.

The rules require that the expert divulge the facts on which his or her opinion is based by stating:

> The facts or data in the particular case upon which an expert bases an opinion or inference may be those perceived by or made known to the expert at or before the hearing. A technical expert can be hired by the plaintiff or the defendant. In addition, if the court believes that the information provided by the experts for the plaintiff and defense is insufficient, the court can appoint its own expert witness.

As stated earlier, the technical expert is qualified by knowledge, skill, experience and training. The qualifications of an expert were specified long before the Federal Rules of Evidence. A quotation from Jacob Leuopold in 1726, translated by Hoff and Geddes (1962), may be timely. Equating a mechanic of that time as a technical expert, Leuopold stated:

> A mechanic ought to be a person who not only understands well and thoroughly all handicrafts, such as wood, steel, iron, brass, silver, gold, glass, and all such materials to be treated according to the arts, and who knows how to judge on physical principles, how far each according to its nature and property is adequate or suitable to withstand and endure this or that, so that everything receives its necessary proportion, strength, and convenience, and neither too much nor too little is done in the matter; but he must also be able to

arrange according to mechanical sciences or rules for any required proportion, or effect according to present or proposed force or load; for which purpose he must also have learned from geometry and arithmetic all that is necessary for calculation of the parts of the machine. And when he desires thoroughly to understand his profession, he must have a complete grasp of all the arts and professions for which he will have to make and invent machines; for otherwise he knows not what he is doing, and has also no power to improve anything, or invent anything new, such as is chiefly demanded of a mechanic. But above all he has to be a born mechanic, so that he shall not only be skilled in invention by natural instinct, but shall also grasp with little trouble all arts and sciences, in such a way that it may be said of him: what his eyes see, that also his hands are able to do; and that love of his art lets him avoid no trouble, labor, or cost, because throughout his whole life he has daily to learn something new and to experiment.

9.6 Technical Expert Roles

A technical expert can be used in two ways: (1) as a fact witness and (2) as an expert witness. In the former case, the expert provides facts, not opinions. Facts are derived from published papers, books, patents, documents etc. along with perhaps a summary of existing knowledge that is accepted by those in the field. On the other hand, the expert witness does the same and, using this information, provides an opinion based on facts, training, and experience. Interestingly enough, in the courtroom, it is only the expert witness and the jury who are entitled to provide an opinion. The judge acts as a chairperson or gatekeeper who guides the proceedings that lead to exposition of the truth. In those cases where there is no jury, the judge can render an opinion based on the facts established by the attorneys and witnesses for the plaintiff and the defense.

The single most important talent that an expert witness must have is the ability to teach technical material to nontechnical people, namely, the judge and jury. Prior to this activity he or she has been teaching the attorney who hired the expert. The better informed the attorney, the better he/she is able to frame questions to achieve delivery of the facts, know what to emphasize and know how to shoot down opponents who attempt to bring in confusing, misleading, or irrelevant material. There is no substitute for a good rapport with the attorney who engaged your services.

Irrespective of for whom the expert witness serves, he or she has only credibility and time to sell and is expected to know all of the relevant facts of the case up to the time of filing of the complaint. Information originating after this time is inadmissible. He or she must have read and understood all of the pertinent material such as the complaint, interrogatories, depositions, reports, exhibits, manuals, published papers, monographs, patents (and file history) if applicable and should be familiar with the technology, competing technology, as well as history of the technology prior to the case. In addition, his or her education, experience and publications need to support credibility as an expert in the case in question. Most importantly, you need to know how your opinion fits with your attorney's theory of the case. Also you need to know the qualifications of the opposing expert and the points that he or she are likely to raise.

In testimony, be sure that you are interrogated about your credentials. Don't let your attorney allow the opposing attorney to stipulate your credentials because they will not be heard by the judge or jury. It is essential that knowledge of your qualifications and expertise be known to those who are going to pronounce judgment.

It is essential that an expert present relevant and reliable evidence. Relevance is easily recognized; reliability is tested by the *Daubert* and *Kumho* criteria, which are discussed in the section dealing with the admissibility of evidence which is information that proves or disproves and alleged fact.

The court reporter is an important person to a testifying expert because it is she or he who enters the expert's words into the official record, be it a deposition or during trial. With very little effort the court reporter can become your ally, thereby insuring that all of your words will be in the record accurately. I have found that by taking a few minutes with the reporter before the proceedings begin produces great results and pays off later when the transcript is proofed by me. I first give the reporter my card so that she or he can contact me later when the transcript is being prepared. I also give the reporter a sheet containing the technical terms that I may use. This list also includes names of authors or persons who I may cite. I also provide the attorneys with the list. Finally, during testimony, glance at the reporter to see if you are speaking too rapidly. It is also courteous to ask the reporter if you are speaking clearly. These few simple considerations will make the reporter your friend—and save you time later when you are delivered the transcript for proofreading and correction.

During deposition or in court, personal traits and body language are very important. Be professional and dress conservatively. Before testifying, be sure that you discuss hypothetical questions with your attorney. Also ask if he or she knows the points to be made by the opposing expert. Listen carefully to the questions; ask for a repetition or rephrasing if you have any doubt as to the meaning. Use exhibits if they will help you explain your point.

Don't let the opposing attorney lead you away from your area of expertise. Just say, "that is beyond my area of expertise." When answering questions, establish eye contact with the jury, or the judge if it is a bench trial, because they make decisions. Speak clearly and avoid technical terms; if you have to use them, explain their meaning and significance. Use easily understood analogs, e.g. electric current is like water flowing in a hose. Always be ready to explain the basis for your opinion and relate it to the question being asked. Even if the same question is asked over and over again, answer it in the same way calmly because the attorney who does this is trying to rattle you and make you inconsistent. Be courteous even if the attorney is trying to badger you. Do not get angry; smile frequently to give the impression that you are enjoying your performance. Being an expert witness is an important job with great rewards for those who can separate the facts from the obfuscation and confusion.

Typically, an attorney will telephone you, describe the case and ask if you are qualified in the area. If so, your CV and list of publications will be requested. The attorney will then send you a copy of the complaint and other relevant documents. When they arrive, you read them carefully and identify all of the possible scenarios for and against your attorney's client. Meanwhile the attorney engaging you will have developed a tentative theory which may or may not coincide with the best choice that you have made. If not, the attorney will discuss the strength and weakness of your choice. Finally a course is plotted and preparations for a written report or a deposition are made.

In cases where there are multiple defendants, and you are serving for the defense, it is often unclear which defendant is the most vulnerable. Although there may be multiple defense experts, I have never encountered pooling of experts. You serve only the attorney that hired you. Moreover, I have never encountered direct communication between experts on the same side.

9.7 Admissibility of Evidence

There are four cases that are cited that pertain to the admissibility of evidence: (1) *Frye*, (2) *Daubert*, (3) *Joiner* and (4) *Kumho*. The differences between them are subtle but important and relate to the type of evidence. Evidence is defined as "that which tends to prove or disprove something." However the essential feature is relevance of the evidence, which is defined in the Federal Rule of Evidence (401) as "relevant evidence means evidence having any tendency to make the existence of any fact that is of consequence to the determination of the action more probable or less probable than it would be without the evidence."

The 1923 *Frye* case dealt with the accuracy of indirect blood-pressure measurement which gave rise to the "general acceptance rule." Briefly it states that the information from which a deduction is made must be sufficiently established to have gained general acceptance in the particular field in which it belongs. Although a useful concept, the general-acceptance rule has been largely superseded.

The 1993 *Daubert* rule derived from a case involving an undesirable side effect of a drug. The rule states that all scientific evidence or testimony admitted is not only relevant, but reliable. Four factors are involved: (1) whether the principle has been tested, (2) whether the principle has been published in a peer-reviewed publication, (3) the error rate associated with the principle, and (4) whether the principle has achieved general acceptance.

It is clear that the *Daubert* criteria deals with scientific matters. However all evidence does not come under the scientific umbrella.

The *Joiner* (1997) case involved the possibility that a chemical was carcinogenic. The court was concerned with the need that an expert explain how and why he or she applied their methodology to reach their opinion. In other words, the Court was not concerned so much with whether the expert's testimony met the four tests as set forth in *Daubert*, but rather, whether the expert's opinions were "connected" closely enough to the underlying methodology in reaching those opinions. In other words, the expert must explain that accepted methodology was used in rendering an opinion.

The 1999 *Kumho* case involved a tire that blew out causing injury. It was claimed that the tire was defectively designed or manufactured. The trial was lengthy and revealed that there were criteria of importance other than the four identified in *Daubert*. The case was appealed to the Supreme Court which held that the basic "gatekeeping" obligation of the trial judge applies not only to "scientific" testimony, but to all expert testimony. The Court based its finding on the plain language of Rule 702 and stated that:

> If scientific, technical, or other specialized knowledge will assist the trier of fact to understand the evidence or to determine a fact in issue, a witness qualified as an expert by knowledge, skill, experience, training, or education, may testify thereto in the form of an opinion or otherwise.

The Supreme Court noted that the rule makes no relevant distinction between "scientific" knowledge and "technical" or "other specialized" knowledge, and that the rule makes clear that such knowledge might become the subject of expert testimony. The Court noted that it is the Rule's word "knowledge," not the words (like "scientific") that modify that word, that establishes a standard of evidentiary reliability.

In other words, the *Kumho* case recognizes that technical information can be used for opinion basing, providing the methodology used is generally accepted by those in the particular field.

9.8 Copyrights

Federal law (17 U.S.C.§ 101 et seq.) allows authors to control the use of their works for a limited time. Once that time period has expired, the public is allowed to freely use the works without paying royalties or obtaining permission from the copyright holder.

The work must be an original work of authorship that is fixed in a tangible medium of expression. The word "copyright" or © is no longer required to identify copyright work. A copyrighted work is protected from the moment of fixation. A work is "fixed" when it is sufficiently permanent or stable to permit it to be perceived, reproduced, or otherwise communicated for a period of more than transitory duration. Works created on or after January 1, 1978 are protected for a term of the life of the author plus seventy years. If the work is a product of a corporate author, then the protection is for the shorter of ninety-five years from publication or 120 years from creation.

Eight categories of works are copyrightable:

1. literary, musical and dramatic works
2. pantomimes and choreographic works
3. pictorial, graphic and sculptural works
4. sound recordings
5. motion pictures and other AV works
6. computer programs
7. compilations of works and derivative works
8. architectural works

The following cannot be copyrighted:

1. ideas, procedures, methods, systems and processes

2. titles, names, short phrases, and slogans
3. facts, news, and research
4. works produced by United States government employees

Exemptions

The purpose of the fair use exemption is to allow the public to use copyrighted works under certain circumstances without paying royalties or obtaining permissions. Fair use is determined by applying a four-factor analysis that balances the rights of the copyright holder with that of the public.

Categories:

Fair Use	Favors Permission
1. nonprofit	1. commercial
2. educational	2. for profit
3. personal	3. entertainment
4. teaching	4. large amount
5. criticism and comment	5. heart of the work
6. scholarship and research	6. major effect
7. news reporting	7. work is made available to world
8. small amount	
9. no effect	
10. licensing/permissions unavailable	

If the balance weighs in favor of fair use, then the work can be used without permission. However, if the balance weighs against fair use and other exemptions do not apply, then permission must be obtained to use the work. Educational use is not automatically fair use. The fair use analysis must be applied to each use of a work. Fair use is technology neutral so the analysis may be used for any medium.

9.9 Patents

A. Introduction

Considerable litigation is associated with infringement and invalidation of a patent for a device and technical expert witnesses are hired by both the plaintiff and defendant. The following will address some of the more important issues related to patent infringement and patent invalidation. Briefly, infringement involves making, using, or selling a product or a method covered by claims in an issued patent. Invalidation seeks to show that the art described in the issued patent was known previously or obvious to one of ordinary skill in the art at that time the invention was made.

A U.S. patent is a contract between the inventor and the people of the U.S. represented by the U.S. Patent and Trademark Office. The right conferred upon the inventor is the right to exclude others from making, using, or selling that which is covered in the claims of the patent. Such rights are really restricted rights in the sense that the patentee is not given the right to do anything except exclude others from making, using, or selling the invention for a limited time. In exchange for these rights granted by the government, the inventor is required to provide a complete disclosure of the invention. This is the inventor's value surrendered as part of the contractual agreement. Public disclosure of the invention is made when the patent issues; nowadays the patent is valid for twenty years from the filing date.

Section 101 of the Patent Act of 1952, 35 U.S.C. §101, provides that "[w]hoever invents or discovers any new and useful process, machine, manufacture, or composition of matter, or any new and useful improvements thereof," may obtain a patent on the invention or discovery. The threshold of utility is not high. An invention is "useful" under section 101 if it is capable of providing some identifiable benefit. "To violate §101 the claimed device must be totally incapable of achieving a useful result." It has been stated that inventions that are "injurious to the well-being, good policy, or sound morals of society" are unpatentable. As examples of such inventions, Justice Story listed "a new invention to poison people, or to promote debauchery, or to facilitate private assassination." Courts have continued to recite Justice Story's formulation. But the principle that inventions are invalid if they are principally designed to serve immoral or illegal purposes has not been applied broadly in recent years. For example, years ago courts invalidated patents on gambling devices on the ground that they were immoral. Clearly, the social values of the times may influence interpretation.

The following questions are asked and must be answered for the subject matter to be patentable.

1. Is it a new and useful improvement process, machine, manufacture or composition of matter?
2. Is it a new and useful improvement thereof?
3. Is the subject matter capable of producing some desirable benefit?

4. Would it have been obvious to one of ordinary skill in the art, prior to the filing date, to combine the elements in the way that they are combined in the patent and described in the claims?

It is not to suggest that §101 has no limits or that it embraces every discovery. The laws of nature, physical phenomena and abstract ideas have been held not patentable. Thus, a new mineral discovered in the earth or a new plant found in the wild is not patentable subject matter. Likewise, Einstein could not patent his celebrated law that $E = mc^2$, nor could Newton have patented the law of gravity. Such discoveries are "manifestations of . . . nature, free to all men and reserved exclusively to none."

A patent can be issued when an inventor creates new living things; this is the basis for patents on genetically engineered living organisms. The courts have ruled that new living organisms created by man which are markedly different from any found in nature and having the potential for significant utility are patentable because they do not represent nature's handiwork.

The fact that one product can be altered to make it look like another is in itself a specific benefit sufficient to satisfy the statutory requirement of utility. Moreover, it is not at all unusual for a product to be designed to appear to viewers to be something it is not. For example, cubic zirconium is designed to simulate a diamond, imitation gold leaf is designed to imitate real gold leaf, synthetic fabrics are designed to simulate expensive natural fabrics, and imitation leather is designed to look like real leather. In each case, the invention of the product or process that makes such imitation possible has "utility" within the meaning of the patent statute, and indeed there are numerous patents directed toward making one product imitate another.

Virtually gone are the days when an invention describes an entirely new discovery. Rather, modern inventions relate to a nonobvious way of combining prior art to solve a problem or create something new and useful. Perhaps the best way of describing the eligibility for a patent appears in the 1952 modification of the patent act which states, "under section 101, a person may have invented a machine or manufacture which may include anything under the sun that is made by man."

B. Anatomy of a patent

An issued patent identifies the inventor(s), title, the filing date, the issue date, and the patent number as well as the name of the examiner(s), the filing attorney(s) and assignee (if any). It also contains a list of relevant prior publications and patents, as well as an abstract. The specification, which is the text of the patent, contains figures and a brief description of each. Frequently there is a background section that describes prior art and procedures and shows how this invention solves a prior problem. A detailed description follows with a reference to the numbered items in the figures. Typically, several methods are presented for use of the invented technology and the preferred embodiment (or embodiments) are described. The patent concludes with the claims, which describe the material that constitutes the invention. The specification must support all claims.

The filing date is important because only technology prior to this date is relevant. Typically, it usually requires about two years from the filing date for the patent to issue.

The inventor usually writes a description of the invention and the abstract; the patent attorney casts the text into patent language and composes the claims. A patent draftsman composes the figures, which contain no text; the various items in the figures are identified by numbers. There are no figure legends or a table of numbers to identify the items in the figures; this information is found only in the specification.

C. Infringement

It is the obligation of the owner of a patent (or the licensee) to prove that claims or elements in the claims of his or her issued patent are infringed by an accused infringer. The infringed claims are identified by number and the litigation begins. Sometimes the number of infringed claims is reduced as the attorneys communicate. If an accused product fails to include even a single element (or its equivalent) of a claim, there can be no infringement of that claim either literally or under the doctrine of equivalents. In other words, the plaintiff must prove by a preponderance of the evidence that at least one of the cited claims and the elements therein are infringed. Thus, it is interpretation of the claim language that becomes the central focus and the doctrine of equivalents is frequently invoked.

D. Doctrine of equivalents

Briefly this doctrine states that infringement exists if the accused infringing product or process does substantially the same function in substantially the same manner and accomplishes substantially the same result as that afforded by the patent claims. *Webster's Dictionary* defines substantial as "of a corporeal or material nature, real or actual, of ample or considerable amount, quantity, size, etc." However, the courts have not ruled on this definition. What constitutes equivalence must be determined in the context of the patent, the prior art, and the particular circumstances of the case. An important part of an infringement case is court rulings in prior cases that may take precedent.

E. Establishing infringement

In establishing infringement, each element in a claim is considered material and essential, and for infringement to be present, each element or its equivalent must be found in the accused device. (*Lemelson* 752 F. 2d at 1551; *Becton Dickson & Co. v. C.R. Bard, Inc.*, 922 F. 2d 792, 798 Fed. Cir. 1990).

Literal Infringement of a patent claim is found when the accused device literally incorporates all the limitations of a patent claim. (*Hi-Life Products v. American National Water Mattress Corp.*, 842 F. 2d 323, 325 Fed. Cir. 1988).

Inevitably, considerations of validity or infringement require one to interpret the language of the patent claims. Several factors may be considered to interpret the claims, such as

1. the prosecution history of the claim
2. the specification of the patent
3. the language of other claims
4. the usage of the terminology in the art

(*McGill, Inc. v. John Zink Co.* 736 F. 2d 666, 673–676, Fed. Cir. 1984); cert. denied, 469 U.S. 1037 1984). However, a claim should be interpreted so that, if possible, it does not read on prior art. (*Lewmar Marine, Inc. v. Barient, Inc.*, 827 F. 2d 744, 749 Fed. Cir. 1987); cert. denied, 98 L. Ed. 2d 253 (1988); (*ACS Hosp. Sys., Inc. v. Montefiore Hosp.* 732 F. 2d 1572, 1577 Fed Cir. 1984).

Also, no infringement can exist by following the exact teachings of the prior art, (*Pennwalt Corp. v. Durand-Wayland Inc.*, 833 F. 2d 931, 934 note 1,) or by practicing obvious variations of the prior art, (*Wilson Sporting Goods Company v. David Geoffrey & Assoc.*, 904 F. 2d 677, 685 Fed. Cir. 1990).

The general rule is that a dependent claim cannot be infringed if the independent claim on which it depends is not infringed.

Where claim limitations are written in means-plus-function or step-plus-function language, the patent claim is construed to cover the corresponding structure, material or acts described in the specification and equivalents thereof. (35 U.S.C. §112, paragraph 6; *Pennwalt*, 833 F. 2d at 934.)

Specifically, 35 U.S.C. §112, paragraph 6 states an element in a claim or a combination may be expressed as a means or step for performing a specified function without the recital of structure, material, or acts in support thereof, and such claim shall be construed to cover the corresponding structure, material, or acts described in the specification and equivalents thereof. In *Pennwalt*, the Federal Circuit confirmed that means-plus-function clauses cannot be interpreted without reference to the specification. Therefore, Section 112, paragraph 6, rules out the possibility that any and every means which performs the function specified in the claim literally satisfies that limitation. While encompassing equivalents of those disclosed in the specification, the provision, nevertheless, acts as a restriction on the literal satisfaction of a claim limitation. (*Dateline Corp. v. Micro Technologies, Inc.*, 813 F. 2d 1196, 1201, 1 USPQ2d 2052, 2055, Fed. Cir. 1987.)

For literal infringement of a claim containing a means-plus-function limitation to be found, the accused device must perform exactly the function specified in the means-plus-function recitation. If the function is not performed, no literal infringement can be found. (*Pennwalt*, 833 F. 2d at 934, *Intellicall, Inc. v. Phonometrics Inc.*, 952 F. 2d 1384, 1389 Fed. Cir. 1992.)

If the accused device performs the specified function, the analysis with respect to literal infringement requires a further determination. One must then resort to the specification to determine what range of structures are covered by the means-plus-function element. Where the issue is raised, it is part of the ultimate burden of proof of the patent owner to establish, with respect to a claim limitation in means-plus-function form, that the structure in the accused device which performs that function is the same as or an equivalent of the structure disclosed in the specification.

Often the issue of interchangeability of components is raised when infringement is being argued. Obviously, if an important component in the alleged infringing device is interchangeable with a component in the invention, it is difficult to argue that there is no infringement. However, if the component in the alleged infringing device, when substituted into the invented device, will not perform and achieve substantially the same result, noninfringement can be argued (see below).

As stated previously, the doctrine of equivalents pertains to the infringing device performing substantially the same function in substantially the same way and producing substantially the same result. However, there is a distinction between the doctrine of equivalents and an "equivalent" under Section 112. Paragraph 6 Section 112 and the doctrine of equivalents has something in common. The word "equivalent" in Section 112 invokes the familiar concept of an insubstantial change, which adds nothing of significance. In the context of Section 112, an equivalent results from insubstantial change, which adds nothing of significance to the structure, material, or acts disclosed in the patent specification. A determination of Section 112 equivalence does not involve the equitable tripartite test of the doctrine of equivalents. As the court has stated, "the sole question under Section 112 involves comparison of the structure in the accused device which performs the claimed function to the structure in the specification. In sum, Section 112, paragraph 6, and the doctrine of equivalents have separate origins and purposes. Section 112, paragraph 6, limits the broad language of means-plus-function limitations in combination claims to equivalents of the structure, materials, or acts in the specification. The doctrine of equivalents equitably expands exclusive patent rights. (*Valmont Industries, Inv. v. Reinke Mfg. Co. Inc.*, 983 F.2d 1039, 1043–44, Fed. Cir. 1993)

As noted above, patent infringement may also be found on the basis of the Doctrine of Equivalents. Under this doctrine, an accused product that does not literally infringe a claim may yet be found an infringement if it performs substantially the same function, in substantially the same way to obtain the same result as the claimed product or process. (*Graver Tank & Mfg. v. Linde Air Products Co.*, 339 U.S. 605, 608, 70 S. Ct. 854, 856, 94 L.Ed. 1097, 1950)

The test for infringement under the doctrine of equivalents has recently been reinstated by the Court of Appeals for the Federal Circuit in *Hilton Davis Chemical Co. v. Warner-Jenkinson Company, Inc.* Appeal 93–1088, decided August 8, 1995. In *Hilton Davis*, the Federal Circuit explicitly held that "the substantiality of the differences between the claimed and accused products or processes [is] assessed according to an objective standard.

The court in *Hilton Davis* stated that in applying the doctrine of equivalents, it is often enough to use the function-way-result test described in *Graver Tank*. However, the Federal Circuit went on to state that the function-way-result test is not necessarily the only test to be used in a doctrine of equivalents analysis, especially in a technically complex case. Other factors that may be considered by the fact-finder include the following:

1. Whether persons reasonably skilled in the art would have known of the interchangeability of an ingredient or element not contained within the claim;

2. Evidence of copying; when an attempt to copy occurs, the fact-finder may infer that the copyist, presumably one of some skill in the art, has made a fair copy, with only insubstantial changes;
3. Evidence of attempts to design around patent claims; when a competitor attempts to design around patent claims, the fact-finder may infer that the competitor, presumably one of skill in the art, has designed substantial changes into the new product to avoid infringement.

Finally, the *Hilton Davis* court clearly stated that the fact-finder must consider all evidence relevant to substantiality of the differences in making a doctrine of equivalents determination. The Supreme Court's reliance in *Graver Tank* on factors other than function, way, and result endorses consideration of all evidence relevant to the substantiality of the differences. Because equivalence, in the patent law, is not a prisoner of formula [339 U.S.] at 609, the available relevant evidence may vary from case to case. When a trial record presents only evidence of function, way, and result, an application of the doctrine will necessarily rest on function, way, and result alone. When a record presents other evidence relevant to the substantiality of the differences, however, the fact finder must consider it.

Application of the doctrine of equivalents is limited in several respects. Under the doctrine of prosecution history estoppel, a patentee is precluded from asserting any equivalent that would encompass subject matter that was surrendered during prosecution to overcome rejections based on the prior art. (*Hughes Aircraft*, 717 F.2d at 1362). Thus, application of prosecution history estoppel requires an examination not only of what was surrendered, but also the reason for surrender as well. (*Hi-Life Products v. American Nat. Water Mattress*, 842 F.2d 323, 325, Fed. Cir. 1988.)

As noted in *Perkin Elmer Corp. v. Westinghouse Electric Corp.* (822 F 2d. 1528, 1532 (Fed. Cir. 1987), a court may not, under the guise of applying the doctrine of equivalents, erase a plethora of meaningful structural and functional limitations in a claim on which the public is entitled to rely in avoiding infringement. . . . Though the doctrine of equivalents is designed to do equity, and to relieve an inventor from a semantic straightjacket when equity requires, it is not designed to permit wholesale redrafting of a claim to cover non-equivalent devices, i.e., to permit a claim expansion that would encompass more than an insubstantial change.

F. Invalidation

A second line of defense that an alleged patent infringer may take is to show that the issued patent that is allegedly infringed is invalid. Often efforts to prove noninfringement and invalidity progress simultaneously. For the patentee, the possibility of discovering that his or her patent may be invalid is troublesome. Before discussing invalidity, it is appropriate to view the duties of a patent examiner to show what underlies granting a patent.

A patent application receives very close scrutiny by one or more examiners; however, it is only the primary examiner who can grant or deny a patent. Patent examiners have special knowledge, training and skills which are aided by an enormous amount of cross-indexed documents. The U.S. Patent and Trademark Office has access to 30 million documents, more than 5 million U.S. patents, 3 million foreign patents and a library of 120 million publications. A primary examiner will have trained at a patent academy and had seven years of on-the-job training to back up his or her decision to issue or deny a patent. However, before issuing a patent, the examiner has responded to the applicant via documents known as "office action." In the absence of prior art turning up in the search, the primary examiner must judge whether the invention is not obvious to one of ordinary skill in the art. It is often this situation that is attacked by those seeking to invalidate a patent.

From the foregoing, it is clear that the absence of prior art and nonobviousness to one or ordinary skill in the art, in full view of the prior art, are what make an invention patentable. Thus, invalidation must address these issues and the burden of proof of invalidation lies with the alleged infringer.

If an inventor, either willfully or negligently, fails to disclose material prior art to the examiner, a case for invalidation can be made, particularly if it can be shown that the inventor possessed such information. I remember one case in which an inventor desired to obtain FDA approval for the sale of a medical device and avoid lengthy clinical testing by stating in the FDA application that the inventor's device was substantially the same as an FDA-approved device. The interesting fact is that the FDA-approved device was in use before the inventor filed for a patent.

Other ways of showing that an inventor may have concealed important background information is to read his or her publications and those cited in the patent. In addition, it is useful to read the papers that appear in the references of the papers identified in the patent. Bibliographic thoroughness requires that all relevant references must have been read and understood.

Dealing with the issue of "obvious to one of ordinary skill in the art" is more difficult and requires knowledge of the state of the art when the invention was made. It also requires a knowledge of how others solved the same problem as claimed in the invention. Although there are other legal issues associated with invalidation, in the final analysis, interpretation of the submitted evidence is subjective; therefore, it is necessary to produce evidence that is easily understood by a judge and jury. This is especially important because every patent carries a presumption of validity that can only be overcome by clear and convincing evidence.

Regarding the concept of "one of ordinary skill in the art," I have encountered a case in which an attorney claimed that the expert was one of "extraordinary skill in the art" and that, because of this, the expert's opinion was not representative of "one of ordinary skill in the art." Dealing with this situation required very careful documentation of the skill of a typical worker in the field at the time of filing the patent application.

Another aspect of invalidation relates to the claim language which must be supported by the specification. If not, it can be argued that the claim is invalid. The services of a claims-construction expert are needed in such a case.

Importantly, it is essential that the contribution of each inventor be identified with one or more elements in the claims. Merely paying for filing a patent does not grant inventorship rights because such an act contributes nothing to the technology of the invention and raises the issue of invalidation.

G. Claims chart

During litigation over patent infringement, it is customary to compose a claims chart which consists of two columns on a page. The left-hand column identifies the patent claim number(s) and the element(s) in the claim that are infringed. In the right-hand column, directly opposite, is a description of the manner in which the accused device or process infringes the claim element(s). In this way, it is easy to argue infringement or defend noninfringement. The same type of chart can be used to argue invalidation.

9.10 Discovery

During discovery, the pretrial time, both sides are pressed to acquire pertinent information. During this time it is unwise to write anything down that could reveal your opinion. What I have found to be very useful is to compose a table of contents for each document that I have read and staple this table to the document. In this way, I can gain easy access (by page number) to any fact or statement made that is pertinent to the case. When evidence is contained in scientific papers, I index each in the same way to identify where the useful information is to be found. The availability of such inventories makes it easy to refresh one's memory, write a report and prepare for deposition and the courtroom.

9.11 The Report

Rule 26 of the Federal Rules of Civil Procedure gives a detailed account of the requirements for the report of an expert witness and this document should be consulted. The essence of this rule is as follows:

> Except as otherwise stipulated or directed by the court, this disclosure shall, with respect of a witness who is retained or specially employed to provide expert testimony in the case or whose duties as an employee of the party regularly involve giving expert testimony, be accompanied by a written report prepared and signed by the witness. The report shall contain a complete statement of all opinions to be expressed and the basis and reasons therefore; the date or other information considered by the witness in forming the opinions; any exhibits to be used as a summary of or support for the opinions; the qualifications of the witness, including a list of all publications authored by the witness within the preceding ten years; the compensation to be paid for the study and testimony; and a listing of any other cases in which the witness has testified as an expert at trial or by deposition within the preceding four years.
>
> These disclosures shall be made at the times and in the sequence directed by the court. In the absence of other directions from the court or stipulation by the parties, the disclosures shall be made at least 90 days before the trial date or the date the case is to be ready for trial or, if the evidence is intended solely to contradict or rebut evidence on the same subject matter identified by another party under paragraph (2)(B), within 30 days after the disclosure made by the other party. The parties shall supplement these disclosures when required under subdivision (e)(1).

Although Rule 26 requires provision of considerable information, much of it will have been requested by the hiring attorney long before a final written report is requested. Often during pursuit of a case, a report is requested by the attorney that you serve. While it is true that attorneys use the same English language as we mortals, they use it differently and punctuate long sentences differently. Therefore, the report has to be in the form that is unambiguous to the opposing lawyer and judge. Whereas, when the expert collects and interprets the facts, it requires a collaborative effort between an expert witness and an attorney to get the report in a form and style understandable to all attorneys. For example, suppose that X was the critical item that caused injury. An attorney would state that the accused did not know X and should have, or if the accused knew X, it was disregarded and it was this disregard that caused the accident that caused the injury. From the foregoing, the expert witness must recognize that his or her facts and evidence must be assembled and presented in a style that is very different from that used in scientific reports and publications. I have found that the best way to start a report is by a telephone conversation with the attorney that you serve. Then a rough draft is composed by you and either read to the attorney or sent to him or her by e-mail or FAX. This iterative process may continue four or five times before the final report is created. Meeting with your attorney in person to collaborate on the report is very desirable, but this is rarely possible. Remember that this report is made available to opposing counsel. Unlike Perry Mason trials in which a new piece of evidence appears first in court, in the real world, both sides work from the same body of evidence; what makes it interesting is to see how different interpretations are placed on the same evidence. Be aware that your report is a statement of your opinion and, along with any deposition, it will be used in the courtroom. As a result of the *Daubert v. Merrell Dow* case in 1993, scientific evidence is required to support your expert opinion. For example, the expert's opinion must be supported by scientific reasoning and methodology that is generally accepted in the expert's particular scientific community. Obviously, the scientific data must be reliable. Stated differently, general scientific knowledge and published literature are needed to justify, to a reasonable certainty, your expert opinion. Obviously, it is necessary to show that the cited scientific knowledge and published literature apply directly to this case.

Although there is no standard form for the final report, it must contain certain key pieces of information. Most importantly, the report must inventory all case documents examined by you. The final report must provide a summary of the basis for the lawsuit, i.e., a description of the accident, the basis for a patent infringement etc. Finally, the report states your opinion and the basis for it.

Because your report will be read by those who do not know your qualifications, a brief outline of your educational background and experience are needed. You should state that you are familiar with all of the scientific and practical aspects of the case. Relevant papers, chapters and books that you have published are assets. Likewise the patents that you hold should be cited, especially if the case involves a patent. Then you must list the documents that you used in forming your opinion. You may include an appendix of exhibits, including your CV.

The following is an illustrative example:

Robert L. Brown
Rouge, Weiss & Azul
0001 Highwater Street
Schwartbert NWT
H270–A66–WL20

RE: Blanco vs. Knife & Omnihospital

Dear Mr. Brown,

Before describing the injury case involving Mr. Blanco, I will summarize my credentials; my CV and list of publications are appended to this report.

I have a bachelor's and master's degree in electrical engineering and a Ph.D. in physiology. I am a certified clinical engineer, a member of the National Society for Professional Engineers, a fellow in the National Academy of Forensic Engineers and hold a Texas license. I have been an expert witness for twenty years and have been deposed many times and have testified in court about ten times.

I have published twenty-four scientific papers on electrosurgery and have written three books that contain chapters on electrosurgery. My most recent book, "Medical Device Accidents," deals extensively with electrosurgical accidents like the one involved in this case.

I have examined the following documents that pertain to this case:

1. Surgeon Knife's report
2. Operating room record
3. Anesthesia record
4. Incident Report
5. Deposition of Dr. Right
6. Deposition by Dr. Fence
7. Medical records of Blanco
8. Complaint

Brief Description of Incident:

On 9/31/92, Jason Blanco, a thirty-year-old male, underwent endoscopic surgery to remove his gallbladder. The operation was performed under general anesthesia by Dr. Knife, a staff surgeon at the Omnihospital. Electrosurgery was used to cut and coagulate and the dispersive electrode was on the anterior right thigh. A standard model X225P dispersive electrode was used which has been used by this hospital for the last five years. During the surgery, Knife noted that at the start of the operation, cutting and coagulation were satisfactory; but later, cutting and coagulation were both a little "slow". Therefore, the surgeon requested more output from the electrosurgical unit. The operation progressed without incident and was completed successfully in 2.5 hours. However, when the drapes and the electrosurgical electrode were removed, it was noted that there was a 3 × 3-cm burn on the right thigh, characterized by second- and third-degree (fullthickness) burns. On consultation with the family, debridement and skin grafting were decided upon and performed successfully the next day by Dr. Right.

Analysis: The function of an electrosurgical dispersive electrode (Bovie pad) is to provide a safe return path for the electrosurgical current to the electrosurgical unit (ESU). It does so by providing a large area of contact with the skin. A typical dispersive electrode is 4 × 6 in. (10 × 15 cm). There is an AAMI/ANSI standard of performance for such electrodes and all that are available commercially must meet this standard. If the skin contact area is reduced, all of the current is forced to pass through a smaller area (current crowding); the current density (mA/cm^2) will be high and skin heating will occur. The amount of heating depends on the current density (squared), and how long it flows, which depends on the number of activations of the ESU.

In relating these facts to the Blanco incident, note that the burn measured 3 × 3cm, which is much smaller than the size of a typical electrosurgical electrode (10 × 15 cm); therefore, the area of skin contact was small, favoring heat production. If we use the burn area ($3 \times 3 = 9\ cm^2$) as the effective contact area, this area is only 6 percent of the area of a typical dispersive electrode ($150\ cm^2$).

In addition, during the operation, the surgeon requested more output from the ESU. This is consistent with the development of a small area of contact which would increase the resistance and require a higher output setting on the ESU, which was requested by Dr. Knife.

Dr. Fence, expert for the defendant, argues that the electrode was defective, but provides no proof. The fact that the hospital has been using the same type of electrode for the last five years without incident argues against a defective electrode. Also, the fact that cutting and coagulation difficulties were not present earlier in the procedure argues against a defective electrode and points to partial dislodgement of the electrode during the operation.

In summary, the electrode contact area with Blanco's skin was small, which caused current crowding, and it was the current crowding that produced the heating that produced the second- and third-degree burns. When a surgeon encounters poor cutting and coagulating, good practice requires that the dispersive electrode and all cables to the ESU and the ESU be checked before proceeding.

Respectfully submitted,
Pietro Amaretto, PhD, PE, etc.
State License Number
Social Security Number

In a report or an affidavit, it is useful to keep the door open to accommodate new, unanticipated, admissible evidence that may come in the future. Therefore, it may be of value to consider inclusion of the following sentence: "I reserve the right to modify or change the opinions and conclusions upon the discovery of additional information, facts, and other circumstances discovered during dependency of any litigation relating to this matter."

Attorneys rely heavily on precedents and I have found that it is often possible to bring a case to a climax without the need of a report by scouring the published literature to find prior publications that deal directly with the events in the present case. For example, I have found papers that describe a medical device accident that is the same as the one being litigated. However, it is not enough to find such publications; it is necessary to identify in them the relevant paragraphs or statements. Attorneys take such material seriously and its presentation has often resulted in prompt settlement.

9.12 The Deposition

The deposition of an expert is an interrogation taken under oath by the opposing attorney. All questions and answers are recorded by a court reporter. Prior to the deposition, make a list of all documents that you have examined that pertain to the case because you will be asked for this information. Just before the deposition begins, take a few minutes with the court reporter to identify technical terms and their spelling, as well as abbreviations and acronyms. This investment in time will pay off later when you proofread your sworn deposition. I also give the court reporter my business card which lists my phone number, FAX number and e-mail address. I also tell the reporter to call me if I can help when he or she is preparing a transcript of the deposition.

The attorney who hired you is present at the deposition. The objective of the opposing attorney is to discover your opinion, which you guard carefully. In other words, the opposing attorney wants to know what you think by asking artfully composed questions which are answered truthfully without commentary; give nothing away. You have no obligation to educate the opposing attorney. If his or her questions are unclear or misleading, ask for a repetition or a rephrasing. Although your attorney will object to some questions, these objections are usually only for the record. Occasionally, some questions violate the rules of procedure and are objected to strenuously. Try to avoid giving a strong conclusion at this time because you may be dealing with limited data. By trial time, new admissible information may be adduced which may or may not modify your opinion. Also recognize that some new evidence may not be admissible. Proofread the typed deposition and remember that the opposing attorney can use this document in court; therefore, you must be consistent. During cross-examination, never guess or speculate; merely state, "I do not remember" or, "I do not know." You can tell how you are progressing by watching the yellow legal pad that the examining attorney uses. Remember that a good attorney will know the answers to all questions that he or she asks. These questions and often the answers are on the yellow legal pad; this is why it is useful to note how often and when the attorney consults the legal pad.

Sworn depositions can be taken anywhere. Typically, they are taken in the offices of the attorney for the defense or plaintiff. Sometimes a deposition is videotaped. I have been deposed in a meeting room in an out-of-town hotel agreed upon by the attorneys. I have had my deposition taken via a conference telephone call. In such a case, the attorney that I serve was with me and all relevant documents and exhibits were present at both sites. This method is very convenient and quite inexpensive, in view of the high cost of air travel and time loss due to travel.

9.13 Chronology of a Case

Lawsuits do not progress swiftly, nor do all cases go to trial. It is reliably estimated that more than 95 percent of all lawsuits are settled out of court. However, it is rarely possible to predict those that will proceed to trial. Even if a trial date is set, it may be delayed for weeks or months. Even if the trial date is changed several times, it is still not possible to predict that a trial will be held. I have experienced settlement of a lawsuit before testifying on the first day of trial. Nonetheless, if a trial date is set, be fully prepared to testify in the courtroom then.

The time course of a lawsuit often shares what I call the airport syndrome "hurry up and wait." Typically, an attorney has about one half dozen active cases— all with differing urgencies. Witnesses have to be interrogated, documents have to be located and analyzed, depositions have to be taken and court hearings have to be scheduled. A technical expert may enter early or late in these proceedings and often is asked for a prompt preliminary opinion. Frequently, the expert hears nothing and wonders what, if anything, is going on. A phone call to the attorney will solve this problem and may reveal that you need to be in court in three weeks, or, as is more usual, the trial has been set for a date that is about ten months in the future. I have one case that is two years old and another that is more than four years old; with both it is impossible to estimate a trial date. Such a situation is usually frustrating to a technical expert who is used to solving problems with dispatch. However, take it easy on your ulcers and blood pressure. Develop a tolerant attitude because the process is not likely to change soon—nor can you change it!

9.14 The Courtroom

The courtroom belongs to the judge who is always addressed as: "your Honor." He or she alone controls all of the proceedings, an example of which occurred recently in a Chicago courtroom. Someone in the courtroom was carrying a cell phone which rang. The judge had this person arrested and put in jail overnight for disturbing the courtroom proceedings. This story made the six o'clock news.

Typically the litigants, witnesses, attorneys, court reporter, bailiff and sometimes a law clerk are present and all rise when the judge enters. There may be some business or announcements before the jury is called in.

When appearing in court, your dress and deportment can have an important effect on the judge and jury. Dress conservatively; do not wear sports clothes, sandals or jeans. You will be surrounded by professionals who dress professionally. Get a haircut and wear clothes that do not create the impression that you belong to a cult. Be confident in your body movements and speech and act in a way that is consistent with your professional standing.

Despite the fact that the witness box is a stressful site for the expert witness, the courtroom is an exciting place where the truth is sought. An enormous amount of information is produced by the attorneys for the plaintiff and defense. There is a considerable amount of information in the behavior of the participants (judge, jury, attorneys, and witnesses). Body language abounds and communicates much information to the sensitive observer. There is considerable information in the time taken to respond to questions as well as how the response is delivered. As is well known, many attorneys can conduct themselves in a threatening or conciliatory manner, depending on what suits them. It can be said that courtroom proceedings can be characterized as a shower of information.

When you take the witness stand, you will be sworn to tell the truth. Greet the judge. Ask if you are speaking loudly enough for the court reporter and jury. Tell the court reporter that you will spell any technical or unfamiliar terms. At the break check with the court reporter to inquire if he or she needs any clarification.

In the courtroom, the role of the expert witness is that of a teacher who is relaxed and has obvious enthusiasm for his or her specialty. Judges and jurors are nontechnical people, by and large, and it is the duty of the expert to translate technical material into simple and easy-to-understand concepts. If you feel your message is not getting across, ask the judge if you are going to fast for the jury or the reporter; he or she will tell you. Remember that you are there to present factual information and modesty has no place, nor has arrogance in this process. There is no better witness than one who believes fervently in his or her views and sticks to them.

Because trials usually occupy many days, it is useful to recognize the limited ability of the human mind to remember. Table 9.1 summarizes the important facts and shows the percent retention of information at one and five days for three different modes of communication. Obviously the spoken word alone is an inadequate teaching mode. Visual aids improve retention; however integration of verbal testimony with visual aids improves retention to 85 percent at one day and 55 percent at five days.

Table 9.1
Retention Time for Different Presentation Modes

PRESENTATION TYPE	Percent retention at	
	1 day	5 days
Verbal testimony alone	60%	30%
Visual aids alone	70%	50%
Verbal and visual aids	85%	55%

I have found that charts, large illustrations, models, videotapes, and demonstrations in the courtroom are very effective. However, never schedule a demonstration if there is even the slightest chance of failure—make a videotape of the demonstration under conditions that you control. Whenever possible, bring enough of these exhibits so that the judge and jury can examine them.

When interrogated, be relaxed; present your answers to the jury, not the attorney. Engage the jury with eye contact and maintain their attention. Be animated, enthusiastic, and show that you are happy to be there to reveal the truth. The first few minutes of direct examination are the most important because your attorney is guiding you with his questions and these are designed to help make your points. This is your chance to tell your story. A good attorney will not ask you a leading question, which is one that contains the answer. This is called "leading the witness" and will be objected to. The cross-examiner will try to discredit you, confuse you, and show that you are inconsistent in every way that he or she can. One technique is to ask the same question at different times using different words. Don't become angry; the attorney is trying to rattle you. Just give the same answer each time.

9.15 Attorney Styles

Opposing attorneys use many techniques to get you confused or to attempt to make you say things that you don't mean. From my experience, I have described such attorneys as follows:

Loudmouth shouts his or her questions at you, which is a tactic designed to rattle or intimidate you. The best defense is to give your answer in a soft, confident voice; this will expose Loudmouth's strategy. Give your answer by directing your attention to the jury or judge, not to Loudmouth.

Binary is the type of attorney who demands a yes-or-no answer to each question. Binary uses this technique to filter the information that you can provide. Binary often interrupts your answers, demanding the yes-or-no answer. The best way of dealing with Binary is to look at the judge or jury and say, "A yes-or-no answer will not reveal the truth."

The Assumer is an attorney who directs the expert to assume something that is very likely contrary to his or her opinion. Beware of the Assumer; he or she will build on the assumption and coax you to agree. On occasion I have refused to join in the assumption, stating that it is too hypothetical or speculative. Only on one occasion has the judge requested me to assume. I balked stating that the assumption would go contrary to my belief.

The Fisherman, who is looking for information, is an attorney who asks questions that are barely relevant and usually call for an affirmative response. The questions often deal with what a prudent person would do or think. By this strategy the Fisherman is trying to cloud the issue by showing how often you agree. A jury could begin to think that you are inconsistent or agree, in general, with Fisherman. You must make your answers bring the questioning back to the central issue—or show tactfully that the central issue is not being addressed.

Double Negative is an attorney who uses two negatives in each question. For example, "Do you not think that X would not do that?" Because such questions are confusing to the jury and may even cause the expert to unknowingly misunderstand or slip, I have flatly refused to answer such questions and request rephrasing the question without the double negatives; I have always been accommodated.

Beware of the Machine Gun attorney who is one who repeats the same question many times in rapid fire. He or she knows something that will reveal that you are inconsistent. A typical question is, "You never said (or did) X?" He or she knows you did and is waiting for you to say that you never said (or did) X. The best answer is "I don't recall."

The Incrementer is an attorney who wants you to move away from something you believe in by asking incremental questions. For example, in one case that I had, a dimension X was not quite specific, but obvious to a prudent person. The attorney said could it be 90 percent of X, then 50 percent of X, etc. I refused to play his game and told him so and that my answer stands as given previously.

9.16 Payment for Services

As stated previously, lawsuits do not proceed with the speed of sound. In accident cases I am called as an expert witness, typically two years after the incident. I have had similar experiences with patent-infringement and trade-secret cases. During this time attorneys for both sides have been accumulating information and documents. A point is reached when an attorney wants an expert to evaluate the information, often as quickly as possible via a telephone conversation. At this point it is prudent to describe your evaluation as preliminary because more information is likely to appear as witnesses are deposed. This starts an ongoing process in which the expert starts to devote time periodically to the case; this makes it necessary to establish a schedule for billing. Many experts bill on a monthly basis; but this is not always practical because a lawsuit does not proceed at a uniform rate. Often, months pass with no activity. Sometimes attorneys offer a retainer; keep track of it and your time spent. At the outset identify your hourly rate for time spent for (a) office work, (b) for deposition, and (c) for court testimony. Keep a work log.

Colleagues of mine have reported to me a situation which is troublesome that relates to billing. Typically, at the outset, an attorney will inquire about your hourly charges and request a curriculum vitae and list of publications. It is important to identify those publications that pertain to the case at hand. Also important is identification of experience that you have had in the area of the present case. By providing this information, the attorney can identify your value to the case at hand. I have been told that some attorneys use your curriculum vitae and publication list to arrange a settlement and often do not report back to the expert. As a result, some expert witnesses charge for sending their curriculum vitae and list of publications. Fortunately, I have not had such an experience.

The trial is over or a summary judgment has occurred, or the parties have had a settlement conference and the lawsuit is ended. Now you need to be paid. Perhaps you have had an advance, perhaps you have billed periodically during the litigation, or perhaps you elected to wait until the suit is over; this latter is not to be recommended. The following paragraphs refer to the financial aspects of the activities of an expert witness.

Regarding remuneration for services rendered, there is no standard method. Some attorneys provide an advance as a retainer, usually $500 to $1000. Because lawsuits may carry on for years, it is wise to submit an invoice periodically. It is often easy to identify when critical phases have passed. I usually submit an invoice after each phase. The invoice identifies the litigants, the time covered by the services, and any expenses incurred. Meanwhile, you retain your work log in case of need to prove activity. The invoice includes my name, degrees, social security number, and license numbers.

In providing payment, there are two types of procedure. With one, the attorney or his or her law firm issues a check on its account. With the other, the attorney sends your invoice to the organization that hired the law firm. This procedure delays payment considerably. In one case that I had, it took six months to be paid. To keep the issue alive, I submitted (to the law firm) an invoice each month, marking them second notice (with date), third notice (with date), etc. The final (sixth) invoice carried the dates of all six invoices and was such an embarrassment that payment was received and the second notice was attached to the check! The message here is "erosion will ultimately win."

Sometimes an attorney neglects to respond to your invoices and a phone call will discover the reason. In problem cases you may suggest an installment plan for payment. Somewhat less attractive is to request payment for a reduced amount within seven days. You may elect to settle via the small claims court.

My experience with the small claims court was very educational. If the law firm's offices are in another city or state, you may hire an attorney in that location to file your suit. To do so, he or she must have a copy of your work log as proof of services rendered. However, some states require that the plaintiff appear in small claims court. Other states will allow the plaintiff to be represented by a local attorney. You should inquire about the local rule.

You may elect to file a complaint for unprofessional conduct with the Bar Association in the state where the delinquent attorney has his office. I pursued this route once to try and force debt payment. Not only did the state Bar Association find the delinquent attorney not guilty of unprofessional conduct, but they warned me (in writing), that if I divulged this action, the attorney could file a civil suit against me! I will not try this approach again.

In 1996 the National Academy of Forensic Engineers (NAFE) published a very useful handbook entitled Business and Financial Practices for Forensic Engineers. In it are chapters on the code of ethics for forensic engineers, risk management, insurance for errors and omissions (E and O), record keeping, financial management, fees and collection thereof and marketing your services. This 102-page book contains a wealth of information derived from the practice of forensic engineering.

9.17 Expert Witness Malpractice

Very frequently the testimony of an expert witness provides the critical information in a judgment for the plaintiff or defendant. Obviously there are two parties concerned with the performance of experts: the party that hires the expert to testify and the opposing party; their goals are at odds. The hiring party wants effective testimony as measured by a beneficial effect on the judge and jury. The opposing party wants the expert discredited and the testimony stricken. Dissatisfaction by either party is clearly not evidence of malpractice. As in other malpractice actions, it must be found that the expert performed below the standard for the profession he or she represents and that this substandard performance caused the party's harm. Thus, the party claiming malpractice must show both the standard for such experts and that, but for the expert's deviation from the standard, the party would have prevailed. However, unlike other malpracticing professionals, the expert witness occupies a privileged place in the legal system.

9.18 Expert Witness Immunity

There are two types of witness immunity: immunity against criminal prosecution based on the testimony and immunity against civil liability for harm caused by the testimony. If a witness lies on the stand or in deposition, the witness may be prosecuted for the crime of perjury. All witnesses at all times, irrespective of any immunity claims, are subject to perjury charges if they lie in sworn testimony. Witnesses may also be prosecuted for crimes that they admit to in testimony, unless the government has granted them immunity for testimony. In the case of perjury and admitted crimes, the prosecutions are brought by government prosecutors and not by the parties to the lawsuit.

It is imperative that an expert witness not be subjected to litigation because the party who retained the expert is dissatisfied with the substance of the opinion rendered by the expert. An expert witness must be able to articulate the basis for his or her opinion without fear that a verdict unfavorable to the client will result in litigation, even where the party who has retained the expert contends that the expert's opinion was not fully explained prior to trial.

9.19 Liability

Expert witnesses have always been subject to prosecution due to perjury for false testimony. The liability of expert witnesses extends to include negligence in the preparation of testimony; therefore it is advisable to seek insurance coverage for these situations. The most convenient type of policy is known as "errors and omissions" (E&O). Typically the insurance company agrees to pay on behalf of the insured all sums which the insured shall become legally obligated to pay as compensatory money damages as a result of claims first made against the insured and reported to the company during the policy period by reason of any act, error or omission in professional services rendered or which should have been rendered by the insured or by any person for whose acts, errors or omissions the insured is legally liable and arising out of the conduct of the insured's profession.

Regarding settlement, the policy usually states that with respect to the insurance afforded by this policy, the company shall defend any claim or suit against the insured seeking compensatory money damages to which this insurance applies, even if any of the allegations of the suit are groundless, false or fraudulent. It is agreed that the company may make such investigation and settlement of any claim or suit as it deems expedient; but the company shall not be obligated to pay any claim or judgment or to defend or continue to defend any claim or suit after the applicable limit of the company's liability has been exhausted by payment of judgments, settlements or claims expenses.

With respect to the claims procedure, the policy typically states that the insured shall, as a condition precedent to their right to the protection afforded by this insurance, give to the company as soon as practicable, notice (a) of any claim made against them, or (b) on the receipt of notice from any person of an intention to hold the insured responsible for the results of any breach of duty, or of an incident or circumstances likely to give rise to a claim hereunder, and shall in any case, upon request, give the company such information as the company may reasonably require.

The cost of E&O insurance is moderate for a typical expert witness. The rates vary among insurance companies. Many professional societies have arrangements with insurance companies that offer special rates to their members.

9.20 Where to Find Information

A. Medical device accidents

Attorneys and expert witnesses always want to know if the accident under investigation is common or rare, or if there are precedents that could effect a judgment. Such background information is not always easy to locate. There are many sources of information on medical device accidents. As stated earlier, Medical Device Reports (MDRs), now called Manufacturer and User Device Experience (MAUDE), which describe an accident, are available from the Food and Drug Administration (FDA). Institutional medical records, the Incident Report, and depositions obtained from those present at the time of the accident contain valuable information. Another useful source of FDA information is the 510K application for permission to sell a device that is substantially the same as one on the market. The IDE (Investigational Device Exemption) and the PMA (Premarket Approval) are FDA documents that assure that safety and efficacy considerations were met so that limited clinical trials of new medical devices are allowed.

A book by Gendron (1988) contains descriptions of a large number of different types of medical accidents and includes references to original sources. In some cases, the court rulings are provided. The book by Shepherd (1992) also contains accident descriptions and identifies the types of questions that should be asked to investigate the accident to determine the cause. A monograph by Geddes (1995), which deals with the response of living tissue to the passage of direct current and low- and high-frequency alternating current, also contains descriptions of medical device accidents due to such currents. A book by Pearce (1985) contains many examples of electrosurgical accidents and in a chapter in a recent book by Fish (2000) describes many electrical accidents and includes many medical accidents. The Emergency Care Research Institute (ECRI) maintains a very large data base on medical accidents. ECRI also publishes a journal entitled Health Devices that contains accident reports. Several journals describe medical accidents, among these are *Medical Malpractice Verdicts, Settlements and Experts* and *The Forensic Examiner.* SEAK Inc. hosts many expert witness conferences that deal with medical malpractice and accidents.

Information on accidents related to anesthesia is available from the American Society of Anesthesiologists, which maintains a closed claims database. A wide variety of accidents that occurred during anesthesia are described therein. In addition, the Wood Library—Museum of Anesthesiology also maintains a data base of anesthesia accidents.

Published papers on accidents can be accessed through a library search of key words. Although the practice of listing key words is of more recent origin, the references in the recent publications provide the trail to previous accidents of the same type. Library sources include Medline and Web of Science. In addition a worldwide listing of government agencies concerned with medical devices appears along with references in this chapter.

B. Medical device standards

Before the FDA was given authority to regulate medical devices in 1976, the various professional societies had made recommendations for minimum performance of devices. In parallel with these activities, several industrial standards-promulgating groups, notably, the National Fire Protection Association and the Underwriters Laboratory, concerned themselves with the safety of medical devices. Now there are mandatory standards for efficacy and safety for medical devices which resulted from the activities of the FDA device classification panels. The Association for the Advancement of Medical Instrumentation (AAMI), in collaboration with the American National Standards Institute (ANSI), maintains a file of the latest AAMI/ANSI standards for the safety and efficacy of medical devices. The American Society for Testing Materials (ASTM) has promulgated performance standards for certain medical devices. The Electronic Industries Association (EIA) concerns itself with the safety of medical devices. There are many professional organizations in the U.S. that concern themselves with promoting safe medical equipment. The analog of the FDA in Canada is the Canadian Standards Association (CSA) and in Europe, the International Electrotechnical Commission (IEC); both promulgate medical device standards. The IEC has a wider range of performance standards than is required in the U.S., and when a U.S. standard is absent, the IEC standard is often cited. In addition to AAMI, ANSI, and ASTM, a wide variety of standards documents can be obtained from Global Engineering Documents. In the reference list to this chapter is a worldwide listing of government agencies concerned with the safety and efficacy of medical devices.

C. Legal documents

There are two enormous data bases that cover the legal aspects of medical mishaps, as well as a wide variety of other subjects, including patents and patent infringement cases. The LexisNexis data base serves sixty countries and has 7,300 databases and adds 9.5 million documents each week. Both legal and nonlegal information is available. The West Publishing Co. operates the WestDoc data base and contains federal and state case law entries. Attorney editorial services can be provided and a nominal charge is levied for each case, there being no subscription fees. LexisNexis and WestDoc are the data bases that attorneys search.

References

AAMI—Association for the Advancement of Medical Instrumentation. 3330 Washington Blvd., Arlington, VA 22201-4598.

American Hospital Association (AHA). 840 North Lake Shore Drive, Chicago, IL 60611.

American National Standard Institute. 1430 Broadway, New York, NY.

American Society of Anesthesiologists. 520 N. Northwest Highway, Park Ridge, IL 60068-2573. http://www.asahq.org/.

American Society for Quality Control. 161 West Wisconsin Ave., Milwaukee, WI 53203.

Argentina: Av. De May 869 Buenos Aires Republica, Argentina, Tel. 54-11-4340-0800, Fax: 54-11-4340-4578.

Australian Therapeutic Goods Administration. P.O. Box 100, Woden A Act. 2606 Australia.

Brazil: Ministry of Health. http://www.saude.gov.br/.

Bruley ME. Accident and forensic investigation. In Medical Devices. 1966. Van Gruting CWD, Ed. Elsevier Science BV, Amsterdam, The Netherlands.

Canadian Standards Association. 235 Montreal Rd., Ottawa, Ontario, Canada K1A 0L2.

Electronic Industries Association (EIA), Health Care Electronics Section. 2001 Eye Street, N.W., Washington, D.C. 20006.

Emergency Care Research Institute (ECRI). 5200 Butler Pike, Plymouth Meeting, PA 19462.

Finland: Ministry of Social Affairs and Health. (STM, sosiaali-ja terveysministeriö) Postal address, P.O. Box 33, FIN-00023 Government Finland, Telephone: +359 9 1601, fax: +358 9 160 4126 (registry).

Fish, R. In Nabours RF, Electrical Injuries. Lawyers & Judges Publ. Co., Tucson, AZ, 2000.

Food and Drug Administration. 5600 Fisher's Lane, Rockville, MD 20857.

Food and Drug Administration. Center for Devices and Radiological Health, 12720 Twinbrook Parkway, Rockville, MD 20857.

Forensic Examiner. American College of Forensic Examiners, 2750 E. Sunshine St., Springfield, MO 65804.

France: Manufacturer's Association. Agence Francaise de Securite Sanitaire des Produits de Sante, 143/147 bd Anatole France, 93285 St. Denise Cedex, France, Telephone: 33 1 55 87 37 02.

France: Direction des Hôpitaux, Bureau des Dispositifs Medicaux, 8 rue de segur, 75350, Paris 075P.

Geddes LA. Handbook of Electrical Hazards and Accidents. 1995. CRC Press, Boca Raton, FL.

Gendron FC. Unexplained Patient Burns. 1988. Quest Publishing (now Lippincott-Raven Press), Brea, CA.

Germany: Federal Institute for Drugs and Medical Devices. Friedrich-Ebert-Allee 38, 53113 Bonn, Germany, Phone: +49 0228 207 30.

Global Engineering Documents. Clayton, MO.

Hoff HE and Geddes LA. The beginnings of graphic recording. ISIS. 1962, 53, Part 3(173):287–324.

IDE (Investigational Device Exemption). See Food and Drug Administration.

International Electrotechnical Commission (IEC). Centre du Service Clientele (CSC), Commission Electrotechnique Internationale, 3 rue de Varembe, Case postale 131, CH1211-Geneve 20 (Geneva) Suisse (Switzerland).

Italy: Ministry of Health. Rome, Italy, Health Informative System/Prevention Department, General Manager: Dr. Fabizio Oleari, 3rd Unit-Infectious diseases and international prophilaxys, Chief: Dr. Dina Caraffa De Stefano, National Epidemiological Observatory, Address: Via Sierra Nevada, 60-00144 Rome, Italy.

Japan: Ministry of Health and Welfare. http://www.mhlw.go.jp/english/.

Lexis-Nexis. 9443 Springboro Pike, PO Box 933, Dayton, OH 45401.

Library Searches: Web of Science. http://www.webofscience.com (fee required).

MAUDE—See Food and Drug Administration.

MDR—See Food and Drug Administration.

Medical Malpractice Verdicts, Settlements and Experts. 901 Church St., Nashville, TN, 37203-3411.

National Academy of Forensic Engineers. 174 Brady Avenue, Hawthorne, NY 10532.

National Electrical Code: National Fire Protection Association (NFPA), PO Box 9145, Quincy, MA 02269-9959.

National Library of Medicine. http://www.nlm.nih.gov/.

National Fire Protection Association. 470 Atlantic Ave, Boston, MA 02210.

Netherlands: Ministry of Health, Welfare Support. Visiting address: Parnassusplein 5, 2511 VX The Hague. Mailing address: PO Box 20350, 2500 EF The Hague, The Netherlands. Health Council of The Netherlands. Visiting address: Parnassusplein, 2511 VX The Hague, The Netherlands. Mailing address: P.O. Box 16052, 2500 BB The Hague, The Netherlands.

New Zealand: Medsafe New Zealand Medicines and Medical Safety Authority, P.O. Box 5013, Wellington, New Zealand.

Norway: Ministry of Health Board of Health. Office: Einar Gerhardsens plass 3. Postal Address: Postboks 8011 Dep, N-0030 Oslo, Norway.

Pearce JA. Electrosurgery. 1985. Chapman Hall, London.

PMA (Premarket Approval)—See Food and Drug Administration

SEAK, Expert Witness Conferences. SEAK Inc., S. Babitsky, Falmouth, MA.

Shepherd MD. Shepherd's System for Medical Device Investigation and Reporting. 1992. Quest Publishing (now Lippincott-Raven Press), Brea, CA.

Simpson K. Forensic Medicine. 1974. Williams and Wilkins, Baltimore, MD, p 362.

South Africa: The Department of Health. Private Bag X828, Pretoria, South Africa 0001, Tel: +27 12 312-000, Fax: +27 12 3238-6299.

Sweden: Medical Products Agency. Box 26, S-751 03 Uppsala, Sweden.

Taiwan: Ministry of Health. http://www.doh.gov.tw/english/.

UK (Great Britain) Medical Devices Agency. Department of Health, London, England UK.

Underwriters' Laboratories Inc., 207 East Ohio Street, Chicago, IL 60611.

United States Department of the Interior. Bureau of Mines, Washington, D.C.

United Stated Department of the Navy. Bureau of Ships (Navships), Washington, D.C.

West Publishing Company. 620 Opperman Drive, PO Box 64779, St. Paul, MN 55164-0779. Webmaster. westdoc@westpub.com.

Wood Library. Museum of Anesthesiology, 520 Northwest Highway, Park Ridge, 60068-2573. ASA Web page: http://www.asahq.org and e-mail to: WLM@asahq.org.geddes.pap.techexp.5/27.

About the Author

Leslie Alexander Geddes was born in Scotland and educated in Montreal (McGill University) and Houston, Texas (Baylor Medical College). He has two degrees in electrical engineering and a Ph.D. degree in physiology and a D.Sc. honoris causa. He has published twenty-two books, over 750 scientific papers and has twenty-five issued U.S. patents. He is a fellow in the American College of Cardiology and several other scientific societies. He is listed in *Who's Who* and the *National Directory of Expert Witnesses*. He is a registered professional engineer (Texas #10170), a certified Clinical Engineer and a member of the National Academy of Engineering, the National Society of Professional Engineers and the National Academy of Forensic Engineers (Fellow).

Dr. Geddes has been an expert witness for over twenty years, specializing in medical device accidents and patent infringement and invalidation.

Index

activation time, 64, 364
active electrode, 74–75, 138–141, 143, 149–150, 155–156, 158–159, 164–168, 171, 184–185, 187, 209, 211, 303, 306, 337–338

B

C

D

E

F

J

K

L

M

N

O

P

R

S

U

V

W

Nursing Malpractice

Second Edition

Edited by Patricia W. Iyer, R.N., M.S.N., L.N.C.C.

The best in its field has now been updated to bring you even more inside information on the field of nursing. An outstanding reference for the attorney or claims adjustor investigating a nursing malpractice claim, the second edition of *Nursing Malpractice* brings you a wealth of information and resources to use in bringing a case to trial. Comprehensive and full of inside information, Ms. Iyer's book covers the spectrum of the nursing process—from patient admittance to lawsuit. Packed with tips and techniques for finding the missing loophole, this volume reveals typical ways in which nurses try to cover up their mistakes, and shows how nurses are caught in a difficult position between insurance company lawyers and hospital procedures. It details the defendant nurse's daily routine, whether as a surgical nurse or nurse-supervisor in a nursing home setting, giving a comprehensive feel for all the actions which fall under a nurse's responsibility.

online table of contents

www.lawyersandjudges.com/5104

Topics include

- Foundations of nursing practice
- Roots of nursing malpractice
- An inside look at today's health care environment
- Nursing documentation
- Obstetrical malpractice issues
- Neonatal malpractice issues
- Pediatric malpractice issues
- Emergency care malpractice issues
- Critical care malpractice issues
- Perioperative nursing malpractice issues
- Nurse anesthesia malpractice issues
- Psychiatric nursing malpractice issues
- Medical surgical malpractice issues
- Subacute and long term care malpractice issues
- Managed care malpractice issues
- Home care malpractice issues
- Medication errors
- Investigation of billing fraud
- The plaintiff attorney's perspective
- The defense attorney's perspective
- The legal nurse consultant
- Working with expert witnesses
- Life care plans
- Vocational expert
- Economist expert
- Pain and suffering
- Trial consulting
- Demonstrative evidence
- Crafting effective themes for a nursing malpractice case

Product #5104. 8 ½" × 11", casebound, 864 pages plus 16 color plates, 2001.

About the editor

Patricia W. Iyer, R.N., M.S.N., L.N.C.C., has extensive experience as a legal nurse consultant, giving testimony, and helping lawyers for both sides. Ms. Iyer is a medical surgical nurse expert witness and president of a legal nursing consulting firm. She received her diploma in nursing from Muhlenberg Hospital School of Pennsylvania in Philadelphia. Ms. Iyer has coauthored six nursing textbooks.

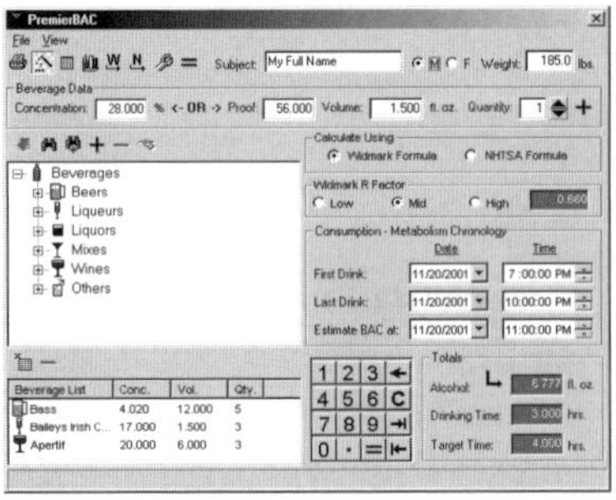

PremierBAC™

David N. Dresser

Accurately calculate blood alcohol levels instantly!

This software program makes it a snap to calculate blood alcohol concentration. Written by the author of *Basic Vehicle Motion Analysis*, this software has been designed with accident reconstructionists and lawyers in mind. It can calculate the person's peak blood alcohol concentration, the person's BAC after a specified time after the last drink, and it also gives you the option of using the two industry-standard equations for better accuracy.

Here is how it works. You provide the person's sex and weight, and either type in the fluid ounces and proof of the drinks, or select common drinks like brand-name beers or daiquiris from a list. The list of common beverages includes their serving size and proof so you don't have to know either of those things! You can request a BAC from a specific time since last drink, as well. Next, you choose from the two standard equations for calculating BAC: the Widmark or the NHSTA equation. You can easily perform both equations for the same person to verify accuracy. After the necessary information is entered, you will see the person's peak BAC and BAC after your specified time period. If you prefer to use the equations without the wizard to help you calculate the amount of alcohol in various drinks, you can do that too! This program is very versatile and contains very useful help screens to guide you on your way.

According to creator David Dresser, some unique aspects of the software that make PremierBAC accurate and versatile include:

- PremierBAC makes it possible to calculate blood alcohol concentration values using both of the currently prevailing formulas: the Widmark formula and the formula developed by Dr. Moskowitz and promoted by the National Highway Traffic Safety Administration (NHTSA). Thus, it is possible to easily compare and contrast the values determined by each of these equations.
- It is possible to alter (tweak) values such as metabolism rates and absorption rates, if desired, to suit a particular subject.
- PremierBAC provides a printout that can be filed for later use, without recalculation, and which can be used as a deposition or trial exhibit.
- PremierBAC permits the user to use drink-alcohol concentration data that is included in the database of the program, and permits the user to modify, delete or add to the data base.

Product #5606. CD-ROM is Windows 95/98® compatible and works best with 32MB RAM and a Pentium® processor. Software is nonreturnable. 2002.

P.O. Box 30040 • Tucson, Arizona 85751-0040

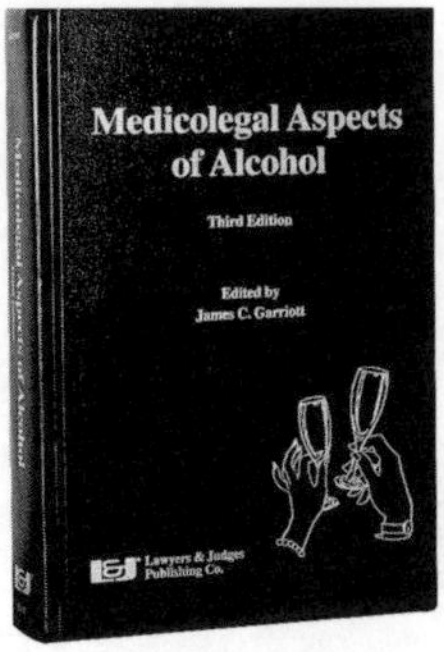
Medicolegal Aspects of Alcohol
Third Edition
Edited by
James C. Garriott
Lawyers & Judges Publishing Co.